AGRICULTURAL TRADE LIBERALIZATION

IMPLICATIONS FOR DEVELOPING COUNTRIES

EDITED BY
IAN GOLDIN AND ODIN KNUDSEN

ORGANISATION FOR ECONOMIC CO-OPERATION AND DEVELOPMENT
THE WORLD BANK

Library of Congress Cataloging-in-Publication data

Agricultural trade liberalization : implications for developing countries / Ian Goldin. Odin Knudsen, editors.
  Includes bibliographical references.
  ISBN 0-8213-1527-7
  ISBN 92-64-13366-6 (OECD)
  1. Produce trade—Government policy. 2. Produce trade —Developing countries. 3. General
Agreement on Tariffs and Trade (Organization) I. Goldin. Ian, 1955-   .II. Knudsen, Odin.
HD9000.6.A545 1990
382'.41—dc20   90-7155
                                                                                       CIP

Pursuant to article 1 of the Convention signed in Paris on 14th December 1960, and which came into force on 30th September 1961, the Organisation for Economic Co-operation and Development (OECD) shall promote policies designed:

- to achieve the highest sustainable economic growth and employment and a rising standard of living in Member countries, while maintaining financial stability, and thus to contribute to the development of the world economy;
- to contribute to sound economic expansion in Member as well as non-member countries in the process of economic development; and
- to contribute to the expansion of world trade on a multilateral, non-discriminatory basis in accordance with international obligations.

The original Member countries of the OECD are Austria, Belgium, Canada, Denmark, France, the Federal Republic of Germany, Greece, Iceland, Ireland, Italy, Luxembourg, the Netherlands, Norway, Portugal, Spain, Sweden, Switzerland, Turkey, the United Kingdom and the United States. The following countries became Members subsequently through accession at the dates indicated hereafter: Japan (28th April 1964), Finland (28th January 1969), Australia (7th June 1971) and New Zealand (29th May 1973).

The Socialist Federal Republic of Yugoslavia takes part in some of the work of the OECD (agreement of 28th October 1961).

The Development Centre of the Organisation for Economic Co-operation and Development was established by decision of the OECD Council on 23rd October 1962.

The purpose of the Centre is to bring together the knowledge and experience available in Member countries of both economic development and the formulation and execution of general economic policies; to adapt such knowledge and experience to the actual needs of countries or regions in the process of development and to put the results at the disposal of the countries by appropriate means.

The Centre has a special and autonomous position within the OECD which enables it to enjoy scientific independence in the execution of its task. Nevertheless, the Centre can draw upon the experience and knowledge available in the OECD in the development field.

The World Bank is a multilateral development institution whose purpose is to assist its developing member countries further their economic and social progress so that their people may live better and fuller lives. It does so through three related functions: lending funds, providing economic advice and technical assistance, and serving as a catalyst for investment by others.

Publié en français sous le titre :
LIBÉRALISATION
DES ÉCHANGES AGRICOLES

The findings of this study are the results of research supported by the World Bank and the OECD Development Centre. The interpretations and conclusions expressed herein, however, are entirely those of the authors of individual papers and should not be attributed in any manner to the World Bank, to its affiliated organizations, or to members of its Board of Executive Directors or the countries they represent. Nor do they necessarily represent the views of the OECD or of the governments of its Member countries.

The cover design represents the levels of support for agriculture by region. It is based upon data from the OECD, the World Bank and the United States Department of Agriculture.

This book is based on an international symposium held in Paris from 5th to 6th October 1989. The symposium was jointly organised by the World Bank and the OECD Development Centre as part of each institution's research on agricultural policy, developing country trade, and international economic trends.

TABLE OF CONTENTS

PART I
PARTIAL EQUILIBRIUM MODELS

PART II
GENERAL EQUILIBRIUM MODELS

PART III

ANALYTICAL ISSUES

PART IV

DISCUSSANT NOTES

PART V

CONCLUSIONS

PREFACE

We are all aware that agriculture is important to developing countries as a source of income, employment and export earnings. To a far greater extent than in OECD countries, agriculture is central to the economic performance of developing countries and the livelihood of their inhabitants. Rural societies in developing countries are directly dependent on the agricultural sector and urban dwellers rely on agriculture to provide food security and sustainable economic growth. Furthermore, many developing countries heavily rely upon the export earnings from agriculture or are highly dependent on food imports. Given the fact that the poorest and most threatened communities and countries are typically the most highly dependent, the resolution of pressing global agricultural policy and trade issues is critical to sustainable development and poverty alleviation.

Trade barriers and subsidisation have distorted world markets and undermined developing country agriculture while contributing to the instability of commodity prices and adding a politically induced uncertainty to world markets. While the rules and disciplines of GATT have had a major impact on trade in manufactured goods, the reality of agricultural trade has been vastly different; agricultural protectionism in the OECD countries has risen steadily during the last two decades. The associated explosion in budgetary costs and agricultural production has burdened OECD taxpayers and penalised developing country farmers. Simultaneously, it has been associated with increased friction between the principal trading groups within the OECD: the United States, the European Community and Japan. The Uruguay round of multilateral negotiations is currently entering its final stages. These multilateral negotiations are amongst the most critical and complex ever on international trade. The issue of agriculture is on the centre-stage, providing a crucial opportunity to subject agricultural trade to the rules of the GATT.

The Uruguay Round negotiations offer a major opportunity but also a challenge. For developing countries, successful GATT negotiations would provide them with an opportunity to compete on a more equal footing in international agricultural trade. Yet it also raises concerns on how international food prices and trade will react to a freer trading regime and which countries will lose and which will gain from possible outcomes. It is important that governments and international institutions understand the possible implications of agricultural liberalization. In particular, it is necessary to consider what the price and trade effects of a successful resolution of the liberalization will be. If grain and other prices rise, how severe will be the implications for developing countries that are net food importers? For net exporters, what are the possible opportunities, and will liberalization increase the imperatives for specialisation or diversification? Furthermore what will be the implications to government fiscal revenues and expenditures?

The contributions to this volume were presented to a symposium co-convened by the OECD Development Centre and the World Bank in October 1989. They represent the "state of the art" regarding the modelling of the implications of agricultural trade liberalization for developing countries. They provide important perspectives for developing country as well as OECD country policy makers involved in the multilateral negotiations. Simultaneously, they provide a basis for assessing the future research agenda, and for providing policy guidance to multilateral agencies.

We hope that this volume will provide direct impetus to the Uruguay process while simultaneously adding fresh insights for the research agenda. We believe that it is one step in the process of enhancing the opportunity for developing countries to meet the challenge of trade liberalization for the promotion of their development.

Louis Emmerij	Michel Petit
President	Director
Development Centre	Agriculture and Rural Development
OECD	World Bank
Paris	Washington

ABBREVIATIONS

AGE	applied general equilibrium (model)
AIDS	almost ideal system (in import demand functions)
BLS	Basic Linked System
CAP	Common Agricultural Policy (of the European Community)
CCC	Commodity Credit Corporation (US agency for farm loans)
CES	constant elasticity of substitution
CET	constant elasticity of transformation
CGE	computable general equilibrium
CPI	consumer price index
CSE	Consumer Subsidy Equivalent
DME	developing (country) market economy
ERP	effective rate of protection
ERS	Economic Research Service of the US Department of Agriculture
ETA	excise tax adjustment
FAN	Food and Agricultural Network
FAO	Food and Agriculture Organization
FIQ	fixed import quota
GAMS	General Algebraic Modelling System (a computer program)
GATT	General Agreement on Tariffs and Trade
GE	general equilibrium (model or analysis)
GLS	Grains, Livestock and Sugar (model)
GSP	Generalized System of Preferences
GYPR	A mechanism or multiplier used in the RUNS model
IC	industrialised country
ICO	International Coffee Organisation
ICCO	International Cocoa Organization
IFPRI	International Food Policy Research Institute
IIASA	International Institute for Applied Systems Analysis
IME	industrial market economy
IMF	International Monetary Fund
LDC	developing country
LST	lump sum taxes
MDC	market developed country
MTM	Ministerial Trade Mandate (model of the OECD)
MVP	marginal value product
MWC	marginal welfare cost (of tax collection)
NPR	nominal protection rates

OECD	Organisation for Economic Co-operation and Development
PIK	payment in kind
PPF	production possibility frontier
PSE	Producer Subsidy Equivalent
ROW	rest of the world
RS	rent seeking
RUNS	Rural Urban North South (model)
SAM	social accounting matrix
SUF	social utility function
SWOPSIM	Static World Policy Simulation (model of the Economic Research Service of the US Department of Agriculture)
TDE	Trade Distortion Equivalent
TLIB	Trade Liberalization (model of the US Department of Agriculture)
USDA	United States Department of Agriculture
WALRAS	World Agricultural Liberalization Study (of the OECD)
WDR	World Development Report (annual report of World Bank)

INTRODUCTION

by

Ian Goldin and Odin Knudsen

The Purpose

This book provides analytically based insights into the possible effects of agricultural trade liberalization on developing countries and thus gives impetus to the agricultural negotiations in the Uruguay Round. It offers perspectives and estimates on the price, trade, production and consumption implications of agricultural trade liberalization for and within developing countries resulting from OECD-country and global liberalization. It aims to extend the understanding of both developing- and OECD-country participants in the Uruguay Round negotiations on the potential benefits and costs of agricultural liberalization and to stimulate more research into this important topic.

The contributions to this volume represent the "state of the art" of the modelling of agricultural trade liberalization and its impact on world trade and in particular on developing countries. The aim of these contributions is to take stock of the possible outcomes, examine the differing assumptions that drive these results and comparatively assess their conclusions. This examination provides the basis for extracting the policy implications of the models.

The Policy Issues

In recent years, agricultural support and protection has come to the fore of the international political agenda. In the developed countries, much of the attention has centred on the trade disputes between the United States, Japan and the EC. Invariably, these disputes focus on the question of agricultural incomes policies, subsidies, protection, and market access. Prolonged protection of agricultural producers in many OECD countries over the past decades has severely distorted national and international resource use as well as agricultural markets and prices.

Most developing countries have been unable to afford the budgetary costs and political ramifications of extensive agricultural support and protection. Indeed, the evidence suggests that developing country agriculture has generally been exposed to net taxation. This has retarded agricultural growth and investment with negative consequences for rural incomes.

The growing pressure for reforming developing country agricultural policies in favour of policies for more sustainable growth and less government intervention in prices and trade has coincided with the convening of what is the most critical and also most complex set of negotiations ever on international trade. The GATT is currently entering the final phase of the Uruguay Round of negotiations. For developing countries, those concerning agricultural and tropical product trade are amongst the most critical.

The liberalization of agricultural trade is generally agreed to be a vital step to the development of a more efficient and equitable international allocation of agricultural production. However, while many developing countries stand to benefit from this process, others may suffer considerable loss, at least in the short term. The examination of the implications of agricultural trade liberalization for developing countries is thus important both in terms of the identification of the potential beneficiaries of the process as well as the potential losers.

In addition to the international redistributive implications, all countries will experience shifts in their domestic income distributions, due to the differential impact of the changes on producers and consumers. Net effects on countries are inadequate to assess the full consequences of liberalization since within each country the implications of the differential consequences and the feasibility of compensation for those who stand to lose is also of analytical importance.

Analytic Approaches

Research on the implications of agricultural trade liberalization is unusual in the extent of its reliance on modelling. In contrast to the standard economic approach to the analysis of policies, the research on trade liberalization has relied on the simulation of world scenarios through the use of analytic models. These models are used as tools to provide guidance on the key outcomes: what happens to the structure and pattern of production; whether prices go up or down; whether trade increases or declines; and who benefits and who loses from the change in policies. Because the actual interaction of policies with trade and agricultural production and consumption is extremely complex, these models necessarily involve simplifications. The key challenge facing economists interested in assessing the ramifications of trade liberalization is how best to distil the complexity of the world agricultural economy into a form which allows manageable models while at the same time remaining sensitive to the critical economic relationships.

In each model, theoretical concepts are moulded into operational systems through simplifying assumptions. Parameters and coefficients are specified which determine the interrelationship of key variables. Advances in modelling and computing technology have facilitated increased complexity in the specification of these interrelationships. Nevertheless, the most complex specifications still capture only a stylised reflection of reality; the specification of assumptions and of parameters and the translation of theory into manageable quantitative systems is the art of building models.

The choice of variables, assumptions, and relationships differentiates the models. Two broad frameworks have been adopted in the modelling of trade liberalization. The first is widely labelled the "partial equilibrium" approach, the second, the "general equilibrium" approach. For those uninitiated into contemporary economic terminology, partial equilibrium denotes those methods which are more sectoral specific in nature and which examine particular sectors or commodities in the economy while generally ignoring interrelationships with other sectors or the macroeconomy. General equilibrium models, by contrast, examine the economy as a whole and the interaction between sectors. These models tend to include a number of important determinants of the macroeconomy such as savings, employment and income. Theoretical rigour is reflected in the extent to which these models follow microeconomic concepts of behaviour, particularly by adhesion to utility as the basic principle and permitting welfare analysis.

The partial equilibrium models are different from general equilibrium models in their focus on individual sectors, and/or commodities in the economy. Thus the partial equilibrium approach to trade liberalization tends to examine the impact of changes in policies regarding specific agricultural commodities with the remaining sectors of the economy not changing. As a consequence, these focus on efficiency gains in the sector analysed, but not on the effects on incomes, relative prices and indirect efficiency effects.

14

By incorporating assumptions regarding the responsiveness of supply and demand to changes in prices, mainly through the use of price elasticities, the partial equilibrium models offer perspectives on the implications for domestic and international agricultural markets of alternative agricultural policies. Because of their sector specific nature, they generally abstract from the spillover effects to and feedback from other parts of the economy. However, recently, some partial equilibrium models have been extended to incorporate general equilibrium elements, such as income and foreign exchange, although whether these attempts to provide general equilibrium complements to partial models are theoretically sound is disputable.

General equilibrium models, by explicitly modelling the non-agricultural economy, allow the analysis of both efficiency and income effects throughout the economy. Thus, for example, general equilibrium models allow the examination of the impact on manufactured exports of changes in agricultural protection and of the income and demand changes which follow a policy shift. However, such analysis, as the contributions in Part II of this book reveal, rests on assumptions regarding the nature of these linkages, for example, how different wage rates and returns to capital in the different sectors of the economy are modelled. While general equilibrium approaches are intuitively more appealing and in principle permit a full specification of both income and efficiency effects, their limitations, not least in terms of the modelling effect and resources required, make them a complement, but not a substitute for the partial equilibrium approaches, such as those presented in Part I of this book.

The Papers

This book begins with a retrospective paper by Tom Hertel on the results of past modelling of the effects of agricultural trade liberalization. The evolution of agricultural trade modelling is presented as the review advances from the initial relatively simple partial equilibrium models to the increasingly complex general equilibrium models developed in recent years. This development has mirrored an evolution in the literature from a concentration on the implication of agricultural trade reform among the major players, notably the United States and the EC, towards incorporating the implications of policy reform in developing countries. Following this historical retrospective on the past modelling efforts, the book presents substantively new efforts built on these early works or representing novel approaches. The book is divided into three main parts: the first on the sector specific models of a partial equilibrium nature; the second on the general equilibrium models and the final on modelling issues. A concluding chapter draws policy implications and points to a modelling agenda for future work.

PART I: PARTIAL EQUILIBRIUM MODELS

The first paper in this section is by Anderson and Tyers, who are among the leading proponents of the partial equilibrium approach. Their model differs from a number of the other partial equilibrium models in its use of a dynamic framework, its incorporation of technological change and in exploring the effects of liberalization on price stability. For their contribution to this volume, they have retained their traditional focus on grains, livestock and sugar. Whereas most of the other partial equilibrium models are comparative static in nature, the Anderson and Tyers' approach traces dynamic changes along the adjustment path.

The second paper in Part I is that of Zietz and Valdés. In the early 1980s, Valdés and Zietz took the lead in the application of partial equilibrium models to the analysis of the implications of trade liberalization for developing countries. The partial equilibrium model presented in this volume is an extension of their earlier work. It adds to their previous models by its explicit incorporation of commodity interdependence and the long-run effects of productivity growth on domestic production and of income growth on demand.

In considering the issue of trade liberalization from a partial equilibrium perspective, the approach of Zietz and Valdés is close in spirit to that of Anderson and Tyers. The Zietz and Valdés model also simulates the adjustment path but ignores the complexities of the adjustment to the new equilibrium, assuming that all long-run changes occur simultaneously in the base period. By contrast, the OECD and USDA partial equilibrium models are more comparative static in nature, simply comparing a base and an end point without specification of the adjustment path.

The OECD Ministerial Trade Mandate (MTM) model was the first to embrace the notions of Producer and Consumer Subsidy Equivalents (PSE, CSE) with analysis which aimed to quantify effects of agricultural reform by OECD countries. The MTM model presented in this volume is an extension of the OECD MTM world agricultural model developed for the Trade Mandate study. However, whereas the original study contained a single region for all developing countries, the present study, as explained in the chapter by Moreddu, Parris and Huff, extends this analysis to examine the policies and the impacts of trade liberalization for eight developing countries and regions, accounting for about 25 per cent of the world production and consumption of the 19 commodities included in the MTM model.

In common with the MTM model, the Static World Policy Simulation (SWOPSIM) model developed by the Economic Research Service (ERS) of the United States Department of Agriculture (USDA) is based on a partial equilibrium comparative static system. The SWOPSIM modelling framework was developed by Roningen and others and has been adapted by Krissoff, Sullivan and Wainio to examine explicitly how the agricultural sectors of developing countries might be affected by an ending of government intervention in agriculture in OECD countries. It further considers how the agricultural sectors in developing countries may be affected if their governments devalue their currency to estimated free market equilibrium levels. They also incorporate in one of their simulations an income multiplier originating from the growth in agricultural income. Both the incorporating of exchange rate and income effects in a partial equilibrium framework is controversial.

In addition to their development of the SWOPSIM model, the USDA (ERS) has provided another contribution to this volume in the form of their analysis of the tropical beverages — cocoa, coffee and tea. Despite their importance to developing countries, the paper by Mabbs-Zeno and Krissoff for the first time specifically examines the issue of tropical beverages and trade liberalization. Their paper examines how government policies have affected the global distribution of tropical beverage production, processing and trade. It presents quantitative estimates of how the markets in tropical beverages would have appeared after medium-term adjustments if government policies affecting trade were removed and 1986 conditions otherwise prevailed.

PART II: GENERAL EQUILIBRIUM MODELS

The section on general equilibrium begins with an introductory overview by Sherman Robinson. He notes that over the past decade, the application of computable general equilibrium (CGE) models to the analysis of trade liberalization has focussed interest on questions of the structural impact of different trade regimes in developed countries. The increased attention given to agriculture and trade in CGE modelling reflects the importance of agriculture in the GATT negotiations. It also reflects the increased importance of trade for developing countries. In his review of recent developments in CGE modelling, Robinson provides both an introductory explanation of the crucial elements in general equilibrium modelling and a review of some of the principal models and their shortcomings.

Following on from Robinson's overview, the results of four different general equilibrium models of trade liberalization are presented in this volume. The first general equilibrium model

..s by Fischer, Frohberg and Parikh and others under the auspices of the Food and Agriculture Programme (FAP) of the International Institute for Applied Systems Analysis (IIASA). Their Basic Linked System (BLS) distinguishes nine agricultural and one non-agricultural commodity and consists of 20 detailed national models and 14 country-group models, covering the entire world system. The analysis of trade liberalization includes the removal of cost reducing subsidies and area set-aside measures in addition to border price wedges, to the extent that those for agricultural commodities deviate from wedges in non-agricultural trade. Several trade liberalization scenarios are presented in this volume; the first assumes trade liberalization in OECD countries, the second unilateral trade liberalization by the European Economic Community (EC) and the third unilateral liberalization by the United States. All three are simulated over the period 1981 to 2000, with protection removed in the first five years, and compare the liberalization scenarios with projections which assume that prevailing trade policies are not altered.

Another general equilibrium model — by Burniaux, Waelbroeck and others — follows the IIASA contribution to this volume. Their model, which they have dubbed RUNS (Rural Urban North South), like most general equilibrium models, is a barter model from which money is absent (it is thus not suitable for the description of money supply policies or of nominal price or wage rigidities). RUNS provides an indication of the change in the economy with capital accumulation and as it responds to exogenous population growth and technical change. A feature of RUNS is its specification of the agricultural sector and the distinctions between the rural and urban economies. For the paper presented here, the RUNS model simulated separately the impact of changes in protection in the EC and the OECD on food and agriculture in the South.

The economy-wide effects of agricultural liberalization on the OECD countries are the focus of the World Agricultural Liberalization Study (WALRAS) from the OECD. The two main objectives of the WALRAS project have been to highlight the key interactions between agricultural and non-agricultural sectors and to quantify the efficiency and welfare effects of OECD countries' policies. Although the developing countries are not modelled in any detail — they enter the model as the Rest of the World (ROW) — the model provides useful insights for policy makers concerned with the implications of trade liberalization for developing countries through its detailed modelling of OECD policies on world trade and prices.

The Loo and Tower paper addresses directly the issue of the heterogeneity of developing countries in a similar general equilibrium context. They explore the impacts of changed agricultural export taxes in low income less developed countries on the welfare, revenue and food consumption aspects of their economic performance. In adapting their model for this volume, they calculate the optimum combinations of different types of policy instruments and show how cost/benefit ratios and tax policies can be utilised for the maximisation of the success of policies of agricultural liberalization.

The Sadoulet and de Janvry paper in another archetypical representation of developing countries provides a new elaboration by further extending the decomposition of developing countries. They focus exclusively on low income cereal importing countries. These are the most vulnerable to the anticipated cereal price rises resulting from trade liberalization. For them, a key issue is how the price effects of higher cereal (import) prices will be transmitted to average incomes. The model distinguishes further between those low income cereal importers that have high substitution in imports and those with low substitution. They also explore the effect of the level of government expenditure on the outcomes of trade liberalization.

PART III: MODELLING ISSUES

The paper by Whalley and Wigle is the first in the section on modelling issues. It aims to emphasize how the subtleties of domestic agricultural support programmes need to be brought into models of trade liberalization and how the reliance on comparisons of border prices seriously undermines many existing modelling efforts. To illustrate this point, Whalley and Wigle focus on how an inclusion of domestic agricultural policies influences the sign of terms of trade effects. They evaluate the implications for developing countries of alternative possible wheat policy liberalizations. Both unilateral United States and multilateral simulations are conducted which endogenize participation in set-aside programmes. A comparison of the results with some of the other models suggests that the results may well be opposite from the conventional thinking as regards the terms of trade, with important implications for developing countries.

The issues of domestic policies and the response of governments to new world prices are taken up by Hammer and Knudsen. Their concern is the extent to which the policy response of developing countries to trade liberalization is likely to determine the nature of the impact of the liberalization process. Using several multi-market models, their paper examines possible developing country responses to agricultural liberalization in the developed economies through simulating the policy options faced by three typical middle income developing countries: an agricultural exporter (Argentina), an agricultural importer (Tunisia) and a country which is both an importer and exporter (Senegal).

The analysis by Rausser, Rose and Irwin addresses the issue of linkage between macro variables and world commodity prices. Their approach is to use a theoretical and empirical framework to examine the mechanisms by which monetary, fiscal, and debt policies can impact on commodity prices. While their paper is outside the strict modelling framework, they add an interesting viewpoint to the discussion of the impact of trade liberalization by emphasizing the effect of real exchange rate and interest rate changes in determining aggregate commodity price indices.

PART IV: COMMENTS AND CONCLUSION

The final section of this volume includes a number of commentaries. These are primarily concerned with the methodological issues associated with the existing models and with the implications for policy analysis and for the future modelling agenda of the papers presented in this volume. These issues are taken up in the conclusion, which after reviewing the differing modelling perspectives highlights the implications — both for policy and for future research — of the papers presented in the volume.

Chapter 1

AGRICULTURAL TRADE LIBERALIZATION AND THE DEVELOPING COUNTRIES: A SURVEY OF THE MODELS[1]

by

Thomas W. Hertel

INTRODUCTION

The past decade has seen a considerable increase in the discussion and analysis of agricultural trade liberalization. Prolonged protection of producers in the industrialised market economies (IMEs) coupled with slower income growth in the developing countries have combined to result in a global glut in the market for many farm products. Export subsidies designed to dispose of this surplus have further depressed world prices. As a result (abstracting from the temporary relief offered by the 1988 US drought), the budgetary costs of IME farm policies have escalated. While these expenditures have been the most visible evidence of the crisis in global agricultural trade, there have been significant repercussions in the developing countries as well. Since 1977, the food trade balance of the developing countries has deteriorated markedly (World Bank, 1986, p. 11). The combination of depressed world prices and developing country policies which tax agriculture relative to industry have discouraged farm output and hence lowered rural incomes. Because the majority of the world's poorest households depend on agriculture and related activities for their livelihood, this recent turn of events is especially alarming.

One response by a number of international organisations has been to commission quantitative analyses designed to measure the degree to which farm policies have contributed to the crisis in agricultural trade. Enthusiasm for such research has received a substantial boost by the high profile which agriculture has played in the Uruguay Round of the GATT negotiations. Not surprisingly, these analyses have tended to focus on the implications of policy reform among the "major players" in these negotiations, especially the European Community (EC) and the United States (Valdés and Zietz; Tyers; Tyers and Anderson; Roningen and Dixit; and Burniaux and Waelbroeck). However, recently researchers have turned their attention toward the potential implications of policy reform in the developing countries (Parikh *et al.*, Krissoff *et al.*). Since the data, models, and treatment of policies in the developing country liberalization studies are necessarily more rudimentary at this stage, and since the GATT negotiations are focussed primarily on IME policies, this survey will emphasize the impact of IME liberalization on the developing countries.

This paper is arranged roughly in order of increasing complexity of models, beginning with single commodity models, progressing through the partial equilibrium, multicommodity analyses, and ending with a discussion of the general equilibrium studies. Coverage is limited to published studies available prior to the conference upon which this book is based.

SINGLE COMMODITY ANALYSES

The first comprehensive analysis of the effects of developed country agricultural policies on the developing countries was that of Valdés and Zietz (1980). Their methodology is simple, straightforward and well-documented. It also covers more countries and commodities than any subsequent effort. Thus it merits some attention.

There are two steps in the Valdés and Zietz study. The first involves determining the world market price effects of a 50 per cent reduction in protection levels by OECD countries. Since the approach is single commodity and partial equilibrium in nature, market price effects are independent for each of the 99 commodities considered. Thus the authors solve 99 different market clearing conditions for the price increase necessary to clear each market of the excess demand generated in the OECD countries as a result of liberalization. These are reported in Table 7 of their study and range from 0.4 per cent (milled rice) to 15.7 per cent (wine). (About three-quarters of the price increases reported fall between 2 per cent and 10 per cent.)

The second step in the Valdés and Zietz analysis involves analysing the impact of these world price increases on the 56 developing countries disaggregated in the study. For this, the authors return to the individual country supply and demand equations (assuming a unitary price transmission elasticity between world and domestic prices) and work out the resulting changes in export revenue and import expenditures, as well as estimating the subsequent change in welfare. Focussing first on those cases where developing countries are net exporters, Valdés and Zietz find that export earnings increase by 11 per cent over 1975-77 levels, or by approximately $3 billion. They note that this is roughly equal to total foreign aid provided to developing countries in 1977. (The largest revenue increases are in sugar products and beef.) Since some of these price increases come at the expense of added domestic resource costs and reduced consumption levels, the gain in welfare for developing countries as exporters is less, and is placed at $1 billion/year.

Valdés and Zietz also find that import expenditures fall by $700 million as a result of increased production of import competing commodities and a reduction in their consumption. This translates into a welfare loss of $580 million/year. In the lowest income developing countries, these welfare losses are primarily associated with increases in the world price of wheat.

As the authors are careful to point out, there are a number of important limitations to their analysis. First, they have assumed full transmission of the world price increases into the developing countries. However, there are many policies which currently insulate domestic producers and consumers from world price changes. As a result, projected increases in developing country foreign exchange earnings and aggregate welfare may be too high.

A second limitation has to do with those cases where production patterns have been so distorted that some OECD countries have become self-sufficient in potentially importable products. In this case, the method used for calculating the world price effects of liberalization by the OECD countries will not reflect potential increases in demand from these sources. This problem is likely to be most severe in the semi-processed sectors where tariff escalation is common[2].

Since Valdés and Zietz do not capture the input-output relationships between raw and processed products, they also do not capture the full protective impact of tariffs which rise with the level of processing (Golub and Finger). If an agro-processor can import raw material at the world price and enjoys a high level of protection on its output, then the resulting effective rate of protection (ERP) can be astronomical[3]. Thus it is likely that the Valdés and Zietz study underestimates gains in developing country agro-processing on two counts: first by not taking account of the contribution of self-sufficient countries to excess demand for the product and, secondly, because the full effects of escalating tariffs on existing imports of semi-processed products are not accounted for.

The third major limitation of their study, also identified by Valdés and Zietz, is the absence of cross-price effects in demand and supply. They argue that this omission will lead to an overstatement of the likely trade changes, since the impact of a particular price shock will be spread out across competing commodity markets. They attempt to adjust for this by using smaller trade elasticities. In some sense one can think of these as "total", as opposed to partial elasticities. If all prices rise together, the impact on the supply of a given commodity will be approximated by the sum of the own- and cross-price elasticities in a given supply equation. Provided they are substitutes, the total elasticity will be smaller, as will the resulting trade elasticity. Valdés' and Zietz' intuition about the role of cross-price effects in this type of experiment is confirmed in a paper by Tyers (1985) who shows that eliminating cross-price effects in a multicommodity trade model tends to overstate the trade effects of EC liberalization in agriculture.

MULTIPLE COMMODITY TRADE MODELS

In addition to introducing cross-price effects in supply and demand, Tyers (1985) and various other papers by Anderson and Tyers, introduce the possibility of sluggish price transmission. Also stock accumulation, motivated by stochastic production, is treated. Thus they are able to look at the implications of agricultural trade liberalization by the OECD countries for market volatility as well as mean prices (Anderson and Tyers, 1988). Their model focuses on grains, livestock products and sugar. They disaggregate the world into 30 producing/consuming regions and project world prices and policies from a 1980-82 base up to 1995, based on behavioural equations and underlying trends.

After analysing the impact of domestic pricing policies in the early 1980s, they conclude that Japan and the EC contributed significantly to world price instability by insulating their domestic markets. By contrast, US policies added slightly to world price stability due to their tendency to boost average grain stocks. Unfortunately, simulation of their model in its full, dynamic-stochastic environment is very costly, and so Anderson and Tyers frequently convert it to a long-run comparative static model. This is done by simply using the long-run elasticities and solving the model twice — once with the policies in place and once with them removed. This is also more in the spirit of the other partial equilibrium studies under review here.

In their long-run experiments, Anderson and Tyers (1988) consider (successively), liberalization in the twelve EC countries, Japan, the United States, and finally, all industrial market economies. They do this for two levels of protection, first that observed in 1980-82 and, secondly, the higher levels of protection which their model projects for 1995. They find that EC policies in grains, livestock and sugar are the most damaging to developing country producers, followed by those of Japan and then the United States[4]. Upon removal of these IME policies, developing country producer welfare is projected to rise by $26 billion in 1980-82 and $50 billion in 1995 (all figures are in 1985 dollars).

Since the developing countries are net importers of the temperate zone products considered in this partial equilibrium analysis, they lose more as consumers than they gain as producers. Thus net economic welfare in the developing countries falls by $2.3 billion and $13.5 billion, respectively, under 1980-82 and 1995 liberalization by the OECD countries. However, as a consequence of the higher world prices, they move from a projected 1995 self-sufficiency ratio of 95 per cent to one of 104 per cent. That is, after liberalization by the OECD countries they become net exporters of grain, livestock and sugar products.

This same basic story of rising world prices — and hence producer gains and overall welfare losses in the developing countries — is told in a number of other multicommodity models that have analysed the question of IME liberalization in agriculture (OECD; Roningen and Dixit; and Parikh et al.). For example, using a 1986/87 base year, Roningen and Dixit estimate that

IME liberalization would lead to an aggregate increase in world prices of 22 per cent, of which 46 per cent and 26 per cent would be contributed by the EC and the United States, respectively. A useful cross-model comparison of these world price effects is provided by Magiera and Herlihy. Those authors show that, once one has controlled for the assumed level of price support, results from these different multicommodity models are quite similar. Furthermore, regardless of the base year, the largest world price increases come in dairy products, followed typically by ruminant meats, and sugar.

Most of the multicommodity, partial equilibrium analyses to date have focussed primarily on the industrial market economies, with little disaggregation of the developing countries and the tropical product markets which they supply (Tyers and Anderson, 1988; Roningen and Dixit, 1989; OECD). Exceptions include the IIASA effort (to be discussed below) and a recent paper by Krissoff, Sullivan and Wainio, both of which have considerable developing country country detail but neither of which disaggregates tropical products. Krissoff, Sullivan and Wainio take the same basic model employed by Roningen and Dixit and break out 24 developing countries. They find that under IME liberalization — with complete price transmission into the developing countries — foreign exchange revenues increase by $11.5 billion (half of this arises in Latin America). Argentina, Brazil and Mexico experience particularly large increases in net export revenues. Asian developing countries increase net exports of rice, with India, Indonesia and Bangladesh shifting from net importer to net exporter status, while Africa and the Middle East suffer a $400 million decline in their net export revenue. These authors also consider the impact on world prices, net agricultural trade, and welfare as a result of simultaneous liberalization in the developing countries. With a few exceptions, this leads to improved agricultural trade balances and increased welfare among the developing countries.

A CRITIQUE OF THE PARTIAL EQUILIBRIUM STUDIES

A major limitation of the partial equilibrium trade models is their lack of economic structure. They are driven by reduced form supply-demand elasticities which cannot be easily related back to specific assumptions about consumer preferences, production technology and factor mobility. This makes it difficult to interpret the results of these models and leaves open the possibility of theoretical inconsistencies.

Many of the researchers using such models are keenly aware of these limitations, and some have taken steps to address them. For example, the OECD model has incorporated complete feed demand systems based on cost minimisation, subject to nested CES production technologies. Their researchers have also been experimenting with complete farm supply and demand systems based on multiproduct, restricted profit functions. In the same vein, the US Department of Agriculture's SWOPSIM model now incorporates some symmetry restrictions on its cross-price elasticities. Also, some attention has been paid to deriving a more complete supply-demand system for the US component of that model.

In order to illustrate the value of imposing additional structure on these models, consider the question of supply response. How are we to interpret the reduced form supply elasticities in these partial equilibrium models? Do they represent the optimal quantity response conditional on exogenous factor prices? Or are some factors (implicitly) held in fixed supply over the time horizon of the simulation? What is the source of increased supply response as we move from the short run to the long run in a model like that of Tyers and Anderson? Presumably this reflects an increased ability to adjust input levels in response to changed output prices, but what kind of factor market adjustment is implied? The reduced form supply equations do not permit us to answer directly any of these questions. However, it is possible to deduce indirectly partial answers to these questions. In order to do so, a slight digression is necessary.

The Normal Case: A Benchmark for Evaluating Cross-price Elasticities

Consider the simple case of supply response from a region producing two crops: grains and oilseeds. For illustrative purposes, assume that in the short run input levels cannot be varied. This means that any decrease in grain output, following a decrease in the grain support price, must work to the advantage of oilseeds supply. Essentially the sector is constrained to move around a fixed transformation frontier, such as that denoted by T_1 in Figure 1.1. Assume that production shifts from point E to E'_1 as a result of diminishing the grains support price. This means that the short-run cross-price elasticity of supply between grains and oilseeds must be negative. Furthermore, with all factors fixed, it must be equal in absolute value to the own-price elasticity in order to preserve zero degree homogeneity of supply (in prices).

As the time horizon lengthens, provided the new relative price ratio denoted by the slope of P'_1 and P'_2 persists, resources will leave the farm sector. This causes the transformation frontier to shift inward to T_2. The absolute size of this contraction effect increases as the number of potentially variable inputs increases. In the long run, it is reasonable to argue that virtually all inputs are somewhat variable in supply. As a consequence, farmers would leave the sector, the capital stock would fall, and some land would move into other uses. It is conceivable that the shift from T_1 to T_2 would be large enough to cause a reduction in both wheat and coarse grains output (e.g. E'_2). This would imply a cross-price elasticity of supply which was *positive*, not negative! We will call this the case of "gross complementarity", whereby the qualifier "gross" indicates that it includes both contraction and substitution effects. Of course, these arguments are fully symmetric and apply equally, for example, to the case where a price increase for grains results in an increased long-run supply of oilseeds.

While the result of gross complementarity may at first seem rather implausible, it turns out to be a fairly common occurrence in empirical work. For example, a recently published matrix of supply and demand elasticities for US agriculture shows that all output-output interactions and all input-input interactions exhibit gross complementarity (Ball). Theoretically, it may be shown that, as input fixities are successively relaxed, any substitution relationships tend to become less significant, and gross complementarity becomes more likely (Hertel, 1987b). This makes sense, since in the long run the farm sector competes more with the non-farm sector for resources and less within itself. In other words, the contraction trade effect eventually dominates the transformation effect.

A rigorous proof of the necessity of gross complementarity in the context of a long-run profit function is developed by Sakai. He bases this on four relatively weak restrictions on the farm sector's technology — which he terms the "normal case". In addition to implying gross complementarity among all outputs and among all inputs, the normal case also predicts non-regressive input-output relationships. This result is really just a generalisation of earlier work by Hicks, Morishima and Rader who worked with the single output case and demonstrated the necessity of gross complementarity among inputs in the situation of either: (a) constant returns to scale; or (b) cooperant inputs[5].

Implications for Models of Trade Liberalization

The "normal case" provides a useful benchmark for evaluating the implications the cross-price elasticities, specified in various partial equilibrium models of trade liberalization. As noted above, given the incomplete specification of these supply equations, it is impossible to know whether these supplies are conditional on factor quantities or factor prices. In the former case, the liberalizing economy moves from E to E'_1 in Figure 1.1, while in the latter case it moves from E to E'_2. Thus a helpful rule of thumb for interpreting the model results is to examine the sign and relative magnitude of the cross-price elasticities of supply. If substitution relationships are dominant, then we might infer that the economy is moving more or less along a transformation frontier such as T_1 in Figure 1.1. If gross complementarity is evident (i.e. positive cross-price elasticities of supply) then we may safely infer that a significant expansion effect is present.

All of the partial equilibrium trade models for which I have been able to obtain supply elasticity matrices specify negative cross-price elasticities of supply[6]. Even the "long-run" supply elasticities for the EC, reported in the appendix of Tyers (1985) exhibit strong substitution relationships. Furthermore, there is no evidence that this relationship diminishes in importance as one moves from the short to the long run.

Tyers' (1985) EC elasticities of supply for wheat and coarse grains are shown in Table 1.1. The ratio of own- to cross-price elasticities in the wheat supply equation is equal to –2 in both the short and long runs. (This factor of proportionality is simply the inverse of the partial adjustment coefficient associated with wheat supply in their model.) Similarly, this ratio in the case of coarse grains is –2.67 in both the short and the long runs. The persistence of strong substitution effects in the long run suggests a limited role for expansion effects, since any shift, such as that from T to T' in Figure 1.1, will change the magnitude and possibly even the sign of the ratio of own- to cross-price elasticities. Rather than reflecting a shift in the transformation frontier, it appears that the difference between the short and long runs in this model is really a matter of increasing the price responsiveness of a stationary frontier. This is suggested by the dotted curve in Figure 1.1, labeled T^*.

While it may be the case that expansion effects do not dominate transformation effects in some regions, for some commodities, I believe there is strong evidence that they do in many cases, once one permits a sufficient proportion of total inputs to vary in supply. For example, in the Ball study cited above, all inputs, with the exception of self-employed labour, are treated as variable. As a consequence, the entire (11x11) matrix of elasticities satisfies sign restrictions implied by Sakai's normal case, i.e. gross complementarity and non-regressivity.

If this is correct, and the partial equilibrium trade models are simply moving agriculture around a relatively fixed transformation frontier, then they will definitely understate the consequences of trade liberalization for:

a) Resource movement out of (or into) agriculture;

b) Aggregate supply response; and hence

c) Welfare changes.

The price support policies of most OECD countries look far less damaging to the global resource allocation between the farm and non-farm sectors when they result primarily in a different mix of production. However, as the authors of many of the papers reviewed above have noted, in the long run we expect an entirely different pattern of investment, and hence, of agricultural production possibilities in both the IMEs and the developing countries, if price supports are permanently removed.

In order to focus more clearly on the issue of farm/non-farm resource allocation, let me now turn to those studies which have attempted to make this link explicit.

FROM PARTIAL TO GENERAL EQUILIBRIUM ANALYSIS

Creating a Residual Sector

The first step in moving from a partial to a general equilibrium framework involves closing the model with respect to all other goods. Having done this, we may then require household income to equal outlays which, at the national level, is tantamount to imposing a balance of payments equilibrium. The shortest route to this goal involves simply expanding the transformation frontier in Figure 1.1 to include not only all agricultural goods, but also a non-agricultural aggregate. This is essentially the approach adopted by Horridge and Pearce, who begin with the model of Tyers and Anderson, and close it by adding a residual product. (In this case the residual includes some farm as well as non-farm products, since the basic partial equilibrium model only treats grains, livestock and sugar products.)

The actual procedure used by Horridge and Pearce for completing the model is logical and straightforward. They take the (7x7) matrices of long-run commodity supply and demand elasticities from Tyers and systematically impose symmetry restrictions on them. This involves changing lots of parameters, and they do so in a manner which minimises a quadratic loss function. The authors then use food/non-food separability, homogeneity and symmetry restrictions to retrieve the final column and row of elasticities corresponding to "all other" goods. Thus this residual includes both those agricultural goods not treated by Tyers, as well as all non-agricultural goods. The resulting model satisfies all of the basic general equilibrium restrictions at the benchmark equilibrium shares.

Simulation of this general equilibrium model yields no big surprises (Horridge and Pearce). First round effects of removing agricultural protection are bound to be quite similar to the partial equilibrium results, since the authors have adopted the Tyers elasticities (in slightly modified form). The second round effects in this model are essentially terms of trade effects. These are small because the residual product's share is very large, and it is assumed homogeneous in trade so that export demand curves for this aggregate commodity are very flat.

Does the finding of Horridge and Pearce mean that these partial equilibrium trade models provide a good approximation of the "true" general equilibrium outcome? This is unclear, since factor movements between the farm and non-farm sectors still have not been fleshed out. By adopting an aggregate production possibility frontier approach, and imposing the same substitution-laden cross-price effects in agriculture, the authors likely understate the shift in the agricultural transformation frontier (T_1 to T_2) shown in Figure 1.1.

By contrast, the IIASA model also has a residual, "non-agricultural" sector. However, that model deals explicitly with resource flows between the farm and non-farm economies. Thus in their analysis of agricultural trade liberalization by the OECD countries, Parikh et al., project a substantial reallocation of labour and capital between the farm and non-farm sectors, particularly in the OECD countries themselves. There is a downsizing of the agricultural sector in Japan and the EC, while Canada, and to a lesser extent New Zealand and Australia, enlarge their productive capacity. The effect on Canadian livestock production is particularly dramatic, with capital and labour increasing by 35 per cent and 30 per cent, respectively[7].

Parikh et al. project a mixed impact on developing countries following liberalization in agriculture by the OECD countries. Higher agricultural prices generally cause additional resources to remain in the farm sector. This is most significant for Argentina, where the projected amount of agricultural labour in the year 2000 is 15 per cent higher as a result of this experiment. Similar figures for Nigeria and Mexico are 5 per cent and 6 per cent, with other developing countries experiencing less of a shift. In the case of Nigeria, this increased investment has a sufficiently large impact on agricultural output to eventually offset the effect of higher priced imports. However, in most of those developing countries which are net importers of food, higher prices translate into IIASA projections of lower real incomes and more hungry people.

Based on the multicommodity, partial equilibrium results discussed here, one would expect the opposite to apply in the case of net exporters of food. However, Brazil, Mexico and Turkey all experience declines in real income under the IIASA projections. This counterintuitive result is explained by the authors (p. 127) who argue that the observed marginal productivity of labour is much higher in the non-agricultural than in the farm sector in these economies. This means that any policy which forces labour out of agriculture will tend to improve these countries' real

GDP, as projected by this model. Thus, when Brazil liberalizes its agricultural policies and agricultural producer prices rise by 20 per cent (p. 189), GDP falls. Is this a reasonable result? It certainly deserves close scrutiny, since it flies in the face of most contemporary analyses of agriculture as a potential engine of economic development.

First of all, one must ask why the marginal value product (MVP) of labour (measured at domestic prices) might differ between the two sectors. There may be several reasons for this, including:

a) Labour quality differences;

b) Differences in the quality and cost of living;

c) Urban wage rigidities with coexistent unemployment; and

d) Disequilibrium in the allocation of labour between the two sectors.

Parikh *et al.*, assume that (d) applies, so that the wage gap narrows over time in their long-run simulations. Since they do not permit unemployment in their model, everyone who leaves agriculture is presumed to find productive employment in the non-farm sector. However, it is hard to envision such wage disparities persisting, over two decades, if these higher paying jobs were really available to rural-urban migrants.

A more satisfactory labour market specification might have individuals making their migration decision based on the ratio of expected returns in the two sectors, whereby the urban wage would take into account the probability of being unemployed (Harris and Todaro; Clarete and Whalley). It would also need to be skill-level adjusted and deflated for the higher urban cost of living. All of these factors (a-c) help explain why one might observe aggregate MVP differentials between the rural and urban sectors. Furthermore, once accounted for, they could result in a model in which adjusted MVPs were equated in both sectors. In this case, the movement of resources from farm to non-farm sectors does not result in marginal welfare losses. On the contrary, once the resource-pull effects of high non-agricultural protection levels are accounted for, the adjusted agricultural MVP of labour at world prices may exceed its counterpart in industry (Loo and Tower). These possibilities will be explored in detail later.

Disaggregating the Non-agricultural Sector

In an attempt to evaluate the impact of the Common Agricultural Policy (CAP) on the world economy, Burniaux and Waelbroeck (1989) implement a model with 13 agricultural products and four non-agricultural commodities (fertilizer, capital goods, other manufactures, energy and services). Nicknamed "RUNS", it breaks up each regional economy into two sectors: rural (i.e. agricultural) and urban (i.e. everything else). As in the IIASA model, econometric price transmission equations play an important role in determining domestic price policies — only now domestic farm prices respond to changes in urban prices as well as world farm product prices. The authors argue that this captures the role which income parity considerations play in determining farm policies. The authors also introduce explicit real wage rigidities in the urban sector, which in turn gives rise to urban unemployment.

Liberalization of the CAP in the RUNS model has two important effects. First, agricultural output in Europe falls, causing sizable increases in the world price of all food products. Secondly, the combined effect of lower European domestic food prices and increased food imports into Europe causes an expansion in manufacturing output and exports, and the world price of these products falls. The impact on rural populations in the developing countries is clearly positive, with higher farm output prices and possibly lower input prices leading to increased incomes. However, the urban sectors are hurt on two counts: first by higher wage costs and secondly by lower world prices for competing imports. Only in the case of Latin

America do the authors project that the increase in rural demand for domestic output would be sufficient to offset these effects and increase urban value added.

Both the RUNS model and the IIASA model rely heavily on reduced form representations of policies as price transmission equations. When combined with sluggish adjustment in the factor markets, it is rather difficult to sort out the net "resource pull" effect of existing public policies on the marginal value product of resources at world prices. In the next section this issue, and the resulting implications for developing country incomes when the farm/non-farm terms of trade change, will be investigated. To keep things simple, it will be done in a one-country framework.

SINGLE REGION, GENERAL EQUILIBRIUM ANALYSIS

Taking the world price effects of industrial market economy agricultural policy liberalization as given, we may consider the economy-wide impact of this price shock in greater detail. This is the general equilibrium analogue to the second stage of the Valdés and Zietz (1980) analysis, whereby the implications of projected world price increases for agricultural supply and demand are examined on a country-by-country basis. However, now the constraints imposed by a finite resource base and balance of payments equilibrium will play a role. This is the framework adopted by Loo and Tower who set about to demonstrate what kinds of gains are possible in a general equilibrium environment, once the structure of pre-existing policies are taken into account. In a way this work may be viewed as an attempt to quantify many of the arguments in favour of agricultural liberalization in the 1986 *World Development Report*. They focus on three particular mechanisms which include:

a) Terms of trade effects;

b) Public sector financing effects; and

c) Resource allocation effects.

Terms of Trade Effects

The terms of trade effects in Loo and Tower's model are measured as the change in foreign exchange earnings, evaluated at initial net export levels. Thus countries which are net exporters of agricultural products will, by definition, experience a terms of trade gain. These gains are available, regardless of whether or not the country in question chooses to transmit the price shock to the domestic economy. The country's surplus agricultural resources have simply become more valuable at world prices. Since five of the six groups of developing countries under consideration in the Loo and Tower paper are net exporters of farm and food products, the aggregate terms of trade effect is positive. It amounts to 16 per cent of their $26 billion total real income gain for developing countries, or approximately $3.2 billion at estimated 1985 prices.

Government Financing Effects

The second source of developing country gains enumerated in the Loo and Tower study are those related to the excise tax which is used to meet whatever public sector budget requirements are left unmet after trade and production taxes have been collected. They vary this tax rate in order to hold public sector spending constant. When world agricultural prices increase and the value of exports and imports increase, so too do tariff revenues. Thus the excise tax rate may be reduced, so that real income gains follow from increased consumption of the taxed products.

Excise tax effects account for about a third of their estimated $26 billion gain in aggregate real income to developing countries as a result of agricultural trade liberalization.

Gains from Resource Reallocation

The final, and most important, source of gain to the developing countries in the Loo and Tower analysis is that which arises from the reallocation of resources from a positively to a negatively protected sector. Postulated effective rates of protection (ERPs) for export agriculture range from –5 per cent (India) to –40 per cent in the poorest countries. (Except for these poorest countries, the ERP for domestic agriculture is set equal to zero.) By contrast, the assumed ERP for domestic industry ranges from 25 per cent in the upper middle income countries to 100 per cent in the poorest countries. (Export industries have an ERP of zero, except in the cases of India and the oil exporter aggregate.)

By reallocating domestic resources from a sector in which less than a dollar's worth of resources at domestic prices is required to earn more than a dollar's worth of foreign exchange, to a sector where the opposite is true, sizable gains are possible. These resource allocation gains may be illustrated with the help of Figure 1.2[8]. The total resource (labour) endowment in the economy is measured along the horizontal axis, and equals $\overline{L}$. Its allocation between agriculture (L_A) and industry (L_I) is determined by equating the after tax wage rate at domestic prices. This amounts to finding the intersection of $A0$ and $I0'$, which occurs at L_0. Furthermore, as a result of taxing agricultural exports and protecting import competing industry, agriculture exhibits a higher marginal value product (MVP) at world prices ($A*0$) while industry exhibits a lower one ($I*0'$).

In the initial equilibrium position, there is a deadweight loss equal to the area between $I*0$ and $A*0$. This "Harberger triangle" is shaded using vertical lines (DWL) and indicates lost real income resulting from the excessive allocation of resources to industry. Since Loo and Tower cast the developing countries as passive actors in the agricultural trade liberalization exercise, these same basic intersectoral distortions remain in place throughout their analysis.

The increase in world agricultural prices is introduced into Figure 1.2 as an upward shift in $A*0'$ to $A*'0'$. If the particular developing country in question either:

a) Failed to transmit this price signal to their domestic markets, or

b) Failed to reallocate labour in response to the higher MVP in agriculture, then there would be no resource allocation gains.

The only benefits would be due to the terms of trade improvement (provided this developing country is a net exporter of agricultural products), as well as any associated public sector financing effects.

Loo and Tower assume that the price increase is indeed fully transmitted to the domestic economy, resulting in an equiproportional upward shift in $A0'$. For ease of illustration here it has been assumed that the new intercept, A', coincides with $A*$. Thus the new MVP at domestic prices is equal to the previous MVP at world prices. This induces a reallocation of labour in favour of agriculture. The new equilibrium, at which point the MVP of labour at domestic prices is equated in both sectors, is given by L_0'.

Of course the optimal labour allocation, which is determined by equating MVPs at world prices, also shifts as a result of the price shock from $L*$ to $L*'$ and so a new "Harberger triangle" is created. It can be seen that if the labour allocation had remained at L_0, the new cost of domestic distortions would be very large indeed. However, by adjusting to L_0', the domestic economy is able to realise resource reallocation gains equal to the horizontally shaded trapezoid (RAG). This effect accounts for 50 per cent of Loo and Tower's estimated real income increase for the developing countries, as a result of industrial market economy liberalization in agriculture. Furthermore, due to the postulated pattern of protection, these gains arise in each of the six groups of developing countries. Because the resource reallocation gains dominate the terms of trade effects, all developing country groups are projected to gain, regardless of their net trade position in agriculture.

Comparison with the IIASA Results

Before discussing the limitations of the Loo and Tower analysis, it is useful to contrast their portrayal of resource allocation gains with those implicit in the IIASA model for several key countries. This is done in Figure 1.3, which preserves the previous MVP of agriculture at world prices but suppresses the MVP at domestic prices.

(Since the labour market in IIASA does not require the domestic price MVPs to be equated between sectors, these lines no longer serve a purpose.) Also, the world price MVP of labour in industry has been vastly increased to reflect the assertion that labour is more productive in industry than in agriculture, in the initial equilibrium position depicted by L_0 (Parikh *et al.*, pp. 126-27). Thus the optimal allocation of labour for this group of developing countries, according to the IIASA model, is given by L^*. Hence the country has too much of its resources in agriculture.

When world agricultural prices increase, shifting A^*0' to $A^{*'}0'$, the IIASA model's factor market adjustment equations predict a larger agricultural labour force (L'_0) in the long term. However, given the position of L^*, rather than moving the economy towards the optimal allocation of labour, the opposite is now occurring. Thus it is conceivable that the deadweight loss actually increases ($DWL'>DWL$). In fact, this seems to be what happens in the IIASA model for Brazil, Mexico and Turkey. In these countries $DWL'-DWL$ exceeds the terms of trade gains, leaving them *worse off* as a result of liberalization by the OECD countries in agriculture.

As noted above, the problem with the IIASA model is that the observed marginal productivity of labour in industry only relates to those factors which are actually employed. In equilibrium, this will always be higher than the MVP of labour in the rural sector, as long as there is a higher probability of unemployment in the urban sector. This is because potential migrants presumably discount the urban wage rates to account for the fact that they are by no means assured of a job.

Further Discussion and Evaluation of Loo and Tower

In evaluating the Loo and Tower results, several potential criticisms must be considered. First of all, how realistic is it to have labour moving *back* into agriculture? Isn't the trend worldwide one of resource movements out of agriculture? In response to this, it is important to bear in mind the *comparative static* nature of this experiment. Everything else is held constant, including the rate of labour migration attributable to other factors such as technical change and disparities in public services. Thus what we are really talking about is a slowing down of the underlying pattern of rural-urban migration, not a reversal of this phenomenon.

A second potential criticism has to do with the fact that the postulated world price changes are based on a partial equilibrium view of the world. As agricultural policies in the IMEs are liberalized, resources move out of farming into other uses. A symmetric, general equilibrium treatment of the IMEs would necessarily include a *decline* in the relative price of industrial products. As noted above, this is in fact what is predicted by the RUNS model.

When the relative price of industrial products falls at the same time as agricultural prices rise, there is an additional terms of trade improvement for the net agricultural exporting developing country. This represents the decline in the cost of imports required to satisfy domestic demand. Once again, there is an accompanying resource allocation effect which reflects the further movement of resources into the higher marginal value product use.

There is yet another general equilibrium effect which is ignored in Loo and Tower's one country analysis. This is the income gain in the developed economies as a result of an improved allocation of resources between agricultural and non-agricultural sectors. These gains would be considerably larger than the developing country income gains, since these countries will actually be removing distortions. Income growth in the IMEs translates into increased demand for imports and so this may be seen as an additional source of gains to developing countries from IME liberalization in agriculture.

Of course the Loo and Tower analysis is based on the assumption of full employment. How would their findings be affected by the existence of a pool of surplus labour? This depends on the source of unemployment in the economy. Consider, for example, a Harris-Todaro type of specification in which urban wage rigidities result in an unemployment equilibrium where the rural wage is equated to the urban wage, deflated by the probability of unemployment. In this case a rise in the agricultural MVP at domestic prices results in a decrease in the equilibrium level of urban unemployment. In terms of Figure 1.2, this translates into a lengthening of the horizontal axis. Furthermore, since the increased agricultural labour force does not come at the expense of the industrial sector, the area RAG now extends down to the horizontal axis. As a consequence, the resource allocation gains in such a model would be even larger than those estimated by Loo and Tower.

A final potential criticism of the Loo and Tower results stems from the fact that their postulated effective rates of protection are largely "best guesses", which probably vary considerably across countries within each of the six aggregate regions. One source of additional information on agricultural protection is provided in a recent comparative study of agricultural price policies in developing countries (Krueger, Schiff and Valdés). They report nominal protection rates (NPRs) for a group of sixteen export crops in an equal number of countries. Their "direct" NPRs — measured as a domestic/world price wedge — ranged from +34 per cent to –31 per cent and averaged –11 per cent over the 1980-84 period[9].

If there were either (a) no purchased inputs in agriculture, or (b) domestic/world variable input price ratios of the same proportion, then these direct NPRs would also equal the effective rates of protection (ERPs), which is the measure reported by Loo and Tower. While it is true that many developing countries subsidise agricultural inputs, such as credit and fertilizer, Krueger et al. note that "initial inspection suggests that most input subsidies were inframarginal" (p. 258). Thus it is likely that average effective rate of protection for the sample of export crops discussed by Krueger et al. is more negative than the average NPR reported above.

Krueger et al. also report NPRs for 16 import competing products from the same group of countries, over the 1980-84 period. These rates of protection ranged from +118 per cent to –21 per cent and averaged +21 per cent. The presence of significant *positive* protection for import competing agriculture and the great diversity in these NPRs suggests the need for further regional disaggregation and systematic analysis of the role of assumed ERPs in generating resource allocation gains for the developing countries following IME liberalization in agriculture.

CONCLUDING COMMENTS

In his survey of recent studies of agricultural trade liberalization, Bruce Gardner ends on a rather pessimistic note. He finds little consistency in the estimated world price effects of IME liberalization across different studies. Furthermore, he argues that in the specific case of rice, simulation results made absolutely no contribution towards understanding what happened immediately following implementation of the 1985 US Farm Bill. My assessment of what is basically the same group of studies, is more optimistic. Given their rather different structures and assumptions, the relative uniformity of world price effects *once one has controlled for the assumed level of support* (Magiera and Herlihy) is striking. That is, due to the dramatic variation in measured farm subsidies over the decade of the 1980s, the base year chosen seems to explain most of the differences across studies (Roningen and Dixit). In light of this fact, more attention needs to be paid to developing a common set of alternative policy scenarios for modellers to draw upon in their diverse analyses.

Where large discrepancies in projected world price effects persist, this is often due to the way policies are modelled. As has been pointed out by a number of authors, many farm sector interventions cannot be adequately represented with *ad valorem* equivalent subsidies and taxes (Gardner, 1989; Kilkenny and Robinson; and Whalley and Wigle in this volume). This is particularly true when liberalization is only partial, and programmes involve multiple interventions, e.g. simultaneous tariffs and quotas (Clarete and Whalley), or voluntary participation, e.g. the US grains programmes (Rutherford, Whalley and Wigle). In these cases explicit modelling of public policies should yield a high payoff, both in terms of model accuracy, and in the ability to address realistic policy liberalization measures. The latter will invariably boil down to "tinkering" with existing programmes.

However, before we devote too much effort to refining model projections of commodity price changes, much more attention must be devoted to factor market adjustments. This will entail "getting behind" the reduced form supply equations which predominate in the agricultural trade literature. Two models may yield similar commodity price projections, while predicting (explicitly or implicitly) vastly different things in the factor markets. Alternatively, two models may yield different world commodity price projections, yet differ little in their factor market implications. The latter is likely the case for alternative models of the US grains programmes where, depending on the relative strength of the acreage reduction and incentive price effects, output may go up or down. Yet the factor market implications of simultaneously releasing idled acreage and lowering target prices are mutually reinforcing. Both serve to lower land rents and encourage a reduction in the use of variable inputs.

The primary motivation for focussing on factor market adjustment is that this is what lies at the heart of the IME farm problem (Johnson). As long as excess resources are retained in agriculture, there will be a tendency for them to earn less than a competitive rate of return. This in turn gives rise to pressure for more government subsidies, which contribute to a further reluctance to adjust out of agriculture. Yet it is only by facilitating such adjustment that long-run gains, offered by an improved allocation of the world's resources between the farm and non-farm economies, can be realised.

Figure 1.1. **IMPLICATIONS OF A REDUCTION IN THE SUPPORT PRICE FOR GRAINS**

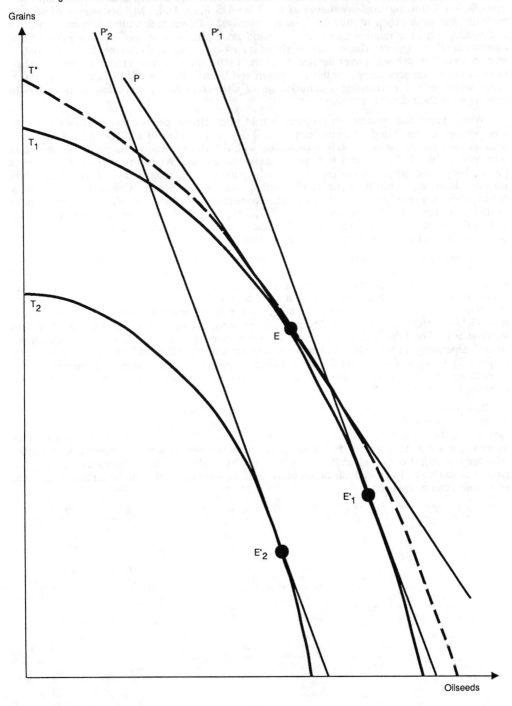

Figure 1. 2. **RESOURCE REALLOCATION GAINS IN THE LOO AND TOWER MODEL**

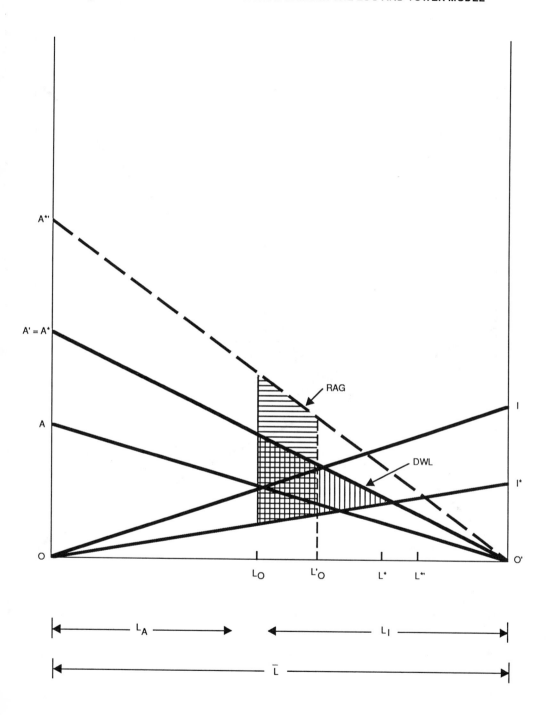

Figure 1. 3. **DEADWEIGHT LOSS IN THE IIASA MODEL**

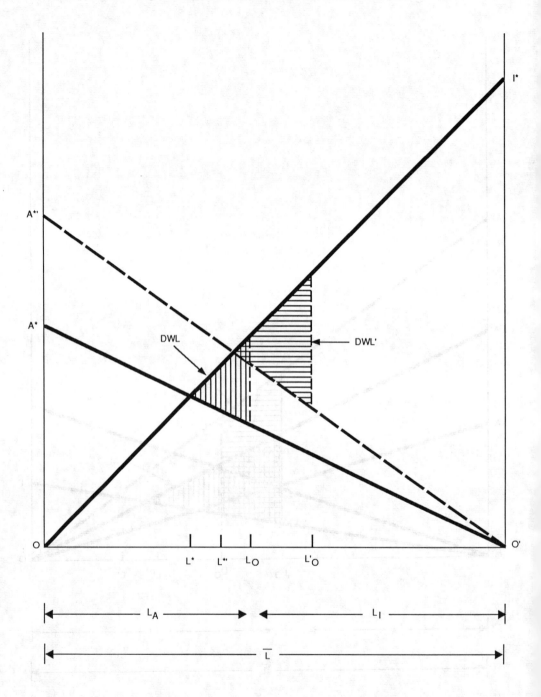

Table 1.1

SHORT AND LONG RUN REDUCED FORM SUPPLY ELASTICITIES FOR THE EC

Commodity	Elasticity of supply with respect to price of:		
	Wheat	Coarse grains	Ratio[1]
Wheat			
Short run	0.30	-0.15	-2.0
Long run	0.90	-0.45	-2.0
Coarse grains			
Short run	-0.15	0.40	-2.67
Long run	-0.34	0.91	-2.67

1.   This is the ratio of own- to cross-price elasticities.

Source : Tyers (1985), Appendix Table A.3.

NOTES AND REFERENCES

1. The author would like to thank Phil Abbott, Barry Krissoff, Tom Loo and Ed Tower for their comments on portions of an earlier draft of this paper.

2. Despite modest reductions in tariffs following the Tokyo Round, tariff escalation persists, and in some cases has worsened (Cable, pp. 172-174). Also, substantial non-tariff barriers remain (World Bank, 1986, p. 126).

3. In this regard, the *1986 World Development Report* cites the case of Sweden in 1969-70 where the ERP for soybean oil was as high as 1 480 per cent!

4. Their results may overstate the cost of sugar policies to the developing countries as a group, since quota rents are not accounted for.

5. For a further discussion of these issues, see Hertel (1987a).

6. One exception is SWOPSIM's treatment of the dairy sector. Since butter and dairy powder are joint products, these outputs are treated as complementary. But this is not evidence of an expansion effect, since the outputs are "net" complements in this case.

7. This massive increase results from the elimination of production quotas (dairy production increases by 108 per cent). Given evidence of significant, unexploited scale economies in Canadian dairy production (Moschini), it is not at all clear that such large increases in labour and capital would be required in the absence of production quotas.

8. This basic figure is taken from the paper by Loo and Tower. It has been simplified here, for purposes of exposition.

9. It should be noted that Krueger, Schiff and Valdés *do find* substantial evidence of *indirect* negative protection for all agricultural commodities as a result of systematic exchange rate overvaluation. This issue is not addressed by Tower and Loo, who take the initial policy configuration in the LDCs as given. By considering the effect of (a) eliminating import tariffs and export taxes, and (b) eliminating exchange control regimes and import licensing mechanisms which sustain an overvalued exchange rate, Krueger *et al.* derive a new, "equilibrium" exchange rate. Using this to link domestic and international prices, they calculate indirect protection rates which average about −30 per cent. This dominates the direct effects reported above. However, it penalises all tradable sectors, not just agriculture.

BIBLIOGRAPHY

ANDERSON, K. and R. TYERS, "Liberalizing OECD Agricultural Policies in the Uruguay Round: Effects on Trade and Welfare", *Journal of Agricultural Economics,* 39, 1988.

BALL, V.E., "Modeling Supply Response in a Multiproduct Framework", *American Journal of Agricultural Economics,* 70(4), 1988.

BURNIAUX, J.M. and J. WAELBROECK, "The Common Agricultural Policy of the European Community and the World Economy: A General Equilibrium Analysis", in the IIASA Conference Proceedings, 1989.

CLARETE, R. and J. WHALLEY, "Interactions Between Trade Policies and Domestic Distortions in a Small Open Developing Country", *Journal of International Economics,* 24, 1988.

GARDNER, B., "Agricultural Protection in Industrial Countries", paper presented at the conference, Global Protectionism: Is the U.S. Playing on a Level Playing Field?, Lehigh University, May 22-23, 1989.

GARDNER, B., "Some Recent Studies of Agricultural Trade Liberalization", invited paper, XX International Conference of the IAAE, Buenos Aires, Argentina, August 24-31, 1988.

GOLUB, S.S. and J.M. FINGER, "The Processing of Primary Commodities: Effects of Developed-Country Tariff Escalation and Developing-Country Export Taxes", *Journal of Political Economy,* 87(3), 1979.

HARRIS, T. and M. TODARO, "Migration, Unemployment and Development: A Two Sector Analysis", *American Economic Review,* 60, 1970.

HERTEL, T.W., "Estimating Substitution and Expansion Effects: Comment", *American Journal of Agricultural Economics,* 69(1), 1987a.

HERTEL, T.W., "Inferring Long-Run Elasticities from a Short-Run Quadratic Profit Function", *Canadian Journal of Agricultural Economics,* 35, 1987b.

HORRIDGE, M. and D. PEARCE, "Modeling the Effects on Australia of Interventions in World Agricultural Trade", IMPACT Preliminary Working Paper No. OP-65, University of Melbourne, 1988.

JOHNSON, D.G., "Excess Capacity: The Evil of Modern Agricultural Policy", paper presented at the annual meetings of the AAEA, East Lansing, Michigan, 1987.

KILKENNY, M. and S. ROBINSON, "Modeling the Removal of Production Incentive Distortions in the U.S. Agricultural Sector", invited paper, XX International Conference of the IIAE, Buenos Aires, Argentina, August 24-31, 1988.

KRISSOFF, B., J. SULLIVAN and J. WAINIO, "Opening Agricultural Markets: Trade and Welfare Implications for Developing Countries", mimeo, ERS/USDA, 1989.

KRUEGER, A.O., M. SCHIFF and A. VALDÉS, "Agricultural Incentives in Developing Countries: Measuring the Effect of Sectoral and Economywide Policies", *World Bank Economic Review,* 2(3), 1988.

LOO, T. and E. TOWER, "Agricultural Protectionism and the Less Developed Countries", in *Macroeconomic Consequences of Farm Support Policies,* A.B. Stoeckel, D. Vincent, and S. Cuthbertson (eds.), Durham, North Carolina: Duke University Press, 1988.

MAGIERA, S.L., and M.T. HERLIHY, "A Technical Comparison of Trade Liberalization Model Results", draft manuscript, Economic Research Service, US Department of Agriculture, Washington, DC, 1988.

MOSCHINI, G., "The Cost Structure of Ontario Dairy Farms: A Microeconometric Analysis", *Canadian Journal of Agricultural Economics*, 36, 1988.

ORGANISATION FOR ECONOMIC CO-OPERATION AND DEVELOPMENT (OECD), *National Policies and Agricultural Trade*, Paris, 1987.

PARIKH, K.S., G. FISCHER, K. FROHBERG, and O. GULBRANDSEN, *Towards Free Trade in Agriculture*, Laxenburg, Austria: Martinus Nijhoff Publishers, 1988.

RONINGEN, V.O. and P.M. DIXIT, *Economic Implications of Agricultural Policy Reform in Industrial Market Economies*, USDA Staff Report No. AGES 89-36, Washington, DC, 1989.

RUTHERFORD, T.F., J. WHALLEY, and R.M. WIGLE, "Capitalization, Conditionality, and Dilution: Land Prices and the U.S. Wheat Program", unpublished manuscript, CSIER, University of Western Ontario, 1989.

SAKAI, Y., "Substitution and Expansion Effects in Production Theory: The Case of Joint Production", *Journal of Economic Theory*, 9, 1974.

TYERS, R., "International Impacts of Protection: Model Structure and Results for EC Agricultural Policy", *Journal of Policy Modeling*, 7(2), 1985.

TYERS, R. and K. ANDERSON, "Distortions in World Food Markets: A Quantitative Assessment", background paper for the *World Development Report, Washington, D.C.: The World Bank*, 1986.

VALDÉS, A. and J. ZIETZ, *Agricultural Protection in OECD Countries: Its Costs to Less-Developed Countries*, research report 21, Washington, DC: IFPRI, 1980.

WHALLEY, J. and R. WIGLE, "Endogenous Participation in Agricultural Support Programs and Ad Valorem Equivalent Modeling", unpublished manuscript, CSIER, University of Western Ontario, 1989.

WORLD BANK, *World Development Report 1981*, Washington, DC, 1981.

WORLD BANK, *World Development Report 1986*, Washington, DC, 1986.

Part I

PARTIAL EQUILIBRIUM MODELS

Chapter 2

HOW DEVELOPING COUNTRIES COULD GAIN FROM AGRICULTURAL TRADE LIBERALIZATION IN THE URUGUAY ROUND

by

Kym Anderson and Rod Tyers

INTRODUCTION

There is a commonly held presumption that if markets for temperate food products were to be liberalized as a result of the Uruguay Round of multilateral trade negotiations, developing countries would be harmed. The basis for this view is that, as a group, developing countries are net importers of those food staples and so would be worse off with liberalized trade because food prices in international markets would be higher.

It is intended to show that for a number of reasons this is too restrictive a view of the effects of including agriculture in the Uruguay Round. In fact it is quite possible the majority of developing countries would be net beneficiaries of such a liberalization.

The first section of the paper uses standard economic analysis to demonstrate key steps in the conceptual argument leading to that opposite conclusion. It begins with the conventional, static, partial equilibrium view, adds distributional and risk considerations, and then raises further issues that add increasingly to the probability that developing countries as a group could gain from the inclusion of agriculture in the Uruguay Round. No one empirical model is available to illustrate all of the steps in the argument. However, the second section of the paper draws on results from a dynamic, stochastic, multicommodity, partial equilibrium model of world food markets to illustrate at least some of the points made in Section 2.1. These results show that even when attention is confined just to the markets for temperate food staples, it is plausible that virtually all developing countries could benefit from a global liberalization of those markets and that the vast majority of the world's poor would be better off. The third and final section points to areas where more complex quantitative models could contribute further to our empirical understanding, before drawing out some policy implications of the analysis.

CONCEPTUAL STEPS IN THE ARGUMENT

The Conventional View of Effects of Food Trade Liberalization by OECD Countries

Figure 2.1 depicts the conventional view of what would occur if the advanced industrial countries alone liberalized their protectionist policies towards food trade. Suppose that following the international price rise the domestic producer and consumer prices in a food-importing developing country rose from P_0 to P_1. (Throughout the P refers to the price of food relative to

41

the price of other tradables. For the moment assume there are no distortions in the developing country.) Then producer surplus would rise by area *abfg* while consumer surplus would fall by area *acdg*. The net loss to this economy therefore is seen as area *bcdf*.

However, it need not be the case that this developing country continues to be a net food importer. Suppose, for example, that the post-liberalization price is P_2 rather than P_1. In that case it is possible that the country's loss would be less than if the price rose only to P_1. The required condition is that area *fde* is less than area *eih*, and the net welfare loss in this case is area *bce* less area *eih*. It therefore follows that if the international price rose sufficiently, this country could even be a net beneficiary. If it rose to P_3, for example, the net gain would be area *ejk* less area *bce*.

Needless to say, an undistorted developing country which is a net food exporter at the pre-liberalization price gains unequivocally from liberalization. If P_2 and P_3 were the pre- and post-liberalization prices, for example, then the net gain to that exporting country would be area *hijk* if the price change is fully transmitted. (If none of the change was transmitted to the domestic market, the gain would be confined to the export tax revenue which is *hi* multiplied by the international price rise P_2P_3.)

Risk Considerations Associated with Stability of Markets

If OECD countries were to liberalize fully their food markets, this would mean reductions in the degrees to which they export their domestically generated market instability and insulate their domestic market from international price fluctuations. The net effect of several large countries liberalizing in this way would be a reduction in the degree of fluctuation in international food prices. Insofar as developing countries transmit those fluctuations to their own domestic markets, and insofar as their food producers and consumers are averse to risk, welfare in those countries would be enhanced by the reduction in food price instability that would follow from the reductions in protectionism and insulation in OECD countries.

Distributional Considerations within Developing Countries

To focus only on the net national welfare change obscures the important fact that there are large welfare transfers between groups within each developing country. Typically, the gain to producers and the loss to consumers, following a rise in international food prices that would result from agricultural trade liberalization in OECD countries, will be much greater than the net change in national welfare which, in the absence of distortions in the developing country, is simply the difference between these two. This is especially so if a developing country is and remains close to self-sufficiency in food products. Additionally, in most low-income countries the number of people who are net sellers of food is well above the number who are net buyers of food, and the former group is usually poorer on average than the latter group. Thus in terms of numbers of people affected and in terms of income inequalities, a food price rise might well be judged to be an improvement in social conditions.

Dynamic Effects through Induced Innovations

The above comparative static view ignores the dynamics of innovation. It is likely that the rate of induced technical change in a sector is positively related to the sector's expected mean level of profitability (Ruttan, 1982; Alston, Edwards and Freebarin, 1988). It is probably also negatively related to the expected variability of profits through time. Therefore the permanent reduction of protection which would lower domestic food price levels (and perhaps their stability) in industrial countries on the one hand, and the once and for always increase in the level and stability of food prices in developing countries on the other, following a liberalization of OECD agricultural policies, is likely to boost agricultural productivity growth in developing countries while slowing it in industrial countries. (This would be especially so if some of the gains to OECD countries from their trade liberalization were to be redistributed in the form of increased foreign aid to agricultural research programmes in developing countries.)

The welfare effects of this situation in a developing country are shown in Figure 2.2, where it is assumed that:

a) The rise in the average international price for food and the greater stability of that price level has induced a shift in the country's food supply curve, for example from S to S';

b) The net effect of the faster shift of food supply curves in developing countries as a group, the slower shift in the food supply curves of industrial countries, and the increased excess demand for food in industrial countries because of their food policy reform, is to raise the mean level of the international price of food; and

c) The increase in the international price is passed on to the domestic food market in the developing country.

In the case of a food-importing developing country faced with a rise in the price of food from P_0 to P_1, consumer welfare is still reduced by area $acdg$ in Figure 2.2, but producer welfare is increased not just by area $abfg$ but also by area mqf less the amortized cost of the research which generated the shift in the supply curve (assuming producers paid for that research). It is possible that the gain in producer welfare could outweigh the loss in consumer welfare in this dynamic case, *even if the country were to remain a net food importer.* This would be the case if area mqf minus the amortized cost of research exceeded area $bcdf$, which is more likely the larger the shift in the supply curve and the smaller the cost of the investment required to generate that shift, all other things being equal.

For the food-exporting developing country, dynamic considerations simply add further to their positive net benefit from the international food price rise.

To examine the trade and welfare effects for developing countries as a group vis-à-vis industrial countries, it is helpful to use Figure 2.3 which depicts the international market for food. In the absence of liberalization the excess supply curve for OECD or industrial countries is ES_I and the excess demand curve for developing countries is ED_D. (Centrally planned Europe is ignored to simplify the diagram.) With liberalization in the OECD countries, their excess supply curve is assumed to shift to ES_I' after full adjustment and normal technical change. As a result the international food price is P' rather than P. If this were the end of the story, developing countries as a group would lose in the case illustrated because, even though they have switched from being net importers to being net exporters of food, the welfare triangle ced is less than abc (c.f. the individual developing country effect of a shift from P_0 to P_2 in Figure 2.1). But what if, in the process of moving to a new long-run equilibrium following liberalization, technical change were to be faster in developing countries and slower in the OECD countries than assumed above? In that case there is a higher probability of developing countries being net gainers. For example, suppose the OECD countries' curve shifted not to ES_I' but to ES_I'' and the developing countries' curve shifted to ED_D'' in Figure 2.3 because of changes in the inducement to innovate or import superior technologies from abroad. Then the international price would be P'' (which could be higher or lower than P'). In this case if area fgh exceeded area abc by more than the amortized cost of extra agricultural research, developing countries would have gained.

Not mentioned to date is the effect of liberalization on national income levels and their growth rates, which in turn affect the demand for food. Since food products valued at the farmgate account for less than 5 per cent of national income and expenditure and have a low income elasticity of demand in the advanced industrial countries, this second round effect on the ES_I'' curve can be ignored. For developing countries it would not be insignificant, however.

43

Higher national incomes would ensure the ED_D'' curve was somewhat steeper and further to the right in Figure 2.3 (given that the income elasticity of demand for food is positive and the price elasticity of food demand declines as incomes rise in developing countries). But higher incomes also would affect the demand for other tradables and for non-tradable goods and services, a point which is taken up below.

What if Developing Countries also Liberalized their own Food Markets?

So far it has been assumed that developing countries do not distort their own food markets. To the extent that they in fact do, the economic gains to developing countries could be even greater if those distortions also were to be removed. In the case of foods grown in temperate zones, developing countries on average (across all countries and commodities) probably keep the domestic price level closer to the international price level than OECD countries but still above it at official exchange rates (Tyers and Anderson, 1986, and Table 2.1 below). Thus a liberalization of those markets as well would raise further the international price of temperate foods in aggregate. In addition, there would be the usual gains to each liberalizing country from removing differences in rates of assistance/taxation between the various food markets *within* its food sector.

Furthermore, if all developing countries reduced their market-insulating behaviour, the instability of international food prices would be reduced even more than if just OECD countries were to liberalize. While the latter may raise the extent of price fluctuations in the developing countries that currently have the most insulated food markets, it would reduce fluctuations in the somewhat more open, less insulated economies. Whether food consumers or producers in developing countries would be better or worse off depends on whether the change in the terms of trade more than or less than offsets the effect on domestic prices of eliminating the country's own food policy. The net change in national economic welfare also depends on whether prices in other sectors are distorted and whether the net distortion in the relative domestic price of food is increased or decreased, a point to which we now turn.

What if Developing Countries Liberalized their Industrial and Foreign Exchange Markets as Well?

The World Bank/IFPRI study led by Krueger, Schiff and Valdés (1988) shows clearly that agricultural production is effectively taxed and food consumption subsidised in developing countries not so much directly but rather in indirect ways, particularly via manufacturing protection policies and overvalued official exchange rates. According to the Krueger *et al.* estimates, these indirect ways of lowering the relative price of food much more than offset the positive effect on the food sector of export taxation of non-food primary products. Reducing the latter distortions would give a tremendous boost to farmers in developing countries, and alone would be sufficient to turn many food-importing poor countries into food exporters. In the absence of these policy distortions in non-food sectors such developing countries (i.e. those with a natural comparative advantage in food production) would gain unequivocally from the international price change that would accompany agricultural trade liberalization by OECD countries. However, in the presence of price distortions in non-agricultural sectors they may not gain.

This point is illustrated easiest with the help of the general equilibrium diagram in Figure 2.4. The slope of line PC represents the pre-liberalization international price of other tradables relative to food. If the developing economy is distorted by, for example, trade restrictions which alter its domestic price ratio to the slope of the tangent at P', then instead of producing at P and consuming at C, as it would under free trade, this country produces at P' and consumes at C'. This means instead of *exporting* the quantity PE of food and importing EC other tradables, the economy *imports* $C'E'$ food and exports $E'P'$ other tradables. And its overall welfare is lower than it would be in the absence of its own trade restrictions, as indicated by the indifference curve through C' being below that through C. In this situation, an increase in the relative price of food internationally, from the slope of lines PC or $P'C'$ to the slope of line $P'C^0$ (or $P''C''$), decreases welfare for this developing country if its government chooses to maintain the original domestic price ratio. This is shown by the move in the consumption bundle to C^0, which is on a lower indifference curve than is C'. Had this economy not used trade restrictions, on the other hand, its welfare would have *increased*, while production would have shifted from P to P'' and consumption from C to C'', the latter representing a higher level of national welfare than at C. That is, a trade-restricting developing economy of the sort depicted in Figure 2.4 would be worse off as a result of agricultural trade liberalization by the OECD countries simply *because of its own policy choice*; a reform of its own policies would ensure it benefitted in a comparative static sense from liberalization of food policies in industrial economies.

Three caveats are worth noting at this point. The first is that if some of the increase in the relative price of food internationally is transmitted to the domestic market, and/or domestic price support for other tradables is lowered, then it is possible for this country to gain from that relative price change, *even if the developing country remains an importer of food*. In terms of Figure 2.4, all that is required is for P' to move sufficiently towards P, as a result of the higher relative price of food domestically, such that the new consumption point to the left of the new production point along a ray parallel to $P'C^0$ is on a community indifference curve further from the origin (but still within the production possibility curve) than the curve through C'. As Tyers and Falvey (1989) have pointed out in a somewhat different context, an important determinant of whether a distorting country gains from a change in its terms of trade is the extent to which that country insulates its domestic market from that relative price change in the international marketplace.

The second caveat is a corollary to the first: *even if the country would be a net food importer under free trade* and has anti-food sector policies in place, it is possible to benefit from liberalization by OECD countries which worsens its terms of trade, if enough of the increase in the relative price of food internationally is transmitted to its domestic market and/or domestic price support for other sectors is lowered enough. This is a specific example of one of Bhagwati's (1971) general points that apparently paradoxical outcomes are possible in a distortion-ridden economy.

Thirdly, if the developing country's own policy bias against the food sector is not sufficient to have shifted it from being a food exporter to a food importer, then that country would benefit from an increase in the relative price of food internationally. This is the case even if none of that increase is transmitted to the domestic market or if there is no reduction in price support for other tradable sectors.

Another useful way to illustrate the general equilibrium gains on the production side of the developing economy from an increase in the international price of food is with the help of the beaker diagram in Figure 2.5. If we assume both the food sector and the aggregate of other sectors each employ a specific factor plus intersectorally mobile labour, then the value of marginal product of labour curve in the food sector with origin O_F can have superimposed on it the mirror image of a similar curve for all non-food sectors with origin O_{NF} positioned such that the length of the horizontal axis represents the economy's total labour supply. If VMP_F and VMP_{NF} are the two sectors' labour demand curves at domestic prices, then at full employment $O_F L$ units of labour will be employed in the food sector and $L O_{NF}$ in non-food production. Should the international price of food rise, the VMP_F curve shifts to VMP_F', (and the more so the more the price rise induces farm productivity growth), which encourages labour to move from non-food to food production. In the absence of distortions the welfare gain on the production side is area *abcd* — which may be more or less than the loss to food consumers from the higher price, depending on whether the country is a net exporter or importer of food.

However, suppose established non-food policies have raised the domestic price of non-food above the international price such that the social value of marginal product of labour curve for the non-food sector is only VMP^*_{NF}. In that case the gain to society on the production side includes not just area *abcd* but also area *befc*, the latter being the difference between the private and social values of the LL' units of labour in the non-food sector. If these non-food policies also were to be liberalized, an additional $L'L^*$ units of labour would transfer to food production and there would be a further welfare gain, area *cfg*. It is therefore possible that a food-importing country, whose food consumers lose more from the higher food price than food producers gain (*viz.* area *abcd*), may nonetheless be better off because area *befc* with or without area *cfg* exceeds the difference between the food consumers' loss and the food producers' gain[1]. These areas, incidentally, play an important role in the general equilibrium results reported in Loo and Tower (1989).

Liberalizing Trade in Tropical Agricultural Products

If OECD countries also liberalized their import restrictions on tropical agricultural and forest products (particularly processed products), it is even more likely that food-importing developing countries would be net beneficiaries. This is because many of them are net exporters of tropical agricultural products. In terms of Figure 2.1, if P_2 was the pre-liberalization price of tropical farm products and P_3 the post-liberalization price, the developing country would gain area *hijk* from the international price rise.

Such a liberalization on the part of OECD countries also might encourage developing countries to reduce their discrimination against these products. Currently, many tropical countries tax their exports of these products not only directly but also indirectly by way of the industrial protection and exchange rate overvaluation policies mentioned in the previous section. Furthermore, such developing and OECD country tropical product reforms would increase the prospects of developing countries gaining from agricultural trade liberalization by OECD countries under the Uruguay Round. The comparative static argument can be seen from Figure 2.4 simply by changing the title of the vertical axis to "all agricultural and forest products".

What if Non-agricultural Trade also is Liberalized in the OECD Countries?

It needs to be kept in mind that agricultural trade reform is not being considered in isolation. Manufacturing and service sector trade negotiations are also part of the Uruguay Round, including trade in labour-intensive manufactures and processed primary products. Thus even the developing countries with the greatest comparative disadvantage in food production might consider supporting agricultural trade liberalization in the Uruguay Round in return for concessions in the form of, for example, lower barriers in OECD countries to imports of processed tropical products or light manufactures from developing countries. With the current Multifibre Arrangement expiring in July 1991, the time is ripe for seeking improved market access for textiles and clothing in particular. Should that eventuate, it would also have the feedback effects of expanding the demand for natural fibres which would in turn help farmers in numerous developing countries, including Bangladesh (jute), Egypt (cotton) and Southern Cone countries (wool).

If trade is liberalized globally in non-agricultural products as well as in farm products, then instead of the change in the international terms of trade moving from the slope of line *PC* to that of *P"C"* as in Figure 2.4 for trade liberalization only in food, it would be less or may even be in the opposite direction. Computable general equilibrium models of the world economy as a whole are needed to estimate the possible direction and extent of such changes, early prototypes of which have been developed by John Whalley and his colleagues and by Burniaux and Waelbroeck (1985). Ideally they would be models with growth included endogenously so that the growth-stimulating impacts of liberalization are captured (Helpman, 1988). And they would of course also include non-tradable sectors to capture endogenously the indirect effects of the above adjustments on the real exchange rate, to which we now turn by way of a conclusion to this section.

Indirect Effects through Adjustments in the Market for Non-tradables

The possibility of a developing country gaining from agricultural trade liberalization by the OECD countries is amended further when one considers the indirect effects of such liberalization on the market for non-tradables in that country.

Consider Figure 2.2 again, which shows the partial equilibrium effect of an innovation induced by an international price-raising liberalization affecting food products. The liberalization by OECD countries benefits food producers in this developing country. The spending of that income growth, however, will shift to the right the income-compensated demand curves not only for food (to D' in Figure 2.6 which reproduces Figure 2.2) but also for other tradables and for non-tradable goods and services (assuming they are substitutes for food in final consumption, apart from the possibility they are inputs into food production). In a slightly different context this has been labelled the "spending effect" of the boom in the agricultural sector (Corden, 1984). These rightward shifts in the demand curves for non-food products are additional to the shifts due to the rise in the price of food. The sum of these two changes is represented by the shift from D to D' in Figure 2.7 for non-tradables and in Figure 2.8 for non-food tradables.

A second point to note from Figure 2.6 is that the quantity of mobile resources used in the production of food is likely to have expanded with output increasing from Q to Q'. This increased demand for mobile resources bids up their price (see the earlier Figure 2.5) and thereby raises the supply curve in other sectors, as does the diversion of investable resources to agricultural research. This "resource-movement effect", to use Corden's (1984) term, is represented by the shift from S to S' in Figure 2.7 for non-tradables and in Figure 2.8 for non-food tradables.

Since non-tradables by definition must be produced domestically, such changes require the price of non-tradables (relative to the price of non-food tradables) to rise from P_n to P'_n in Figure 2.7. The quantity of non-tradables may increase or decrease depending on the relative extent of the supply and demand curve changes.

These changes in the market for non-tradables have two effects on tradables markets. The net incomes of producers of non-tradables will increase from area *abc* to area *ade*, which shifts rightward the demand curves for food and other tradables (as well as for non-tradables) — a shift that is additional to the rightward shift in those demand curves due to the increase in the price of non-tradables insofar as they are substitutes for tradables. And if there is a bidding up of the price of mobile resources to attract them into non-tradables production, this raises costs of producing tradables and thereby shifts upward the supply curves for food and for other tradables. These shifts are represented in Figures 2.6 and 2.8 by the shift from D' to D'' and from S' to S''. The quantity of food produced domestically is thus Q'' which is more than before the liberalization (Q), while the quantity of food consumed is now C'' which may be more or less than the original consumption level C. Net imports of food must necessarily be less, however, because the value of non-food exports with which to pay for food imports has shrunk: export revenue is now P_T multiplied by $C''_T Q''_T$ instead of P_T multiplied by $C_T Q_T$ (see Figure 2.8), and since the price of food imports has risen the volume of food imports must shrink to an even smaller proportion than $C''_T Q''_T / C_T Q_T$ of QC for the trade balance to be restored. That is, net imports of food are even smaller once these indirect effects are taken into account than when only the direct effects on the food sector are considered. Since in what follows only the food sector effects are included, it should be kept in mind that the analysis below understates the reductions in net food imports.

ESTIMATING THE MAGNITUDE OF THE DIRECT EFFECTS

A Multicommodity Model of World Food Markets

Numerous models are now available for estimating the magnitude of these various effects. One of the early models developed for this type of policy analysis is by Rod Tyers (1984, 1985). It has since been updated and revised a number of times, including for reports published by the World Bank and the Trade Policy Research Centre. As it happens, though, most of its applications to date have focussed on industrial country interests (e.g. Anderson and Tyers, 1984, 1986, 1987, 1989; Tyers and Anderson, 1986, 1988; and Tyers and Falvey, 1989). It is a dynamic, stochastic, multicommodity simulation model of world food markets involving the major traded staples: wheat, coarse grain, rice, meat of ruminants (cattle and sheep), meat of non-ruminants (pigs and poultry), dairy products and sugar. These seven commodity groups account for about half of world food trade (edible oils and beverages account for most of the rest) and one tenth of global trade in all commodities. This grain, livestock products and sugar (GLS) model is not a general equilibrium model, in that markets for other tradable goods, services and physical and financial factors of production and for non-tradables are excluded, so currency exchange rates have to enter as exogenous variables. So too do productivity growth rates. Offsetting these drawbacks, however, are the model's following features:

— It is global in coverage, involving 30 countries or country groups spanning the world, so that the international as well as the domestic effects of policy or structural changes in one or more countries or commodities can be determined endogenously;

— It incorporates the cross effects in both production and consumption between the interdependent grain, livestock product and sugar markets;

— It has a dynamic mode, in which the effects of policy or structural changes in a particular year can be simulated for every subsequent year, as well as a static equilibrium mode which can simulate the effects of those changes after any desired degree of adjustment (full adjustment, for example, being provided simply be using the long-run elasticities, as illustrated below);

— It is stochastic in that production uncertainty is included via probability distributions associated with each commodity's production level;

— Stockholding behaviour is endogenous, based on empirical analysis of stock level responses to price and quantity changes in each country; and

— Policy is endogenous to the extent that price transmission equations are used to incorporate the two key features of each country's food price policies, namely, the protection component, which raises the trend level of food prices faced by domestic producers and consumers around which prices fluctuate, and the stabilisation component, which allows trade fluctuations to limit the degree to which domestic prices change in response to shifts in domestic supply or in international prices.

Production behaviour is represented by Nerlovian reduced form partial/adustment equations which are log-linear, resulting in constant supply elasticities. In dynamic mode, production in each country is subject to random disturbances from the distribution of residuals to the fitted production equations and to exogenously set productivity growth rates which shift out the supply curves each year. Allowance is also made for the effect on production of land set-aside policies such as those used in the United States during the 1980s.

Direct human consumption is assumed to be characterised by income and price elasticities of demand which are set to decline slightly over time as incomes grow. The demand for livestock feed is based on input-output coefficients for each livestock product which again are assumed to change over time as the proportion of livestock output that is feed-based changes.

Policies affecting domestic prices are incorporated via econometrically estimated price transmission equations for each country and commodity. These equations capture both the protection and the stabilization components of food price and trade policies. They are based on estimates of reduced form Nerlovian partial/adjustment equations which distinguish short-run from longer-run elasticities of price transmission. Separate elasticities are used for producer and consumer prices. In general, even the long-run price transmission elasticities are less than unity, reflecting the prevalence of non-tariff protection instruments in food markets. In the face of volatile and declining real prices in international commodity markets, governments limit the extent to which both the long-run trend and the short-run changes in domestic prices follow those of international prices. The smaller the short-run elasticity of price transmission in relation to its long-run counterpart, the greater the degree of market insulation and the more sluggish is the eventual transmission of any sustained change in the international price. In a few extreme cases domestic prices are completely insulated, which means both the short- and long-run elasticities of price transmission are zero.

The estimated welfare effect of a policy change has four components. The benefit to food consumers is the expected Hicksian equivalent variation in income; the benefit to food producers is the expected change in producer surplus; the government revenue benefit is the expected net budgetary effect of food producer, consumer and trade taxes and subsidies; and the storage benefit is the expected increase in profits from stockholding. All benefits are evaluated assuming risk neutrality. These are thus partial equilibrium measures only: whether the total general equilibrium effects are larger or smaller depends crucially on whether there are other distortions in the economy which affect food markets.

Structurally, the model is simply a set of expressions for quantities consumed, produced and stored, each of which is a function of known past prices and endogenous current prices. The dynamic version of the model is solved iteratively by starting from the 1980-82 base period and beginning each subsequent year with the assumption that all prices are the same as those in the preceding year, generating random disturbances in production and calculating new production, consumption and closing stock levels in each country. The resulting excess demands are then totalled and international prices adjusted to move world markets towards clearance. The procedure is then repeated until a satisfactory degree of market clearance has been achieved for each commodity. Thus the model selects that series of international and domestic prices, production, consumption, and closing stock levels which simultaneously clear all markets in each successive year, from 1983 to 1995. Once 100 simulations of this type have been completed, each using a different set of generated random disturbances from the distributions of each error term, forecast means and standard deviations are calculated for all key variables in the model for each year of the simulation period. The solution procedure is conventional, but it is not based on a standard software package. It is described in more detail for an earlier version of the model in Tyers (1984, 1985) and for the version used here in an appendix of Tyers and Anderson (forthcoming).

Extent of Distortions in World Food Markets

Any estimate of the effects of a future liberalization of trade in agriculture necessarily has to be forecast-dependent. That is, the model used first has to forecast a reference scenario for the world economy, against which liberalization scenarios can be compared. In the present case in which the GLS model forecasts to 1995 from a base period of 1980-82, a wide range of reference cases could be produced by altering assumptions about productivity growth rates on the supply side, about income and population growth rates on the demand side, and about the various elasticities of demand, supply and price transmission. Also important are the estimates of the distortions in food markets in the base years and the assumptions made about how government policies respond to changing market conditions over the forecast. For the reference case used to produce the results we have published in recent years, the GLS model forecasts that the average real international food price by 1995 would decline to 54 per cent of the (very high) 1980-82 level. This scenario assumes developing countries retain their relatively low rates of transmission of international price changes to their domestic markets even in the long run. A consequence of this is that developing countries are forecast to have domestic prices somewhat above border prices on average by 1995.

It is possible, however, that developing country governments, which so often favour consumer interests over farmers, would during a long period of low international prices, transmit more of the change in those prices to their domestic markets than they have tended to do in the past. The net import demand for food by developing countries would be greater in that case, which would reduce the decline in real international food prices. The extreme case would be where they fully transmit those changes in the long run, thereby returning their nominal protection coefficients in long-run equilibrium to those of the base period. In this alternative reference scenario the price level by 1995 is forecast to decline to 69 per cent instead of 54 per cent of the 1980-82 level.

These two forecasts are on the lower and upper bounds of other recent forecasts. The World Bank (1989, Table 3), for example, forecasts that real international food prices in 1995 will be 60 per cent of the 1980-82 level. And the US Department of Agriculture forecasts that grain and soybean prices for the year 2000 will be about 70 per cent of the 1980-82 level, while sugar, meat and dairy prices will be somewhat higher (Roningen, Dixit and Seeley, 1989)[2]. Thus the first set of results presented below, which uses the standard reference run with imperfect price transmission, is compared with a second set of results based on the assumption of perfect price transmission in the long run for developing countries and hence lower domestic food prices in those countries and higher international prices.

The domestic-to-border price ratios (or nominal protection coefficients in the case of producer prices) to be used are shown in Table 2.1 for all countries and country groups represented in the GLS model. These are the forecast protection coefficients for 1995 under the standard and alternative reference runs. The forecast ratios for the alternative reference case involving full price transmission are similar for developing countries to those in the 1980-82 base period; furthermore, 1995 protection coefficients in OECD countries are closer to 1980-82 levels in the alternative reference case because international prices fall less over the forecast period in that case[3].

Food prices are affected by government policies not only directly but also indirectly via overvalued (or undervalued) exchange rates and industrial protection policies. The latter are of comparatively minor importance in OECD countries but, as Krueger, Schiff and Valdés (1988) and others have stressed, they have typically had sizable negative effects on relative food prices in developing countries. Based on the Krueger et al. estimates of these indirect effects for 17 developing countries, and in the absence of reliable estimates for other countries, we have categorised developing countries into one of three groups: those with no net indirect distortions affecting agriculture (South Korea and Taiwan); those with non-food policies which are equivalent to an additional effective tax of 15 per cent on food prices (Bangladesh, Brazil, China, India, Indonesia, North Africa and the Middle East, South Africa and Thailand); and those whose non-food policies are equivalent to an additional effective tax of 30 per cent on food prices (all other developing countries). The domestic-to-border price ratios shown in Table 2.1 are the GLS model's estimates of the distortion to food prices without and then with the above amounts included to account for the indirect distortions. Even with the indirect distortions included these ratios are still not as much below unity as is assumed in Loo and Tower (1989) and Zietz and Valdés (1989). Thus results generated with these parameters can be expected to be less likely to show developing countries gaining than these other recent studies.

What Table 2.1 suggests is that the OECD countries' policies are highly protectionist towards farmers and hurt consumers and taxpayers, whereas the staple food prices of developing countries are somewhat closer to but still above international prices converted at official exchange rates. By contrast, tropical export crops and other primary exports are often heavily taxed by developing countries. If our adjustments for policies which indirectly affect food prices are correct, the second and fourth columns of Table 2.1 indicate that policies in total are likely to be neutral to or, in many cases, negative towards farmers and in favour of food consumers in developing countries.

Effects of Agricultural Trade Liberalization

Two sets of results are presented here for the year 1995. The first is based on the standard reference scenario using the price transmission elasticities estimated from past price data. The second assumes eventually full transmission on the part of developing countries of the decline in international food prices over the 1980-1995 period. Since the latter is probably an over-correction to the limited adjustment assumed in the standard reference case, these two sets of results can be considered upper- and lower-bound cases with the most likely situation being somewhere in between.

For each set of results the relevant reference case is compared in turn with three alternative scenarios, each with either:

a) Exogenously set price-independent farm productivity growth, or

b) Productivity growth which is also affected by the producer price.

In the latter case the price-independent rate of shift of the supply curve is assumed to be an extra five percentage points by 1995 for each 10 per cent by which the producer price increases, and vice versa for price decreases. This adjustment is similar to increasing all long-run supply elasticities by 0.5 in terms of their net trade impact. A justification for expecting the long-run elasticity to be greater is that this is assumed to be a permanent and unprecedented change in world food policies which stimulates developing countries to reduce their current under-investment in agricultural research and causes high levels of investment in agricultural research by OECD countries to be cut back in crops for which there are strong price incentives.

The three alternative scenarios are as follows:

1) Complete liberalization of food policies in all OECD countries;

2) Complete liberalization of food policies not only in all OECD countries but also in all developing countries; and

3) Same as for (2), except liberalization of other trade and exchange rate policies in developing countries as well.

The first of these alternative scenarios corresponds to the first four of our conceptual steps, the second to the fifth step, and the third to steps six and seven, at least insofar as non-food policies directly affect food prices domestically. Steps eight and nine cannot be addressed with the GLS model. The motivation for considering scenario (3) is that OECD countries are pressuring developing countries to undertake such reforms to improve the latter group's prospects for repaying their loans to the former and they may intensify that pressure through the Uruguay Round negotiations.

The results presented in Table 2.2 are derived using the standard reference case involving imperfect long-run price transmission, building on results presented in an earlier paper (Tyers, 1989a); those in Table 2.3 assume developing countries eventually fully transmit the declines in international food prices expected over the forecast period to 1995. To simplify the presentation, the changes in centrally planned Europe are not included in the tables, and the details for the various countries and commodities are discussed later in the chapter.

The first point, from row 2 of Table 2.2, is that if food policies of OECD countries were completely liberalized, international food prices would rise 30 per cent. Food self-sufficiency in 1995 would be 92 instead of 105 per cent in OECD countries, and self-sufficiency in developing countries would be 104 instead of 95 per cent. While this change would enhance welfare for food-sector agents in the OECD countries by an estimated $48 billion per year (in 1985 dollars), it would in this scenario yield a net decline for those agents in developing countries, by $13 billion, despite the fact that developing countries become slight net exporters of food as a result of the higher international prices following liberalization by OECD countries. This is the conventional result discussed in the first conceptual step and is similar to that obtained by other modellers (e.g. OECD, 1987; Valdés, 1987; Parikh et al., 1988; and Roningen and Dixit, 1989).

The above scenario 1a assumes productivity growth is independent of producer price changes. With the alternative assumption used in scenario 1b, which has an effect similar to assuming long-run supply elasticities are greater by 0.5, supplies and hence self-sufficiency ratios in OECD countries are less and those in developing countries are greater. The net change in world supply is only a small positive amount so that international food prices are similar in both scenarios (28 instead of 30 per cent greater than in the reference case). However, the welfare effects for developing countries are very different. Ignoring the change in the cost of agricultural research needed to alter the productivity growth rates, the welfare results suggest food-sector agents in OECD countries would be slightly better off (with consumers benefitting more than producers lose from the slightly lower price in scenario 1b compared with 1a), but food-sector agents in developing countries would hardly lose at all (only $2 billion per year in scenario 1b compared with a $13 billion loss in scenario 1a).

Thus far we have simply repeated the results presented Tyers (1989a). We now extend the analysis, along the lines discussed above on dynamic effects through induced innovations. Should developing countries also liberalize their own food policies but leave their other distortionary policies in place, as in scenarios 2a and 2b, the lowering of their (on average positive) nominal protection rates to zero further boosts the international price for food. This has the effect of encouraging production and discouraging consumption in all countries, so the self-sufficiency ratios are similar in this second set of scenarios as in the first. It turns out that welfare improves even more for OECD countries when they are joined by developing countries in liberalizing food policies, by an extra $12 to $14 billion per year. The welfare of food-sector participants in developing countries, however, is much greater in this set than in the first set of scenarios. There would also be gains in efficiency of resource use (area *befc* in Figure 2.5) and indirect effects via the market for non-tradables (see above, "Indirect Effects through Adjustments in the Market for Non-tradables") that are not captured in this partial equilibrium model.

Suppose, however, that developing countries also were to liberalize their other trade and exchange rate policies and thereby remove the indirect distortions affecting food prices. If our projected domestic-to-border price ratios in columns 2 and 4 of Table 2.1 are accurate, and if it can be assumed that there are no net shifts of the food demand and supply curves as a result of general equilibrium adjustments, then the corresponding projected effects on prices, self-sufficiency and welfare are as for scenarios 3a and 3b in Table 2.2. The boost such a reform would give to developing country farmers ensures international food prices would be higher by less than would be the case without the removal of those indirect disincentives. It also ensures greater food self-sufficiency in developing countries and more food import dependence in OECD countries, especially if productivity growth is positively correlated with producer price changes to the extent growth productivity is positively related to the price changes. OECD countries (which would be net importers) would gain even more in this pair than in the previous two pairs of scenarios, by a further $3 billion to $5 billion per year. And the benefit to food-sector participants in developing countries would be similar in this set as in the previous set of scenarios, the domestic food price change being similar in the two cases after the different adjustments to international prices. However, it should be recalled that there is an additional gain in resource efficiency in this case that is not captured in this partial equilibrium model, represented by area *cfg* in Figure 2.5, not to mention the gain to consumers from the lowering of non-food prices.

Thus even with this standard reference case, it appears unlikely that many developing countries would lose from agricultural trade liberalization by OECD countries in the Uruguay Round if productivity growth is positively correlated with producer price changes to the extent assumed. Of course, if developing countries were to respond to the opportunity provided by food market liberalization of OECD countries by also liberalizing their own policies, they would be substantial net gainers in aggregate welfare terms as measured here.

Turning to the alternative reference case in which developing countries are assumed to transmit fully the decline in international prices expected through 1995, the above conclusion is strengthened further. In particular, in scenarios 1a and 1b of Table 2.3 in which food policies of OECD countries alone are liberalized, developing countries gain from the liberalization, unlike in the cases presented in Table 2.2. In terms of Figure 2.3, areas *dce* and *hfg* both exceed area *abc* in the case of Table 2.3 results, whereas neither did in Table 2.2. International food prices rise by less than in Table 2.2 because the degree of protection of agriculture is less in this reference case (see Table 2.1; and see also Table 2.4 for the commodity detail of those price changes), but except in scenarios 1a and 1b the effects on self-sufficiency and welfare are much the same as for Table 2.2. That is, both OECD and developing countries can expect to each gain up to $60 billion per year just from food sector adjustments to these policy changes alone; gains from adjustments by consumers and producers in other sectors would be additional. The gain to developing countries could be even greater, of course, if OECD countries chose to give some of their $60 billion gain to developing countries in the form of aid.

These effects are broken down by groups and by region in Tables 2.5 and 2.6, at least for scenarios 1b and 3b from Table 2.3. As one would expect from liberalization of just OECD country food policies (Table 2.5), developing country consumers of food lose and farmers gain from the consequent rise in international food prices. Insofar as farmers make up the majority of households in developing countries and are poorer than their urban counterparts, this redistribution would constitute an improvement in equity within those countries. Furthermore, the majority of developing countries/country groups specified in the model are net gainers from food policy reform by OECD countries in this scenario. That is, the net gain of $11.5 billion per year to developing countries as a group is not simply the result of a few large net exporters gaining at the expense of the rest. Moreover, gains accrue to some countries that otherwise would be net importers of these foods, namely, Pakistan, Mexico, and those grouped under Other Asia and Other Sub-Saharan Africa. This, together with the result that no developing country has to spend any more foreign exchange on food than in the reference case, comes about because of the assumed transmission of the change in international food prices to developing country markets and because its positive impact on farm production and productivity growth more than outweighs its impact on consumers.

If developing countries also liberalized their own distortionary policies (Table 2.6), food consumers in numerous developing countries would become beneficiaries because international prices are projected to fall slightly. It is true that farmers in some developing countries are slight net losers in this scenario, but they are the farmers currently enjoying agricultural protection and so are relatively well off anyway. Virtually all countries are better off in a net welfare sense, even without measuring the benefits outside the food sector; the only ones to lose are those whose trade tax revenue has been reduced significantly. It should also be noted that many of the

53

gaining countries remain substantial net food importers, as shown in column 2 of Table 2.6, even though developing countries would spend $104 billion less (in 1985 dollars) on food imports net of export in this case.

Risk Considerations

Another important benefit from food policy liberalization concerns the year-to-year fluctuations around the trend level of food prices. Because many countries transmit only a fraction of international price changes to their domestic market, especially in the short run, and they export some of their own domestic market fluctuations as well, international prices are much less stable than they would be under free trade.

Using the stochastic version of the GLS model, the extent of the effects of policy insulation can be seen by comparing the coefficients of international food price variation in the standard reference case with what those coefficients would be in the absence of current food policies. The final column of Table 2.7 shows that about 25 per cent of the fluctuation in international food prices is attributable to the stabilization aspects of the EC's Common Agricultural Policy. The United States, by contrast, has been a slight contributor to stability in international markets as a result of its stockpiling policies. Overall, however, the food policies of OECD countries in total are responsible on average for one third of the degree of fluctuations, and considerably more to instability in the wheat, beef and dairy product markets.

The great degree of fluctuation in international food prices is one of the reasons why developing countries insulate their domestic markets. Their own stabilization policies also contribute up to about one third of the degree of fluctuation (two thirds in the case of rice and sugar)[4]. That is, if both OECD and developing countries were to liberalize their markets fully, international food price fluctuations might be only one third as great as we currently observe. This is less than the actual fluctuations in many domestic markets of developing and other countries, suggesting that such countries could do without the stabilization component of their food policy entirely, if only other countries would do likewise.

Insofar as producers and consumers are risk averse, any reduction in fluctuations of prices they face would be a further benefit from liberalization in addition to the benefits already discussed.

CONCLUSIONS AND POLICY IMPLICATIONS

The GLS model used in this study is but one of many available now to address the issue at hand. Despite sharing with some others the limitations of partial equilibrium analysis, the model is nonetheless useful in providing illustrative empirical support for all of the points developed in the first section of the paper that the model is capable of addressing. The first of those points is that when the effect of liberalization on the inducement to invest in new technologies is allowed for, developing countries that might otherwise have been losers from liberalization by the OECD countries can become gainers, *even if they are net importers of food*. Second, the number of developing countries in that category will be larger the more developing countries are prompted by OECD country liberalization to reform their own policies affecting their food prices. And, such countries can gain *even if they remain net importers of food*. Third, the income redistribution within developing countries between food consumers and producers, as a result of liberalization, is likely to improve equity. And fourth, risk-averse actors in relatively open economies would be better off because, following liberalization, international food prices would fluctuate less — indeed less than in all but the currently most insulated of economies.

These points could be made stronger, and further points added, with the use of more complex models. One conceptually simple amendment would be to add to the GLS model three (or more) other sectors: other agriculture, other tradables, and non-tradables. This is something the USDA has done recently with its SWOPSIM model (Krissoff and Ballenger, 1988), although that model lacks the stochastic and dynamic features of the GLS model and so cannot measure the effects on market stability and the paths of adjustment to reform[5]. The main advantage of such an amendment to the current GLS model is that it would ensure consistency by requiring, for example, expenditure to equal income and the value of each country's exports to equal the value of its imports.

Another alternative is to build on the pioneering CGE work of Burniaux and Waelbroeck (1985), Burniaux, Delorme et al. (1988), Loo and Tower (1989), Parikh et al. (1988) and John Whalley and his colleagues, Trela and Wigle (1987). Those studies aim to represent the world in a traditional global general equilibrium framework. It is true that the greater risk of specification errors in general equilibrium as compared with partial equilibrium models may more than outweigh the benefits of including non-agricultural sectors, as Gardner (1989) has warned. This is especially true if non-tradables are not included as a separate sector, which has been a shortcoming of IIASA's work to date (Parikh et al., 1988). However, with sufficient effort such problems could be overcome. Typically these models will lack the quantitative detail of agricultural commodity markets that characterises the available multicommodity partial equilibrium models, and they may be subject to aggregation bias[6]. However, they have the virtues not only of internal consistency and of including the indirect income effects mentioned above but also of including explicitly the factor markets (Hertel, 1989). Moreover, the new trade and growth theories now beginning to be incorporated in dynamic CGE models, involving imperfect competition and economies of scale, offer more scope for modelling whole economies realistically, and with them will come the capacity to demonstrate with greater clarity and precision the pervasiveness of the gains from trade liberalization[7].

If it is true that not only the world economy but also developing economies and especially their farmers would be better off if food policies were liberalized under the Uruguay Round, it remains to convince developing country governments to support agriculture's inclusion on the GATT agenda. It may be insufficient to demonstrate that their economies would benefit, namely by showing that their farmers could gain more than their food consumers would lose, for many of these governments clearly have chosen unilaterally to forego economic benefits by adopting trade and exchange rate policies which harm their farmers. They have done this presumably because those policies yield political benefits to the governments which more than outweigh the political costs (Anderson and Hayami, 1986; Anderson, 1989). Therefore another approach is needed.

It happens that OECD countries would benefit more if developing countries joined them in liberalizing their food markets than if they abstained. They would benefit not just in a net economic welfare sense but also politically in that producer prices in OECD countries would not have to fall as much if developing countries also reformed their food price policies (compare the international price changes in scenarios 1 and 2 in Table 2.2 or Table 2.3)[8]. Nor would OECD country export prices of manufactured goods fall as much if resources in developing countries are attracted back into agriculture, resulting in an increase in net imports of manufactured goods from OECD countries (Burniaux and Waelbroeck, 1985; Mathews, 1985). In addition, OECD countries would enjoy greater stability in international food prices. Developing countries might stress these facts in their negotiations with OECD countries, and seek from them some liberalization of other markets of interest to developing countries such as tropical primary and processed products and textiles, clothing and footwear.

Figure 2.1. **COMPARATIVE STATIC PARTIAL EQUILIBRIUM EFFECTS ON A FOOD-IMPORTING ECONOMY OF A HIGHER INTERNATIONAL PRICE FOR FOOD**

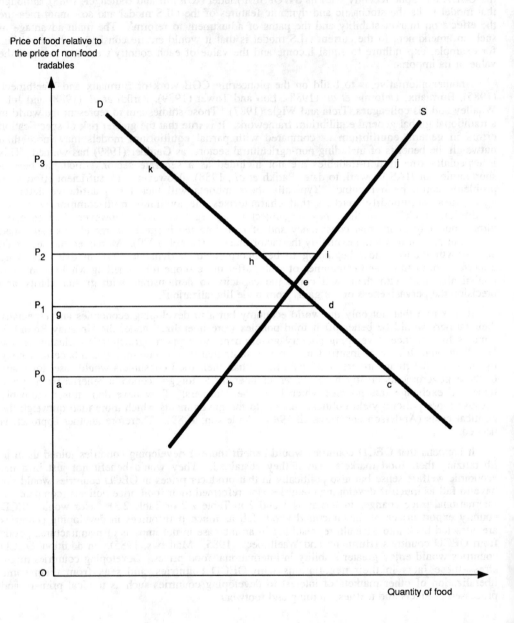

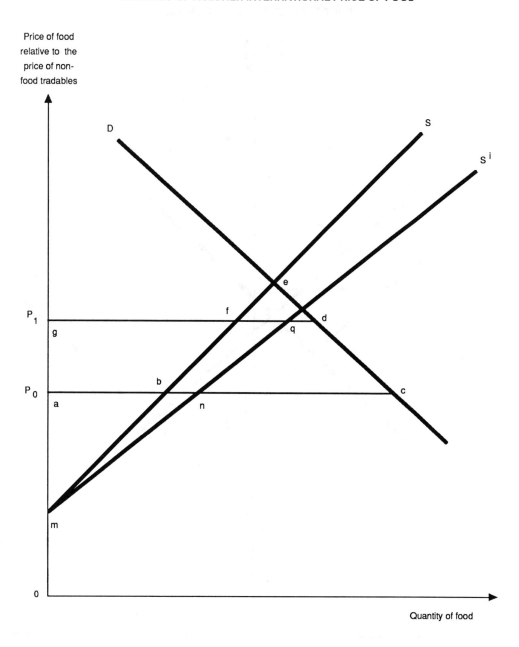

Figure 2.3. PARTIAL EQUILIBRIUM EFFECTS ON THE INTERNATIONAL FOOD MARKET AND ON WELFARE IN DEVELOPING COUNTRIES OF LIBERALIZING FOOD POLICIES BY OECD COUNTRIES

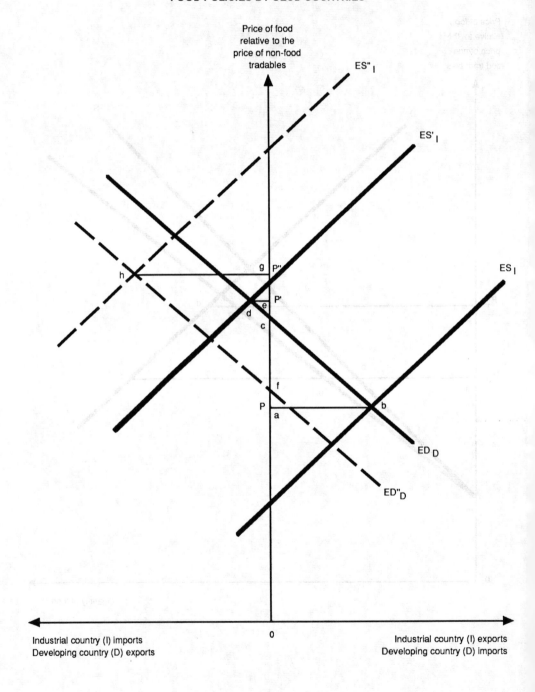

Figure 2. 4. **GENERAL EQUILIBRIUM EFFECTS IN A DEVELOPING COUNTRY OF A HIGHER INTERNATIONAL PRICE FOR FOOD WITH AND WITHOUT REFORM OF ITS OWN NON-FOOD POLICIES**

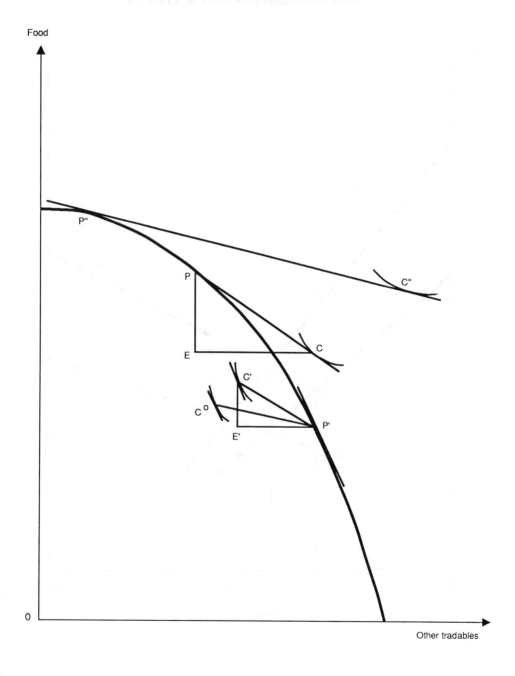

Figure 2. 5. PRODUCTION EFFICIENCY GAINS RESULTING FROM INTERNATIONAL AND DOMESTIC PRICE CHANGES IN A DEVELOPING COUNTRY

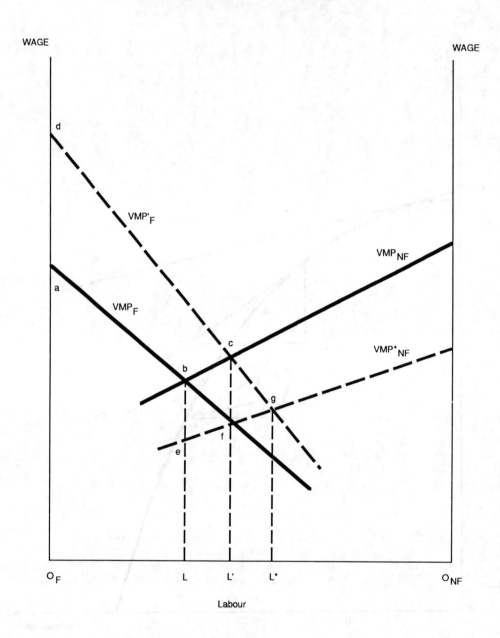

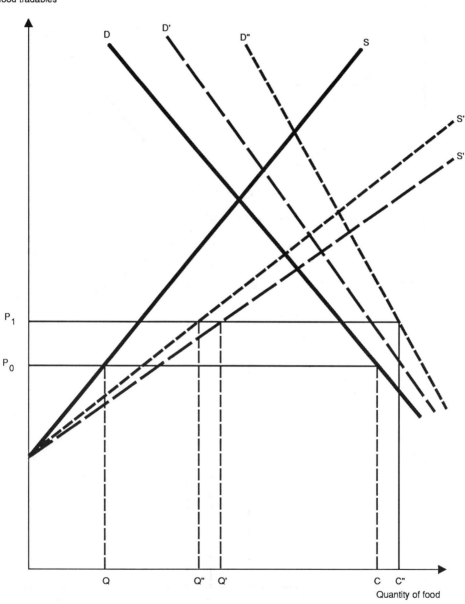

Figure 2. 6. **FEEDBACK EFFECTS FROM THE MARKET FOR NON -TRADABLES IN A FOOD-IMPORTING ECONOMY OF A HIGHER INTERNATIONAL PRICE FOR FOOD**

Price of food relative to the price of non-food tradables

Quantity of food

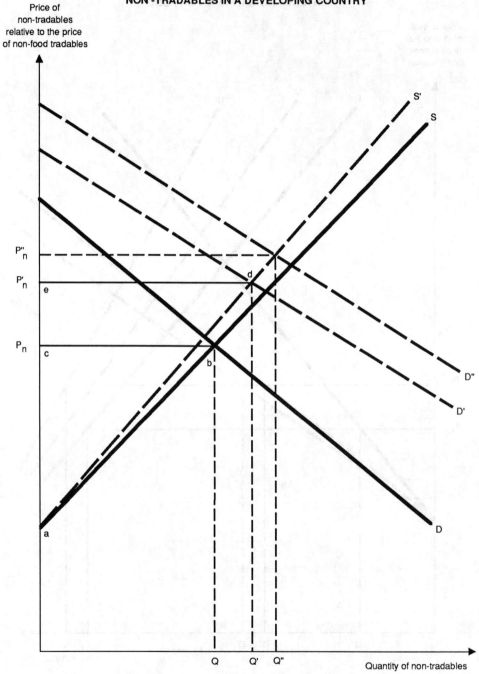

Figure 2. 7. **EFFECT OF LIBERALIZING FOOD POLICIES BY OECD COUNTRIES ON THE MARKET FOR NON -TRADABLES IN A DEVELOPING COUNTRY**

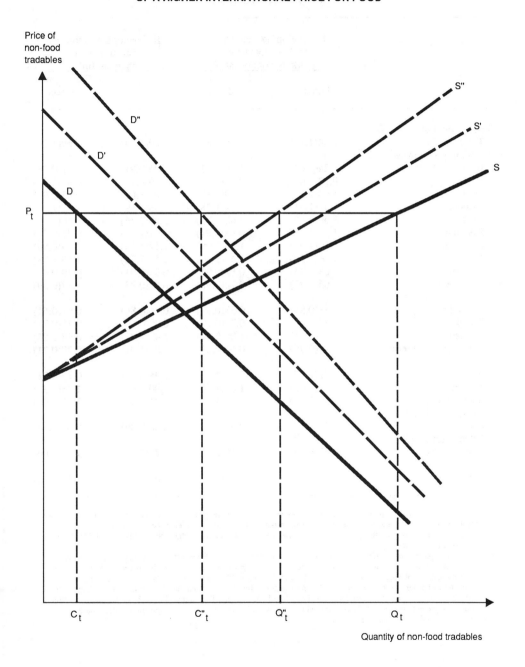

Table 2.1

PROJECTED AVERAGE DOMESTIC-TO-BORDER PRICE RATIOS FOR FOOD PRODUCTS[1]: 1995

	If developing countries insulate domestic markets somewhat		If developing countries transmit price changes fully	
	Direct	Direct plus indirect	Direct	Direct plus indirect
OECD countries[2]				
Total	1.84(1.86)	1.84(1.86)	1.69(1.74)	1.69(1.74)
Developing countries[3]				
Bangladesh	1.24(1.64)	1.06(1.41)	0.96(0.91)	0.81(0.78)
China	0.97(1.01)	0.82(0.86)	0.99(0.95)	0.82(0.82)
India	1.63(1.57)	1.39(1.33)	1.05(1.01)	0.87(0.87)
Indonesia	1.57(1.51)	1.34(1.28)	1.33(1.19)	1.12(1.02)
Korea, Rep.	3.60(2.99)	3.60(2.99)	2.60(2.36)	2.60(2.36)
Pakistan	1.35(1.38)	0.98(1.01)	1.12(1.07)	0.77(0.79)
Philippines	1.50(1:55)	1.05(1.09)	1.14(1.15)	0.79(0.80)
Taiwan	1.45(1.39)	1.45(1.39)	1.53(1.38)	1.53(1.38)
Thailand	1.03(1.14)	0.88(0.97)	0.93(1.01)	0.79(0.87)
Other Asia	1.05(1.27)	0.74(0.90)	0.82(0.83)	0.57(0.59)
Argentina	0.83(0.84)	0.58(0.59)	0.86(0.86)	0.61(0.61)
Brazil	0.84(0.84)	0.72(0.72)	0.90(0.90)	0.76(0.77)
Mexico	1.52(1.41)	1.06(0.99)	1.47(1.22)	0.98(0.85)
Other Latin America	0.86(0.90)	0.60(0.63)	1.00(1.01)	0.70(0.71)
Egypt	2.02(1.97)	1.73(1.67)	0.98(0.95)	0.76(0.81)
Nigeria	2.36(2.42)	1.65(1.70)	1.90(1.88)	1.33(1.32)
South Africa	1.35(1.40)	1.15(1.19)	1.24(1.23)	1.01(1.05)
Other Sub-Saharan Africa	1.30(1.36)	0.92(0.96)	0.86(0.88)	0.60(0.62)
Other North Africa & Middle East	2.57(2.46)	2.18(2.09)	1.26(1.24)	1.05(1.06)
Total	1.27(1.37)	1.04(1.12)	1.05(1.04)	0.84(0.86)

1. The ratio of domestic producer (consumer) prices to comparable prices at the country's border for grains, meats, milk products and sugar, averaged using production valued at border prices as weights.
2. Here, and in the rest of the paper, Turkey is included as one of the "Other North Africa and Middle East" developing countries.
3. The developing country ratios in columns 2 and 4 include the indirect effect of overvalued exchange rates and of direct distortions to other tradable sectors' prices (most notably through industrial protection). Based on estimates published by Krueger, Schiff and Valdés (1988) and others, the adjustments to the direct domestic-to-border price ratios involved reducing them by 0.15 for Bangladesh, Brazil, China, Egypt, India, Indonesia, other North Africa and Middle East, South Africa and Thailand and by 0.3 for all other developing countries (except Korea and Taiwan for which, as with OECD countries, no adjustments were made).

Source: Tyers and Anderson (forthcoming).

Table 2.2

EFFECTS OF REMOVING FOOD PRICE DISTORTIONS ASSUMING INCOMPLETE PRICE TRANSMISSION IN DEVELOPING COUNTRIES: 1995

	Percentage change in international price of food	Food self-sufficiency (production as a % of consumption)		Change in net economic welfare[1], in constant $ billion (1985) per year	
		OECD countries	developing countries	OECD countries	developing countries
Reference	-	105	95	-	-
1. Liberalize OECD country food policies					
a. Exogenous productivity growth	31	92	104	51	-13
b. Price-responsive productivity growth	28	85	108	52	- 2
2. Liberalize OECD and developing country food policies					
a. Exogenous productivity growth	46	93	102	60	17
b. Price-responsive productivity growth	33	84	107	64	58
3. Liberalize OECD and developing country food policies and developing country non-food policies					
a. Exogenous productivity growth	28	84	109	63	12
b. Price-responsive productivity growth	15	74	119	69	60

1. Welfare here refers only to agents in the food sector; welfare of agents in non-food sectors may also change.

Source: GLS model simulation runs.

65

Table 2.3

EFFECTS OF REMOVING FOOD PRICE DISTORTIONS ASSUMING FULL LONG-RUN PRICE TRANSMISSION IN DEVELOPING COUNTRIES: 1995

	Percentage change in international price of food	Food self-sufficiency (production as a % of consumption)		Change in net economic welfare[1], in constant $ billion (1985) per year	
		OECD countries	developing countries	OECD countries	developing countries
Reference	-	109	92	-	-
1. Liberalize OECD country food policies					
a. Exogenous productivity growth	13	89	105	53	1
b. Price-responsive productivity growth	12	83	111	51	12
2. Liberalize OECD and developing country food policies					
a. Exogenous productivity growth	16	93	102	56	29
b. Price-responsive productivity growth	1	81	111	59	64
3. Liberalize OECD and developing country food policies and developing country non-food policies					
a. Exogenous productivity growth	0	84	109	58	24
b. Price-responsive productivity growth	-3	74	118	61	56

1.   Welfare here refers only to agents in the food sector;   welfare of agents in non-food sectors may also change.

Source: GLS model simulation runs.

Table 2.4

EFFECTS OF DIFFERENT LIBERALIZATIONS ON INTERNATIONAL PRICES OF VARIOUS STAPLE FOODS: 1995

(Per cent change from reference case)

	Wheat	Coarse grain	Rice	Rum. meat	Non-rum. meat	Dairy prod.	Sugar	Weighted average
With insulation by developing countries								
1. OECD country food policy liberalization								
a. price-independent productivity growth	25	3	18	43	10	95	22	30
b. price-dependent productivity growth	19	2	2	39	8	90	27	28
2. OECD and developing country policy liberalization								
a. price-independent productivity growth	51	16	41	41	-2	124	41	46
b. price-dependent productivity growth	36	9	17	26	-8	111	28	33
3. OECD country food policy liberalization and developing country food and non-food policy liberalization								
a. price-independent productivity growth	32	2	19	23	-12	99	19	28
b. price-dependent productivity growth	20	-4	-5	7	-20	87	6	15
With no insulation by developing countries								
1. OECD country food policy liberalization								
a. price-independent productivity growth	10	2	5	30	6	39	7	13
b. price-dependent productivity growth	9	2	3	24	6	37	9	12
2. OECD and developing country food policy liberalization								
a. price-independent productivity growth	15	5	-6	24	-2	80	5	16
b. price-dependent productivity growth	1	-5	-27	4	-12	66	-10	1
3. OECD country food policy liberalization and developing country food and non-food policy liberalization								
a. price-independent productivity growth	1	-8	-21	8	-12	60	-12	0
b. price-dependent productivity growth	1	-7	-25	-2	-17	56	-19	12

Source: GLS model simulation runs.

Table 2.5

EFFECTS ON INDIVIDUAL COUNTRIES OF REMOVING FOOD PRICE DISTORTIONS BY OECD COUNTRIES ASSUMING FULL LONG-RUN PRICE TRANSMISSON IN DEVELOPING COUNTRIES AND PRICE-DEPENDENT PRODUCTIVITY GROWTH: 1995[1]
[Constant (1985) $ billion per year]

	Food self-sufficiency (production as a % of consumption		Change in net foreign exchange earnings	Change in economic welfare within the food sector relative to the reference case for		
	Reference after complete liberalization		from food trade	Consumers of food	Producers of food	Net welfare[2]
OECD Countries	109	83	-113.2	202.2	-155.6	51.1
Developing Countries						
Bangladesh	61	70	0.8	-0.7	0.6	-0.0
China	104	117	16.2	-6.6	13.5	3.2
India	84	99	11.5	-9.5	10.3	-1.0
Indonesia	103	112	1.3	-0.9	1.1	-0.4
Korea, Rep.	65	73	0.5	-1.4	1.3	-1.3
Pakistan	84	116	5.0	-2.5	3.4	0.9
Philippines	104	114	0.6	-0.3	0.4	0.2
Taiwan	81	88	0.3	-0.4	0.4	-0.2
Thailand	156	173	1.3	-0.4	0.6	0.5
Other Asia	63	71	2.3	-1.8	1.1	0.1
Subtotal			39.8	-24.5	32.7	2.0
Argentina	173	213	5.8	-1.1	2.7	3.9
Brazil	156	186	9.1	-2.2	5.7	4.9
Mexico	95	120	3.7	-1.8	3.5	0.4
Other Latin America	182	226	9.3	-1.7	5.3	6.2
Subtotal			27.9	-6.8	17.2	15.4
Egypt	30	38	0.6	-1.4	0.6	-1.1
Nigeria	48	57	0.7	-0.9	0.6	-0.6
South Africa	62	78	1.2	-1.3	1.1	-0.5
Other Sub-Saharan Africa	45	57	3.9	-2.5	1.6	0.6
Other North Africa and Middle East	46	58	5.1	-8.5	5.9	-4.3
Subtotal			11.5	-14.6	9.8	-5.9
Total	92	111	79.2	-45.9	59.7	11.5
World total[3]	100	100	-26.6	162.3	-87.5	65.0

1. This scenario corresponds to scenario 1b in Table 2.3 in which only food policies in OECD countries are liberalized.
2. The effect on taxpayers and food stock-holders as well as on food producers and consumers are included in the net welfare measure, but general equilibrium welfare effects in non-food sectors are not included.
3. Includes centrally planned Europe.

Source: GLS model simulation runs.

Table 2.6

EFFECTS ON INDIVIDUAL COUNTRIES OF REMOVING ALL FOOD PRICE DISTORTIONS
ASSUMING FULL LONG-RUN PRICE TRANSMISSION IN DEVELOPING COUNTRIES
AND PRICE-DEPENDENT PRODUCTIVITY GROWTH: 1995[1]
[Constant (1985) $ billion per year]

	Food self-sufficiency (production as a % of consumption		Change in net foreign exchange earnings from food trade	Change in economic welfare within the food sector relative to the reference case for		
	Reference	after complete liberalization		Consumers of food	Producers of food	Net welfare[2]
OECD Countries	109	74	-143.6	250.0	-193.9	61.0
Developing Countries						
Bangladesh	61	70	1.6	-0.6	0.4	0.9
China	104	122	20.1	-3.4	20.0	15.2
India	84	98	11.1	-9.9	8.3	0.2
Indonesia	103	60	-6.7	5.5	-4.8	2.2
Korea, Rep.	65	14	-8.3	15.2	-6.5	6.5
Pakistan	84	141	8.0	-4.2	6.4	2.6
Philippines	104	119	0.7	-0.1	0.4	0.2
Taiwan	81	42	-1.9	2.9	-2.3	0.8
Thailand	156	159	-0.4	0.4	0.4	-0.5
Other Asia	63	116	15.0	-7.8	8.2	4.7
Subtotal			39.2	-2.0	30.5	32.8
Argentina	173	345	15.2	-3.4	13.9	7.3
Brazil	156	215	11.8	-3.6	11.1	3.7
Mexico	95	115	2.6	-1.5	1.1	1.4
Other Latin America	182	226	14.4	-3.8	13.8	4.4
Subtotal			44.0	-12.3	39.9	16.8
Egypt	30	43	1.9	-1.3	1.1	1.0
Nigeria	48	27	-2.7	3.2	-1.4	0.6
South Africa	62	59	0.3	0.3	-0.2	-0.2
Other Sub-Saharan Africa	45	113	20.4	-8.9	9.2	6.6
Other North Africa and Middle East	46	48	1.1	0.3	0.6	-1.3
Subtotal			21.0	-6.4	9.3	6.7
Total	92	118	104.2	-20.7	79.7	56.3
World total[3]	100	100	-27.0	226.8	-110.0	120.3

1. This scenario corresponds to scenario 3b in Table 2.3 in which food policies in both industrial and developing countries are liberalized along with non-food policies which affect incentives in the food sector of developing countries.
2. The effect on taxpayers and food stock-holders as well as on food producers and consumers are included in the net welfare measure. However, it needs to be kept in mind that this is only the gain from the staple food sector; as well there will be gains in other sectors from the liberalization of non-food trade policies and from liberalizing the foreign exchange market, but the latter cannot be measured completely with a partial equilibrium model.
3. Includes centrally planned Europe.

Source: GLS model simulation runs.

Table 2.7

EFFECTS OF FOOD POLICY LIBERALIZATION ON INSTABILITY OF INTERNATIONAL FOOD PRICES

	Wheat	Coarse grain	Rice	Ruminant meat	Non-rum meat	Dairy prod.	Sugar	Weighted average
Coefficient of variation before liberalization	0.58	0.53	0.38	0.24	0.08	0.26	0.36	0.34
Coefficient of variation after liberalization in:								
European Community	0.39	0.45	0.32	0.15	0.08	0.13	0.28	0.26
United States	0.60	0.64	0.36	0.17	0.10	0.27	0.31	0.35
All OECD countries	0.33	0.47	0.28	0.07	0.08	0.11	0.25	0.23
All OECD and developing countries	0.15	0.23	0.09	0.04	0.05	0.06	0.07	0.11

1. Weights based on 1980-82 share of each commodity group's exports in the total value of world exports of these commodities.

Source: Anderson and Tyers (1989, Table 5.1).

NOTES AND REFERENCES

1. This possibility is even greater if Harris-Todaro type unemployment exists in the developing country because of a high minimum urban wage which attracts would-be workers to the towns and cities in the hope of getting one of those highly paid jobs. If the institutionally set urban wage did not change, a shift out of the food sector's value of marginal product curve would attract some of the urban unemployed back to now-better-paid farm jobs while leaving employment in the non-farm sector unchanged, thereby raising national product even more. The required modifications needed for Figure 2.5 to demonstrate this can be found in Corden (1974, Ch. 6).

2. See also Johnson *et al.* (1989). These forecasts — which are a continuation of the past long-term trend (Grilli and Yang, 1987) — contrast with those in the Food and Agriculture Organization's 1979 report *Agriculture: Toward 2000*, which forecasts traded food prices to rise. The latter are what Parikh *et al.* (1988) follow in constructing their reference scenario.

3. It is true that *ad valorem* tariff equivalents are not always the most appropriate way to represent some policies (Whalley and Wigle, 1988), and in fact US land set-aside and stockpiling policies are modelled separately from price policies in the GLS model. For most countries and commodities, however, domestic-to-border price comparisons capture most of the distortions involved. The main exceptions are where production quotas are binding, as with EC and Canadian milk output.

4. The improved world price stability under free trade assumes perfect price transmission in all markets. In practice, however, large developing countries such as India and China have internal transport and other cost barriers which would prevent the achievement of full price equality across all regions, so the above may overstate the extent of stability thus derived.

5. The latter was not included in the present paper for space reasons.

6. An example of possible bias is in Loo and Tower's (1989) model, in which all agricultural production is in one aggregate sector. This makes it a net export sector for virtually all developing countries. The authors assume the sector is subjected to export taxes. Necessarily, then, if OECD countries liberalize "agriculture", the consequent international price rise will make developing countries better off. The gain will be partly due to resources being attracted from the other protected sectors to agriculture and partly via other instruments which are assumed to have much higher collection or by-product distortion costs. However, a reform of OECD country farm policies would be confined to temperate food staples, of which developing countries are net importers and which (according to our data) on average are priced above international price levels at official exchange rates. If Loo and Tower had split agriculture into "temperate staple food" and "other agriculture", a rise in the international price of staple food would probably have been measured as welfare reducing for developing countries. The loss would result partly from the attraction of agricultural resources from the taxed "other agriculture" export sector to the staple food sector, and partly from the need to raise more tax revenue via more costly instruments than trade taxes, following the decline in food import tax revenue and "other agriculture" export tax revenue. That is, a more disaggregated Loo and Tower model that confined itself to the same simulation as our first scenario in Table 2.2 would be likely to generate the same conventional outcome, namely, that developing countries would lose from OECD country food trade liberalization.

7. The new theories are summarised in, for example, Helpman (1988), while a survey of empirical applications can be found in Richardson (1989). The subsequent big challenge will be to integrate these economic models with models of the environment, given the strong link between economic activity and the state of the environment (Young 1988; Lutz and Young 1989).

8. Although not reported in this paper, the GLS model also generates the change in national economic welfare which is not the simple sum of welfare changes of food producers, consumers and taxpayers but rather a weighted sum. The weights, derived as implicit policy preferences, are biased in favour of food producers in OECD countries and food consumers in developing countries. They are based on political market theory (Anderson 1989) and on the estimates of distortions in Table 2.1 (see Tyers 1989b). The printouts show the weighted welfare change for OECD countries to be more favourable by several billion dollars per year if developing countries also reform their food policies than if only OECD country food policies are liberalized.

BIBLIOGRAPHY

ALSTON, J.M., G.W. EDWARDS and J.W. FREEBARIN, "Market Distortions and Benefits from Research", *American Journal of Agricultural Economics*, 70 (2), May, 1988.

ANDERSON, K., "Rent-seeking and Price-distorting Policies in Rich and Poor Countries", Seminar Paper No. 428, Institute for International Economic Studies, University of Stockholm, January, 1989.

ANDERSON, K., Y. HAYAMI and others, *The Political Economy of Agricultural Protection: East Asia in International Perspective*, Sydney, Boston and London: Allen and Unwin, 1986.

ANDERSON, K. and R. TYERS, "European Community Grain and Meat Policies: Effects on International Prices, Trade and Welfare", *European Review of Agricultural Economics*, 11(4), 1986.

ANDERSON, K. and R. TYERS, "Agricultural Policies of Industrial Countries and Their Effects on Traditional Food Exporters", *Economic Record*, 62(179), December, 1986.

ANDERSON, K. and R. TYERS, "Japan's Agricultural Policy in International Perspective", *Journal of the Japanese and International Economics*, 1(2), June, 1987.

ANDERSON, K. and R. TYERS, *Global Effects of Liberalizing Trade in Farm Products*, Thames Essay No. 55, Aldershot, England: Gower for the Trade Policy Research Centre, 1989.

BHAGWATI, J., "The Generalized Theory of Distortions and Welfare", in *Trade, Balance of Payments and Growth*, edited by J. Bhagwati, *et al.*, Amsterdam: North-Holland, 1971.

BURNIAUX, J.M., D. DELORME, I. LIENERT, J.P. MARTIN and P. HOELLER, "Quantifying the Economy-wide Effects of Agricultural Policies: A General Equilibrium Approach", Working Paper No. 55, Department of Economics and Statistics, OECD, Paris, July, 1988.

BURNIAUX, J.M. and J. WAELBROECK, "The Impact of the CAP on Developing Countries: A General Equilibrium Analysis", in *Pressure Groups, Policies and Development*, edited by C. Stevens and J. Verloren van Themaat, London: Hodder and Stoughton, 1985.

CORDEN, W.M., *Trade Policy and Economic Welfare*, Oxford: Clarendon Press, 1974.

CORDEN, W.M., "Booming Sector and Dutch Disease Economics: Survey and Consolidation", *Oxford Economic Papers*, 36, 1984.

GARDNER, B., "Recent Studies of Agricultural Trade Liberalization", in *Agriculture and Governments in an Interdependent World*, edited by A. Maunder and A. Valdés, London: Dartmouth for the IAAE, (forthcoming).

GRILLI, E.R. and M.C. YANG, "Primary Commodity Prices, Manufactured Goods Prices, and the Terms of Trade of Developing Countries: What the Long Run Shows", *World Bank Economic Review*, 2(1), January, 1988.

HELPMAN, E., "Growth, Technological Progress and Trade", NBER Working Paper No. 2592, May, 1988.

HERTEL, T.W., "Quantifying the Effects of Agricultural Trade Liberalization on the LDCs: A Survey of the Models", elsewhere in this volume.

JOHNSON, S.R., W.H. MEYERS, P. WESTHOFF and A. WOMAK, "Agricultural Market Outlook and Sensitivity to Macroeconomic, Productivity and Policy Changes", in *Agriculture and_Governments in an Interdependent World*, edited by A. Maunder and A. Valdés, London: Dartmouth for the IAAE, (forthcoming).

KRISSOFF, B. and N. BALLENGER, "Agricultural Trade Liberalization in a Multi-sector World Model: Implications for Select Latin American Countries", Paper presented to the 20th International Conference of Agricultural Economists, Buenos Aires, August 1988.

KRUEGER, A.O., M. SCHIFF and A. VALDES, "Measuring the Impact of Sector-specific and Economy-wide Policies on Agricultural Incentives in LDCs", *World Bank Economic Review*, 2(3), September, 1988.

LOO, T. and E. TOWER, "Agricultural Protectionism and the Less Developed Countries: The Relationship Between Agricultural Prices, Debt Servicing and the Need for Development Aid", in *Macroeconomic Consequences of Farm-Support Policies*, edited by A.B. Stoeckel, D. Vincent and S. Cuthbertson, Durham: Duke University Press, 1989.

LUTZ, E. and M. YOUNG, "Agricultural Policies in Industrial Countries and Their Environmental Impacts: Applicability to and Comparisons With LDCs", mimeo, Environment Department of the World Bank, Washington D.C., July, 1989.

MATHEWS, A., *The Common Agricultural Policy and the Less Developed Countries*, Dublin: Gill and Macmillan, 1985.

OECD, *National Policies and Agricultural Trade*, Paris: Organisation for Economic Cooperation and Development, May, 1987.

PARIKH, K.S. G. FISCHER, K. FROHBERG and O. GULBRANDSEN, *Towards Free Trade in Agriculture*, Amsterdam: Mortimers Nijhoff for the International Institute for Applied Systems Analysis, 1988.

RICHARDSON, H.D., "Empirical Research on Trade Liberalization with Imperfect Competition", *OECD Economic Studies*, 12, Spring, 1989.

RONINGEN, V.O. and P.M. DIXIT, *Economic Implications of Agricultural Policy Reform in Industrial Market Economies*, ERS Staff Report AGES 89-36, Washington, D.C.: U.S. Department of Agriculture, August, 1989.

RONINGEN, V.O., P.M. DIXIT and R. SEELEY, "Agricultural Outlook for the Year 2000", *Agriculture and Governments in an Interdependent World*, edited by A. Maunder and A. Valdés, London: Dartmouth for the IAAE, (forthcoming).

RUTTAN, V.W., *Agricultural Research Policy*, Minneapolis: University of Minnesota, 1982.

TRELA, I., J. WHALLEY and R. WIGLE, "International Trade in Grain: Domestic Policies and Trade Conflicts", *Scandinavian Journal of Economics*, 89(3), 1987.

TYERS, R., "Agricultural Protection and Market Insulation: Analysis of International Impacts by Stochastic Simulation", Research Paper No. 111, Australia-Japan Research Centre, Canberra, May, 1984.

TYERS, R., "International Impacts of Protection: Model Structure and Results for EC Agricultural Policy", *Journal of Policy Modelling*, 7(2), 1985.

TYERS, R., "Developing-Country Interests in Agricultural Trade Reform", *Agricultural Economics*, 3, 1989a.

TYERS, R., "Implicit Policy Preferences and the Assessment of Negotiable Trade Policy Reforms", Seminar Paper 89-01, Centre for International Economic Studies, University of Adelaide, May, 1989b.

TYERS, R. and K. ANDERSON, "Distortions in World Food Markets: A Quantitative Assessment", background paper No. 22, prepared for the World Bank's *World Development Report 1986*, mimeo, Washington, D.C., January, 1986.

TYERS, R. and K. ANDERSON, "Liberalizing OECD Agricultural Policies in the Uruguay Round: Effects on Trade and Welfare", *Journal of Agricultural Economics*, 39(2), May, 1988.

TYERS, R. and K. ANDERSON, *Disarray in World Food Markets*, Cambridge: Cambridge University Press, forthcoming.

TYERS, R. and R. FALVEY, "Border Price Changes and Domestic Welfare in the Presence of Subsidized Exports", *Oxford Economic Papers*, 41(2), April, 1989.

VALDÉS, A., "Agricultural in the Uruguay Round: Interests of Developing Countries", *World Bank Economic Review*, 1(4), September, 1987.

VALDÉS, A. and J. ZIETZ, *Agricultural Protection in OECD Countries: Its Cost to Less-Developed Countries*, Research Report 21, Washington, D.C.: International Food Policy Research Institute, 1980.

WHALLEY, J. and R.M. WIGLE, "Endogenous Participation in Agricultural Support Programs and Ad Valorem Equivalent Modelling", NBER Working Paper No. 2583, May, 1988.

WORLD BANK, "Half-Yearly Revision of Commodity Price Forecasts", mimeo, Washington, D.C., 11 July, 1989.

YOUNG, M.D., "The Integration of Agricultural and Environmental Policies", paper presented to the 18th European Conference of Agricultural Economists, Copenhagen, 1-4 November, 1988.

ZIETZ, J. and A. VALDÉS, "International Interactions in Food and Agricultural Policies: The Effect of Alternative Policies", Technical Paper No. 2, OECD Development Centre, Paris, April, 1989.

Chapter 3

INTERNATIONAL INTERACTIONS IN FOOD AND AGRICULTURAL POLICIES: EFFECTS OF ALTERNATIVE POLICIES

by

Joachim Zietz and Alberto Valdés

PURPOSE AND SCOPE OF STUDY

The purpose of this study is to identify how long-run changes in agricultural productivity and overall income growth as well as alternative economic policies of developing countries and industrialised countries will affect agricultural production, consumption, and trade flows of both groups of countries.

Compared with the OECD-MTM modelling effort, the focus of this study is not restricted primarily to the effects of OECD country agricultural policies on other OECD countries. The emphasis is rather on the ramifications that changes in OECD agricultural policy may have on developing countries. Equally important for this study is the question of how changes in economic policy and, in particular, in agricultural policy, in developing countries would affect, through their impact on world prices, both developing countries themselves and industrialised countries.

Similar to the OECD-MTM modelling effort, the current study employs a multicountry multicommodity model, where commodity interdependencies enter via cross-price elasticities. In contrast to the OECD-MTM model, however, the present study is long-run in focus in the sense that productivity and per capita income growth are modelled explicitly. Furthermore, the study provides considerably more detail for developing countries.

The next section provides a descriptive overview of the formal world trade model that is used to investigate the following three questions:

a) How can the world market for key food products be expected to evolve in the long run if current economic policies continue in industrialised and developing countries?

b) How will trade liberalization and hence lower output levels for agricultural products in OECD countries affect world markets and hence developing countries?

c) What is the likely effect on world markets, OECD countries, and developing countries of alternative development strategies in developing countries, and in particular, a move towards a more export-oriented policy in agriculture?

This presentation of the formal model is followed by a detailed description of the data, their sources and transformations. The model's simulation results are then presented in the following section along with an interpretation in terms of the three central questions posed above. The study ends with a summary of the main results and suggestions for further research.

DESCRIPTION OF THE MODEL

The analysis is based on a nonspatial price equilibrium model of the world grain, soybean, and meat markets. The model is comparative static in nature and, largely, partial equilibrium. The model is built around constant elasticity demand and supply functions rather than explicit utility and production frontiers. All demand and supply relationships are modelled in terms of percentage changes from a base period. In that sense, the model is in the Johansen (1960) tradition of model building.

The model can handle n commodities and m countries simultaneously. Commodity interdependence is introduced through the use of cross-price elasticities of demand and supply. Long-run trend factors enter the model via income and population effects on the demand side and productivity growth on the supply side. Some rudimentary general equilibrium effects are incorporated for developing countries. In particular, to take into account the importance of the agricultural sector for many developing countries, the overall growth rate of income as measured by gross domestic product (GDP) is modelled as a function of model endogenous changes in agricultural growth in most agriculture-based developing countries.

The model is an extension of Valdés and Zietz (1980) and Zietz and Valdés (1986) in that commodity interdependence is modelled explicitly and long-run effects of productivity growth on domestic production and of income growth on demand are incorporated. The model is close in spirit to that of Tyers and Anderson (forthcoming) and also Roningen et al. (1988). It goes beyond these models in that the demand for feed as derived from livestock production is separated from food demand. In the latter sense the model resembles the OECD's (1987) MTM model. The current study goes beyond the above studies as well as the modelling effort by IIASA (Parikh et al., 1988) in that the latest available information on the price incentives facing farmers in developing countries is incorporated in a Producer Subsidy Equivalent (PSE)-like measure.

Some Preliminaries

All absolute or percentage changes are defined over the model's time horizon (T). As the percentage changes to be handled by the model are potentially large, model equations based on logarithmic differentiation are inappropriate because of the inherent approximation errors. Rather than using a stepwise solution procedure, where the data are updated between each pair of steps as suggested in Dixon (1982)[1], the percentage changes are simply calculated using the discrete changes formula which generates exact results for arbitrarily large changes[2]. Hence, for a Cobb-Douglas function such as

$$c = A\, p^n\, q^x,$$

the percentage change in c (dc/c) is calculated as

$$dc/c = (1 + dp/p)^n\ (1 + dq/q)^x - 1$$

rather than by the common approximation formula

$$dc/c = n\, dp/p + x\, dq/q.$$

All model equations depend, either directly or indirectly, on the percentage world price changes of the n commodities that are considered. Hence, there are only n independent equations. As the model is highly nonlinear due to the use of the exact changes formula, it cannot be solved by simple matrix routines. Hence, the choice of solution algorithms reduces to one of following three types: fixed-point methods, techniques that make use of the derivatives of the excess demand function, and simple tatonnement processes, where the prices are adjusted in response to excess demand. The latter method is implemented in this paper: the model is solved by Gauss-Seidel for a vector of n world price changes.

The model is comparative static in nature, yet it is used for a forecast exercise. As the model ignores the complexities of the adjustment path to the new equilibrium, it assumes that all long-run changes occur simultaneously at the base period. All exogenous changes are translated into excess demands at the base period and the model is projecting the price adjustment needed to eliminate these excess demands. In reality, obviously growth cannot be regarded as imposed in a single year. It is a complex evolutionary process. However, it can be shown that a comparative static model very closely approximates the results to be obtained from a sequence model with explicit time and permanent market clearing, as long as one assumes that all growth rates are constant over the model's time horizon and not excessively large[3].

Production

The absolute change in domestic production of crop i in country k (dq_{ik}) is derived as

$$dq_{ik} = q0_{ik} \left[\Pi_j (1 + php_{jk})^{sijk} (1 + qh_{ik}) - 1 \right]$$

$i=1,...,n,\ k=1,...,m$ (except beef)

where

dq_{ik}=absolute change of production of commodity i in country k

$q0_{ik}$ =base period production of commodity i

php_{jk}=percentage change in producer price of commodity j

$sijk$=cross-price elasticity of production between commodities i and j

qh_{ik}="price-constant" percentage change of production of commodity i.

The value for the price-constant percentage change of production of commodity i is derived from the average annual exogenous growth rate of production yields (rq_{ik}) as

$$qh_{ik} = \exp(rq_{ik} T) - 1$$

$i=1,...,n,\ k=1,...,m.$

Price changes for commodities that are used as feed clearly affect the profitability of beef production. Hence beef production is made a function of the percentage change in feed cost. As the relative price of alternative feeds changes, profit maximising beef producers will shift their feed consumption, as far as substitution possibilities exist, towards the relatively inexpensive feed products. For all countries, the feedback from feed prices to beef production is incorporated through a feed-cost term that is added to the above determining equation for production for i=beef. As a result, the absolute change in beef production is given as

$$dq_{ik} = q0_{ik} \left[\Pi_j (1 + php_{jk})^{sijk} (1 + qh_{ik}) (1 + phfc_k)^{efck} - 1 \right]$$

i=beef, k=i,...,m

where $phfc$ represents the percentage change in feed cost given cost minimisation behaviour of beef producers and where efc is the elasticity of beef production with respect to feed cost. The value of qh_{ik} for beef is derived from the predicted change in livestock production for each country k. Details of the derivation are given in the data section.

The percentage change in feed cost $(phfc)$ is calculated as

$$phfc_k = \left[\Sigma_i p0c_{ik} (1 + phc_{ik}) f0_{ik} \Pi_j (1 + phc_{jk})^{efbijk} / \Sigma_i p0c_{ik} f0_{ik} \right] - 1,$$

$k=1,...,m$

where

$p0c_{ik}$=price of feed i to beef producers of country k in base period

phc_{ik}=percentage change in consumer price of feed commodity i

$efbijk$=cross price elasticity of demand, in beef production, between feed i and j, country k.

The base year price of feed i to beef producers in country k $(p0c_{ik})$ is derived as

79

$$p0c_{ik} = pw0_i \, (\, 1 + cse0_{ik}\,),$$

$i=1,...,n; \; k=1,...,m$

where $pw0_i$ is the base year world price of commodity i and $cse0_{ik}$ stands for the base year consumer subsidy equivalent for commodity i in country k.

Domestic Utilisation

Domestic utilisation of commodity i,j ($i,j=1,...,n$) in country k ($k=1,...,m$) consists of food consumption, feed consumption, and other uses, such as seed and waste.

Food consumption

The absolute change in food consumption over the model's time horizon is determined by

$$dc_{ik} = c0_{ik} \, [\, \Pi_j \, (1 + phc_{jk})^{eijk} \, (1 + nh_k) \, (1 + ynh_k)^{eiyk} - 1],$$

$i=1,...,n, \; k=1,...,m$

where

dc_{ik}=absolute change of food consumption of commodity i in country k

$c0_{ik}$=base period food consumption of commodity i in country k

phc_{ik}=percentage change in consumer food price of commodity i in country k

$eijk$=cross-price elasticity of demand between product i and j, country k

nh_k=expected percentage change in population of country k

ynh_k=expected percentage change in real per capita income of country k, calculated as
$(1 + yh_k)/(1 + nh_k) - 1$

$eiyk$=income elasticity of food demand for commodity i in country k.

The percentage changes identified by nh_k and yh_k are derived from the corresponding average annual percentage growth rates (rn_k and ry_k) and the model's time horizon (T) as

$$nh_k = exp \, (rn_k \, T) - 1 \quad \text{and}$$

$$yh_k = exp \, (ry_k \, T) - 1$$

$k=1,...,m,$

where *exp* denotes exponents.

Feed consumption

Feed demand is derived demand. As such it depends on the level of livestock production, the production technology utilised, and relative feed prices. Livestock production technology as well as production levels are subject to change, especially so for developing countries experiencing significant growth in per capita income such as, for example, South Korea and Taiwan (Sarma, 1986). Production also reacts to changing trends in consumption. Important in this respect has been the shift away from ruminant meats towards non-ruminant meats, i.e. pig and poultry. As non-ruminants are dependent on significantly larger rations of feed grain than ruminants such as cattle and mutton and lamb, a shift towards ruminants implies, *ceteris paribus*, an increase in feed demand.

Feed consumption, as defined in this model, consists of feed for all types of meats, i.e. for beef, which is one of the commodities explicitly incorporated in the model, and of feed for other meats that are not treated explicitly in this model (i.e. pork, poultry, mutton and lamb)[4].

The fact that none of the meats apart from beef is modelled explicitly in this study causes a potential problem because the level of meat production is decisive for feed demand. In order to avoid a serious underestimate of feed demand and hence of changes in the markets for feed grains, it appears mandatory to include meat production at least in a rudimentary form in the model. A simple yet fairly realistic way to do this is to make the percentage change in total meat production a function of the forces that determine meat demand in the long run, i.e. per capita income and population growth. Historical data, as assembled for example in Sarma and Yeung (1985), appear to support this simple approach. They show not only that meat production is highly correlated with meat consumption across countries but also that the growth rates of production and consumption are almost identical. In other words, trade plays a negligible role as a way to balance meat consumption and production for the vast majority of countries. This stylised fact is incorporated in the model in that trend meat production is made, in a direct way, a function of demand parameters. In particular, for meat importing countries, the predicted percentage change in meat production in country k over the model's time horizon ($louh_k$) is derived as

$$louh_k = [(1 + ynh_k)^{elyk} - 1] + nh_k \qquad\qquad k=1,...,m$$

where $elyk$ is the elasticity of per capita meat production with respect to per capita income that is calculated for this purpose[5]. For the meat exporting countries or regions, i.e. Australia, New Zealand, Argentina, and the remainder of Latin America, world averages are used for ynh, ely, and nh rather than country specific values indexed by k.

The long-run shift in consumption from ruminant meats to non-ruminant meats, mentioned above, is captured in the present model by a feeding ratio that is assumed to grow over time as the production share of non-ruminants to ruminants increases. The expected feeding ratio ($frat$) T years from the base period is approximated by attaching a constant growth factor to the base period ratio between total feed use of cereals (and soybeans) and the level of total meat production,

$$frat_k = (tf0_k / lou0_k) \, exp \, (gfr_k T) \qquad\qquad k=1,...,m$$

where

$tf0_k$=base period feed consumption of cereals and soybeans in country k, all livestock

$lou0_k$=base period meat production in country k

gfr_k=predicted average annual percentage change of the feeding ratio in country k

T=time horizon of the model.

Given the predicted percentage change in meat production and in the feeding ratio, the change in feed consumption of commodity i in country k is given as

$$df_{ik} = [f0_{ik} \, \Pi_j \, (1 + phc_{jk})^{efijk} / tf1_k] frat_k \, lou0_k \, (1 + louh_k) - f0_{ik} \qquad i=1,...,n,\ k=1,...,m$$

where

df_{ik}=absolute change in feed consumption of commodity i for all livestock

$f0_{ik}$=base period feed consumption of commodity i, all livestock

$tf1_k$=total feed consumption (all i) in year $t+T$, based on relative price changes alone, i.e.

$$tf1_k = \Sigma_i f0_{ik} \, \Pi_j (1 + phc_{jk})^{efijk}$$

phc_{jk}=percentage change in price of commodity j to livestock producers

$efijk$=cross-price elasticity of feed demand between commodities i and j,

and where all variables and parameters are indexed by country k.

The above equation determining the change in feed demand for commodity i in country . represents a compromise solution for several reasons. First, as mentioned above, the percentag change in meat production is used as a proxy for the percentage change in livestock productior Second, feed demand is based on total meat production rather than being decomposed b individual meat product. As feed demand for cereals, soybeans, and other feeds varie considerably by meat product, a decomposition of feed by meat product would clearly b preferable. However, there are no data on feed use by meat or livestock product (Sarma, 1986) for most developing countries. Third, by defining *lou* in terms of total meat, there is no direct link between the model's predictions of beef production and the above equation determining feed demand. Given the unavailability of feed data by meat product, however, adding this feedback from beef production to feed demand is not considered worth the added complication that it would introduce. Fourth, it has to be realised that meat production or its predicted change over time is dependent solely on the income elasticity of meat demand and population growth. The relative price of meats is assumed to remain unchanged over the model's time horizon and hence to have no effect on meat production. Finally, total meat production does not depend in any way on changes in input costs. Changes in the relative prices of feeds affect meat production only insofar as they alter the share of alternative feeds in total feed consumption. But a rise in feed costs will not lower meat production as it will beef production in the model[6].

Other domestic demand components

Other domestic uses are comprised of seed and waste. Since seed and waste are lumped together in the data that are being used, this number can be large for some commodities even if production is minimal but consumption is large. Hence, assuming a constant ratio of this composite of other uses to production does not make sense for each country and commodity. After studying the available data, the following assumptions are made.

For industrialised countries (ICs), seed and waste are assumed to be a constant proportion of production for wheat and coarse grains and a constant proportion of food and feed consumption for rice and soybeans. Other uses of wheat and coarse grains in developing countries are defined as those for rice and soybeans for industrialised countries[7].

More formally

$$do_{ik} = dq_{ik}\, rat_{ik} \qquad i=\text{wheat and coarse grains, } k=\text{ICs}$$

$$do_{ik} = (dc_{ik} + df_{ik})\, rat_{ik} \qquad i=\text{rice and soy, } k=1,...,m$$

$$do_{ik} = 0 \qquad i=\text{beef and sugar, } k=1,...,m,$$

where

rat_{ik}=constant ratio of seed and waste to production or food and feed consumption.

It may be added that assuming constant ratios between other uses and production or food and feed consumption poses a potential problem: price changes as well as advances in technology could very likely change these ratios, especially in the long run. In many countries, better reporting could also significantly affect these numbers.

Price Transmission

The production decisions of farmers in country k depend on the real net price received relative to their costs of production. The real net output price received by farmers depends on the world market price, tariff and non-tariff barriers to trade, the real exchange rate, product and trade taxes, marketing costs and the rate of inflation as measured by the consumer price index. The costs of production depend, among other factors, on the prices of input factors and government subsidies.

For OECD countries, all government interventions on the price or cost side are captured by the concept of Producer Subsidy Equivalents (PSEs) (OECD, 1987). For most countries, government interventions tend to give farmers a Positive Subsidy Equivalent. For most developing countries, PSEs and Consumer Subsidy Equivalents (CSEs) are measuring only nominal protection rates[8]. However, in contrast to the methodology of previous studies, the PSE measure includes not only the effect on incentives of direct government interventions in agriculture but also the indirect effects resulting from import protection outside of agriculture. As reported in Krueger, Schiff, and Valdés (1988), these indirect effects that can be traced to protection of domestic industry and exchange rate overvaluation make up a very considerable part of the incentive effect of economic policy to farmers. They tend to provide farmers in many developing countries not only with a negative level of protection for exportables but also for importables.

Removing these indirect effects that have their origin outside of agriculture will clearly have less of an influence on agricultural production than eliminating the direct effects that are specific to agriculture. The reason is that the removal of exchange rate overvaluation and protection in import competing industries will expand all sectors producing exportables and other unprotected importables, not just agriculture. Over time, the simultaneous expansion inside and outside of agriculture is likely to put pressure on capital, labour, and other resources, with input prices rising and thereby eliminating part of the impulse resulting from the initial elimination of production disincentives. These secondary effects could be significant if the sector producing exportables is potentially large. However, even if increased production of exportables and other importables outside of agriculture will limit the potential expansion of agriculture, it is unlikely to eliminate all expansionary effects of removing the indirect disincentive effects. Zero production effect in agriculture would presume that the resources freed in the formerly protected industries and in the non-tradable sector flow exclusively to non-agriculture. This appears to be a far-fetched assumption. In addition, one would expect to see foreign investment to increase in the wake of liberalization, a development which would further help relieve the internal constraints on investment. In sum, although it appears unrealistic to give direct and indirect effects equal weight in their impact on agricultural production, completely ignoring the indirect effects seems to be similarly unrealistic. Hence, rather than simply adding up direct and indirect effects in the calculation of PSEs, the indirect effects would have to be discounted relative to the direct effects, a point taken up again in the data notes.

In calculating the percentage change of prices received by producers for commodity i in country k, it is assumed that all factors other than those captured by PSE or the equivalent concept used for developing countries remain constant[9]. This applies in particular to quality factors, transportation costs, and changes in a country's underlying inflation rate. Under those assumptions, the percentage change in producer prices can be written as a function of the percentage change in world price and PSE as

$$php_{ik} = (1 + pwh_i)(1 + pse1_{ik}) / (1 + pse0_{ik}) - 1 \qquad i=1,\ldots,n,\ k=1,\ldots,m$$

where

php_{ik}=percentage change in producer price of commodity i, country k

pwh_i=percentage change in world price of commodity i

$pse0_{ik}$=PSE for commodity i in country k before policy change

$pse1_{ik}$=PSE for commodity i in country k after policy change.

The percentage change in consumer prices is calculated in a way equivalent to that of producer prices. Consumer Subsidy Equivalents (CSEs) are used instead of PSEs. In contrast to the calculation of PSEs, CSEs are treated in the common way. They incorporate only direct effects, that is incentives or disincentives specific to the commodity.

$$phc_{ik} = (1 + pwh_i)(1 + cse0_{ik}) / (1 + cse1_{ik}) - 1 \qquad i=1,\ldots,n,\ k=1,\ldots,m$$

where

phc_{ik}=percentage change in consumer price of commodity i

$cse0_{ik}$=CSE for commodity i before policy change

$cse1_{ik}$=CSE for commodity i after policy change.

Both equations above assume that domestic producer or consumer prices change in tandem with the world price for constant levels of PSE and CSE. This assumption implies full transmission of world price changes. This clearly makes little sense in a short-run analysis for countries such as those of the European Community (EC) that largely insulate the domestic markets from world price changes through the use of variable import levies or similar devices. It is also questionable for many developing countries. For instance, Krueger, Schiff, and Valdés (1988) report that, for a sample of 18 developing countries during the period 1960 to 1984, direct price policies by governments managed to reduce producer price variability by 27 per cent for export goods and by 31 per cent for import goods relative to the variability of world market prices.

For a long-run analysis such as this, however, the assumption of full price transmission appears more acceptable. After all, what counts for a long-run analysis is not whether a country manages to insulate domestic prices from the fluctuations of world market prices around their trend, but whether the trend of domestic prices deviates from the trend of world market prices. Full insulation of the domestic market in the long run would imply that the two trends diverge systematically. However, this appears to be quite unrealistic an assumption for most countries because it would be very costly, even for a relatively rich country group such as the EC. Hence, for a long-run analysis, it seems more realistic to assume that domestic output levels and thus also trade are adjusting to trend changes in world market prices and quantities traded. This has been the case in recent years for the EC's Common Agricultural Policy (CAP), as it has been modified through a variety of restrictions on price guarantees to cope with the pressures of inflating agricultural budgets[10]. Complete transmission of world price changes can therefore be interpreted as assuming that what remains constant is not the EC's CAP or the US farm policy of 1985 but rather the process of adapting the CAP and the US farm policy to cope with the pressures of inflating agricultural budgets. Full price transmission, in other words, implies that the CAP and the US farm policy are presumed to continue to evolve in the sense that methods of containing production growth will develop over time. The same applies to agricultural policies in developing countries[11].

The Dependence of GDP Growth on Growth in Agriculture

Changes in development strategy in developing countries are likely to have a strong influence not only on the agricultural sector or, even more limited, on the specific commodity groups that are explicitly considered in this study. They are likely to have significant effects also on industrial development. Although modelling the influence of development strategy on overall growth in some detail is far beyond the scope of this study, ignoring it altogether is certain to underestimate the impact of a change in economic policy. As a compromise solution, this study makes two simplifying assumptions. First, agricultural growth is equal to the average endogenous (simulated) growth rate of this study's commodities, following economic liberalization. Second, the growth rate of income (GDP) as predicted from historical trends ($r0_y$) is modified by a fraction of the difference between the model endogenous growth rate of agriculture (r_a) and its historical growth rate ($r0_a$). As far as economic liberalization in developing countries leads to an increase in the growth rate for agriculture compared to its historical mean, it is assumed to increase the growth rate of GDP. The higher growth rate of income, in turn, stimulates human consumption of cereals and meats, including beef. As meat consumption is directly linked to meat production, a rise in income translates into larger meat production and hence increased consumption of grains and soybeans for feed. In equation form, the average annual growth rate of income (r_y), which enters food and feed demand, is assumed to be given as

$$r_y = r0_y + \alpha(r_a - r0_a)$$

where α is a parameter relating agricultural growth to GDP growth and where r_a is calculated as

$$r_a = [1 + (1/n) \, \Sigma_i \, dq_i \, / q0_i \,]^{1/T} - 1$$

where country subscript k has been left out for clarity.

The above modification of the exogenously predicted growth rate of income applies to all developing countries and country groups for which the share of agricultural GDP to total GDP exceeds one third or for which more than a third of all export earnings derives from the agricultural sector. In practice, this means that only three developing countries or country groups are excluded from this modification of the overall growth rate of income. They are Egypt, South Korea, and the country group identified as North Africa/Middle East.

Market Clearing

Simultaneous equilibrium in all n markets requires that the model's n excess demand functions equal zero. Excess demands are expressed in terms of net exports as

$$dx_{ik} = dq_{ik} - dc_{ik} - df_{ik} - do_{ik} \qquad \text{\small $i=1,...,n$ and $k=1,...,m$}$$

where do_{ik} identifies changes in waste and seed, as explained above. As stock changes are not entering the excess demand function, they are implicitly assumed to be constant.

Given world market equilibrium in the base period, equilibrium in period T requires that the sum of the absolute changes in net exports for all m countries equals zero for each of the n commodities, i.e.

$$\Sigma_k \, dx_{ik} = 0 \qquad \text{\small $i=1,...,n$}$$

If world stock changes are different from zero in the base period, setting stock changes constant means either constant stock accumulation or drawing down. Although stock accumulations are sensible as production grows, the stock changes in the base period are not necessarily optimal. The problem of stock changes in the base period is handled in this comparative static model in the same way as any other exogenous change, for example those deriving from income or productivity growth. Stock accumulations in the base period are interpreted as excess supply that is eliminated through appropriate changes in the world price.

This modifies the above world market equilibrium condition to

$$\Sigma_k \, dx_{ik} + d \, (stocks \,)_i = 0 \qquad \text{\small $i=1,...,n$}$$

where $d(stocks)$ identifies the sum of base period stock changes for all countries except China and the centrally planned economies of Eastern Europe. The existence of stock changes in the base period in combination with the above modification of the model's equilibrium condition also requires a reinterpretation of exports at the individual country level. In particular, if actual net exports in the base period ($xact0$) are given by

$$xact \, 0_{ik} = q0_{ik} - c0_{ik} - f0_{ik} - o0_{ik} - d(stocks \,)_{ik} \qquad \text{\small $i=1,...,n$ and $k=1,...,m$}$$

then the actual net export level at the end of the model's time horizon is

$$xactl \,_{ik} = xact \, 0_{ik} + dx_{ik} + d(stocks \,)_{ik} \qquad \text{\small $i=1,...,n$ and $k=1,...,m$.}$$

Hence, the change in net exports in the case of stock changes in the base period and the modified world equilibrium condition will be

$$dxact \,_{ik} = dx_{ik} + d(stocks \,)_{ik} \qquad \text{\small $i=1,...,n$ and $k=1,...,m$}$$

in this model. Clearly, the world equilibrium condition remains defined in terms of dx_{ik}.

Commodities, Countries, Base Period

As requested in the terms of reference, the study covers six commodities: wheat, coarse grains, rice, beef, sugar, and soybeans. A category called "all meats" is also included in the model, although it is not treated symmetrically to the other commodities.

The world is divided into 22 countries and country groups, of which ten are industrialised countries or country groups according to the FAO classification and 12 are developing. The definition of the groups of industrialised countries follows largely the OECD classification, i.e. the European Community combines in its EC-10 definition Belgium/Luxembourg, Denmark, France, Germany, Greece, Ireland, Italy, the Netherlands, and the United Kingdom; the "Mediterranean Countries" include Malta, Portugal, Spain, and Yugoslavia; the "Nordic Countries" consist of Finland, Iceland, Norway, Sweden, and Switzerland. The group "Other developed countries" includes Israel and South Africa. Australia, Austria, Canada, Japan, New Zealand, and the United States enter the model as individual countries.

The following developing countries are modelled separately: Argentina, Brazil, Egypt, India, South Korea, Nigeria, Pakistan, and Turkey. All remaining developing countries are grouped together into the regions Asia, North Africa/Middle East, Sub-Saharan Africa, and Latin America. The regional classification follows that of IFPRI (Paulino, 1986).

China and the centrally planned economies of Eastern Europe (Albania, Bulgaria, Czechoslovakia, the German Democratic Republic, Hungary, Poland, Romania, and the USSR) are not incorporated in the model[12]. This implies that their exports and imports are assumed to remain at base year levels for each year of the model's time horizon. The main reason for treating China and the centrally planned economies as exogenous relative to the world market is the very unpredictable nature of their future development and, hence, export and import behaviour. For example, China is in the middle of significant changes regarding economic policy. After a strong movement towards freer markets, this process seems to be under review. At the same time, the Soviet Union appears to be ready to divert resources from government consumption towards private consumption. To what extent these trends will continue and/or pick up momentum is highly uncertain. But as both economic entities are large relative to the world market, internal structural changes can have significant effects for the world market. To model their behaviour by relying on continuing trends for domestic consumption and production or for exports and imports could lead to predictions that are far off the mark.

The specified time horizon of the model is 20 years, the base period is 1981-83. The latter is chosen because the comparable data set on production and supply utilisation for wheat, rice, and coarse grains for later years has not been completed or released yet by IFPRI.

Definition and sources of model variables and parameters

The base year data on production and consumption for all commodities are simple averages of the years 1981-83. The basic input data on food and feed consumption, production, waste and seed for wheat, rice, and the coarse grains are derived from the Agricultural Supply/Utilization Accounts Tape of the Food and Agriculture Organization of the United Nations. All data are in raw equivalents. The consumption of processed products, such as bread, is converted back into the consumption of its basic ingredients, as, for example, wheat. Food consumption data on beef and sugar are derived from FAO production and trade yearbooks as production plus imports minus exports. Total domestic utilisation of soybeans is calculated as domestic production plus imports minus exports of soybeans plus imports minus exports of soymeals and soycakes, with the latter two converted back to soybean equivalents. Approximate values of the conversion factors and the shares of food, feed, seed and waste use in total domestic utilisation are obtained from various issues of the FAO Food Balance Sheets.

The values for total meat production in the base period (*lou0*) are taken from a printout provided by FAO (June 26, 1988). The product (meats) is identified as commodity 2944 of the FAO Agricultural Statistics.

Most of the elasticities are drawn from estimates by other researchers. In particular, all price elasticities of demand and supply for industrialised countries match those used in the OECD-MTM model (OECD, 1988a). This applies to price elasticities of food demand and supply as well as to feed demand. Price elasticities of demand and supply for developing countries are taken from a variety of sources, including Parikh *et al.* (1988) and its various prior IIASA documents, Scandizzo and Bruce (1980), Tyers and Anderson (1986), USDA (1986), Valdés and Zietz (1980), and Zietz and Valdés (1986). Feed demand elasticities for all livestock (*efij*) are constructed for each industrialised country or country group as simple averages of the feed demand elasticities for individual livestock categories for that country[13]. Feed demand elasticities for beef (*efbij*) as well as the feed cost elasticity of beef production are taken from the MTM model without any modification. For countries and country groups that are not treated separately in the MTM model, feed demand elasticities for all livestock (*efij*) are equated to those of the EC or Australia, depending on which country provides a better match with respect to the production structure. The New Zealand feed demand elasticities for beef as well as the corresponding feed cost elasticity are used for all developing countries. This choice reflects the fact that, as in New Zealand, most cattle in developing countries are grass-fed rather than raised on grains.

Estimates of average annual changes in feeding ratios are calculated from data provided by Sarma (1986, Table 26). In particular, *gfr* is found as the difference between the average annual growth rate of cereal feed use between 1966-70 and 1976-80 and the corresponding growth rate of livestock output. For industrialised countries the value of *gfr* is set uniformly at 0.5 per cent per annum.

Per capita income elasticities of demand are predominantly from Parikh *et al.* (1988) and its various prior IIASA documents, Sarma (1986), Sarma and Yeung (1985), and USDA (1986). An upper limit of unity is imposed on all income elasticities for cereals. Income elasticity estimates of livestock production with respect to per capita income (*ely*) are derived from a regression on a cross section of 52 developing countries for the year 1985. The estimated regression equation is given by

$$lou/n = 66.2 + .019Y - .000003Y^2 + .0017 \; area + regional \; dummies$$

$$(5.3) \quad (3.4) \quad (-2.9) \quad (1.5)$$

$$R^2 = .71 \qquad F(12, \; 39) = 7.8$$

where *lou* represents 1985 livestock production in 1 000 mt, defined as the sum of all meat production, fresh milk production divided by ten, and hen egg production[14]. Variable *n* represents population in millions. Y and Y^2 are per capita income and its square, respectively, and area, the land area of each country included in the sample[15]. The intercept term holds for the countries in the southern part of Latin America. The dummy variables for all other regions are negative and lower the intercept term by a value between 45 and 66. For industrialised countries, the parameter *ely* is set equal the maximum of two times the value of the income elasticity of beef demand and 0.5, which closely approximates the average value of *ely* for developing countries.

Data on PSEs for OECD-countries come from OECD (1988b). CSE values are derived from OECD (1987) values by assuming the ratio between PSEs and CSEs remained approximately the same between 1979-81 and 1981-83. PSE and CSE measures for the group

"Others" are derived from the data for South Africa given in USDA (1988). For South Korea, India, and Nigeria, the values substituting for PSEs and CSEs are also taken from USDA (1988)[16]. All other values are derived from the nominal protection rates reported in Krueger, Schiff, and Valdés (1988). Although these rates are nominal as opposed to real rates of protection, they include both direct and indirect effects of protection on agriculture. The direct effects derive from tariffs, quotas and other intervention measures directly aimed at agriculture. The indirect effects result from currency overvaluation and protection of non-agriculture. As figures are available for only 18 countries and two commodities at this time [information on more commodities will be released in Krueger, Schiff, and Valdés (forthcoming)], the information on the direct and indirect incentive effects of prices for all other countries, country groups, and commodities are best-guess averages of the data available so far. The values substituting for the PSE and CSE values for developing countries are derived from the given data in Krueger, Schiff, and Valdés (1988) as follows. First, the six commodities analysed in this study are grouped into importables and exportables for each of the developing countries or country groups defined in this study. Second, for exportables and importables separately, PSEs are derived as the sum of the direct effect and one half the indirect effect[17]. For the four developing country groups included in the study, PSEs are calculated as simple averages of PSEs for those countries in the country group that are covered in Krueger, Schiff, and Valdés (1988). CSEs are approximated by setting them equal to the direct effect given in Krueger, Schiff, and Valdés (1988).

Information on expected average annual growth rates of population is taken from World Bank (1987, Table 27). The growth rates refer to the time period 1985 to 2000. The expected average annual growth rate of income is set at 2.5 per cent for most industrialised countries. Slightly different rates are used for Austria, Japan, and New Zealand to take into account differences in expected growth potential compared to this average. Income growth rates for developing countries ($r0_y$) are generally derived as a simple average of the average annual growth rates of GDP for the time periods 1965-80 and 1980-85, as reported in World Bank (1987, Table 2). Expected growth rates of agriculture are determined in an analogous way.

Average annual growth rates of productivity (rq_{ik}) are based on simple log-linear time trend regressions of yields for wheat, coarse grains, and rice. The regressions cover the years 1961-83. Due to the difficulty of obtaining consistent time series of real producer prices for most developing countries, the regressions do not control for changes in producer prices. Hence rq_{ik} and therefore qh_{ik} may contain the effect of changes in producer prices. But as few developing countries have followed a constant price policy for food products over the complete sample, the calculated growth rate may not be overly biased. The situation is somewhat different for OECD countries. The price-constant growth rate of yields and production may be less likely to be captured by a simple log-linear time trend. Hence the estimated exogenous rates of growth of production may be more biased than the one for developing countries.

The estimates of the above growth rates are adjusted as follows:

a) Insignificant or negative trend coefficients are converted to zero; and

b) Trend growth rates for production are substituted for trend growth rates in yields for countries and crops for which the growth in yields exceeds that in production.

The latter is the case, for example, in coarse grains for the country group identified as Asia. Hence the rate of growth of production (3.7) is substituted for the rate of growth of yields (8.8). There are a number of reasons for this somewhat more cautious approach[18].

Exogenous production growth is dependent both on the ability to increase arable land and on the introduction of new technologies to raise the productivity of existing land. Both are difficult to handle for forecasting purposes. Simply extrapolating past trends may lead to large forecast errors, especially over a long time horizon. Forecast problems exist for developed as well as for developing countries.

One important question in this context is to what extent productivity increases are independent of price changes. This age-old question is far from resolved. Genetic improvements, the rate of yield change due to more intensive use of fertilizer, and the yield change induced through other types of chemicals, machines, improved irrigation, etc. can all be assumed to depend on price incentives, although, of course, to a varying extent and over different time horizons. Fertilizer use is considered to be quickly price responsive, while genetic improvements respond rather slowly by comparison. If one assumes, as in this paper, that there will be more emphasis on the containment of production growth in industrialised countries, in particular in the EC, one can doubt whether the rate of growth in productivity experienced over the past 30 years will be maintained in the future. In addition, there is growing concern about the effect of the so-called "greenhouse" effect, especially how it could affect the North American plains.

Extrapolating past yield growth seems particularly treacherous for developing countries. The "Green Revolution" led to significant production growth in the 1960s and early 1970s. At the moment, however, the momentum seems to have been lost[19]. Also, there is no similar technological breakthrough in sight. Although new developments in biotechnology could revive the momentum, there appears to be little they will contribute to production in the developing world in this century[20]. Significant resources are required for biotechnology applications. Even if one assumes that these resources could be provided in industrialised countries, the technology does not transfer readily to developing countries. This is because biotechnology applications must be specifically designed for the target environment.

Developing countries face another problem in their effort to increase food production. In recent years, environmental stress has become apparent in Sub-Saharan Africa as well as in countries as diverse as India, Indonesia, Mexico, and a number of others. Soil erosion, receding water tables and increasing competition of agriculture with industry for water resources are alarming signs[21].

The average annual price-constant growth rates for sugar and soybean production are derived from yield averages as given in the FAO production yearbook for 1961-65 and 1984-86. Beginning and end years are modified in a number of cases to take into account the decrease in growth rates in more recent years[22]. For beef, the average annual growth rate of production is derived as a function of the predicted percentage change in total meat production, which is identified as *louh* in the model. The relationship between rq_{ik} and *louh* is given by

$$rq_{ik} = \sigma_k (1 + louh_k)^{1/r} \qquad \text{for } i=\text{beef} \quad k=1,\dots,m$$

where parameter σ is set to unity for all industrialised countries and where σ varies between 0.71 for Latin America and 0.84 for North Africa/Middle East. The values of σ are calculated based on data on average annual growth rates of beef and total meats as reported in Sarma and Yeung (1985, p. 26).

The parametric link between GDP growth and agricultural growth is based on a regression on a cross section of developing countries similar to that employed for the estimation of the parameter *ely* described above. The basic idea behind the regression is described in some detail in Hwa (1986). The estimated equation is given by

$$\hat{Y} = 1.3 - .03\,\hat{K} + .59\,\hat{L} + .20\,\hat{X} - .02\,\hat{P} + .81\,\hat{A} + 7.0\,OILD$$

$$(1.1) \quad (-.6) \quad (1.8) \quad (3.7) \quad (-2.0) \quad (6.7) \quad (4.5)$$

$$R^2 = .86 \quad - \quad F(6,\ 21) = 21.9$$

where $\hat{Y}, \hat{K}, \hat{L}, \hat{X}, \hat{P}$ and $\hat{A}$ represent, respectively, average percentage changes in annual growth rates, between 1970 and 1979, of gross domestic product, the country's capital stock, its labour force, exports, its GNP deflator, and of its agricultural sector. All data are from Hwa (1986, Annex Table 2). *OILD* is a dummy variable that equals unity for oil exporting countries. The equation is estimated on a sample of 28 countries for which either one of two conditions holds:

89

a) The share of agricultural exports in total exports exceeds 30 per cent, or

b) The share of the agricultural sector in GDP surpasses 30 per cent.

RESULTS OF MODEL SIMULATIONS

The model described above is used to identify the impact of changes in the agricultural policies of both OECD countries and developing countries. To be able to distinguish clearly these policy-induced changes from those that can be attributed to the growth of productivity, population, and other trend factors, the model is simulated first without any policy changes. This simulation serves as the base-line run.

Base-Line Model Projections

The base-line run of the model with base year 1981-83 projects prices and quantities for all six commodities 20 years into the future. The results of the base-line run can be summarised in a number of ways. They are presented in aggregate form in Tables 3.1 through 3.7.

Table 3.1 reports the predicted changes in real world prices over the model's time horizon. For the purpose of comparison, the predictions of some other studies are also presented. From a methodological viewpoint, the study by Roningen *et al.* (1988) is the closest to our approach. Similar to the present study, it is a nonspatial world trade equilibrium model that is essentially partial equilibrium in nature[23]. Both studies assume for the reference run that world price changes will feed back one for one into the markets of all industrialised countries. Unlike Roningen *et al.*, this study also assumes that world prices will be fully transmitted to producers and consumers in all developing countries. The econometric studies cited in Table 3.1 by Mitchell (1988) and Lord (1988) are also partial equilibrium in nature. In contrast to this study and the one by Roningen *et al.*, price transmission in the econometric studies is governed by constant parameters that are based on estimates of historical performance. For the purpose of predicting future developments, the historical trend is assumed to continue. This means, *inter alia*, that the Common Agricultural Policy of the EC and the US farm policy as contained in the 1985 Farm Bill are presumed to remain unchanged[24]. The IIASA study (Parikh *et al.*, 1988) consists of linked country-specific general equilibrium models. Of all the models cited, it is the most general in its approach. All studies except the present try to model explicitly the likely behavior of China and the centrally planned economies of Eastern Europe.

All cited studies have two things in common with the present one. They predict lower real grain and higher beef prices for the year 2000. The disagreement among studies on real price changes is the lowest for the heavily traded commodities wheat and coarse grains. It is substantial for most other commodities, even to the extent that there is no agreement as to the direction of change of real prices for three out of the six commodities[25].

Table 3.2 provides some clues for explaining some of the differences in predicted world price changes. For example, it shows that there are only small differences between the present study and that by Mitchell (1988) in the predicted rates of growth of both rice consumption and production in developing countries, by far the main market for this commodity. The studies differ, however, in the predicted production and consumption changes in industrialised countries, with Mitchell projecting a decline in both and the present study projecting positive growth. Although rice production and consumption in industrialised countries is minimal compared to that in developing countries, they appear to cause a large difference in the predicted price change for rice. A partial explanation is provided by the thinness of the rice market (Siamwalla and Haykin, 1983): even small differences in predicted quantities traded can lead to large differences in predicted world price changes.

Table 3.2 also provides some insight into the underlying causes of the predicted world price changes in beef and sugar. Lagging production growth in industrialised countries appears to be the main reason behind the very strong rise in world beef prices predicted by IIASA compared to the present study. The possibly surprising rise in sugar prices projected in this study results mainly from very strong demand growth in developing countries. One can be certain in this connection that substituting larger supply elasticities into the model, especially for developing countries, could reduce the resulting price increase substantially.

Tables 3.3 and 3.4 illustrate how the differences among studies in predicted world price changes and growth rates of quantities affect the estimated levels of production, domestic utilisation and net exports for the year 2000. It is apparent from Table 3.3 that the predictions for cereal production and domestic utilisation in developing countries vary considerably among models when compared to those for industrialised countries. The predictions of the present study for both developing country consumption and production of cereals are somewhat above the average for the studies referenced in Table 3.3. This is especially true for domestic utilisation, although it does not apply to its subcomponents food and feed consumption. Notice, for example, that this model's predicted feed demand of developing countries matches almost exactly that by Sarma (1986), a study that concentrates on this component of domestic consumption. Similarly, there is a very close match between the results of the present study and those of FAO for both developing country food and feed consumption. Yet this still leaves a substantial difference in total domestic utilisation. This can be traced to a substantially larger seed and waste component in domestic utilisation in the present study compared to FAO's[26]. Corresponding to the larger figures for domestic utilisation the present model also projects a larger cereal gap than the other studies. For example, the cereal gap without China is almost equal to the one projected by Mitchell for all developing countries including China. Similarly, it is twice the size of the low estimate by Paulino (1986). However, the cereal gap is only about 30 per cent higher than the one projected by the IIASA project.

Table 3.4 translates the cereal gap in developing countries evident from Table 3.3 into levels of self-sufficiency for each type of cereal and for cereals as a whole. Again some comparisons to other studies are provided. Except for rice, the model predicts a marked drop in self-sufficiency ratios for cereals. The reduction is particularly pronounced for coarse grains. Self-sufficiency ratios are predicted to fall somewhat more in this study than in the other cited studies. The one exception is rice. The overall levels of cereal self-sufficiency, however, do not differ significantly among studies. The consensus appears to be that self-sufficiency levels in cereals will drop by about 10 percentage points between the early 1980s and the year 2000.

Table 3.5 provides a breakdown of the cereal gap and self-sufficiency levels by region. It also identifies what the cereal gap implies for the cereal import bill of developing countries. The absolute level of cereal imports is predicted to triple for Asia and North Africa/Middle East by the year 2000 compared to the early 1980s. For Sub-Saharan Africa and Latin America, cereal imports are projected to increase fivefold. The large percentage increase in cereal imports, however, does not necessarily imply a large drop in self-sufficiency levels. The latter drop only slightly for Asia and Latin America. But for North Africa/Middle East and Sub-Saharan Africa the model projects a rather dramatic drop in self-sufficiency levels. Sub-Saharan Africa is also the region that is likely to experience by far the largest increase in its cereal import bill, whereas the cereal import bill is predicted to rise only marginally for Asia.

Tables 3.6 and 3.7 provide the base-line results for beef, sugar, and soybeans. Quantities of production, consumption, and trade as well as corresponding self-sufficiency ratios are provided for both industrialised and developing countries. The main directions of change are the same for all three commodities: self-sufficiency levels grow for industrialised countries and they fall for developing countries. The only exception to this is soybeans in Sub-Saharan Africa where self-sufficiency levels are predicted to grow rather than fall.

Central to the model simulations that are supposed to capture the effect of a change in OECD country policies towards lower output levels are the assumptions that are made with respect to how the reduction in output comes about. Is the output reduction associated with a decrease in PSEs or is a policy of acreage reduction pursued without a change in border protection? For the purpose of the model simulations it is assumed that all changes come about as changes in PSEs and CSEs. Furthermore, it is accepted that a change in PSEs and CSEs translates one for one into changes in trade volumes. As explained in some detail in Zietz and Valdés (1988), this may be quite unrealistic because there is no unique correspondence between changes in PSEs and in trade. Even if one ignores this potential problem, there still remains the question of how PSEs will be reduced. Will PSEs be decreased by an equal percentage across-the-board for all OECD countries and all commodities, or will the highest PSEs be reduced the most? To make the simulations as comparable as possible to those of other studies, PSEs and CSEs are varied in ways for industrialised countries. The model is used to simulate reductions in PSEs and CSEs of 10, 50, and 100 per cent.

The resulting world price changes corresponding to these alternative reductions are given in Table 3.8. Also given in this table are the results of a number of other studies. A 10 per cent reduction in PSEs and CSEs in industrialised countries causes a rather significant increase in the world price of sugar and beef. The orders of magnitude of these predicted price changes relative to those of the other commodities are similar to those of the OECD (1987) study. This also applies to the price changes for rice, whereas the predicted change in the world price of wheat is significantly different from that of the OECD study. Coarse grain and soybean prices are projected to decline more in the OECD study. The price changes in wheat, rice, beef, and sugar predicted for the 50 per cent scenario correspond rather closely to those of Valdés and Zietz (1980). Real prices of coarse grains and soybeans, however, are predicted to decline rather than rise in the present study. For both commodities, interdependencies in feed demand play a fairly large role. These were not modelled explicitly in Valdés and Zietz (1980).

Eliminating support levels as measured by PSEs and CSEs altogether leads to changes in world prices that are fairly modest compared to the predictions of the other studies quoted in Table 8. An exception is sugar. The price increases for wheat and coarse grains for one of the simulations of Tyers and Anderson (1987) are also fairly close to those of the present study. Overall, the results of complete liberalization appear to be close in spirit to what one would expect from the OECD model. This is not very surprising since many of the price elasticities are taken from that model. To explain the fairly large differences in predicted world price changes among models, one has to address the issue of base or reference periods. Model predictions are quite sensitive to the values of PSEs and CSEs. These values, however, can vary considerably over time. Hence, the choice of the base period is fairly crucial for the model's predictions of world price changes. This has been demonstrated in some detail by Zietz and Valdés (1986) for sugar. It is also apparent in Table 3.8. The differences in the two model simulations reported by Tyers and Anderson (1987) are largely the result of different protection levels.

The model simulations that capture the effects of alternative development strategies of developing countries on home and world agricultural markets assume a policy change towards export promotion. In the context of the present model this is interpreted to mean changing the modified PSE values (as developed from the information in Krueger, Schiff, and Valdés 1988) to zero[27]. At the same time, all CSE values are also set at zero.

Two policy simulations are conducted for the developing country liberalization scenario. The first one assumes that only developing countries liberalize. The second simulation combines liberalization in developing countries with complete trade liberalization in all industrialised countries. The effect of these two alternative liberalization scenarios on world prices is given in Table 3.9. Liberalization in developing countries alone is predicted to drive world prices down considerably. With the exception of beef, world prices drop by more than 10 per cent. These results are totally different from those of the IIASA model. The main reason for this discrepancy is that the latter study considers only border distortions, that is tariffs and quotas. All other distortions, Consumer Subsidy Equivalents and the indirect effect of protection in non-agriculture on agriculture, are kept constant. Indirect effects are also left out in the study by Tyers and Anderson (1987).

The large negative protection rates accorded to agriculture in developing countries are predicted to have a more significant effect on world prices than protection in industrialised countries. The two exceptions are beef and sugar, the two commodities for which protection rates are significant in industrialised countries. It is not surprising to find that, for these two commodities, the world price effects of global liberalization are the closest for all three studies quoted in Table 3.9. Overall, the strong world market effects of incentive structures of developing countries that are unfavourable to their agricultural production may well be the biggest surprise of this study.

Tables 3.10 through 3.14 provide information on how the predicted price changes associated with the various liberalization scenarios translate into changes in trade quantities, self-sufficiency levels and cereal import needs.

Table 3.10 shows the predicted change in net exports by developing countries which results from setting producer and consumer support levels to zero in industrialised countries. Liberalization by the latter causes an increase in net exports of developing countries in all commodities except for coarse grains and soybeans. Similar findings are reported by Tyers and Anderson (1987). The results by IIASA show significantly larger export changes in wheat and rice than either this study or the one by Tyers and Anderson (1987). Furthermore, developing countries are predicted to increase rather than reduce coarse grain exports in the IIASA study.

Liberalization by developing countries is predicted to increase net exports of coarse grains, rice, and sugar. Net exports of wheat are unaffected in the aggregate and beef and soybean exports decline. Again it is not surprising that the IIASA model predicts effects that are opposite in sign given IIASA's definition of liberalization by developing countries.

Table 3.11 demonstrates that liberalization in either industrialised or developing countries does not dramatially change the import needs of developing countries for wheat and coarse grains. They remain large under any scenario. Trade flows of the other commodities are affected more significantly. But trade flows in these other commodities are small when compared to those of wheat and coarse grains.

Table 3.12 reports self-sufficiency levels of industrialised or developing countries for all commodities and trade liberalization scenarios. Compared to the base line simulations, trade liberalization tends to improve self-sufficiency levels of developing countries in all commodities except soybeans. However, the improvement generated by trade liberalization is not enough to compensate for the decrease in self-sufficiency ratios predicted to materialise up to the year 2000. The long-run forces of growth in productivity, population, and per capita income appear to dominate the effect of trade liberalization for all commodities with regard to self-sufficiency levels. The fact that trade liberalization can reverse only part of the downward trend in self-sufficiency levels, however, may underestimate the overall benefit of liberalization. As detailed later in this chapter, the full effects of trade liberalization on developing countries are unlikely to be captured by a model that covers only six commodities but leaves out most of the agricultural products that generate the bulk of their foreign exchange earnings.

Table 3.13 is a supplement to Table 3.12 in the sense that it provides a breakdown of self-sufficiency levels of developing countries by region. All commodities and liberalization scenarios are covered. Table 3.14, in contrast, concentrates on their cereal import needs. It demonstrates that cereal imports and the cereal import bill of developing countries as a group are predicted to drop under all liberalization scenarios. The reduction is most dramatic for the scenarios that include developing country liberalization. For the latter two cases Asia as a group

93

is even projected to generate export earnings from cereal exports that exceed in magnitude the cereal import bill under the base-line simulation run. Cereal import needs are predicted to increase slightly for Sub-Saharan Africa and Latin America under liberalization. The cereal import bill of Sub-Saharan Africa, however, decreases under the two liberalization runs that include developing country liberalization. The opposite is true for the cereal import bill of Latin America. It decreases only for the case of liberalization in the industrialised countries.

Some Qualifying Interpretations of the Simulation Results

There are a number of caveats to keep in mind regarding the assumed policy changes and their predicted results. First, domestic policy reforms for a particular country are difficult to model in a global trade model such as this. The success of liberalization depends on a number of favourable conditions. As the experience with the Southern Cone countries has demonstrated, the liberalization steps have to be taken in the proper sequence and be timed right to be successful[28]. In addition, there is ample evidence from African countries that price policy reform alone is not sufficient to spur economic activity. On the contrary, higher prices could lead to little change in economic activity of farmers if the expected increase in cash income cannot be transformed into the desired consumer goods. The income effect of higher prices may, in other words, just compensate for or even outweigh their substitution effect[29].

A global trade model such as this that is limited to six agricultural products is unlikely to be the proper instrument to identify complex domestic policy changes. This applies, for example, to purely domestic policies aimed at raising self-sufficiency levels for basic food crops. To capture such policies adequately in a model, one would have to take into account not only the relationship between food crops and competing cash crops but also the impact of possibly reduced foreign exchange earnings on the entire economy. This would require incorporating a sufficient number of cash crops in the model as well as some representation of the non-agricultural sector. How this can be done for countries that are grouped together in such aggregates as Asia or Latin America is an open question. It therefore appears that intricate domestic policy reforms are better modelled within the context of general equilibrium country models rather than in global trade models. A large number of commodities of potential economic interest to developing countries have not been discussed in this study. These include primary tropical products, such as beverages, oilseeds other than soybeans, and groundnuts, as well as temperate-zone commodities in which there is considerable potential for growth[30]. In particular, horticultural products offer excellent possibilities for generating employment and for increasing foreign exchange earnings (Islam 1988).

Another group of commodities which have not been discussed here are processed agricultural products. Like horticultural products, they also could contribute significantly to growth in employment and foreign exchange earnings. Structural adjustment policies in developing countries along the lines assumed in the model simulations are likely to provide a strong incentive to develop the production and marketing of processed products if, at the same time, OECD countries manage to lower their import barriers on these goods. The study of the trade of processed agricultural goods and its potential effect on economic growth in developing countries as well as OECD countries is clearly in its infancy. Yet this is where a large part of the potential benefits of structural adjustment in developing countries toward a more export-oriented economic policy and trade concession by OECD countries could be most important for long-run economic growth.

In short, the focus on traditional temperate-zone agricultural products may seriously underestimate the long-run gains to developing countries following an export-oriented policy when there is lower protection in agricultural products in OECD countries.

Another qualification relates to potential data problems, in particular the data on feed grain substitutes. Although soybean consumption for feed has been included in this study, all other feed grain substitutes have not. Yet they are of considerable importance in the case of the EC and also for certain developing countries that supply them (e.g. cassava from Thailand). Hence actual tariff harmonization between feed grains and feed grain substitutes may lead to results that are somewhat different from those generated by the model. A more elaborate feed grain subsector would have to be incorporated into the model to capture the potential changes more adequately (see OECD, 1988a). Yet this is clearly beyond the scope of the present modelling exercise.

CONCLUSIONS AND OUTLOOK

The simulations and a comparison of the results with other studies have shown that there is a fairly large degree of uncertainty regarding the development of world prices of food commodities over the next 20 years or so. There appears to be a consensus, however, that real prices of wheat and coarse grains are likely to continue to fall, whereas the real prices of beef are going to rise.

The base-line simulations have shown that despite large differences in predicted prices among various studies, there appears to be less controversy about the level of production, consumption, and net trade, in particular in cereals. This conclusion is essentially independent of the type of modelling effort, be it a simple trend forecast, an econometric model, a partial equilibrium world trade model or a linked applied general equilibrium model. The convergence of predicted magnitudes of production, consumption, and trade seems to be particularly high with regard to industrialised countries. There is much less certainty about the forecasts for developing countries. It seems that the modelling of developing countries' reactions would require considerably more work.

This need is all the more important because of the considerable impact that the economic policies of developing countries seem to have on world trade and prices of agricultural products. In fact, the major surprise of this study may well be the predicted dominance on world prices of the large negative protection rates by developing countries compared to positive protection in industrialised countries. As demonstrated in this study, a removal of the disincentive effects of negative protection is likely to lead to an increase in self-sufficiency levels of cereals and other products. In addition, there appears to be no evidence that trade liberalization will increase the cereal import bill of developing countries. On the contrary, as a group and for all regions except Latin America the cereal import bill will either remain constant under trade liberalization or decrease. This also applies for Sub-Saharan Africa.

Further investigation of the role of trade liberalization appears to be highly desirable. For that purpose, the current modelling effort would have to be extended in a number of ways. Apart from including more commodities in the study and updating the data, it seems that a thorough comparison with other similar modelling efforts is highly desirable. Such an exercise should, however, go beyond a comparison of simulation results, as done in this paper. One would like to make some comparisons of the underlying assumptions regarding crucial elasticity values. A first step in this direction may be possible using the input data for the USDA model. Running a model with alternative input data and comparing the results could help clarify the differences among models. It would also put any discussions on modelling strategies on a more solid basis.

Table 3.1

PREDICTED LONG-RUN CHANGES IN WORLD PRICES

(Base year to approximately 2000)

Studies	Base	Wheat	CGs	Rice	Beef	Sugar	Soya
Present study	1982	-16.5	-13.7	20.5	1.4	62.9	-2.3
Other studies[1]							
Roningen et al.[2]	1986	-8.8	-9.6	-7.0	10.2	-5.3	-9.8
IIASA (Parikh et al.)	1980	-8.0	-10.0	1.0	53.0	..	..
Lord	1984	..	-22.5	..	63.4	50.1	65.9
Mitchell	1987	-23.0	-16.4	-13.4	..	..	-31.6

1. China and the CPEs are treated on par with other countries rather than assuming that their net imports and stock changes remain constant at base period levels.
2. Roningen et al. use oilseeds and products instead of soybeans.

96

Table 3.2

PREDICTED AVERAGE ANNUAL GROWTH RATES OF QUANTITIES
Circa 1980-2000

	Production		Utilisation		Domestic net export	
	ICs	LDCs	ICs	LDCs	ICs	LDCs
Present study:						
Wheat	1.7	2.7	1.1	3.2	2.6	4.5[1]
Coarse grains	2.7	2.0	2.2	3.1	5.7	10.8[1]
Rice	1.1	2.4	0.6	2.4	3.5	5.7[1]
Beef	1.6	2.1	1.2	2.8	30.8	..
Sugar	2.4	1.6	-0.1	2.9	20.1	..
Soybeans	1.6	1.4	1.3	3.3	14.4	-2.1
Mitchell[2]:						
Wheat	2.4	3.0	1.4	3.5	5.0	5.0[1]
Coarse grains	1.7	1.8	1.8	2.4	12.2	8.5[1]
Rice	-0.3	2.3	-1.3	2.4	15.2	24.3[1]
Soybeans	3.4	4.3	3.3	4.2	-13.1	4.5
IIASA[3]:						
Wheat	2.8/1.1	3.3	1.9		3.0	
Coarse grains	2.4/1.4	2.1	1.7		3.7	
Rice	3.4/0.7	2.9	2.1		3.4	
Beef	0.9/1.0	2.8	1.5		2.8	

1. Imports increase in this case.
2. Figures for developing countries include China.
3. First column gives growth rates for North America and Oceania and growth rates for all remaining industrialised countries; consumption and export columns give global growth rates, for all countries combined.

Table 3.3

CEREAL PRODUCTION, DOMESTIC UTILISATION AND NET IMPORTS IN THE YEAR 2000

	Present Study		Mitchell (1988)		IIASA (1988)		Paulino (1986)	FAO AT2000	Sarma (1986)
	ICs	LDCs	ICs	LDCs	ICs	LDCs	LDCs	LDCs	LDCs
			(millions)	(tonnes)					
Production	886	763	832	1 270[1]	829	656	787	679	..
Domestic utilization	648	935	593	1 246[1]	640	788	867	851	..
Food	94	565				488	575	..	
Feed		471	233				379[2]	276[2]	245
Net imports	-238	173	-229	177[1]	-189	132	80	136	..

1. China is included in the figures.
2. Includes feed and other uses, such as seed and waste.

Table 3.4

**CEREAL SELF-SUFFICIENCY OF DEVELOPING COUNTRIES
IN 1981-83 AND THE YEAR 2000**

		2000		
	1981-83	This study	Mitchell[1] (Per cent)	IIASA
Wheat	76	68	73	73
Coarse grains	95	76	85	79
Rice	100	99	99	98
All cereals	92	82	86	83

1. The figures include China.

Table 3.5

CEREAL IMPORT NEEDS BY DEVELOPING COUNTRY REGION: 1981-83 to 2000

	Import level 1981-83	Import level 2000	Percentage change in import bill	Self-sufficiency 1981-83	2000
	(Million metric tonnes)				(Per cent)
All developing countries	48	173	174	92	82
Asia	10	30	29	97	94
North Africa/Middle East	28	86	143	70	51
Sub-Saharan Africa	8	44	350	84	55
Latin America	2	12	293	99	92

Note: The figures exclude China.

Table 3.6

PRODUCTION, DOMESTIC UTILISATION, NET IMPORTS OF BEEF, SUGAR, AND SOYBEANS IN 2000

	Beef	Sugar (Million tonnes)	Soybeans
Industrialised countries:			
Production	31	46	74
Domestic utilisation	29	28	70
Net imports	-3	-18	-4
Developing countries:			
Production	19	88	28
Domestic utilisation	21	98	21
Net imports	3	10	-7

Note: The balance of net imports is absorbed by the centrally planned economies and China.

Table 3.7

SELF-SUFFICIENCY OF INDUSTRIALISED AND DEVELOPING COUNTRIES IN BEEF, SUGAR, AND SOYBEANS: 1981-83 AND 2000

	Beef		Sugar		Soya	
	1981-83	2000	1981-83	2000	1981-83	2000
			(Per cent)			
All industrialised countries	100	109	102	167	100	106
All developing countries	100	88	115	90	194	132
Asia	97	77	105	80	49	38
North Africa/Middle East	78	65	46	30	24	16
Sub-Saharan Africa	97	86	109	62	83	131
Latin America	106	99	162	157	353	270

Note: The figures exclude China.

Table 3.8

CHANGES IN WORLD PRICE RELATIVE TO BASE-LINE RUN RESULTING FROM TRADE LIBERALIZATION IN INDUSTRIALISED COUNTRIES

Percentage reduction in PSEs and CSEs	Wheat	CGs	Rice	Beef	Sugar	Soya
Present study:						
10 per cent	0.4	-0.1	0.2	0.9	1.5	-0.3
50 per cent	2.0	-0.7	0.9	4.9	7.6	-1.5
100 per cent	3.5	-2.8	1.7	10.5	15.0	-4.0
Other studies:						
OECD-1987 (10%)	-0.1	-0.3	0.1	1.5	1.0	-1.0
Valdés/Zietz-80 (50%)	4.9	2.1[1]	0.4	6.8	7.7[2]	1.0
IIASA (100%)	18.0	11.0	21.0	17.0	..	..
Tyers/Anderson-87[3] (100%)	9.0	3.0	10.0	21.0	10.0	..
Tyers/Anderson-87[4] (100%)	25.0	3.0	18.0	43.0	22.0	..
Roningen et al. (100%)	25.9	18.8	18.1	17.3	31.0	6.8
Zietz/Valdés-86[5] (100%)	12.1	11.0	..	17.4	18.2	..

1. Maize.
2. Raw sugar.
3. Based on protection levels of 1980-82.
4. Based on projected protection levels for 1988.
5. The reported price increases are simple averages of the various alternative model simulations reported in Table 1 of Zietz and Valdés (1986); the estimates are based on 1979-81 protection levels.

Table 3.9

**CHANGES IN WORLD PRICE RESULTING FROM TRADE LIBERALIZATION
IN DEVELOPING COUNTRIES AND ALL COUNTRIES**

100 per cent reduction in PSEs and CSEs in	Wheat	CGs	Rice	Beef	Sugar	Soya
Present study:						
Developing countries	-13.6	-20.9	-21.8	2.9	-12.1	-11.5
All countries	-11.7	-24.4	-21.1	13.3	0.8	-15.9
IIASA:						
Developing countries	5.0	4.0	1.0	-3.0	..	..
All countries	23.0	13.0	16.0	11.0	..	..
Tyers/Anderson-87:						
All countries	10.0	2.0	-8.0	13.0	-1.0	..

Table 3.10

ABSOLUTE CHANGE FROM BASE LINE RUN IN NET EXPORTS OF DEVELOPING COUNTRIES UNDER VARIOUS LIBERALIZATION SCENARIOS

	Wheat	CG	Rice	Beef	Sugar	Soya
			(Million tonnes)			
Present study:						
ICs-liberalize	8.8	-11.6	4.0	0.8	5.1	-0.9
LDCs-liberalize	0	16.1	2.5	-1.8	2.5	-4.0
All-liberalize	8.9	1.7	6.4	-0.7	7.8	-5.3
IIASA:						
ICs-liberalize	11.1	1.3	9.1	1.8	..	..
LDCs-liberalize	-11.0	-10.0	-0	0.3	..	..
Tyers/Anderson:						
ICs-liberalize	4.9	-2.3	4.0	2.9	2.9	..

Note: Liberalization means complete removal of all PSEs and CSEs. Liberalization is superimposed on the base line results.

Table 3.11

**IMPORTS OF DEVELOPING COUNTRIES IN THE YEAR 2000
UNDER VARIOUS LIBERALIZATION SCENARIOS**

	Base line run	Liberalization by		
		ICs (Million tonnes)	LDCs	All
Wheat	86.8	78.1	86.8	77.9
Coarse grains	82.4	93.7	66.3	80.7
Rice	3.5	-0.5	1.0	-2.9
Beef	2.5	1.7	4.3	3.2
Sugar	9.7	4.6	7.2	1.9
Soybeans	-6.8	-5.9	-2.8	-1.5

Note: The figures exclude China. Liberalization means complete removal of all PSEs and CSEs. Liberalization is superimposed on the base line results.

Table 3.12

SELF-SUFFICIENCY OF INDUSTRIALISED COUNTRIES AND DEVELOPING COUNTRIES: 1981-83; BASE-LINE AND LIBERALIZATION RUNS

	Cereals	Wheat	CG	Rice (Per cent)	Beef	Sugar	Soya
1981-83:							
Industrialised countries	124	178	107	108	100	102	100
Developing countries	92	76	95	100	100	115	194
Base-line results:							
Industrialised countries	137	189	122	128	109	167	106
Developing countries	82	68	76	99	88	90	132
Industrialised countries liberalize:							
Industrialised countries	136	185	124	104	106	143	107
Developing countries	82	71	73	100	92	95	127
Developing countries liberalize:							
Industrialised countries	134	195	118	113	115	155	112
Developing countries	84	69	81	100	82	93	111
All liberalize:							
Industrialised countries	134	190	121	91	112	133	113
Developing countries	84	72	77	101	86	98	106

Note: The figures exclude China. Liberalization means complete removal of all PSEs and CSEs. Liberalization is superimposed on the base line results.

Table 3.13

SELF-SUFFICIENCY OF DEVELOPING COUNTRIES BY REGION: 1981-83, BASE-LINE AND LIBERALIZATION RUNS: 2002

	Cereals	Wheat	CG	Rice (Per cent)	Beef	Sugar	Soya
1981-83 averages:							
Asia	97	86	94	102	97	105	49
North Africa/ME	70	67	75	69	78	46	24
Sub-Saharan Africa	84	29	95	66	97	109	83
Latin America	99	83	106	97	106	162	353
Base-Line run:							
Asia	94	87	77	104	77	80	38
North Africa/ME	51	52	46	77	65	30	16
Sub-Saharan Africa	55	18	64	40	86	62	131
Latin America	92	63	102	95	99	157	270
Industrialised countries liberalize:							
Asia	94	89	72	105	85	86	37
North Africa/ME	52	55	43	79	67	32	15
Sub-Saharan Africa	54	19	63	41	89	65	128
Latin America	92	66	100	96	102	164	261
Developing countries liberalize:							
Asia	98	87	87	107	44	83	25
North Africa/ME	54	58	46	75	72	32	17
Sub-Saharan Africa	53	14	66	33	83	64	130
Latin America	92	58	107	82	104	160	299
All liberalize:							
Asia	98	89	81	108	49	89	24
North Africa/ME	54	61	42	76	75	34	16
Sub-Saharan Africa	52	15	64	34	86	66	126
Latin America	91	60	105	83	107	167	287

Note: The figures exclude China. Liberalization means complete removal of all PSEs and CSEs. The figures for the base line results and the various liberalization scenarios are predictions for the year 2002, i.e. 20 years from the base year.

Table 3.14

CEREAL IMPORT NEEDS BY DEVELOPING COUNTRY REGION UNDER VARIOUS LIBERALIZATION SCENARIOS: YEAR 2000[1]

	All LDCs	Asia	NA/ME	Sub-Sah. Africa	Latin America
Base line run					
Import level (million tonnes)	173	30	86	44	12
Cereal import bill (% change)	174	29	143	350	293
Industrialised countries liberalize					
Import level (million tonnes)	171	29	85	45	13
Cereal import bill (% change)	157	-56	137	352	287
Developing countries liberalize					
Import level (million tonnes)	154	11	81	48	14
Cereal import bill (% change)	106	-204[2]	88	322	384
All liberalize					
Import level (million tonnes)	156	10	81	49	14
Cereal import bill (% change)	93	-267[2]	81	323	383

1. The figures exclude China. The percentage change in the cereal import bill is calculated with reference to the cereal import bill of 1981-83.

2. Export earnings exceed the import bill in the reference period.

NOTES AND REFERENCES

1. Valdés and Zietz (1980), for example, used a two-step procedure for their calculations. It is not clear to what extent the approximation problem is taken into account in the work of Tyers and Anderson (forthcoming) or Roningen, *et al.* (1988).

2. This method is also used in Zietz and Valdés (1986). For large changes, use of the discrete changes formula clearly makes a difference for the results. Ignoring the problem of large changes can easily lead to odd results. Although changing model parameters can eliminate these results in most cases, it is unlikely to be a satisfactory approach.

3. As an empirical matter, the size of the growth rates and the time horizon used in this model provide for very good approximations to what one can expect from an explicit sequence model.

4. A more complete model would also include livestock products to determine feed demand, in particular milk and eggs. Restricting the coverage of livestock products to meats will not introduce a significant error in the present model as long as one can assume that production of meats, milk and eggs is following a rather similar growth path.

5. Details of the elasticity derivations are given in the data section.

6. Clearly, most though not all of the above simplifying assumptions regarding meat production can be avoided if one extends the model to cover ruminants, non-ruminants, and dairy production, rather than restricting the commodity coverage to beef.

7. Other uses of soybeans for Argentina and Brazil are defined as other uses of wheat for developing countries.

8. More detail on the construction of the protection measures for developing countries is provided in the data section.

9. For simplicity of exposition, PSE is used to identify both measures in what follows.

10. Compare, for example, the discussions in Commission of the European Communities (1988).

11. In some countries, part of the pressure for adjustment may originate from outside the country, for example, from the intervention of international lending organisations such as the World Bank or the International Monetary Fund.

12. For the purpose of comparison, the basic input data for both China and the centrally planned economies are included in a data appendix (not published here).

13. Feed demand elasticities for rice are set to unity for lack of better information, cross-price elasticities with respect to other feeds to zero.

14. Compare Sarma (1968) for the rationale of dividing fresh milk production by a factor of 10.

15. Data on meat production are from the FAO printout mentioned earlier, data on milk and hen egg production from the 1986 *FAO Production Yearbook.* Per capita income levels for 1985 and land area are taken from the *World Development Report 1987.*

16. To allow model calculations to proceed, it was decided to convert the PSE figure of −1.5 quoted for Nigeria in USDA (1988) to −0.9.

17. Although it is unclear to what extent the indirect effect translates into output changes, simply restricting the PSE measure and hence the output effect to the direct effect appears too conservative.

Setting the PSE measure equal to the simple sum of direct and indirect effect, however, is likely to lead to an overestimate of the output effect.

18. The more cautious approach advocated here constrasts with the rather more optimistic predictions for output growth by Anderson and Herdt (1988). As part of a simple model for cereal output growth, they assume that yields of cereals will grow at an average annual rate of 2.65 on non-irrigated land and of 3.57 on irrigated land. Area is predicted to grow between 0.5 and 1 per cent per annum, respectively. Overall then, output growth amounts to 3.16 per cent per annum on non-irrigated land and 4.54 per cent on irrigated land. These predictions assume constant relative prices.

19. Compare World Watch Institute (1988).

20. For more detail, see the discussion in Anderson and Herdt (1988).

21. Compare World Watch Institute (1988).

22. In the case of soybeans, for example, the growth rate in yields for Australia and the country category identified as "Others" is calculated on the period between 1974-76 and 1984/85. Average annual growth rates of sugar yields are generally calculated for the period covering the years 1961-65 to 1979-81.

23. We ignore, for the moment, the endogenous feedback of agricultural growth on the growth rate of GNP in this study.

24. See, in particular, the study by Mitchell based on the World Bank Model.

25. It is not clear, however, whether Lord uses real prices in the case of soybeans. If not, there is a good chance that all studies predict real soybean prices to decline towards the year 2000.

26. As mentioned earlier, it may be unrealistic to assume that seed and in particular waste will grow in fixed proportion with production of consumption. Changes in technology or relative price changes may very well reduce the waste component of domestic utilisation. If that is true, the present study would overestimate total domestic utilisation for the year 2000.

27. Ideally, one would want to run another simulation that sets the value to 0.1, that is, a value identical to that proposed for developed countries. However, to do this, detailed information would have been required from Krueger, Schiff, and Valdés (forthcoming).

28. See, for example, the discussion in Congdon (1985).

29. Compare Bevan et al. (1987) on the importance of this point for two East African countries.

30. Compare, for example, the trade liberalization study by Valdés and Zietz (1980) on the quantitative importance for developing countries of tropical products vis-à-vis temperate zone products.

BIBLIOGRAPHY

ANDERSON, K., Y. HAYAMI, and M. HONMA, "Growth of Agricultural Protection" in Anderson, Kym, and Yujiro Hayami (eds.), *The Political Economy of Agricultural Protection*, London: Allen and Unwin, 1986.

ANDERSON, J.R. and R.W. HERDT, "The Impact of New Technology on Foodgrain Productivity to the Next Century", in A. Maunder and A. Valdés (eds.), *Agriculture and Governments in an Interdependent World*, proceedings of the XX International Conference of Agricultural Economists, Aldershot, England: Dartmouth, 1989.

BEVAN, D., A. BIGSTEN, P. COLLIER, and J.W. GUNNING, *East African Lessons on Economic Liberalization*, Thames Essays No. 48, Aldershot, England: Gower for the Trade Policy Research Centre, 1987.

CENTRE FOR INTERNATIONAL ECONOMICS, *Macro-economic Consequences of Farm-support Policies*, overview of an International Program of Studies, Canberra, 1988.

CLEMENTS, K.W. and L.A. SJAASTAD, *How Protection Taxes Exporters*, Thames Essay No. 39, London: Trade Policy Research Centre, 1984.

COMMISSION OF THE EUROPEAN COMMUNITIES, "Disharmonies in EC and US Agricultural Policy Measures," Luxembourg, 1988.

CONGDON, T.G., *Economic Liberalization in the Cone of Latin America*, Thames Essay No. 40, London: Trade Policy Research Centre, 1985.

FAO, "Agricultural Protection and Stabilization Policies: A Framework of Measurement in the Context of Agricultural Adjustment," C 75/Lim/ 2, Rome, October 1975.

FAO, *Agriculture: Toward 2000*, Rome, 1981.

FAO, "Agricultural Supply/Utilization Accounts Tape, 1984," Rome, 1984.

HWA, E.-C., "The Contribution of Agriculture to Economic Growth — Some Empirical Evidence," paper presented at the 8th World Congress of the International Economic Association, New Delhi, India, December 1986.

ISLAM, N., "World Trade in Horticultural Products: Performance of Developing Countries," Washington, DC: International Food Policy Research Institute, mimeo, June 1988.

KRUEGER, A.O., M. SCHIFF, and A. VALDÉS, "Agricultural Incentives in Developing Countries: Measuring the Effect of Sectoral and Economywide Policies", *The World Bank Economic Review*, Vol. 2, No. 3, September 1988.

KRUEGER, A.O., M. SCHIFF, and A. VALDÉS, *The Political Economy of Agricultural Pricing Policies: Country Studies*, 5 volumes, Baltimore, Maryland: John Hopkins University Press, forthcoming.

LORD, M.J., "The Outlook for Trade in Agricultural Commodities", in A. Maunder and A. Valdés (eds.), *Agriculture and Governments in an Interdependent World*, proceedings of the XX International Conference of Agricultural Economists, Aldershot, England: Dartmouth, 1989.

MAHE, L.P. and C. TAVERA, "Bilateral Harmonization of EC and US Agricultural Policies," Economic Development Center, University of Minnesota, August 1988.

MCCLATCHY, D. and S. CAHILL, "Cross-Commodity Trade Effects of Agricultural Policies: Some Implications for the GATT", in A. Maunder and A. Valdés (eds.), *Agriculture and Governments in an Interdependent World*, proceedings of the XX International Conference of Agricultural Economists, Aldershot, England: Dartmouth, 1989.

MITCHELL, D.O., "The Outlook for Trade in Agricultural Commodities," in A. Maunder and A. Valdés (eds.), *Agriculture and Governments in an Interdependent World*, proceedings of the XX International Conference of Agricultural Economists, Aldershot, England: Dartmouth, 1989.

NOGUES, J.J., A. OLECHOWSKI, and L.A. WINTERS, "The Extent of Nontariff Barriers to Imports of Industrial Countries," World Bank Staff Working Papers, No. 789, Washington, D.C., February 1986.

OECD, "Agricultural Policies, Markets and Trade: Monitoring and Outlook 1989," draft report of Annex IV, Agricultural Policy and Trade Developments in the Developing Economies: Implications for OECD, (AGR/APM(89)1, AGR/TC/WP(89)1, Paris, January 1989.

OECD, "MTM Model Specification and Elasticities," Committee for Agriculture, AGR(88)7, March 1988a.

OECD, "Rapport sur le Suivi et les Perspectives des Politiques, des Marchés et des Échanges Agricoles," Paris, May 1988b.

OECD, *Agricultural Policies, Markets and Trade: Monitoring and Outlook 1988*, Paris, 1988c.

OECD, *National Policies and Agricultural Trade*, Paris, 1987.

PARIKH, K.S., G. FISCHER, K. FROHBERG, and O. GULBRANDSEN, *Towards Free Trade in Agriculture*, Laxenburg, Austria: Martinus Nighoff Publishers, 1988.

PAULINO, L.A., *Food in the Third World: Past Trends and Projections to 2000*, Research Report 52, Washington, DC: International Food Policy Research Institute, June 1986.

RONINGEN, V.O., P.M. DIXIT, and R. SEELEY, "Agricultural Outlook for the Year 2000: Some Alternatives", in A. Maunder and A. Valdés (eds.), *Agriculture and Governments in an Interdependent World*, proceedings of the XX International Conference of Agricultural Economists, Aldershot, England: Dartmouth, 1989.

SARMA, J.S., *Cereal Feed Use in the Third World: Past Trends and Projections to 2000*, Research Report 57, Washington, D.C.: International Food Policy Research Institute, December 1986.

SARMA, J.S. and P. YEUNG, *Livestock Products in the Third World: Past Trends and Projections to 1990 and 2000*, Research Report 49, Washington, D.C.: International Food Policy Research Institute, April 1985.

SCANDIZZO, P.L. and C. BRUCE, "Methodologies for Measuring Agricultural Price Intervention Effects," World Bank Staff Working Paper No. 394, Washington, D.C.: IBRD, June 1980.

SCHIFF, M.W., *An Econometric Analysis of the World Wheat Market and Simulation of Alternative Policies, 1960-80*, Economic Research Service, Washington, D.C.: US Department of Agriculture, October 1985.

SIAMWALLA, A. and S. HAYKIN, *The World Rice Market: Structure, Conduct, and Performance*, Research Report 39, Washington, D.C.: International Food Policy Research Institute, June 1983.

TANGERMANN, S., T.E. JOSLING, and S. PEARSON, "Multilateral Negotiations on Farm-support Levels," *The World Economy*, Vol. 10, No. 3, September 1987.

TYERS, R. and K. ANDERSON, "Distortions in World Food Markets: A Quantitative Assessment," background paper for the *World Development Report 1986* of the World Bank, mimeo, January, 1986 (revised and expanded version forthcoming as book by Cambridge University Press).

TYERS, R. and K. ANDERSON, "Global Interactions and Trade Liberalisation in Agriculture," University of Adelaide, revised mimeo, April, 1987 (forthcoming in Ray, A. and Johnson, D. Gale (eds.), *Economic Policies and World Agriculture*).

USDA, "Estimates of Producer and Consumer Subsidy Equivalents: Government Intervention in Agriculture, 1982-86," Agriculture and Trade Analysis Division, Economic Research Service, ERS Staff Report No. AGES880127, Washington, D.C., April 1988.

USDA, "Embargoes, Surplus Disposal, and U.S. Agriculture," Economic Research Service, Agricultural Economic Report 564, Washington, D.C., December 1986.

USDA, "Government Intervention in Agriculture: Measurement, Evaluation, and Implications for Trade Negotiations," Foreign Agricultural Economic Report 229, Economic Research Service, United States Department of Agriculture, Washington, D.C., April 1987.

VALDÉS, A., "Agriculture in the Uruguay Round: Interests of Developing Countries," *The World Bank Economic Review*, Vol. 1, No. 4, September 1987.

VALDÉS, A. and J. ZIETZ, *Agricultural Protection in OECD Countries: Its Cost to Less Developed Countries*, Research Report 21, Washington, D.C.: International Food Policy Research Institute, December 1980.

WORLD BANK, *World Development Report 1987*, Oxford University Press, for the International Bank for Reconstruction and Development, New York, 1987.

WORLDWATCH INSTITUTE, *State of the World 1988*, Annual Report, Washington, 1988.

YOTOPOULOS, P.A., "Middle-Income Classes and Food Crises: The 'New' Food-Feed Competition", *Economic Development and Cultural Change*, Vol. 33, No. 3, 1985.

ZIETZ, J. and A. VALDÉS, "The Costs of Protectionism to Developing Countries: An Analysis for Selected Agricultural Products," World Bank Staff Working Papers 769, Washington, D.C.: IBRD, January 1986.

ZIETZ, J. and A. VALDÉS, *Agriculture in the GATT: An Analysis of Alternative Approaches to Reform*, Research Report 70, Washington, D.C.: International Food Policy Research Institute, November 1988.

Chapter 4

AGRICULTURAL POLICIES IN DEVELOPING COUNTRIES AND AGRICULTURAL TRADE[1]

by

Catherine Moreddu, Kevin Parris and Bruce Huff

INTRODUCTION

The report, *National Policies and Agricultural Trade*[2], concluded that a reduction in assistance to agricultural producers and consumers in the OECD countries would in general increase world prices and thus have a mixed impact on developing countries, depending on their agricultural trade balance. Nonetheless, the higher world prices should induce the developing countries to increase domestic agricultural production. The Ministerial Communiqué in May 1987 noted the benefits of higher prices from agricultural policy reforms for developing country agricultural exporters, while at the same time providing more appropriate market signals to developing country importers. More detailed analysis of these impacts was not possible as the Ministerial Trade Mandate (MTM) model included only one aggregate region covering all developing countries. In addition, as no estimation of assistance was included for this region, the impact of policy changes in developing countries on OECD countries and on developing countries themselves could not be analysed.

The impact of OECD country agricultural policy reform on the developing countries has been an important issue in the current Uruguay Round of trade negotiations. The OECD MTM world agricultural model developed for the Trade Mandate study contained a single region for all the developing countries. The present study extends this analysis to examine the policies and the impacts of trade liberalization for eight developing countries and regions, accounting for about 25 per cent of the world production and consumption of the 19 commodities included in the MTM model.

While this analysis represents an important contribution to the policy research and debate with respect to the developing country issue, it does not represent an exhaustive study of all the aspects of the problem. For example, further research would be required to assess, particularly, the intersectoral linkages which are much more important in the developing than in the OECD countries. Furthermore, the exclusion of tropical products from the MTM model understates the extent of the benefits which would accrue to these countries if the OECD countries liberalized their import policies for these products as well as for the temperate zone products.

Agriculture is a major component of the economy in most developing countries. Changes in domestic and international commodity markets have considerable consequences for their economies. Thus the impact of the intersectoral linkages are relatively more important in developing countries than in OECD countries.

This project draws upon and complements the ongoing analysis of the OECD's Agriculture Directorate which monitors OECD country agricultural trade relations with developing countries, providing annually a document to the Committee for Agriculture (most recently, see Annex IV of *Agricultural Policies, Markets and Trade — Monitoring and Outlook*[3]). The results of this analysis will improve the quantitative analysis of developing and OECD country interlinkages and agricultural policy assessment.

The objectives of this project were firstly to improve the understanding of agricultural policies across a range of developing countries and their implications for agricultural trade, and secondly to identify the domestic and international commodity market impacts from trade liberalization in OECD and developing countries.

To carry out the analysis to achieve the above project objectives involved extending the basic structure of the OECD agricultural trade model and obtaining the data for commodity markets and trade, the behavioural parameters and the domestic agricultural and trade policies for the specific developing countries.

The inclusion of individual developing countries with estimates of their domestic assistance allowed closer examination of the possible consequences of reduced OECD country assistance on these countries and permitted, for example, the comparison of effects on richer versus poorer developing countries, and agricultural exporters versus importers. In addition, by varying the assistance to producers and consumers in these developing countries, changes in world prices and in commodity supply-utilisation in OECD countries could be observed.

While there are a number of ways in which the existing MTM model might be extended, it was decided to keep new modelling and data work to a minimum, in order to fulfill these work requirements in a timely manner with limited resources. Nevertheless, the work constitutes a significant expansion of the analytical capacity of the Secretariat. The most significant change in model structure was to allow a feedback of changes in farm income on demand for agricultural commodities, one of the important intrasectoral linkages. The existing commodity coverage was maintained even though some additional commodities would be of interest in the context of OECD/developing country trade. As regards country coverage, the disaggregation of the developing countries was increased to eight new countries or regions, in addition to the nine OECD countries or regions, a Centrally Planned Economies group and the rest of the developing countries as a group. Table 4.1 presents the country and commodity coverage of the model.

To ensure comparability with current analysis for the OECD area, the 1982-85 base period was chosen. For the developing countries, the supply/utilisation and price data were drawn from FAO sources following a careful transformation to ensure consistency with the existing data used for the OECD countries. Behavioural parameters for the model and policy data were drawn mainly from recently published literature. Behavioural data were, as much as possible, consistent with the medium-term, partial static framework of the MTM model. Finding subsidy equivalent estimates for developing countries which were consistent with OECD work proved to be more difficult than originally anticipated.

Three criteria were employed in drawing up the list of eight new developing countries or regions to be included. One criterion was the importance of the country as an agricultural producer/consumer, reflecting also a representative mix of importers/exporters and types of domestic policy support measures. A second criterion was the availability of appropriate data on agricultural assistance levels and behaviour parameters for use in the model (demand-supply elasticities). A third criterion was whether the countries were covered by other parts of the OECD Secretariat examining relations with developing countries (e.g. Development and Cooperation Directorate, Development Centre, Trade Directorate, Economics and Statistics Department, North/South Group). Using these criteria, it was proposed that developing countries be represented by the following countries and regions: China, Brazil, India, Mexico, Argentina, Thailand, South Korea and Sub-Saharan Africa[4].

These countries, except for Sub-Saharan Africa, figure prominently among the ten largest developing country producers, exporters and importers of the main commodities included in the

MTM model. China, Brazil, India, Mexico, Argentina and Thailand are large producers, consumers or traders. South Korea is a particularly large importer of cereals, sugar and soybeans and, in addition, is representative of the "newly industrialised developing countries". At the other end of the spectrum are members of the Sub-Saharan Africa group, chosen, in contrast to South Korea, to represent the low income developing countries.

The addition of these eight countries and regions substantially enhances the coverage of world consumption and production in the commodities which are specifically modelled. As shown in Figure 4.1, production coverage rises substantially for rice (from 6 to over 70 per cent) and the oilseeds (to include about 90 per cent). Twenty-five per cent or more of the world market was also added for pork, sheep, wheat, coarse grains and sugar. The additional developing countries provide a similar increase to global coverage in the case of consumption (Figure 4.2). Largest increases are in those same commodities reported above for production increase. These countries represent a mix of importers (five countries) and exporters (three countries) and provide a range of agricultural policy approaches. As a result of their contribution to the world market, these additional countries could be considered as representative of the developing countries.

A large body of literature was reviewed by the Secretariat to obtain behavioural parameters for the model. Five studies were examined in more detail as they provide internationally comparable, rather than country specific, elasticity estimates. Of these studies elasticities from the FAO[5] and USDA[6] studies were most suitable for the analysis because of the similarity of the commodity and country coverage.

For estimates of domestic assistance to agricultural producers in the developing countries, the USDA study (Gardiner *et al.*) is particularly helpful as the methodology employed closely follows that used by the OECD in its estimates of assistance for OECD countries. Two other sources, FAO (FAO, no date) and Anderson-Tyers[7], do not provide Producer Subsidy Equivalent and Consumer Subsidy Equivalent (PSE/CSE) estimates directly but, with some manipulation, the nominal rates of protection which are given can be converted into the element of PSEs. It was not possible in all cases to extend the analysis to other forms of support which would include direct transfers to producers from budgetary sources, such as deficiency payments, input subsidies or extension services. In general, these are small relative to price effects in most developing countries.

The third criterion considered in drawing up the list of countries was the country coverage of other OECD work. Work of particular relevance to this proposal is being done by the Development Centre, the Trade Directorate, the North/South Group and the Development Co-operation Directorate.

In the next section, there is a description of the agricultural markets and types of policy assistance including estimates of PSE/CSEs for each of the 8 countries and 12 commodities covered in this study. In the section after that, there are details of the MTM model structure, the method used to account for the demand impact from income changes in agriculture and the policy experiments undertaken in this study. Also, there is a presentation of data sources used in the study. In the next section, the results of the analysis are presented. In the final section, there is a summary and conclusions.

Agricultural Policies in Developing Countries

Introduction

In an increasing number of developing countries, a structural adjustment programme is now being implemented, or is in the planning process, to establish an environment for sustainable development. Developing country governments, with encouragement from the international community, are giving high priority to changing domestic agricultural policies and also seeking the diversification of commodity exports. These reforms have been introduced in many instances where countries have secured an IMF/World Bank loan, the structural adjustment facility, for balance of payments support which is usually provided conditionally on the implementation of a structural adjustment programme and macroeconomic policy reform.

Agricultural policies in many developing countries are widely believed to be biased against domestic production of food crops in favour of imports of staple foods in order to secure low prices for urban consumers. This is sometimes accomplished by the use of food subsidies. Moreover, many countries also have agricultural pricing policies biased in favour of cash/export crops, while in other cases producer returns for export crops are depressed by the use of export taxes, overvalued exchange rates, or by the ill-functioning of state marketing boards. Agencies such as the IMF, however, advise, or stipulate, the adoption of a more market-oriented approach as part of a loan programme. This may involve eliminating food subsidies, reducing government intervention in agriculture, liberalizing agricultural trade and reforming macroeconomic policies to help provide incentives for farmers such as devaluing the exchange rate and reducing inflation. Those developing countries which have provided incentives to agriculture and supportive macroeconomic policies, such as Indonesia, Malaysia and Thailand, are considered more successful in raising agricultural production and the rate of growth in agricultural exports than those developing countries that have not adopted these reforms, notably many countries in Sub-Saharan Africa, although the latter group of countries has been particularly affected by drought and wars (Table 4.2).

The role of developing countries in the GATT Uruguay Round is likely to be much more significant, in the context of agriculture, than in previous rounds. This is due to a variety of factors, including the fact that a number of developing countries are major exporters of products that compete with OECD countries, for example, in cereals, oilseed products, sugar and beef markets. Also, some major developing country agricultural importing countries, for example South Korea and Mexico, which are seeking to expand their exports of manufactured goods to the OECD countries region, at the same time wish to protect their domestic agricultural sectors on the basis that they need to improve their food self-sufficiency level. In some of these cases, however, there is growing pressure in GATT to question their status as developing countries which qualify for preferential trade treatment across the board, while in turn OECD agricultural exporting countries are keen to gain easier access to such markets, partly to correct the growing trade imbalances that have occurred in markets like South Korea.

It should be emphasized that the motivation for protection in developing countries can be quite different from that of most OECD countries. Protectionist policies are normally implemented to meet three objectives in developing countries: the ease of collection of government revenue, balance of payments support and infant industry protection. Moreover, the recent growth in export promotion policies by developing countries must be seen against a background of low commodity prices, current account deficits and arrears in debt servicing obligations.

The PSE/CSEs in developing countries

PSE/CSE measures for all developing countries, not just the modelled developing countries, show that in general developing countries mainly tax agricultural producers while they subsidise directly or indirectly food consumers. Furthermore, while developing countries tend to provide substantially less support for agricultural producers than developed countries, there is nevertheless wide variation in assistance levels depending on the country and commodity considered.

Of the eight developing countries/regions considered in this report, for two countries, South Korea and Mexico, the percentage PSE measured for all products was about double that of the OECD average percentage PSE for 1982-85 of 27 per cent, although comparable to some OECD countries with high levels of assistance (see Figure 4.3). Argentina, India and Thailand, however, over the period 1982-85 had negative PSEs, while Brazil, China and Sub-Saharan Africa had PSEs which were positive but close to zero. At the individual commodity level for the modelled developing countries, PSEs were in general negative for meat, except poultry, and for sugar. On the other hand, cereal crops, except rice, had positive PSEs, as was the case for milk.

It is beyond the scope of this document to examine in detail the policy background of the eight countries/regions and the 13 modelled commodities for which PSE measures were calculated. The remainder of this section focuses on the policy aspects for those commodities and countries which were expected to be the most important in the model simulations during the 1982-85 period, the results of which are analysed below.

Livestock policies

Government incentives to livestock production in developing countries have generally benefitted intensive poultry/pig production located in areas close to urban centres, and neglected small-holder ruminant and non-ruminant production in rural areas. Illustrative in this study is the 100 per cent PSE for pork and poultry in Mexico compared with a zero measure for beef and sheepmeat, and similarly in Brazil the PSE for poultry is 6 per cent in contrast to a negative beef PSE of –59 per cent.

Poultry development plans in particular have aimed to satisfy urban meat demand at a low price, encourage the substitution of meat imports domestically produced poultry by sometimes enforced through import restrictions, and in some cases even develop exports. Governments have assisted poultry producers through low interest loans and producer price subsidies, encouraged the entry of multinational investment through reduced tax and other incentives, and in some cases granted export subsidies/credits to assist the growth in trade. Indeed the use of poultry subsidies by *Brazil* for example are considered to impede the exports of some other developing country poultry exporters who are attempting to develop trade outlets without government assistance. Brazil, since 1986, has begun to reduce subsidies to poultry producers and traders as a contribution to the government's austerity programme instituted as part of the IMF's condition to restructure Brazil's debt.

The explanation for a negative PSE for *pork in China* is similar to that for poultry in Brazil. The Chinese central government has adopted a policy of feed input subsidies to producers and indirect food subsidies through providing increased wages to industrial workers and low retail pork prices via export controls to help maintain per capita consumption levels of pork. Since the review period of this study, 1982-85, China has entered a cautious phase of price liberalization, with urban food prices having risen in 1986 and 1987 by as much as 25 to 30 per cent. Since pork amounts to 88 per cent of all meat production in China and 94 per cent of red meat consumption, the price of pork in China is an extremely sensitive political issue. Thus it is unclear to what extent the authorities are willing to risk the consequences of following free market dictates and leaving recent market reforms intact.

Although generally *beef* PSEs for the modelled countries are negative, *South Korea* has a large positive PSE for beef. In a drive for self-sufficiency, South Korea has actively encouraged beef production by use of producer and input subsidies and strict border restrictions on imported beef through the use of quotas. In view of South Korea's long history of protecting its agricultural sector and other parts of the economy, as well as the development of a large trade current account surplus since 1985, tensions have emerged with some of its major trading partners. Indeed, a large part of South Korea's trade surplus is with the United States and the EC and frustration has built up on the part of these and other OECD countries attempting to export agricultural products. Recent government attempts to liberalize the South Korean agricultural market have been met with considerable resistance from the domestic farm lobby.

Other *beef* producers/traders, notably *Argentina* and *Brazil*, have a large negative PSE. In these countries the national beef policies have been designed to raise tax revenue for the state; in the case of Argentina mainly through taxing exports, and in Brazil through beef producer taxes. Beef production and exports from Argentina and Brazil have declined over the 1980s. In an effort to reverse this decline and as part of these countries' recent economic reform programmes the beef producer/export taxes have been reduced. Even so, the governments of both countries have stated clearly that they perceive the major problem afflicting their beef producers and traders is the beef export subsidy policies of mainly the EC, and also the protectionist beef import policies in most OECD countries.

Cereal policies

The long-run demand for *cereal imports* by developing countries is affected by the rate of economic and population growth, changes in the level of per capita disposable incomes, the extent of foreign exchange reserves to purchase imports, the degree of shifting consumption patterns in favour of livestock production and the level of international cereal prices. For an increasing number of developing countries, however, a growing influence affecting the growth of cereal imports is government policy intervention. Hence with controlled producer and consumer prices associated with the use of trade and exchange rate policies, cereal imports have been the major instrument of food policy in developing countries to balance food supply and demand.

In examining trends in *wheat imports* by developing countries up to the early 1980s, Byerlee considers that policy interventions by a number of countries are sufficient to account for much of the growth and variability in wheat imports. Byerlee[9] notes that:

> Consumer subsidies alone account for a large share of wheat imports. Taking the large wheat importers alone (over 500 000 tonnes annually), the weighted average subsidy on wheat in 1981 was over 50 per cent of consumer prices. Even assuming a relatively inelastic demand (–0.33), wheat imports by this group of countries would be at least one third lower if market prices prevailed. These countries together make up well over half of commercial wheat imports by the Third World.

Thus the work of Byerlee and other researchers suggests that a significant share of cereal imports by developing countries is accounted for by direct government interventions in cereal markets.

Brazil, a major developing country importer of cereals, especially wheat, introduced an explicit subsidy in 1972 to make up the difference between what millers had to pay for wheat and the price at which they had to sell their flour on the market. Coupled with the persistent overvaluation of the Brazilian cruzeiro since the 1950s, which further benefitted cereal consumers, the demand for wheat grew rapidly in Brazil. At the same time the government offered guaranteed prices to stimulate domestic wheat production which at times, depending on exchange rate changes, have been double border price levels. Even so, the effect of the wheat production subsidies has been swamped by the effect of the consumer subsidies and, since the mid-1970s, net wheat imports grew rapidly in Brazil. The wheat PSE for Brazil used in this study was 61 per cent.

During the 1980s the Brazilian economy was seriously affected by growing economic problems including an increasing debt burden. To meet some of the IMF's conditions to restructure Brazil's debt, the government instituted a structural adjustment programme which incorporates a number of policy reforms that affect agricultural trade including trade liberalization and the removal of subsidies, especially consumer subsidies. In the case of cereal imports, devaluation of the cruzeiro since 1986 and elimination of the wheat consumer subsidy in April 1988 is thought likely to reduce demand. Indeed, imports of wheat/flour were 2.8 million tonnes in 1986/87 and are forecast at 2 million tonnes in 1988/89. Given the fact that Brazil's austerity economic reform programme is likely to remain in effect for the foreseeable future, or at least until the debt burden is eased, it seems possible that cereal imports, wheat particularly, will continue to be modest over the medium term.

While in general the developing countries that are net importers of cereals and some other crop products have high positive PSEs, for the net exporters of cereals and other crops, such as Argentina and Thailand, the PSEs for these commodities are frequently negative. Between 1982-85 the PSEs were negative for most of Argentina's export crops, including wheat, coarse grains and soybeans; indeed in 1983 the export tax on wheat was 25 per cent and 15 per cent on maize and sorghum. Since the early 1980s, however, as part of the IMF structural adjustment programme for the Argentine economy, the government has made a number of important policy changes which also affect the country's cereal producers and exporters.

Argentina eliminated its cereal export taxes in December 1987 and, although not yet implemented, these are reportedly to be replaced with taxes on agricultural land. The imposition of a land tax could lead to the utilisation for cereal production of grazing land which is at present left idle for much of the year. In addition, transport costs are also to be lowered in an effort to make Argentina's cereal exports more competitive on world markets.

The impact of lowering cereal export taxes since 1983 on Argentina's volume of cereal exports is difficult to determine, although in 1983/84 Argentina's wheat exports peaked at 9.7 million tonnes and are expected to decline to 3.1 million tonnes in 1988/89 with a similar pattern of decline for coarse grain exports. The lower wheat exports after 1983/84 reflect, in part, lower producer prices. At the same time, poor weather conditions in the last several years have adversely affected cereal yields, and the grain area harvested has been in constant decline for the past decade. Indeed, much of the reduction in cereal area has been offset by a more or less corresponding increase in the oilcrop area, especially soybeans and sunflowerseed, reflecting the trend towards a more favourable oilseed-cereal price ratio.

According to Sarris[10], if Argentina allowed its wheat producer price to rise to world levels domestic production would increase by over 16 per cent, although this does not take into account cross-commodity effects of liberalization. The Argentine government has emphasized that the principal cause of low international wheat prices during the 1980s was due to the export subsidy policies of mainly the United States and the EC.

Rice and maize exports account for the importance of *Thailand as a cereal exporter*. Rice provided 56 per cent of the total volume of cereal exports between 1985/86 and 1987/88, and over the same period about 30 per cent of world rice exports, it being the world's largest rice exporter. Like Argentina, Thailand taxes its rice producers/exporters and Sarris (1987) estimates that the unilateral liberalization of Thai rice policies would probably lead to a 2 per cent increase in domestic production. The main policy problem facing Thai agriculture, in particular cereal exporters, is the lack of budgetary resources to finance subsidies and thus maintain their market share in the face of the competition on world cereal markets from subsidised cereal exports.

China and India also intervene in their domestic *rice markets*, with the objective of stabilizing domestic rice prices for consumers. As a result of this intervention consumer rice prices in these countries are substantially below world market prices, at least over the review period of the study. As the simulations of this study reveal, the OECD countries' rice policies have a limited impact on the world market in comparison with developing countries' rice policies. This is not so surprising, however, given that in most OECD countries rice is only a marginal food, while in China, India and many other developing countries rice is a major staple food.

Since 1985/86 *China's net imports of cereals* have risen sharply, reaching just over 10 million tonnes for both 1987/88 and 1988/89; this growth is related to a number of factors including the recent liberalization of the economy and consequent increases in demand for meat and, hence, derived demand for feed. The growth in China's net cereal imports has led a number of analysts to suggest that this marks the beginning of expanding net cereal imports into China over the 1990s. Other researchers are much more cautious in extrapolating from recent import trends, assuming that a large part of recent cereal imports has been encouraged by low world prices and assistance from exporters, such as the US Export Enhancement Program. Given the political importance attached to having achieved cereal self-sufficiency in China, the prospect of a medium- to long-term decline in the nation's cereal self-sufficiency would appear politically unacceptable. On the other hand, if China were able to sustain a surplus on its current trade surplus, perhaps by expanding manufactured exports or by increasing its invisible earnings such as through tourism, then the country could be in a position to afford increased food imports. However between 1984 and 1988, China's foreign trade balance was continually in deficit.

The OECD Ad Hoc Group of Experts on East/West Economic Relations in Agriculture, at their meeting in June 1988, drew the conclusion that the Chinese target of producing 500 million tonnes of cereal by the year 2000 was realistic. But with a population of close to 1.3 billion, China would still be short of grain and would either have to slow down the growth of feed grain consumption or otherwise turn to massive imports. However, some experts expressed more optimism for China's grain production capacity but emphasized that even with grain production of about 500 million tonnes by the year 2000, the country would still be facing a relatively poor food supply situation.

Sub-Saharan Africa

The role of *Sub-Saharan Africa* in international trade of the commodities examined in this study is small compared to the other developing countries. It is nevertheless important to consider the region in view of its chronic food security problems and acute poverty. Sub-Saharan Africa's current account deficit between 1985 and 1986 grew from $9 billion to $16 billion, the terms of trade declined by 26 per cent, export earnings dropped from $64 billion to $46 billion, the debt service ratio increased from 25 per cent to nearly 30 per cent and there was a reduction in real terms of net capital resource inflows. For most of Sub-Saharan Africa, the short-term prospects for non-oil commodity prices and rising debt servicing obligations offers little hope for an immediate recovery. The gloomy outlook for Africa is even more serious given the food security problems faced by some countries in the region.

The *food security situation* in Sub-Saharan Africa is forecast to deteriorate. This development is based upon expected reductions in international food aid shipments and international cereal stocks. Following the sharp decline in cereal stocks in 1987/88, world ending stocks in 1988/89 were further reduced to a level FAO considers to be somewhat below the minimum to safeguard world food security. Moreover, with the rise in food commodity prices, together with the forecast of continued deterioration in low income developing countries' terms of trade and balance of payments deficit, their ability to pay for additional commercial food imports is in doubt.

The extent to which liberalization of international agricultural markets would be beneficial to Sub-Saharan Africa and other low income food deficit countries is generating an intense debate. Indeed, the reopening of the debate on poverty and famine, partly stimulated by A.K. Sen's work in the early 1980s, has emphasized the complexity of the relationship between the price of food and hunger. Briefly stated, it is not clear that a long-term decline in the world price of food will necessarily benefit all the hungry or even the majority of them. Kanbur[11] comments that a decrease in the price of food benefits net buyers at the expense of net sellers. But the hungry consist of both net sellers and net buyers of food. Added to this is the complication that many of the net buyers of food rely on net sellers of food for employment. Thus the overall outcome of a decline in food prices in terms of aggregate poverty will depend on how poverty is distributed between net food sellers and buyers.

OECD-Developing Country Agricultural Trade Policy Concerns and Actions

The *trade concerns* in OECD-developing country agricultural relations from a developing country perspective relate to the protection of major import markets, especially the increasing use of non-tariff barriers to trade. In addition, the use of domestic and export subsidies to alleviate OECD country domestic agricultural problems, the instability of international commodity prices, and the severely depressed state of international agricultural markets are also of concern.

Equally, from an OECD country point of view the major concerns for many agricultural importing countries relate to the stability and level of international commodity prices, exchange rate policies and security of supplies. OECD exporting countries are increasingly concerned that developing countries are protecting their agricultural sectors through import barriers and also that some developing country agricultural exporters are competing "unfairly" on world markets through the use of various export promotion policies.

Most of these concerns in OECD-developing country agricultural trade relations provide the basis for trade liberalization discussions in the context of the new GATT Uruguay Round. While a number of recent trade policy actions have tended to heighten OECD-developing country trade tensions, including the continued use of export subsidies by some OECD countries and the dumping of certain agricultural products in OECD country markets by a few developing countries, other recent policy actions point in the direction of trade liberalization.

Many developing countries have embarked on a policy of trade liberalization as part of their domestic structural adjustment programmes, including the reduction of import barriers on agricultural products and elimination of agricultural import subsidies and export taxes. At the same time, some OECD countries have offered new concessions to their Generalised System of Preferences covering agricultural products and also the complete liberalization of trade barriers affecting most developing countries' tropical product exports to OECD countries as part of the "fast track" reforms in the Uruguay Round.

In conclusion, there can be little disagreement that improving the prospects for OECD-developing country agricultural trade relations depends on a combination of growth-oriented development policies in developing countries, the easing of developing countries' debt problems, and a supportive international environment, including expanding aid flows and moving towards the liberalization of international agricultural and other trade barriers. It is clear that in each of these areas — development, debt and trade — more needs to be done by OECD countries, but also by developing countries themselves, as emphasized by Ministers at the OECD Ministerial meetings in 1987 and 1988 and also in other international forums.

IMPLEMENTATION OF THE MODEL

Methodology

The model devised for this analysis is an extension of the one developed for the Ministerial Trade Mandate (MTM model) as described in Annex IV of *National Policies and Agricultural Trade* (OECD, 1987). It retains the same features: it is a near linear, medium-term partial equilibrium comparative static model of agricultural production, consumption and trade and of domestic and foreign market prices. It is a "medium-term" model because the model's parameters are calibrated to estimate the impact after about five years of an initial change in an exogenous variable. The model is "partial equilibrium" because it does not explicitly incorporate as endogenous many of the variables which can influence agriculture such as consumer income, agricultural input prices, exchange rates and interest rates. Finally, the model is "comparative static" in nature in that it measures the impact of a policy shock over a five-year period, but ignores the path of adjustment during the intervening period. In order to keep down costs and because the analysis focuses principally on the OECD countries, the list of commodities covered is unchanged (see Table 4.1). The number of countries represented individually has, however, been increased: certain developing countries previously included in the "Rest of the World" or "Centrally Planned Economies" groups (e.g. China) are now specified individually. Those countries for which data are easily available and which have an impact on production, consumption and world trade are listed in Table 4.1. It is now possible, therefore, to study the impact of a policy change in an OECD country on a specified developing country and vice versa.

Furthermore, the demand equation specification has been improved by the inclusion of a response to change in farm income represented here by the change in the net value of production of modelled commodities. This response has been introduced for all the countries in the model but it is likely to be significant only in those where agriculture makes a substantial contribution to GNP and where the elasticity of demand with respect to income is strong, such as the developing countries. Its omission from the original MTM model, representing only OECD countries, was thus justified.

The new MTM-LDC model thus enables an analysis of the impacts on production, consumption, world trade and prices of a liberalization of agricultural support, measured by PSE/CSEs. It should be borne in mind when interpreting the results that this model is subject to the same limitations as its predecessor. The results show the consequence of a reduction in base period assistance levels at the end of a medium-term adjustment period (about five years), other factors such as technology, macroeconomic factors, aid to other sectors, population, etc., being held constant. The responses noted over a short period depend on short-term elasticities and the form of assistance, which itself depends on the support system in operation in the various countries. It is important, also, to distinguish between the initial reductions in effective prices and the final impacts of these price changes.

Various sensitivity tests were carried out using as a basis of comparison the simulations conducted with the aid of the MTM-LDC model. These are described in the Annex to this chapter. A 10 per cent reduction in PSEs/CSEs in the OECD was examined first, using two price elasticity sets: those from the FAO and those from the USDA. The impact of this simulation on world reference prices was compared to that obtained for the same simulation using the previous MTM model, the characteristics of which are described in *MTM Model Specification and Elasticities*[12].

For the analysis discussed here, the USDA elasticities were used, with the 10 per cent reduction in PSEs/CSEs in the OECD countries implemented, taking the MTM-LDC model as the reference simulation. The effects on world prices, production, consumption and trade between the OECD countries and the developing countries of a 10 per cent reduction in PSEs/CSEs in all modelled countries will be compared with the effects of such a reduction applied only in the OECD countries. The influence of developing country agricultural support on world markets can thus be deduced, as well as the interactions between OECD and developing countries.

Finally, an increase of 10 per cent in developing country revenue stemming from a shock exogenous to agriculture, for example an oil price or development assistance change, will be simulated, and its impact on world reference prices and developing country demand will be analysed.

Data Sources

The data currently used for the OECD countries are an average for the period 1982-85 and are derived from the following sources. The commodity balances are drawn from the OECD database, the behavioural parameters are presented in *MTM Model Specification and Elasticities*, and the PSE/CSEs are set out in Tables 13 to 19 of Annex 1 to Agricultural Policies, *Markets and Trade — Monitoring and Outlook* (OECD, 1989).

For the developing countries selected, data similar to that for the OECD countries were collected and the averages for the period 1982-85 were calculated. The commodity balances were drawn from FAO statistics and correspond to OECD data. However, only total consumption of cereals has been calculated for the developing countries since it was difficult to obtain data on animal feed consumption per livestock category.

The behavioural data required for this study could be drawn from several sources. Since their country and commodity coverage was sufficiently wide, we chose the FAO World Food Model and the USDA Trade Liberalization Model (TLIB, USDA, forthcoming) as the source of elasticities for the products covered. The USDA-derived elasticities correspond more closely to the MTM model specifications with regard to dairy products and the substitutions represented are more extensive than in the FAO model.

As in the previous model, world reference prices are equivalent to the world trade unit value taken from the FAO Trade Yearbook[13]. The 1982-85 average of annual exchange rates for national currencies/dollars is drawn from the International Financial Statistics published by the IMF.

Several synthetic sources can be used for evaluating domestic prices and agricultural support levels in developing countries, but the ones used are those listed in Table 4.3. They were chosen on grounds of availability, reliability and closeness to the period studied. Preference was given to the Producer and Consumer Subsidy Equivalents calculated by the USDA using the OECD methodology. Adjustments of the undervaluation of exchange rates have not been incorporated. For most of the commodities covered, the prices and rates of protection used in the TLIB model for 1984 are available, excluding rapeseed and wool in all countries and animal products in Thailand. Combined with the producer prices in the FAO database, or in their absence with the unit value of trade calculated on the basis of FAO or UN data for the 1982-85 period, these 1984 rates of protection provide an approximation of the price support component of the PSE/CSE.

In the case of Sub-Saharan Africa, the rates of protection given by Tyers and Anderson for the period 1980-82 were used for animal products. In other cases, they were not used because their period of application did not coincide with that of this study. Krueger, Schiff and Valdés[14] have published nominal percentage protection rates for the years 1982-1984, generally concerning countries and commodities already covered by the USDA, which we preferred to use since they are more detailed. To obtain more specific data, a country by country analysis of agricultural policies would be necessary.

To incorporate endogenous demand response to changes in farm income the income-related demand elasticities in the FAO World Food Model were used. To take account of the fact that the modelled agricultural products constitute only part of national income, these elasticities were multiplied by the contribution of agriculture to GDP given by the FAO in *State of Food and Agriculture*[15] and by the share of modelled products in total production, which is estimated at 50 per cent for the developing countries.

RESULTS OF THE ANALYSIS

Impact of a Ten Per Cent Reduction in Assistance in Each Country

Using this simulation, the contribution which both the OECD and the modelled developing countries could make to multilateral trade liberalization can be studied. The changes in world prices stemming from a 10 per cent PSE/CSE reduction in the OECD countries alone, then in all modelled countries, are compared, as is production, consumption and trade of OECD countries and of the modelled developing countries.

Impact on world reference prices (see Figure 4.4)

As previously described in *National Policies and Agricultural Trade* (OECD, 1987), in the OECD countries, agricultural production support is generally positive. When support in OECD countries only is reduced domestic producer prices and production fall. On the world market prices for livestock products rise. However, animal feed prices decline as the states set-aside is also reduced and livestock numbers and hence feed demand is lower.

If, however, support is also reduced in the modelled developing countries, livestock product prices would not rise in all cases. Since some of these developing countries tax producers, particularly livestock producers, a 10 per cent reduction in the negative PSEs of these countries would bring a rise in domestic prices which increases production and reduces consumption.

In the case of beef, the increase in modelled developing country exports, particularly by Brazil and Argentina, more than offsets the decline in OECD exports. The world price of beef thus falls slightly. Similarly, for sheepmeat, reduced taxes in Argentina and China significantly limit increases in the world price. China dominates the world pork market, and higher domestic producer prices, combined with the lower price of animal feed, causes world pork prices to fall. The world price of rice also falls, largely due to reduced producer taxation in China.

With the exception of animal feeds such as manioc, corn gluten feed, other energy-rich and protein-rich feeds, the difference in the change in world prices for other commodities under the two simulations is only slight, either because the OECD countries dominate the market, as is the case with dairy products, poultry, coarse grains, soybeans and wool, or because data on developing country support for these commodities were not available (rapeseed, wool). However, the reduction in developing country support further accentuates the fall in the above-mentioned animal feed prices because OECD animal production, and particularly pork production, is reduced due to its falling price, thus less feed is required.

It is clear from this comparison that if the selected developing countries take part in a multilateral liberalization of agricultural policies world reference prices would be somewhat lower than if only OECD countries instituted agricultural reforms. Importing countries would therefore benefit from this. It is nevertheless necessary to make a more thorough study of these results, particularly with regard to production, consumption and trade in these countries, to be able to assess the ultimate consequences of such a policy.

OECD and developing country production and consumption impacts

In both scenarios, aggregate OECD country production falls slightly for all commodities because domestic prices are reduced (see Figure 4.5). On the other hand, in some developing countries domestic prices rise, depending on whether their PSEs/CSEs are reduced and, if they are reduced, whether they represent assistance or taxes. Thus the change in developing country production varies according to commodity and simulation (see Figure 4.6).

If agricultural reform occurs only in OECD countries with policies unchanged in the developing countries but assuming that the world price changes are passed back to their domestic markets, then domestic prices in developing countries will increase for animal products and decrease for the products used in animal feed such as wheat, coarse grains and soybeans. A 10 per cent PSE/CSE reduction in developing countries as well as in OECD countries, on the other hand, will also affect domestic price trends, depending on the sign and amount of the PSE/CSE. Where the PSE/CSE is positive for the developing country group, the increase in production is either more limited (milk), or switches to a decline (poultry), or an existing decline is accentuated (coarse grains, soybeans). Beef, pork and sugar experience more significant rises in production since for these commodities taxes are reduced (Figure 4.6).

Under these two simulations, livestock and sugar producers in the modelled developing countries enjoy a relatively substantial increase in domestic prices whereas producer prices for cereals and soybeans are lower than in the reference period.

Reduced assistance in OECD countries generally increases agricultural production in each of the modelled developing countries since increased animal production more than offsets the fall in cereal and soybean production. The only exception is Sub-Saharan Africa where, of the commodities covered in the model, coarse grains form an important part of agriculture and food, thus overall agricultural production falls (Figure 4.7).

When assistance is also reduced in the selected developing countries, those countries where the average PSE is negative will find that their production will increase in line with the size of the tax reduction (Figure 4.7). For example, the rise in production represents an increase in production of 1.6 per cent in Argentina and 0.3 per cent in China, India and Thailand. In the other countries, where the average PSE/CSE is positive, production is reduced, by 2.5 per cent and 1.4 per cent respectively in Mexico and South Korea, countries where average assistance is fairly high. A reduction in assistance to agriculture in the developing countries would not seem to favour producers. However, when world prices are taken into consideration an examination of the changes in production shows that this is not the case for all developing countries.

In certain countries, however, producers are taxed in order to provide the State with revenue. At the same time, consumers often enjoy lower food prices. Even if this is not the primary aim, it represents an important social measure in countries where household expenditure on food is very high and where consumer reaction to price and income variations is relatively strong. In examining overall consumption in these countries, the importance of human consumption in this aggregate must be borne in mind. In addition, it was noted that animal feed consumption in developing countries is not represented separately in the model in the same way as for the OECD countries.

In the OECD countries, lower livestock numbers result in lower feed use and thus a decline in consumption of wheat, coarse grain, soybeans and other livestock feeds. Consumption of other commodities rises as a result of lower domestic prices (see Figure 4.8). For the developing countries, however, feed consumption depends solely on price variations. Thus the rise in world prices for red meat, sugar and rice experienced on national markets results in lower feed consumption in developing countries (see Figure 4.9). For beef, sheepmeat and to a lesser extent sugar, this reaction is reinforced by the cut in producer taxes on these commodities. On the other hand, when PSEs/CSEs are reduced in these countries, the rise in the price of poultry, coarse grains and soya is accentuated. When policy changes occur only in the OECD countries, wheat consumption falls slightly whereas according to price movements, it ought to increase. The reason for this would appear to be substitution of wheat by coarse grains, the price of which has fallen even further. In this simulation, the effects of PSEs/CSEs are more powerful than the repercussions of world price changes only in the case of pork, in which case consumption falls along with the world price.

From the point of view of consumers in the specified developing countries, the only positive effect of reduced assistance to agriculture will be to increase poultry and coarse grain consumption. Consumption of other commodities will fall, in particular beef, notably in Argentina and Brazil. Nevertheless, it is probable that if the response of animal feed consumption to livestock production changes was represented, overall cereal and soybean consumption would increase more sharply.

Consumption of the modelled commodities will fall in Argentina and, to a lesser extent, in China, India and Thailand (see Figure 4.10). In Argentina, the consumption of most products falls except for pork. In countries whose consumption levels increase generally it would be for cereals and soybeans. In Mexico and Brazil, there would also be rises in pork and poultry consumption, and in Sub-Saharan Africa in rice consumption. In the latter group of countries, staple products are not taxed. Overall, consumption of animal products, in particular ruminants, is most depressed. From the results for production and consumption, it can be expected that the developing countries' net exports of animal products will be larger, and of cereals will be smaller.

Impact on developing country trade

When assistance to agriculture is reduced the principal effect of changes in production and consumption in the specified developing countries is a reduction in their imports of dairy products, sugar and rapeseed, and an increase in their exports of rice, beef, sheepmeat and pork. Furthermore, their substantial wheat deficit increases while their coarse grain and soybean surpluses decline. The repercussions of these volume movements on the net trade of the specified developing countries depend on the countries' starting position and the relative importance of each commodity in agricultural trade.

The modelled developing countries, taken as a group, are small net exporters of all the commodities in question in value terms. However, there exist very different situations for each country (see Figure 4.11). Three of the countries selected are net exporters; namely Argentina, Brazil and Thailand. Argentina has the largest agricultural trade surplus in value terms; particularly for cereals, soybeans and beef. Brazil is also a major exporter of soybeans and beef as well as sugar. Thailand mainly exports rice, manioc and coarse grains. All the other specified developing countries record a net trade deficit for the commodities covered in the model. The largest deficit in terms of value is that of Sub-Saharan Africa, largely accounted for by cereals and rice. China and India import large quantities of wheat but also import milk, sugar and wool. Lastly, Mexico and South Korea import most of the commodities in question, in particular cereals.

When agricultural support is reduced in all countries, the overall developing country trade surplus increases (see Figure 4.12). Exporting countries' net trade either remains constant (Thailand) or improves (Argentina, Brazil), whilst in the net importing countries changes in trade offset one another. Some deficits widen (Mexico, South Korea, Sub-Saharan Africa) and others narrow (China, India). Argentina and Brazil become net importers of pork but the increase in their net exports amply offsets this trend; with beef and sugar exports increasing in both cases, and soybeans and sheepmeat only for Argentina. Reduced domestic producer taxes are largely responsible for the increased surpluses, particularly in Argentina. On the other hand, in Thailand, where the level of support is relatively low, the movements of the various products offset one another.

The net trade position of each modelled developing country for the commodities included in the MTM-LDCs model is shown in Table 4.4. The first column indicates the base period position and the second the change arising from the 10 per cent reduction in PSE/CSEs in all the modelled countries. The overall net imports of India and especially of China fall because their net exports, in particular of meat, increase. This is most noticeable in the case of pork exports from China and stems from the reduction in producer taxes affecting its production. In India higher rice exports and lower sugar and wheat imports make a substantial contribution to its fall in net imports. Net imports in other countries increase, most significantly in Mexico where reduced support for pork and poultry production exacerbates the agricultural trade deficit. South Korea, which subsidises the production of most of its commodities, imports larger quantities of many crop products, in particular rice. The fall in world rice and cereal prices is also responsible in South Korea and in Sub-Saharan Africa for the worsening agricultural trade deficit.

An improved trade balance after reductions in agricultural support can be expected only in those countries where animal production is in surplus or is substantial compared to the cereals sector. The predominance of animal products in the change can be explained by their greater price elasticities for supply and demand, and by their high price in relation to other commodities. Export revenue will therefore increase in these countries.

Reduced agricultural taxes or assistance can give rise either to losses or gains for government budgets. For example, in Argentina, Brazil or China, where export taxes are reduced, the shortfall for government budgets may be substantial. In general this shortfall is difficult to calculate, since we do not always know the type of policy involved or the procedures by which it is applied. In the case of Argentina, where most PSE/CSEs take the form of export taxes, the loss represents approximately $25 million. Those countries with significant agricultural support levels, on the other hand, show budgetary savings.

The reform of the agricultural sector only in the modelled developing countries is not a very realistic policy scenario. Nevertheless, there is interest in assessing the implications of such reforms in these countries on the OECD countries. The impact of this reform is illustrated in Figure 4.13. There would be a decline in most world commodity prices (except poultry), especially for the red meats. As a result, there would be a decline in red meat, coarse grains and rice production, and a shift towards the production of milk and poultry in the OECD countries. In the developing countries, there would be less milk, poultry, soybean and coarse grain production, but increased production of red meats, wheat, and sugar. Overall production would decline marginally in the OECD countries. In the developing countries, there would be an increase in production in Argentina, but a decline in Mexico, Brazil and South Korea (Figure 4.14).

Impact of a Ten Per Cent Reduction in Positive Producer Assistance

In the OECD countries, PSEs were almost always positive. However, in many of the developing countries, PSEs were negative. Translating the reduction of PSEs in terms of a GATT scenario, it was considered that only positive PSEs should be reduced. Countries could continue to tax their agriculture. A scenario was run where only the positive PSEs were reduced in the OECD and modelled developing countries[16]. In this scenario, because these domestic taxes on production were not reduced, world production would be lower than in the case where they were reduced (Figure 4.15). For all commodities, world prices would be higher when negative PSEs were not reduced. In fact, world prices in this scenario would be generally higher than in the scenario where only the OECD countries reduced PSEs. The commodities for which prices were slightly lower were beef, sheepmeat and sugar.

Impact of a Ten Per Cent Increase in Income in Developing Countries

Increased consumption by developing countries is often held to be one of the possible solutions for absorbing agricultural surpluses on world markets. If purchasing power constraints could be eased there is indeed potential for consumption to increase. That is why an attempt has been made in this model to represent demand response to changes in agricultural production which bring about income changes. During the simulations described above, overall agricultural consumption in the developing countries specified increased only slightly in relative terms (0.3 per cent when all assistance is reduced) and an income response is not perceptible in percentage terms to any degree of precision.

Although the agricultural commodities considered account for a greater share of total income in the developing countries than in the OECD countries, this does not amount to more than 18 per cent because fruits and vegetables and tropical products are not taken into consideration in the model. The repercussions of change in agricultural production are thus fairly slight. Therefore the demand effect of an exogenous increase in income was tested and a 10 per cent increase in developing country income was simulated.

When developing country income increases by 10 per cent most countries consume approximately 2 per cent more in terms of value, whereas overall consumption in the OECD countries drops slightly (see Figure 4.16). All the specified developing countries react to the same extent except for Argentina and Sub-Saharan Africa, which represent the two extremes of per capita income levels amongst the selected countries. Argentina has a relatively high per capita income level, and demand reacts only slightly to income change, whereas consumption in the poorer group of African countries increases by more than 6 per cent.

World commodity prices increase as a result of this fairly major income shock. The increased world prices for animal products and rice are due solely to the reaction of consumption to increases in income. On the other hand, the greater use of cereals for animal feed in OECD countries also has an effect. For example, the income elasticity for coarse grains is weak (and sometimes negative) in developing countries so they do not consume more of these commodities. Yet because of larger livestock numbers their price increases. For the same reasons, the increase in livestock feed prices is relatively large.

This income shock imposed is substantial compared to trade liberalization, which explains its major consequences on developing country consumption and world prices. Nevertheless, it provides a relative order of magnitude for assessments of the consequence of oil-price, exchange-rate or development assistance changes for agricultural commodities.

Sensitivity Tests of Elasticities

In the original development of the MTM model, an assumption of 0.2 was made for all of the demand and supply elasticities for the rest of the world (OECD, 1988). In the development of the MTM-LDCs model, a search was made for these elasticities for the modelled developing countries. It was noted that these elasticities, on average, were substantially larger than those previously assumed for all developing countries. Hence a sensitivity test was made by increasing the supply and demand elasticities for the rest of the world in the MTM-LDCs model by 200 per cent (to 0.6) to note their effect on the liberalization results.

The results of this sensitivity test of increasing the rest of the world (i.e. the non-modelled developing countries) responsiveness show that this change has only a very small impact on the world prices for the policy liberalization scenarios (Figure 4.17). If the OECD and the modelled developing countries reduced their PSE/CSEs by 10 per cent, world price changes would be slightly smaller if the larger elasticities were used for the non-modelled developing countries (as compared to the base set of elasticities). The exception to this situation would be for the non-cereal feeds whose prices would decline slightly more. The larger elasticities for non-modelled developing countries would therefore result in slightly lower production of livestock (except for pork) and sugar and slightly higher cereal production.

SUMMARY AND CONCLUSIONS

The consequences for developing countries of the reform of agricultural policies in OECD countries has been an issue of concern. In order to assess the implications of such reforms, the Secretariat expanded the scope of the MTM model to include individual specifications for eight developing countries. These countries represented the most important importers and exporters, as well as a diverse mixture of producer and consumer policies, and both middle income and low income countries. These countries substantially increased the commodity coverage of the modelled countries in the MTM-LDC model.

The Secretariat used the MTM-LDC model to assess the impact of agricultural policy reform using a 10 per cent reduction in PSE/CSEs both for (a) the OECD countries, and (b) the OECD and developing countries. From this analysis, the impact on production, consumption and trade of the individual developing countries was assessed in addition to the world price implications.

If agricultural assistance (including acreage set-aside restrictions) is cut back *only* in the OECD countries, and if the induced world price changes are reflected in the domestic prices of modelled developing countries, then their animal products and sugar production would increase while cereal and soybean production would decrease. This would result in a slight rise in value of output for each modelled developing country. There would also be little variation in consumption for these developing countries, with the exception of Argentina where domestic consumption will fall significantly. As a result, the net trade position of these developing countries will improve by $770 million. From this point of view, Argentina and Brazil would stand to gain the most because of the importance of their meat production.

If the modelled developing countries also participate in reducing agricultural support, world prices would be noticeably lower for all commodities (except poultry) and significantly lower for red meats and cereal substitutes than in the previous scenario. Nevertheless, modelled developing country production would still increase for most commodities except poultry, coarse grains and oilseeds. Sugar, beef and especially pork production in the modelled developing countries would increase more if the developing countries as well as the OECD countries institute agricultural reforms, since support levels for many products in these countries are negative. OECD countries would experience a decline in net exports of some $1 477 million while the modelled developing countries would have an additional net export surplus of $1 438 million. Individual country results, however, vary from those for all modelled developing countries. The increased surplus comes from larger net exports from Argentina, and reduced net imports from China and India. These are offset by larger net imports by South Korea, Sub-Saharan Africa and Mexico. The internal position of the modelled developing countries would also differ among countries. The most important production changes would be found in Mexico and South Korea where agricultural assistance levels are very high and production would decline sharply, while the opposite would occur in Argentina as agriculture is highly taxed. Production would decline in Sub-Saharan Africa and marginally in Brazil. On the other hand, consumption generally would increase, significantly in Mexico and marginally in Brazil, South Korea and Sub-Saharan Africa, but would decline significantly in Argentina.

Consumption declines would be largest for beef, sheepmeat, sugar and milk. In general, the developing country urban food consumers have proportionally greater political influence than in OECD countries and it may be politically difficult to institute the types of changes which affect consumers.

The analysis discussed here has been carried out using data and policy information for the period 1982-85. The PSE/CSE figures for the OECD countries have substantially increased since this period. If there has been a similar increase for the developing countries, then the impacts of liberalization in these countries will be also larger. Recent policy developments in some of these developing countries have been conditioned to a large extent by the problems associated with high levels of debt (e.g. Argentina, Mexico and Brazil), with drought (e.g. Sub-Saharan Africa) or low commodity prices (e.g. Thailand). Hence the results of agricultural policy reform for more recent time periods may differ somewhat from those obtained in this study.

Estimates of the production and net trade impact for developing countries of the agricultural policy reform are undoubtedly less reliable than those for the OECD countries, reflecting the quality of the underlying data involved in the operation of the MTM model. Other specific data problems include PSE/CSE estimates which have been derived using official exchange rates. Many of these countries have overvalued exchange rates which would imply smaller PSEs and larger CSEs. Exchange rate policies were not considered as part of the agricultural policy package. Since the overvaluation of the exchange rate was not included as part of the PSE, this gives a downward bias to the trade impacts of agricultural policy reform. Moreover, under rapid inflation rates, four-year average prices are very difficult to calculate. In some cases data on government expenditures were not available to include in PSE/CSE calculations. As the magnitude of results depends on PSE/CSE estimates, much additional work remains to refine these results.

Those tropical products not now included in the MTM model accounted for about 35 per cent of total agricultural exports from developing countries in 1982-85. Reduction in OECD country CSEs would result in an additional increase in net exports from developing countries. Since import duties on unprocessed tropical products are low and there is only a small response to prices in the OECD and exporting countries, only a small increase in imports would be anticipated. Nevertheless, the addition of tropical products and many of the important fruit and vegetable products would likely further increase the estimated benefits of OECD country agricultural policy reform to developing countries. As few estimates have been made of the economic parameters in these markets, the exact magnitude of these changes is difficult to anticipate.

Because agriculture is such an important part of the economy of developing countries, it was anticipated that changes in farm income arising from trade liberalization could therefore have a significant impact on food consumption. This analysis allowed an evaluation of the magnitude of the increased domestic consumption from improved farm revenue. The study found, however, that the impact of these changes was generally small.

This study indicates that the reform of agricultural policies in OECD countries would encourage additional production in seven of the eight represented developing countries (the exception is Sub-Saharan Africa) without reducing consumption in most of these developing countries (the exceptions are India and Argentina). On the other hand, if the developing countries reform agriculture as well, production declines in several countries, notably Mexico and South Korea; whereas in a country like Argentina it expands considerably. In the developing countries, economic growth and development are much more dependent on the performance of the agricultural sector than are the OECD countries. In general, it is much more important to ensure the most efficient use of resources in agriculture when it forms a large part of the economy. Thus, though some of the adjustment problems may be politically difficult, the benefits appear much greater than for OECD countries.

Figure 4.1. **PERCENTAGE SHARES OF 1982 / 1985 WORLD PRODUCTION**

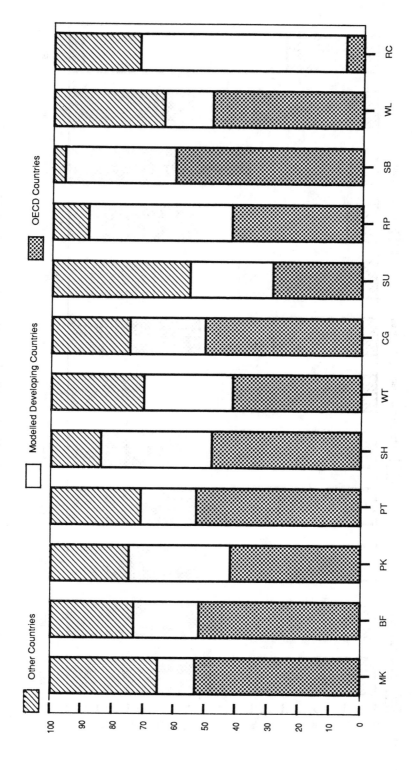

This graph shows the percent of world supply covered by the model: OECD + Modelled Developing Countries; and the percentage not modelled: Other Countries. The addition of the eight-country developing country group has substantially increased modelled market coverage.

Figure 4.2. PERCENTAGE SHARES OF 1982 / 1985 WORLD CONSUMPTION

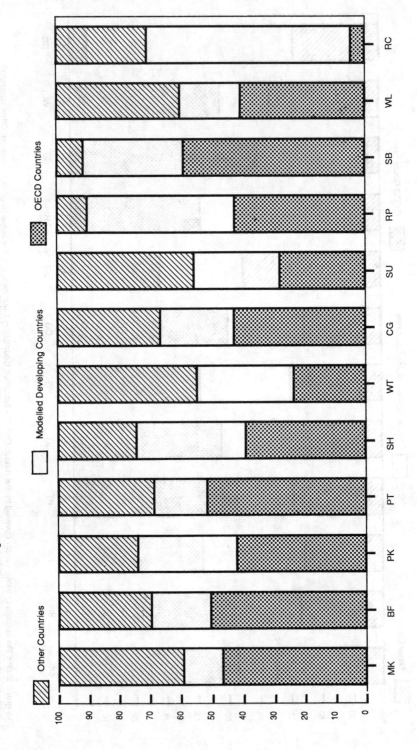

This graph shows the percent of world supply covered by the model: OECD + Modelled Developing Countries; and the percentage not modelled: Other Countries. The addition of the eight-country developing country group has substantially increased modelled market coverage.

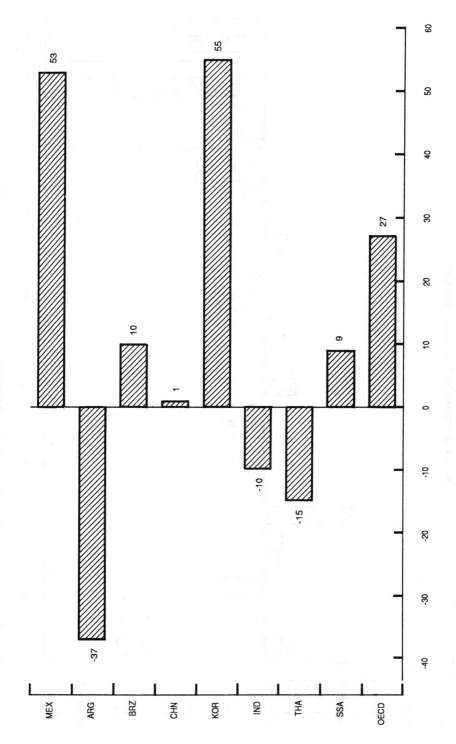

Figure 4.3. PERCENTAGE PSE OF ALL MODELLED COMMODITIES BY COUNTRY

See Table 1 for country codes.

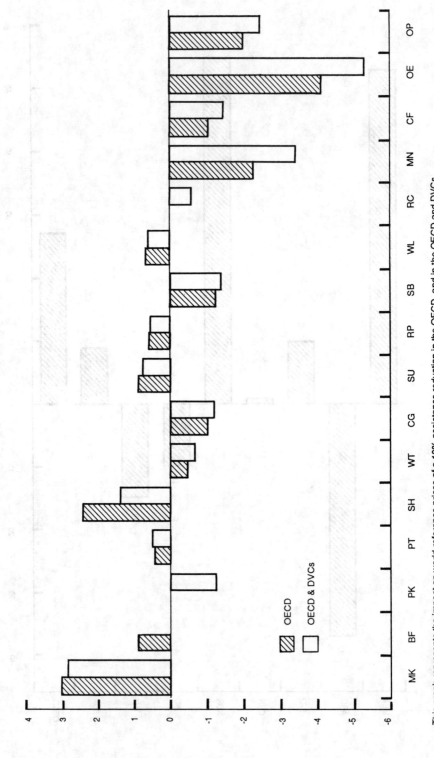

Figure 4.4. PERCENT CHANGE IN 1982/85 WORLD PRICES RESULTING FROM A 10% REDUCTION IN OECD AND IN OECD & DVC ASSISTANCE

This graph represents the impact on world reference prices of a 10% assistance reduction in the OECD, and in the OECD and DVCs. The difference between the two bars is therefore the impact of a 10% reduction in DVC assistance only. See Table 1 for codes.

Figure 4.5. **PERCENT CHANGE IN OECD PRODUCTION RESULTING FROM A 10% REDUCTION IN OECD AND OECD & DVC ASSISTANCE**

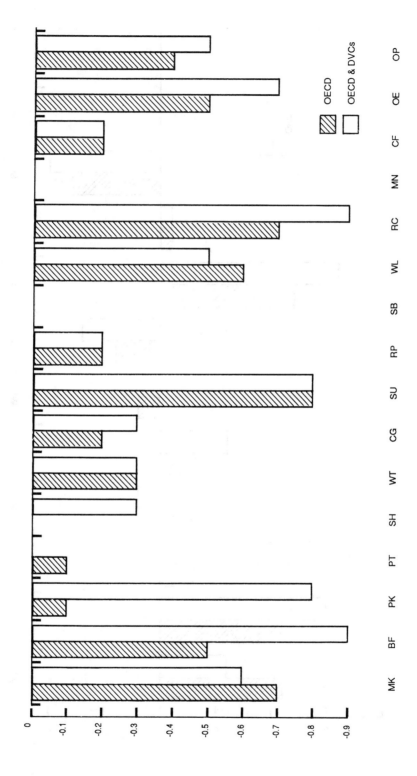

This graph represents the impact on 1982 / 1985 OECD production levels of a 10% reduction in assistance in the OECD and in the OECD & DVCs. See Table 1 for product codes.

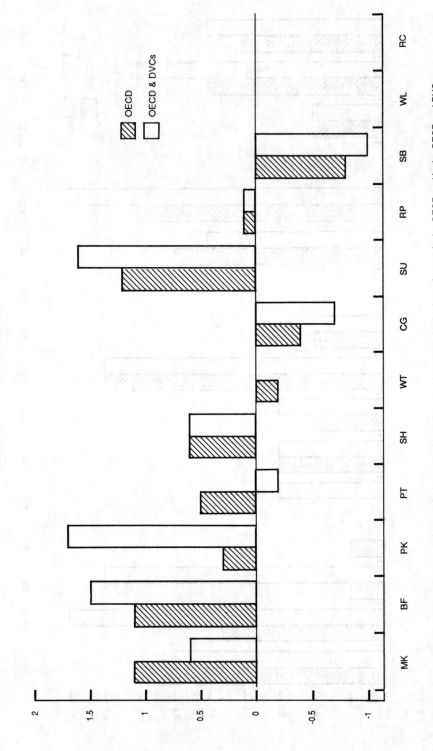

Figure 4.6. PERCENT CHANGE IN DVC PRODUCTION RESULTING FROM A 10% REDUCTION IN OECD AND OECD & DVC ASSISTANCE

This graph represents the impact on 1982 / 85 developing group production levels of a 10% reduction in assistance in the OECD and in the OECD and DVCs. See Table 1 for product codes.

Figure 4.7. **PERCENTAGE CHANGE IN THE VOLUME OF PRODUCTION DUE TO A 10% REDUCTION IN ASSISTANCE IN OECD AND IN OECD & DVCs**

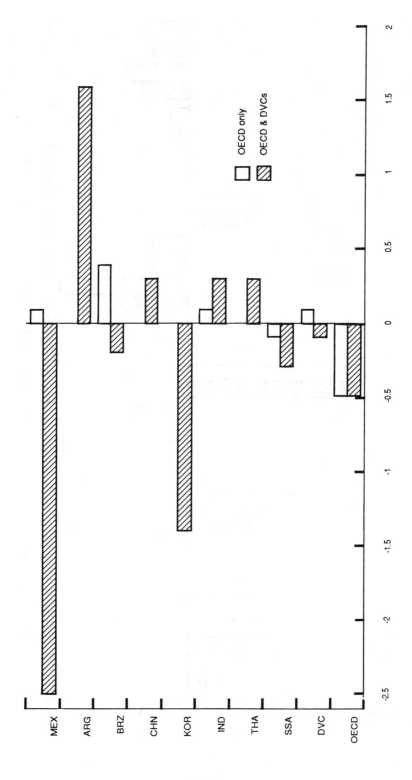

This graph represents the percentage change in the volume of production of modelled products, by country, during 1982 / 85. See Taable 1 for country codes.

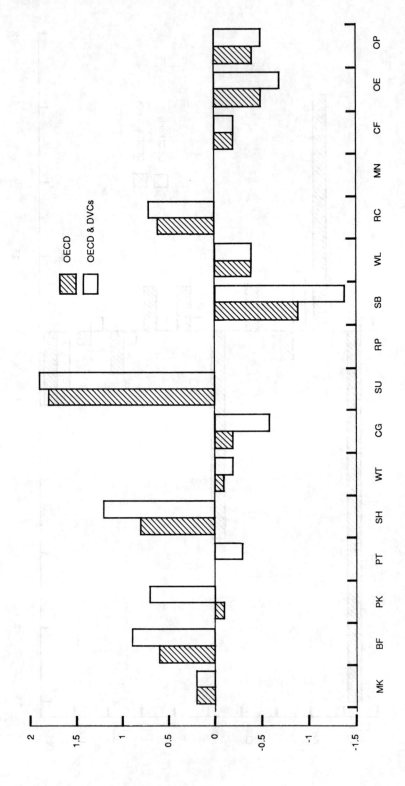

Figure 4.8. PERCENT CHANGE IN OECD CONSUMPTION RESULTING FROM A 10% REDUCTION IN OECD AND OECD & DVC ASSISTANCE

This graph represents the impact on 1982/85 OECD consumption levels of a 10% reduction in assistance in the OECD and in the OECD and DVCs. See Table 1 for product codes.

Figure 4.9. **PERCENT CHANGE IN DVC CONSUMPTION RESULTING FROM A 10% REDUCTION IN OECD AND OECD & DVC ASSISTANCE**

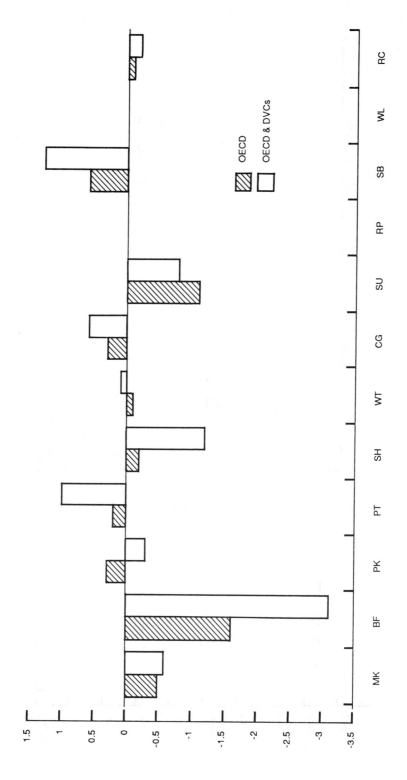

This graph represents the impact on 1982 / 85 developing group consumption levels of a 10% reduction in assistance in the OECD and in the OECD and DVCs. See Table 1 for product codes.

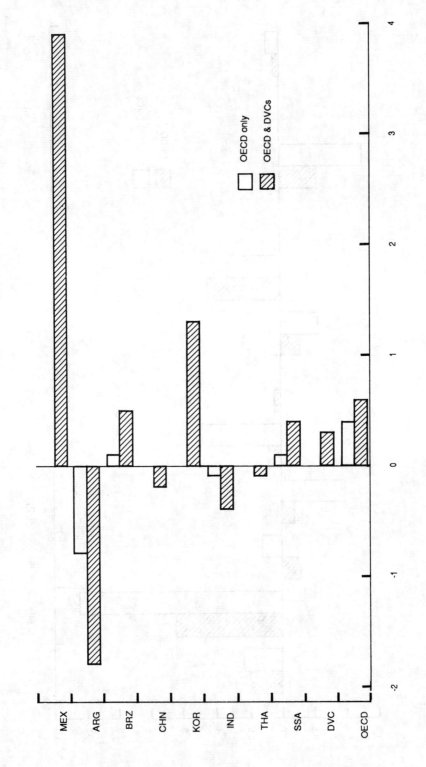

Figure 4.10. PERCENTAGE CHANGE IN THE VOLUME OF CONSUMPTION DUE TO A 10% REDUCTION IN ASSISTANCE IN OECD AND IN OECD & DVCs

This graph represents the percentage change in the volume of consumption by country resulting from a 10% reduction in OECD assistance (shown by the first bar), and in all modelled countries assistance (represented by the second bar), during 1982 / 85.

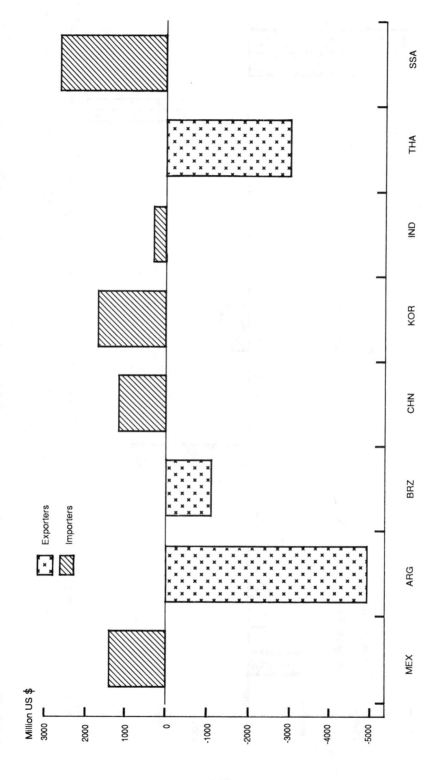

Figure 4.11. **VALUE OF MODELLED DEVELOPING COUNTRIES NET IMPORTS : 1982 / 85**

This graph represents the net trade value of modelled products by developing country during 1982 / 85.
See Table 1 for country codes.

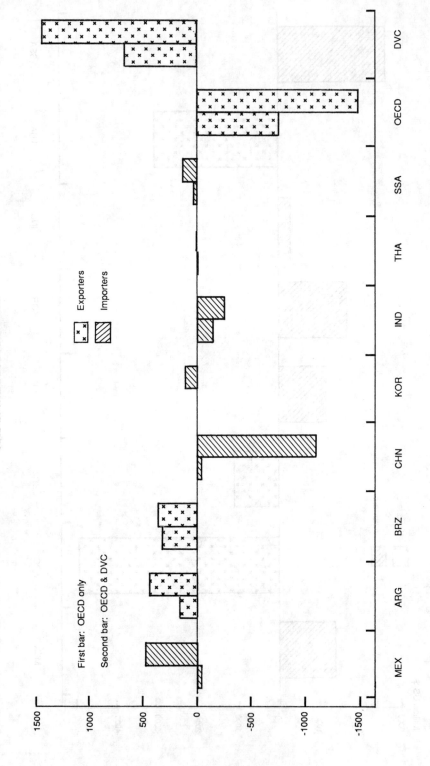

Figure 4.12. NET TRADE VALUE CHANGES DUE TO 10% ASSISTANCE REDUCTIONS IN THE OECD ALONE, AND IN THE OECD AND DVCs

The two bars in each pair represent the change in net trade value of modelled commodities by country resulting from a 10% reduction in OECD assistance, and in OECD & DVC assistance, respectively, during 1982/85. See Table 1 for country codes.

Figure 4.13. **IMPACT ON THE WORLD REFERENCE PRICE OF A 10% ASSISTANCE REDUCTION
IN DEVELOPING COUNTRIES**

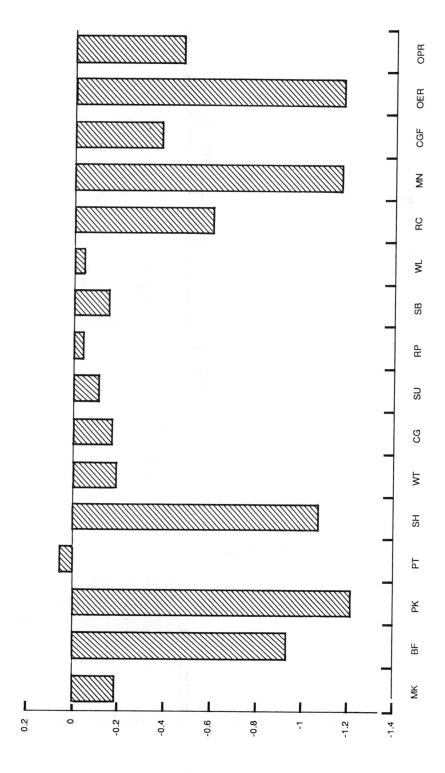

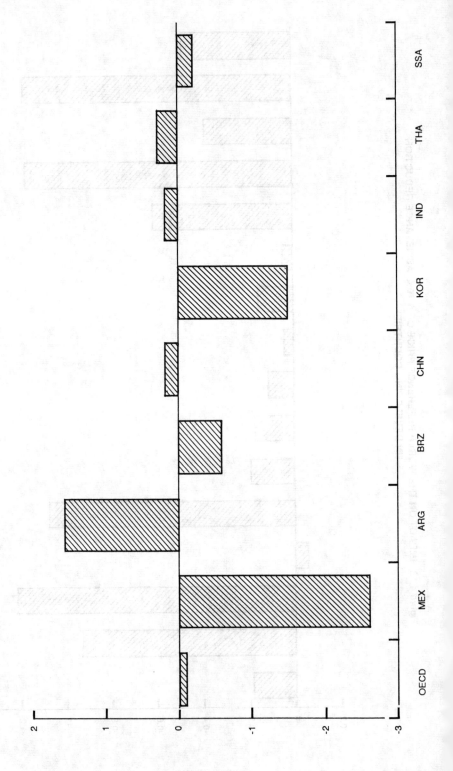

Figure 4.14. IMPACT ON PRODUCTION OF A 10% ASSISTANCE REDUCTION IN DEVELOPING COUNTRIES

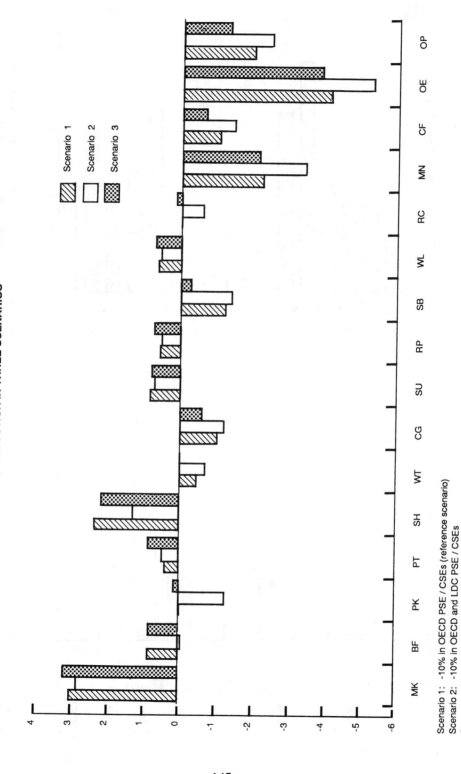

Figure 4.15. **IMPACT ON WORLD REFERENCE PRICES OF A 10% ASSISTANCE REDUCTION IN THREE SCENARIOS**

Scenario 1: -10% in OECD PSE / CSEs (reference scenario)
Scenario 2: -10% in OECD and LDC PSE / CSEs
Scenario 3: -10% in OECD and LDC positive PSE / CSEs only

Scenario 1
Scenario 2
Scenario 3

147

Figure 4.16. **10% EXOGENOUS INCREASE IN INCOME**

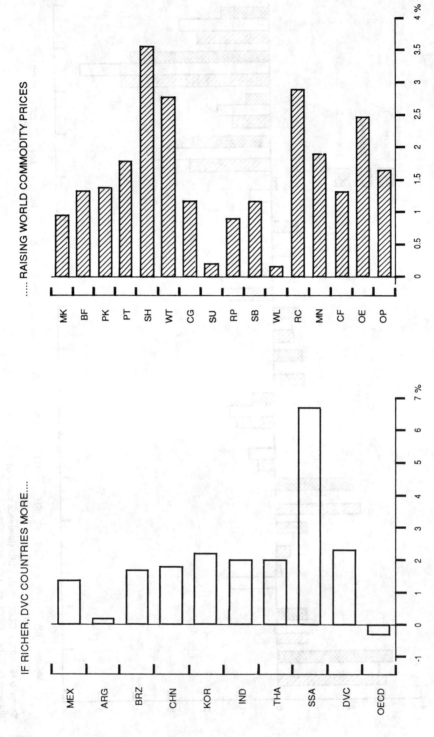

IF RICHER, DVC COUNTRIES MORE....

This graph represents the percent change in the volume of consumption of modelled products, by DVC country, resulting from a 10% exogenous increase in income in the eight modelled developing countries for the period 1982 / 85.

.... RAISING WORLD COMMODITY PRICES

This graph represents the percent change in world reference prices of specified products resulting from a 10% exogenous increase in income in the eight modelled developing countries in the period 1982 /85.

Figure 4.17. PERCENT CHANGE IN 1982 / 85 WORLD PRICES RESULTING
FROM A 10% REDUCTION IN OECD & DVC ASSISTANCE

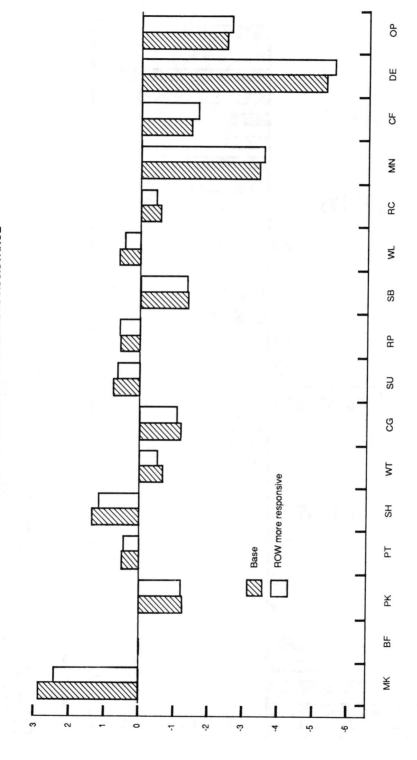

This graph represents the impact on world reference prices of a 10% assistance reduction in the OECD and DVCs.
The base supply and demand elasticities for the "rest of world" are 0.2; the high response assumption is 0.6.
See Table 1 for codes.

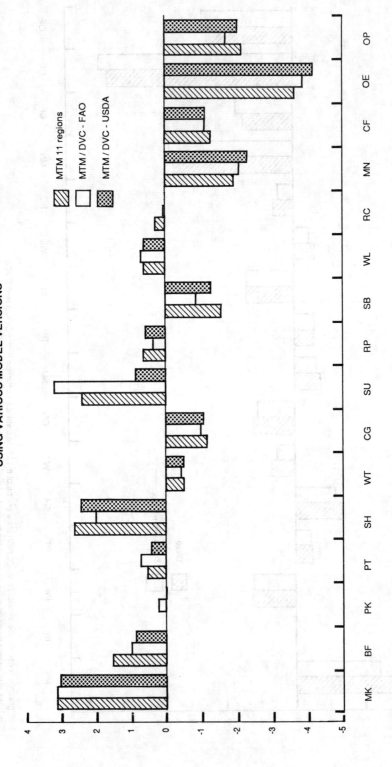

Figure 4.18. PERCENTAGE WORLD PRICE CHANGES OECD AD VALOREM SCENARIO
USING VARIOUS MODEL VERSIONS

MTM 11 REGIONS: See Agriculture Policies, Markets and Trade, 1989.
MTM / DVC - FAO: OECD / DVC model w / FAO elasticities.
MTM / DVC - USDA: OECD / DVC model w / USDA elasticities.
Each group of three bars represents the percentage change in world reference prices due to a 10% reduction in OECD assistance,
resulting from four different model versions.
See Table 1 for product codes.

Table 4.1

MTM MODELLED COUNTRIES AND PRODUCT GROUPS

OECD GROUP

DEVELOPING GROUP

CAN: Canada
AUS: Australia
EEC: European Economic Community
USA: United States
AUT: Austria
NZL: New Zealand
JPN: Japan
NOR: Nordic Group
MED: Mediterranean Group

MEX: Mexico
ARG: Argentina
BRZ: Brazil
CHN: China
KOR: South Korea
IND: India
THA: Thailand
SSA: Sub-Saharan Africa Group
DVC: 8-country grouping above

OTHER

CPE: Centrally Planned Economies
RST: Not otherwise specified

PRODUCT CODES

MK: Dairy products
BF: Beef
PK: Pork
PT: Poultry
SH: Sheepmeat
WT: Wheat
CG: Coarse grains
SU: Sugar

RP: Rapeseed
SB: Soybeans
WL: Wool
RC: Rice
MN: Manioc
CF: Corn gluten feed
OE: Other energy-rich feed
OP: Other protein-rich feed

Table 4.2

CHANGES IN DEVELOPING COUNTRIES AGRICULTURAL PRODUCTION AND TRADE: 1970-1986

	Indices of food and agricultural production				Growth rates of total agricultural trade[1]				Share of agriculture total		
	Total production		Per capita		Exports		Imports		Exports[1]	Imports[1]	GDP[2]
	1975-77	1984-86	1975-77	1984-86	1970-80	1980-85	1970-80	1980-85	1983-85	1983-85	1985
		(1979-81 = 100)			(Growth rates % per annum)				(Percentage)		
Developed market economies	92	106	93	103	5.7	0.7	2.0	2.5	11	11	3
All developing countries	89	119	96	108	1.8	3.3	8.0	1.7	14	14	20
Sub-Saharan Africa	95	112	107	96	-2.2	0.4	6.6	1.6	26	17	34
North Africa/West Africa	91	112	102	98	-2.6	-0.1	12.7	6.1	5	18	17
East and South Asia	87	125	95	113	4.0	4.4	5.4	-1.8	18	11	19
China	84	133	89	125	0.5	15.7	11.1	-13.8	16	10	33
India	93	122	101	111	2.4	-3.2	-2.7	7.6	28	14	31
South Korea	98	112	104	103	7.6	4.6	9.7	2.9	2	11	14
Thailand	87	120	95	109	9.2	7.2	7.5	2.7	50	6	17
Latin America	89	111	97	99	2.7	3.8	8.3	-3.2	30	14	15
Argentina	92	107	98	98	6.2	7.6	0.7	-9.5	72	6	12
Brazil	87	117	95	105	1.7	5.6	12.7	-5.2	39	9	13
Mexico	84	110	94	96	-1.1	3.0	18.3	-4.3	7	20	11

1. Trade is expressed in value terms.
2. These data are taken from the IBRD, see sources below. For Iran and Iraq, figures are for 1978. The classification of regional country groupings does not correspond exactly with those of FAO.

Sources: FAO, Agriculture: Toward 2000 (Revised version, 1987), for trade data, see Appendix Table 3, July 1987, Rome.
FAO, Monthly Bulletin of Statistics, for production indices, Vol. 10, Table 1, April 1987, Rome.
IBRD (World Bank), World Development Report 1987, for GDP data, Table 3, pp. 206-207, June 1987, Washington.

Table 4.3

SOURCES OF PSE/CSEs AND PRICE ESTIMATES

	Mexico	Argen-tina	Brazil	China	South Korea	India	Thai-land	Sub-Sahar. Africa
Milk	3	3	3/4	3/4	1	3/4	6	5
Beef	4	3	1	2	1	4	6	5
Pork	3	3	3	2	1	4	6	5
Poultry	4	3	1	3	1	6	2	5
Sheepmeat	4	3	4	2	4	4	6	5
Wheat	1	1	1	3	1	1	3	1/3
Coarse grains	1	1	1	3	1	4	2	1/3
Sugar	4	3	3	3	3	4	3	1/3
Rapeseed	6	6	6	6	6	1	6	5
Soybeans	1	1	1	3	1	1	2	3
Wool	6	6	6	6	6	6	6	6
Rice	2	3	1	2	1	1	1	1/3
Eggs	4	4	3	6	1	6	6	6

1. Producer prices and PSEs/CSEs drawn from USDA, *Estimates of Producer and Consumer Subsidy Equivalents: Government Intervention in Agriculture 1982-86*, ATAD-ERS-USDA, Staff Report No. AGES 380127.
2. Producer prices drawn from the FAO database and the protection rates used in the TLIB model for 1984 (Gardiner and Roningen, forthcoming).
3. Unit trade value calculated on the basis of FAO and UN data and the protection rates used in the TLIB model for 1984.
4. Prices and protection rates of the TLIB model.
5. Unit trade value and protection rates (Anderson and Tyers, 1986).
6. Not available.

Table 4.4

NET IMPORTS BY DEVELOPING COUNTRIES: 1982-85
(Million $)

| | OECD modelled products (1982-85) (1) | 10 per cent PSE/CSE reduction in all countries | |
		Absolute change of (1) (2)	Relative change % (2)/(1)
Mexico	141	479	34.0
Argentina	-4 915	-439	8.9
Brazil	-1 093	-360	32.9
China	1 193	-1 107	-92.8
South Korea	1 717	113	6.6
India	311	-251	-80.7
Thailand	-3 003	-8	0.3
Sub-Saharan Africa	2 674	135	5.0
Total	-1 706	-1 438	84.3

In Column (1), a negative value indicates net exports and a positive value net imports.

In Column (2), a negative value for a net exporter represents increased net exports, whereas for a net importer, it represents reduced net imports.

Source: OECD.

Annex I

COMPARISON OF THE DIFFERENT MODEL VERSIONS

In order to establish a new basis for comparison, the simulation of a 10 per cent reduction in PSEs/CSEs in the OECD countries was conducted using the new MTM-LDC model. This was compared with previous results from the 11 region MTM model. The world reference price changes are shown in Figure 4.18. The first bar was obtained with the 11 region MTM model. This corresponds to that published in the Monitoring report. The second and third bars show the results obtained with the MTM-LDC model, using the FAO and USDA elasticities respectively. These results will now be compared and the differences explained, and the final results will be considered a reference basis for further simulations carried out using the MTM-LDC model.

The results of the scenario for a 10 per cent reduction in agricultural assistance using the 11 region model indicate that animal product prices increase whilst livestock feed prices fall and cereal prices decline slightly.

The same simulation was carried out using the MTM-LDC model, measuring developing country response first with the FAO elasticities and then with the USDA elasticities. These new results do not conflict with the previous ones. In general, with the exception of animal feed, the incorporation of a developing country response in the model weakens the impact on world prices of a 10 per cent reduction in OECD country PSEs/CSEs. If the price rise is transmitted to national markets in developing countries without any policy change on their part, they will increase their production and reduce their consumption, which acts as a brake on world price rises.

This reaction is even stronger if the commodity plays an important role in the developing countries under consideration in relation to the OECD countries. This is particularly the case with rice: 66 per cent of world production is consumed in the developing countries covered (China: 38 per cent) and only 5 per cent in the OECD countries. For the same reason, the fall in the world price of soybeans is smaller. Reduced beef exports by OECD countries are almost offset by increased exports by Argentina and Brazil. As a result the world beef price rises less than in the MTM model. The different price movements for sugar can be explained by the fact that in the FAO version the elasticities for this product are equivalent to zero, whereas in the USDA version they are stronger than those used in the MTM model for the rest of the world. The greater fall in livestock feed prices is due to a reduction in feed use in the OECD countries because of smaller rises in world prices for animal products. In the future, the MTM-LDC model will be used with the USDA elasticities since these cover a larger number of commodities and substitutions between these commodities, and this simulation will serve as a basis for reference.

155

Annex II

DEVELOPING COUNTRIES' ELASTICITIES

TLIS (USDA) PRICE ELASTICITIES

The own- and cross-price total demand and supply elasticities are those used by the USDA in its "Trade Liberalization Model" (Gardiner and Roningen, forthcoming).

GENERAL COMMENTS

Each of the countries of the MTM study is covered by the USDA model. In the case of the Sub-Saharan Africa group, the USDA distinguishes between Nigeria on the one hand, and "Other Sub-Saharan African Countries" on the other. The price elasticities which have been used for Sub-Saharan Africa thus correspond to weighted averages (of production or, depending on circumstances, of total consumption) of the price elasticities for Nigeria and "Other Sub-Saharan African Countries".

The list of the commodities covered by the USDA is, to a large extent, similar to that covered by the MTM model. However, some differences should be noted:

a) The naming system of the USDA in terms of dairy products is slightly less detailed. The USDA treats as separate products only: fresh milk, butter, cheese and milk powder. Thus it was decided to use the same price elasticities for whole and skimmed milk powder; that is, the supply and demand elasticities for milk powder used by the USDA.

b) For oilseeds, the USDA treats soybeans and "other oilseed grains" separately. The price elasticities presented in the tables for supply and demand of rapeseed grains are those given for "other oilseed grains".

c) Finally, the Secretariat has obtained elasticities of demand for cereals (wheat and coarse grains) with respect to the prices of oilseed meals. In this case, the demand considered is total demand, i.e. demand for animal feed is included. These elasticities, weighted by the share of animal feed in the use of each cereal, have thus been taken as cross-price elasticities for cereals with respect to oilseeds.

NOTES AND REFERENCES

1. This paper draws on work carried out in the OECD Agricultural Directorate, but in particular the authors would like to express their gratitude for the help and advice of Matthew Harley and Chantal Le Mouël.

2. OECD, *National Policies and Agricultural Trade*, OECD, Paris, 1987.

3. OECD, *Agricultural Policies, Markets and Trade — Monitoring and Outlook*, OECD, Paris, 1989.

4. The Sub-Saharan Africa group includes all African countries, except South Africa and the North African countries, namely Algeria, Morocco, Tunisia, Egypt, Libya and Western Sahara.

5. FAO, "The FAO World Food Model, Model Specification," supplement to *FAO Agricultural Commodity Projections to 1990*, ESC/4186/4, FAO, Rome.

6. W. Gardiner, V.O. Roningen and K. Liu, *Elasticities in the Trade Liberalization (TLIB) Model*, US Department of Agriculture, ERS Staff Report, Washington (forthcoming).

7. K. Anderson and R. Tyers, *Distortions in World Food Markets: A Quantitative Assessment*, January 1986.

8. A large part of this section draws on recent work completed by the OECD Directorate for Food, Agriculture and Fisheries concerning OECD trade relations with developing countries, including: *Agricultural Trade Relations with Developing Countries*, Annex 3 to the report "Agricultural Policies, Markets and Trade: Monitoring and Outlook; *Trade in Cereals and Feeds: Recent Developments and Policies*, document presented to the OECD 1988 Group on Cereals, Animal Feeds and Sugar; *Trade in Meat and Meat Products: Recent Developments, Outlook and Policy Review*, document presented to the OECD 1988 Group on Meat and Dairy Products.

9. D. Byerlee, "The Political Economy of Third World Food Imports: The Case of Wheat", *Economic Development and Cultural Change*, Vol. 35, No. 2, pp. 307-28, January 1987.

10. A.H. Sarris, "Domestic Price Policies and International Distortions: The Case of Wheat and Rice", *Economic Notes*, No. 2, pp. 5-35, 1987.

11. S.M. Kanbur, "Global Food Balances and Individual Hunger: Three Themes in an Entitlements Based Approach", *Warwick Economic Research Papers*, No. 227, University of Warwick, Coventry, United Kingdom, April 1987.

12. OECD, *MTM Model Specification and Elasticities*, Paris, 1988.

13. FAO, *Trade Year Book*, FAO, Rome.

14. A. Krueger, M. Schiff and A. Valdés, *Measuring the Impact of Sector-Specific and Economy-Wide Policies on Agricultural Incentive in LDCs*, paper presented at the American Economics Association meeting, Chicago, January 1988.

15. FAO, *State of Food and Agriculture*, Rome, 1985.

16. The corresponding CSEs were also left unchanged in this scenario.

Chapter 5

DEVELOPING COUNTRIES IN AN OPEN ECONOMY: THE CASE OF AGRICULTURE[1]

by

Barry Krissoff, John Sullivan and John Wainio

INTRODUCTION

Two separate but interrelated sets of economic reforms could have significant effects on the agricultural sectors in the developing countries with market economies (DMEs). The first set of reforms are those currently being negotiated by parties to the General Agreement on Tariffs and Trade (GATT) in the Uruguay Round of multilateral trade negotiations. A final agreement is not expected until the conclusion of the negotiations in late 1990, so the exact nature of these reforms remains speculative. At the completion of the mid-term review of the negotiations in early 1989, most countries agreed to short-term measures of freezing agricultural support and to the long-term objective of a substantial and progressive reduction in tariff and non-tariff import barriers and trade distorting subsidies, and a reduction and harmonization of health and sanitary standards across countries.

The DMEs have been relatively passive participants in past multilateral trade rounds. In this round, however, the opportunity to increase their agricultural exports by gaining access to industrialised country markets has been a strong incentive for DME exporters to take an active role in the current negotiations. For those DMEs which are dependent on food imports, on the other hand, interest in the current negotiations revolves around a concern that their consumers will be adversely affected should world prices rise as a result of the elimination of export subsidies in the industrial market economies (IMEs).

The second set of economic reforms are distinct in that they are unilateral, not multilateral, reforms and are not agricultural specific but economy-wide reforms. They stem from the debt crises currently facing many of the DMEs. During the 1970s, the long-term external debt of a number of DMEs grew at a rapid pace, raising serious concerns about their ability to meet repayment obligations and to attract additional international credit to finance future development. In the 1980s, the World Bank and the International Monetary Fund began urging developing countries to pursue more prudent macroeconomic policies as a condition of future loans.

The cornerstone of this macroeconomic reform often consists of removing distortions in the debtor country's currency exchange rate. Such distortions in the exchange rates of DMEs are neither rare nor insignificant. An overvalued currency is effectively a tax on exports and a subsidy to imports. Devaluing alters relative prices across countries. Imports into the devaluing country become more expensive relative to domestic goods while its exports become more competitively priced in international markets. Hence, imports contract while exports expand.

For the heavily indebted DMEs, the ability to attract additional foreign credit is closely tied to the ability to earn foreign exchange. Since, for many of these countries agricultural commodities are the main exports, simply devaluing the exchange rate may not be enough to bring about significant increases in export earnings if there is not also an accompanying agricultural reform in the IMEs to provide a market for these exports.

The objectives of this study are:

a) To examine how the agricultural sectors of the DMEs might be affected should there be an elimination of government policies which influence agricultural markets; and,

b) To provide a preliminary examination of the effects on their agricultural sectors should the DMEs also elect to devalue their currency exchange rates to estimated free market levels.

The paper proceeds by first presenting the simulation model used to conduct the analysis, second by explaining the relationships of the partial equilibrium framework used here compared to a general equilibrium framework, and third by presenting the results from each simulation experiment.

The Model Structure

The world model used for this analysis is based on the Static World Policy Simulation (SWOPSIM) modelling framework. SWOPSIM models are characterised by four basic features: (a) static, (b) nonspatial, (c) partial equilibrium, and (d) net trade models. (For more details on the structure of SWOPSIM models, see Roningen, and Roningen and Dixit.) The world model includes 22 commodity groups and is made up of 36 linked country or regional models, 25 of which represent countries or regions in the developing world (see Appendix Tables 5.A1 and 5.A2).

For each country/region i and commodity j (or k) in the model, a demand and supply function is specified

$$D_{ij} = D_{ij} (CP_{ij}, CP_{ik}) \tag{1}$$

$$S_{ij} = S_{ij} (PP_{ij}, PP_{ik}) \tag{2}$$

where CP_{ij} and PP_{ij} are the domestic incentive prices facing consumers and producers of commodity j.[2] CP_{ik} is the cross-product consumer price for commodity k (for all relevant k's); PP_{ik} is an input and/or product substitute or complement producer price with respect to commodity j. Trade is the difference between domestic supply and total demand

$$T_{ij} = S_{ij} - D_{ij}. \tag{3}$$

Domestic incentive prices depend on the level of consumer and producer support wedges (CSW_{ij} and $PSWij$) and world prices denominated in local currency

$$CP_{ij} = CSW_{ij} + F (E_i * WP_j) \tag{4}$$

$$PP_{ij} = PSW_{ij} + G (E_i * WP_j) \tag{5}$$

where CSW_{ij} and PSW_{ij} depend on the level of government support in each country, as measured by Producer and Consumer Subsidy Equivalents ($PSEs/CSEs$). The PSE/CSE is a broader measure of policy support than the nominal rate of protection. It includes direct income payments, input, marketing, and structural assistance as well as market price support. (A subsidy is positive support and a tax is negative support.) E_i is the exchange rate defined as local currency (i) dollar and WP_j is the world reference price of commodity j. The functional relationships, $F( )$ and $G( )$, allow a specification of world to domestic prices to be less than or equal to 1, depending on price transmission coefficients. If the developing country's government

160

wants to protect its consumers from a 10 per cent world price increase, for instance, then consumer (and producer) prices may rise by less than 10 per cent.

World markets clear when net trade of a commodity across all countries is equal to 0. For commodity j, this occurs when

$$\sum_{i=1}^{n} T_{ij} = \sum_{i=1}^{n} S_{ij} - \sum_{i=1}^{n} D_{ij} = 0 \tag{6}$$

The commodity supply and demand equations are parameterized to reproduce 1986 base period data for each countries' supply, demand, prices, and trade. When a change is made in the support wedges or the exchange rates, the model recalculates domestic supply and demand levels, rebalancing world trade, production, consumption, and prices in the process. The pattern of prices and quantities observed in the base period is then compared to the pattern which emerges from the model.

General Equilibrium Considerations

The structure of the model presented above is similar to other partial equilibrium models which have examined liberalizing agricultural trade (see OECD, Tyers and Anderson, Roningen and Dixit). One shortcoming of this approach, particularly for developing countries, is the exclusion of an income effect generated by world trade liberalization. Since agriculture is such a large component of many DMEs, a change in income in this sector may have significant effects on the economy. Mellor writes that income generated by prospering farmers augments rural purchasing power, reduces unemployment and underemployment of labour, and promotes economic growth in the rural economy. Thus agricultural trade liberalization could enhance productivity, expand the developing country agricultural sector, and advance economic development and growth throughout the entire economy.

In order to capture the income effect, the demand equation (1) is modified to include economy-wide income, Y_i (and the accompanying income elasticity, in constant elasticity form):

$$D_{ij} = D_{ij} (CP_{ij}, CP_{ik}, Y_i) . \tag{1'}$$

Increases in commodity prices resulting from trade liberalization lead farmers to expand agricultural output, thus resulting in an increase in agricultural income and in effective demand. The imbalances generated by new demands influence prices, which continue to adjust until world and domestic markets attain new market clearing levels.

The alternative assumption regarding changes in income can be illustrated in a general equilibrium framework. Specifically, a production possibility surface is depicted for a developing country in Figure 5.1, where two goods are produced, agriculture and non-agriculture. The agricultural sector is proxied by aggregating the 22 commodity SWOPSIM set. The developing country is assumed to be an importer of agriculture and an exporter of non-agriculture (on the whole, developing countries are importers of the commodities found in our model). Line *P1* represents world agricultural prices relative to world non-agricultural prices, assuming free trade. It is tangent to the production possibility frontier (PPF) at point *1* and tangent to a social utility function (SUF) at point *F*. Line *P2* represents agricultural prices which are lower than *P1* due to IME government intervention in agricultural markets. It is tangent to a *PPF* at point *2* and to a SUF at point *G*.

If all available resources and technology are employed in the developing country economy, that is, there are no distortions in factor or output markets, then production would take place at point *2*, given IME support to agriculture. An IME liberalization causing commodity price increases would lead to a reallocation of resources to agriculture and consequently, agricultural production would increase and non-agricultural production would decline to point *1*. Agricultural imports and non-agricultural exports would fall for the developing country importer. There would be a welfare loss as indicated by the movement from point *G* to point *F*. (The general equilibrium qualitative result suggested by Figure 5.1 is consistent with the quantitative model results of the International Institute for Applied Systems Analysis (IIASA). They indicate a welfare loss for countries that import large quantities of food, such as Brazil, Mexico, Egypt, and Indonesia. IIASA also suggests a loss in gross domestic product for these countries because the gains in the agricultural sector are not sufficient to offset the losses in the non-agricultural sector.)

In our partial equilibrium framework the effects on the non-agricultural sector of IME agricultural trade liberalization are less clear. One simple approach is to assume that there is a decline in non-agricultural production, which is not measured, and therefore, the effect of an IME agricultural liberalization on DMEs' overall GNP is ambiguous. Another approach is to assume that the increase in agricultural income due to trade liberalization generates increases in food and non-food consumption, investment and productivity. Under these conditions, there is a rightward shift in the PPF and the DME economy may be producing at point *3* (Figure 5.1). In Mellor's terminology there would be an income multiplier and linkage effect from the agricultural to non-agricultural sector, generating more employment and expanding agricultural and non-agricultural production. It is this latter approach that we pursue in the simulation exercises by including income in the demand function and using an income multiplier.

To this point our discussion on general equilibrium considerations has assumed that there are no macroeconomic distortions in the developing country economy. However, there is considerable evidence that overvaluation of exchange rates has adversely affected developing country agricultural trade. In a World Bank study, Krueger finds that the indirect economic policies affecting producer returns to agriculture (mainly exchange rate misalignments and protection to the non-agricultural sector) are always negative in the 18 countries studied.

Overvaluation of exchange rates is equivalent to a tax on tradable goods relative to non-tradables. That is, the relative price between traded and non-traded goods is lower than it would be when exchange rates are in equilibrium. Since the agricultural commodities in our partial equilibrium model are all traded goods (with the exception of dairy milk), then overvaluation adversely affects agricultural production relative to non-traded goods production. Hence, we consider both IME agricultural trade and DME exchange rate liberalization in the simulation exercises.

The Four Simulation Experiments

In the first three simulation exercises (IME1, IMEY2, and IMEY3), we remove all IME agricultural support while DME support is kept in place. The price transmission coefficients are assumed to equal one for all IME and DME countries. Assumptions underlying IME1, IMEY2, and IMEY3 differ as to the effect on aggregate income. In IME1, demand equation (1) is utilised so that there is no feedback from the agricultural sector to aggregate income. The results from this experiment are compared to the base period to illustrate the effects on developing countries of IME liberalization.

In IMEY2 we model changes in agricultural income (dYA_i) endogenously by:

a) Approximating the change in agricultural income with the change in agricultural GDP (calculated as the domestic market price times quantity supplied less an estimate for the intermediate use of grains, soybeans, and manufactured milk);

b) Adding the change in agricultural income to the economy-wide base level income, $dYA_i + Y_i$; and

c) Utilising demand equation (1') which includes the income term.

In effect, we are assuming an income multiplier of one. The results of IME1 and IMEY2 can be compared to determine the effects of the inclusion of the income term in the demand functions.

A change in farm income also can impact on the rural sector by changing the demand for goods and services of the non-agricultural sector. Income gains could accrue to non-agriculture, a movement from point *1* to point *3* in Figure 5.1. In IMEY3, changes in agricultural income are modelled endogenously with a multiplier effect of three assumed for all of the developing countries and regions, $(3*dYA_i) + Y_i$, excluding the newly industrialised Asian economies of Taiwan, South Korea, and East Asia (Singapore and Hong Kong). The size of the income multiplier was an arbitrary choice; it was included to reflect how developing country economy-wide income may improve with agricultural trade liberalization and how this may feedback to the agricultural sector through increases in the demand for food.

In the fourth exercise (IMEYX4), exchange rate values are realigned to their estimated free market levels and IME agricultural policies are removed. The income effect with the multiplier of one is maintained so that a comparison of IMEY2 and IMEYX4 reveals the influence of changes in exchange rates. The E_i's in equations (4) and (5) are exogenously changed to reflect the level of distortion in a country's exchange rate. These levels of distortion are taken from estimates provided in Cowitt's *World Currency Yearbook*. They are based on exchanges observed in black markets, and thus, may differ from free market rates if there is a premium associated with participating in an illegal activity. In this case, they would magnify the level of exchange rate distortion and could lead to overestimated values of production, consumption, and trade in IMEYX4.

Changes in World Prices

Average world prices, weighted across all 22 commodities, increased 16 per cent when IME government support to the agricultural sector (experiment IME1) was removed from the model. This compares to price increases of 18, 21, and 10 per cent, respectively, in the experiments with an income term (IMEY2), an income multiplier (IMEY3), and an exchange rate shock (IMEYX4). These price increases are consistent with other studies, including those by Roningen and Dixit, who report an average world commodity price increase of 22 per cent from an IME liberalization simulation using the same commodity coverage[3].

Table 5.1 shows the percentage change in individual world commodity prices needed to clear world commodity markets in each of the four model simulations. In all four cases, dairy product prices show, by far, the steepest increases relative to 1986 base prices, reflecting the extensive use of producer subsidies and consumer taxes in the dairy sectors of the IMEs. Sugar and wheat are two other commodities which experience significant increases in prices when IME government programmes for these commodities are eliminated in the model.

When the effects of these price increases are factored into the economies of the DMEs via an income term (IMEY2), DME consumers demand larger quantities of agricultural commodities (relative to IME1), which places additional upward pressure on commodity prices. This is especially true for rice, soyoil, other oilseeds and products, cotton, and sugar; markets where the developing country share of world consumption is large (see the top portion of Table 5.A3). When this income effect is enhanced via an income multiplier (IMEY3), we begin to see effects on world livestock, dairy, and feed prices, as well. Even though the DMEs do not currently account for large shares of world consumption in these commodities, their demand for them is relatively income elastic, when compared to the IMEs. Therefore, when income in the DMEs is significantly increased we begin to see a large enough demand response in these commodities to affect world prices.

In experiment IMEYX4, with developing country exchange rates realigned to estimated free market levels, increases in world prices are considerably less than those observed in the three previous experiments. The smaller world price increases reflect the significant overvaluation of national currencies by governments in the developing world. Should IMEs liberalize their agricultural markets while DMEs are simultaneously devaluing their currencies, the domestic prices of agricultural commodities (in fact, of all traded goods) in the DMEs should rise considerably, thus encouraging further production and less consumption. With expanded world production and contracted world consumption, there is less pressure for world prices to increase as a result of increased excess demand in the IMEs.

The bottom of Table 5.A3 shows the extent to which the DMEs in this study would have to devalue their currencies to be at estimated free market levels. In Nigeria, for example, the government would have to pay Nigerian exporters converting dollars into naira 3.7 times the amount they paid them in 1986. In the 17 individual developing countries included in our model, ten were estimated to have overvalued currencies in 1986, six to have market determined rates, and one, South Korea, was estimated to be slightly undervalued. The eight DME regional models are all denominated in dollars, so no changes were made in their exchange rate.

Changes in Agricultural Production and Consumption

As a group, the DMEs' agricultural production increases by successively larger percentages above the base level in each of the four experiments: 3.3, 4.0, 5.6, and 7.2 per cent, respectively (Table 5.2). On an individual country/region basis, however, this is not always the case (quantity increases in each country were weighted by value of production in the base year to get an average across all commodities). In IME1, given the world price increases resulting from simulating an IME liberalization, all of the DMEs show increases in production. Those DMEs with relatively elastic supply schedules, particularly in commodities that show marked price increases, should experience significant increases in production (more than 5 per cent). The commodity composition of production in each country, in the base year, also has an effect on the total change in quantities produced reported in Table 5.2.

Scenarios IMEY2 and IMEY3, are designed to show how these increases in production can lead to income gains in the economy, and that the increasing effective demand that this generates can lead to further increases in production. Results in these scenarios depend not only on the elasticities of supply and the composition of production, but also on the importance of these commodities in the country's overall economy. The greater the percentage of GDP that these commodities contribute in a country, the greater the income effect to the economy from increases in output and the greater the impact of the income term and income multiplier in the demand equations. For example, India, Pakistan, and Bangladesh have over 13 per cent of their GDP accounted for by the 22 commodities modelled here and experience some of the largest agricultural production responses, approximately 7, 12, and 11 per cent, respectively.

Scenario IMEYX4 produces the largest supply responses in the DMEs, approaching 50 per cent in Nigeria and 60 per cent in Bangladesh, as exchange rates are realigned to estimated free market levels. In countries such as Venezuela, Nigeria, Egypt, and Bangladesh, this realignment requires large devaluations, thus resulting in large increases in domestic prices and large increases in production[4]. In those countries/regions which we do not show as having an overvalued currency we see either production decreases or production increases which are smaller than those observed in the three previous experiments. This is because, in effect, their currencies are being valued upward vis-à-vis those DMEs that are devaluing.

On the consumption side, results show a reduction in quantity demanded of 2.6 per cent for the DMEs as a result of higher domestic prices due to IME liberalization (IME1, Table 5.3). The decline in demand is not as large in IMEY2 (1.6 per cent), even with higher world price increases, because of the feedback provided through the income term in the demand equations.

Consumption prospects for nearly all of the DMEs are considerably brighter when the income multiplier effect is introduced in IMEY3. Overall, the DMEs are estimated to increase their consumption of these commodities by 1.6 per cent. Exceptions are those countries in which the production of commodities in our model accounts for only a small percentage of total GDP, such as Nigeria. Consumption actually decreases further when we include an income multiplier in the demand equations in these countries, as the effect of the higher world prices generated in IMEY3 dominates the effect of increasing income in the demand equations. Declines in consumption are also observed in the newly industrialised economies of East Asia. In their case, we assumed that the income multiplier would not be greater than one, so for these countries decreases in consumption are a function of higher consumer prices.

In the Asian countries of India, Pakistan, Bangladesh, Indonesia, Thailand, and the Philippines, the 22 commodity groups included in our model accounted for more than 10 per cent of total GDP in the base period (see Table 5.A3). Thus income generated by an expanding agricultural sector provides the purchasing power needed to increase food consumption across a large section of the economy. Quantity demanded in these countries increases over what it was in the base year. Other countries or regions that demonstrate modest increases in consumption are Egypt, other Sub-Saharan Africa, and the Middle East/North African non-petroleum producing countries.

In scenario IMEYX4, consumption declines an average of 3.5 per cent in the DMEs. Here the exchange rate adjustment magnifies the increase in consumer prices due to IME liberalization. Quantity demanded drops sharply in those countries which maintained highly overvalued currencies in 1986. We stress again, however, that the magnitude of the overvaluation assumed in our model could very well be overestimated due to the premium generally associated with observed black market exchange rates. In addition, if prices remain flexible in the long run, continued output growth in other DMEs should eventually put downward pressure on prices. In the short and medium term, however, food deficient countries may need increased food aid should the IMEs liberalize their agricultural sectors.

Changes in Agricultural Trade

Substantial improvements in the net agricultural trade balances for the developing countries occur in each of the simulation exercises (Table 5.4). Initially, developing country gross agricultural exports equal $25 billion and gross imports equal $35 billion (valued at 1986 world reference prices). For the developing country exporter, the greater volume of exports and the higher world prices result in additional foreign exchange revenues. For the developing country importer, the smaller import volume mitigates the negative balance of trade impact of higher world prices. The importing country may face a higher or lower food import bill depending on import demand elasticities.

With the opening of markets in IME countries (IME1), we find that foreign exchange revenue from the net sale of agricultural exports by developing countries expands nearly $12 billion. In scenarios with the income term (IMEY2, IMEY3, and IMEYX4), agricultural trade balances are affected by two counteracting forces: increases in prices and increases in incomes. As discussed earlier most commodity prices rise, thus stimulating production, discouraging consumption, and therefore, enhancing the volume of net exports. The increases in income generated by increases in agricultural production, however, have a demand expanding effect, so that agricultural commodity trade expands; demand elasticities with respect to income are positive in general. Since DMEs have higher income elasticities and relatively larger income improvements than do the IMEs, they demonstrate greater increases in demand. Therefore, we would expect these countries to have less of an improvement in their overall trade balances under simulation IMEY2 compared to simulation IME1 where the income effect is not included. This is even more true in IMEY3. We find that developing countries' agricultural trade balances improve by $11 and $8 billion in IMEY2 and IMEY3, respectively.

India is a country that illustrates how the agricultural balance of trade can differ in IMEY2 and IMEY3 relative to IME1. India gains nearly $4 billion in its agricultural trade balance in IME1, while in IMEY3 the gain is less than $100 million. Agriculture is a key sector in the Indian economy, substantially contributing to income. The 22 commodity groups in our model account for 21 per cent of total GDP in the Indian economy. In the case of IMEY3 (given an income multiplier of three), when commodity prices and domestic production increase, the value of agricultural income increases by 33 per cent, and total income is augmented by nearly 21 per cent. This large overall income increase leads to significantly greater domestic demand and, consequently, less net exports.

Although most developing countries/regions attain smaller trade revenue gains in moving from scenarios IME1 to IMEY2 and IMEY3, several Latin American and Asian agricultural exporters experience gains in trade. This is due to the increase in world demand by both industrialised and other developing countries for beef, grains, and sugar produced by Argentina, Brazil, Mexico, and Central America and the Caribbean, and for rice, other oils, and sugar produced by Thailand, Malaysia, and the Philippines.

In scenario IMEYX4 the ten developing countries whose currencies are devalued in the model show strong improvement in their net trade; exports become more competitively priced and imports become more expensive. As a group, developing countries' agricultural trade balances improve $24 billion in IMEYX4, over twice the gain experienced in IMEY2. Thus the macroeconomic exchange rate factor has at least the same effect on developing countries' agricultural trade position as an IME liberalization.

The trade gain is realised mainly by eight countries — Mexico, Brazil, Argentina, Venezuela, Nigeria, Egypt, India, and Bangladesh — the countries with the most misaligned currencies. Argentina and Brazil each increase their agricultural net exports by over $5 billion and Mexico improves its agricultural trade position by $2.7 billion, thus accounting for most of the $15 billion trade gains of Latin American countries. Nigeria, Egypt, India, and Bangladesh achieve agricultural trade gains of $1.3, $1.8, $3.2 and $2.7 billion. (The developing countries not modelled individually, such as other Sub-Saharan Africa, do not have an adjustment for exchange rate misalignment. As a consequence, relative prices across countries may be biased depending on any exchange rate misalignment in these regions.)

Changes in Gross Domestic Product

Gross Domestic Product is a measure of aggregate economic activity and is often interpreted as a living standard, albeit an imperfect one. We calculated GDP in constant dollar terms to provide a measure of the welfare effects of trade and exchange rate liberalization. Our results indicate that GDP changes in the DMEs, as a whole, are very similar in scenarios IME1 and IMEY2, increasing by 1.3 and 1.6 per cent, respectively (Table 5.5). The gains are considerably higher in the IMEY3 scenario (6.3 per cent) because of the income multiplier effects, while they are dampened when exchange rate distortions are removed (1.1 per cent).

Not surprisingly, a critical factor in determining the magnitude of GDP increases is the share of modelled agricultural GDP relative to economy-wide GDP. The more important these commodities are in the overall GDP of a country and the larger the increase in agricultural product in the simulation exercises, the larger the increases are in total GDP. For the developing

166

countries as a whole, agriculture is a primary sector of the economy, accounting for a significant percentage of total GDP. The World Bank estimates the importance of agriculture in the structure of total production as approximately 35 per cent for low and middle income developing economies and 10 per cent for upper middle income economies. For many of the DMEs, the commodities included in our model account for only a fraction of agricultural GDP, the bulk of which comes from the production of tropical commodities. We estimate that the commodities we have modelled are equal to about 7 per cent of total GDP in the developing world. Hence, we substantially understate the value of agriculture in many developing economies.

Our commodity coverage is more complete in Asia and Latin America than in the Africa and Middle East regions. As such, the Asian GDP gains are about 3 per cent, the gains in Latin America about 2 per cent, while those in Africa and the Middle East equal less than 1 per cent (IMEY2). Gains are 11, 6, and 3 per cent for Asia, Latin America, and Africa and the Middle East, respectively, in IMEY3, while the corresponding figures in IMEYX4 are 1, 2, and less than 1 per cent, respectively.

Individual country gains are very skewed depending on the importance of the modelled agricultural sector to the total economy, as well as the agricultural supply elasticities and the magnitude of the exchange rate shock. The countries achieving the largest growth in GDP in IMEY3 are: Argentina, 12 per cent; India, 21 per cent; Pakistan, 19 per cent; and Bangladesh, 24 per cent. When the exchange rate scenario is run (IMEYX4) these increases drop significantly: Argentina, 5 per cent; India, 3 per cent; Pakistan, 2 per cent; and Bangladesh, 12 per cent.

CONCLUSIONS

In this paper we examine the effects on developing countries of removing market distorting agricultural policies in the industrial market economies and of aligning developing country exchange rates to estimated free market levels. A few key points emerge from our simulations of these changes. First, with the opening of agricultural markets in the IMEs, world prices tend to increase, as expected. Our results indicate an average increase in world commodity prices of around 16 per cent. Prices of dairy products, sugar, and wheat experience the largest price increases, reflecting high levels of support for these commodities in the IMEs. When explicit recognition of income increases are accounted for in the agricultural trade liberalization experiments, there is additional pressure on prices to rise. However, a realignment of developing country exchange rates, to offset an overvaluation of currency values in the base year, tends to offset the income effect so that the average world commodity price increase is only 10 per cent.

Second, domestic price increases provide the incentives to developing countries' farmers to increase output. Domestic prices rise due to world price increases resulting from IME liberalization, domestic demand pressures generated from income increases, and currency devaluations. On average, developing country production expands over 7 per cent when agricultural markets are freed from IME intervention and exchange rate misalignment is corrected in developing countries. Argentina, Brazil, Mexico, Venezuela, Egypt, Nigeria, and Bangladesh, the countries with large currency overvaluations, show substantial production gains.

Third, consumers face higher domestic prices due to trade and exchange rate liberalization. This results in a decline in food consumption in countries that already may be suffering from underconsumption. Developing countries' consumers buy over 3 per cent fewer agricultural goods than before liberalization. The distribution though is highly skewed, particularly when exchange rates are altered; demand falls everywhere, but the decline is greatest where devaluation is most extreme. However, when the income multiplier is assumed equal to three, increases in the purchasing power of DME consumers outweigh the effect of higher domestic prices, and developing countries' consumption increases by nearly 2 per cent.

Fourth, developing countries improve their agricultural trade balances, and thus, as a group, switch from being net importers to net exporters of these commodities in three of the four experiments. The trade gains are largest when exchange rate realignment is simulated, smallest when an income multiplier of three is assumed.

Fifth, our results indicate that GDP increases for the developing countries by 6 per cent when the income multiplier assumption is adopted. For countries where the commodities included in this model make up a significant portion of total GDP, the gains are considerably higher: for example, Argentina, India, Pakistan, and Bangladesh achieve growth of at least 12 per cent. However, overall GDP increases are significantly smaller, perhaps negligible, in the scenarios without the multiplier assumption.

What then are the policy implications that can be drawn from this study? The first is that substantial gains could accrue to the agricultural sector in the DMEs should the IMEs liberalize their agricultural sectors and producers in DMEs be allowed to benefit from higher world prices. The DMEs would increase their production of temperate agricultural commodities while improving their overall balance of trade. Since agriculture is the primary sector in most DMEs, the stimulus from higher world prices would have an impact on the entire economy. For the heavily indebted DMEs, the increased foreign exchange from improvements in the balance of trade would ease the burden of servicing their debt.

On the negative side, urban consumers in the DMEs would suffer real income losses because of the higher food prices. This outcome raises significant concerns for countries already having difficulty meeting the food needs of their populations. In the short term, these countries may require increased food aid from the IMEs. Since production in the IMEs will be declining as a result of eliminating agricultural support, the issue of food aid availabilities in a liberalized world agricultural environment should not be taken lightly.

There are many limitations to our study and, at the very least, some should be mentioned. We have included in our commodity coverage only the more important traded temperate and sub-tropical products. The proportion of the agricultural sector modelled relative to its actual size crucially influences the findings. Even within this subset of agricultural goods there are data shortcomings and uncertainty regarding parameter estimates. Other limitations are the crude estimation of exchange rate misalignments and assumptions regarding the agricultural/ non-agricultural linkages. Finally, concerns about changes in parameter values when substantial policy shocks occur are relevant but cannot easily be addressed. These are but some of the factors which have a bearing on the results.

Figure 5. 1. **PRODUCTION POSSIBILITY FRONTIER**

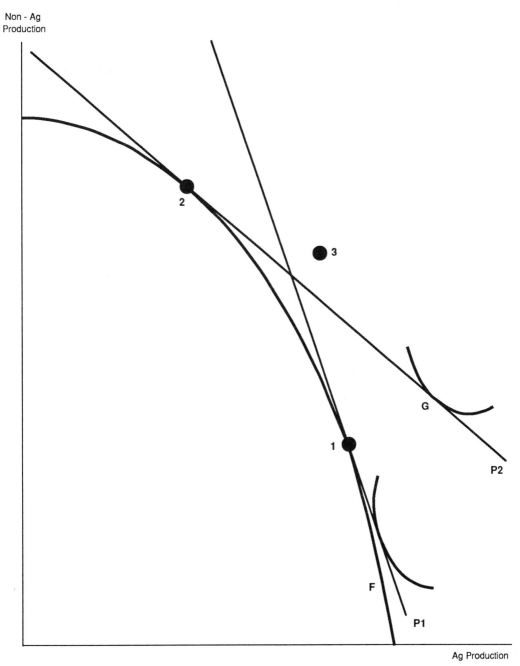

Non - Ag
Production

Ag Production

Developing Market Economy, Agricultural Importer

169

Table 5.1

WORLD PRICE PERCENTAGE CHANGES FROM 1986 BASE

	Alternative scenarios*			
	IME1	IMEY2	IMEY3	IMEYX4
Beef and veal	16	16	17	7
Pork	12	12	14	8
Mutton and lamb	25	26	30	21
Poultry -- meat	16	16	18	11
Poultry -- eggs	6	6	8	-1
Dairy -- fresh milk	0	0	0	0
Dairy -- butter	84	85	91	79
Dairy -- cheese	37	38	40	31
Dairy -- milk powder	81	81	82	74
Wheat	27	29	34	23
Corn	22	23	26	19
Other coarse grains	16	17	20	8
Rice	11	14	22	-5
Soybeans	-2	-1	1	-11
Soymeal	-3	-3	-1	-10
Soyoil	4	7	17	-6
Other oilseeds	8	13	24	3
Other meals	0	3	9	-5
Other oils	7	12	27	1
Cotton	8	14	23	4
Sugar	29	32	39	15
Tobacco	3	6	12	-1
Average	16	18	21	10

Notes : *Scenario assumptions

	IME DME Liberalization		Income term	Income multiplier	Exchange rate realignment
IME1	Yes	No	No	No	No
IMEY2	Yes	No	Yes	Yes(1)	No
IMEY3	Yes	No	Yes	Yes(3)	No
IMEYX4	Yes	No	Yes	Yes(1)	Yes

Table 5.2

SUPPLY QUANTITY PERCENTAGE CHANGES FROM 1986 BASE

	Alternative scenarios[*]			
	IME1	IMEY2	IMEY3	IMEYX4
Mexico	4.4	4.7	5.6	10.9
Central America and Caribbean	4.6	5.1	6.3	2.3
Brazil	3.2	3.5	4.3	11.8
Argentina	5.4	6.0	7.5	17.1
Chile	3.2	3.7	4.7	5.7
Venezuela	3.9	4.1	4.6	28.8
Other Latin America	4.2	4.7	6.0	1.9
Latin America average	4.1	4.5	5.5	11.7
Nigeria	3.6	4.2	5.7	48.4
Kenya	6.9	7.3	8.2	5.8
Other Sub-Saharan Africa	2.5	3.2	4.8	1.1
Egypt	2.4	2.7	3.5	18.0
Middle East & North Africa (oil)	4.3	4.6	5.5	3.2
Middle East & North Africa (other)	3.1	3.5	4.5	2.2
African/Middle East average	3.1	3.6	4.7	7.9
India	3.2	4.1	6.8	3.6
Pakistan	6.0	8.4	11.8	2.9
Bangladesh	5.3	6.6	10.5	58.7
Indonesia	2.5	3.2	5.1	1.8
Thailand	4.1	4.8	6.6	0.8
Malaysia	1.1	1.6	2.7	-0.2
Philippines	2.2	2.6	3.7	0.6
South Korea	1.5	1.7	2.4	-1.8
Taiwan	1.9	2.1	2.6	0.6
Other East Asia	3.1	3.3	3.6	2.0
Other Asia	2.4	3.1	4.9	-0.6
Asian average	3.0	3.8	5.9	3.7
Rest of world	0.3	0.5	1.1	-0.4
Developing country average	3.3	4.0	5.6	7.2

Notes :

[*]Scenario assumptions

	IME Liberalization	DME	Income term	Income multiplier	Exchange rate realignment
IME1	Yes	No	No	No	No
IMEY2	Yes	No	Yes	Yes(1)	No
IMEY3	Yes	No	Yes	Yes(3)	No
IMEYX4	Yes	No	Yes	Yes(1)	Yes

Table 5.3

DEMAND QUANTITY PERCENTAGE CHANGES FROM 1986 BASE

	Alternative scenarios[*]			
	IME1	IMEY2	IMEY3	IMEYX4
Mexico	-3.2	-2.9	-2.2	-6.3
Central America & Caribbean	-2.3	-2.2	-1.6	-0.4
Brazil	-2.2	-2.0	-1.4	-7.6
Argentina	-3.2	-2.6	-1.0	-8.1
Chile	-2.5	-2.6	-2.9	-4.3
Venezuela	-1.7	-1.5	-1.1	-12.6
Other Latin America	-2.9	-2.1	-0.1	-1.1
Latin America average	-2.7	-2.3	-1.4	-6.3
Nigeria	-2.3	-2.4	-2.5	-21.0
Kenya	-3.9	-3.6	-2.8	-2.4
Other Sub-Saharan Africa	-2.0	-1.3	1.5	-0.8
Egypt	-2.5	-1.8	0.4	-13.5
Middle East & North Africa (oil)	-2.9	-3.0	-3.1	-2.1
Middle East & North Africa (other)	-1.2	-0.7	0.6	-0.4
African/Middle East average	-2.2	-1.9	-0.6	-4.7
India	-3.1	-0.4	7.6	-1.5
Pakistan	-2.6	0.1	8.3	-0.1
Bangladesh	-3.2	-0.9	8.5	-18.8
Indonesia	-1.9	-1.4	1.5	-1.6
Thailand	-1.3	-0.8	1.5	-0.3
Malaysia	-1.7	-2.0	-1.6	-0.1
Philippines	-1.9	-1.2	1.5	-0.4
South Korea	-1.3	-1.2	-1.6	0.4
Taiwan	-1.6	-1.7	-2.3	-0.6
Other East Asia	-2.5	-2.9	-3.8	-1.4
Other Asia	-1.4	-0.7	2.6	0.5
Asian average	-2.4	-0.8	4.4	-1.3
Rest of world	-9.4	-9.8	-10.5	-7.0
Developing country average	-2.6	-1.6	1.6	-3.5

Notes :

[*]Scenario assumptions

	IME Liberalization	DME Liberalization	Income term	Income multiplier	Exchange rate realignment
IME1	Yes	No	No	No	No
IMEY2	Yes	No	Yes	Yes(1)	No
IMEY3	Yes	No	Yes	Yes(3)	No
IMEYX4	Yes	No	Yes	Yes(1)	Yes

Table 5.4

AGRICULTURAL BALANCE OF TRADE CHANGES FROM 1986 BASE
(Million $)

	Base	Changes from base			
		Alternative scenarios[*]			
		IME1	IMEY2	IMEY3	IMEYX4
Mexico	-1 221	1 110	1 132	1 157	2 718
Central America & Caribbean	637	550	594	693	251
Brazil	2 600	1 580	1 694	1 904	5 302
Argentina	3 627	2 334	2 439	2 681	5 415
Chile	-82	45	51	61	89
Venezuela	-416	207	200	182	1 582
Other Latin America	146	625	616	567	220
Latin American total	5 291	6 451	6 726	7 245	15 577
Nigeria	-431	87	90	90	1 344
Kenya	-85	47	43	32	39
Other Sub-Saharan Africa	542	399	442	399	185
Egypt	-1 981	-44	-100	-277	1 772
Middle East & North Africa (oil)	-6 422	-1 144	-1 214	-1 407	-896
Middle East & North Africa (other)	-992	301	282	189	191
African/Middle East total	-9 369	-354	-457	-974	2 635
India	-184	3 696	2 907	93	3 209
Pakistan	521	608	603	386	208
Bangladesh	-370	295	241	-59	2 695
Indonesia	-57	390	421	386	300
Thailand	1 193	458	502	612	102
Malaysia	2 240	151	301	718	-27
Philippines	549	254	283	322	67
South Korea	-1 626	-94	-129	-169	-290
Taiwan	-1 177	68	50	34	27
Other East Asia	-1 966	-145	-175	-234	-65
Other Asia	-282	314	310	161	-94
Asian total	-1 159	5 995	5 314	2 250	6 132
Rest of world	-4 864	-502	-513	-538	-349
Developing country total	-10 101	11 591	11 070	7 983	23 995

Notes :   [*]Scenario assumptions

	IME	DME	Income	Income	Exchange rate
	Liberalization		term	multiplier	realignment
IME1	Yes	No	No	No	No
IMEY2	Yes	No	Yes	Yes(1)	No
IMEY3	Yes	No	Yes	Yes(3)	No
IMEYX4	Yes	No	Yes	Yes(1)	Yes

173

Table 5.5

GROSS DOMESTIC PRODUCT CHANGES FROM 1986 BASE

	Base GDP (Million $)	Alternative scenarios*			
		IME1	IMEY2	IMEY3	IMEYX4
			(Percentage change)		
Mexico	186 635	1.3	1.4	5.0	1.6
Central America & Caribbean	80 212	1.1	1.3	4.9	0.6
Brazil	270 026	1.3	1.3	5.0	1.4
Argentina	78 798	4.0	3.2	11.9	4.5
Chile	16 882	1.4	0.8	2.8	0.7
Venezuela	48 003	1.1	1.2	4.0	2.4
Other Latin America	78 329	1.8	2.0	7.4	0.9
Latin American total	758 885	1.6	1.6	5.8	1.7
Nigeria	73 683	0.4	0.5	2.2	1.5
Kenya	6 921	1.6	1.8	6.1	1.3
Other Sub-Saharan Africa	108 011	1.1	1.4	6.4	0.5
Egypt	56 453	1.4	1.7	6.3	2.7
Middle East & North Africa (oil)	542 158	0.2	0.3	1.0	0.2
Middle East & North Africa (other)	117 146	1.4	1.6	6.1	0.9
African/Middle East total	904 372	0.6	0.7	2.8	0.6
India	219 063	3.5	5.1	20.8	2.7
Pakistan	32 409	3.5	4.5	18.7	1.9
Bangladesh	15 839	3.8	4.9	24.1	11.8
Indonesia	71 916	1.6	2.2	11.2	0.1
Thailand	40 146	1.6	2.1	9.3	0.1
Malaysia	25 778	1.0	1.1	6.8	-0.1
Philippines	29 945	2.2	2.2	9.7	0.5
South Korea	95 108	0.4	0.7	0.9	-0.1
Taiwan	73 270	0.7	0.7	0.9	0.2
Other East Asia	54 795	0.1	0.1	0.1	0.1
Other Asia	72 850	1.6	2.1	10.2	-0.2
Asian total	731 119	1.9	2.7	11.1	1.2
Developing country total	2 394 376	1.3	1.6	6.3	1.1

Notes :   *Scenario assumptions

	IME DME Liberalization		Income term	Income multiplier	Exchange rate realignment
IME1	Yes	No	No	No	No
IMEY2	Yes	No	Yes	Yes(1)	No
IMEY3	Yes	No	Yes	Yes(3)	No
IMEYX4	Yes	No	Yes	Yes(1)	Yes

174

Table 5.A1

PRODUCT GROUP AND COUNTRY CODING

CODE	PRODUCT GROUP	CODE	PRODUCT GROUP
BF	BeeF and veal	CG	other Coarse Grains
PK	PorK	RI	RIce
ML	Mutton and Lamb	SB	SoyBeans
PM	Poultry -- Meat	SM	SoyMeal
PE	Poultry -- Eggs	SO	SoyOil
DM	Dairy -- fresh Milk	OS	Other oilSeeds
DB	Dairy -- Butter	OM	Other Meals
DC	Dairy -- Cheese	OO	Other Oils
DP	Dairy -- milk Powder	CT	CoTton
WH	WHeat	SU	SUgar
CN	CorN	TB	ToBacco

	COUNTRY/REGION		COUNTRY/REGION
	Developed Countries		Sub-Saharan Africa & Middle East
US	United States	NG	NiGeria
CN	CaNada	KY	KenYa
EC	European Community	AF	Other sub-saharan AFrica
WE	other Western Europe	EG	EGypt
JP	JaPan	MP	Middle East/N. Africa -- oil
AU	AUstralia	MO	Middle East/N. Africa -- other
NZ	New Zealand		
SF	South AFrica		
	Centrally Planned		Asia
EE	Eastern Europe	ND	INDia
SV	Soviet Union	PK	PaKistan
CH	CHina (Peoples'	BG	BanGladesh
	Republic)	DO	InDOnesdia
		TH	THailand
	Latin America	ML	MaLaysia
		PH	PHilippines
MX	MeXico	SK	South Korea
CA	Central America/	TW	TaiWan
	Caribbean	EA	other East Asia
BZ	BraZil	OA	Other Asia
AR	ARgentina		
CL	ChiLe		
VE	VEnezuela		
LA	other Latin America		
RW	Rest of World		

Table 5.A2

COUNTRY COMPOSITION OF REGIONAL AGGREGATES

Region	Country composition of regional aggregates
EC	Denmark, France, Federal Germany, Greece, Ireland, Italy, Belgium/Luxembourg, Netherlands, United Kingdom, Spain, Portugal
WE	Austria, Finland, Iceland, Malta, Norway, Sweden, Switzerland
EE	Albania, Bulgaria, Czechoslavakia, German Democratic Republic, Poland, Hungary, Romania, Yugoslavia
MP	Syria, Iraq, Iran, Kuwait, Qatar, Saudi Arabia, United Arab Emirates, Oman, Bahrain, Algeria, Tunisia, Libya
MO	Turkey, Cyprus, Lebanon, Israel, Gaza, West Bank, Jordan, North Yemen, South Yemen, Morocco
LA	Bolivia, Colombia, Ecuador, Paraguay, Peru, Uruguay
CA	Belize, Costa Rica, El Salvador, Honduras, Guatamala, Nicaragua, Panama, Bahamas, Bermuda, Cuba, Dominican Republic, Haiti, Jamaica, Trinidad and Tobago, Barbados, Bonaire, Curaçāo, French West Indies, Guadeloupe, Martinique, Turcs and Caicos, Cayman Islands, Aruba, British West Indies, Leeward-Windward Islands, St. Kitts, Netherlands Antilles, Antigua, Nevis, Montserrat, British Virgin Islands, Grenada, St. Vincent, St. Lucia, Dominica, Guyana, French Guiana, Suriname
AF	Angola, Benin, Botswana, Burkina Faso, Burundi, Cameroon, Cape Verde, Central African Republic, Chad, Comoros Republic, Congo, Djibouti, Equatorial Guinea, Ethiopia, Gabon, Gambia, Ghana, Guinea, Guinea-Bissau, Ivory Coast, Lesotho, Liberia, Madagascar, Malawi, Mali, Mauritania, Mauritius, Mozambique, Namibia, Niger, Réunion, Rwanda, Sao Tomé/Principe, Seychelles, Sierra Leone, Somalia, Senegal, Sudan, Swaziland, Tanzania, Togo, Uganda, Zaïre, Zambia, Zimbabwe
EA	Hong Kong, Singapore
OA	Afghanistan, Bhutan, Brunei, Burma, Cambodia, Fiji, Laos, Mongolia, Nepal, North Korea, Sri Lanka, Viet Nam

Table 5.A3

SELECTED DEVELOPING COUNTRY CHARACTERISTICS

Domestic Share of Commodity Consumption in Base Period

Beef	23	Other coarse grain	25
Pork	8	Rice	57
Mutton and lamb	31	Soybeans	32
Poultry meat	24	Soymeal	20
Poultry eggs	21	Soyoil	36
Dairy milk	17	Other oilseeds	41
Dairy butter	19	Other meals	29
Dairy cheese	15	Other oils	49
Dairy powder	21	Cotton	42
Wheat	32	Sugar	48
Corn	26	Tobacco	29

	Percentage of GDP accounted for in model	Exchange rate adjustment factor
Latin America		
Mexico	6	1.25
Brazil	7	1.5
Argentina	13	1.4
Venezuela	6	2.4
Chile	3	1.2
Africa and Middle East		
Egypt	7	2.5
Nigeria	2	3.7
Kenya	5	1.0
Asia		
India	21	1.1
Pakistan	13	1.0
Bangladesh	22	2.7
Indonesia	13	1.1
Thailand	11	1.0
Malaysia	8	1.0
Philippines	14	1.0
South Korea	4	0.9
Taiwan	5	1.0

Sources: World Development Report, 1988; World Currency Yearbook, 1986.

NOTES AND REFERENCES

1. A debt of thanks is owed to Vern Roningen, who provided the framework on which this analysis is based. The research assistance of Liana Neff is also gratefully acknowledged. Reviews by Steve Magiera, Jerry Sharples, Praveen Dixit, Steve Haley, and Mary Bohman were also appreciated. Views expressed are those of the authors and not necessarily those of USDA.

2. The supply and demand equations are specified in constant elasticity form in the SWOPSIM framework. Other conditions and restrictions regarding the supply and demand functions can be found in Roningen, and Dixit and Roningen. The data set is published in Sullivan, Wainio, and Roningen.

3. Roningen and Dixit assume a price transmission of 0.5 for the developing countries, while we assume a price transmission of one. With complete transmission of world price increases, there is a larger supply response from the developing countries, and thus the world price increases needed to clear world markets of the excess demand in the IMEs as a result of liberalization are less in our model (16 per cent) than in the Roningen and Dixit model (22 per cent).

4. Keep in mind that these changes are simulated to take place over a period of more than one year. The elasticities in this model are medium-term ones, reflecting a time of adjustment of five to seven years.

BIBLIOGRAPHY

BALASSA, B., "Agricultural Policies and International Resource Allocation", *Journal of Policy Modeling*, 10 (2), Summer 1988.

COWITT, P., *World Currency Yearbook, 1986*, New York: International Currency Analysis, Inc., 1987.

KRUEGER, A., "Some Preliminary Findings from the World Bank's Project on the Political Economy of Agricultural Pricing", paper presented at the XX International Conference of Agricultural Economists, Buenos Aires, Argentina, 24-31 August 1988.

MELLOR, J., "Agricultural Development in the Third World: The Food, Development, Foreign Assistance, Trade Nexus", paper prepared for the 1988 World Food Conference, European Parliament, Brussels, Belgium, April 6-8 1988.

ORGANISATION FOR ECONOMIC CO-OPERATION AND DEVELOPMENT (OECD), *National Policies and Agricultural Trade*, Paris, 1987.

PARIKH, K.S., G. FISCHER, K. FROHBERG, and O. GULBRANDSEN, *Towards Free Trade in Agriculture*, Laxenburg, Austria: Martinus Nijhoff Publishers, 1988.

RONINGEN, V.O., "A Static World Policy Simulation (SWOPSIM) Modelling Framework", Staff Report AGES860625, Economic Research Service, US Department of Agriculture, Washington, DC, July 1986.

RONINGEN, V.O., and P. DIXIT, "Economic Implications of Agricultural Policy Reform in Industrial Market Economies", Staff Report AGES89-36, Economic Research Service, US Department of Agriculture, Washington, DC, August 1989.

SULLIVAN, J., J. WAINIO, and V. RONINGEN, "A Database for Trade Liberalization Studies", Staff Report AGES89-12, Economic Research Service, US Department of Agriculture, Washington, DC, March 1989.

TYERS, R. and K. ANDERSON, "Distortions in World Food Markets: A Quantitative Assessment", background paper for the World Bank's *World Development Report*, Washington, DC., July 1986.

VALDÉS, A., "Agriculture in the Uruguay Round: Interests of Developing Countries", *World Bank Economic Review*, 1(4), 1987.

US DEPARTMENT OF AGRICULTURE, *Estimates of Producer and Consumer Subsidy Equivalents: Government Intervention In Agriculture*, Staff Report No. AGES880127, Economic Research Service, US Department of Agriculture, Washington, DC, April 1988a.

US DEPARTMENT OF AGRICULTURE, *Global Review of Agricultural Policies*, Staff Report No. AGES880304, Economic Research Service, US Department of Agriculture, Washington, DC, May 1988b.

WORLD BANK, *World Development Report*, 1986.

Chapter 6

TROPICAL BEVERAGES IN THE GATT[1]

by

Carl Mabbs-Zeno and Barry Krissoff

INTRODUCTION

The Uruguay Round of the General Agreement on Tariffs and Trade (GATT) is apparently taking a view of agricultural policy reform similar to the one international lending agencies have taken in recent years by seeking reduced government intervention. Agricultural liberalization has lagged behind liberalization in other sectors within the GATT. In the mid-term review of the Uruguay Round, most participants agreed to reduce tariffs on tropical products and to liberalize tropical product markets in a parallel fashion to the eventual agreement on other agricultural products.

The analysis to date of agricultural reform proposals at the GATT has seldom focussed on tropical product markets. Where tropical products have been considered, the analysis usually views only the primary product level. The developing countries, however, are often dependent on tropical products whose markets are likely to respond to liberalization differently from those of most temperate commodities. Furthermore, the developing countries also have special interest in the effects of policy reform on the amount of processing that occurs within their borders. More processing of commodities before export serves employment and industrialisation goals.

This paper focuses on liberalization in tropical product markets and on the incentives in the producing countries for processing some of the most traded tropical products. It examines how government policies affected the global distribution of tropical beverage production, processing, and trade. More specifically, it presents quantitative estimates of how markets in cocoa, coffee and tea would have appeared after medium-term adjustments if government policies affecting trade were removed and 1986 conditions otherwise prevailed.

Tropical products constitute an important portion of world agricultural trade. Even if those that compete fairly well with temperate products are excluded from the classification (such as rice, cane sugar, and oilseeds), they still accounted for 28 per cent of world food and fibre exports in 1986. Nearly all exports of these commodities originate in developing countries (Figure 6.1).

Tropical beverages, including coffee, tea and cocoa[2], accounted for about 70 per cent of world trade among food and fibre commodities that compete little with temperate agriculture (Figure 6.2). In 1986, the value of coffee trade alone amounted to $16 billion, exceeding even the $14 billion wheat trade, although coffee trade ranks just below wheat in most years. In 38 of the 53 countries whose tropical products export value comprised 10 per cent or more of their merchandise export value, coffee, tea or cocoa was their leading export in 1986.

Processing Chain

Each of the three tropical beverages has a distinctive processing chain that includes stages which can be accomplished without sophisticated industrial infrastructure. Each commodity offers potential for adding more value to its traded form than is typically coming from producer countries today.

Cocoa is only grown in the tropics at elevations below 1 000 feet. A tree requires up to five years before it produces commercially, and it may produce for 50 years, achieving peak yields at ages 10-15 years. Beans are dried immediately after harvest, and may be stored for a year in tropical climates or up to three years in a cooler climate. Regardless of their final use, all beans are roasted and shelled, leaving a waste product used as fertilizer, mulch or fuel, weighing about 20 per cent of the original dry weight. The next step is grinding into liquor, sometimes called paste, which is packaged into solid blocks. The liquor may be used directly in chocolate or it may receive further intermediate processing into a fatty component, called butter, and a dry cake, each component constituting about half the weight of the liquor from which it was made. The butter is used in various industries, but most of it goes into chocolate. The cake is further processed into the powder used in cocoa beverages. Blending of chocolate for final consumption is highly differentiated among manufacturers, but the technology necessary to produce marketable, standardized versions of liquor, butter, and powder has long been accessible to cocoa-producing nations (Riedl, 1978).

Coffee is generally grown on sloped land in the tropics, often in drier areas than would support cocoa. A coffee tree requires three years before bearing commercially, and it follows a biennial cycle of high- and low-yielding years over a 50-year lifetime. Several varieties are grown, each with distinctive requirements and flavours. The cherry, consisting of about 70 per cent water, may be immediately depulped to yield "washed" parchment coffee or it may be sun-dried and then depulped to yield a lower quality "dry" parchment. A fermentation process removes the remaining mucilage before grading and sun-drying the parchment to reduce moisture content from over 50 per cent to about 12 per cent, requiring over a week. This parchment is hulled to remove the silver skin and cured to produce green coffee. The green coffee may be blended before roasting and grinding, resulting in a further 15 per cent loss in weight and a 3 per cent moisture content. Blending is especially important prior to roasting for certain varieties of coffee and this requirement inhibits roasting in countries that specialise in those varieties. Some coffee is further processed into a soluble or "instant" form weighing 33 per cent of its green bean equivalent. Soluble coffee, however, yields about twice as much brew as roast coffee from an equal green bean equivalent. About 10 per cent of coffee is decaffeinated, mainly from cheaper beans, providing a caffeine by-product used in cola beverages and medicines.

Tea requires high rainfall to be productive but it can tolerate periods of drought. It produces leaves commercially three to four years after planting and reaches maturity at nine or ten years, beginning a long period of fairly constant productivity, perhaps 40 years or more. Maintenance and harvesting of tea plants is particularly labour intensive. In processing, the tea is first partially dried or "withered" before crushing the leaves to begin fermentation. Eventually the tea is "fired" to stop fermentation and dried to a 3 per cent moisture content. Storage in humid climates is limited to a few years because tea is hygroscopic, absorbing moisture from the air. Tea is often blended and packaged without further processing, but some is bagged and a small quantity is processed into a soluble form.

Production and Trade

Brazil and Côte d'Ivoire are the largest cocoa producers, together providing about half of world production. The seven largest producers provided about 85 per cent of the world total in

1986 when the 2 million tonnes of bea.. production were valued at about $4.3 billion (Table 6.2). Most of the trade from the cocoa producing nations was in the form of beans rather than partially processed products. About 75 per cent of the beans received minimal processing before export, 10 per cent was exported as liquor, and 15 per cent was exported as butter or powder. Brazil, Ecuador, and Côte d'Ivoire together account for over 90 per cent of liquor exports. Over half of the beans and a third of the liquor went to the European Community (EC). Just under half of the world's liquor trade was imported by the United States.

Processed forms of cocoa, like any commodity, must be more valuable per unit of weight than less processed forms. The international price of liquor in 1986 was about 1.23 times the price of beans, accounting for a loss of 20 per cent in weight, the value of by-products, and the cost of processing. The value of cake and butter from a quantity of liquor was 1.05 times the value of the liquor at 1986 prices, but 80 per cent of the value was in the butter, even though it constitutes only 47 per cent of the weight. Liquor prices are about twice powder prices, one half butter prices. These price ratios resulted in value distributed among cocoa producer exports of 75 per cent in beans, 7 per cent in liquor, and 18 per cent in butter or powder.

Brazil and Colombia are the largest coffee producers, together providing about 40 per cent of world output. Brazilian production in 1986 was well below the normal range of variation, so the coffee analysis in this paper is based on average data for 1984-86. During that period, the output of the 14 largest producers was about 80 per cent of the world total of 5.3 million tonnes (Table 6.3). Nearly 95 per cent was exported in green bean form and less than 0.5 per cent as roast coffee. Mexico was the only major producer exporting roasted coffee with nearly 6 per cent of its trade in roast form. The EC also had significant roast exports, but they totalled less than Mexico's. Brazil is the largest exporter of soluble coffee, with 12 per cent of its exports as soluble. Imports of the EC and the United States together account for 75 per cent of world coffee trade.

The price of roasted coffee in international markets was about 3.5 per cent greater than the price of the green beans from which it was made. Soluble coffee was priced 40 per cent higher than its green bean equivalent. Since soluble coffee makes twice as much brew as its green bean equivalent, the price ratio apparently reflects a considerable premium for quality in brew made directly from roast.

Sri Lanka and India are the largest tea exporters, together producing 46 per cent of world trade. The eight countries included in this study account for 93 per cent of world exports of black tea (Table 6.4). China is the second largest producer behind India and, like India, it consumes most of its production[3]. Nearly 20 per cent of world tea imports for consumption went to Britain in addition to substantial imports destined for re-export. Another 40 per cent of imports goes to Poland, the United States and the countries situated in the region from Egypt to Pakistan.

Government Policies

The governments of most cocoa producing countries actively affected producer prices within their respective countries in 1986. The ratios of producer prices to international prices, evaluated at official exchange rates and adjusted for location and quality, ranged from 0.24 in Malaysia to just over 1.0 in Nigeria. When overvalued exchange rates are considered in the analysis, however, the Nigerian ratio falls to 0.3 and the major producing countries range from 0.2 in Ghana to 0.5 in Brazil. Apparently cocoa farmers in all countries were receiving half or less of the international price. Relatively small subsidies are given to producers in some countries in the form of low cost inputs, like pesticide in Nigeria and credit in Colombia, but the reduced farmgate price on output probably represents most of the effects of government agricultural policy.

The differences *among countries* in their agricultural policies are unlikely to explain much of the differences in their production levels. Cocoa production generally competes for resources within national borders, so the differences in government intervention among commodities *within a country* contribute to how resources are allocated among commodities. A farmer seldom faces an opportunity to grow cocoa in another country even though that country may have more favourable policies. In cases like West Africa, where Ghana's farmers receive one fifth and Nigerian farmers receive one third the international price, there is an incentive for smuggling into Côte d'Ivoire where producers receive one half the world price.

The importing countries generally offer reduced tariffs to developing countries on cocoa imports under their Generalized System of Preferences (GSP) as authorised by the GATT. Since all cocoa producing countries are qualified for GSP, the apparent attempt to offer preferences had little effect. Perhaps these provisions blocked re-exports through developed countries. Almost no importers placed tariffs on beans from developing countries. The EC, Japan, New Zealand, and Finland placed moderate tariffs on liquor. Nearly all importers placed larger tariffs on cake or powder imports, and several also placed tariffs on butter. The overall pattern of tariffs shows moderately higher levels for more processed forms of cocoa, a tendency called tariff escalation.

Several European countries, including some EC members, also have internal taxes on cocoa and cocoa products. These ranged from 6-21 per cent among the ten countries cited by the International Cocoa Organization (ICCO). All countries with such taxes applied them to beans as well as the partly processed forms of cocoa. Only Spain had lower internal taxes for beans than for the processed forms while Germany, Italy, and the Netherlands had lower internal taxes on powder than on other forms.

Since 1972 the ICCO has attempted to influence cocoa trade. It has relied principally on a buffer stock arrangement to stabilize international prices but has actually exerted little control over the market. Since 1981 it has not been supported by either the United States or Côte d'Ivoire, greatly weakening its potential to intervene.

The governments of most coffee exporting nations, as with cocoa exporters, usually intervened in trade to extract revenue by holding producer prices well below international levels. Two exceptions were Ecuador and Guatemala where producer prices were only 10 per cent less than international prices at their border, probably reflecting only the cost of marketing and internal transportation. Brazil and Kenya moderately taxed their producers with prices about 17 per cent below export value. Other major exporters offered their farmers prices 40-70 per cent below international prices at their borders. As with all exports, the international price would be higher if evaluated at equilibrium, rather than official, exchange rates in economies with an officially overvalued currency. Overvaluation acted as a tax on processed as well as primary products.

Most of the major tea producing nations also effectively taxed their tea exports. Currency overvaluation was especially important in China, Malawi, and Bangladesh while being fairly important in India and Indonesia. Even at official exchange rates, China and Malawi paid particularly low prices to producers. When producer prices were adjusted to account for currency overvaluation in each exporting country, only Argentina supported tea producers, only Kenya paid farmers approximately the international price for their tea, and only Indian farmers effectively paid small taxes.

METHOD OF ANALYSIS

Separate models with similar frameworks are developed for cocoa, coffee, and tea. Each model contains policy variables that represent sectoral policies and foreign exchange policies in each major exporter and importer. The cocoa and tea models are based on 1986 prices, policies, production, and trade while the coffee model relies on a 1984-86 base. Two simulations were analysed for each commodity. First, all policies in the developed economies were removed. While this scenario exceeds the liberalization accepted at the mid-term review of the current GATT negotiations, complete removal of tariffs remains a long-term GATT objective. Second, all policies in the developing countries were removed, representing a long-term objective stressed by the International Monetary Fund, the World Bank, and by domestic pressures relating to balance of payments. Although the models are not linear, liberalization by all governments would yield results about equal to the sum of the two partial liberalizations.

Simplifying Assumptions

Like all economic models, the models used here depend upon simplification of reality in order to focus attention on salient features of the economies under study. The version adopted for analysis represents a balance between:

a) Including elements that significantly contribute to the outcome; and

b) Reducing the number of elements that complicate understanding the workings of the system.

Most of the simplifications accepted here extend to all three commodities under study although a few are specific to one market.

Many of the opportunity costs associated with changing production are not considered. In reality, each country faces a different set of likely alternative uses for resources initially or potentially occupied in production and processing of tropical beverages. Other crops might substitute freely for coffee in one country while another country has only poor substitutes. Similarly, capital and labour compete with non-agricultural industry better in countries with relatively developed infrastructure than in the poorest countries. Another opportunity cost shared in production of these commodities is the yield from existing trees when production is reduced. Considerable investment is required to bring trees to maturity, so producers are reluctant to destroy them without confidence of better long-term returns from an alternative enterprise. The model results presented here are intended to represent a medium-term outcome of policy reform, so the supply response is not fully constrained by the supply inelasticity associated with tree crops.

The nature of the processing subsector is simplified in several ways. Since the models use net trade for each country, there is no explicit allowance for re-exporting. Re-exports of tropical beverages occur widely within the EC, but, by treating the EC as a unit, the model greatly reduces global re-exports. Processors based in importing countries probably play an important role in production through their control of trade institutions and market power. With the focus here on government reforms, the role of multinationals is considered too distracting for inclusion in the models. The value of by-products, such as caffeine from coffee and fertilizer from cocoa, is ignored because it is too small to affect the results significantly.

Among the simplifications peculiar to a particular commodity model, the most conspicuous is probably failure to specify processed forms of tea. Blended, bagged, and soluble tea are traded, but their shares in world tea trade are even smaller than those of processed forms of cocoa and coffee, and processed tea is especially poorly documented in international databases. The coffee market in reality is separable into submarkets of various grades which are generally poor substitutes in both production and consumption. Price differences between countries due to the quality of coffee they produce or to their distance from importers are captured through adjustments in the estimates of policy intervention rather than through the structure of the models. Since grades are often blended before roasting, and since various qualities tend to come from different countries, there is an incentive, not expressed in the models, for a consuming nation to do its own roasting.

185

Another major simplification is that the coffee model does not specifically recognise the International Coffee Agreement of the International Coffee Organisation (ICO). The Agreement established quotas during the base period for this analysis (1984-86). The present study focuses on national policy rather than international institutions, but the Agreement's effect is modelled elsewhere (Akiyama and Varangis, 1989). That research found the main effect of the Agreement before 1986 was a buildup of stocks although other effects may have been significant more recently.

Model Structure

The models developed for this analysis are based on the Static World Policy Simulation (SWOPSIM) framework (Roningen, 1986). It is a simple framework that assumes that the structure of global agricultural markets is competitive. For each country or region (i), and primary commodity (j) or processed product (k) in the model, demand (D) and supply (S) functions are specified:

$$D_{ij} = D_{ij}\,(CP_{ij}, PP_{ik}) \tag{1}$$

$$S_{ij} = S_{ij}\,(PP_{ij}) \tag{2}$$

$$D_{ik} = D_{ik}\,(CP_{ik}) \tag{3}$$

$$S_{ik} = S_{ik}\,(PP_{ik}, CP_{ij}) \tag{4}$$

where $CP_{ij,k}$ and $PP_{ij,k}$ are the incentive prices facing consumers and producers respectively[4]. An increase in the price of commodity k raises the quantity supplied of commodity k and the derived demand for commodity j. Similarly, a decrease in the price of commodity j increases the quantity demanded of commodity j and the output supply of commodity k. Net trade (T) is the difference between domestic supply and total demand for any j (or k):

$$T_{ij} = S_{ij} - D_{ij}\,. \tag{5}$$

Domestic incentive prices depend on the level of consumer and producer support wedges (CSW_{ij} and PSW_{ij}) and world prices denominated in local currency:

$$CP_{ij} = CSW_{ij} + E_i * WP_{ij} \tag{6}$$

$$PP_{ij} = PSW_{ij} + E_i * WP_{ij} \tag{7}$$

where E_i is the exchange rate defined as local currency per dollar and WP_{ij} is a world reference price in dollars.

World markets clear when net trade of a commodity across all countries is equal to 0. For commodity j, this occurs when

$$\sum_{i=1}^{n} T_{ij} = \sum_{i=1}^{n} S_{ij} - \sum_{i=1}^{n} D_{ij} = 0\,. \tag{8}$$

The models consider technical and economic relationships between the primary and processed products by imposing restrictions on the parameters in equations (1) through (4). In the cocoa model, four primary and processed products are modelled: beans, liquor, butter, and cake. Beans are an input into liquor, butter, and cake, with the latter two products subject to a physical, joint-product constraint. The demand for beans and the supply of the products are functions of consumer incentive prices for beans and the producer incentive prices for liquor, cake, and butter. Symmetry and homogeneity conditions are imposed on these derived demand

and supply equations which reduce the number of independent parameter estimates. Higher product prices raise the quantity produced of liquor, cake, and butter as well as the quantity demanded of beans. In the actual technical process, cake and butter are produced from liquor and not directly from the bean as we have modelled. Although liquor is modelled for "final supply," liquor can be demanded for "final use" or as an input producing butter and cake. The model allows for this relationship by expressing demand for liquor and supply of cake and butter as functions of the prices of the three products. Higher cake and butter prices raise production of these products and the quantity demanded of liquor[5].

In the coffee model, green, roasted, and soluble are specified in green bean equivalents. Green beans are modelled as an input into roasted coffee, specified by a derived demand equation for green beans and a supply equation for roasted coffee as functions of both the consumer incentive price for green beans and producer incentive price for roasted coffee. Again, symmetry and homogeneity conditions are imposed. Roasted coffee is modelled as an input into soluble coffee, and as a final product for consumption (and therefore homogeneity conditions are not imposed)[6].

Data were drawn critically from a variety of sources including principally the Food and Agriculture Organization of the United Nations, the Foreign Agricultural Service of the US Department of Agriculture, and the respective international organisations for each commodity[7]. All sources were examined for each datum and the most credible were used. Detailed investigations of each exporting nation's policies were required to quantify their effects during the base period[8]. Elasticities were based loosely on Adams and Behrman (1976, 1984) for cocoa and coffee, and on Akiyama and Trivedi (1987) for tea.

Hypotheses

The models present alternative, static equilibria in tropical beverage markets. The model structures require certain apparent outcomes from the simulations. In fact, the models were structured intentionally to retain certain relationships among production, consumption and trade variables. These relationships thus constitute hypotheses about how the commodity markets would function. Economic theory guided the formation of the hypotheses, the hypotheses guided the structure of the models, and the data entered in the models led to the "results," that is, the quantitative estimates of the effects built into the system.

Given that policies in nations producing tropical beverages typically tax their producers, the likely effect of removing those policies is opposite that of removing policies in temperate-product producing nations where subsidies are more common (see Dixit and Roningen, 1989; Krissoff, *et al.*, 1989). When taxes are removed, effective producer prices rise (equation 7), production rises (equation 2), and international prices fall.

Since the only policies representing importing countries in the models are tariffs, removal of their policies would lower consumer prices (equation 6), raise quantity demanded (equations 1 and 3), raise international prices, and raise the value of trade. The proportion processed before export from the primary product producer (i.e. the developing country) would rise because removing the higher tariffs on processed products would raise their demand and international prices more than those of primary products.

With government policies expressed as effects on producer prices, the country with the lowest initial producer price has the lowest marginal costs, and will gain most from multilateral liberalization. Countries with the lowest producer prices in the models are those with the heaviest taxes. Removal of all taxes would benefit the farmers in these countries most, generating the strongest increase in production and, hence, trade revenue.

The change in proportion of production that is processed in developing countries following developing country liberalization is determined by the policy structure. The models used here assumed that policies allowed processors to buy primary products at international prices, adjusted for exchange controls, if any. A typical producing nation is modelled with a marketing board that buys from producers at a controlled price but sells to the highest bidder, that is, sells at market price. Producer prices may have been held below international prices before liberalization but processors did not gain from this. Their costs are lower than producers' in developed nations only by transportation cost. Of course, their exported output is also reduced in value by its transportation cost. Removal of developing country policies lowers the relative price of the primary product, so processing becomes more profitable and more product is processed in developing countries.

RESULTS

All three tropical beverages had weak, escalating tariffs by importers and strong taxes on primary products by producing countries so the production and trade responses to policy liberalization are similar for each commodity. The simulations showing removal of policies in developed countries indicate an increase in revenue to producer nations. Liberalizing the policies of producer nations, in contrast, would result in a decline in value of trade of 26 per cent. Simultaneous liberalization of policies in all countries is approximately equal to the sum of these two simulations, that is, a 25 per cent reduction in trade value (Table 6.1). This loss in trade revenue for producers of tropical products resulting from global trade liberalization is about $4 billion. The trade revenue loss results from the export demand elasticities facing the major exporters as a group. These are –0.7, –0.3, and –0.6 for cocoa beans, green coffee, and tea, respectively. They imply that changes in trade revenue have the same sign as changes in international prices following global liberalization.

Despite the substantial net decline in revenue from these products, developing country revenue from processed products was approximately stable in the simulations. Removal of developed country policies raised trade revenue from partially processed forms of cocoa and coffee by 21 per cent to $2 billion. Removal of developing country policies reduced trade value by 18 per cent to $1.5 billion. Global liberalization would be expected to raise trade value in processed tropical beverages only slightly.

Eliminating developed country policies, which now favour trade in the form of beans, would raise incentives to process cocoa in developing countries. The price of beans would remain essentially constant with developed country liberalization while liquor prices would rise 6 per cent, cake prices by 24 per cent, and butter prices by 2 per cent. Value traded in beans would fall slightly overall, due mainly to a decline in Brazil's revenue from bean exports.

If developing countries liberalize their policies, the price of beans would fall 44 per cent, with the partially processed product prices falling 31-38 per cent. As with developed country liberalization, developing country liberalization yields relatively low value in bean trade and a higher proportion of beans processed in developing countries.

The redistribution of cocoa production and processing following liberalization is heavily influenced in the model simulations by the market share of producing countries in the base year. Brazil's trade revenue would rise the most with developed country liberalization in absolute ($30 million) and percentage (4.6 per cent) terms because it is best able to take advantage of improved prices in partially processed cocoa. Brazil's trade losses following developing country liberalization, however, would be 37 per cent, about average for producers, since revenue from processed forms of cocoa fare about as well as that from cocoa beans in this scenario.

Developed country liberalization of policies affecting coffee trade would raise the price of roasted and soluble coffee by about 4 per cent while leaving green bean prices nearly unchanged. Trade in roasted coffee would rise 15-fold but still be only 2 per cent of the value traded as green beans. India and Brazil would capture the largest improvements in trade revenue, both actually reducing green bean export value in order to increase processing.

Developing country liberalization would reduce the prices of green beans by 35 per cent and those of processed forms by lesser amounts, 19 per cent for roasted and 10 per cent for soluble coffee. With revenue from trade in roasted coffee rising sevenfold among developing countries, revenue from processed coffee would rise 10 per cent overall. This gain would be more than offset by a decline of 29 per cent in revenue from green bean trade coming mainly from the largest two producers, Brazil and Colombia. Gains in revenue would be experienced by relatively small trading countries whose initial producer taxes were large, such as Ecuador, Uganda, and Zaire. In these countries, the removal of producer taxes more than outweighed the international price decline while their increased quantity of production had relatively little effect on prices.

Liberalization of developed country policies affecting tea had little effect on either production or prices since there are few tariffs on tea. Removing developing country policies reduced the international price in the simulation model by 27 per cent and trade revenue by 12 per cent, the smallest decline of the studied commodities. China and Malawi would increase their trade revenues because they had the largest tax on their producers and their production increase would therefore be large relative to the price decline. India and Kenya would lose relatively large portions of their market share while Argentine trade would fall nearly 80 per cent.

CONCLUSIONS

Processing of tropical beverages is a potential source of growth in developing countries now exporting primary beverage commodities. Trade liberalization by developed countries or by developing countries would promote processing of coffee and cocoa in developing countries. The policies of developed countries are biased against imports of processed forms of cocoa and coffee, but removing those policies leads to relatively small changes in prices and traded quantities. Current policies in developing countries constrain processors by restricting quantities produced and raising the international price of unprocessed inputs. Policy liberalization, however, would lower trade revenue in both primary and processed products among exporters of these commodities due to large reductions in international prices. Furthermore, governments would no longer directly extract revenue from this trade.

The distribution of costs and benefits from trade liberalization among developing countries depends on the distribution of current policies. Liberalization by developed countries mainly improves the trade balance of developing countries already supplying processed forms of cocoa and coffee. Removal of developing country policies improves the trade balance of those removing the most oppressive policies. Since liberalization by all developing countries reduces prices enough that global trade revenue in tropical beverages falls, the countries that benefit from multilateral liberalization would benefit even more from unilateral liberalization.

Goals other than improving trade revenue clearly contribute to policy design, but trade revenue is receiving emphasis among debtor nations, many of which export tropical beverages. Government revenue losses with trade liberalization by developing countries will be a major concern to policymakers. In contrast to staple food crops, tropical beverages give small cause for concern about domestic consumer losses arising from increased local prices. The major attraction to developing country liberalization is the contribution to long-term development associated with increased processing before export. There is evidence in the simulations reported here that substantial trade revenue benefits in some countries now taxing production accompany global liberalization in cocoa, coffee, and tea. However, the predominant effects are losses incurred in government revenue and losses in trade revenue for the producing nations as a group. Each exporter of tropical beverages needs to evaluate the implications of various policy reforms for meeting its goals.

Table 6.1

**EFFECTS OF TRADE LIBERALIZATION ON EXPORT REVENUE
OF SUPPLIER NATIONS**

Commodity	Export revenue			Prices		
	Base levels	Non-LDC policies removed (Million $)	LDC policies removed	Base levels	Non-LDC policies removed ($ per	LDC policies removed tonne)
Cocoa						
Subtotal	3 784	3 872	2 636			
Bean	2 827	2 797	1 887	2 139	2 145	1 202
Liquor	289	308	216	2 636	2 783	1 826
Cake	116	158	87	1 075	1 332	666
Butter	552	609	446	4 672	4 763	3 197
Coffee						
Subtotal	10 795	11 083	7 981			
Green	10 112	10 166	7 215	2 850	2 869	1 857
Roast	15	222	132	2 950	3 082	2 378
Soluble	668	695	634	4 022	4 175	3 611
Tea	1 238	1 242	1 096	1 529	1 531	1 112
Total	15 817	16 197	11 713			
Primary[1]	12 939	12 963	9 102			
Processed[1]	1 640	1 992	1 515			

1. Excludes tea.

Table 6.2

EFFECTS OF TRADE LIBERALIZATION ON COCOA EXPORTS

Country/region	Net export volume			Net export value		
	1986 levels	Non-LDC policies removed	LDC policies removed	1986 levels	Non-LDC policies removed	LDC policies removed
		(1 000 tonnes)			(Million $)	
Côte d'Ivoire						
Bean	465	462	494	995	993	594
Liquor	24	24	24	63	67	44
Cake	35	37	38	38	49	26
Butter	25	26	28	117	125	88
Ghana						
Bean	198	198	318	424	425	382
Liquor	4	4	4	11	11	8
Cake	0	0	1	0	0	1
Butter	8	8	9	37	39	28
Brazil						
Bean	134	125	104	287	268	126
Liquor	51	52	53	134	144	96
Cake	39	45	47	42	60	31
Butter	44	48	52	206	227	167
Malaysia						
Bean	106	106	156	227	228	187
Liquor	1	1	1	3	3	2
Cake	8	8	8	9	11	6
Butter	11	11	11	51	53	36
Cameroon						
Bean	90	89	94	193	192	113
Liquor	4	4	4	11	11	7
Cake	8	8	9	9	11	6
Butter	4	4	5	10	21	15
Nigeria						
Bean	60	58	78	128	125	94
Liquor	1	1	3	3	3	5
Cake	5	6	9	5	8	6
Butter	10	11	13	47	51	41
Ecuador						
Bean	38	37	175	81	80	210
Liquor	31	32	36	82	88	66
Cake	2	2	3	2	3	2
Butter	2	2	3	9	10	10
Rest of world						
Bean	230	227	150	492	486	181
Liquor	-7	-7	-7	-18	-19	-12
Cake	10	12	13	11	16	9
Butter	16	17	19	75	83	61

Table 6.2 (continued)

Total						
Bean	1 321	1 302	1 569	2 827	2 797	1 887
Liquor	109	111	118	289	308	216
Cake	107	118	128	116	158	87
Butter	120	127	140	552	609	446

Table 6.3

EFFECTS OF TRADE LIBERALIZATION ON COFFEE EXPORTS

Country/region	Net export volume			Net export value		
	Base levels	Non-LDC policies removed (1 000 tonnes)	LDC policies removed	Base levels	Non-LDC policies removed (Million $)	LDC policies removed
Brazil						
Green	848	841	698	2 417	2 413	1 295
Roast	0	24	50	0	73	119
Soluble	120	120	127	483	502	456
Colombia						
Green	617	620	677	1 758	1 779	1 257
Roast	0	4	1	0	12	2
Soluble	13	13	13	52	54	47
Indonesia						
Green	292	78	347	832	841	644
Roast	0	2	3	0	8	7
Soluble	0	6	0	0	0	0
Côte d'Ivoire						
Green	219	221	296	624	634	550
Roast	0	0	1	0	1	2
Soluble	13	13	13	52	54	49
Mexico						
Green	190	190	180	542	545	334
Roast	12	16	5	35	49	11
Soluble	0	0	0	0	0	-1
Guatemala						
Green	152	152	155	433	437	287
Roast	0	0	4	0	3	9
Soluble	0	0	0	0	0	0
El Salvador						
Green	147	148	230	419	424	427
Roast	0	1	3	0	2	8
Soluble	3	3	3	12	13	12
Uganda						
Green	142	143	355	405	411	659
Roast	0	0	1	0	0	3
Soluble	0	0	0	0	0	1
Costa Rica						
Green	110	110	136	314	317	252
Roast	0	1	2	0	2	4
Soluble	0	0	0	0	0	0
Kenya						
Green	109	109	104	311	314	193
Roast	0	0	0	0	0	1
Soluble	0	0	0	0	0	0

Table 6.3 (continued)

Zaire						
Green	91	92	171	259	264	317
Roast	0	1	2	0	1	6
Soluble	0	0	0	0	0	0
Ecuador						
Green	86	86	209	245	247	388
Roast	0	1	9	0	2	21
Soluble	0	10	12	40	42	42
Cameroon						
Green	81	82	102	231	234	190
Roast	1	1	1	3	3	3
Soluble	0	0	0	0	0	0
India						
Green	80	80	83	228	228	154
Roast	0	2	3	0	7	8
Soluble	6	6	6	24	25	23
Rest of world						
Green	384	376	144	1 094	1 078	268
Roast	-8	18	-30	-24	59	-72
Soluble	1	1	1	4	5	5
Total						
Green	3 548	3 328	3 887	10 112	10 166	7 215
Roast	5	71	55	15	222	132
Soluble	156	172	175	668	695	634

Table 6.4

EFFECTS OF TRADE LIBERALIZATION ON TEA EXPORTS

Country/region	Net export volume			Net exports value		
	1986 levels	Non-LDC policies removed	LDC policies removed	1896 levels	Non-LDC policies removed	LDC policies removed
		(1 000 tonnes)			(Million $)	
Sri Lanka	208	208	235	318	319	262
India	200	201	198	306	307	220
Kenya	116	117	90	179	179	100
China	104	103	216	158	158	240
Indonesia	79	79	103	121	121	115
Argentina	36	36	11	55	55	12
Malawi	40	38	105	58	58	117
Bangladesh	28	28	27	43	43	30
Total	811	810	985	1 238	1 242	1 096

1. Total includes only countries listed in table. Rest of world is a net importer in this model.

NOTES AND REFERENCES

1. The authors acknowledge the able assistance of Liana Neff in running the models.

2. Although cocoa is usually consumed in non-beverage form, it is conventionally classified as a "tropical beverage".

3. No major producers of cocoa or coffee are also major consumers of those products.

4. The supply and demand equations are specified in constant elasticity form in the SWOPSIM framework.

5. The five equations reflecting the technical relationships in supply:

$$LT = 0.8 * Be \qquad (F_1)$$

$$LT = LF + LI \qquad (F_2)$$

$$Bu = (0.17/0.14)\, LF \qquad (F_3)$$

$$LI = Ck + Bu \qquad (F_4)$$

$$Ck = (0.47/0.53)\, Bu \qquad (F_5)$$

where LT, LF, and LI are total, final and intermediate use of liquor, Be is bean, Bu is butter and Ck is cake production. Equations (F_1) and (F_5) are based on physical relationships, equation (F_3) on the assumption that all liquor and butter are used in uniform proportions (14 per cent liquor and 17 per cent butter) to make chocolate, and (F_2) and (F_4) are definitional. Supply data are adjusted to ensure that the conditions in equations (F_1) to (F_5) were met. Given the supply and net trade data set, demand was calculated as a residual. Analogous procedures were used for coffee and tea.

6. The four equations reflecting the technical relationships in the coffee supply model are:

$$G = 1.19\, R \qquad (F_6)$$

$$G = 2.50\, S \qquad (F_7)$$

$$RT = RF + RI \qquad (F_8)$$

$$RF = X_i * RT \qquad (F_9)$$

where RT, RF, and RI are total, final, and intermediate use of roasted coffee. Technical relationships are given in equations (F_6) and (F_7) in which R is roasted, G is green bean, and S is soluble quantity. Equation (F_9) sets a proportion (X_i) of roast coffee being supplied as soluble consumption. For the United States the proportion was 0.2, for other developed countries, 0.1, and for developing countries, 0.05.

7. Specific data sources are listed in the references at the end of this report.

8. Some of these investigations are being published in reports edited by Mabbs-Zeno and Trapido.

BIBLIOGRAPHY

ADAMS, G.F. and J.R. BEHRMAN, *Econometric Models of World Agricultural Commodity Markets*, Cambridge, Massachusetts: Ballinger Publishing Company, 1976.

ADAMS, G.F., and J.R. BEHRMAN, *Commodity Exports and Economic Development*, Lexington, Massachusetts: Lexington Books, 1984.

AKIYAMA, T. and P.K. TRIVEDI, *A New Global Tea Model*, World Bank Working Paper, No. 17, Washington, D.C., 1987.

AKIYAMA, T. and P. VARANGIS, *Impact of the International Coffee Agreement's Export Quota System on the World's Coffee Market*, World Bank Working Paper, WPS 148, Washington, D.C., 1989.

FOOD AND AGRICULTURE ORGANIZATION, United Nations, *Production Yearbook*, various issues.

FOOD AND AGRICULTURE ORGANIZATION, United Nations, *Trade Yearbook*, various issues.

FOREIGN AGRICULTURAL SERVICE, US Department of Agriculture, Attache reports, various issues.

FOREIGN AGRICULTURAL SERVICE, US Department of Agriculture, *Commodity Report*, various issues.

INTERNATIONAL COFFEE ORGANIZATION, *Stocks, Production and Availability of Coffee in Exporting Member Countries*, Agreement No. 11/88 (E), Rev. 1, 1988.

INTERNATIONAL TEA COMMITTEE, *Annual Bulletin of Statistics*, 1989.

KRISSOFF, B., J. SULLIVAN and J. WAINIO, "Opening Agricultural Markets: Trade and Welfare Implications for Developing Countries", mimeo, Economic Research Service, US Department of Agriculture, Washington, D.C., 1989.

MABBS-ZENO, C.C., ed., *Government Intervention in the Agriculture of Africa and the Middle East*, ERS Staff Report, Economic Research Service, US Department of Agriculture, Washington, D.C., forthcoming.

RIEDL, O, "The Manufacture of Cocoa Mass — A Challenge for Developing Countries", *Review for Chocolate, Confectionery, and Bakery*, Vol. 3, No. 4, December 1978.

RONINGEN, V.O., *A Static World Policy Simulation (SWOPSIM) Modeling Framework*, ERS Staff Report No. AGES860625, Economic Research Service, US Department of Agriculture, Washington, D.C., July 1986.

RONINGEN, V.O. and P.M. DIXIT, *Economic Implications of Agricultural Policy Reforms in Industrial Market Economies*, ERS Staff Report No. AGES89-36, US Department of Agriculture, Washington, D.C., August 1989.

TRAPIDO, P., ed., *Government Intervention in the Agriculture of Latin America*, ERS Staff Report, Economic Research Service, US Department of Agriculture, Washington, D.C., forthcoming.

Part II

GENERAL EQUILIBRIUM MODELS

Chapter 7

ANALYSING AGRICULTURAL TRADE LIBERALIZATION WITH SINGLE COUNTRY COMPUTABLE GENERAL EQUILIBRIUM MODELS

by

Sherman Robinson

INTRODUCTION

The current round of multilateral trade negotiations, the Uruguay Round of the GATT, has focussed policy interest on questions of the structural impact of different trade regimes in developed and developing countries. Given that the GATT negotiations, at the request of the United States, started with agriculture, there has been active work using multisectoral models to explore the impact of different domestic and international agricultural policy regimes on various economies. While linear models can capture many of the important linkages between agriculture and the rest of the economy, most recent work has used nonlinear, price endogenous, computable general equilibrium (CGE) models.

In both developed and developing countries, CGE models have become part of the standard tool kit of policy analysts. One strand of work has focussed on efficiency questions in neoclassical welfare analysis — what might be called triangle counting. These models, by design, have stayed close to the neoclassical paradigm. A second strand of work, largely applied to developing countries, has focussed on structural issues. What is the impact of different choices of development strategy on growth, structural change, and the distribution of income? Given macroeconomic shocks, how do different choices of "structural adjustment" policies affect the economy? Given various rigidities, distortions, and market imperfections characteristic of developing countries, how do these countries react to different policy instruments? These models have introduced a variety of "structuralist" features designed to capture institutional rigidities characteristic of developing countries. In analysing the impact of different trade liberalization scenarios, CGE models have been built that draw on both strands of work.

While the neoclassical paradigm has provided the fundamental theoretical underpinning for trade-focussed CGE models, there has also been work to extend the empirical models to include recent theoretical advances in trade theory. This paper will review some of the recent work using CGE models to address issues of trade policy, especially the analysis of liberalization scenarios. The review is more issue-centred than country-centred and will discuss work on both developed and developing countries. After presenting a core CGE model, there will be a discussion of the limitations of models which stick to the neoclassical paradigm and some examples of models that incorporate rent seeking, externalities, and imperfect competition[1]. Then the empirical results from existing models used to analyse the impact of agricultural liberalization are reviewed. Given these results, and the evolution of the GATT negotiations, recent developments in the formulation and use of policy-focussed CGE models are discussed. The review is selective, presenting examples of recent work rather than trying to provide a broad survey[2].

A SINGLE COUNTRY, TWO-SECTOR, THREE-GOOD, TRADE MODEL

De Melo and Robinson (1989a) present a simple single country, two-sector, three-good model that can be seen as an extension of the Salter-Swan (or Australian) trade model[3]. In this "1-2-3" model, the country produces two commodities: (1) an export good, E, which is sold to foreigners and is not demanded domestically, and (2) a domestic good, D, which is only sold domestically. The third good is an import, M, which is not produced domestically. The model has no factor markets. The country is small in world markets, facing fixed world prices for exports and imports.

The 1-2-3 CGE Model

The model equations are set out in Table 7.1. Equation 1 defines the domestic production possibility frontier and gives the maximum achievable combinations of E and D that the economy can supply. The function is assumed to be concave. In multisector CGE models, it is specified as a constant elasticity of transformation (CET) function for each sector. The constant $\overline{X}$ defines aggregate production and is assumed fixed. Since there are no intermediate inputs, $\overline{X}$ also corresponds to real GDP. The assumption that $\overline{X}$ is fixed is equivalent to assuming full and efficient employment of all primary factor inputs in a model with factor markets[4]. In addition to the production possibility frontier, the economy faces a second constraint: the value of imports cannot exceed the value of exports plus exogenous foreign borrowing. This balance of trade constraint is given by equation 18.

Equation 2 defines a composite commodity, Q, made up of domestic goods and imports, which is consumed by a single consumer. In CGE models, Q is usually a constant elasticity of substitution (CES) function of D and M at the sectoral level[5]. Assuming that the single consumer in the model gains utility from Q, welfare is maximised when the amount of Q in the economy is maximised. In this model, Q defines total absorption[6].

Equations 1, 2, 16, and 18 together suffice to define a simple CGE model. Equation 16 adds the assumption that supply equals demand on the market for the domestic good, D. Figure 7.1 presents the model in graphs. The production possibility frontier is given in quadrant IV. The balance of trade constraint is given in quadrant I, setting $\pi^m = \pi^e = 1$ and $\overline{B} = 0$ for convenience. Quadrant III captures equation 16. The consumption possibility frontier in quadrant II is the locus of points that satisfy the three constraint equations in quadrants I, III, and IV. The market equilibrium is given at point C, where absorption Q is maximised. Solution prices are given by the slopes of the tangent lines at the production point P and the consumption point C.

The rest of the equations in Table 7.1 complete the description of the model, including prices as endogenous variables and explicit income and expenditure constraints for the single household, government, and the rest of the world. To complete the macro specification, the model adds savings and investment, with all savings done by the single household. There are also three price-wedge tax instruments. The government collects indirect taxes and tariffs, pays export subsidies, and transfers any net balance in a lump-sum fashion to or from the single household.

Equations 4 and 5 give the efficient export and import ratios as functions of relative prices. Equations 13 and 14 define the corresponding prices (P^x and P^q) of aggregate output X and the composite good Q. They are the cost-function duals to the first-order conditions embodied in equations 4 and 5. P^x essentially defines the GDP deflator, while P^q defines the consumer price index for the CES composite good, which will also be a CES function.

Equation 3 defines consumer and investment demand for the composite good. In this model, it merely states that all income is spent on the single composite good, and could be omitted. However, in a multisector model, this equation defines how consumers allocate consumption expenditure across goods and how aggregate investment is spent on capital goods. There is a vast literature on systems of consumer demand as functions of relative prices and income. In the simple model, equation 3 can stand in for a more complex system of expenditure equations and does reflect an important property of all complete systems — the value of the goods demanded must equal aggregate expenditure.

Equations 6 to 9 determine the income flows in the economy. The model has four actors: a producer, a household, government, and the rest of the world. Equation 6 determines government revenue and equation 7 determines household income. Equations 8 and 9 divide household income between consumption and savings. The nominal flows among the actors can be tabulated in a Social Accounting Matrix (or SAM), which is presented in Figure 7.2.[7] The SAM shows the circular flow of income and expenditure in the economy. Each cell represents a payment from a column account to a recipient in a row account. The SAM is square and, following the conventions of double-entry bookkeeping, each actor's accounts must balance — income must exactly equal expenditure. Thus column sums in the SAM must equal the corresponding row sums.

The SAM defines six accounts, one for each actor, one for savings and investment, and an additional "commodity" account. The commodity account keeps track of absorption, which equals the value of domestic products sold on the domestic market, D, and imports, M. The producer account pays out total revenue to households and government down the column and sells goods on the domestic and foreign markets along the row. The column sum equals gross domestic product (GDP) at market prices, which includes indirect taxes. GDP at factor cost equals $P^x \cdot X$. Export subsidies are seen as a payment by government to producers. Exports and imports in the account for the rest of the world are valued in world market prices times the exchange rate.

In Table 7.1, the price equations define relationships among eight prices. There are fixed world prices for E and M; domestic prices for E and M; producer and consumer prices for D; and prices for the two composite commodities, X and Q. Equations 1 and 2 are linearly homogeneous, as are the corresponding dual price equations, 13 and 14. Equations 3, 4, and 5 are homogeneous of degree zero in prices — doubling all prices leaves real demand and the desired export and import ratios unchanged[8]. Since only relative prices matter, it is necessary to define a numeraire good whose price is set exogenously. Equation 15 defines the numeraire price as the GDP deflator, a common choice in applied models.

Equations 16 to 20 define the market-clearing equilibrium conditions. Supply must equal demand for D and Q, the balance of trade constraint must be satisfied, aggregate savings must equal aggregate investment, and the government account must balance. The complete model has 20 equations and 19 endogenous variables. The five equilibrium condition equations, however, are not all independent. The model satisfies Walras' Law and it can be shown that if any four of the five equations are satisfied, then the fifth must also hold. So, any one of them can be dropped, and the resulting model is exactly identified.

De Melo and Robinson (1989a) analyse the properties of this model in some detail and argue that it is a good stylisation of most recent single country, trade-focussed, CGE models. The assumption of product differentiation on both the import and export sides is very appealing for applied models, especially at the levels of aggregation typically used. The specification is a theoretically clean extension of the Salter-Swan model and gives rise to normally shaped offer curves. The exchange rate is a well-defined relative price (the shadow price on the balance of trade constraint). If the domestic good is chosen as numeraire, setting P^d equal to one, then the exchange rate variable, R, corresponds to the "real" exchange rate of neoclassical trade theory: the relative price of tradables (E and M) to non-tradables (D). Trade theory models often set R to one, with P^d then defining the real exchange rate. For other choices of numeraire, R is a monotonic function of the real exchange rate[9].

In Table 7.1, the balance of trade is specified exogenously. The model then determines the equilibrium value of the real exchange rate. Alternatively, one could specify the exchange rate as an exogenous variable and solve for the equilibrium value of the balance of trade. What the model determines is an equilibrium relationship between the balance of trade and the real exchange rate. The model, however, can only determine relative prices. The implication is that a macro economist is free to specify any two, but only two, of the following three variables: the balance of trade, the nominal exchange rate (R), and any price index (the numeraire in the CGE model).

Extending the CGE model to include many sectors, sectoral production functions, intermediate goods, factor markets, many consumers, and macro-balances is relatively straightforward. For example, to move to many sectors, just add sector subscripts to all the output and price variables. The CET production possibility frontier is now interpreted as a sectoral export transformation function describing the relative degree of difficulty in producing goods for the domestic market versus the export market. Similarly, the import aggregation function describes the degree of substitution in demand between imports and domestically produced goods within the same sectoral category. The CGE model can also easily accommodate downward-sloping world demand curves for sectoral exports by adding an equation specifying a functional relationship between E and π^e.[10]

Product Differentiation and Trade Theory

The standard neoclassical trade model, with all goods tradable and all tradables perfect substitutes with domestic goods, has long been a staple of trade theory, but yields wildly implausible results in empirical applications[11]. Empirical models that reflect these assumptions embody "the law of one price," which states that domestic relative prices of tradables are set by world prices. Such models tend to yield extreme specialisation in production and unrealistic swings in domestic relative prices in response to changes in trade policy or world prices. Empirical evidence indicates that changes in the prices of imports and exports are only partially "transmitted" to the prices of domestic goods in the same sector categories. In addition, such models cannot exhibit two-way trade in any sector ("cross hauling"), which is often observed in empirical data at fine levels of disaggregation.

The addition of non-tradables, as in the Salter-Swan model, is a theoretical improvement, but with limited empirical applicability. Even looking at an input-output table with over 500 sectors, there are very few sectors which are purely non-traded; i.e. with no exports or imports. So defined, non-traded goods are a very small share of GDP; and, in models with 10-30 sectors, there would be at most only one or two non-traded sectors. Furthermore, the link between domestic and world prices does not depend on the trade share, only on whether or not the sector is tradable.

The picture is quite different in models with imperfect substitutability and transformability. In this case, all domestically produced goods that are not exported (D in Table 7.1) are effectively treated as non-tradables. The share of non-tradables in GDP now equals one minus the export share, and all sectors are treated symmetrically. A pure non-traded sector is one in which the share parameters in the import aggregation and export transformation functions are both zero. In effect, the specification extends and generalises the Salter-Swan model, and makes it much more empirically relevant.

As de Melo and Robinson (1985) show, the link between domestic and world prices depends critically on the trade shares, both for exports and imports. For given substitution and transformation elasticities, domestic prices are more closely linked to world prices the greater the export and import shares. The net effect of this specification is a very realistic insulation of the domestic price system from changes in world prices. The links are there, but they are not nearly as strong as in the standard neoclassical trade model. Also, the model naturally accommodates two-way trade, since exports, imports, and domestic goods in the same sector are all distinct.

For a single country model, the CES and CET functions capture the reasonable notion that it is not "easy" to shift trade shares in either export or import markets. Given that each sector has eight associated prices, the model provides for a lot of product differentiation. The assumption of imperfect substitutability on the import side has been widely used in empirical models. Note that it is equally important to specify imperfect transformability on the export side. Without imperfect transformability, the law of one price would still hold for all sectors with exports. In the 1-2-3 model, both import demand and export supply depend on relative prices[12].

The specification of imperfect substitutability on the import side has been criticised in the context of multicountry models because it implies that every country has market power, leading to the potential for national welfare gains from imposing trade restrictions. What is a reasonable approximation for a single country model has become something of an embarrassment in multicountry models designed to analyse the gains from trade liberalization. While attention has focussed on the elasticities of substitution, the share parameters in the CES functions are really at the root of the problem. In a multi-country model, the assumption of fixed sectoral share parameters in every country largely determines the volume and direction of world trade, with price changes only affecting shares at the margin. It is probably more correct to view trade shares as evolving over time in response to shocks and policy changes, with short-run import aggregation functions sliding along long-run functions that have much higher substitution elasticities. The problem for multicountry models is to understand why and how these shares change over time in ways that do not depend only on shifts in relative prices.

In single country models, the CES formulation for the import-aggregation function has been criticised on econometric grounds[13]. It is certainly a restrictive form. For example, it constrains the income elasticity of demand for imports to be one in every sector. In both single country and multi-country models, it is probably time to explore other formulations, while maintaining the fundamental assumption of imperfect substitutability. Other functional forms are certainly available. For example, Hanson, Robinson, and Tokarick (1989) estimate sectoral import demand functions based on the almost ideal demand system (AIDS) formulation. They find that sectoral expenditure elasticities of import demand are generally much greater than one in the United States, results consistent with estimates from macroeconometric models. Factors other than relative prices appear to affect trade shares, and it is important to start doing research on what they might be and how they operate.

TRADE POLICY AND WELFARE

Since Adam Smith, much of the literature in trade theory has explored the benefits of free trade and the welfare costs of protection. The development of CGE models permitted the empirical estimation of the welfare costs of protectionist policies in a general equilibrium framework. In analysing the implications of agricultural liberalization, it is important to keep in mind the lessons learned from past work with trade-focussed models. This section reviews recent work with such models.

One of the intriguing results from the now rather large body of empirical work is that the costs of engaging in protectionist policies, or the gains from removing them, are relatively small. In a recent conference volume, Srinivasan and Whalley (1986) compare studies of trade liberalization in a variety of single country and multicountry CGE models. In their summary, they note that the welfare gains from trade liberalization are relatively small, seldom amounting to as much as 1 per cent of GNP. They cite Harberger's discussion of the welfare costs of distortions, which can be summarised in the often-quoted proposition that "triangles are smaller than rectangles." They also note that, at least in developed countries, the reforms being modelled are not really dramatic. In the conference volume, for example, each paper explored the impact of a 50 per cent cut in tariffs. Since the initial levels of tariffs in many countries such as the United States are fairly low, one might expect that aggregate welfare effects of halving them would be small. However, more dramatic changes in protection also yield small welfare effects. In a recent 30-sector CGE model of the United States, Hanson, Robinson, and Tokarick (1989) explore the impact of a protectionist policy where the United States adds an across-the-board 50 per cent tariff to existing tariffs in all sectors. The experiment is designed to measure the structural impact of a complete failure of the current round of GATT talks, with the United States imposing protection similar to the 1930 Smoot-Hawley tariff. The structural results are dramatic, but aggregate GDP falls by only about 0.25 per cent.

The result that the static welfare costs from misallocation of resources due to price-wedge distortions are small in a competitive general equilibrium model represents one of the robust properties of CGE models. Substitution possibilities in production, consumption, and trade endow the economy with a great deal of adjustment flexibility. When markets work and factors are fully employed, even large price-wedge distortions can be vitiated by substitution possibilities, with little effect on aggregate welfare.

Two points should be noted about this result. First, the term "small" must be evaluated in terms of the problem being analysed. Work with CGE models focussing on tax issues indicates that welfare losses from "inefficient" tax systems can be a large share of total tax revenue. Consider a "project" which involves redesigning the tax system to raise the same amount of revenue more efficiently — that is, with less deadweight losses. Such a project can easily have a social rate of return of 20-50 per cent, where the denominator is aggregate tax revenue. For the United States, such welfare gains amount to billions of dollars, which should certainly justify work with CGE models in the US Treasury.

Second, while price-wedge distortions may generate small aggregate welfare losses, their impacts on the sectoral structure of resource allocation, production, and trade tend to be more significant. In general, political pressure groups are organised by sector and care about the impact of policy on the relative position of their sector in the economy[14]. The closer one gets to actual policy makers, the more evident is the interest in measures of the structural impact of policies, rather than measures of aggregate welfare. Any positive analysis of policy needs to take this concern into account.

Especially in developing countries, much of the work with CGE models evaluating the impact of policies in an operational environment has tended to reflect these concerns about structure. For example, the extensive work on CGE models of "structural adjustment" at the World Bank has tended to focus on issues of resource allocation and "expenditure switching" rather than aggregate welfare. This concern for analysing the structural impact of policy changes is also evident in the recent work on trade liberalization.

Optimal Tariff Policy

Some of these problems with neoclassical CGE models are nicely illustrated by work on optimal tariff policy in the presence of a government revenue constraint. A standard rule of thumb in policy analysis is that countries should equalise their tariff rates across sectors. A policy of equal tariffs across sectors is best, getting the prices right and yielding a level playing field. Given the existence of differentiated tariffs and a revenue constraint, it is desirable to move in the direction of equalising tariffs. This "uniformalist" position certainly represents the conventional wisdom at the World Bank and has been forcefully advocated by writers such as Harberger (1988), Balassa et al. (1982), and Krueger (1985).

From the public finance literature, we know that in the presence of non-removable distortionary taxes, equalising tariff rates is not optimal. Chambers (1989) provides a good

206

survey of the theoretical arguments[15]. Dahl, Devarajan, and van Wijnbergen (1986) discuss a theoretical model of the issue and provide an empirical application with an eight-sector CGE model of Cameroon. Devarajan and Lewis (1989) discuss a similar application using a 13-sector CGE model of Indonesia and Devarajan, Lewis, and Robinson (1989) illustrate the empirical issues using an extension of the two-sector, three-good model described above that includes a fourth good, an imported intermediate input.

In these models, the method used is to include the CGE model as constraint equations in a nonlinear programming model. The objective function is the utility function of the single consumer and is defined to be consistent with the expenditure functions in the CGE model. Then various tax instruments are specified as variables rather than fixed parameters, so the CGE model no longer has a unique solution. The programming problem is solved by finding the set of tax instruments that yields a market equilibrium with maximum welfare.

From these studies, the answer is that, in a second-best world, a policy of equal tariffs across sectors is not optimal. The results from the theory of public finance carry over into empirical models. Moreover, a policy of moving towards equal tariffs from an existing situation of unequal tariffs is not generally welfare improving. Based on the empirical results from the latter two studies, a better rule of thumb would be to recommend that tariff rates for intermediate and capital goods be very low or zero, and certainly much less than the tariff rates for consumer goods[16].

These empirical results do not imply that the World Bank should cease recommending that countries move towards equalising tariff rates. In a world of rent seeking and administrative capacity constraints, it is probably a good idea to simplify tariff rate structures. However, tariff equalisation cannot be justified on the basis of static efficiency gains in the neoclassical model, either theoretical or empirical, once realistic second-best constraints are introduced. The neoclassical competitive general equilibrium model is a powerful tool, but it is also important to describe how the world actually works, not just how it would work in some first-best Platonic form.

In these optimal-policy applications, large variations in policy instruments yield small changes in aggregate welfare. While it is clearly optimal to use differentiated tariffs, the improvement in aggregate welfare is not all that large. One might argue that simplifying the structure of tariffs would save a lot of administrative costs and reduce rent seeking, and that the resulting benefits might well exceed the welfare losses arising from tariff equalisation. While persuasive, this argument turns the neoclassical model on its head and would probably not appeal much to the proponents of uniform taxation. It would appear that they are being hoist with their own petard.

Rent Seeking, Imperfect Competition, and Externalities

Quantitative controls on imports have been a characteristic feature of trade regimes in many developing countries. The seminal article on rent seeking by Krueger (1974) was motivated by her experience in Turkey, where pervasive quantitative controls generated enormous gains to particular groups. Those developing trade-focussed CGE models of developing countries were strongly influenced by these "stylised facts." The first of the World Bank "structural adjustment" CGE models, the Dervis-Robinson model of Turkey, incorporated quantity rationing of imports and rent-seeking behaviour[17]. In the last decade, the majority of CGE models applied to developing countries have focussed on issues of trade and structural adjustment, and many of them have incorporated quantitative restrictions and rent seeking.

The empirical results from this literature indicate that the rents generated by policies to restrict imports are indeed large, sometimes amounting to 10-15 per cent of GDP[18]. These results raise a number of issues for policy analysis and modelling: (a) Who gets the rents? (b) How do we model the trade regime? and (c) What are the efficiency losses due to rent seeking?

The first two questions are closely related. Dervis, de Melo, and Robinson (1981) compare the distributional impact of two import rationing regimes: a fixprice regime where import demanders receive a direct allocation of imports which they cannot sell and a flexprice regime where there is, in effect, a market in quota certificates[19]. In their model, typical of semi-industrial countries, imports consist largely of intermediate inputs and capital goods, with very few consumer goods. Thus producing sectors are the agents most directly affected by the trade regime. Under fixprice rationing, sectors receive fewer imported intermediate inputs and capital goods than they desire, but get them at far lower prices than they would be willing to pay. Producers thus receive the rents, since they pay less than market-clearing prices for the imports they use, and so are subsidised by the trade regime. In an environment where imports must be reduced (say, in response to a decline in foreign investment or a balance of payments crisis), import-dependent producers will tend to favour quantity rationing over a flexible exchange rate regime because they gain a great deal from the implicit subsidies.

Under flexprice rationing, all users are assumed to pay the premium-ridden price for imports, so rationed imports are efficiently allocated across competing uses. The rationing is implemented by an *ad valorem* equivalent premium. However, the allocation of the premia rents must be handled separately. In a CGE model, they appear as an explicit flow which must be allocated to agents in the economy. They are computed by applying a supplemental tariff whose proceeds must be allocated to agents other than the government. Figuring out who gets these rents in the first instance is important for policy analysis, since it largely determines the impact effect of any change in policy. The CGE model also traces out the indirect effects, which will work themselves out through changes in equilibrium prices and quantities.

The existence of quantitative restrictions raises the issue of spillover effects. How do agents in the economy behave, given the quantity rationing? Is the rationing scheme incentive compatible? Dervis, de Melo, and Robinson (1982) note the problem and argue that because of the special characteristics of their model it is relatively unimportant in their case. Grais, de Melo, and Urata (1986), drawing on the notion of "virtual prices" introduced by Neary and Roberts (1980), solve explicitly for the agents' behaviour on the non-rationed markets. By "reoptimising", given the quantity constraints, their model captures the spillover effects in a theoretically satisfying way.

The final question is whether the existence of "chaseable rents" induces efficiency losses through rent seeking behaviour. Bhagwati and Srinivasan (1980) generalise the notion, using the term "revenue seeking," and argue that the magnitude of the efficiency losses will equal the value of the rents. Grais, de Melo, and Urata (1986) make this assumption, and find that rent seeking efficiency losses amounted to over 5 per cent of GDP in Turkey in 1978, in the midst of their foreign exchange crisis. In the references cited in footnote 18, a variety of assumptions are made about efficiency losses as a share of total rents. There is no obvious answer, since one can easily think of quota allocation schemes that will generate no rent seeking. In general, one would expect that there would be an initial period of intensive rent seeking while the institutional rules determining the allocation of rents are settled[20]. After that, there should be no more efficiency losses from rent seeking associated with import quotas than with any other government entitlement programme[21].

The literature on rents and rent seeking when there is extensive import rationing has certainly identified an effect where the numbers are large. Pervasive import rationing, however, occurs rarely. In the studies cited earlier, such rationing was usually a short- to medium-term policy response to a crisis situation. More common, in developing and developed countries, is sectoral protection over a long period which is intended to restrict foreign competition. In this environment, there are potential welfare losses because protection induces non-competitive behaviour. If, in addition, the affected industries are subject to scale economies, then potential welfare losses from protection, and the potential benefits from liberalization, can be quite large.

The interaction between oligopolistic behaviour, scale economies, and import protection in developed countries is an area of active research in trade theory. There are some CGE models of developed countries incorporating these effects[22]. Work in developing countries is surveyed by de Melo (1988) and Devarajan and Rodrik (1989). Condon and de Melo (1986) build a stylised three-sector CGE model loosely based on Chile to illustrate the potential effects. In their model, with import rationing, scale economies in manufacturing, and imperfect competition (but no rent seeking), the welfare costs of import rationing in the manufacturing sector amount to 13-17 per cent of national income. In a similar, but more disaggregated, model of Cameroon, Devarajan and Rodrik (1989) generate a much smaller number for welfare costs, around 2-3 per cent of GDP.

The models appear to provide a reasonable description of parts of the manufacturing sector in a number of developing countries. In addition to coexisting firm-level scale economies and imperfect competition, many developing countries are also characterised by scale economies that appear to be external to the firm. There is some very recent work with theoretical long-run growth models incorporating Marshallian externalities that attempt to explain long-run development. See, for example, Lucas (1988) and Romer (1986). These models, in effect, introduce increasing returns to scale at the economy-wide level, while maintaining constant returns to scale at the level of the firm. They thus do not require any assumptions about imperfect competition to generate equilibrium growth paths[23]. While much of this literature appears to be inspired by long-run historical industrialisation in the currently developed countries, some of the externality mechanisms they discuss are potentially relevant for developing countries, especially when considering the role of manufacturing exports[24].

AGRICULTURAL TRADE LIBERALIZATION

The earlier work on trade-focussed CGE models yields a number of lessons for those analysing agricultural trade liberalization. First, do not expect to find large welfare gains from models sticking close to the neoclassical paradigm. In the long run, with flexible prices and all factors fully employed, market economies appear able to substitute around most problems and distortions. The welfare gains, however, may be large in comparison to the "costs" of the policy change (e.g. the change in government revenue). Second, the sectoral structure of resource use, output, exports, imports, and income will be very sensitive to policy choices. Third, existing structural rigidities which limit the capacity of the economy to adjust will generate significant differential returns or rents and also affect the sectoral structure of income. For example, existing distortions in the operation of factor markets or quantitative constraints on trade may generate significant potential gains from changes in policy. Analysis of the impact of policy should incorporate any existing institutional rigidities. Welfare analysis will then necessarily involve comparisons among second-best situations.

Work on using CGE models to analyse the impact of agricultural trade liberalization has been underway for a few years. This section provides some background on the policy environment that motivated much of this research, briefly reviews the empirical results, and discusses where the next generation of models is heading, given the current state of the GATT negotiations.

At the beginning of the Uruguay round of GATT negotiations, the United States insisted that agriculture be discussed first and that domestic policies, as well as border policies, should be brought under the GATT. The initial US proposal was that the major trading partners should dismantle all domestic agricultural programmes — i.e. complete liberalization. The underlying view was that liberalization would generate higher prices on world markets, which would offset the losses to farmers from the removal of the programmes. Trade liberalization, at least for agricultural exporters, would be a substitute for domestic farm programmes.

The initial round of modelling work sought to analyse the impact on various countries and on the world economy of complete agricultural liberalization. Work focussed on two scenarios: unilateral liberalization (in which the country removes all programmes, but no one else does) and multilateral liberalization. These scenarios were analysed with a variety of modelling methodologies. Hertel (1989a,b) surveys many of the CGE models and some of the empirical results. Stoeckel, Vincent, and Cuthbertson (1989) edited a collection of papers describing analysis of common liberalization scenarios with single-country CGE models of various countries. The most elaborate models were developed for the United States and Australia[25]. There is much less work with single country models of developing countries[26]. Burniaux *et al.* (1989) describe the results from a set of small, single country CGE models of the OECD countries, tied together in a world model called WALRAS. Results from other, non-CGE models are surveyed by Baker, Hallberg, and Blandford (1989) and Gardner (1988). The results from a USDA world model are presented in Roningen and Dixit (1989).

Policy interest centred on a few key questions (in descending order of importance). What happens to the agricultural sectors? What happens to the rest of the economy, especially sectors linked to agriculture, either upstream or downstream? What is the net impact on the government budget? What is the impact on aggregate welfare?

The main empirical results are robust across different methodologies. In most countries, and certainly in the United States, trade liberalization is not a substitute for existing programmes supporting agriculture. Even under the most optimistic world-market scenarios, with significant rises in world prices, income gains from higher market prices do not offset income losses due to removal of agricultural programmes. From the results of the OECD WALRAS models, only in New Zealand does the agricultural sector gain under multilateral liberalization[27].

The welfare effects, while small relative to GNP, are generally positive and represent a significant share of the change in programme costs. In the United States, for example, Robinson, Kilkenny, and Adelman (1989) find that removal of a $20-30 billion agricultural programme leads to about a $10 billion increase in real GDP (in 1982 dollars). Part of this gain comes about because of removal of land set-asides, increasing the total supply of a primary factor. Capital and labour move out of agriculture, with gains to the non-agricultural sectors. As a group, grain importing developing countries lose from trade liberalization, while grain exporters gain. Within all developing countries, specific groups of poor people who are net buyers of cereals lose[28].

In general, intersectoral linkages and general equilibrium effects are significant. For example, in the United States, about half of the benefits of programmes aimed at agriculture accrue to other sectors through forward and backward linkages[29]. In Australia, Higgs (1989) finds that protection granted to the manufacturing sectors has indirectly taxed agriculture, and if all trade policies were removed, agriculture would actually gain. Similarly, Stoeckel (1985) finds that the Common Agricultural Policy (CAP) in the European Community has hurt the industrial sectors and contributed to increased unemployment.

The empirical results from past work have generated a need for new approaches. Given that trade liberalization is not a substitute for existing agricultural programmes in virtually all countries, it is necessary to consider proposals for partial liberalization. The current position of the United States is to eliminate all "distorting" agricultural programmes, but allow "non-distorting" programmes that serve to maintain the incomes of farmers[30]. This change in focus has a number of implications for modellers, and the next generation of work is already underway to analyse more complicated liberalization scenarios. The next section discusses the implications of this new policy focus on model specification.

Modelling Issues

There have been a number of recent surveys of different technical specifications for trade-focussed CGE models[31]. In particular, Hertel (1989b) has surveyed the treatment of agriculture in existing CGE models, focussing on issues of aggregation, specification of technology (including the treatment of land), time horizon, the operation of factor markets, and the modelling of agricultural policies[32]. Without duplicating Hertel's survey, here the focus will be on two modelling issues that arise from the recent change in policy focus: the treatment of agricultural programmes and the need for forward-looking analysis.

As part of the work to support the GATT negotiations, the OECD organised work to measure the size of existing agricultural programmes. After much debate, two *ad valorem* measures were agreed on: a Consumer Subsidy Equivalent (CSE) and a Producer Subsidy Equivalent (PSE). Data on PSEs and CSEs have been tabulated for a number of countries[33]. The standard approach, with a few exceptions, has been to model the programmes as an *ad valorem* price wedge, analogous to an indirect tax or subsidy[34]. The model is estimated or calibrated for some base year with the wedges in place, then a liberalization scenario is simulated by simply setting all the wedges to zero and resolving the model. One problem with this approach is that the PSE and CSE measures include the cost of all programmes to support agriculture. While some of these programmes affect incentives, some do not. The modelling issue is to decide which programmes affect incentives, and hence can be treated as a incentive wedge, and which programmes should be treated as lump-sum transfers, with no effect on production or consumption incentives[35].

Even granting our ability to distinguish programmes which affect supply decisions from those which do not, the use of *ad valorem* equivalents raises problems. Programmes to support agriculture around the world are not, in fact, administered as *ad valorem* wedges. In virtually all countries, agricultural policies involve a complex mix of programmes. For example, Kilkenny and Robinson (1988) classify US agricultural policies into five broad categories, with benefits depending on instruments such as fixed target prices and loan rates, land "set aside" requirements (with voluntary participation by farmers), government stock accumulation, import quotas, and export subsidies. Only the last, export subsidies, are set in terms of an *ad valorem* measure[36]. The question is how accurate will be empirical estimates of the impact of liberalization scenarios when this complex mix of programmes is approximated by a few *ad valorem* wedges? It may be reasonable to use such an approximation when the experiment is to simulate complete liberalization; i.e. eliminating all programmes and hence setting all wedges to zero[37]. However, in the current policy environment, we must analyse the impact of partial liberalization scenarios and movement towards non-distorting agricultural support programmes. The policy challenge is to design such programmes. Policy models must reflect existing institutional arrangements and be capable of incorporating alternative policies, if they are to be useful in supporting the next phase of policy work[38].

In the first round of work on analysing the impact of agricultural liberalization, modellers used a comparative static approach. The model is first "benchmarked" on a base year, preferably as recent as possible, and is designed to reflect the policies in place at that time. Most models use 1986, but some start from 1982 or even 1977. Analysis proceeds by changing policy variables and/or exogenous parameters and then comparing the results with the benchmark solution. The models are used as simulation laboratories, allowing controlled experiments to sort out the empirical importance of changes in policies. While this approach yields useful information for policy makers, it also has serious limitations. The impact of the current round of trade negotiations will not start to be felt until the early 1990s, and policy makers need to estimate the impact of their current decisions five to ten years into the future. If they are to support such analysis, policy models also need to be forward-looking.

Two US CGE models have been used in forward-looking analyses of alternative agricultural trade policy scenarios. Robinson, Kilkenny, and Adelman (1989) use a ten-sector model to examine alternative scenarios for 1991, and Hanson, Robinson, and Tokarick (1989) use a 30-sector model to explore alternative scenarios for 1995. In order to make forward projections, these models incorporate projections of all their exogenous variables and time-varying parameters. Their results must then be seen as conditional on these exogenous projections. Important exogenous variables that must be projected include: aggregate labour force; aggregate capital stock; sectoral total factor productivity; world prices of exports and imports and/or shifts in world demand functions for US exports; agricultural policy parameters such as target prices, loan rates, and land set-asides; and key macro aggregates such as the balance of trade and the government deficit and/or aggregate investment.

In making forward projections, the models cited above drew on sector specific and macro "base-line projections" developed by the USDA and on similar exercises done by other groups[39]. The CGE model results turn out to depend critically on the underlying macro scenario. The 1981-85 period in the United States was characterised by high real interest rates, increasing federal deficits, growing trade deficits, and significant real appreciation of the exchange rate. US agriculture suffered in these circumstances, with declining shares in export markets and increasing costs of government programmes to support agricultural incomes[40]. Most macro analysts project a reversal of these trends over the next five to ten years, with reductions in the federal deficit, a shift in the trade balance back to surplus, and significant real depreciation of the exchange rate. This macro scenario implies a significant increase in US exports, with exports growing much faster than GNP.

Given the macro scenario, the CGE models are solved to determine the implications for sectoral production, employment, prices, income, exports, and imports. The models are specified so that the balance of trade and government deficits are exogenous variables (close in spirit to the model given in Table 7.1). Both the CGE and macro base lines project a successful expansion of US exports, including agriculture. Certainly the incentives for producers to increase exports are already strengthening and should strengthen further over the next few years. A legitimate question is to consider to what extent the assumptions of the macro models and the CGE models about the evolution of export markets are valid. How will world markets absorb the increase in US exports? What will happen to the structure of world trade? These are questions best considered within the framework of multicountry models of world trade. However, the US model results indicate that the United States will be attempting to increase exports and will actively contest world markets for agricultural goods, regardless of the outcome of the GATT negotiations. This is an important message for trade negotiators.

The CGE results also indicate that the cost of agricultural support programmes will decline over time. These results are sensitive to assumptions about agricultural supply responses and the speed of macro adjustment, especially the improvement in the trade balance. If output were to grow faster than projected, or exports expand less rapidly, then domestic prices would be lower and the programmes would cost more. Even with these qualifications, the projections indicate that the United States may be moving into a period analogous to the 1970s, where real depreciation was accompanied by improved agricultural performance and reductions in the cost of government support programmes. If so, then the US negotiating stance in the GATT is stronger. Over the next decade, the United States should be under less budgetary strain from agricultural programmes than the European Community.

The macro and CGE results indicate a continued strong US interest in furthering the current round of trade negotiations. To re-establish macro balance, the United States must expand exports. Expanding exports in a world environment of liberalized trade would be much easier than in an environment of increasing protectionism. Indeed, a collapse of the current GATT negotiations might generate an economic environment of shrinking world trade akin to that of the 1930s. Hanson, Robinson, and Tokarick (1989) simulate a scenario in which the United States lapses into a protectionist environment. The results indicate that the structural adjustments required in the United States would be very difficult, even ignoring the likely results of additional macro adjustment problems and increased unemployment.

Forward-looking projections with these models indicate that the approach should be fruitful. However, it imposes new demands on models. In particular, given the importance of the macro scenarios, there is a real need for work to integrate macro phenomena into CGE models. This is an area of active research, especially in developing countries[41]. Much of the existing work along these lines has been motivated by issues of structural adjustment in developing countries in the face of shocks such as the need for debt repayment or large swings in international prices (such as oil prices). There is some recent work in this vein that incorporates asset markets and endogenous macro variables in CGE models that also incorporate income distribution[42]. In view of the past dramatic changes in the world macro environment, and the likelihood of equally dramatic future changes, research to incorporate such changes in policy analysis with multisector models is very important.

CONCLUSION

The analysis of trade liberalization has generated an active body of work with multisectoral, computable general equilibrium models. This work has drawn heavily on earlier work with trade-focussed CGE models designed to analyse issues of structural adjustment in developing countries. The core of most single country, trade-focussed CGE models can be seen as an extension of the Salter-Swan "Australian" model of a small, open economy producing both tradables and non-tradables. The addition of assumptions about imperfect substitution and transformability between goods produced for the domestic and world markets represented a considerable advance, certainly in empirical realism. The resulting models, however, are still theoretically very much in the neoclassical paradigm.

While these CGE models have proven useful in policy analysis, they have also demonstrated the need for further work extending the modelling framework. One strand of work has sought to improve the specification of the models in addressing issues related to agriculture and trade liberalization, while remaining within the structure of neoclassical general equilibrium theory. Work in this strand has sought, for example, to improve model specification of agricultural technology, factor markets, and the operation of agricultural programmes. A second strand of work with CGE models has sought to incorporate phenomena such as rent seeking, imperfect competition, scale economies, and externalities which extend the paradigm. Future models seeking to analyse issues relating to agricultural trade liberalization could fruitfully draw on some of this work.

The development of CGE models for analysing agricultural liberalization has been strongly influenced by the policy concerns expressed in the GATT negotiations. As the negotiations move into the next phase, policy models need to reflect the changing concerns. To support the ongoing negotiations, future models will need to be forward-looking, incorporate the actual implementation of agricultural policies, provide a framework for considering the impact of different macro scenarios, and consider the links between agriculture and the rest of the economy.

Figure 7. 1. **THE 1 - 2 - 3 MODEL**

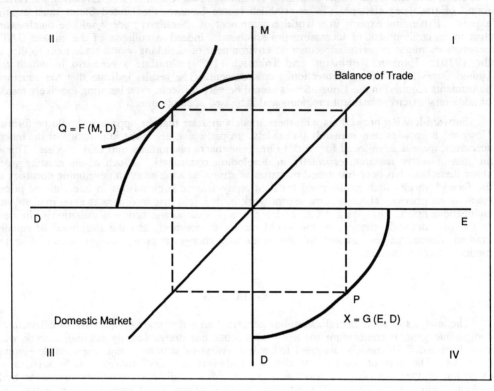

Figure 7.2

SOCIAL ACCOUNTING MATRIX FOR THE CGE MODEL

Receipts	Expenditures						Total
	Commodity	Producer	Household	Government	Capital	World	
Commodity			C		Z		$P^q \cdot Q^D$
Producer	$P^t \cdot D^D$			$\tilde{T}^e$		E	$P^t \cdot D^D + P^e \cdot E$
Household		$P^x \cdot X$		G		$R \cdot B$	Y
Government	$\tilde{T}^m$	$\tilde{T}^d$					$\tilde{T}^m + \tilde{T}^d$
Capital account			S				S
World	M						M
Total	$P^q \cdot Q^S$	GDP	Y	$G + \tilde{T}^e$	Z	$E + R \cdot B$	

Definitions:

$$M = R \cdot \pi^m \cdot \bar{M}$$

$$E = R \cdot \pi^e \cdot \bar{E}$$

$$\tilde{T}^m = t^m \cdot R \cdot \pi^m \cdot \bar{M}$$

$$\tilde{T}^d = t^d \cdot p^d \cdot D^d$$

$$\tilde{T}^e = t^e \cdot R \cdot \pi^e \cdot \bar{E}$$

$$GDP = P^x \cdot X + \tilde{T}^d$$

All other variables are defined in Table 1.

215

Table 7.1

TWO-SECTOR, THREE-GOOD, CGE MODEL

Real flows

(1) $X = G(E, D^S)$

(2) $Q^s = F(M, D^D)$

(3) $Q^D = C/pq + Z/pq$

(4) $E/D^s = g_2(P^e, P^d)$

(5) $M/D^D = f_2(p^m, p^t)$

Nominal flows

(6) $T = t^m \cdot R \cdot \pi^m \cdot M +$
$t^d \cdot P^d \cdot D^d -$
$t^e \cdot R \cdot \pi^e \cdot E$

(7) $Y = P^x \cdot X + R \cdot \bar{B} + G$

(8) $C = \bar{s} \cdot Y$

(9) $S = Y - C$

Accounting identities

(i) $P^x \cdot X \equiv P^e \cdot E + P^d \cdot D^S$

(ii) $P^q \cdot Q^S \equiv P^m \cdot M + P^t \cdot D^D$

(iii) $P^q \cdot Q^D \equiv Y$

Prices

(10) $P^m = (1 + t^m) \cdot R \cdot \pi^m$

(11) $P^e = (1 + t^e) \cdot R \cdot \pi^e$

(12) $P^t = (1 + t^d) \cdot P^d$

(13) $P^x = g_1(P^e, P^d)$

(14) $P^q = f_1(P^m, P^t)$

(15) $P^x = \bar{P}$

Equilibrium conditions

(16) $D^D - D^S = 0$

(17) $Q^D - Q^S = 0$

(18) $\pi^m \cdot M - \pi^e \cdot E = \bar{B}$

(19) $Z - S = 0$

(20) $T - G = 0$

Endogenous variables

E:	Export good
M:	Import good
D^S:	Supply of domestic good
D^D:	Demand for domestic good
Q^S:	Supply of composite good
Q^D:	Demand for composite good
P^e:	Domestic price of export good
P^m:	Domestic price of import good
P^d:	Producer price of domestic good
P^t:	Consumer price of domestic good
P^x:	Price of aggregate output
P^q:	Price of composite good
R:	Exchange rate
T:	Net government revenue
G:	Net government expenditure
Y:	Total income
C:	Aggregate consumption
S:	Aggregate savings
Z:	Aggregate investment

Exogenous variables

π^m:	World price of import good
π^e:	World price of export good
t^m:	Tariff rate
t^e:	Export subsidy rate
t^d:	Indirect tax rate
$\bar{s}$:	Average savings rate
X:	Aggregate output
$\bar{P}$:	Numeraire price index
$\bar{B}$:	Balance of trade

NOTES AND REFERENCES

1. This part of the review draws heavily on Robinson (1989a).

2. Robinson (1989b) provides a general survey of work with multisector models of developing countries. De Melo (1988), Roland-Holst and Tokarick (1989), and Whalley (1989) provide complementary surveys of trade-focussed CGE models. Devarajan (1989) surveys CGE models of taxation and natural resources applied to developing countries. Hertel (1989b) surveys recent work on including agriculture in CGE models. Shoven and Whalley (1984) review earlier work with tax and trade models applied to developed countries.

3. See Saler (1959) and Swan (1960).

4. Indeed, it can be shown that if we were to specify separate Cobb-Douglas production functions for D and E which depend on, say, capital and labour, then the implied production possibility frontier is locally a CET function. See Devarajan, Lewis, and Robinson (1989).

5. In a multisector model, we disaggregate by sectors and assume that imports and domestic goods in the same sector category are imperfect substitutes, following Armington (1969).

6. The model would be unchanged if we defined a utility function with total absorption, Q, as the only argument.

7. Pyatt and Round (1985) provide a good introduction to SAMs and a number of examples of their uses.

8. For the demand equation, one must show that nominal income doubles when all prices double, including the exchange rate. Tracing the elements in Equations 6 and 7, it is easy to demonstrate that nominal income goes up proportionately with prices.

9. Dervis, de Melo, and Robinson (1982), Chapter 6, discuss this relationship in detail.

10. This approach can be seen as a reasonable approximation for a single country model. In multicountry models, of course, endogenizing world prices presents a number of problems.

11. Empirical problems with this specification have been a thorn in the side of modellers since the early days of linear programming models. For a survey, see Taylor (1975).

12. Dervis, de Melo, and Robinson (1982) specified a logistic export function in place of equation 4 in Table 1. It can be shown that their logistic function is locally equivalent to the function that is derived from the CET specification.

13. See, for example, Allston *et al.* (1989).

14. Recent work with "specific factors" models in international trade also tends to support the view. See, for example, Magee (1978) who argues that political pressure for import protection in the United States is organised along industry lines rather than, say, by ownership of factor of production (as would be predicted by the Stolper-Samuelson model). Work with CGE models supports this view. Empirically, even large shocks tend to have little effect on economy-wide wage-rental ratios, but large effects on the sectoral composition of value added. Hanson, Robinson, and Tokarick (1989) discuss the issue in a model of the United States.

15. He is the one that used the term "uniformalist". Dixit (1985) and Mitra (1986) also discuss the theory as applied to trade policy in open economics.

16. This particular result depends on the nature of the second-best initial situation. In the small model, we assume that the indirect tax rate on the domestic good is less than optimal.

17. That model was developed in 1978 for a World Bank mission in Turkey, and is described in Dervis, de Melo, and Robinson (1982).

18. Representative studies include: Dervis, de Melo, and Robinson (1982, Turkey); Lewis and Urata (1984, Turkey); Condon, Robinson, and Urata (1985, Turkey); Ahmed *et al.* (1985, Egypt); Clarette and Whalley (1986, Philippines); Kis, Robinson, and Tyson (1989, Hungary); and Robinson and Tyson (1985, Yugoslavia). See also de Melo (1988).

19. In their model, the fixprice regime is modelled directly, not by using an *ad valorem* equivalent.

20. Robinson and Tyson (1985) argue that the disruption caused by the introduction of extensive import rationing in Yugoslavia may well have led to short-term efficiency losses that exceeded the value of the rents.

21. Note that one has to be careful in defining what constitutes an efficiency loss. A bribe is a lump-sum transfer and involves no efficiency loss. When James Watt lobbied the US Department of Housing and Urban Development, some part of his fee represented a bribe. The only efficiency loss was the social opportunity cost of his time, which was probably not that large.

22. See Harris (1985), Cox and Harris (1985), de Melo and Tarr (1989), and work in progress by Burniaux and Waelbroeck (1989). Dixon (1978) was an early contributor to this literature and provided some suggestive calculations for Australia, although not in a full CGE model.

23. Although Romer (1988) specifies a model with imperfect competition and externalities arising from investment in R&D. See also the survey by Krugman (1989).

24. Helpman (1988) surveys some of the externality models and relates them to recent work in trade theory. De Melo and Robinson (1986b) present a model with externalities linked to exporting which is designed to capture the major features of manufacturing export-led growth in many semi-industrial countries.

25. See, for example Higgs (1986, 1989); Hertel and Tsigas (1988); Hertel, Thompson, and Tsigas (1989); Robinson, Kilkenny, and Adelman (1989); and Kilkenny and Robinson (1989).

26. See Loo and Tower (1989) and Sadoulet and de Janvry (1989). The archetype models by Sadoulet and de Janvry represent a major advance in CGE modelling of agriculture in developing countries in terms of specification of agricultural technology, sectoral disaggregation, and the incorporation of income distribution effects.

27. Burniaux *et al.* (1989), Table 11a.

28. See Sadoulet and de Janvry (1990).

29. See Kilkenny and Robinson (1989).

30. The current official position of the United States, apparently, is that this was their position all along.

31. See the references cited in footnote 2.

32. De Janvry and Sadoulet (1987) survey the treatment of agriculture in CGE models of developing countries.

33. See US Department of Agriculture, Economic Research Service (1988).

34. The exceptions are:

    a) CGE models of the United States by Kilkenny and Robinson (1988, 1989); Robinson, Kilkenny, and Adelman (1989); and Hanson, Robinson, and Tokarick (1989); and

    b) A linked set of CGE models of EC countries and the Common Agricultural Policy (CAP) by Harrison, Rutherford, and Wooton (1989).

    These models incorporate the various programmes explicitly, albeit in a fairly stylised way. The US models were developed at the USDA and are implemented with the GAMS software. The core model is described in Robinson, Hanson, and Kilkenny (1989) and the software is described in Brooke, Kendrick, and Meeraus (1988).

35. The terminology used was "coupled" versus "decoupled" programmes. For coupled programmes, benefits are related to output, and hence affect production decisions by farmers. Decoupled

programmes have no effect on production decisions. Rausser and Wright (1987) proposed developing measures of producer incentive equivalents (or PIEs).

36. See Newman, Fulton, and Glaser (1987) for a comparison of agricultural policies in the United States and the European Community.

37. Kilkenny and Robinson (1988) compare models using the *ad valorem* approach and explicit modelling of programmes, and show that even when simulating complete liberalization, the *ad valorem* modelling approach leads to errors in estimating the impact of policy changes.

38. Whalley and Wigle (1989) and de Gorter and Fisher (1989) present models that endogenize the decision by farmers to participate in programmes which require the farmer to "set aside" land from production. While suggestive, these approaches have not yet been implemented within a CGE model.

39. The USDA macro model is described in Malley (1989). In addition to USDA base-line projections, detailed sectoral productions are given in Food and Agricultural Policy Research Institute.

40. Adelman and Robinson (1988) use a CGE model to analyse the impact of macro shocks in the 1982-86 period on US agriculture.

41. Robinson (1989a, b) discusses the theoretical issues and surveys recent models.

42. This work is in response to recent policy interest in the distributional impact of World Bank and IMF structural adjustment and stabilization packages. See, for example, Bourguignon, Branson, and de Melo (1989). De Janvry, Fargeix, and Sadoulet (1989) present a model of Ecuador in this tradition which has a more detailed specification of income distribution and the agricultural sectors.

BIBLIOGRAPHY

ADELMAN, I. and S. ROBINSON, "Macroeconomic Shocks, Foreign Trade, and Structural Adjustment: A General Equilibrium Analysis of the United States Economy, 1982-1986", in Colin Carter and Walter Gardiner, eds., *Elasticities in International Agricultural Trade*, Boulder, Colorado: Westview Press, 1988.

AHMED, S., A. BHATTACHARYA, W. GRAIS, and B. PLSEKOVIC, "Macroeconomic Effects of Efficiency Pricing and the Public Sector in Egypt", Staff Working Paper No. 726, World Bank, 1985.

ALLSTON, J. M., C. A. CARTER, R. GREEN, and D. PICK, "Whither Armington Trade Models", *American Journal of Agricultural Economics*, forthcoming.

ARMINGTON, P., "A Theory of Demand for Products Distinguished by Place of Production", *IMF Staff Papers*, Vol. 16, 1969.

BAKER, D., M. HALLBERG, and D. BLANDFORD, "U.S. Agriculture Under Multilateral and Unilateral Trade Liberalization — What the Models Say", Paper A.E.&R.S. 200, Department of Agricultural Economics and Rural Sociology, The Pennsylvania State University, University Park, Pennsylvania, 1989.

BALASSA, B. *et al.*, *Development Strategies in Semi-Industrial Countries*, Baltimore, Maryland: Johns Hopkins University Press, 1982.

BHAGWATI, J. and T.N. SRINIVASAN, "Revenue-Seeking: A Generalization of the Theory of Tariffs", *Journal of Political Economy*, Vol. 88, 1980.

BOURGUIGNON, F., W. H. BRANSON, and J. de MELO, "Adjustment and Income Distribution: A Counterfactual Analysis", Working Paper No. 2943, National Bureau of Economic Research, April, 1989.

BROOKE, A., D. KENDRICK, and A. MEERAUS, *GAMS: A User's Guide*, Redwood, California: The Scientific Press, 1988.

BURNIAUX, J.-M. and J. WAELBROECK, "Preliminary Results of Two Experimental Models of General Equilibrium with Imperfect Competition", paper presented at the Fourth IIASA Task Force Meeting on Applied General Equilibrium Modeling, Laxenburg, Austria, August 23-25, 1989.

BURNIAUX, J.-M., F. DELORME, I. LIENERT, J.P. MARTIN, and D. van der MENSBRUGGHE, "Economy-Wide Effects of Agricultural Policies in OECD Countries: Final Results", draft paper, Economics and Statistics Department, OECD, Paris, 1989.

CHAMBERS, R.G., "Tariff Reform and the Uniform Tariff", preliminary draft, May 1989.

CLARETTE, R. and J. WHALLEY, "Equilibrium in the Presence of Foreign Exchange Premia", University of Western Ontario, processed.

CONDON, T. and J. de Melo, "Industrial Organization Implications of QR Trade Regimes: Evidence and Welfare Costs", processed, Country Economics Department, The World Bank, 1986.

CONDON, T., S. ROBINSON, and S. URATA, "Coping with a Foreign Exchange Crisis: A General Equilibrium Model of Alternative Adjustment Mechanisms", *Mathematical Programming Study*, No. 23, issue edited by Alan Manne under the title *Economic Equilibrium: Model Formulation and Solution*, 1985.

COX, D. and R. HARRIS, "Trade Liberalization and Industrial Organization: Some Estimates for Canada", *Journal of Political Economy*, Vol. 93, No. 1, 1985.

DAHL, H., S. DEVARAJAN, and S. van WIJNBERGEN, "Revenue-Neutral Tariff Reform: Theory and an Application to Cameroon", discussion paper No. 1986-25, Country Policy Department, The World Bank, May, 1986.

DERVIS, K., J. de Melo, and S. ROBINSON, "A General Equilibrium Analysis of Foreign Exchange Shortages and Adjustment Mechanisms in a Developing Economy", *Economic Journal*, Vol. 91, December, 1981.

DERVIS, K., J. de MELO, and S. ROBINSON, *General Equilibrium Models for Development Policy*, Cambridge: Cambridge University Press, 1982.

DEVARAJAN, S., "Taxation and Natural Resources in Computable General Equilibrium Models of Developing Countries", *Journal of Policy Modeling*, Vol. 10, No. 4, 1989.

DEVARAJAN, S. and J.D. LEWIS, "Structural Adjustment and Economic Reform in Indonesia: Model-Based Policies versus Rules of Thumb", HIID Development discussion paper, Harvard University, in D. Perkins and M. Roemer, eds., *Reforming Economic Systems*, forthcoming.

DEVARAJAN, S. and D. RODRIK, "Trade Liberalization in Developing Countries: Do Imperfect Competition and Scale Economies Matter?" *American Economic Review*, May 1989.

DEVARAJAN, S., J.D. LEWIS, and S. ROBINSON, "Policy Lessons from Two-Sector Models", Kennedy School of Government, Harvard University, processed, 1989.

DEWATRIPONT, M. and G. MICHEL, "On Closure Rules, Homogeneity, and Dynamics in Applied General Equilibrium Models", *Journal of Development Economics*, Vol. 26, No. 1, June 1987.

DIXIT, A., "Tax Policies for Open Economies", in A. Auerbach and M. Feldstein, eds., *Handbook of Public Economics*. New York: North-Holland/Elseveir, 1985.

DIXON, P.B., "Economies of Scale, Commodity Disaggregation and the Costs of Protection", *Australian Economic Papers*, June, 1978.

FOOD AND AGRICULTURAL POLICY RESEARCH INSTITUTE, "FAPRI United States and World Agricultural Outlook", Staff Report No. 2-89, Iowa State University and University of Missouri-Columbia, April 1989.

GARDNER, B., "Some Recent Studies of Agricultural Trade Liberalization", in A. Maunder and A. Valdés (eds.), *Agriculture and Governments in an Interdependent World*, proceedings of the XX International Conference of Agricultural Economists, Aldershot, England: Dartmouth, 1989.

de GORTER, H. and E.O.N. FISHER, "The Dynamic Effects of Agricultural Subsidy Programs in the United States", working papers in Agricultural Economics, No. 89-9, Department of Agricultural Economics, Cornell University, Ithaca, New York, 1989.

GRAIS, W., J. de MELO, and S. URATA, "A General Equilibrium Estimation of the Effects of Reductions in Tariffs and Quantitative Restrictions in Turkey in 1978", in Srinivasan and Whalley (below), 1986.

HANSON, K., S. ROBINSON, and S. TOKARICK, "United States Adjustment in the 1990's: A CGE Analysis of Alternative Trade Strategies", working paper No. 510, Department of Agricultural and Resource Economics, University of California, Berkeley, California, 1989.

HARBERGER, Arnold, "Reflections on Uniform Taxation", paper presented at the 44th Congress of the International Institute of Public Finance, Istanbul, August 1988.

HARRIS, R., "Applied General Equilibrium Analyses of Small Open Economies with Scale Economies and Imperfect Competition", *American Economic Review*, Vol. 74, No. 5, 1985.

HARRISON, G.W., T.F. RUTHERFORD, and I. WOOTON, "The Common Agricultural Policy of the European Communities", Department of Economics, University of New Mexico, Albuquerque, New Mexico, 1989.

HELPMAN, E., "Growth, Technological Progress, and Trade", *Austrian Economic Papers*, Vol. 15, No. 1, 1988.

HERTEL, T.W., "Agricultural Trade Liberalization and the Developing Countries: A Survey of the Models", in this volume.

HERTEL, T.., "Applied General Equilibrium Analysis of Agricultural Policies", paper prepared for the NBER Conference on Applied General Equilibrium Analysis, San Diego, California, September 8-9, 1989.

HERTEL, T.W. and M.E. TSIGAS, "Factor Market Implications of Trade and Policy Liberalization in United States Agriculture", paper prepared for the IATRC Symposium on "Bringing Agriculture into the GATT", Annapolis, Maryland, August 19-20, 1988.

HERTEL, T.W., R.L. THOMPSON, and M.E. TSIGAS, "Economywide Effects of Unilateral Trade and Policy Liberalization in United States Agriculture", in Stoeckel, Vincent, and Cuthbertson (below), 1989.

HIGGS, P.J., "The Taxation of Australian Agriculture Through Assistance to Australian Manufacturing", in Stoeckel, Vincent, and Cuthbertson (below), 1989.

HIGGS, P.J., Adaptation and Survival in Australian Agriculture, Melbourne: Oxford University Press, 1986.

de JANVRY, A. and E. SADOULET, "Agricultural Price Policy in General Equilibrium Models: Results and Comparisons", American Journal of Agricultural Economics, Vol. 69, No. 2, May 1987.

de JANVRY, A., A. FARGEIX, and E. SADOULET, "Economic, Welfare, and Political Consequences of Stabilization Policies: A General Equilibrium Approach", paper prepared in support of the World Development Report 1990, World Bank, Washington, DC, 1989.

KILKENNY, M. and S. ROBINSON, "Modeling the Removal of Production Incentive Distortions in the United States Agricultural Sector", in A. Maunder and A. Valdés (eds.), Agriculture and Governments in an Interdependent World, proceedings of the XX International Conference of Agricultural Economists, Aldershot, England: Dartmouth, 1989.

KILKENNY, M. and S. ROBINSON, "Economywide Implications of Agricultural Liberalization in the United States", USDA/ERS Staff Report, forthcoming.

KIS, P., S. ROBINSON, and L.D. TYSON, "Computable General Equilibrium Models for Socialist Economies", in L. Bergman, D.W. Jorgenson, and E. Zalai, eds., General Equilibrium Modeling and Economic Policy Analysis, New York: Basil Blackwell, 1989.

KRUEGER, A.O., "The Political Economy of the Rent-Seeking Society", American Economic Review, Vol. 643, No. 3, 1974.

KRUEGER, A.O., "The Experience and Lessons of Asia's Super Exporters", in V. Corbo, A. Krueger, and F. Ossa, eds., Export-Oriented Development Strategies: The Success of Five Newly Industrializing Countries, Boulder, Colorado: Westview Press, 1985.

KRUGMAN, P.R., "Industrial Organization and International Trade", in R. Schmalensee and R. Willig, eds., Handbook of Industrial Organization, Amsterdam: North-Holland, forthcoming.

LEWIS, J. D. and S. URATA, "Anatomy of a Balance of Payments Crisis: Application of a Computable General Equilibrium Model to Turkey, 1978-1980", Economic Modelling, Vol. 1, No. 3, July, 1984.

LOO, T. and E. TOWER, "Agricultural Protectionism and the Less Developed Countries: The Relationship between Agricultural Prices, Debt Servicing Capacities, and the Need for Development Aid", in Stoeckel, Vincent, and Cuthbertson (below), 1989.

LUCAS, R.E., Jr., "On the Mechanics of Economic Development", Journal of Monetary Economics, Vol. 22, 1988.

MAGEE, S.P., "Three Simple Tests of the Stolper-Samuelson Theorem", in P. Oppenheimer, ed., Issues in International Economics, Oriel Press, 1978.

MALLEY, J.R., "Analysing Alternative Economic Policies with a Small Multi-Country Macroeconomic Model", Journal of Mathematical and Computer Programing, forthcoming.

de MELO, J., "Computable General Equilibrium Models for Trade Policy Analysis in Developing Countries: A Survey", Journal of Policy Modeling, Vol. 10, No. 4, 1988.

de MELO, J. and S. ROBINSON, "Product Differentiation and Trade Dependence of the Domestic Price System in Computable General Equilibrium Trade Models", in Theo Peeters, Peter Praet, and Paul

222

Reding, eds., *International Trade and Exchange Rates in the Late Eighties*, Amsterdam: North-Holland, 1985.

de MELO, J. and S. ROBINSON, "Product Differentiation and the Treatment of Foreign Trade in Computable General Equilibrium Models of Small Economies, *Journal of International Economics*, forthcoming.

de MELO, J. and S. ROBINSON, "Productivity and Externalities: Models of Export-Led Growth", Trade Policy Division, Country Economics Department, The World Bank, processed, 1989.

de MELO, J. and D. TARR, "A General Equilibrium Analysis of United States Foreign Trade Policy", World Bank, April, processed, 1989. MITRA, Pradeep, "Revenue Raising Tariffs: Theory and an Application to India", Country Economics Department, The World Bank, processed, 1986.

NEARY, J.P. and K. ROBERTS, "The Theory of Household Behaviour Under Rationing", *European Economic Review*, Vol. 13, 1980.

NEWMAN, M., T. FULTON, and L. GLASER, "A Comparison of Agriculture in the United States and the European Community." Foreign Agricultural Economic Report No. 233, US Department of Agriculture, Economic Research Service, Washington, DC, 1987.

PYATT, G. and J.I. ROUND, eds., *Social Accounting Matrices: A Basis for Planning*, Washington, DC: The World Bank, 1985.

RAUSSER, G. and B. WRIGHT, "Alternative Strategies for Trade Policy Reform", working paper prepared for the Benjamin E. Lippincot Symposium on Policy Co-ordination in World Agriculture, April 22-24, University of Minnesota, 1987.

ROBINSON, S., "Computable General Equilibrium Models of Developing Countries: Stretching the Neoclassical Paradigm", working paper No. 513, Department of Agricultural and Resource Economics, University of California, Berkeley, California, 1989a.

ROBINSON, S., "Multisectoral Models", in H.B. Chenery and T.N. Srinivasan, eds., *Handbook of Development Economics*, Amsterdam: North-Holland, 1989b.

ROBINSON, S. and L.D. TYSON, "Foreign Trade, Resource Allocation, and Structural Adjustment in Yugoslavia: 1976-1980", *Journal of Comparative Economics*, Vol. 9, 1985.

ROBINSON, S., K. HANSON, and M. KILKENNY, "The Structure and Properties of the USDA/ERS Computable General Equilibrium (CGE) Model of the United States", Staff Report, Economic Research Service, US Department of Agriculture, forthcoming.

ROBINSON, S., M. KILKENNY, and I. ADELMAN, "The Effect of Trade Liberalization in Agriculture on the U.S. Economy: Projections to 1991", in Stoeckel, Vincent, and Cuthbertson (below), 1989.

ROLAND-HOLST, D., and S.P. TOKARICK, "General Equilibrium Modeling for Trade Policy: An Overview", Research Division, Office of Economics, US International Trade Commission, Washington, DC, November, 1989.

ROMER, P., "Increasing Returns and Long-Run Growth", *Journal of Political Economy*, Vol. 94, 1986.

ROMER, P., "Endogenous Technological Change", Economics Department, University of Chicago, processed, 1988.

RONINGEN, V.O. and P.M. DIXIT, "Economic Implications of Agricultural Policy Reform in Industrial Market Economies", USDA Staff Report No. AGES 89-36, Washington, DC, 1989.

SADOULET, E. and A. de JANVRY, "Growth and Welfare Effects of a GATT Agreement in Agriculture on the Low Income Countries: An Integrated Multimarket-General Equilibrium Analysis", in this volume.

SALTER, W., "Internal and External Balance: The Role of Price and Expenditure Effects", *Economic Record*, Vol. 35, 1959.

SHOVEN, J., and J. WHALLEY, "Applied General Equilibrium Models of Taxation and International Trade: An Introduction and Survey", *Journal of Economic Literature*, Vol. 22, September, 1984.

SRINIVASAN, T.N. and J. WHALLEY, eds., *General Equilibrium Trade Policy Modeling*, Cambridge, Massachusetts: MIT Press, 1986.

STOECKEL, A.B., *Intersectoral Effects of the CAP: Growth, Trade, and Unemployment*, Canberra: Australian Government Publishing Service, 1985.

STOECKEL, A.B., D. VINCENT, and S. CUTHBERTSON, eds., *Macroeconomic Consequences of Farm Support Policies*, Durham, North Carolina: Duke University Press, 1985.

SWAN, T., "Economic Control in a Dependent Economy", *Economic Record*, Vol. 36, 1960.

TAYLOR, L., "Theoretical Foundations and Technical Implications", in C.R. Blitzer, P.B. Clark, and L. Taylor, eds., *Economy-Wide Models and Development Planning*, London: Oxford University Press, 1975.

U.S. DEPARTMENT OF AGRICULTURE, Economic Research Service, "Estimates of Producer and Consumer Subsidy Equivalents: Government Intervention in Agriculture, 1982-86", USDA/ERS, Staff Report No. AGES880127, Washington, DC, 1988.

WHALLEY, J., "General Equilibrium Trade Modelling Over the Last Five Years", paper presented at the NBER Applied General Equilibrium Conference, San Diego, California, September 8-9, 1989.

WHALLEY, J. and R. WIGLE, "Endogenous Participation in Agricultural Support Programs and *Ad Valorem* Equivalent Modeling", CSIER, University of Western Ontario, 1989.

Chapter 8

WOULD DEVELOPING COUNTRIES BENEFIT FROM AGRICULTURAL TRADE LIBERALIZATION IN OECD COUNTRIES?

by

Klaus Frohberg, G. Fischer and K.S. Parikh

INTRODUCTION

In this paper, we analyse the impact of agricultural trade liberalization by OECD countries on developing countries. Results of three different scenarios are presented. The scenarios differ in the assumption about what countries liberalize; all OECD countries, the European Community alone, and only the United States. Results of these scenarios are also published elsewhere by Parikh *et al.* (1988) and discussed there in detail. Here we look at the results more from the perspective of developing countries.

This paper is organised in the following way. The next section provides a brief discussion of the model used for the current analysis. Thereafter, the results of the three scenarios are described. The paper ends with some concluding remarks.

A Brief Description of the Basic Linked System and the Implementation of Agricultural Trade Liberalization

The Basic Linked System (BLS) of IIASA consists of a set of national and regional models linked through trade and capital flows. The 20 detailed national models designed for policy analysis which are included comprise approximately 80 per cent of the world's agricultural production, trade, land availability and population. The remaining part of the global food and agriculture system is divided into 14 regions, each of which is represented by a simplified model, called hereafter the country-group model.

The model system is of the general equilibrium type both at the national and international level. Exchange equilibria are established with the system, i.e. production does not adjust when exchange takes place. Money is assumed to be neutral. Care has been taken in modelling the responses of various economic actors in the system; i.e. of governments, producers and consumers. There is a mutual dependence in the behaviours of these actors which is built in through several linkages and through the imposition of the accounting identities of quantity and financial flows. The system covers the entire global economy and hence there are no unaccounted-for supply sources and demand sinks.

Among the global models used for studying the impact of agricultural trade liberalization the BLS is one of the few which have been estimated econometrically using time series data. Among the general equilibrium models it is the only one which is so estimated.

Models are often put together synthetically, using estimates found in the literature and/or by benchmarking the parameters to one year's data. Although econometric estimation does not guarantee that the model specification represents correctly the important economic relations, at least one is assured that the structure chosen is consistent with past observation over a larger and richer data set covering many years. With benchmarked parameters one is less likely to find out if the chosen specification is inappropriate or whether it is consistent with observed data.

Of course, estimating a model as large as the BLS must be done in several stages. The BLS was estimated in a modular way, i.e. each national model was estimated independently of the other national models. Within a national model, several subsystems were identified for estimation most often requiring nonlinear, simultaneous equation estimation techniques.

Most models are based on time series obtained from FAO's Supply Utilisation Accounts, National Income Accounts and the World Tables of the World Bank.

Prices are endogenously calculated in the model system for the domestic markets and the world market. Both producers and consumers respond to changes in relative prices. The government in each country has a range of policy instruments at its disposal. These are taxes, income transfers, input subsidies, procurement, rationing, and a set of instruments dealing with international trade.

The specifications of the BLS are basically in the tradition of neoclassical theory. Its dynamic features recognise that all factor allocations cannot adjust instantaneously when economic conditions change. Once committed to a certain economic activity, capital cannot be easily shifted to other uses. Much of agricultural capital is specific to this sector. Hence it is not allowed to move between agriculture and non-agriculture in the BLS. Investment allocation between the sectors, however, does depend on the marginal returns in the two sectors and thus through accumulation does affect the capital stock over time.

Also in agriculture, capital is not easily reallocated between different uses. A plough cannot be used to milk a cow, though a cowshed can be converted for storing grain. This observation is supported by the relatively low returns to scale that were obtained as estimates for capital used in various agricultural production activities even though constant returns to scale were imposed for the agricultural sector as a whole for all three primary factors considered in the BLS; i.e. for land, labour and capital.

Labour is also not as mobile and labour markets are not as perfect as always to find employment where its marginal value product is highest. Many factors contribute to this behaviour (skill differences, institutional constraints, closed shops, cost of migration-like searching for a new job and employing a new person, etc.) which might be conveniently summarised as transaction cost. These factors also explain some of the differences between returns to labour in agricultural and in non-agricultural activities obtained as estimation results. Another determinant of these differences is the assumption that full employment exists in both sectors. The time series used for estimation consists of total manpower in agriculture and non-agricultural activities including unemployment, disguised or not. The share of unemployment in each of the two time series is not known.

The specification of the labour migration function includes both expected average income of labour in agriculture relative to non-agriculture (expected income parity) and expected relative marginal value products of labour as determining factors. The higher the expected income disparity in agriculture and the lower its expected marginal return relative to that in non-agricultural activities the more labour leaves agriculture. As with the other functions in the BLS, these labour migration functions have also been estimated. It is therefore not surprising to find in results obtained from simulations up to the year 2000 that migration is not strong enough to equalise expected marginal returns to labour between agriculture and non-agriculture because the differences were "observed" over the entire estimation period. In this respect, the BLS deviates from most computable general equilibrium models which stipulate that labour is allocated to equate marginal returns in all sectors of the economy. This is obtained in the BLS only within agriculture.

Needless to say, a more elaborate specification of the labour market could take account of the unemployment situation in the economy. Yet it is not clear that this would alter the essential results of the model simulations. The discrepancy found in marginal returns over the historical period is likely to further influence migration behaviour, also under trade liberalization. Not all of the national models have the same structure. Among those with a different structure are the models for China, the CMEA, India and the United States. The China model has been constructed on a limited information basis and is used mainly for consistency checking. It therefore does not provide all desired characteristics for an in-depth analysis of Chinese policies and is not used for such purposes. The CMEA model is an aggregated version for all European CMEA countries including the Soviet Union. It is a model which focuses on the long-term prospects of these countries and includes many features to characterise the planning aspects of their economies. The Indian model determines supply by allocating land, fertilizer and capital to the various commodities and demand by distinguishing ten expenditure classes. The consumption pattern of each class is described by a Linear Expenditure System. The US model includes a conventional supply module for output determination and a Linear Expenditure System for calculating the consumption levels.

The following countries are represented in the BLS by models with a common structure: Argentina, Australia, Austria, Brazil, Canada, Egypt, Indonesia, Japan, Kenya, Mexico, New Zealand, Nigeria, Pakistan, Thailand, Turkey and the European Community. The EC is modelled by aggregating all member countries except Greece, Portugal and Spain which are included in one of the country group models.

Out of the 14 country-group models 13 are comprised of developing countries only. The grouping of these models is based on geographic considerations, and their likely behaviour on the international market which is based on the country's income level and whether the country is an exporter or importer of nutrients for human consumption. In this way, five models have been identified for Africa, three for Latin America, three for Far East Asia, and two for Near and Middle East Asia. In principle, these country-group models follow an exogenously specified supply and demand pattern which was taken from scenario B of the FAO study *Agriculture: Toward 2000*. Deviations from those trends are possible, however, if the price structure at the world market changes from the base year. For this purpose own- and cross-price elasticities of supply and demand derived from results of detailed models for developing countries are introduced in all 14 country-group models.

The model system provides annually calculated information on quantities produced, demanded, traded and stockpiled, on sets of prices, input use and allocation, and on macroeconomic variables. Table 8.1 lists the commodities in which international trade is carried out and their composition.

The analysis of trade liberalization in this study is restricted to removal of distortions between trade prices and domestic prices of the agricultural commodities. The scenarios do not remove all distortion-creating measures from all markets and production activities. Thus they move towards free trade and not to total trade liberalization, so that one should characterise them as freer trade scenarios.

For some countries, additional changes are introduced. In the case of the United States, land set aside programmes are also removed in the scenarios in which it liberalizes trade. The wedges which exist between the consumer and producer prices for wheat, coarse grain, and bovine and ovine meat in Japan and for wheat in Nigeria are also set to zero when these countries liberalize; and in Canada the quota imposed on dairy production in the reference run is removed when it liberalizes. The dairy quota of the EC is not included in the model. The monetary compensatory amounts (MCAs) that are given to member countries of the EC under its Common Agricultural Policy (CAP) are still implicitly included in the producer prices as the EC

227

is treated as one aggregated country. The kind of distortion resulting from this is very difficult to assess. Since the MCAs are small in comparison to the EC's protection against third countries, one might argue that their impact is not very drastic. This is especially so if one works with the hypothesis that the MCAs only distort the (absolute) price levels between the EC member countries but not the relative prices of agriculture, which are the same in all member countries of the EC.

Thus in our analysis of trade liberalization where these calculated tariff equivalents are removed, only the supports given at the border are abolished. The supports given to domestic production or/and consumption are not affected by the removal of tariff equivalents. This holds for all types of domestic assistance, e.g. input subsidies, storage subsidies, production quotas (except Canada), consumer subsidies, transportation subsidies, marketing licensing, export credits, and insurance.

Trade liberalization is partial in our analysis in yet another sense. Agricultural trade liberalization is achieved in the scenarios by removing protection from agricultural commodities only. As reliable information on the protection of non-agricultural activities is not available, it is not removed from that sector.

Results of Three Scenarios of Agricultural Trade Liberalization

The trade liberalization scenarios are simulated over the years 1981 to 2000 in annual increments and assessed relative to a reference scenario which describes future events under the assumption that past policies, especially trade policies, are continued. A discussion of the reference scenario can be found in Parikh et al. (1988).

The level of agricultural protection is not constant over time in the reference scenario. If the policy objective of a government is to maintain constant domestic prices and the world market prices decrease over time, the tariff rates are reduced over time. In the BLS, domestic price policies are assumed to incorporate a number of policy objectives such as levels of self-sufficiency in different commodities and parity of income from farming to income from other activities. The relative weights given to these objectives are reflected in the estimated coefficients of price transmission functions. These functions relate relative prices on the world market, past relative prices on the domestic market and self-sufficiency ratios to domestic relative prices. Such characterisations of government policies imply that when world market prices change substantially due to OECD countries' agricultural trade liberalization a non-trade liberalizing country does not necessarily transmit fully these changes to its domestic prices. The results of the liberalization scenarios reflect the level of protection which the reference scenario has built in. In general, protection levels expressed as tariff equivalents are lower in the later years of the time period under investigation than what they are for the earlier years. Also, the relatively high level of protection observed during the mid-1980s is not reflected in the reference scenario.

One may also note that in the BLS, part of the difference between the border price and domestic producer price is accounted for by domestic transportation cost. This difference remains even when the country liberalizes agricultural trade since domestic transportation cost is not a tariff and is not removed.

Not for all years are simulation results presented. We emphasize the year 2000, the last year of the simulation. This is 15 years after an assumed liberalized trade in agricultural products becomes effective. To indicate the dynamic adjustments to trade liberalization, some tables also report on the situation simulated for 1990, i.e. five years after the free trade is introduced.

As indicated above, the scenarios discussed in this report deal with a partial removal of distortions. While trade distortions in agriculture are removed, those in non-agriculture and all

228

domestic distortions are left in place. For such a partial liberalization it is possible that the welfare outcome is inferior to the situation with all distortions in place. A more detailed discussion on this point is given in Parikh *et al.* (1988). The arguments brought forward in this respect are mainly of a static nature. In dynamic situations, an initial improvement might turn into a loss with the passing of time. This is conceivable when a large country substantially increases its global export share for a commodity for which it cannot impose an optimal tariff under free trade.

Agricultural Trade Liberalization in OECD Countries

The following OECD countries are assumed to liberalize agricultural trade: Australia, Austria, Canada, EC, Japan, New Zealand, and the United States, for which explicit models exist in the BLS. Turkey is excluded from liberalization as one of the less developed OECD countries. The other OECD countries are included in a country group model and also are assumed to liberalize.

With trade liberalization by OECD countries the average world market prices of agriculture products relative to non-agriculture would be higher by 9 per cent by the year 2000 compared to the reference run (see Table 8.2). This modest *average* rise is strongly influenced by the very small increase in the price of the commodity group "other food" which has a high aggregation weight at the world market and has relatively low protection in OECD countries. This aggregate consists mainly of fruits, vegetables, fats and oils, sugar and tropical products. In fact, for the commodities of primary importance to the producers in OECD countries, such as cereals, protein feed, and bovine and ovine meat, the increases in world market prices compared to the reference scenario are of the order of 10-20 per cent and, for dairy products, more than 30 per cent.

While in this scenario the trade liberalizing OECD countries set their domestic agricultural prices equal to their levels at the world market, taking into account transportation cost and quality and compositional differences, the developing countries are assumed to follow the same price policies as in the reference scenario. This implies that price transmission from world market to domestic markets remains unaltered. But both price and protection levels may change.

This indeed is the case if one compares the relative changes of agricultural to non-agricultural prices reported in Table 8.3 with those in Table 8.2. Although the weights used at national levels to calculate an aggregate price for agriculture differ from those employed for the world market and hence, create a problem of comparing price changes, developing countries can be seen as not transmitting fully the increase of agricultural prices onto their domestic markets. Only Argentina and Kenya follow a price policy of transmitting approximately the entire world market price increases. Most developing countries improve the domestic terms of trade of agriculture only marginally. This price policy influences substantially the impact of this scenario on developing countries' growth.

The macroeconomic indicators given for different countries in Table 8.3 show how agricultural trade liberalization by OECD countries affects patterns of development. Since agricultural GDP is a small part of the economies of OECD countries, the increase in the relative price of agriculture resulting from trade liberalization has a relatively small impact on savings and real investment. The changes in total investment, and consequently in total capital, are very small and so are the adjustments in factor allocation between agriculture and non-agriculture. Thus, GDP in OECD countries improves by 0.3 per cent or less, except for New Zealand, whose GDP in 2000 increases by 1.6 per cent over the reference run value. Agriculture captures a higher share of total GDP in New Zealand than in other OECD countries and the increases in world prices are especially strong for commodities for which New Zealand has a high export share.

The overall response of value added in developing countries to a liberalization of agricultural trade in OECD countries is modest and not even of uniform direction. In some developing countries, a reorientation of factor allocation in favour of agriculture, as suggested by changes in relative prices, does not positively influence economic growth. But one should also bear in mind that the measure "GDP at prices of 1970" is likely to be somewhat biased due to index number problems. This is supported by the observation that evaluated at current prices GDP does not contract in those cases in which constant GDP declines, although one would expect the latter to move in the opposite direction.

Global GDP calculated at 1970 world prices increases by 0.22 per cent in the year 2000. Though 0.22 per cent seems to be a small amount, it is not negligible. Valued at 1980 dollars, this would amount to $31 billion, whereas official development assistance given by OECD countries in 1980 was around $27 billion. The gain for the OECD countries in GDP valued at 1980 world prices is 0.57 per cent in 2000, which is nearly $50 billion. At these prices, the loss for developing countries is 0.02 per cent of GDP or $1 billion in 2000. The remaining difference is borne by centrally planned economies.

The small effect on global GDP at constant prices is also an outcome of the fact that agriculture in the OECD countries is a small part of the economy. The efficiency gains to be realised by removing agricultural trade distortions may be expected to be small. Though in the trade liberalization scenario all border distortions for agriculture were removed, the non-agricultural sector included as a single aggregate in the model does not capture the gains that could be realised by reallocating factors among the different subsectors of non-agriculture.

Associated with the higher agricultural world market prices under OECD trade liberalization is an expansion of world agricultural production and trade. Though production increases are observable for all agricultural commodities except non-food agriculture, the changes are rather modest (see Table 8.2). The largest increase is observed for bovine and ovine meats and reaches only 3.3 per cent in the year 2000. In spite of sizeable changes in world prices, these small changes in production reflect the fact that demand for human consumption, particularly in the OECD countries, where the major price changes take place, is price inelastic. As discussed above the income changes between the reference scenario and the OECD trade liberalization scenario are not very substantial. Thus changes in demand between the two scenarios are small, and so are the corresponding increases in production at the global level.

Production changes in OECD countries, however, are substantial, particularly in those which are highly protected. The OECD countries with low levels of protection and the developing countries increase their agricultural production to fill the gap created by output reduction of the highly protected OECD countries. In terms of agricultural GDP, the OECD countries with low protection gain more than twice as much as all developing countries together. This implies farm incomes change as well.

Brazil, Mexico and Turkey, all with agricultural self-sufficiency ratios exceeding 1.0, indicate an increase in the volume index of agricultural output but a decline in total value added. The explanation of this unexpected result can be found in the fact that labour migration out of agriculture is slowed down in these countries although the marginal product of labour is higher in non-agricultural activities than in agriculture. These differences in marginal product, which get narrowed over time, are historically observed and reflect various rigidites in labour mobility between sectors. The historically "observed" incentives to migrate out of agriculture get smaller in the trade liberalization scenario compared to the reference run. Therefore, a smaller number of people leave agriculture to find jobs in the non-agricultural sector. Looked at from the other side, prices fall in non-agriculture relative to agriculture making it less attractive for agricultural labour to migrate.

The modest increases at the global level in production are associated with much larger increases in trade levels. This is as one would expect, since liberalization should increase specialisation by countries, exploiting their comparative advantage and leading to larger trade.

As the major OECD countries remove protection, leading in general to lower domestic agricultural prices, domestic demand increases and domestic supplies fall, with imports increasing to fill the gap. Higher world market prices for agricultural products reduce imports by developing country importers, as their demand falls and domestic production increases to the extent that world market prices are transmitted to consumers and producers in these countries. The sum total of the outcome is a considerable change in the volume of agricultural trade for most countries and commodities, as is seen in Tables 8.2 and 8.3. Global trade expands in all commodities except wheat and coarse grains. The most striking percentage change occurs in rice trade. Global rice exports increase by 37 per cent in 2000, mainly as a result of higher imports by Japan. Since in this model different varieties of rice are not distinguished, an implicit assumption is made that either other countries will supply the type of rice Japanese like to eat or that the Japanese consumers will develop tastes for other types of rice. The world trade in animal products also increases by 12-35 per cent in 2000.

The most significant shift in the world trade pattern is that the highly protected OECD countries reduce agriculture exports and increase their agricultural imports when all OECD countries liberalize agricultural trade (see Table 8.4). One would expect that the OECD countries with low protection would export a large part of the additional production stimulated by the higher prices under trade liberalization. However, this is the case only for wheat and protein feed. For bovine and ovine meat, as well as dairy products, exports even fall. The reason is that for these products the United States has a high protection. When trade is liberalized, the lower beef and milk prices stimulate consumption in this country by more than 10 per cent. Because of the large volumes this more than offsets the fall in demand in other low-protected OECD countries.

The developing countries as a group are thus able to export more of their traditional agricultural products — rice and other food — at higher prices. They also reduce their imports of wheat, coarse grain, and dairy products, and turn rice imports into exports; as a result, their agricultural trade surpluses in 2000 are nearly tripled compared to the reference scenario.

The increased volume of agricultural trade also results in increased trade of non-agriculture since the overall trade balance for each country is assumed to be not very responsive to changing world market conditions. In particular the developing countries as a group are able to expand significantly (by 21 per cent) their imports of the aggregate non-agricultural products under OECD country trade liberalization. Also, the EC and Japan must export considerably more of this aggregate to pay for the higher bill of agricultural imports.

Trade liberalization by OECD countries may be expected to improve incomes and welfare in these countries, though one cannot rule out the possibility that some of them may actually be worse off. The non-OECD countries, themselves not liberalizing their agricultural trade, are affected mainly through changes in their terms of trade, which can become significant as world market prices for some commodities show substantial changes. Another question is to what extent the developing countries can take advantage of the changed world market conditions for their domestic policies.

In comparing the welfare of a country in alternative situations as represented by the two scenarios, the problems of finding a satisfactory measure or a consistent indicator are almost insurmountable. We have therefore used a range of macroeconomic and welfare indicators for comparison including gross domestic product at prices of 1970, parity of farm income to non-farm income, equivalent income, consumption cost, per capita calorie intake, and the number of people hungry. Whether a country gains or loses cannot always be determined unambiguously.

Values of these indicators are reported on in Table 8.3. For ease of comparison they are qualitatively summarised in Table 8.6. It should be noted that not all the indicators are available for all the national models. In terms of equivalent income or cost of consumption the gains or losses in the year 2000 are rather small. The largest changes in equivalent income are a 2.6 per cent loss for Indonesia in 1990 and a 2.1 per cent gain for Argentina in 2000.

Brazil, Mexico, Egypt and Turkey show losses in terms of all indicators and must be considered as clear losers under trade liberalization by OECD countries. Similarly, Indonesia is a loser since it either indicates negative impacts or insignificant changes in all indicators.

India should also be considered a loser, on balance, as it loses on all indicators except GDP. The very small improvements in the latter may be considered to be negligible as all the consumer and social welfare indicators show losses.

By contrast, Kenya shows a clear gain in all indicators and so does Nigeria. Argentina may be considered a qualified gainer since improvements do occur in the consumer welfare indicators. The increase in hunger affects a relatively small number of people since the projected level of hunger in the reference scenario is very small. In principle, Argentina should be able to help the poor who become worse off, from the large income gains at the aggregate level.

Pakistan and Thailand gain on some indicators and lose on others, and thus they are not unequivocal gainers or losers.

The welfare gains of OECD countries are easy to understand. These countries remove distortions, and thus domestic resources are allocated more efficiently. These gains in production efficiency are not lost due to adverse changes in terms of trade as a consequence of trade liberalization. Terms of trade improve for all OECD countries except the EC and Japan, for both of which equivalent income and consumption cost comparisons are still favourable, since efficiency gains outweigh these losses.

Austria, which also has relatively high protection, does not gain significantly in production, but enjoys a considerable improvement of its terms of trade. The food price index remains almost unchanged, and thus consumers benefit, as reflected in equivalent income and consumption cost comparisons.

The United States has relatively low nominal protection rates, but specific commodity programmes provide a much greater degree of protection, and hence the adjustments in the United States are somewhat similar to those in highly protected countries. It shows increases in value added, improving terms of trade, and declining food prices. US consumers thus gain.

Australia and Canada are the only OECD countries (except Turkey, which does not liberalize in this scenario) that show losses in equivalent income. Even though the losses are very small, Canada's loss is surprising.

The per capita calorie intake indicator does not suffer from the index number problem to the same extent as the GDP measure does. Values of this indicator for the group of developing countries are shown in Table 8.5. The average per-capita calorie intake in the developing countries decreases under agricultural trade liberalization by OECD countries, and consequently the incidence of hunger increases (see also Table 8.3). Thus, for the developing countries as a group, agricultural trade liberalization by OECD countries is not attractive from a nutritional point of view unless additional efforts are undertaken to minimise the negative impact on the poor in these countries.

The extent of the adverse impact on developing countries is small enough that compensation schemes could be devised to ensure that the incidence of hunger does not increase under agricultural trade liberalization by the OECD countries. Nonetheless, the results do show that the trade policies of the developed countries affect the developing countries and that a balanced outcome in trade negotiations is desirable.

232

A removal of the EC's protectionist policies leads to a price increase on the world market of about 5 per cent (Table 8.7). This effect is more pronounced in the initial years after introduction of the new policies than in later years after other countries have time to adjust to the new situation. All relative agricultural prices increase, with the largest rise occurring in dairy products (about 15 per cent), the commodity the EC protects most. It is therefore not surprising that bovine and ovine meat indicates the next largest price increase, because in many member countries of the EC the dual-purpose cow is prevalent; i.e. the production of milk and beef is interwoven so that assistance to dairy production also means assistance to beef production. The price of wheat also increases above the average in 2000. This is again not surprising, since the EC has a rather high share of total volume traded in this product. The world market prices of all other commodities increase, but less than average.

There is a contraction of trading in grains as a result of the reduction of the EC's exports of wheat and imports of coarse grains. Dairy products are traded substantially less in the initial period. This is a result of the rather sharp drop in the EC's dairy exports, which is not taken up by other countries. Initially, many importing countries increase their dairy production, reducing global trade, but over the long run the dairy trade increases. As can be seen from Table 8.7, production contracts as well, but by a very small amount.

The largest percentage increase in trade volume is shown for bovine and ovine meat. Again, this is a direct impact of the EC, which imports considerably more of this commodity because of lower production and higher demand.

Production at the global level changes only marginally. Also total consumption does not change significantly. Since many countries shield their domestic prices from world price changes, demand is rather price inelastic and income does not change noticeably in the developing countries, where income elasticity of food is high. Therefore production cannot increase. The non-EC countries need the price increase on the world market as an incentive to increase their production to compensate for the output reduction in the EC. Even for those commodities that are largely used as feed (coarse grains and protein feed), no substantial change in global demand can be observed. The quantities used as feed change by less than 1 per cent (coarse grains up and protein feed down). This indicates that the shift in production of animals does not lead to a drastic change in feeding ratios.

The effect of trade liberalization by the EC on developing countries may be broadly summarised as follows (see Table 8.9). In terms of equivalent income, consumption cost and number of people hungry, the developing countries lose from such a policy whereas the developed countries gain. However, there are a few exceptions to this more general observation. Argentina, Nigeria, and Pakistan gain in equivalent income but the number of people hungry increases in these countries, while Kenya gains by having fewer people hungry and with respect to consumption cost. Among the developed countries, Austria and Japan lose with respect to equivalent income.

If one looks for an explanation of why the developing countries are in general worse off under EC trade liberalization, then one must first note that for all of them the agricultural price rise observed on the world market is transmitted to their domestic markets, but in varying degrees (see Table 8.8). As a result of this price stimulation, value added by agriculture increases. However, the response of total GDP to an agricultural price increase is mixed. In only two developing countries (Kenya and Nigeria) is this response positive, in most it is insignificant, and in some it is even negative. Among the latter are Brazil, Egypt, Mexico and Turkey. In those countries the increase in agricultural GDP is more than offset by a decrease in non-agricultural GDP. The reason is that agriculture's increased competitiveness attracts more resources, which are drawn from non-agricultural activities although their marginal productivity is higher in this sector. This behaviour reflects the reverse of what happened in the past when resources were retained in agriculture in spite of a higher return in non-agriculture.

The higher agricultural prices lead also to an increase in food prices. Lacking additional income, this amounts to a lowering of calorie intake (see Table 8.8). Therefore the number of hungry people rises.

From a trade point of view, it is interesting to see that the terms of trade improve under EC trade liberalization for almost all developing countries (See Table 8.8). Brazil, Egypt, Indonesia, and Nigeria are exceptions to the rule. All four of them have a very low self-sufficiency ratio for wheat (the ratio for Indonesia and Nigeria is zero). As already mentioned, wheat has the largest price increase of all crops on the world market, and only dairy products show a greater rise.

A large share of the changes in the ECs trade pattern is claimed by the United States. This underlines the importance of the United States as an exporter of agricultural products, but also the competition between the EC and the United States for shares of the world market. It is especially interesting that the United States expands its wheat exports while it reduces those of coarse grains. This can be explained by the improvement of the wheat price relative to that of coarse grains, as observed in the world market. Accordingly, US wheat production is increased while US coarse grain output remains unchanged. Since animal production is increased, and with it consumption of grains as feed, the new export pattern results. However, the United States cannot prevent the world market prices of the two grains from diverging rather strongly under EC trade liberalization, attaining a difference comparable to their distant past historical levels. The export subsidies for wheat that the EC grants its exporters depress the wheat price on the world market in the reference scenario.

A similar observation can be made for dairy products. The relative price increase for dairy products on the world market under EC trade liberalization is a result of the drop of the export restitutions. The changed volumes of dairy products traded by the EC cannot be compensated for by other countries, although all countries except India react with an increase in dairy production, especially the United States. But as mentioned earlier, the assumption that Canada does not change the policy of supply management to remain just self-sufficient does also contribute to the rise of the world market prices. If Canada were to mobilise its production potential for dairy products, the price increase would be smaller. In addition, it is to be noted that the EC model did not incorporate a dairy quota for production when the reference run was made and hence might overstate quantities exported.

Overall, the impact of an agricultural trade liberalization by the EC on growth of developing countries is small. Only a few countries gain, among them Argentina, Kenya, Nigeria and Pakistan. Within these countries, income in agriculture increases relative to non-agriculture.

Unilateral Trade Liberalization by the United States

By and large, the changes in world market prices follow the protection levels that are imposed by the United States in the reference run. The removal of a positive (negative) protection measure decreases (increases) the domestic price and hence stimulates (reduces) domestic demand while simultaneously cutting (increasing) production. As a result, the world market prices increase (decrease) but with differences in magnitude depending on the response of the other countries to a world market price change. The only exception to this rule is non-food agriculture. In spite of a change in the US trade position from an exporter to an importer, other countries respond to the changed structure of all world market prices, and the world market price of agriculture declines. On the average, world prices increase by 5 per cent under US agricultural trade liberalization (see Table 8.10).

The price changes translate into only small production adjustments. Global production of all agricultural products except bovine and ovine meat is hardly changed. In other words, global output responds only marginally to price changes. This, of course, is also influenced by the elasticity of transmission of world market price variations to domestic prices.

Bovine and ovine meat is one of the products generating significant changes in global trade. All other commodities are traded globally at approximately the same volume. The 25 per cent increase in the volume of bovine and ovine meat traded globally is caused mainly by the United States, which imports 163 per cent more than in the reference run. This increase of imports comes partly (70 per cent) from additional exports and partly (30 per cent) from decreased imports by other countries, mainly developing ones. Argentina provides half of the additional exports (0.8 million tonnes), which makes developing countries as a group net exporters of bovine and ovine meat in 2000 under this scenario. The increased world market price leads to a 4 per cent higher production and a 1 per cent lower consumption in this group.

Dairy products also show a substantial change in trade pattern. The United States becomes an importer of these commodities. The export share of the United States is largely gained by the EC and by New Zealand, the latter exporting an additional 1.3 million tonnes of dairy products, but also by a number of developing countries, especially India, which switches from being an importer to an exporter. Canada continues to remain absent from the world market because of its policy of self-sufficiency. All other commodities show much smaller changes in their trade pattern. The United States increases its exports and its world market shares of wheat and coarse grains because of the reduction in feed use. The additional exports are mainly imported by developing countries.

Table 8.11 shows the changes occurring in each country. In general, the overall adjustments are relatively small. As can also be seen from Table 8.12, most developing countries either lose or do not indicate changes in their welfare measures. Based on equivalent income and GDP, gains are shown for Argentina, Nigeria and Pakistan. On the other hand, neither of these three countries can improve their hunger problem. Farmers in most developing countries are relatively better off in comparison to those engaged in non-agricultural activities under a unilateral trade liberalization in agricultural products by the United States.

Summarising Comments

OECD countries as a whole as well as the EC and the United States protect their agriculture. World market prices increase when these countries liberalize agricultural trade. Global efficiency gains due to a better allocation of resources are relatively small. In absolute terms, trade liberalization by OECD countries leads to a gain of approximately $50 billion at 1980 prices per year, which is the equivalent of 20 per cent of their agricultural GDP. The gains, by and large, accrue to the countries that liberalize. The impact on growth of developing countries is small, even 15 years after agricultural trade was liberalized.

Under a unilateral liberalization by either the EC or the United States, farmers in the liberalizing country lose relative to those engaged in non-farming activities. In the OECD country free trade scenario farmers in the EC and in Japan also lose in parity. The developing countries, in general, are worse off though some developing countries do gain. Higher world market prices of cereals and ruminant products hurt many food importing developing countries. Their terms of trade decrease making it more difficult for them to import the food necessary to maintain their level of nutrient intake. Hunger increases in many of these countries. Though this increase is rather small, any worsening is unacceptable.

To offset the negative effects occurring in some of the developing countries those countries which benefit could transfer some of their gains to the needy ones. If these transfers would be targeted to the low income groups, such a policy should be more effective in helping the poor than one in which the rich countries protect their agricultural sector. Of course, some redistributive policies in the OECD countries may be necessary, as well, if the income disparity widens between the farming and non-farming populations.

The increase in agricultural world market prices observed for all three scenarios presented in this paper indicates that nominal tariffs are not a good indicator of what the compensation would have to be to protect farm income. For example, in 2000 the EC policy protects agriculture in the reference scenario by 40 per cent on the average. When OECD countries liberalize their agriculture trade, farm income in the EC drops by only 7 per cent.

We will end with a note on further use of the BLS. With the passage of time, this model system — as any other model — becomes less relevant for policy analysis unless it is updated. Such efforts were under way at the time this report was written. Most national models are re-estimated with some modifications in the specifications if necessary. The US model is being completely revised. The country-group models are being updated using the FAO's revised study, *World Agriculture Toward 2000* (1988). For the purpose of using the BLS to strengthen their own capabilities for policy analysis and to analyse further international policies six research institutes joined in the Food and Agriculture Network (FAN).

Table 8.1

COMMODITIES AND UNITS USED IN INTERNATIONAL TRADE

Commodity aggregate	Main components	Type of measurement
Wheat		Physical weight
Rice, milled		Physical weight
Coarse grains		Physical weight
Bovine and ovine meat		Carcass weight
Dairy products		Milk equivalent
Other animals	Pork, poultry, eggs fish	Protein equivalent
Protein feed	Oilcakes, fish/meat meal	Protein equivalent
Other food	Oils, fats, sugar, vegetables, fruits, coffee, cocoa, tea	Unit value of exports (expressed in $) averaged over the period 1969-70
Nonfood agriculture	Clothing fibre, industrial crops	Averaged over the period 1969-70
Nonagriculture	All nonagricultural outputs	1970 domestic prices (expressed in $)

Table 8.2

PERCENTAGE CHANGES IN WORLD MARKET PRICES[1], GLOBAL NET EXPORTS AND GLOBAL PRODUCTION IN 2000 DUE TO OECD COUNTRY TRADE LIBERALIZATION
(Relative to the reference scenario)

	Relative prices	Net exports[2]	Production
Wheat	18	-2	0.5
Rice	21	37	1.2
Coarse grains	11	-5	1.7
Bovine and ovine products	17	35	3.3
Dairy products	31	13	1.9
Other animal products	-0	17	0.8
Protein feed	13	5	2.0
Other food	5	10	0.2
Nonfood agriculture	-2	5	-1.5
Nonagriculture	--	17	-0
Total agriculture[3]	9	--	--

1.   Relative to the nonagricultural price.
2.   Sum of net exports.
3.   Price weighted by production.

Note: +0 = small positive change.
            -0 = small negative change.
            -- = non relevant or not calculated

Table 8.3

PERCENTAGE CHANGES OF SOME MACROECONOMIC AND WELFARE INDICATORS IN 1990 AND 2000
UNDER OECD COUNTRY TRADE LIBERALIZATION
(Relative to the reference scenario)[1]

Indicator[2]	Argentina		Australia		Austria		Brazil		Canada		Egypt	
GDP70	0.1	+0	0.3	0.3	0.2	-0	-0.3	0.2	-0.1	0.1	-0.4	-1.1
GDPA70	8.1	13.9	1.7	2.5	-1.1	1.5	0.8	1.0	16.6	7.2	1.5	2.1
GDPNA70	-0.7	-1.4	0.2	0.1	0.2	-0.1	-0.3	-0.2	-0.5	-0.1	-0.8	-1.6
AG HCons at P70	-1.5	-0.5	-0.1	0.8	1.5	1.3	-0.3	-1.1	-1.9	-1.2	-0.1	-0.3
NAG HCons at P70	1.2	2.8	-0.5	-0.2	0.3	0.1	-0.9	-0.9	0.1	0.1	-0.4	-1.6
Trade deficit 70	-4.6	-3.2	-1.0	0.1	-7.4	1.3	0.5	-7.6	0.5	1.5	-3.0	-1.2
AG trade deficit 70	32.9	35.0	4.2	3.1	19.2	-31.7	-281.8	33.5	24.3	7.7	-86.1	-115.6
Trade/GDP at WP	57.7	57.6	22.5	23.2	44.6	42.9	-2.7	20.6	51.1	21.3	15.7	29.7
GDPA at WP70	8.1	11.1	1.8	1.3	2.2	5.4	4.1	2.4	5.2	2.0	3.0	5.5
Investment	2.7	2.0	1.8	1.2	0.3	0.3	+0	0.6	0.4	0.5	1.0	-0.5
Total capital	1.0	1.5	0.6	0.9	+0	0.3	0.1	0.3	0.1	0.1	0.4	0.1
AG vol. index WP70	8.1	12.5	2.0	1.7	-0.9	1.8	3.7	2.2	12.6	4.8	3.0	5.4
Net calories produced	7.9	-10.9	0.5	-12.6	-15.8	-21.9	7.7	5.1	-19.4	-13.4	3.3	7.0
Agricultural capital	10.4	20.4	9.4	13.7	-0.8	2.0	9.8	7.3	21.2	8.6	3.3	6.2
Agricultural labour	7.8	14.7	1.4	4.3	-1.7	2.1	0.8	0.3	19.8	6.2	1.4	1.8
Total acreage	10.3	1.4	-0.5	-0	+0	-0	4.4	3.3	2.4	2.8	0.4	3.2
N fertilizer	12.6	28.2	29.0	8.6	-8.4	-5.2	3.7	2.1	15.4	-1.7	3.7	6.5
P_n/P_n	17.3	12.1	22.6	14.5	1.1	7.5	7.8	11.3	15.5	11.3	8.5	5.4
Crop price index	7.9	6.7	-6.4	-8.2	-10.3	-7.7	5.6	7.9	8.6	8.0	8.0	5.3
Food price index	13.5	7.7	18.1	12.1	-1.2	0.6	5.8	7.0	6.5	6.5	4.9	3.0
Terms of trade	19.4	19.8	16.8	19.7	23.6	52.9	-1.6	7.2	29.8	18.9	-2.7	-5.6
AG SSR	8.1	9.3	-0.8	-1.0	-1.6	1.0	4.1	2.5	-0.2	-2.5	2.8	5.8
Parity	17.4	11.0	22.6	12.2	1.6	6.8	7.7	12.1	12.2	12.1	8.0	5.7
Equivalent income	0.7	2.1	-0.5	-0.1	0.4	0.2	-0.9	-0.9	-0.1	-0	-0.3	-1.2
Calories/capita	-0.9	-0.3	0.3	0.5	0.3	0.3	-0.5	-0.9	-0.8	-0.4	-0.2	-0.5
Protein/capita	-1.2	-0.6	0.3	0.6	0.4	0.3	-0.4	-1.1	-1.3	-0.4	-0.2	-0.5
Number hungry	18.4	6.7	-	-	-	-	12.3	10.1	-	-	-	-

Table 8.3 (continued)

Indicator[2]	India		Indonesia		Japan		Kenya		Mexico		New Zealand	
GDP70	0.2	0.1	-0.1	0.1	0.2	0.3	0.9	1.8	-1.0	-2.1	1.4	1.6
GDPA70	0.1	0.1	0.3	0.4	-5.7	-5.2	2.8	5.3	1.9	3.6	10.3	14.0
GDPANA70	0.2	0.1	-0.3	-0	0.3	0.4	0.6	0.6	-1.2	-2.4	+0	-0
AG HCons at P70	+0	-26.2	-0.2	-0.1	5.2	4.8	2.4	2.3	-1.3	-0.7	1.8	2.3
NAG HCons at P70	0.2	0.2	-7.8	-3.5	0.6	0.8	0.3	2.6	-0.8	-2.1	3.8	3.5
Trade deficit 70	-1.1	0.4	1.9	0.9	6.6	4.1	-4.4	-1.4	-3.5	-4.3	-15.9	123.0
AG trade deficit 70	18.7	211.9	-1.7	-2.6	38.8	48.9	-8.6	13.8	59.1	75.8	14.3	23.2
Trade/GDP at WP	3.9	5.7	13.8	3.9	41.8	44.7	-4.9	8.0	15.4	22.5	36.0	37.5
GDPA at WP70	-0.1	0.1	0.1	0.3	-2.3	-3.8	0.1	4.6	2.4	4.4	10.9	15.4
Investment	-0.5	0.3	1.1	0.6	-0.9	-0.4	5.6	5.1	-0.3	-2.1	7.4	5.6
Total capital	–	–	0.4	0.5	-0.4	-0.6	2.2	3.8	+0	-1.0	2.7	4.5
AG vol. index WP70	-0.1	0.1	0.2	0.3	1.0	1.4	0.1	4.4	2.4	4.2	7.9	12.5
Net calories produced	0.2	0.7	0.3	0.6	283.7	130.9	-0.8	4.9	12.2	15.9	9.5	20.5
Agricultural capital	–	–	1.2	2.0	-12.6	-21.9	6.5	11.8	2.4	3.4	17.1	29.9
Agricultural labour	–	–	0.1	-0	-3.8	-5.4	+0	+0	2.8	6.1	1.0	2.6
Total acreage	+0	-33.0	+0	+0	-10.6	-6.0	–	–	-0	-0	–	–
N fertilizer	0.8	3.9	0.1	0.7	-32.3	-46.1	-4.7	1.6	10.0	8.6	-7.3	-2.5
P_t/P_n	4.6	3.0	3.2	2.3	-36.1	-35.3	14.8	10.6	4.6	-0.7	25.2	15.8
Crop price index	–	–	2.3	1.9	-41.7	-42.1	7.5	4.7	5.5	1.0	7.4	6.1
Food price index	–	–	1.8	1.4	-18.8	-19.2	12.9	10.4	2.1	-0.4	10.6	9.1
Terms of trade	11.1	14.6	-16.5	-8.6	-9.3	-9.7	8.2	4.3	5.1	1.4	24.2	16.6
AG SSR	0.5	0.6	0.1	0.3	-7.9	-8.7	-1.8	2.6	3.6	4.7	7.2	10.9
Parity	2.5	1.3	3.4	2.7	-37.3	-35.2	17.6	15.7	3.1	-3.4	36.6	28.5
Equivalent income	-0.5	-0.2	-2.6	-1.5	1.1	1.1	–	–	-0.9	-1.9	–	–
Calories/capita	-0.7	-0.9	-0.1	+0	4.2	3.8	1.9	1.8	-0.8	-0.5	0.4	0.5
Protein/capita	-0.8	-1.0	-0.2	-0.1	3.6	3.7	2.3	2.1	-1.4	-0.9	0.4	0.5
Number hungry	3.1	5.6	1.0	+0	–	–	-8.1	-8.8	12.4	8.8	–	–

Table 8.3 (continued)

Indicator[2]	Nigeria		Pakistan		Thailand		Turkey		United States		EC	
GDP70	0.8	1.2	0.3	-0.1	0.1	0.1	-0.3	-0.1	+0	0.1	0.1	0.2
GDPA70	3.0	6.5	2.0	3.2	1.6	2.7	5.7	3.1	1.4	1.8	-3.0	-7.1
GDPNA70	0.1	0.1	-0.3	-1.2	-0.2	-0.3	-1.2	-0.6	+0	0.1	0.2	0.4
AG HCons at P70	-0.3	0.3	-1.8	-0.5	-0.9	-0.6	-0.1	-0.5	0.5	3.0	2.0	1.4
NAG HCons at P70	1.7	2.9	4.5	2.6	2.0	1.7	-0.1	0.3	0.4	1.1	0.1	0.2
Trade deficit 70	-0.9	0.8	-2.4	-0.1	-3.2	-0.6	0.2	-2.4	2.9	2.3	3.5	3.0
AG trade deficit 70	-14.4	-20.8	-118.0	-147.2	14.5	23.2	29.0	13.6	4.6	1.9	42.7	46.8
Trade/GDP at WP	-7.6	-13.1	7.4	8.0	16.2	22.8	21.5	11.6	24.9	23.5	17.7	24.0
GDPA at WP 70	-2.5	5.9	2.8	3.9	4.0	5.8	4.0	1.0	2.0	2.6	-3.0	-7.3
Investment	2.7	2.2	1.8	0.2	2.6	1.2	-0.1	1.3	--	--	-0.2	-0
Total capital	1.2	2.2	0.5	0.5	0.7	1.0	0.5	0.8	--	--	-0.1	-0.1
AG vol. index WP70	2.6	6.1	3.3	4.1	2.9	4.4	4.2	2.1	1.7	1.8	-4.4	-8.4
Net calories produced	3.2	5.9	8.6	8.1	9.1	10.2	7.1	4.3	5.6	9.3	-15.5	-11.0
Agricultural capital	3.9	8.5	2.1	3.4	4.2	7.3	6.6	4.7	--	--	-1.8	-5.4
Agricultural labour	2.2	4.8	1.1	2.4	+0	+0	2.7	0.9	--	--	-5.8	-11.7
Total acreage	3.5	4.6	0.4	0.6	--	--	1.3	1.7	2.9	2.5	-1.8	-2.2
N fertilizer	3.4	8.2	13.2	7.8	4.0	5.9	4.2	1.7	--	--	-16.5	-16.9
P_n/P_n	4.8	0.3	4.9	0.6	12.1	7.7	1.4	7.3	2.8	-2.0	-10.5	-8.8
Crop price index	3.9	1.1	4.2	1.5	13.7	10.1	3.9	6.6	--	--	-13.2	-14.6
Food price index	3.0	0.9	3.0	0.6	5.2	2.9	1.3	3.2	0.3	-3.2	-4.2	-3.7
Terms of trade	-10.0	-7.8	11.3	12.0	8.7	6.7	5.7	9.5	3.5	1.7	-9.1	-8.4
AG SSR	2.8	5.9	5.2	4.8	4.0	5.4	3.2	0.9	1.3	0.5	-6.0	-8.6
Parity	3.8	-0.9	5.0	0.6	14.1	10.8	4.3	9.6	2.8	-2.0	-7.7	-4.0
Equivalent income	+0	1.5	1.3	1.0	--	--	-0.1	0.1	--	--	0.3	0.3
Calories/capita	-0.5	0.4	-1.9	-0.6	0.2	-0.1	-0.1	-0.2	--	--	0.8	0.8
Protein/capita	-0.9	-0.4	-1.9	-0.6	+0	-0.2	-0	-0.2	--	--	1.2	0.8
Number hungry	4.0	-47.4	18.8	8.1	-1.3	1.0	1.7	4.6	--	--	--	--

Table 8.3 (continued)

1. The first figure given for each country is for 1990, the second for 2000.
2. GDP70:   GDP at 1970 prices
   GDPA70:   GDP agriculture at 1970 prices
   GDPNA70:   GDP nonagriculture at 1970 prices
   AG HCons at P70: Human consumption of agricultural products at 1970 prices
   NAG HCons at P70: Human demand for nonagricultural products at 1970 prices
   Trade deficit 70: Trade deficit at 1970 prices
   AG trade deficit 70: Deficit in agricultural trade at 1970 prices
   GDPA at WP70:   GDP agriculture at 1970 world prices
   Investment: Real investment
   Total capital: Capital stock at 1970 prices
   Net calories produced: Net calorie production
   N fertilizer: Nitrogenous fertilizer
   P_a/P_n: Agricultural price index relative to nonagriculture
   AG SSR: Agricultural self-sufficiency ratio
   Parity: Agricultural GDP per person engaged in agriculture divided by nonagricultural GDP per person engaged in nonagriculture

Note. +0 = small positive change.
       -0 = small negative change.
       -- = not relevant or not calculated

242

Table 8.4

TRADE PATTERNS IN REFERENCE SCENARIO AND WITH OECD COUNTRY TRADE LIBERALIZATION

(Figures show net exports)

Commodity	Unit	Low-protected OECD[1] RO,[3] 1980	RO, 2000	F-OECD,[4] 2000	High-protected OECD RO, 1980	RO, 2000	F-OECD, 2000	Developing countries[2] RO, 1980	RO, 2000	F-OECD, 2000
Wheat	10^6t	61.2	106.0	116.9	2.4	3.4	-14.2	-35.6	-76.5	-65.4
Rice	10^6t	2.9	6.3	6.7	-2.1	-3.0	-12.6	-1.9	-4.6	4.5
Coarse grains	10^6t	69.1	155.8	153.1	-26.1	-73.5	-69.4	-7.0	-63.8	-62.5
Bovine and ovine	10^6t	0.2	0.7	0.2	-0.9	-1.2	-2.5	-0.3	-0.2	1.6
Dairy	10^6t	4.6	16.2	14.0	8.8	9.0	5.0	-12.7	-23.5	-18.2
Other animals	10^6t	0.4	0.3	0.4	0.2	0.6	0.4	+0	-0.2	-0.2
Protein feed	10^6t	11.2	16.1	17.0	-9.2	-13.8	-15.2	4.6	4.6	5.3
Other food	10^9*	2.1	3.1	3.6	-5.5	-7.6	-11.2	11.4	15.9	19.9
Nonfood agriculture	10^9*	1.1	1.4	1.7	-3.9	-4.2	-4.6	1.8	2.8	2.9
Nonagriculture	10^9*	-13.8	-14.2	-18.1	-5.2	29.2	38.3	0.6	-33.1	-40.1
Agricultural trade balance	10^9*	13.2	21.8	23.1	-9.1	-13.2	-19.9	7.4	5.9	16.1

*   US $ 1970

1.   Includes Australia, Canada, New Zealand and the United States.
2.   Includes China.
3.   RO refers to reference scenario.
4.   F-OECD refers to OECD country trade liberalization.

Note: +0 = small positive change.

243

Table 8.5

PER CAPITA CALORIE INTAKE AND HUNGER IN DEVELOPING COUNTRIES IN REFERENCE SCENARIO AND THEIR PER CENT CHANGES DUE TO OECD COUNTRY TRADE LIBERALIZATION

Indicator	1990		2000	
	Reference scenario	% change for F-OECD	Reference scenario	% change for F-OECD
Calorie intake (kcal/day)	2 510	-0.13	2 640	-0.3
Persons hungry (10^6)	470	3.3	400	3.6

Note: F-OECD refers to OECD country trade liberalization.

Table 8.6

GAINS AND LOSSES ON MACROECONOMIC AND WELFARE INDICATORS FOR 2000 UNDER OECD TRADE LIBERALIZATION
(Relative to the reference scenario)

Countries	GDP70	Parity	Equiv. income	Consump-tion cost	People hungry
USA	G	L	--	G	--
Canada	L	G	L	L	--
Australia	NS	G	L	G	--
New Zealand	G	G	--	G	--
Austria	NS	G	G	G	--
EC	G	L	G	G	--
Japan	G	L	G	G	--
CMEA	L	--	--	ID	--
China	--	--	--	ID	--
Argentina	G	G	G	G	L
Brazil	L	G	L	L	L
Mexico	L	L	L	L	L
Egypt	L	G	L	L	--
Kenya	G	G	--	G	G
Nigeria	G	L	G	G	G
India	G	G	L	L	L
Indonesia	L	G	L	L	--
Pakistan	G	G	G	G	L
Thailand	G	G	--	G	L
Turkey	L	G	L	L	L

Notes:

G, country gains;
L, country loses;
ID, indeterminate;
NS, change not significant;
--, not calculated.

GDP70, GDP at price of 1970; Parity, agricultural GDP per person engaged in agriculture divided by nonagricultural GDP per person engaged in nonagriculture; consumption cost, a comparison of consumption cost between the current scenario and the reference scenario. A gain refers to a situation in which the current consumption bundle is more costly than the bundle of the reference scenario both when evaluated a) at prices of the current scenario; and, b) at prices of the reference scenario. A loss indicates the opposite result.

Table 8.7

PERCENTAGE CHANGES IN WORLD MARKET PRICES[1], GLOBAL
NET EXPORTS AND GLOBAL PRODUCTION IN 2000 DUE TO A
UNILATERAL TRADE LIBERALIZATION BY THE EC
(Compared to the reference scenario)

	Relative prices	Net exports[2]	Production
Wheat	8.7	-2.2	0.6
Rice	1.5	-1.8	0.1
Coarse grains	3.7	-5.0	0.6
Bovine and ovine	6.9	14.4	0.7
Dairy	14.9	1.9	-0.5
Other animal products	5.2	5.2	-0.6
Protein feed	0.3	-0.6	0.2
Other food	2.4	6.7	+0
Nonfood agriculture	2.0	3.1	0.1
Non-agriculture	--	10.1	-0
Total agriculture[3]	4.5	--	--

1.   Relative to the nonagricultural price.
2.   Sum of net exports.
3.   Price weighted by production.

Note: +0 = small positive change.
        -0 = small negative change.
        -- = non relevant or not calculated

246

Table 8.8

PERCENTAGE CHANGES OF SOME MACROECONOMIC AND WELFARE INDICATORS IN 1990 AND 2000 UNDER EC TRADE LIBERALIZATION

(Relative to the reference scenario)[1]

Indicator[2]	Argentina		Australia		Austria		Brazil		Canada		Egypt	
GDP70	+0	+0	0.2	0.2	-0	-0.1	-0	-0.1	-0	-0.1	-0	-0.8
GDPA70	2.7	6.4	2.9	5.2	0.5	1.7	0.2	0.3	3.6	4.9	0.3	1.9
GDPNA70	-0.2	-0.6	-0	-0.1	-0	-0.2	-0.1	-0.1	-0.1	-0.2	-0.1	-1.3
AG HCons at P70	-0.6	-0.2	-0.3	-0.4	0.1	0.1	-0.8	-0.5	0.1	0.3	-0.1	-0.2
NAG HCons at P70	0.4	1.1	0.1	0.2	+0	-0.1	-0.4	-0.3	0.1	0.1	+0	-1.0
Trade deficit 70	-0.6	-0.7	0.6	1.0	3.4	0.8	-3.8	0.8	0.9	1.0	-1.2	0.5
AG trade deficit 70	12.0	16.5	6.8	11.0	-2.4	-21.0	13.2	-136.8	4.9	13.3	-0	-18.5
Trade/GDP at WP	21.5	25.7	13.3	17.0	4.4	-3.5	6.4	-0.6	12.5	21.5	2.6	18.0
GDPA at WP70	3.0	5.4	3.1	4.9	0.1	1.1	0.6	1.8	2.8	4.7	0.5	3.2
Investment	1.1	0.8	0.7	0.6	-0	-0.1	0.3	+0	0.2	+0	0.7	-0.4
Total capital	0.3	0.6	0.2	0.4	-0	-0	0.1	0.1	+0	-0	0.2	0.1
AG vol. index WP70	2.9	5.9	3.1	5.0	0.4	1.3	0.6	1.7	2.9	6.2	0.6	3.3
Net calorie produced	4.1	-3.8	12.5	8.4	2.4	0.9	1.9	2.1	1.8	9.2	1.7	5.0
Agricultural capital	3.6	8.3	3.5	7.9	0.2	1.1	2.1	4.4	4.3	5.7	1.3	3.9
Agricultural labour	2.8	6.8	0.3	1.4	0.5	2.0	0.1	0.3	3.2	6.0	0.3	2.3
Total acreage	4.6	1.4	1.3	+0	+0	-0	1.1	1.7	3.0	1.5	0.4	3.2
N fertilizer	3.4	11.4	23.5	17.3	2.5	2.2	0.4	1.6	3.0	25.1	1.1	4.6
P_f/P_n	7.9	5.4	7.8	5.4	1.5	0.7	5.2	3.8	4.8	2.1	5.2	4.1
Crop price index	4.6	3.1	6.8	6.7	2.1	2.1	3.5	1.9	5.0	3.2	4.3	2.4
Food price index	5.5	3.3	4.9	3.9	0.7	0.5	3.4	2.5	2.1	0.3	2.9	1.7
Terms of trade	8.8	9.1	6.4	5.5	3.9	6.3	1.7	-3.7	7.1	7.9	-0.4	-1.2
AG SSR	3.0	4.4	2.5	4.3	0.2	0.9	0.9	1.7	-0.7	3.3	0.6	3.3
Parity	7.8	4.9	10.7	9.5	1.5	0.4	5.2	3.8	5.2	1.0	4.9	2.9
Equivalent income	0.2	0.9	0.1	0.2	+0	-0.1	-0.4	-0.3	+0	0.1	-0.1	-0.7
Calories/capita	-0.4	-0.2	-0.1	-0.2	0.1	0.1	-0.6	-0.4	+0	0.2	-0.1	-0.1
Protein/capita	-0.4	-0.1	-0.1	-0.2	0.2	0.1	-0.7	-0.4	0.1	0.3	-0.1	-0.1
Number hungry	8.0	3.4	--	--	--	--	6.8	7.8	--	--	--	--

247

Table 8.8 (continued)

Indicator[2]	India		Indonesia		Japan		Kenya		Mexico		New Zealand	
GDP70	0.1	–	-0	+0	-0	-0.1	0.3	0.7	-0.5	-0.8	0.4	0.6
GDPA70	0.1	0.1	0.1	0.2	0.3	1.2	0.7	2.1	0.7	1.8	2.9	4.7
GDPNA70	0.1	–	-0.1	-0	-0	-0.1	0.1	0.3	-0.6	-1.0	+0	+0
AG HCons at P70	+0	0.2	0.1	-0.1	-0	-0.1	0.9	1.0	-0.8	-0.6	0.5	0.7
NAG HCons at P70	0.2	0.2	-2.3	-0.4	-0.2	-0.3	-0	1.2	-0.3	-0.5	1.6	1.4
Trade deficit 70	-0.3	0.7	1.9	0.9	1.7	1.0	-2.3	-0.4	-1.3	-1.4	-5.3	-166.9
AG trade deficit 70	8.4	83.5	1.0	-2.9	-0.6	-3.3	-6.7	5.3	32.7	32.1	4.3	8.4
Trade/GDP at WP	0.9	1.3	5.0	-0.4	4.6	-0.2	-4.0	3.1	5.8	16.1	14.8	14.8
GDPA at WP70	+0	0.1	-0	0.2	-0.1	0.4	-0.6	1.8	1.1	1.9	3.3	5.4
Investment	-0.1	0.4	0.5	0.2	0.1	-0.1	2.6	2.4	+0	-0.8	3.0	2.2
Total capital	–	–	0.1	0.2	+0	+0	0.8	1.7	+0	-0.5	1.0	1.8
AG vol. index WP70	+0	0.1	+0	0.2	-0.3	-0.3	-0.6	1.8	1.1	1.9	2.5	4.7
Net calories produced	0.2	0.4	+0	0.3	-31.9	-17.4	-0.5	1.7	9.9	2.8	2.9	6.1
Agricultural capital	–	–	0.4	0.9	0.4	1.9	2.4	5.3	1.1	2.0	6.0	11.8
Agricultural labour	–	–	0.1	+0	0.5	2.1	+0	+0	1.3	2.1	0.4	1.1
Total acreage	+0	+0	+0	+0	+0	0.8	–	–	-0	+0	–	–
N fertilizer	0.7	1.9	-0.1	0.4	1.4	2.0	-2.7	0.7	6.1	1.9	-2.9	-1.1
P_a/P_n	2.4	1.5	1.7	1.1	4.0	2.7	8.1	5.8	3.5	0.6	13.1	8.4
Crop price index	–	–	1.1	0.5	2.8	1.4	4.5	2.7	3.9	0.7	4.2	2.9
Food price index	–	–	1.0	0.6	2.6	2.0	6.3	4.8	1.6	0.1	5.8	5.2
Terms of trade	4.8	2.8	-5.5	-3.2	-5.1	-2.3	5.1	2.5	3.8	3.9	11.8	7.7
AG SSR	0.2	0.2	-0.1	0.3	0.1	0.6	-1.3	1.0	2.0	2.0	2.0	3.7
Parity	1.4	0.7	1.7	1.2	3.8	1.8	8.7	7.8	2.7	0.3	15.8	12.2
Equivalent income	-0.3	-0.2	-0.6	-0.2	-0.2	-0.2	–	–	-0.4	-0.5	-0.5	–
Calories/capita	-0.2	-0.2	0.2	-0.1	-0	0	0.9	1.0	-0.5	-0.3	0.1	0.2
Protein/capita	-0.3	-0.2	0.1	-0.1	-0.3	-0.3	1.0	1.0	-0.8	-0.6	0.1	0.1
Number hungry	1.1	1.3	-3.1	+0	–	–	-3.7	-4.6	7.4	5.4	–	–

248

Table 8.8 (continued)

Indicator[2]	Nigeria		Pakistan		Thailand		Turkey		United States		EC	
GDP70	0.2	0.2	0.2	+0	-0	0.1	0.1	-0.2	-0	-0	0.1	0.2
GDPA70	0.8	3.3	1.0	1.6	0.2	1.0	1.7	3.6	1.1	2.4	-3.1	-8.9
GDPNA70	+0	-0.1	-0	-0.5	-0	-0.1	-0.2	-0.7	-0.1	-0	0.2	0.5
AG HCons at P70	-0.3	-0	-1.1	-0.5	-0.6	-0.8	-0.4	-0.1	-2.2	-0.8	2.8	1.9
NAG NCons at P70	+0	0.8	2.3	1.4	0.3	0.3	0.3	-0	-0.1	0.1	0.1	0.2
Trade deficit 70	0.8	0.4	-1.0	0.7	-1.4	0.2	-1.0	0.7	1.7	1.3	3.2	2.6
AG trade deficit 70	-4.3	-10.3	-71.5	-83.4	0.3	3.1	10.3	18.3	6.4	4.5	49.3	60.0
Trade/GDP at WP	0.6	-6.5	5.8	4.7	2.4	4.2	5.3	13.3	12.6	12.1	16.9	29.1
GDPA at WP70	0.5	2.7	1.7	2.1	-0.3	0.2	0.7	2.5	0.8	1.3	-2.7	-9.1
Investment	0.8	1.1	1.0	0.1	1.1	0.6	0.9	-0.1	—	—	-0.5	-0.1
Total capital	0.3	1.0	0.2	0.3	0.2	0.4	0.4	0.3	—	—	-0.2	-0.2
AG vol. index WP70	0.5	2.8	2.0	2.2	-0.1	0.6	1.2	2.6	0.9	1.5	-4.6	-10.0
Net calories produced	0.9	2.7	5.9	4.5	0.7	0.1	6.0	4.2	0.5	0.3	-20.7	-18.7
Agricultural capital	0.9	3.8	0.9	1.6	1.2	2.9	2.3	3.8	—	—	-2.4	-7.2
Agricultural labour	0.5	2.2	0.4	1.1	+0	+0	0.3	1.5	—	—	-6.2	-14.9
Total acreage	1.4	2.5	0.5	0.3	-0.4	0.1	1.1	0.7	0.9	0.3	-1.8	-2.2
N fertilizer	0.6	3.7	6.9	4.0	6.0	4.4	1.4	2.8	6.6	3.8	-22.4	-22.7
P_a/P_n	2.2	0.6	2.6	0	4.6	2.1	4.8	0.1	—	—	-16.5	-12.1
Crop price index	1.5	0.8	2.3	0.5	2.9	2.3	3.7	1.8	3.8	1.6	-15.3	-17.8
Food price index	1.5	0.9	1.6	0.1	3.7	2.3	1.9	0.4	7.3	7.2	-7.1	-5.3
Terms of trade	-6.2	-5.3	4.1	3.2	0.1	0.7	5.5	3.2	2.0	1.4	-6.8	-7.5
AG SSR	0.7	2.9	3.1	2.7	6.3	5.6	0.7	2.1	6.6	3.8	-6.7	-10.8
Parity	2.1	0.4	2.9	0.2	—	—	6.3	2.1	—	—	-13.6	-5.7
Equivalent income	-0.3	0.3	0.6	0.5	-0.1	-0.2	0.1	-0	—	—	0.4	0.4
Calories/capita	-0.4	-0.1	-1.2	-0.5	-0.2	-0.3	-0.1	-0.1	—	—	1.2	1.0
Protein/capita	-0.7	-0.3	-1.2	-0.5	0.8	1.7	-0.1	-0	—	—	1.8	1.1
Number hungry	3.4	3.5	11.7	6.9	—	—	3.1	1.6	—	—	—	—

Table 8.8 (continued)

1. The first figure given for each country is for 1990, the second for 2000.
2. GDP70:   GDP at 1970 prices
   GDPA70:   GDP agriculture at 1970 prices
   GDPNA70:   GDP nonagriculture at 1970 prices
   AG HCons at P70:   Human consumption of agricultural products at 1970 prices
   NAG HCons at P70:   Human demand for nonagricultural products at 1970 prices
   Trade deficit 70:   Trade deficit at 1970 prices
   AG trade deficit 70: Deficit in agricultural trade at 1970 prices
   GDPA at WP70:   GDP agriculture at 1970 world prices
   Investment: Real investment
   Total capital: Capital stock at 1970 prices
   Net calories produced: Net calorie production
   N fertilizer: Nitrogenous fertilizer
   P_a/P_n: Agricultural price index relative to nonagriculture
   AG SSR: Agricultural self-sufficiency ratio
   Parity: Agricultural GDP per person engaged in agriculture divided by nonagricultural GDP per person engaged in nonagriculture

Note: +0 = small positive change.
      -0 = small negative change.
      -- = not relevant or not calculated

250

Table 8.9

GAINS AND LOSSES ON SOME MACROECONOMIC AND WELFARE INDICATORS
IN 2000 UNDER EC TRADE LIBERALIZATION
(Relative to the reference scenario)

Countries	GDP70	Parity	Equiv. income	Consump- tion cost	People hungry
US	NS	G	--	ID	--
Canada	NS	G	G	G	--
Australia	G	G	G	G	--
New Zealand	G	G	--	G	--
Austria	NS	G	L	L	--
EC	G	L	G	G	--
Japan	L	G	L	L	--
CMEA	L	--	--	L	--
China	NS	--	--	ID	--
Argentina	G	G	G	G	L
Brazil	L	G	L	L	L
Mexico	L	G	L	L	L
Egypt	L	G	L	L	--
Kenya	G	G	--	G	G
Nigeria	G	G	G	G	L
India	NS	G	L	L	L
Indonesia	NS	G	L	L	--
Pakistan	G	G	G	G	L
Thailand	NS	G	--	G	L
Turkey	L	G	NS	L	L

Notes:

G, country gains;
L, country losses;
ID, indeterminate;
NS, change not significant;
--, not calculated.

For a description of the indicators, see footnote to Table 8.6.

Table 8.10

PERCENTAGE CHANGES IN WORLD MARKET PRICES[1], GLOBAL NET EXPORTS AND GLOBAL PRODUCTION IN 2000 DUE TO UNILATERAL TRADE LIBERALIZATION BY THE UNITED STATES

(Relative to the reference scenario)

	Relative prices	Net exports[2]	Production
Wheat	1.6	2.3	0.6
Rice	0.2	-1.3	-0
Coarse grains	0.8	0.7	1.0
Bovine and ovine meat	14.3	25.2	2.7
Dairy products	39.0	-2.1	1.3
Other animal products	-2.2	0.4	-0.4
Protein feed	0.3	-0.7	0.3
Other food	1.1	2.4	-0.1
Nonfood agriculture	-5.8	-0.4	-1.9
Nonagriculture	--	0.6	-0
Total agriculture	4.6	--	0.2

1. Relative to the nonagriculture price.
2. Sum of net exports.
3. Price weighted by production.

Note: -0 = small negative change.
-- = not relevant or not calculated

Table 8.11

PERCENTAGE CHANGES OF SOME MACROECONOMIC AND WELFARE INDICATORS IN 1990 AND 2000
UNDER US TRADE LIBERALIZATION
(Relative to the reference scenario)[1]

Indicator[2]	Argentina		Australia		Austria		Brazil		Canada		Egypt	
GDP70	+0	-0	+0	0.1	-0	-0	-0.1	-0.1	-0	-0.1	-0.2	-0.2
GDPA70	4.3	9.3	-0.1	1.1	0.3	0.4	0.3	0.1	0.8	1.2	0.4	0.2
GDPNA70	-0.4	-1.0	+0	-0	-0	-0.1	-0.1	-0.1	-0.1	-0.1	-0.3	-0.3
AG HCons at P70	-1.0	-0.5	-0.4	-0.2	+0	+0	0.1	+0	-0.9	-0.6	-0.1	-0.3
NAG HCons at P70	0.4	1.5	-0.2	-0.2	+0	0.1	-0.4	-0.4	-0.1	-0	-0.4	-0.8
Trade deficit 70	-5.1	-2.5	-0.8	0.1	-1.5	0.8	0.5	-0.1	-0.1	0.7	-0.2	0.2
AG trade deficit 70	17.6	22.9	0.8	4.8	-3.4	-8.9	-67.9	4.5	-0.2	3.6	-16.8	-17.3
Trade/GDP at WP	27.3	36.1	4.7	9.1	-1.7	-3.2	-1.3	-0.5	0.2	5.7	1.5	1.4
GDPA at WP70	3.9	7.2	-0.2	2.0	0.4	0.5	1.0	0.3	-1.3	1.2	0.4	0.6
Investment	1.3	1.3	0.4	0.4	+0	-0	+0	0.1	+0	-0	-0.2	-0.2
Total capital	0.5	0.9	0.1	0.3	+0	-0	0.1	0.1	+0	-0	+0	-0.1
AG vol. index WP70	4.1	8.0	-0	2.1	0.2	0.5	0.9	0.4	-0.5	1.6	0.4	0.5
Net calories produced	1.9	-6.6	-4.3	1.1	-1.3	-0.1	2.1	-0.6	-7.2	1.6	-1.0	1.6
Agricultural capital	5.6	12.2	2.1	4.3	0.3	0.5	3.1	2.4	2.4	2.5	0.5	0.4
Agricultural labour	4.5	10.0	0.4	1.4	0.5	0.7	0.3	0.1	2.2	3.0	0.6	0.3
Total acreage	4.1	1.4	-0.3	-0	-0	-0	0.6	0.6	-0.2	0.6	0.3	1.2
N fertilizer	8.2	16.0	-1.5	5.7	-0.3	0.7	-0.4	-0.4	-7.2	4.5	-0	0.7
P_e/P_n	9.2	8.2	5.8	5.8	0.3	0.3	2.8	2.8	1.6	2.3	-0.3	0.1
Crop price index	-0.7	0.4	-0.2	2.2	-0.1	0.7	-0.1	-0.4	-0.7	0.6	-0.6	-0.1
Food price index	8.4	6.4	6.2	6.1	0.1	0.3	2.4	2.4	1.7	1.3	0.2	0.6
Terms of trade	8.2	12.6	4.3	4.4	15.1	20.4	-2.8	1.8	1.2	2.8	-5.1	-7.9
AG SSR	4.3	6.0	0.7	1.0	0.2	0.4	0.9	0.5	1.0	-0.8	0.5	0.9
Parity	8.9	7.3	5.3	5.5	0.1	+0	2.6	3.1	0.2	0.5	-0.7	-0.1
Equivalent income	0.1	1.1	-0.2	-0.2	+0	0.1	-0.3	-0.3	-0.1	-0.1	-0.3	-0.6
Calories/capita	-0.4	-0.2	-0.2	-0.2	+0	+0	-0.1	0.1	-0.4	-0.3	-0.1	-0.3
Protein/capita	-1.1	-0.7	-0.3	-0.3	+0	+0	-0.1	-0.1	-0.7	-0.6	-0	-0.2
Number hungry	8.1	4.5	–	–	–	–	-0.2	1.9	–	–	–	–

253

Table 8.11 (continued)

Indicator[2]	India		Indonesia		Japan		Kenya		Mexico		New Zealand	
GDP70	+0	+0	-0	-0	-0	-0.1	0.4	0.9	-0.2	-0.4	0.9	1.0
GDPA70	0.1	+0	0.1	0.1	0.1	0.7	1.1	2.6	0.3	0.5	6.7	8.5
GDPNA70	-0	+0	-0.1	-0	-0	-0.1	0.1	0.3	-0.2	-0.4	+0	-0
AG HCons at P70	-0	0.1	-0	-0	+0	-0.1	0.7	1.5	0.2	-0.1	1.9	2.8
NAG HCons at P70	+0	0.1	-0.2	-0.4	-0.1	-0.1	-0.2	0.7	-0.2	-0.4	2.4	2.8
Trade deficit 70	-0	0.4	-0.3	0.7	0.2	0.8	-1.4	-1.3	-0.6	-0.4	-9.9	1.5
AG trade deficit 70	1.6	50.8	-1.5	-0.2	-0	-1.5	-8.4	-1.4	0.5	14.9	7.9	13.4
Trade/GDP at WP	-0.7	-0.7	-0.7	0.7	-0.7	-3.6	-5.4	0.4	0.1	4.5	22.7	28.7
GDPA at WP70	0.1	0.1	+0	+0	-0	-0.3	-1.1	0.6	0.2	0.8	6.9	10.0
Investment	+0	0.3	0.1	0.1	-0	-0.1	2.0	3.2	-0.2	-0.3	4.4	4.3
Total capital	--	--	0.1	0.1	-0.1	-0	0.9	2.0	-0	-0.1	1.6	3.1
AG vol. index WP70	0.1	0.1	+0	-0	-0.1	-1.5	-1.1	0.6	0.3	0.8	4.8	8.0
Net calories produced	-0	0.2	-0.1	+0	-1.0	-27.3	-4.5	-0.9	-3.2	3.1	-2.2	8.4
Agricultural capital	--	--	0.3	0.4	0.3	1.1	2.6	6.3	0.4	0.6	10.2	20.5
Agricultural labour	--	--	0.1	+0	0.4	1.0	+0	+0	0.4	1.1	0.7	1.8
Total acreage	+0	+0	-0	+0	-0	0.2	--	--	-0	+0	--	--
N fertilizer	-0.5	0.9	-0.1	-0.1	0.5	1.3	-5.0	-3.5	-0.2	2.4	-9.6	-5.5
P/Pₐ	0.3	0.8	0.3	0.6	-0	0.5	6.5	8.0	0.3	0.3	16.3	15.2
Crop price index	--	--	-0	0.2	0.2	-0.7	-0.4	-0.2	-0.3	-0.3	0.1	1.4
Food price index	--	--	0.3	0.5	-0.5	0.6	7.5	9.5	0.4	0.6	9.4	11.9
Terms of trade	0.6	1.0	-0.8	-1.1	-0.1	-0.6	2.0	2.9	-1.3	0.6	16.1	16.7
AG SSR	+0	0.1	0.1	+0	-0.3	+0	-1.6	-0.6	+0	0.9	3.5	5.5
Parity	0.2	0.4	0.2	0.6	-0.1	0.1	7.5	10.5	0.1	-0.3	23.2	22.6
Equivalent income	+0	-0	-0.1	-0.2	-0.1	-0.1	--	--	-0.2	-0.4	--	--
Calories/capita	0.1	-0	-0	-0	-0.1	-0.1	0.6	1.4	0.1	-0.1	0.3	0.5
Protein/capita	0.1	-0.1	-0	-0	-0.1	-0.1	0.7	1.6	0.1	-0.2	0.3	0.5
Number hungry	-0.7	0.2	0.4	--	--	--	-2.3	6.7	-1.5	1.8	--	--

Table 8.11 (continued)

Indicator[2]	Nigeria		Pakistan		Thailand		Turkey		United States		EC	
GDP70	0.2	0.3	-0.1	+0	-0	-0.1	-0.1	-0.2	0.1	0.1	-0	-0
GDPA70	0.9	1.2	1.0	0.4	-0.3	-0.6	0.7	1.8	-1.2	-0.4	0.3	0.3
GDPNA70	-0	0.1	-0.5	-0.1	-0	+0	-0.3	-0.5	0.1	0.1	-0	-0
AG HCons at P70	+0	+0	-0.6	-0.5	0.1	-0	+0	0.1	3.4	4.1	-0.1	-0.1
NAG HCons at P70	0.1	0.2	1.4	1.2	+0	0.1	0.2	-0	0.1	-0.2	+0	+0
Trade deficit 70	-0.9	0.7	+0	-0.4	0.1	0.4	-0.3	0.3	0.3	1.3	-0.12	0.9
AG trade deficit 70	-4.4	4.7	-55.5	-16.9	0.4	0.8	-0.5	8.4	-8.0	-9.0	-2.3	-2.6
Trade/GDP at WP	-2.8	-1.7	-0.2	-2.3	0.7	1.8	3.6	9.8	1.6	-2.4	-0.9	-0.2
GDPA at WP70	0.8	1.3	1.1	0.1	0.2	0.3	-0.3	1.1	-0.7	-0.6	0.3	0.4
Investment	0.6	0.5	0.2	0.3	-0.2	-0.1	0.1	-0.1	-	-	-0	-0
Total capital	0.4	0.5	0.2	0.1	-0	-0.1	0.2	0.1	-	-	-0	-0
AG vol. index WP70	0.8	1.3	1.2	0.2	+0	-0	0.2	1.4	-0.8	-0.6	0.2	0.4
Net calories produced	0.7	1.3	2.0	-0.1	+0	0.9	-2.4	1.2	2.8	1.9	-1.9	-0.5
Agricultural capital	1.2	1.8	1.2	0.6	-0.1	-0.6	1.6	2.8	-	-	0.4	0.6
Agricultural labour	0.8	1.2	1.6	0.6	+0	+0	0.5	1.4	-	-	1.0	0.8
Total acreage	0.4	1.8	0.2	-0.1	-	-	0.1	0.4	+0	+0	-0.2	-0.1
N fertilizer	1.3	1.5	2.1	1.1	0.1	0.4	-0.5	0.8	-	-	-0.1	1.0
P_s/P_n	0.4	0.3	1.3	1.5	-1.0	+0	1.7	1.7	-5.6	-6.4	0.3	0.9
Crop price index	0.1	0.1	0.2	-0.3	-0.4	0.2	0.3	0.5	-	-	-0.8	0.1
Food price index	0.2	0.2	0.7	1.0	-0.8	-0.3	0.9	0.9	-4.3	-4.7	0.1	0.4
Terms of trade	-2.1	-3.8	-3.3	-3.1	0.1	0.9	3.3	4.8	-12.0	-15.1	2.2	2.7
AG SSR	0.9	-1.8	-0	0.7	-1.3	-0.6	1.9	2.1	-5.6	-6.4	-0.4	0.4
Parity	-0.2	-0.8	-0	0.9	-1.3	-0.6	1.9	2.1	-5.6	-6.4	-0.4	0.4
Equivalent income	+0	0.1	0.3	0.3	-	-	0.1	-0	-	-	+0	+0
Calories/capita	+0	-0	-0.5	-0.4	+0	-0	+0	+0	-	-	+0	-0
Protein/capita	+0	-0	-0.6	-0.4	0.1	-0	+0	+0	-	-	-0.1	-0.1
Number hungry	-0.2	1.0	6.6	3.6	-0.2	0.1	-0.1	-0.1	-	-	-	-

Table 8.11 (continued)

1. The first figure given for each country is for 1990, the second for 2000.

2. GDP70: GDP at 1970 prices
GDPA70: GDP agriculture at 1970 prices
GDPNA70: GDP nonagriculture at 1970 prices
AG HCons at P70: Human consumption of agricultural products at 1970 prices
NAG HCons at P70: Human demand for nonagricultural products at 1970 prices
Trade deficit 70: Trade deficit at 1970 prices
AG trade deficit 70: Deficit in agricultural trade at 1970 prices
GDPA at WP70: GDP agriculture at 1970 world prices
Investment: Real investment
Total capital: Capital stock at 1970 prices
Net calories produced: Net calorie production
N fertilizer: Nitrogenous fertilizer
P_a/P_n: Agricultural price index relative to nonagriculture
AG SSR: Agricultural self-sufficiency ratio
Parity: Agricultural GDP per person engaged in agriculture divided by nonagricultural GDP per person engaged in nonagriculture

Note : +0 = small positive change.
-0 = small negative change.
– = non relevant or not calculated

256

Table 8.12

GAINS AND LOSSES ON SOME MACROECONOMIC AND WELFARE INDICATORS IN 2000 UNDER US TRADE LIBERALIZATION
(Relative to the reference scenario)

Countries	GDP70	Parity	Equiv. income	Consumption cost	People hungry
USA	NS	L	--	G	--
Canada	NS	G	L	L	--
Australia	NS	G	L	G	--
New Zealand	G	G	--	G	--
Austria	NS	NS	G	G	--
EC	NS	G	NS	ID	--
Japan	NS	G	L	L	--
CMEA	L	--	--	G	--
China	NS	--	--	ID	--
Argentina	G	G	G	G	L
Brazil	L	G	L	L	L
Mexico	L	L	L	L	L
Egypt	L	NS	L	L	--
Kenya	G	G	--	G	G
Nigeria	G	L	G	G	L
India	NS	G	NS	G	NS
Indonesia	NS	G	L	L	--
Pakistan	G	NS	G	G	L
Thailand	NS	L	--	G	NS
Turkey	L	G	NS	ID	NS

Notes:

G, country gains;
L, country losses;
ID, indeterminate;
NS, change not significant;
--, not calculated.

For a description of the indicators, see footnote to Table 8.6.

BIBLIOGRAPHY

ALEXANDRATOS, N. (ed.), *World Agriculture Toward 2000*, London: Belhaven Press, 1988.

LINNEMANN, H., J. de HOOGH, M.A. KEYZER and H.D.J. van HEEMST, *MOIRA: A Model for International Relations in Agriculture*, Amsterdam: North-Holland, 1979.

FISCHER, G., K. FROHBERG, M. KEYZER and K.S. PARIKH, *Linked National Models: A Tool for International Policy Analysis*, Dordrecht, Netherlands: Kluwer Academic Publishers, 1988.

PARIKH, K.S., G. FISCHER, K. FROHBERG and O. GULBRANDSEN, *Towards Free Trade in Agriculture*, Dordrecht, Amsterdam: Mortimers Nijhoff Publishers, 1988.

PARIKH, K.S. and W. TIMS, "From Hunger Amidst Abundance to Abundance Without Hunger", Executive Report No. 13, International Institute for Applied Systems Analysis, Laxenburg, Austria, 1986.

Chapter 9

THE FOOD GAP OF THE DEVELOPING WORLD: A GENERAL EQUILIBRIUM MODELLING APPROACH

by

J.-M. Burniaux, Dominique van der Mensbrugghe, and Jean Waelbroeck

INTRODUCTION

The Rural Urban North South (RUNS) model was one of two Applied General Equilibrium (AGE) models built in the Université Libre de Bruxelles with support from the World Bank, that were used for simulations in the fourth, fifth, and sixth World Development Reports[1]. The other model, "Varuna"[2], which is more disaggregated regionally and has a more sophisticated description of non-agricultural protection, has been described in Gunning *et al.* (1982) and Carrin *et al.* (1983).

Both models were designed for sensitivity analysis. The World Bank felt that, thanks to the insights acquired by its staff, it could produce better forecasts of growth of output and trade in developing countries than could a model. Producing those forecasts, however, required lengthy internal discussions that were in some cases as hard fought as negotiations. It would have been wasteful to seek a similar consensus with respect to the possible impacts of such changes in the world environment like higher oil prices or faster growth of OECD countries: this was to be the task of the model. AGE models are as a general rule calibrated to the data of a base year. It was decided that the two built in Brussels would, in addition, be calibrated to reproduce the growth rates of GNP and agricultural production predicted by the Bank's staff. This was done quite straightforwardly, through an iterative procedure that adapts the rates of growth of the productivity of resources used in the agricultural and non-agricultural sectors of the models' various regions.

The initial version of RUNS was built and operated on a CDC Cyber computer in the Université Libre de Bruxelles. The period covered was 1978-1995. It was fortunate that the World Bank also had access to a CDC machine via telecommunication to Minnesota). In shuttling across the Atlantic between the capitals of the United States and of the European Community (EC), we found it quite straightforward to switch from one mainframe to another, as there were few differences in their operating systems. The World Bank staff with which we worked was not used to the CDC, however. There were problems of budgeting. Time on the World Bank-IMF machine did not reflect real computing costs. Such problems could be overcome fairly easily, as the Bank's procedures are quite flexible. The differences in machines were, however, definitely an impediment to transferring the model to the World Bank staff.

Years have passed. The European Community has grown from nine to 12 countries, taking in three countries that used to be included in RUNS' Southern Europe region. Japan's increasing role in world trade and policy has made it imperative to represent that country by an endogenous

259

model, not an exogenous one as in the initial system, while it was necessary to recalibrate trade flows to take account of the growth of exports of manufactures by developing countries.

Last but not least, today's microcomputers are so powerful that transfer of the model to such a machine seemed desirable, to achieve a portability that is not feasible on mainframes and to take advantage of the user friendliness of micros. There would seem to be a large cost in terms of speed. Execution of the programme took three quarters of an hour in 1989 on the Mac 2 microcomputer that was selected, instead of 15 seconds in 1983 on the Minnesota CDC, and probably a fraction of this today. In Belgium, however, we are not working in North American research conditions. In spite of the power of the Cyber, each run cost a whole night in Brussels, two or three at the critical times when students have to hand in their term papers. Computer time is free, but the mainframe is strangled to prevent students and researchers from hogging all the available space, so that logging on gives access to less memory than on a PC.

It was thus decided to say farewell to the mainframe (by now a Cray), to love the portability and user friendliness of the Mac and hate its slowness, and to recalibrate the model to a recent base year. This has required a great deal of work which was not quite completed in time for this conference. Thus the results presented are based on the old mainframe version of the RUNS model.

THE MODEL AND WHAT IT CAN DO

Like video cameras or automobiles, particular features differentiate AGE models. Whoever buys a car knows that what he or she purchases will have four wheels, a motor, and a hand and foot brake. Likewise, the AGE buyer knows that what is offered will have balance equations and optimising producers and consumers, and would be quite surprised if it does not have an Armington system. Thus in this section, we shall only discuss features of RUNS that are "different".

Some Theoretical Problems

What are the model's limitations?

Like the vast majority of applied general equilibrium models, RUNS is a barter model from which money is absent. It is thus not suitable for the description of monetary policies or of nominal price or wage rigidities.

Like the vast majority of AGE models again, the dynamics of RUNS are limited. The model basically lets itself be pushed from one year to the next as the economy accumulates capital and responds to exogenous population growth and technical progress[3]. Models of this type do not incorporate forward-looking dynamics of the type which the rational expectations school has emphasized. They do not even incorporate the more easily handled backward-looking adaptive expectations dynamics.

This feature of the Brussels models actually caused some anguish in the World Bank when the project was designed. In a medium-term model, the rationality of expectations is important, particularly to describe the motivation of investment. We were urged by some, accordingly, not to use a general equilibrium approach but a dynamic linear programming one of the type used in earlier World Bank Research (Goreux and Manne, 1973), and the World Development Report Model by Gupta (Cheetham *et al.*, 1979) which preceded the Brussels ones. Whether rich dynamics are more important than the correct handling of balances of payments, which is the strong point of AGE systems, is a matter of opinion but the modeller cannot have it both ways, since with today's computer technology, it is not possible to solve a truly dynamic model as large as RUNS.

Would this have justified building a far smaller system? "We do not need big models" is a familiar argument in academic circles, but the World Bank felt that substantial disaggregation was needed to make possible fruitful discussions with experts from its regional departments.

That RUNS is a barter model that does not take account of expectations has limited its uses in the turmoil of the debt crisis, because these deficiencies preclude an appropriate representation of what drives the capital account of developing countries. For example, it is not possible to represent properly such crucial events as the squeeze on world money markets that was generated by the combination of the Reagan deficit and Volker tight money policies which, as stressed by World Development Reports at the time, played a role in triggering the debt crisis by "crowding out" developing countries through a sharp rise in interest rates. Such a model also cannot represent adequately the sudden loss of creditworthiness by all developing country borrowers in the summer of 1982, when Mexico defaulted on its debt obligations.

The Description of Agriculture

What AGE models do well, of course, is the less exciting job of analysing long-run developments. It is for that purpose that RUNS was designed and used.

RUNS' distinctive feature is its careful specification of the agricultural sector. This reflected our perception of the fundamental role of agriculture in the development process. This was recognised as early as the early 1920s by the Soviet economist Preobrazhenski (1956), whose ideas are reflected to some extent in the model design.

It was decided that to pinpoint better the forces that drive the rural economy, it and the urban economy should be modelled like distinct countries.

This is difficult to do well. The key problem is that, for want of data, the specification of RUNS identifies too closely the rural economy with agriculture. That economy is not solely agricultural. Everywhere in the world, farming is closely linked to ancillary non-agricultural activities that are almost part of it (for example, trade, transport, simple processing like the ginning of cotton, the crushing of oilseeds, or the milling of rice). Production in these activities rises and falls with that of agriculture.

More importantly from a general equilibrium point of view, farm households in both developed and in developing countries derive a substantial fraction of their income from these and other rural non-agricultural activities which, as a result of the limitations of data, are lumped into the urban sector of the RUNS model. This income goes into the pockets of farmers in the real world, but in the model this money enters the budget constraint of the urban population. The share of this income in the earnings of farmers may rise or fall in response to the evolution of technology and the development of the market. Transport activities, for example, are obviously less important in subsistence economies than in those that are monetised to a greater extent.

This share probably also depends on the economic policies whose impact the model seeks to represent. Thus price policies that encourage farmers to stay on the land may induce the accumulation of excess farm labour, which will tend to seek non-agricultural local employment and to some extent succeed in doing so. This will increase the ratio of non-farm income to the total income of farm households[4]. In such countries as Mexico and Japan, land tenure legislation has made it difficult for farmers to sell their farms, or has guaranteed the benefit of low controlled rents to tenants who had been renting land before a period of inflation.

Even geography matters. A farmer in densely populated Belgium can get an outside job far more easily than one who works in sparsely populated areas of Utah or New Mexico.

For this reason, the model thus misses an important aspect of the farm economy. Improving it in this respect is a high priority (but costly) item in our research agenda. Recognising that farmers have sizable non-agricultural incomes is important because this insulates them to some extent from changes in agricultural prices. The result is a bias in the model: farm incomes are less dependent on agricultural protection than the model suggests[5].

For want of appropriate data again, RUNS assumes that farm investment adjusts to match farm savings, plus an exogenous contribution of public investment to irrigation and other items of rural infrastructure. Net private capital flows between the two parts of the economy are not taken into account. This may make sense for undeveloped economies of Sub-Saharan Africa[6], but is less acceptable for, say, the upper income economies of Latin America, or poor countries such as Pakistan, where a substantial fraction of agricultural income goes to wealthy landowners who are surely sophisticated enough to invest their money wherever the return is highest.

Again this induces a bias. The flow of capital between city and country is obviously responsive to the terms of trade of agriculture. Because it does not recognise that private capital flows between city and country respond to market incentives, the model understates the long-run impact of price policies on farm output. Again the bias probably differs between regions: it is probably small in Africa, and large in Latin America, for example, where rural sectors are highly monetised and where a significant share of farm incomes goes to rich land owners.

The model does provide an adequate representation of the flow of labour between the rural and urban sectors. This is an extremely important phenomenon. Is not the ratio of the agricultural labour force to the total population often used as a rough indicator of the level of development[7]? The relevant equation of the model, inspired by Harris and Todaro's (1970) seminal piece, is based on the work of Mundlak (1979).

We come to the assumptions on competition. Agricultural markets are highly competitive, so that it is not realistic to describe this trade by an Armington (1969) system. To avoid unrealistic behaviour where trade patterns swing wildly from year to year, supply must be made inelastic. The standard technique for achieving this is to use the constant elasticity of transformation (CET) production function (Powell, 1968). This is based on the assumption that the goods which industries sell on the domestic and export markets are not the same, which makes it reasonable to assume a finite elasticity of transformation between them.

This is not an appropriate assumption in agriculture. The rice that Chinese eat and that which they export may not be identical. However, even though there may be categories of broken rice which they eat and which could not be disposed of on world markets, any reasonable guess about the elasticity of transformation between "domestic" and "export" rice must be a very large number.

It is climate and the structure of soil that make supply of agricultural goods inelastic. The law of comparative advantage reigns supreme on the land. Just as great Burgundy cannot be produced in Flanders, for any agricultural product there are certain optimal combinations of soil characteristics and climate.

Describing in full detail this aspect of agriculture would not have been practical. It would have been possible to use a CET whose arguments are the various outputs of the various agricultural sectors. However, this would have implied equal elasticities of transformation between all these goods[8]. This was inappropriate, because econometric evidence suggests that the supply elasticities of the various agricultural goods are far from uniform. The CRESH function[9], a well-known generalisation of the CET, would avoid this problem, but is quite hard to manipulate. We have used instead a specification devised by Burniaux, that is both simple in design and very easy to calibrate to the abundant empirical data that exist on the supply elasticity of the various agricultural products[10].

This may be described as follows. Two conventional variables are defined, representing resources used in animal husbandry and in growing crops. Each is expressed as an input function whose arguments are agricultural inputs such as land, labour, irrigation and so on, and an output function whose arguments are the various goods. Both functions are separable. Setting them equal generates two multi-input multi-output production functions for agriculture's cropping and animal husbandry subsectors[11].

On the input side, the specification of RUNS is closer to technology than production functions of the usual type. On the output side, this search for "technological authenticity" motivated the clear separation of animal and vegetal products. This work resembles the very original MOIRA project (Linneman *et al.*, 1979), possibly because like half of the authors of MOIRA, the author of RUNS is an agricultural economist. Coefficients for the input component of these functions are not readily available in the literature. We used the results of work undertaken for the project by Mundlak and Hellinghausen (1982).

The GYPR Mechanism

We now come to the crucial feature of the RUNS model: the representation of the running socio-political struggle between city and countryside, and of its economic implications for developing country economies. This conditions the model's response to economic shocks[12] and is worth discussing in some detail.

Modern macroeconomics emphasizes the importance of the rigidity of labour incomes. This is a fundamental element of Keynes' thinking, and remains a key feature of recent work in macroeconomics. Malinvaud (1977)[13] and others have worked this idea into a "general equilibrium with rationing" approach which has found followers mainly on this side of the Atlantic. In North America especially, there has been considerable but thus far unsuccessful effort to work out rigorous "microeconomic foundations" of this phenomenon. There is no point in going into details of this work, which sometimes appears to resurrect the ancient art of counting angels that dance on the head of a pin. Whatever their disagreements about nuances economists agree that wages are rigid.

It is important to keep in mind that this rigidity is not just the result of the stubbornness of trade unions, which are often very weak in developing countries. In any event, it is not only wages that are rigid. This is true of all urban labour incomes, through a variety of mechanisms that, for example, even include enshrining privileges of particular interest groups in Brazil's new constitution. In India, with high urban unemployment, trade unions would not be strong if they were not able to muster the vote, or secure, without crucial support from the government when the going gets tough[14]. Riots are dangerous to those in power throughout the developing world and self-employed shoeshine boys in the informal sector can riot as destructively as paid-up trade union members.

However the matter is envisaged, preserving those incomes has been a major political constraint since the days when uprisings by the Roman plebians forced the Senate to grant the poorest citizens a free supply of bread, a privilege which their (often wealthy) descendants preserved for half a millennium. The Parisians who brought the king back from Versailles during the French Revolution were shouting even more loudly for bread than for freedom[15], and the triumph of Solidarnosc in Poland owes a good deal to the price of meat. Paldam (1983) has shown that in Latin America, where there have been sudden falls in real wages, democratic governments and military regimes have been toppled indiscriminately.

Mellor (1976), for example, has emphasized another aspect of the matter in putting forth the intellectually seductive, though slightly vague concept of the food wage. As we understand him, this mainly reflects the impact of nutrition on the productivity of the labour force.

Hence governments everywhere have sought to contain increases in the cost of living and, in particular, the prices of basic food products. There are good arguments in favour of such policies as short-run devices that may make it easier for the economy to adjust to unexpected events, such as sharp rises in food prices on world markets. Increases in agricultural prices are supply shocks which, like oil price increases, squeeze living standards without changing the marginal value product of labour. This triggers a struggle by urban workers to safeguard their living standards which, if successful, squeezes profit margins, and lowers both employment and investment.

The political power of the urban masses has thus made agricultural prices sticky. So has the pressure of farmers at times of low world prices.

Such policies have significant costs. Food aid may help governments to subsidise urban consumption, but securing it may be difficult and may entail politically unattractive concessions. Keeping agricultural prices low may be achieved via subsidies, but they have a high budgetary cost. Shifting to farmers the cost of subsidising urban food makes low farmgate prices necessary, which discourages agricultural production and burdens the balance of payments with imports — a "heads I lose and tails you win" policy.

Downward rigidity of real wages and efforts of governments to keep food prices in line with other prices combine to generate a fundamental mechanism of RUNS which may be christened the "get your prices right" (GYPR) effect. In a barter general equilibrium model, Keynesian unemployment due to inadequate demand cannot exist; unemployment can occur only because the product wage (the ratio of the wage paid to workers to the prices of products sold by their employers) exceeds the market-clearing result. Any event that reduces the gap between the two — that contributes to "getting prices right" — must raise employment and GNP.

In RUNS, therefore, an increase in demand for manufactures does not increase output in direct response to the change in aggregate demand as envisaged by the standard Keynesian theory[16]. Production does adapt to demand, but the increase is mediated by an increase in profitability that induces producers to satisfy the increased inflow of orders.

Likewise supply shocks that raise the product wage will make production less profitable, causing output and employment to fall. If the consumption wage is rigid (if wages are indexed even partially to the cost of living), an increase in any price but that of domestically produced urban goods will raise the cost of living index with respect to the index of producer prices, and hence raise the product wage, in such a way that employment and output are reduced.

The mechanism does not operate everywhere in the same way. In the discussion above, we have stressed the policy tradeoff between the benefits and costs of insulating domestic agricultural prices from world market prices. Countries have reacted in very different ways to this tradeoff. Given the central importance of the GYPR mechanism in RUNS, Burniaux has carried out an extensive investigation of the extent to which governments have allowed fluctuations in world food prices to be passed through to domestic prices[17]. These regressions demonstrate that some countries have adopted "adjusting policies", allowing domestic prices to move in parallel with world prices, while other countries (in South Asia and the European Community with its Common Agricultural Policy) have pursued resolutely "non-adjusting" policies. Within each country, different goods have been treated in different ways: the pricing of tea in India, for example, is more "adjusting" than that of wheat[18].

This somewhat lengthy discussion is warranted by the fact that this mechanism is a key property of RUNS, accounting for the differences between its results and those of other world agricultural models[19]. It also has a significant impact on the results obtained for individual regions, as adjusting and non-adjusting regions respond quite differently to changes in world agricultural prices.

It is worthwhile to sketch briefly the mechanisms involved. When world agricultural prices rise, for example, because of reduced protection in the OECD countries, domestic food prices rise by amounts that depend on the degree to which regions are adjusting or not. These price increases squeeze urban output as workers, in their attempt to maintain their consumption wage, pressure their employers to raise the wage rate above the marginal product of labour (or induce the government to use a variety of devices to achieve this result). This makes production less profitable and induces producers to shed labour by closing down marginal production facilities. Agricultural output increases, however, to a degree that also depends on the extent that regions pursue adjusting policies. This strengthens the balance of payments[20], and offsets the loss in GNP which results from the drop in urban production. Here what matters is the share of agriculture in total output. This offsetting increase in agricultural output matters less in semi-industrialised countries than in those that are less developed.

The distinction also affects long-run economic growth. The "problem of the scissors", stressed in the 1920s by the Soviet economist Preobrazhenski, continues to haunt developing country governments[21]. An acceleration of urban growth increases food demand, and reduces supply by drawing rural workers to city jobs. Either agricultural prices are allowed to rise, which may cause urban unrest, or food imports are bound to rise to an extent that may cause widespread unrest and jeopardise the growth process[22].

These policy patterns also have a crucial impact on world markets for agricultural products. World demand for agricultural products would be virtually inelastic if all countries pursued fully non-adjusting policies[23]. Attempts by countries to insulate themselves from world market price fluctuations contribute to making a vicious circle by reducing the price elasticity of demand on world markets and making these prices even more unstable.

As explained, the assessment of the degree to which various regions pursue adjusting policies is based on econometric estimates. We have made no attempt to compare degrees of wage rigidity. There is a good deal of folklore about this, that emphasizes, for example, the flexibility of real wages in the United States, their rigidity in the "Eurosclerosed" old world[24], and the flexibility of the populations of East Asia in comparison with those of Latin America. As for developing countries, comparisons across countries or regions are even more questionable.

It would have been desirable to confirm statistically a key feature of the RUNS model, but it was thought that an econometric investigation would not prove useful. Wage data are quite poor for developing countries. The figures that exist cover only the formal sector (covering often only large firms), whereas resistance to cuts in real labour incomes exists throughout the urban economy. However, data on other labour incomes are nonexistent. Casual observation suggests that the degree of wage rigidity cannot be characterised by structural relations that are stable enough to be estimated. The rigidity of real labour incomes depends on the general political context. The Mexican government, for example, with a broad and stable political base can adjust wages more easily than a fragile democracy like Brazil. To mention another example, in Italy, after years of debate, a referendum confirmed the government's decision to abolish the long-standing system of wage indexation.

Subject to these doubts, the matter was resolved by a bold guess. The RUNS model covers a period that is long enough to bring about a rather strong adjustment of real wages towards the wage rate that is compatible with labour market equilibrium. In the absence of solid econometric information, it was assumed that the wage rate adjusts by 0.75 per cent to a 1 per cent change in the equilibrium rate when the actual wage exceeds the equilibrium level. It adjusts fully to increases in that rate when the economy is at full employment.

Greater daring was displayed in the representation of the domestic price policies pursued by governments. Here it is possible to use detailed FAO data on domestic and world prices of agricultural commodities. For each country and each commodity, regressions were run expressing changes in domestic prices as a weighted average of changes in world prices and in domestic consumer prices. Aggregating the estimated weights for each region yields the necessary domestic price equations[25].

265

DISCUSSION OF THE SIMULATION RESULTS

Every year since 1974, the World Bank has prepared evaluations of the global outlook of developing countries. The first of these studies, the yearly "Prospects for Developing Countries", had a so-called "restricted" circulation, but was distributed in thousands of copies to civil servants, selected scholars, and members of the governments of member countries. The more ambitious World Development Reports that followed them can be purchased in book shops, and are even more widely known. All of these studies have contained an assessment of the impact of key economic variables on the growth of the developing world. These are:

a) The growth of developed countries;

b) Aid and capital flows from North to South[26];

c) The world price of oil; and

d) Protection by OECD countries against exports from developing countries.

Both the RUNS and the Varuna models have been used to calculate the impact of these variables on the economies of developing countries.

We shall not discuss these results here, since a paper exists that reviews them[27]. The focus will be on a more specific topic: the impact of slow economic growth in the North on the food and agricultural situation in the South[28].

The chief focus of attention will be the by now numerous attempts to project the "food gap" of developing countries, where this gap is represented either by their net imports of grain, or by their net imports of primary food products[29]. All the studies that we know of have concluded that this gap will increase a great deal in coming years. This conclusion has been used to highlight the fact that much greater attention should be paid to the development of the agricultural sector in thinking about the long-run strategies of both individual developing countries, and the agencies whose mission is to provide aid to the South[30].

All this work has been done in a partial equilibrium context or, to be more accurate, using rather simple extrapolation techniques that involve trend projections of agricultural output, and projections of food demand that combine population projections with forecasts of per capita consumption obtained by applying appropriate income elasticities to projections of per capita income. The word "simple" is not used in a derogatory sense: avoiding irrelevant sophistication is necessary in policyo-riented research. The results obtained by the "simple" approach are in any event no more than a starting point for these projections, whose authors use their considerable expertise to modulate the results obtained to express as accurately as possible the prospects of the countries and regions studied.

What this approach cannot easily do is to take into account the impact of the price mechanism, which is quite significant. Experience shows agricultural supply to be quite sensitive to prices. Demand also is dependent on the price of food, even in very poor countries whose inhabitants are close to the subsistence level, because even though the substitution effect of a food price increase may be thought to be small, the income effect is large[31].

Assessing the impact of price changes is of course what the general equilibrium approach is good at. The authors of food gap projections do indicate implicitly, and sometimes explicitly, that they are catastrophe scenarios that must not be allowed to come true. History shows that catastrophes do not occur often. Thanks to the price mechanism, market economies have a remarkable ability to muddle through apparently inextricable difficulties. Prices do change in the process, possibly quite sharply. Groups of individuals suffer, possibly to a shocking extent. However, no sharp breakdown occurs, no catastrophe occurs, in the usual sense of that term, implying a sudden and lasting disintegration of the economic system.

What we shall do is to try to assess how the world would evolve should the job of dealing with the food gap crisis be left to the market. There is reason not to limit ourselves to scenarios where wise policy makers take matters in hand and solve the problems pointed out by their economic advisers. Experience shows that until circumstances force them to do so, politicians do not pay much heed to the pleadings of their advisers. It is therefore interesting to ascertain how the world will evolve if nothing is done to head off the difficulties which the authors of food gap projections have been pointing to.

Does a comparison between the results of RUNS and the food gap projections make sense? We think so. RUNS was initially calibrated to judgement forecasts by the World Bank staff. Its GNP and agricultural output growth rates therefore match the judgement of practical persons whose detailed knowledge of the developing world is on the whole similar to that of the food gap projectors[32].

The model adds three elements to this analysis:

a) It completes the description of the developing economies by providing submodels of their urban sectors;

b) It closes the description of the world economy by providing forecasts of growth of developed countries[33]; and

c) Finally, it specifies a price system that is able to match supply and demand for all commodities, and to bring foreign payments into balance.

In the food gap projections, what happens to the balance of payments is left to the imagination of the reader, who cannot avoid, and indeed is encouraged to entertain an uneasy feeling that the projected gap is so large that balance of payments equilibrium is likely to be unattainable. In the RUNS simulations, this equilibrium is achieved willy-nilly through the impersonal and possibly cruel power of the market. All variables change to achieve this: prices and real incomes, exports and imports of agricultural and non-agricultural goods. The food gap is not an exogenous piece of data: it is represented by endogenous variables that adjust like all the others to bring about general equilibrium.

The RUNS Food Gap Projection in the Base Case

It is important to note that the base case assumptions imply that balance of payments equilibrium is not easy to achieve. The calibration describes a world where GNP growth is quite slow in developed countries, so that they do not offer easy markets to their partners from the South.

Table 9.1 compares our food gap projections with other major forecasts. The difference in results is striking. In the RUNS base case, production in the South increases more rapidly than consumption, a result that is in sharp contrast with the picture provided by the usual food gap projections. As the table shows, it is the demand projection that accounts for most of the difference: the projection of supply is in line with other forecasts[34].

Table 9.2 sheds further light on food prospects. Per capita food consumption grows by 0.77 per cent per annum, a good deal more slowly that is assumed in other projections; it is the urban population that is squeezed. Per capita consumption of that population actually drops. How does this come about?

The basic explanation is that the food gap is too large to be financed by the foreign exchange receipts that developing countries are likely to be able to earn. Low growth in the developed world will affect the prices and volumes of their exports. Capital flows to the South are expected to decline as a result of the debt crisis. The import needs of developing countries, however, will continue to be large. Their underlying rate of growth remains high, generating a need for growing imports of non-agricultural products. Finally, as pointed out by the food gap studies, agricultural imports will tend to be buoyant.

Something has to give. What happens is that the relative price of food rises in developing countries. The real rate of exchange falls[35], stimulating exports and discouraging imports. Because of the assumed wage rigidity, urban unemployment rises, which helps the balance of payments by restricting import demand. Food consumption falls in the cities, as a result both of the fall in employment and of the increase in food prices. This is only partly offset by increased food consumption in the countryside, where farmers consume more food in spite of the shift in relative prices, because this shift improves their income. The scenario is one of urban misery caused by slow income growth in the developed world. The history of recent years, with the numerous urban food riots that have accompanied efforts of developing countries to adjust to balance of payments difficulties, shows that it is not a figment of a computer's imagination.

Agricultural Trade Liberalization with Slow Growth in the OECD Countries

What would be the impact of a widespread liberalization of food protection in the North on the food situation in the South?

An argument that is sometimes put forward is that the North's agricultural protection, because it reduces world agricultural prices, helps to reduce hunger and alleviate poverty in the South. How valid is this in the context of an AGE model such as RUNS?

That agricultural trade liberalization by OECD countries would lift world prices of food is obvious. As a matter of fact, it has similarly been argued by proponents of protection that world agricultural prices are so distorted that it is meaningless to measure protection by comparing world prices of agricultural products with their domestic prices in individual countries, as is done for example in the PSE calculations of the OECD. This point is valid. We shall investigate how important it is by using RUNS to assess the rise in world prices that would occur if the North's agricultural protection was removed.

This price increase will raise the domestic price of food in the South. The impact would be larger in "adjusting" than in "non-adjusting" countries, but there would be an increase everywhere. To the extent that food is felt to be a basic need or that, as argued by John Mellor, workers are more productive when they are adequately fed, this price increase would indeed be an undesirable consequence of trade liberalization. Here again, however, other less obvious mechanisms should be taken into account.

The first is the terms of trade. Important developing regions are net exporters of agricultural products. An increase in their prices therefore improves their terms of trade. This has a positive income effect, which may offset completely or in part the negative effect just described.

The second mechanism has likewise been much discussed. Adelman[36] has argued that higher prices of food, because they increase the incomes of farmers, stimulate their demand for manufactures in a way that is favourable to accelerated industrialisation (on this, see the Agricultural Demand-Led Industrialisation strategy discussed by Adelman, 1984; and Adelman, Burniaux, and Waelbroeck, 1989).

The third is the complex linkage between agriculture and the rest of the economy that is described by the GYPR multiplier described above. Higher food prices inflict a negative supply shock on the cities which, other things being equal, tends to reduce employment and output.

It is clear that an assessment of the impact of agricultural trade liberalization on the developing world must be based on more than the glib remark that since world prices will rise, the poor will suffer. The mechanisms are too complex to be grasped intuitively: a model is needed.

The simulation assumptions are that protection is fully removed in OECD countries, i.e. that domestic agricultural prices in these countries are allowed to fall to the world market level. In the United States, the payment in kind scheme is abolished, bringing back into production 20 per cent of the land (McCalla and Joslings, 1985, p. 169).

It is assumed that developing countries do not participate in this liberalizing process. There will be no pressure on them to do so, as their protection is mostly negative. Why should agricultural exporters press them to abolish import subsidies which induce them to import more? Also, the discussion of the base case has suggested that the politically powerful urban masses will suffer from increases in the relative domestic price of food, and pressure governments to reverse them. Why, in this context, should these governments abolish the negative protection that keeps food cheap?

How much would world food prices rise in response to such a change? This is a question that has exercised the minds of several model builders. It is nice to discover that, as shown by Table 9.3, their results are in broad agreement. Anderson and Tyers 1 contradict the results of other modellers, but reassuringly, Anderson and Tyers 2 do agree with their colleagues' results and ours.

The next table describes the effect of this liberalization on the chief macroeconomic variables in the various regions. The key mechanisms here involve the terms of trade and the quite powerful GYPR multiplier. The terms of trade effect works in favour of developing countries. Europe, which is by a good margin the world's chief importer of agricultural products, suffers a significant terms of trade loss. The GYPR mechanism brings about a strong expansion in the OECD countries, especially in Europe, where GNP increases by 2.8 per cent.

In developing countries, what occurs is more complex. It is interesting that urban value added rises in "adjusting" Latin America. As there is a strong pass through of world to domestic prices, an increase in urban unemployment would be expected. The region is a large net exporter of agricultural products, however. The resulting terms of trade gain causes a favourable income effect which offsets the negative GYPR impact. Latin America has, in addition, significant exports of mining products and manufactures whose world demand benefits from the increase in GNP in the OECD countries.

The rural urban price parity, on the other hand, shifts in favour of agriculture, while the "urban misery" that was predicted in the preceding section becomes worse. This will sharpen the latent conflict between farm and city that plays such a key role in the politics of developing countries. This remark must be qualified by the observation that approximately nine tenths of the absolute poor identified by the World Bank live in the countryside, and that it is to rural areas that higher agricultural prices transfer the purchasing power whose loss causes this urban misery[37].

Can Trade Liberalization for Non-agricultural Goods Offset the Negative Effects of the Liberalization of Agricultural Trade?

The liberalization of agricultural trade is of course only part of the Uruguay Round. The current negotiations, if they are successful, will bring about lower protection for both agricultural and non-agricultural goods.

The "urban misery" that would grow worse if developed countries gave up protection of their agriculture is the consequence of worsened terms of trade of the cities. Reduced protection of non-agricultural goods in the OECD countries would have an opposite effect. By expanding the export markets for goods produced in the cities of the developing world, their terms of trade will improve, making food cheaper and their populations better off.

269

How strong is this effect? Table 9.5 confirms that trade liberalization for non-agricultural goods will operate in the way just described, but suggests that it will offset only to a limited extent the impact of agricultural liberalization. This is not surprising, given that the tariff equivalent of agricultural protection far exceeds the protection rate for non-agricultural products[38].

Trade liberalization has the strong impact on welfare in the liberalizing regions that characterises models with real wage rigidities. OECD countries gain more than the traditional developed agricultural exporters, because the initial level of protection is higher. This enhances the boost that free trade gives to demand for the goods produced in the developing world's cities. The regions that gain are, reasonably enough, the middle-income countries with their well developed industries. Real income in South East Asia in particular grows by almost 1 per cent. The shift in the rural-urban parity ratio is influenced by the type of agricultural policies which the various regions pursue. This explains in particular why the change in the rural-urban income parity in Europe is only half that in the more "adjusting" United States.

One figure merits a special comment, as it illustrates the complexity of this type of model. Non-agricultural trade liberalization in the OECD countries improves the terms of trade of Africa's rural areas, but worsens those of the rural sectors of other developing countries. Our understanding of this difference is the following. The urban sectors of Africa export very little. Thus they derive negligible benefits from non-agricultural trade liberalization and accelerated growth in the OECD countries. As a large exporter, Africa's agriculture benefits from the upswing in world demand that results from trade liberalization.

Does Increased Investment in Agriculture Provide a Solution?

That the model suggests that trade liberalization of agriculture in the South will have a negative impact on the food situation in the cities of the South is of course not a reason to oppose a trade liberalization which, according to RUNS, has a strong positive impact on world GNP. The reason why the impact is negative is that this liberalization reduces world food output and, because of its impact on prices and demand in the North, increases consumption in that area. The right conclusion to draw is that this liberalization should be complemented by a shift in Southern investment in favour of agriculture.

This shift will come about spontaneously to a certain extent. In RUNS, agricultural investment equals rural saving plus an exogenous flow of capital from city to country. As the model is set up, the first component does respond to increases in agricultural prices, the second does not. In the real world, the roughly 15 per cent increase in world prices which trade liberalization brings about would trigger an increase in the flow of capital to agriculture. The loans of international agencies for agriculture[39] would also increase. The World Bank, for example, has a 15 per cent cutoff rate of return for the projects that it finances; more agricultural projects would meet this condition if world prices rose by a seventh.

In addition, we believe that policies should change. Successful liberalization of agricultural trade should be accompanied by a conscious effort to increase investment in agriculture, whether in production facilities, in research, or in such activities as rural education, crop research, and extension services. Indeed, such a shift is desirable even in the absence of agricultural trade liberalization, to alleviate the social tensions that have plagued so many developing countries in recent years.

Table 9.6 assesses the impact of such a shift. The impact is a strong one. A shift in the pattern of investment does make a substantial contribution to solving the problem at hand. In the past, there has been much wasted public investment in agriculture, so that the model result does not justify a mechanical, across-the-board increase in budget funding of such investments. Hopefully, the world has learned enough for such mistakes to be avoided.

The table is also interesting as an illustration of the impact of what Adelman (1984) has christened the "Agricultural Demand Led Industrialisation" strategy. This is positive both for the GNP of developing countries and for their real income (nominal GDP deflated by the price index of consumption). Not all regions gain in the same proportions, however. An improved supply of "wage goods" is more beneficial to semi-industrialised regions, with their large urban sectors, than to the less-industrialised countries in low-income Asia and, especially, in Africa.

In both of the lower income regions, the increase in agricultural investment may choke off the supply of capital to industry to an extent that may be excessive, leading to a sharp increase in the price of urban goods. This reflects the high weight of agriculture in these economies. Additional aid might be necessary to alleviate their difficulties.

The strongly favourable impact on the middle-income countries confirms Adelman's (1984) earlier results. The reader will note that, contrary to what was assumed in her earlier study, the simulation does not use the assumption that technical progress is speeded up when policies that are favourable to agriculture are adopted. The simulation thus implies that even without an assumption that some have criticized, RUNS confirms Adelman's result that agricultural demand-led industrialisation is unambiguously favourable to outward-oriented countries that are past the take-off stage[40].

Table 9.1

A COMPARISON OF FOOD GAP PROJECTIONS

Average yearly growth rates in percentage	FAO[1]	UN[2]	USDA[3]	FAO[4]	MOIRA[5]	Reference scenario 78-86	Reference scenario 87-95
Developing countries							
Population	2.7	2.7	2.7	2.3	2.2	2.3	2.3
Agricultural production (1)	3.3	2.6	3.0	2.7	3.4	3.2	3.6
Agricultural demand (2)	3.6	3.6	3.2	3.7	3.6	3.3	2.8
Gap (1) - (2)	-0.3	-1.0	-0.2	-1.0	-0.2	-0.1	+0.8
			(Centrally planned economies included)			(Centrally planned economies excluded)	
Developed countries							
Population	--	--	0.8	--	0.7	0.5	0.6
Agricultural production (1)	--	--	2.2	--	2.5	1.9	2.0
Agricultural demand (2)	--	--	1.8	--	1.9	1.3	1.4
Gap (1) - (2)	--	--	+0.4	--	+0.6	+0.6	+0.6

1. FAO: FAO, Agricultural commodity projections (1971). These figures are taken from Nagle (1976), p. 74. The period covered is 1970-1980.
2. UN: United Nation World Food Conference, Assessment of the World Food Situation: Present and Future, Rome, 1974. These figures are taken from Nagle (1976), p. 77. The period covered is 1970-1985.
3. USDA: GOL model. These figures are taken from Revel and Riboud (1981), p. 265. The period covered is 1970-1985.
4. FAO: Agriculture toward 2000, FAO. 1979.
5. MOIRA: The Moira de Linnemann, De Hoogh, Keyzer and Van Heemst (1979), p. 309. The period covered is 1966-2009.

Note: Developed countries include socialist countries in projections (3) and (5).

Table 9.2

THE FOOD SITUATION IN THE BASE RUN

	Rural		Urban		Total		Growth rate
	past	projected	past	projected	past	projected	
Poor countries	0.34	0.48	0.79	0.63	0.48	0.53	0.6
Middle income non-oil exporting countries	0.81	1.47	1.35	1.2	1.12	1.32	1.0
Middle income oil exporting countries	0.47	0.63	1.08	1.18	0.77	0.9	1.0
All developing countries	0.44	0.67	1.05	0.94	-0.69	0.79	0.8
Developed countries	1.93	3.86	1.95	2.21	1.95	2.29	0.9

Table 9.3

**IMPACT OF AGRICULTURAL TRADE LIBERALIZATION BY OECD COUNTRIES
ON WORLD PRICES OF AGRICULTURAL PRODUCTS**

	RUNS	IIASA	Anderson/ Tyers 1[1]	Anderson/ Tyers 2[2]
Wheat	15.3	18.0	2.0	20.0
Rice	13.2	21.0	5.0	16.0
Coarse grains	8.5	11.0	1.0	14.0
Sugar	57.0	n.a.	5.0	n.a.
Meats	17.9	17.0	16.2	24.0
Oils	6.1	n.a.	n.a.	n.a.

1.   Anderson and Tyers 1 refers to the figures given in the World Bank (1986).
2.   Anderson and Tyers 2 refers to the figures quoted in Parikh (1986).

Table 9.4

FULL LIBERALIZATION OF AGRICULTURAL PROTECTION IN OECD MEMBER COUNTRIES
[Percentage changes with respect to reference scenario (in 1986 with low agricultural world prices)]

Countries	Real income[1]	Rural value added	Urban value added	Terms of trade	Rural/ urban income	Rural/ urban price parity[2]	Food product.	Food demand[3]	Food per capita rural	Food per capita urban	Food prices[4]
Low income	-0.2	n.a.	n.a.	1.8	n.a.	n.a.	0.1	-0.5	n.a.	n.a.	1.7
Asia (excl. China)	-0.1	0.1	-0.8	3.8	5.0	1.2	0.3	-0.8	1.9	-2.7	2.4
Africa	-0.6	0.1	-1.4	1.0	6.0	4.5	0.2	-0.7	1.8	-2.9	2.5
Middle upper income	0.7	0.3	0.1	1.1	2.8	3.6	0.7	-0.3	1.2	-1.2	3.2
Latin America	1.4	0.9	0.1	7.1	6.8	6.1	1.7	-0.1	2.4	-2.3	6.6
Southeast Asia	0.9	0.2	-0.1	0.8	6.3	6.3	0.5	-1.2	2.4	-2.2	4.2
Oil producers	0.4	-0.1	0.2	0	0.5	0.5	-0.1	0.0	0.3	-0.1	0.4
All developing	0.5	n.a.	n.a.	0.2	n.a.	n.a.	0.4	-0.4	n.a.	n.a.	2.3
OECD	1.6	n.a.	n.a.	-0.8	n.a.	n.a.	-2.4	5.2	n.a.	n.a.	13.7
Europe	2.9	-3.3	2.8	-2.8	-34.0	-26.5	-5.1	8.6	2.2	12.5	-20.3
US, Canada, Oceania	1.1	1.2	0.5	3.0	9.7	10.1	2.3	-0.5	3.6	-1.5	4.1

1. Real income is nominal value added at market prices, deflated by the consumption price index.
2. The real urban price parity is the ratio of the prices of rural and urban value added at factor prices.
3. Total food demand includes feed uses.
4. The food prices is the ratio of an average of food prices to the consumption price index.

Table 9.5

NON-AGRICULTURAL LIBERALIZATION IN OECD COUNTRIES
(Percentage changes with respect to reference scenario)

Countries	Real income	Total value added	Terms of trade	Food production	Food demand	Rural/ urban income parity
Low income	0.1	0	0.9	0	0	n.a.
Asia (excluding China)	0.2	0.1	0.5	-0.1	1.0	-0.2
Africa	0.2	0.1	0.3	0	0	0.2
Middle upper income	0.3	0.1	0.6	-0.1	0.2	-0.2
Latin America	0.1	0	0.7	-0.2	0.1	-0.4
South East Asia	0.9	0.5	0.8	0	0.5	-0.6
Oil producers	0.3	0.1	0.5	0	0.1	0
Total developing	0.2	0.1	0.7	0	0	n.a.
Developed	0.9	0.3	-0.5	0.4	-0.6	n.a.
OECD Europe	1.7	0.6	-1.4	-1.1	0.3	n.a.
US, Canada, Oceania	0.5	0.2	-0.2	0.5	-0.3	0.6

Table 9.6

IMPACT ON KEY VARIABLES OF A SHIFT IN INVESTMENT FROM THE URBAN TO THE RURAL SECTOR IN ALL DEVELOPING REGIONS[1]

Countries	Real income	GNP total	Rural GNP	Urban GNP	International terms of trade
Poor regions	0.2	-1.0	2.5	-2.4	5.3
Asia	1.2	-0.5	2.4	-1.5	8.2
Africa	-2.0	-2.3	2.7	-4.6	1.1
Middle income non-oil exporting	1.4	1.1	7.4	0.4	1.5
Latin America	2.4	2.2	8.8	1.3	1.6
Southeast Asia	1.2	0.5	3.6	0.2	1.1
Mediterranean	0.5	0.3	7.2	-0.4	2.1
Oil exporting	0.0	0.1	3.2	-0.2	0.2
All developing	0.8	0.5	4.8	-0.1	1.3
Developed	1.8	0.6	-1.0	0.7	0.2
Europe	1.3	0.9	0.1	1.0	0.6
North America, Oceania	0.5	0.4	-1.9	0.5	-0.6

1. A 40 per cent increase in agricultural investment in the middle income regions; a 30 per cent increase in the poor ones.

NOTES AND REFERENCES

1. The Rural Urban North South (RUNS) model was developed by Burniaux in his work for a Ph.D. (Burniaux, 1985). A full description of the model is provided in Burniaux (1987).

2. Varuna was the major deity of the Aryans who invaded India. One of his major attributes is assuring order in the Universe, a task that clearly entails a responsibility for general economic equilibrium.

3. The dynamic specification of RUNS is more complex than that of most general equilibrium models, to the extent that the dynamics of the tree crops sector is described in some detail. Even there, the expectations are adaptive, not rational.

4. This has rather clearly taken place in Germany, for example, and is one factor that accounts for why outside activities account for far more than half of the income of Japanese farmers.

5. Not only the model, but government policies neglect to take account of this aspect of rural life. Everywhere, farm parity policies focus on the ratio of agricultural to non-agricultural prices, neglecting to allow for the substantial non-agricultural incomes of farmers.

6. Even in such a country as the Côte d'Ivoire, there has been significant investment in plantations by wealthy city dwellers.

7. The very term "industrialising countries" implies that the driving force in development is a shift of production factors to the industrial sector.

8. Using a multi-level CET would have made the specification more complicated without improving matters very much.

9. Hanoch (1971).

10. Important sources that have been used are Adams and Behrman (1976 and 1984) and Rojko et al. (1978), as well as the remarkable continuing work of the Commodities Division of the World Bank. For a fuller list, see the already cited Burniaux (1987).

11. As already explained, tree crops are modelled distinctly. They use the same resources as other crops, but their inputs are multi-year ones.

12. In particular, it accounts for key differences between the simulation results obtained using RUNS and other world agricultural models.

13. Malinvaud was only one of a group of people who developed this approach to macroeconomic theory of modelling, and was not the first to develop the concept of general equilibrium with rationing. However, there is no point in citing all the basic references here. His name is selected because of the brevity and admirable clarity of exposition of his presentation of those ideas.

14. For example, safeguarding jobs through nationalisation of a number of large textile mills that had gone out of business as a result of the very lengthy strike some years earlier.

15. Historians have judged that Marie Antoinette's "let them eat cake" was not entirely adequate as a policy response to these demands.

16. Which differs from the mechanism that Keynes described. In the General Theory, Keynes provides a very careful discussion of the way in which profits and real wages adapt to a change in demand.

17. A similar effort was a feature of the MOIRA model. In that model, full employment reigns, however, and there is no GYPR mechanism.

18. For another view of the contrast between adjusting and non-adjusting countries, see the interesting paper by Krueger *et al.* (1988).

19. It is, however, very easy to turn off the mechanism: the programme is built so that it can be switched off by changing one flag.

20. I.e., in a model where the current balance of payments is exogenous, the real exchange rate is strengthened.

21. The scissors, much discussed by Soviet economists at the time, refers to the gap between urban and agricultural prices that widens and industrialisation that reduces rural output and increases urban food demand. Stalin solved the problem by collectivization in which as many as 20 million peasants may have died. Today's developing country governments are using gentler methods, but the problem is still in the background of policy making.

22. Stalin of course solved the problem by a non-market approach that involved setting very low farmgate prices, imposing delivery quotas, and killing farmers who disagreed.

23. The price elasticity of demand would not be zero because of income effects. It would be easy to construct examples where it is perverse, i.e., positive and not negative.

24. Econometric studies have not confirmed those beliefs, however. See in particular the thorough study by Gordon (1987).

25. This is similar to the procedure used in the already cited MOIRA model.

26. To be precise, the resource gaps: net capital flows from OECD countries and high income oil exporters to the South, net of the corresponding interest burden.

27. Mercenier and Waelbroeck (1983).

28. The paper takes up and extends the analysis presented by Burniaux in two publications in French (Burniaux, 1983 and 1987).

29. A recent study of this type is Paulino (1986) an IFPRI Research Report.

30. The Paulino study, for example, has served as background to a number of policy papers, dealing with such topics as food policies in the Middle East and North Africa, and the role of food aid in closing the cereals gap.

31. By Engle's Law, food accounts for a large fraction of the expenditures of the poor. An increase in its price has therefore a significant impact on the real value of their earnings.

32. Indeed, World Bank economists have produced internal papers that provide their own projections of the food gap.

33. Some of the food gap projections, the FAO's, for example, also cover developed countries.

34. Not too much should be read into this, however. Remember that the model is calibrated to reproduce the agricultural production forecasts of the World Bank's economists.

35. There is no "rate of exchange" in a barter general equilibrium model, in the usual sense of defining the ratio at which the monies of two countries are exchanged. There is no single way of defining the "real rate of exchange"; a good choice is to use the ratio of the price of urban resources in pairs of countries (of the prices of capital and labour, weighted by the shares of capital and labour in the production function).

36. See for example Adelman (1984), Adelman, Burniaux, and Waelbroeck (1989).

37. The mechanism that operates may be even more complex in countries/regions such as South Asia where, as stressed by de Sadoulet in her paper in this volume, there exists a large landless agricultural labour force. It is quite possible that, although the overall purchasing power of farmers increases, rural wages fail to rise, so that landless workers become poorer.

38. The "Producer Subsidy Equivalent", in OECD jargon.

39. Reduce the outflow in regions where capital moves in the opposite direction.

40. The result is due to special properties of RUNS, in particular on its GYPR mechanism.

BIBLIOGRAPHY

ADAMS, G.F. and J. BEHRMAN, *Econometric Models of World Agricultural Commodity Markets*, Cambridge, Massachusetts: Ballinger, 1976.

ADAMS, G.F. and J. BEHRMAN, *Commodity Exports and Economic Development*, Lexington, Massachusetts: Lexington Books, 1984.

ADELMAN, I., "Beyond Export-Led Growth", *World Development*, Vol. 12, 1984.

ADELMAN, I., J.-M. BURNIAUX, and J. WAELBROECK, "Agricultural Development-Led Industrialisation in a Global Perspective", in J.C. Williamson and V.R. Panchamuki, eds., *The Balance between Industry and Agriculture in Economic Development*, Vol. 2 Sector Proportions, IEA Conference Volumes, London: Macmillan, 1989.

ARMINGTON, P., "A Theory of Demand for Products Distinguished by Place of Production", IMF Staff Papers, 16, 1969.

BURNIAUX, J.-M. "La configuration Nord-Sud du commerce des produits alimentaires : un essai projectif et une expérience d'histoire économétrique", *Recherches Economiques de Louvain*, 49:3, September 1983.

BURNIAUX, J.-M., "Shifting Investment to Agriculture and the Food Dilemma, a General Equilibrium Approach", paper presented to the IIASA Conference on General Equilibrium Modelling, held in Sopron, Hungary, 18-20 June 1984.

BURNIAUX, J.-M., "Chômage, Sous-Nutrition, Croissance : Un Essai d'Interprétation de Quelques Paradoxes de l'Economie Mondiale à l'Aide d'un Modèle d'Equilibre Général", Ph.D. Thesis, Université Libre de Bruxelles, April, 1985.

BURNIAUX, J.-M., Le Radeau de la Méduse : Essai d'Analyse des Dilemmes Alimentaires, Paris: Economica, 1987.

CARRIN, G., J.W. GUNNING, and J. WAELBROECK, A General Equilibrium Model for the World Economy: Some Preliminary Results, 99-119 in B. Hickman ed., *Global International Economic Models*, Amsterdam: North-Holland, 1983.

CHEETHAM, R., SYAMA G., and A. SCHWARTZ, "The Global Framework", *World Bank Staff Working Paper No 355*, September 1979.

FAO, *Agriculture Toward 2000*, Rome, 1980.

GORDON, R.J., "Productivity, Wages, and Prices Inside and Outside of Manufacturing in the US, Japan, and Europe," *European Economic Review*, 31, 1987.

GOREUX, L.M. and A.S. MANNE, *Multi-Level Planning: Case Studies in Mexico*, Amsterdam: North-Holland, 1973.

GUNNING, J.W., G. CARRIN, and J. WAELBROECK, and associates J.-M. BURNIAUX and J. MERCENIER, "Growth and Trade of Developing Countries: A General Equilibrium Analysis", Discussion Paper 8210, CEME, Université Libre de Bruxelles, 1982.

HANOCH, G., CRESH Production Functions, *Econometrica*, 39, 1971.

HARRIS, J.R. and M.P. TODARO, Migration, Unemployment, and Development: A Two-Sector Analysis. *American Economic Review*, Vol. 60, No. 1, 1970.

KRUEGER, A.O., M. SCHIFF, and A. VALDÉS, "Agricultural Incentives in Developing Countries: Measuring the Effects of Sectoral and Economywide Policies", *World Bank Economic Review*, Vol. 2, No. 3, 1988.

LINNEMAN, H., J. DE HOOGH, M.A. KEYZER, and H.D.J. VAN HEEMST, *Moira: A Model of International Relations in Agriculture*, Amsterdam: North-Holland, 1979.

MALINVAUD, E., *The Theory of Unemployment Reconsidered*, Oxford: Basil Blackwell, 1977.

MELLOR, J.W., *The New Economics of Growth: A Strategy for India and the Developing World*, Ithaca, New York: Cornell University Press, 1976.

MERCENIER, J., and J. WAELBROECK, The Sensitivity of Developing Countries to External Shocks in an Interdependent World, Discussion Paper 8338, Institut d'Etudes Européennes de l'Université Libre de Bruxelles, 1983.

MUNDLAK, Y., Intersectoral Factor Mobility and Agricultural Growth, IFPRI, Research Report 6, Washington, DC: International Food Policy Research Institute, 1979.

MUNDLAK, Y. and R. HELLINGHAUSEN, "The Inter-Country Agricultural Production Function: Another View", *American Journal of Agricultural Economics*, Vol. 64, No. 4, November 1982.

NAGLE, J.C., *Agricultural Price Policies*, Saxon House, Lexington Books, 1976.

PALDAM, M., "Industrial Conflicts and Economic Conditions", *European Economic Review*, 20, 1983.

PARIKH, K.S., G. FROHBERG and O. GULBRANDSEN, *Towards Free Trade in Agriculture*, Dordrecht: Martinus Nijhoff, 1988.

PAULINO, L.A., "Food In The Third World: Past Trends and Projections to 2000", *IFPRI Research Report*, 52, June 1986.

POWELL, A. and F. GRUEN, "The Constant Elasticity of Transformation Production Frontier and Linear Supply System", *International Economic Review*, 9, 1968.

PREOBRAZHENSKI, E., *The New Economy*, Oxford: Clarendon Press, 1956.

ROJKO, A., H. FUCHS, P. O'BRIEN and D. REIGER, Alternative Futures for World Food in 1985, World GOL Model, *USDA Foreign Economic Reports* 149, 150, 151, Washington, D.C., 1978.

VALDÉS, A. and J. ZIETZ, "Agricultural Protection in OECD Countries, its Cost to Less Developed Countries", *IFPRI Research Report* 21, Washington: International Food Policy Research Institute, 1980.

WORLD BANK, *World Development Report*, Oxford: Oxford University Press for the World Bank, 1982.

Chapter 10

ECONOMY-WIDE EFFECTS OF AGRICULTURAL POLICIES IN OECD COUNTRIES: A GE APPROACH USING THE WALRAS MODEL[1]

by

Jean-Marc Burniaux, John P. Martin, François Delorme, Ian Lienert and
Dominique van der Mensbrugghe

Agricultural policies in OECD countries have come under increasing scrutiny and criticism in recent years in line with growing imbalances in the markets for the main agricultural products and soaring budgetary support costs. There has been a sharp rise in levels of agricultural assistance in the 1980s, as measured by the Producer (and Consumer) Subsidy Equivalents (PSEs and CSEs), in virtually all OECD countries. For the OECD countries as a whole, the average net percentage PSE rose from 32 per cent in 1979-81 to 50 per cent in 1986/87, before falling back slightly to an estimated 45 per cent in 1988. The overall transfers from consumers and taxpayers associated with agricultural support in the major OECD countries have more than quadrupled in the 1980s, from $61 billion per year in 1979-81 to $270 billion in 1988[2].

In addition to having a major direct impact on the structure of agricultural production, support on such a massive scale has the potential to create serious side effects for non-agricultural sectors. There are a variety of factor- and product-market mechanisms through which such economy-wide effects can occur and any serious assessment of the costs and benefits of agricultural policies must take them into account. Applied general equilibrium (AGE) models are a natural vehicle for doing this since they allow the analyst to take account of all the feedback effects in a consistent manner. The OECD Economics and Statistics Department has developed a set of applied general equilibrium models for six OECD countries/regions with the explicit objective of quantifying the economy-wide effects of agricultural policies in OECD countries. The project is called the World Agricultural Liberalization Study — hereafter referred to as the WALRAS model — and this chapter presents some of its results[3].

The WALRAS project has two main objectives: (a) to highlight the key interactions between the agricultural and non-agricultural sectors; and (b) to quantify the efficiency and welfare effects of OECD countries' policies on the OECD countries themselves. This focus explains why the agricultural sector is not modelled in great commodity detail in WALRAS: there are only two aggregate agricultural goods compared with 18 in the MTM model. It also explains the country/region coverage and the fact that there are no developing countries distinguished separately in the model.

Thus WALRAS cannot be used to provide detailed information on the impact of agricultural liberalization by OECD countries on the developing countries. Nevertheless, it can still provide some useful information to the policy maker on this issue for two reasons. First, it is a consistent world model. Hence, it can serve as a useful check on other world AGE models such as the IIASA and RUNS models, which focus much more on detailed modelling of the agriculture sector and the developing countries but at the expense of a cursory treatment of the links with the non-agricultural sector. In addition, WALRAS includes a seventh region — the Rest of the World (ROW) — which is modelled in less detail than the OECD countries but whose supply response has some important implications for the OECD countries and vice versa.

The chapter is organised into three parts. The first section has a brief overview of the methodology on which WALRAS is based and describes how the complexity of agricultural policy regimes in OECD countries was integrated into the model[4]. The next section reports results from a simulation of a multilateral removal of recent levels of agricultural protection in OECD countries. The final section discusses how these results compare with those from other world AGE models.

OVERVIEW OF THE MODEL

The present version of WALRAS includes six submodels for the major OECD agricultural trading countries/regions — Australia, Canada, EC, Japan, New Zealand and the United States. These individual models are linked together and with a residual aggregate for the ROW via a bilateral world trade submodel. Each country/regional model can be subdivided into five blocks of equations. These are described briefly in turn.

Production

Table 10.1 lists the 13 sectors of the production submodel. Given that the main objective is to quantify the economy-wide effects of agricultural policies rather than their effects on the agricultural sector itself, the sectoral disaggregation of the model was chosen deliberately to highlight the main links between agriculture and the rest of the economy. Nonetheless, it was thought important to identify two farm sectors — livestock and other agriculture (mainly grains) — which use land as a specific fixed factor, separately from the three major food-processing industries — meat, dairy and other food products. The other eight sectors comprise other primary industries, various manufacturing and service industries.

For each sector, a production function describes the technology available to the industry. Given the standard assumptions of optimal cost minimising behaviour, producers choose inputs of primary factors and intermediate goods (domestic and imported) as a function of their relative after tax prices. Once the optimal combination of inputs is determined, sectoral output prices are calculated assuming competitive supply conditions in all markets. Since each sector supplies inputs to other sectors, output prices — which are the cost of inputs for other sectors — and the choice of the optimal combination of inputs are determined simultaneously for all sectors.

Some simplifying assumptions are used in the specification of the sectoral production functions. All non-agricultural sectors are assumed to operate under constant returns to scale, which permits the determination of output prices independently of the level of activity[5]. The primary factors of production are assumed to be in fixed supply to the total economy, fully employed and partially mobile between sectors. Labour and capital are allocated to each industry according to demand and supply, and are paid a price that equates demand with supply.

Land is assumed to be a mobile factor of production between the two agricultural sectors only; it is not modelled as a factor of production in the non-agricultural sectors. This treatment of land implies that the two agricultural sectors are implicitly characterised by decreasing returns to capital and labour.

Moreover, the model incorporates the assumption that labour and capital are less than perfectly mobile between the two farm sectors and the rest of the economy. At the same time, labour and capital are assumed to be perfectly mobile within the farm and non-farm sectors.

This implies that the returns to labour and capital are not equal in all sectors. The reasons for introducing partial factor mobility are threefold:

a) Historical evidence from OECD countries of persistent discrepancies between farm and non-farm returns to factors;

b) Econometric evidence in favour of this hypothesis[6]; and

c) The presumption that ageing of the farm labour force would contribute to lower labour mobility over the horizon of this analysis.

Another element of simplification is the assumption of fixed intermediate inputs per unit of gross output in all sectors. There are, however, two important elements of flexibility in the choices available to producers:

a) The optimal combination of capital and labour — and land in the two agricultural sectors — is variable and depends on the relative prices of these inputs, assuming substitutability between them; and

b) For each intermediate input, producers have the option of buying domestically or importing, depending on relative prices.

Consumption

A single representative consumer is assumed to choose between 13 consumer goods (see Table 10.1). These consumer goods are different from the outputs of the 13 sectors of production, and correspond more closely to the standard groups of products which consumers demand. A matrix of fixed coefficients — a so-called transition matrix — is used to convert goods and services in the production-sector classification into consumer goods and services. Using this matrix, producer prices are translated directly into prices for consumer goods, and the demands for consumer goods can be transformed immediately into demands for producer goods.

It is well known that the demand for certain goods — and in particular for food — does not increase with income as rapidly as for other goods. For this reason, the model of consumer behaviour incorporates different marginal propensities to spend on different goods and services.

Consumers are assumed to have the option of importing the commodities they want to buy. Their optimising decisions are thus separated in two stages: first, given their disposable income and the prices of consumer goods, they decide how much they want to save and how much they want to spend on each type of good or service; and second, they decide, for each of these, what proportions to buy domestically or to import, as a function of relative prices.

Consumers obtain their income from the returns to supplying primary factors of production and from government transfers. In countries where agricultural production quotas are operative, quota rents are assumed to augment farm household income. After paying income taxes, consumers spend a proportion of their disposable income on the purchase of goods and services; the remainder is saved. Saving is assumed to take the form of purchases of investment goods; financial intermediation is not incorporated in the model.

The Role of the Government

The government collects taxes on incomes, intermediate use, outputs, and consumer expenditures, as well as on imports. It also subsidises exports of agriculture and food. All of these taxes and subsidies influence the decisions of economic agents, by changing prices and/or by reducing incomes. Tax revenues collected by the government are a function of the level of economic activity and are therefore calculated endogenously. In addition, household income taxes can be adjusted to compensate for the variations in government net budget positions due to changes in agricultural protection.

Government expenditure is not constrained to be constant at its benchmark level nor equal to revenues. Once the total level of spending is decided, the government allocates it to transfers, which are exogenous in the model, or to the purchase of goods, services, capital and labour. Non-transfer expenditures are functions of relative prices, obtained from an assumption of optimising behaviour by the government.

Foreign Trade

The world trade submodel is based on a set of bilateral trade matrices which describe how price and quantity effects are channelled through world markets, with imports originating in different countries/regions being treated as imperfect substitutes. The use of such a specification — commonly referred to as the Armington (1969) specification — represents a major departure from the typical Hecksher-Ohlin framework. One drawback, however, with the use of the Armington specification in AGE models is that it often leads to strong terms of trade effects following trade experiments. In such a framework, welfare losses due to the imposition of tariffs may be compensated for by terms of trade gains.

Imports have already been mentioned above in the context of producer and consumer behaviour. Given composite import prices, calculated as the weighted average of export prices set by the other countries/regions plus tariffs, the decisions to import by producers and consumers are part of their optimising behaviour.

While most AGE models treat imports and domestic goods as imperfect substitutes, they often assume that exports and domestically sold goods are perfect substitutes. This specification of export supply, however, overstates both the links between export and domestic prices and the responsiveness of exports to demand shifts on world markets. Following the approach developed by Dervis *et al.* (1982) and de Melo and Robinson (1985, 1989), the external closure of WALRAS involves a symmetric assumption of product differentiation for imports and for exports. In each industry, producers are assumed to choose the optimal output-mix between exports and domestic supplies in response to the market-clearing price differential between domestic and export markets.

This specification of export supply — the so-called constant elasticity of transformation (CET) approach — is often justified on aggregation grounds, i.e. many of the broad sectors used in models such as WALRAS group together industries with widely differing export shares. The wider the product coverage of a given sector, the likelier it is that exported goods will be different from domestically sold ones. Hence, it seems justified to assume a lower value of the transformation elasticity for large aggregates, which group together a wide variety of different industries, than for sectors with a more homogeneous coverage. In practice, finite transformation elasticities have only been introduced in the two farm sectors and in three large non-farm sectors in WALRAS — other manufacturing industries, wholesale and retail trade and other private services.

Trade flows depend on both country supplies and foreign export demands, with the latter being determined by export prices from one country relative to its competitors' prices. Since goods are nationally differentiated, each country is assumed to face a downward-sloping demand curve for both its agricultural and industrial exports. Due to the relatively more homogeneous nature of many agricultural products as compared with manufactures, they could be treated as perfect substitutes. However, at the levels of aggregation used in WALRAS, there are considerable intercountry differences between broad categories such as "livestock" or "meat products". The capacity to take account of imperfect substitutability, therefore, seems desirable.

As a result, export prices for any commodity may differ from world prices as well as from prices paid on the domestic market, and a country may both export and import goods in a given sector. In this way the model captures the phenomenon of intra-industry trade. This represents a significant departure from the "small-country assumption" of traditional trade theory in which countries can export any amount of a given commodity at a given price and nothing at a higher price.

Countries can, in principle, run current account surpluses or deficits in the model. The counterpart of these imbalances is a net outflow or inflow, respectively, of capital, which is subtracted or added to the domestic flow of saving. To satisfy the world current account constraint, the counterpart of this net flow in turn has to be reallocated between the other countries/regions. At this stage of development of the model, however, this is done exogenously and no account is taken of net income flows associated with stocks of foreign assets or liabilities.

The model includes a measure of the "real exchange rate", which is defined as the weighted average of domestic factor prices relative to the average world price. Changes in this relative price play a key equilibrating role in the model.

Investment and Saving: Closing the Model

To complete the model, an investment equation is specified. Since there are no financial assets in the model, net saving is allocated entirely to investment goods, and thus the specification of investment is greatly simplified. Savings come from three main sources:

    a)   Private savings, as determined by consumer behaviour;

    b)   Public savings, which correspond to the net budget position; and

    c)   Foreign savings, arising from a current account deficit.

All income generated by economic activity is assumed to be distributed to consumers. Therefore, corporate saving is treated as part of household saving and is dealt with in the consumer submodel. Overall consistency requires making total domestic investment identical to net national savings plus net capital inflows. One possible closure rule would be to allow government and foreign saving to be determined endogenously. A government budget deficit, or a capital outflow as a counterpart of a current account surplus, represents applications of savings, which reduce the amount available for domestic investment.

The closure rule in the WALRAS model can be varied for different simulations. In the standard WALRAS closure, it is assumed that the initial government deficit and base year foreign trade imbalance do not change. If there were to be a change in agricultural policy, the government's deficit could be expected to change. In the model, the marginal income tax rate is adjusted to restore the initial government deficit/surplus position. This approximates revenue neutrality which is considered the appropriate closure to apply to the government sector for long-term simulations. Similarly, it would be unreasonable in the long run to have a changing foreign balance. In the model, adjustment via real factor prices is the mechanism which restores the initial balance of payments position. In the case of exogenous government and foreign trade imbalances, investment is almost entirely savings driven. If these constraints were to be relaxed, changes in the fiscal and external imbalances would be expected to have crucial effects on the aggregate savings-investment picture.

The Rest of the World (ROW) region includes not only the newly industrialising economies and the developing countries but also some OECD countries and the Centrally Planned Economies. In the present version of WALRAS, ROW does not have a full general equilibrium treatment. Instead it is restricted to a set of simple import demand functions which express imports as a function of the ratio between world import prices and ROW factor prices. Export demands to ROW are derived from the bilateral world trade submodel.

The current version of the model considers total demand for agricultural resources in ROW to be endogenous as well as supply, and determined by changes in net trade only, given that the internal demand in ROW is assumed to remain unchanged. This involves solving for an additional equilibrium price: the agricultural factor price in ROW relative to the price of the non-agricultural good which is the numeraire price in the model. The long-run supply elasticity in agriculture in ROW is set equal to the corresponding average elasticity for the OECD countries, which has been calculated at around 2.

Modelling Agricultural Policies in WALRAS[7]

One of the key issues in the WALRAS project has been how to translate the complexity and variety of agricultural policies in OECD countries into a set of policy instruments which can be manipulated easily in the model without doing too much violence to reality. The solution adopted is to represent policies in terms of a set of *ad valorem* wedges between producer and consumer prices, derived in part from OECD data on PSEs and CSEs.

The OECD estimates of PSEs cover support to the producers of 13 temperate-zone commodities, and distinguish the following policies:

a) Market price support

b) Direct payments

c) Reduction in input costs

d) General services and other expenditures

e) Subnational expenditures.

For the purposes of WALRAS, market price support has been converted into a nominal protection ratio which is implemented in the model through a set of *ad valorem import taxes* and *export subsidies*. All remaining policies are treated as a *production subsidy*. The common feature of all these other policies is that they stimulate agricultural production without inducing an increase in consumer prices. On the contrary, if these policies were to be removed, agricultural production would decrease and equilibrium producer and consumer prices would rise. In the model, these subsidies are applied equally to all primary and intermediate inputs of production.

In addition to these price wedges, it was also necessary to incorporate explicitly income flows associated with domestic *quantitative restrictions*, such as land set asides and milk production quotas which have become increasingly prevalent in the 1980s. In the case of the US *land set aside policy*, the amount of land withdrawn from production has been included directly in the policy simulations. To incorporate the effects of milk quotas in the EC, and output quotas for Canadian milk, poultrymeat and egg production, *quotas in the livestock* sector are included. Empirical studies, to the extent that they are available, were used to derive the share of the annual quota rent in the domestic producer price of each commodity. These wedges between the marginal cost of production and the producer price were treated like a fourth factor of livestock production, with an initial price equal to the quota rent that raises producer prices above those determined by marginal costs alone. In simulations of the removal of supply-management policies, i.e. when quota rents are eliminated, farm incomes decline and agricultural output expands depending on the values of the underlying supply and demand elasticities.

Constant *ad valorem* wedges alone are not able to take due account of interacting policies in a world context. Indeed, some countries tend to adjust their protection levels in response to world price changes so as to keep their internal agricultural prices constant. In this case, domestic agricultural supply no longer reacts to world market signals and budgetary expenditures on agriculture usually bear the main brunt of maintaining the gap between domestic and world prices. The EC variable import levy and export subsidy scheme is a classic example of such a system. Similar insulation of domestic from world prices is achieved by Japanese agricultural protection, and by the use of target prices for determining deficiency payments in the United States. In order to deal with this, variable import tariffs, export and production subsidies were introduced in the model. These variable instruments, however, come into play only in simulations of unilateral and partial liberalization.

Finally, agricultural assistance fluctuates from year to year in response to temporary shocks. In order to minimise the effects of temporary fluctuations in support levels, we decided to use three-year averages of the PSEs/CSEs in deriving the policy instruments[8].

Table 10.2 presents information on 1986-88 average levels of protection in the agricultural and food processing sectors. These data illustrate how the systems of protection differ across the six countries/regions, depending upon the net trade position of the country in question with respect to agricultural and food products.

EFFECTS OF A REMOVAL OF THE 1986-88 LEVELS OF AGRICULTURAL PROTECTION IN OECD COUNTRIES

This simulation involves a full multilateral removal of the average 1986-88 levels of agricultural assistance (including the elimination of the US land set asides and supply controls in the Canadian and EC dairy sectors) in the six countries/regions, assuming no change in protection in their non-agricultural sectors and no change in protection in ROW. The standard WALRAS closure rule is applied, namely no change in either the government balance or the current account. The postulated tax rates on private incomes are varied in order to maintain the given levels of the government balance. Equilibrium factor prices adjust to keep current accounts unchanged. A summary of the main results is presented in Tables 10.3a to 10.3c.

Before discussing the results some caveats must be mentioned. First, these results are designed to illustrate the long-run economic effects of current policies; they are not intended to quantify the likely impacts of any multilateral agreement which might be negotiated as part of the Uruguay Round. Second, they are also conditional upon the structure of the model, the choice of benchmark year and key parameter values, and the characterisation of most agricultural policies as *ad valorem* equivalents. Finally, the model does not capture dynamic effects arising though savings-investment decisions; hence it says nothing about the adjustment paths following any reform.

World Market Reactions

Agricultural trade liberalization has two main effects on world trade flows in WALRAS. First, countries which apply high tariff barriers, like the EC and Japan, will increase their demand for agricultural imports from other countries after these barriers have been removed. This *demand effect* serves to increase the world volume of agricultural trade, thereby increasing agricultural production and factor prices in food exporting OECD countries and the rest of the world. Countries which directly subsidise their agricultural exports (like the EC) or compensate their farmers for selling at below marginal costs with direct payments (like the United States and Canada) will now be forced to increase their offer prices on agricultural exports. This, in turn, will drive a further reallocation of the world markets. We refer to this latter effect as a *supply effect*; its magnitude depends on whether products can be substituted for each other on world markets and on the ability of potential agricultural exporters to provide what was previously supplied by OECD countries. This supply effect results in an increase of the real prices for agricultural commodities on world markets.

Therefore, the removal of agricultural protection leads to rises in both world prices and trade volumes of most agricultural and food products. In particular, the removal of the very large import taxes on dairy and on meat products has a major impact on world trade volumes and prices of these products (Chart 10.1).

Output in the Agricultural and Non-agricultural Sectors

In four of the six countries/regions, the agricultural sector contracts as a result of agricultural liberalization, while it expands in the two smaller food exporters, Australia and New Zealand. ROW is also a major gainer on world markets: its exports of agriculture and food products rise by almost 5 and 134 per cent, respectively. Rough estimates suggest this increase in ROW exports corresponds to an increase of nearly 9 per cent in its agricultural output. For the OECD countries as a whole, the output contraction in the two farm sectors is over 13 per cent on average, with above average declines in Japan, the EC and Canada, and a much smaller contraction in the United States.

As capital and labour flow out of agriculture and food processing in the EC, Canada, Japan and the United States in response to falling relative prices, output of non-agricultural sectors expands by 1 to 2 per cent in Canada, the EC and Japan, and by 0.4 per cent in the United States. The converse occurs in Australia and New Zealand, where resources flow out of the non-agricultural sectors into agriculture and food processing in response to improvements in their terms of trade.

While the simulation shows that multilateral liberalization would lead to a decline in output of the agricultural and food processing sectors in the EC and Japan, this result is in line with the findings of similar studies. There is less agreement, however, about what could happen to agricultural output in North America, as will be seen below.

These simulation results need to be seen against the perspective of the relative sizes of the sectors in question. Agriculture and food processing account for only 6 per cent of total GDP of the OECD countries so these results imply a resources shift away from agriculture and food processing towards non-food industries and services equivalent to about 1 per cent of total value added in these countries.

Factor Prices

Along with these changes in output and trade patterns, the model yields significant changes in factor prices and income distribution. Not surprisingly, there are large changes in the rental value of agricultural land, which is specific to the two farm sectors. This declines by 40 to 50 per cent in Canada, the EC, Japan and the United States. There is a small increase in Australia and a sharp rise in land prices in New Zealand. The magnitude of the fall in land prices is correlated directly with both the size of the output contraction in agriculture and the land share in value added — Canada has the third largest land share after the United States, and it records the second largest decline in agricultural output. However, these changes in land prices are overstated since, as presently specified, WALRAS makes no allowance for alternative uses of land outside agriculture. Sensitivity analysis with the Japanese model which allowed for land usage in the non-agricultural sectors, suggested that these changes could be overstated by as much as 40 to 50 per cent[9].

In those countries where the agricultural sectors contract, returns to labour and capital in these sectors also fall, though by much less than the land price. The assumption of partial factor mobility is important here since it means that returns to all three factors in agriculture will fall in all those countries where the sector contracts in response to a decline in relative product prices. The wage rate and the capital rental in the non-agricultural sectors rise in all countries in line with the expansion in industry and services. The converse occurs in Australia and New Zealand.

The Terms of Trade

Changes in the terms of trade (and the real exchange rate) play an important role in determining the outcomes. Under the assumption of an unchanged current account, sharp rises in net imports of agricultural and food products in North America, Japan and the EC have to be counterbalanced by a rise in their net exports of non-agricultural goods to Australia, New Zealand and ROW. Faced with downward-sloping export demand curves, their terms of trade (and real exchange rates) fall. The decline in terms of trade ranges from 3.6 per cent in Japan to 0.2 per cent in the United States. On the other side of the coin, the terms of trade improve for New Zealand by almost 11 per cent, for Australia by 4 per cent and for ROW by 0.8 per cent[10].

Real Income

In order to provide a summary indicator of the impact of agricultural liberalization on consumer welfare, a measure of the change in household real income — the so-called Hicksian equivalent variation — has been computed. This is the increase in income that a consumer would need before the change in relative prices to allow him to reach the welfare levels he actually achieves after agricultural liberalization. It is defined in terms of the utility function of the representative private consumer in the model; government is excluded.

Multilateral liberalization is simulated to improve welfare by 0.9 per cent on average in the six countries/regions, ranging from a real income gain of 0.3 per cent in the United States to 2.7 per cent in New Zealand. To put these estimates into context, they imply that agricultural protection in 1986-88 cost the OECD countries almost $72 billion (measured at 1988 prices and exchange rates) in lost income, over and above any benefits to farmers.

For the world as a whole, this welfare loss is an underestimate of the waste involved in farm-support policies of the OECD countries since it takes no account of the high levels of agricultural protection in other Member countries, which are not modelled specifically, such as the EFTA countries. It also takes no account of any favourable effects on household welfare from falling land prices in urban areas, although sensitivity analysis with the Japanese model suggests that this effect is likely to be small. Finally, it overlooks any welfare gains which many developing countries might realise if OECD countries were to open their markets for agricultural and food products.

One way of identifying the various sources of these real income gains from liberalizing agricultural protection is to calculate the income transfer ratio. Chart 10.2 shows the size of the changes (as a per cent of GDP) for both the agricultural and food processing sector and the non-agricultural sector. The differences between gains and losses (shown within the rectangles in Chart 10.2) reflect the intersectoral structure of each economy, as described by the detailed input-output tables; they provide an estimate of the efficiency gain in production as factors move between the agricultural and non-agricultural sectors. For the average of the six countries/regions, this amounts to 0.6 per cent. The factor reallocation implies overall productivity losses in Australia and New Zealand: the welfare gains for these two countries originate entirely from world market price changes. Agricultural protection has the most negative impact on productivity in Canada. In Japan, however, where agriculture is more labour-intensive, productivity gains are relatively small compared with the benefit to consumers of an improvement in their purchasing power for foods.

COMPARISON WITH SIMILAR STUDIES

While there is a large body of literature on using partial or general equilibrium (GE) models to analyse the costs of agricultural protection, there have only been a few studies which have examined this issue within the framework of a world GE model. Burniaux (1988) used the RUNS model — developed by Burniaux and Waelbroeck (1985) — to analyse the effects of the Common Agricultural Policy. The International Institute for Applied Systems Analysis (IIASA) has developed a very ambitious AGE model to analyse the interactions between the developed and developing countries — see Fischer *et al.* (1988) for details.

Both the RUNS and IIASA models have been applied to assess the consequences of a multilateral reform of farm-support policies at the OECD country level. Differences in results compared with WALRAS illustrate how GE analysis is sensitive to some specific assumptions about model specification and the treatment of policies. First, since WALRAS uses the PSE/CSE measures, together with instruments designed to capture the main supply controls, it is able to accommodate a much richer treatment of agricultural policies compared with the other two models which rely upon a simple nominal tariff rate as their sole policy instrument. Second, WALRAS is a comparative static long-run model whereas the IIASA and RUNS models are multi-period, dynamic models with a medium-run focus. Third, in both IIASA and RUNS models, factor shifts between farm and non-farm sectors are subject to rigidities based on medium-term econometric estimates; the degree of factor immobility is significantly more constraining than that introduced in WALRAS. Fourth, the IIASA and RUNS models also take account of price rigidities for food products, reflecting government action in stabilizing basic commodity prices. Fifth, the IIASA and RUNS models consider agricultural commodities as homogeneous whereas WALRAS treats them as imperfect substitutes. Finally, neither the IIASA nor the RUNS models are based on input-output tables; hence, unlike WALRAS, they are unable to quantify the key intersectoral linkages between the farm sectors and the food processing industries.

In comparison with WALRAS, we can anticipate that these models will exhibit larger demand shifts and lower supply adjustments; i.e. they will be more sensitive to prices. As the RUNS and IIASA models focus more on the farm sectors in developing countries than does WALRAS, part of the difference in results can be explained by a lower response of agricultural output in the Rest of the World. These points will be illustrated below with respect to world market price changes, changes in agricultural output and real income gains (see Table 10.4).

World Market Prices

The three models suggest that although world prices would increase by non-negligible amounts, these simulated increases are far less than the corresponding initial levels of support — initial nominal protection ratios range from 18 per cent (coarse grains) to 197 per cent (milk) in 1978-80 and from 43 per cent (coarse grains) to 242 per cent (sugar) in 1984-86. However, over a period of five to ten years, world market reactions are likely to compensate farmers, at least partially, for the losses incurred from the removal of the support. The corresponding figures from WALRAS suggest that these compensations are likely to be smaller in the long run than they would be over the short to medium term, especially as far as livestock products are concerned.

Unlike the other models, WALRAS describes the equilibrium situation which is reached after the existing potential for reallocation has been fully exhausted. There is, however, some uncertainty relative to the longer-run implications of agricultural reform. On the one hand, dynamic effects through reduced saving and capital accumulation in agriculture should imply further cuts in agricultural supply in the OECD countries, an outcome which would contribute to upward pressure on world market prices. While the RUNS and IIASA models are able to account for such mechanisms, they are ignored in WALRAS. On the other hand, agricultural policies in non-OECD countries are likely to be modified in response to changing world prices as governments would probably be willing to switch resources back to agriculture in order to take full advantage of world market price changes. Hence, price rigidities related to such policies cannot be adequately represented in the longer run by constant transmission elasticities between domestic and world prices, as is the case in the RUNS and IIASA models. Whatever the case, it seems highly implausible that world price increases of up to 30 per cent could persist for more than 20 years given the agricultural potentials currently existing in developing countries, as well as the proven ability of Third World agriculture in shifting resources from one product to another.

Agricultural Output

The simulation outcomes for agricultural output reflect differences in specification of agricultural supply between the three models. In comparison with the IIASA results, WALRAS reports larger cuts in agricultural output in the major food importing countries, namely Japan and the EC, but lower increases in the smaller food exporters, like Australia and New Zealand. This reveals how the assumed degree of supply rigidities in non-OECD countries acts in reallocating the additional demand for agricultural products towards more efficient food exporters and in moderating the output cuts incurred by the highly protected farm sectors in Japan and the EC. Whereas agricultural output in the non-OECD countries is roughly estimated to increase by 8.7 per cent in WALRAS, corresponding changes reported by the other two studies are in the 2-3 per cent range only (with the larger increases being in Latin America: 5.8 in RUNS, 4.6 in the IIASA model).

The more important differences between the three models relate to the simulated outcomes in Canada and the United States. Part of the explanation for the differences refers to the fact that the RUNS and IIASA models simulate removals of support levels around 1980-83 while the WALRAS figures refer to 1986-88 levels of protection. However, using the 1979-81 figures from WALRAS only goes part of the way towards reconciling the results from the various studies: relatively large cuts in farm output are still predicted by WALRAS (7 per cent in Canada, 4 in the United States) whereas the RUNS and IIASA models both predict increases. The contradiction reflects differences in measurement of the levels of support: namely, by not using PSEs/CSEs there is a significant underestimation of the effective level of support in countries such as Canada and the United States, where it mainly takes the form of direct and deficiency payments. The WALRAS results for the United States are corroborated by the findings of three other AGE models of the US economy which have focussed on the issue of agricultural liberalization, using a variety of policy instruments to characterise the policy regime[11].

Real Incomes

Real income gains in WALRAS are in line with those from RUNS as far as food exporting countries are concerned while they exceed significantly the IIASA figures. As expected, real income gains are proportional to the factor outflow from agriculture in countries where such an outflow implies an improvement in overall productivity, namely in all the OECD counties with the exception of New Zealand and Australia (see Chart 10.2). The IIASA model exhibits a lower overall level of factor mobility than either the WALRAS or RUNS models; hence it shows lower efficiency gains and even a slight welfare loss in Canada where the factor reallocation takes place at the expense of non-agricultural industries and services. On the other hand, the small food exporters are expected to benefit from terms of trade improvements and increasing world demand. In the IIASA model, this latter source of welfare gains is completely offset by sharp increases in real food prices as a result of the assumed supply rigidities in the farm sectors. Hence, while household welfare is unchanged, the IIASA results show GDP increases by 1.6 and 0.3 per cent in New Zealand and Australia, respectively.

Estimates of the gains to the EC from the RUNS model look quite optimistic, amounting to a 6.2 per cent increase in real income after 12 years. The explanation for this result is that RUNS allows non-agricultural labour demand to vary endogenously in line with an assumed degree of real wage rigidity. As real food prices decrease because of the removal of agricultural protection, so does the pressure to increase nominal wages, and the equilibrium level of output gets closer to the transformation possibility frontier. These real wage rigidities are partial and assumed to fade out gradually in the longer run. However, the short-run gains induced by these rigidities tend to improve long-run growth as increased saving adds to the capital stock in future periods.

SUMMARY AND CONCLUSIONS

While any approach to measuring the economy-wide effects of agricultural protection is subject to reservations, both on theoretical and measurement grounds, simulations with the WALRAS model suggest that existing levels of agricultural assistance in OECD countries are costly, both to the OECD countries themselves and to many non-OECD countries too. The results suggest that the average 1986-88 levels of agricultural protection could have cost the six OECD countries/regions as a whole 0.9 per cent in lower real household income ($72 billion in 1988 prices and exchange rates). This waste of resources has also to be judged against the small share of agriculture and food processing in most economies: their combined value added accounts for about 6 per cent of total GDP of the OECD countries.

The results from WALRAS, as from any other GE model, are subject to some uncertainty relative to the values of key exogenous parameters and alternative specifications. The sensitivity of the model has been tested for various parameters and the major source of uncertainty relates to the level of the substitution elasticities between domestic and imported goods — see van der Mensbrugghe et al. (1989). The sectoral results are also somewhat sensitive to the ways in which the PSE/CSE data have been used to characterise the agricultural policy regimes in OECD countries — see Martin et al. (1989) for details.

A comparison of the outcomes from the few currently existing world GE models also highlights the importance of taking account of ad hoc rigidities. These relate to agricultural policies in non-OECD countries, supply constraints and restrictions on rural factor mobility and the existence of real wage rigidities in Europe. Although part of the real world, such rigidities are typically ignored in neoclassical GE models on the grounds that they cannot resist market forces in the longer run. Persisting high unemployment rates in some European countries, however, seem to contradict this view, at least insofar as labour markets are concerned. Whatever the case, WALRAS is based on the conservative assumption of an overall high level of flexibility of rural factors, which implies aggregate supply elasticities in agriculture of around 2 in the OECD as well as in the ROW countries. Finally, the results highlight how crucial is the measurement of the various existing agricultural distortions. The use of the PSEs/CSEs indicators in WALRAS leads to outcomes for some countries, like Canada and the United States, which are completely different from those obtained from studies based on nominal protection ratios.

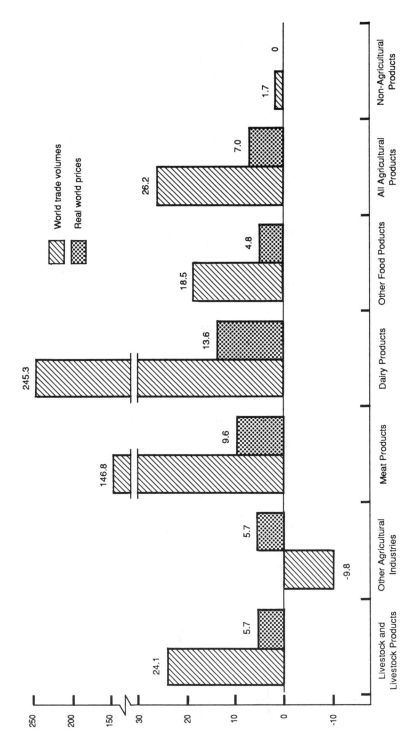

Chart 10.A. **EFFECTS OF MULTILATERAL ELIMINATION OF THE 1986 - 88 LEVELS OF AGRICULTURAL PROTECTION ON WORLD TRADE VOLUMES AND REAL WORLD PRICES BY SECTOR (a)**

(Per cent changes compared with benchmark year)

a) World trade volume changes by sector are calculated as the percentage change of post-simulation aggregate export volumes compared with benchmark aggregate volumes. The sectoral world price changes are calculated as the per cent change in world imports valued at post-simulation prices compared with aggregate world imports valued at benchmark prices.

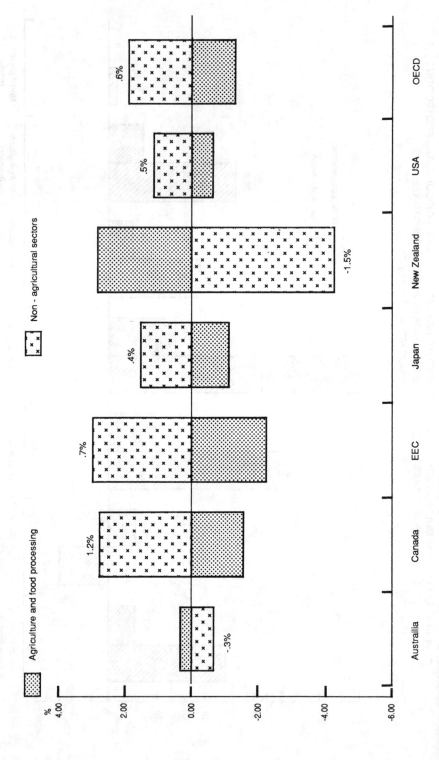

Chart 10.B. REAL INCOME TRANSFER RATIOS FROM THE ELIMINATION OF THE 1986 - 88 LEVELS OF AGRICULTURAL PROTECTION IN THE OECD COUNTRIES (CHANGE IN REAL INCOME AS A PERCENTAGE OF GDP)

Agriculture and food processing

Non - agricultural sectors

296

Table 10.1

THE STRUCTURE OF INDUSTRIES AND DEMAND IN THE WALRAS MODEL

The 13 industries

1. Livestock and livestock products
2. Other agricultural industries
3. Other primary industries[2]
4. Meat products
5. Dairy products
6. Other food products
7. Beverages
8. Chemicals
9. Petroleum and coal products
10. Other manufacturing industries
11. Construction
12. Wholesale and retail trade
13. Other private services

The 17 demand components[1]

1. Bread and cereals
2. Meat
3. Milk, cheese and eggs
4. Other food and non-alcoholic beverages
5. Alcoholic beverages
6. Tobacco
7. Clothing and footwear
8. Gross rents, fuel and power
9. Household equipment and operation
10. Medical care
11. Transport and communication
12. Education and recreation
13. Other consumer goods and services
14. Gross private fixed investment
15. Change in stocks
16. Government expenditure[3]
17. Exports of goods and services[4]

1. The first thirteen items are components of private consumption.
2. Forestry, fishing, mining and quarrying.
3. Includes government investment.
4. Includes re-exports.

Table 10.2

**1986-88 AVERAGE LEVELS OF AGRICULTURAL PROTECTION
IN THE SIX COUNTRIES/REGIONS**

	Small exporters		Large exporters		Large importers[1]	
	Australia	New Zealand	Canada	United States	EC	Japan
PSE[2]	12	18	46	39	50	76
Distribution of protection by sector:						
Agriculture	78.9	99.0	89.4	83.7	42.4	68.6
Food processing	21.1	1.0	10.6	16.3	57.6	31.4
by instrument:						
Import taxes	2.1	0.7	3.9	6.0	25.2	55.1
Export subsidies	19.3	0.3	10.6	8.2	43.7	1.5
Production subsidies	78.6	99.0	85.5	79.7	25.7	42.5
Consumption subsidies	..	..	..	6.1	5.4	0.9
Stockbuilding policies	..	..	..	6.8	..	..

1. The EC was a net importer of agricultural commodities and a net exporter of food in 1980 (the benchmark year).
2. Net total PSEs for all commodities as a per cent of adjusted production.

Table 10.3a

ECONOMY-WIDE AND SECTORAL EFFECTS FROM COMPLETE ELIMINATION OF 1986-88 LEVELS OF AGRICULTURAL SUPPORT IN OECD COUNTRIES

(Per cent changes compared with benchmark year)[1]

	Australia	Canada	EC	Japan	New Zealand	United States	OECD[2]
Aggregate effects							
Household real income	0.8	1.3	1.4	1.1	2.7	0.3	0.9
Real exchange rate[3]	1.5	-1.9	-2.9	-2.2	3.9	-1.6	-2.1
Terms of trade[4]	4.1	-0.7	-3.0	-3.6	10.6	-0.2	-1.7
Total exports[5]	3.0	3.3	7.6	10.7	-0.4	3.5	6.3
Total imports[5]	6.9	6.9	14.9	17.2	9.7	4.6	11.1
Labour re-allocation[6]	1.3	0.8	1.3	0.8	2.3	0.4	0.8
Consumer prices[7]	0.2	1.5	-0.6	-1.9	-1.6	1.0	-0.0
Sectoral effects							
Agriculture							
Output[8]	4.4	-16.7	-18.7	-24.2	7.9	-7.0	-13.6
Producer prices[9]	11.1	9.8	-4.6	-6.9	20.3	4.2	-0.0
Imports[5]	51.0	27.9	-17.4	24.8	48.4	1.7	-4.9
Exports[5]	-30.8	-42.5	-59.7	109.2	-58.2	-5.7	-21.6
Food processing and beverages							
Output[8]	14.6	1.0	-21.3	-13.9	18.9	-2.8	-11.9
Producer prices[7]	5.0	4.0	-1.3	-3.1	10.0	1.8	-0.0
Imports[5]	37.5	156.1	389.5	275.8	16.8	114.7	267.6
Exports[5]	71.1	70.8	-79.6	158.0	42.3	28.8	-20.4
Non-food industries and services[9]							
Output[8]	-0.7	0.9	2.1	1.2	-2.4	0.4	1.1
Producer prices[7]	-0.4	2.3	1.5	0.7	-2.7	0.9	1.1
Imports[5]	5.0	0.2	-2.9	-1.0	8.9	-0.1	-1.1
Exports[5]	-7.4	2.6	13.4	9.1	-18.1	3.0	8.3

Table 10.3a (continued)

1. The benchmark year for the WALRAS model is 1980 or 1981, depending upon the country/region in question. The per cent changes in the variables when the 1986-88 farm-support policies are removed are measured relative to the 1980 (or 1981) levels.
2. Total of the six countries/regions.
3. Defined as the weighted average of domestic factor prices relative to world prices in domestic currency.
4. Export prices including agricultural export subsidies divided by import prices excluding agricultural import taxes.
5. Volumes.
6. Proportion (in per cent) of total labour shifting from one sector to another.
7. Deflated by the GDP deflator at factor cost.
8. Value-added.
9. Including government.

Table 10.3b

EFFECTS OF COMPLETE ELIMINATION OF 1986-88 LEVELS OF AGRICULTURAL SUPPORT IN OECD COUNTRIES ON FACTOR AND PRODUCT PRICES
(Per cent changes compared with benchmark year)[1]

	Australia	Canada	EC	Japan	New Zealand	United States	OECD[1]
Capital rental in agriculture[3]	1.4	-9.6	-8.8	-17.5	4.4	-4.4	-8.9
Wage rate in agriculture[3]	2.8	-8.4	-4.1	-17.0	14.3	-4.7	-5.9
Price of land[3]	4.4	-53.0	-40.3	-44.3	38.7	-41.2	-39.6
Capital rental in non-agricultural sector[2]	-0.5	1.9	0.7	0.7	-2.9	1.0	0.8
Wage rate in non-agricultural sector[3]	-0.1	2.5	1.8	0.8	-3.3	0.8	1.2
Import prices[3]	-1.8	3.9	5.4	4.6	-5.2	1.9	3.8
Export prices[3]	2.2	3.2	2.2	0.9	4.9	1.6	1.9
Domestic food consumption prices[3]	5.2	1.6	-3.0	-5.3	5.8	2.0	-1.6

1. The benchmark year for the WALRAS model is 1980 or 1981, depending upon the country/region in question.
2. Total of the six countries/regions.
3. Deflated by the GDP deflator at factor cost.

Table 10.3c

**EFFECTS OF COMPLETE ELIMINATION OF 1986-88 LEVELS OF
AGRICULTURAL SUPPORT IN OECD COUNTRIES ON THE
REST-OF-THE-WORLD (ROW)**
(Per cent changes compared with benchmark year)[1]

		Rest of the World	
	Terms of trade	Import volumes	Export volumes
Agriculture	-1.0	-6.8	5.3
Food processing	-2.4	-16.7	134.4
Other industry and private services	0.8	4.3	-3.6
Total	0.8	2.7	1.6

1. The benchmark year for the WALRAS model is 1980 or 1981, depending upon the country/region in question.

Table 10.4

EFFECTS OF MULTILATERAL LIBERALIZATION OF AGRICULTURAL POLICIES IN OECD COUNTRIES ON SELECTED VARIABLES: COMPARISON BETWEEN THE WALRAS, IIASA AND RUNS MODELS[1]
(Per cent changes)

	WALRAS	RUNS	IIASA
World prices			
Wheat		24	18
Coarse grains	[17][2]	8	11
Rice		14	21
Meats	10	21	31
Milk	14	n.a.	31
Sugar	n.a.	60	n.a.
Agricultural output			
OECD	-13.5	-4.9	n.a.
EC	-18.8	-17.8	-7.1
Japan	-24.3	-9.2	-5.2
United States	-6.7		1.8
Canada	-16.8		16.6
New Zealand	7.7	11.0	14.0
Australia	4.4		2.5
Real income[3]			
OECD	0.9	1.6-2.7	0.6
EC	1.4	2.9-6.2	0.3
Japan	1.1	n.a.	1.1
United States	0.3		0.0
Canada	1.3		-0.1
New Zealand	2.7	1.1-0.7	0.0
Australia	0.8		-0.1

1. The WALRAS figures refer to the long-term effects of the elimination of the 1986-88 levels of support; the RUNS results refer to the period 1983-95; and the IIASA results refer to the period 1980-2000.
2. Extrapolated from the world price change in the "other agriculture" sector, given that cereals represent one-third of the total world trade volume for "other agriculture" commodities.
3. WALRAS and IIASA figures report household income equivalent variations; RUNS figures are GDP at market prices deflated by the consumer price index.

NOTES AND REFERENCES

1. Special thanks are due to Antonio Borges who acted as a consultant to the WALRAS project. We are also grateful to Isabelle Wanner for outstanding statistical assistance.

2. See OECD (1989) for a detailed discussion of recent trends in agricultural assistance.

3. There have been many partial equilibrium studies of the impact of farm-support policies on agricultural output, trade and welfare. See Winter (1987) for a comprehensive survey of this literature.

4. A more detailed description of these topics and related data and parameter issues can be found in Burniaux et al. (1988, 1989).

5. The assumptions of constant-returns-to-scale technology and perfect competition have, however, been relaxed in the single country model for Canada — referred to as the WALRAS-SE model — in order to explore what differences this could make to the results. This work is described in Delorme and van der Mensbrugghe (1989).

6. Econometric evidence in support of partial mobility of capital and labour between rural and urban sectors is reported in Fischer et al. (1988), p. 129.

7. For a detailed discussion of this issue, see Kienert (1989).

8. Martin et al. (1989) also report simulation results based on longer averages of the PSE/CSE data.

9. See van der Mensbrugghe et al. (1989) for details of the sensitivity analysis.

10. The results are sensitive to the magnitude of the ROW supply elasticity. If the value were set at 8 instead of 2, as is used here, the agricultural and food sectors in the OECD countries would contract more and the welfare gain would be somewhat higher in food importing countries, like Japan and the EC. The ROW terms of trade gain, however, remains equal to 0.8 per cent whatever the level of agricultural responsiveness assumed in ROW.

11. See Hertel et al. (1989), Robinson et al. (1989) and Kilkenny and Robinson (1989).

BIBLIOGRAPHY

ANDERSON, K. and R. TYERS, "Liberalising OECD Agricultural Policies in the Uruguay Round: Effects on Trade and Welfare," *Journal of Agricultural Economics,* Vol. 39, May, 1988.

ARMINGTON, P., "A Theory of Demand for Products Distinguished by Place of Production," *IMF Staff Papers,* 16(1), 1969.

BURNIAUX, J.-M. and J. WAELBROECK, "The Impact of the CAP on Developing Countries: A General Equilibrium Analysis," in C. Steven and J. Verloren van Themat (eds.), *Pressure Groups, Policies and Development,* London, Hodder and Staughton, 1985.

BURNIAUX, J.-M., F. DELORME, I. LIENERT, J.P. MARTIN and P. HOELLER, "Quantifying the Economy-wide Effects of Agricultural Policies: A General Equilibrium Approach," OECD Department of Economics and Statistics working paper No. 55, July, 1988.

BURNIAUX, J.-M., F. DELORME, I. LIENERT, and J.P. MARTIN, "WALRAS — A Multi-sector, Multi-country Applied General Equilibrium Model for Quantifying the Economy-wide Effects of Agricultural Policies," *OECD Economic Studies,* forthcoming.

BURNIAUX, J.-M., "Intersectoral Effects of CAP Trade Liberalisation," in Tarditi, S., K.J. Thompson, P. Pierani and E. Croci-Angelini (eds.), *Agricultural Trade Liberalization and the European Community,* Oxford, Oxford University Press, 1988.

DELORME, F. and D. van der MENSBRUGGHE, "Agricultural Trade Liberalisation Under Imperfect Competition: A Canadian Case Study," *OECD Economic Studies,* forthcoming.

de MELO, J. and S. ROBINSON, "Product Differentiation and Trade Dependence of the Domestic Price System in Computable General Equilibrium Trade Models," in Peeters, T., P. Praet and P. Reding (eds.), *International Trade and Exchange Rates in the Late Eighties,* Amsterdam, North Holland, 1985.

de MELO, J. and S. ROBINSON, "The Treatment of Product Differentiation and its Implications for the Foreign Trade Sector in Computable General Equilibrium Models of Small Economies," *Journal of International Economics,* 27, 1989.

DERVIS, K., J. de MELO and S. ROBINSON, *General Equilibrium Models for Development Policy,* A World Bank Research Publication, Cambridge University Press, 1982.

FISCHER, G., K. FROHBERG, M.A. KEYZER and K.S. PARIKH, *Linked National Models: A Tool for International Food Policy Analysis,* Dordrecht, Kluwer Academic Publishers, The Netherlands, 1988.

HERTEL, T., R.L. THOMPSON and M. TSIGAS, "Economywide effects of Unilateral Trade and Policy Liberalization in U.S. Agriculture," in Stoeckel, A.B., D. Vincent and S. Cuthbertson (eds.), *Macroeconomic Consequences of Farm Support Policies,* Durham, North Carolina, Duke University Press, 1989.

KILKENNY, M. and S. ROBINSON, "Economy-wide Implications of Agricultural Liberalization in the United States," Economic Research Service, U.S. Department of Agriculture, forthcoming.

LIENERT, I., "Quantifying Agricultural Policies in the WALRAS Model," *OECD Economic Studies,* forthcoming.

MARTIN, J.P., J.-M. BURNIAUX, F. DELORME, I. LIENERT, and D. VAN DER MENSBRUGGHE, "Economy-wide Effects of Agricultural Policies in OECD Countries: Simulation Results with the WARLRAS Model," *OECD Economic Studies,* forthcoming.

OECD, *National Policies and Agricultural Trade*, Paris, 1987a.

OECD, *Structural Adjustment and Economic Performance*, Paris, 1987b.

OECD, *Agricultural Policies, Markets and Trade: Monitoring and Outlook 1988*, Paris, 1989.

ROBINSON, S., I. ADELMAN and M. KILKENNY, "The Effect of Trade Liberalization in Agriculture on the U.S. Economy: Projections to 1991," in Stoeckel, A.B., D. Vincent and S. Cuthbertson (eds.), *Macroeconomic Consequences of Farm Support Policies*, Durham, North Carolina, Duke University Press, 1989.

van der MENSBRUGGHE, D., J.P. MARTIN and J.M. BURNIAUX, "How Robust Are WALRAS Results?", *OECD Economic Studies*, forthcoming.

WINTERS, L.A., "The Economic Consequences of Agricultural Support: A Survey," *OECD Economic Studies*, No. 9, Autumn, 1987.

Chapter 11

AGRICULTURAL LIBERALIZATION, WELFARE, REVENUE AND NUTRITION IN DEVELOPING COUNTRIES[1]

by

Thomas Loo and Edward Tower

INTRODUCTION

Less developed countries, particularly the poorest ones, typically impose restrictions on imports of final industrial goods and tax exports of agricultural products. The rationales for such policies are to protect domestic industry, raise nutritional standards, increase industrial employment, improve the terms of trade, raise revenue and alter the income distribution. This paper demonstrates the importance of three second best issues in analysis of agricultural liberalization by developing countries: import tariffs and quotas, rent seeking in the allocation of import licenses, and the cost of raising tax revenues. We use a highly aggregated, full-employment computable general equilibrium model to explore the impacts of changed agricultural policies in low income less developed countries on several aspects of their economic performance: welfare, revenue, and food consumption. It is implemented on the General Algebraic Modelling System (GAMS), and well documented (in appendices, which are available upon request). We consider various interactions of rent seeking with import restrictions, and use the model to calculate for a representative developing country (LDC):

a) Cost/benefit ratios for incremental policy reforms;

b) Optimum welfare, maximum revenue and maximum nutritional export tariffs;

c) Optimum export taxes for alternative degrees of willingness to trade off welfare and nutrition;

d) The sensitivity of optimum welfare export taxes to the degree of foreign aid; and

e) Debt repayment which reform of agricultural export tax policy would make possible without reducing a developing country's welfare.

All of our conclusions are conditional on the particular parameter values assumed and our informed guesses about the tax structure of the group of low income developing countries analysed. Moreover, no one model can adequately describe all developing countries, so limited confidence should be placed on particular simulations. Still, our parameter values reflect reasonable guesses about how the economy functions over a time horizon of approximately three to five years. Also, the sensitivity of our results to alternative specifications for rent seeking and the form of import restrictions have important policy implications. The model demonstrates that agricultural liberalization will be most successful when import restrictions consist of tariffs and least successful when they consist of fixed import quotas with rent seeking prevalent. The paper also demonstrates the types of calculations that we believe to be useful for policy analysis: optimum taxes for alternative policy maker's objective functions and cost/benefit ratios. Our major findings are contained in the "lessons" sprinkled throughout the paper and in the paper's conclusion.

Tariffs, Quotas and Rent Seeking: Intuition

Before presenting the actual model used, we provide in Figure 11.1 a simple version of it, which is enough to illustrate qualitatively what Clarete and Whalley (1988) found for the Philippines and the most important mechanisms operating in our model. The two parts of Figure 11.1 illustrate a small open economy which produces and consumes three goods: an agricultural exportable good AX with an export tax attached, a non-traded good, labour services, which is subject to no distortions, and an imported good J, which is subject to both an import tariff and import quota.

Representing $TAXAX$ as the initial export tax expressed as a fraction of the domestic price, PA:

$$PA = PAX \,/\, (1 + TAXAX)$$

where PAX is the fixed world price. Figure 11.1a shows the domestic excess supply of the agricultural export, S^{AX}, as a function of its domestic price PA^2. Figure 11.1b shows the domestic market for J. Its import tariff is levied at an *ad valorem* rate of $TAXJ$. J is also subject to import licencing, with its import licenses valued at an *ad valorem* premium pegged at QJ. The fixed world price of J is PJ, and the price to domestic buyers of J is PJB whose initial value is PJB_0. D^J shows the excess demand for J as a function of PJB at the initial agricultural export tax. D^J_L is the demand for J after agricultural liberalization, defined as an incremental reduction of the agricultural export tax, $TAXAX$. The agricultural liberalization generates more foreign currency to be spent on J at any price PJB. Thus D^J_L lies incrementally to the right of D^J. Liberalization moves the level of imports from J_0 to J_L.

The welfare gain from the reduction of TAXAX, which raises the domestic price of AX from PA_0 to PA_L and increases the quantity of agricultural exports from AX_0 to AX_L, is given by the area marked A in Figure 11.1a between the domestic excess supply of the agricultural export good and its fixed world price, plus an area in Figure 11.1b.

If the ad valorem equivalent of the import licence premia is kept constant by varying the number of import licenses printed, and there is no rent seeking, with imports of J going to their highest valued use, then there is an additional welfare gain equal to the sum of the shaded areas marked T and Q. This would be the situation, for example, if import licenses were auctioned off.

Suppose the *ad valorem* equivalent of the import licence premia is kept constant as above, but there is rent seeking, which is modelled by queuing for the import licenses. The value of additional time spent in the queue as a result of the liberalization is the area of the additional quota rents denoted by Q. In this case the additional welfare gain is only T, instead of $T+Q$. Thus, the welfare gain associated with agricultural liberalization is less with rent seeking[3] than when it has been suppressed by efficiently distributing the import licenses[4].

As a third possibility, suppose that the import licenses are fixed in quantity, but there is no rent seeking. In this case the price of J to domestic buyers rises to PJB_L, but with trade balanced and imports fixed, exports must also be frozen. Thus S^{AX} is vertical, and there is no welfare change at all.

As a final possibility, suppose that the import licenses are fixed in quantity, and that the quota rents are dissipated in rent seeking. In this case, liberalization again raises the price of J to PJB_L. But this time additional resources equal to R are drawn into rent seeking to acquire the new larger premia, resulting in a welfare loss of R. Moreover, S^{AX} is vertical, so there is no welfare gain on the export side. This set of assumptions leads to the welfare loss, R, shown in Figure 11.1b, implying a welfare loss from liberalization.

This analysis leads us to conclude that the welfare gain from liberalization will be largest when the fixed quota is replaced by a fixed import licence premium and import licenses are distributed in such a way (by auction or lottery with permitted resale) that rent seeking is minimised[5].

These qualitative predictions are precisely what Clarete and Whalley (1988) found for a small open developing economy: the Philippines, using a specific factors model with import and export tariffs and which is similar to our model. They considered various liberalization experiments, including the elimination of export taxes. With no quotas welfare rose by 0.3 per cent. With fixed quotas on only import substitutes, but no rent seeking, welfare rose by 0.11 per cent. With rent seeking added welfare rose by 0.08 per cent. Finally, with fixed quotas covering all imports and no rent seeking, so that the condition for trade balance equilibrium dictated no change in total exports or imports, export liberalization left welfare virtually unchanged (a change of zero per cent). Finally, with rent seeking added export liberalization reduced welfare by 0.2 per cent.

Modeling a Representative Developing Country

We constructed the model and calibrated it for a representative low income developing country as follows[6]. The data describing our country are the parameters which are presented in the World Development Report 1989 (henceforth simply WDR) and describe low income economies other than China and India[7]. The WDR defines "low-income economies" as those with a GNP per capita of $480 or less in 1987[8]. The data used are presented in our Table 11.1.

Figure 11.2 illustrates our model. We assume four sectors. Every production and consumption relationship is assumed to be a nested, constant-returns-to-scale Cobb-Douglas function, so input proportions everywhere depend solely on relative prices. The agricultural sector uses imported materials (ZA) plus land (T) to produce an agricultural composite (TZ) which is combined with labour services (LA) to produce agricultural output (A), some of which is exported (AX) and some of which (AC) is combined with imports, [typically of cereals] (C) to produce a composite commodity called food (F) which is consumed domestically. The industrial sector uses labour (LI) and capital (K) to produce an industrial composite which in combination with imported materials (ZI) is used to produce the industrial good (I), some of which is exported (IX), and some of which is combined with final good imports (J) to produce a good which we refer to as merchandise (M). The mining and petroleum sector (henceforth simply "deposits") uses natural resource endowments, which we refer to as deposits (D), along with labour (LD), to produce a natural resource composite, which is combined with imported materials (ZD) to produce deposits output, (DX), all of which is exported. Finally, the services sector uses labour to produce services (S), all of which are consumed domestically.

Consumption is also nested with consumption proportions depending on relative prices. Merchandise and food combine to produce a goods composite (G) which is consumed along with services. Labour is assumed to be homogeneous when measured in efficiency units and is assumed to be perfectly mobile between agriculture, industry, services and deposits.

All world prices are assumed to be exogenous, except for the world price of agricultural exports, which is assumed to be determined by a constant elasticity foreign excess demand curve. However, throughout the paper except in the section discussing terms of trade, even the world price of agricultural exports is assumed to be fixed. Imports are assumed to be financed by exports plus an exogenously determined level of foreign aid net of debt servicing (AID). Thus the trade deficit equals foreign aid net of debt servicing requirements. Perfect labour mobility between sectors equates wage rates throughout the economy. Flexible wages and prices maintain full employment. All disposable income is spent, so that the trade deficit is equal to the government budget deficit. We assume that the proportions in which various goods and services are consumed domestically are invariant to the income distribution. Also, we assume that the government's consumption function is identical to that of the private sector and that it responds to the same tax-inclusive prices that the private sector does. Thus, we assume that the government adjusts tax rates in order to enable it to finance its initial real consumption level with available tax revenues plus foreign aid net of debt servicing requirements.

We postulated that the only taxes are those on agricultural exports (*TAXAX*), agricultural production for domestic consumption (*TAXAC*)[9], extraction of minerals (*TAXD*)[10], imports of the import-competing final industrial good (*J*, *TAXJ*), exports of the final industrial good (*IX*, *TAXIX*) and consumption of the composite good (*G*, *TAX*). Services are assumed to be tax free. We also recognise that the imported final industrial good is subject to quota protection, with a tariff/quota premium of *TAXQJ*. Some of our simulations assume that the *ad valorem* equivalent of the quota protection is constant. Other simulations assume that the import quota on *J* is fixed.

Some simulations assume that import licenses are given away efficiently, so there is no rent seeking. Other simulations assume that rent seeking drives the net private return to acquiring the licence to zero. We model the rent seeking process as labour queuing for the licenses until the wage rate in queuing is driven down to the wage rate elsewhere in the economy.

We calibrated the taxes as follows. We constructed effective rates of protection (ERP) for our hypothetical country by drawing on information contained in the 1986 and 1987 WDRs and asking experts from the World Bank and elsewhere for their best informed guesses about the ERPs that apply on average to industrial and agricultural goods for domestic consumption and exports[11]. Table 11.2 presents these ERPs and the tax rates calculated from them and the benchmark equilibrium flows. Our figures for ERPs show, based on the 1986 and 1987 WDRs, that the poorer the country is, the lower its ERP for agricultural exports (*ERPAX*) and the higher its ERP on import competing industry (*ERPID*) tend to be. Thus our ERPs are extreme by world standards.

We determined the *ad valorem* tax on agricultural exports to be that rate which would set *ERPAX* at its exogenously determined level given in the top half of Table 11.2. We then set the ad valorem equivalent of tariff plus quota protection on the imported final industrial good (*J*) at that rate which would set *ERPID* at its exogenously determined level. We assumed the subsidy rate on industrial exports and the tax on the production of agricultural goods for domestic consumption which set the corresponding ERPs, *ERPIX* and *ERPAD* equal to their predetermined levels.

Data on tax revenues arising out of international trade is presented in the WDR. We then divided up the protection on *J* into tariff and quota components so that trade tax revenues in the benchmark equilibrium equaled this figure. We postulated that all mining and petroleum exports were taxed via 20 per cent of royalties paid to the fixed factor (a non-distorting tax), and that no additional taxes were levied on this sector. The remaining tax revenues indicated in the WDR were assumed to be collected via a uniform excise tax on the composite consumption good[12].

We recognise that the export tax may substitute for an alternative distorting tax in generating revenue. In our simulations, we used the excise tax. Consequently, we modelled the excise tax so that the marginal welfare cost of tax collection (MWC) from adjusting this tax was consistent with evidence from other sources. There are efficiency costs associated with collecting this tax which are greater than would appear from just looking at the average excise tax wedge. In reality, these consist of administrative costs of tax collection, resources used up in tax avoidance, tax compliance and tax evasion, and resource misallocation costs. To keep the modelling simple, we modelled these as a leak in the tax collection process. We assumed that the excise taxes paid exceed the tax revenue accruing to the government by a factor consisting of bribes to the tax collector and issuers of licenses[13]. Picking an appropriate level for the MWC is tricky, because all governments are currently imposing some taxes with very high MWCs such as tariffs, licencing fees and the inflation tax. Moreover, they have the capacity to collect taxes with negative MWCs such as those on pollution and charges for import licenses, which diminish rent seeking. Ballard, Shoven and Whalley (1985, p. 128) estimate that "The welfare loss from a 1 per cent increase in all distortionary tax rates [in the United States] is in the range of 17 to 56 cents per dollar of extra revenue." Stuart (1984) estimates 24 per cent. Judd (1987) has median estimates of 12 per cent and 21 per cent for the marginal welfare cost of permanent wage taxation, and 42 per cent and 149 per cent of the marginal welfare cost of permanent capital income taxation. We asked two leading practitioners of tax reform in developing countries who estimated 30 per cent and 50 per cent respectively for the *MWC* via the kinds of tax increases that are likely to occur in such countries. Drawing in part on this information, we based all of our calculations on either a zero leak, which implies (according to our simulations with no rent seeking and a fixed import license premium) a *MWC* of 16.6 per cent or a leakage rate of 84.7 per cent of the tax collected, which implies a *MWC* of 50 per cent. Except where noted explicitly, we use a leak of zero.

We calibrated all benchmark flows to correspond to those of Table 11.1 and to be consistent with the distortions of Table 11.2. We treated the imports of fuels and other primary goods, and machinery and transport equipment as intermediate inputs into the three sectors, and apportioned them in proportion to value added in those sectors. Throughout, we assumed that all production and consumption relations are nested Cobb-Douglas, with constant returns to scale.

Table 11.3 presents definitions of the most important notation used.

Properties of the Model

The quantitative results depend strongly on the demand and supply relationships in agriculture, so we present in Table 11.4, the relevant elasticities. These elasticities are generated by the following conceptual experiment. We allowed the world price of agricultural exports to rise by 1 per cent. We held constant all tax and tariff rates and the *ad valorem* equivalent of the quota restriction on imports of final industrial goods. We assumed no rent seeking, and we postulated that the real government budget was kept constant by adjusting lump sum taxes. The elasticity of agricultural production was recorded as the percentage change in domestic agricultural production (A). The elasticity of agricultural exports was recorded as the percentage change in domestic agricultural exports (AX). The elasticity of agricultural consumption was recorded as the percentage change in consumption of A (AC).

The consumption elasticity seems small in absolute value. This is partially due to the fact that a 1 per cent higher agricultural price drives up the wage rate by 0.986 per cent, which in turn drives up the price of services by the same amount, thereby limiting the fall in AC. This serves as a reminder that these are general equilibrium elasticities. An elasticity of agricultural production of 0.63 seems reasonable to us over a several year time horizon. The large agricultural export supply elasticity of 8.13 reflects the fact that trade is small relative to domestic production and consumption, and that export supply is an excess supply. Such a large figure would be relevant only for countries that have no quantitative barriers to exports and are assumed to provide transportation facilities in response to changed excess supplies[14].

The assumption that all world prices are fixed would be relevant only for a country which is flexible enough to adjust its export production, in both agriculture and industry, to take advantage of the best world prices available. Thus the fewer restrictions that are placed on the allocation of resources within the major export aggregates, the more closely the real world approximates our assumption of fixed world prices. In the section on terms of trade we relax the assumption of fixed world prices.

Finally, as a check on the model, we raised all world prices by the same proportion and discovered that no real variables changed. As a second check, we raised all factor supplies and the government's revenue needs by the same proportion and discovered that all prices remained unchanged while all real variables increased by the same proportion as the exogenous changes.

Cost/Benefit Analysis for Incremental Policy Reform

Table 11.5 presents cost/benefit ratios for an incremental reduction of agricultural export tax. In each case we simulated a 1 per cent reduction in the agricultural export tax rate. We denote percentage changes with hats, "^".

Column 1 defines the cost/benefit ratio. Column 2's "Lump Sum Taxes (LST)" simulation assumes that all distorting taxes and quotas, other than the agricultural export tax ($TAXAX$) have been eliminated and that any shortfall or surplus in the government's budget is accommodated by adjusting non-distorting lump sum taxes[15]. While the notion of a lump sum tax is an idealized one, there is an array of relatively distortionless taxes available, such as land taxes and fines for antisocial behaviour. Thus we believe that these LST simulations are useful.

Column 3's "Incremental Lump Sum Taxes (ILST)" simulation assumes that all other taxes and the *ad valorem* equivalent of the import quota are unchanged, and that incremental changes in revenue generated by these distorting taxes are accommodated by adjusting lump sum taxes. It also assumes no leakage in the collection of the excise tax, and as in other columns, unless explicitly noted to the contrary, it assumes away rent seeking.

Column 4's "Excise Tax Adjustment (ETA)" simulation is identical to column 3's, except that any change in real tax revenues is replaced by adjustment in the excise tax rate.

Column 5's "ETA/50 per cent MWC" simulation is identical to column 4's, except that leakage is assumed to occur in collection of the excise tax, raising the marginal welfare cost of tax collection via hiking the excise tax to 50 per cent.

Column 6's simulation is identical to that in column 3 except that the import quota on the final industrial good is fixed.

Column 7's simulation is identical to that in column 4 except that the import quota on the final industrial good is fixed. Finally, column 8 is identical to column 7's except that rent seeking for the import licenses occurs. As noted above, rent seeking is modelled as if labour queues for the import licenses until the implicit wage for queuing is identical to that in the rest of the economy.

Rows 1 and 2 show the percentage changes in utility ($\hat{U}$) and real government revenues ($RE\hat{V}TOT$) due to a 1 per cent cut in the agricultural export tax. In each of the simulations reducing the export tax raises utility and real government revenue. This implies that the current agricultural export tax rate exceeds the levels that maximise utility and real tax revenue in each case. In each case, the export tax reduction increases revenue collected directly from the export tax ($TAXAX$, not shown). The largest increment to utility comes in column 5. The gain is high, because (a) the export tax reduction is accompanied by an increase in imports which now generates more tariff revenue, and (b) this increased tariff revenue makes possible a larger reduction in a highly distorting excise tax.

The increment to utility is smaller when the fixed quota of column 6 applies. This is because increased imports across a tariff/quota wedge are welfare improving, since consumers are willing to pay more for these increased imports than their foreign exchange cost[16]. A fixed quota eliminates this mechanism, so the welfare gain in 6 is smaller. Even with the fixed quota, liberalization raises revenue, so the welfare gain in 7, when the distorting excise tax can be reduced, is slightly greater than in 6. Finally, the welfare gain in 8 is smallest. The reason is that agricultural liberalization in the presence of a fixed import quota raises the domestic relative price of the restricted final good import relative to the wage rate. This drives additional labour into rent seeking, thereby depriving the economy of the incremental rent seekers' labour services. The largest gain in utility is more than a factor of five times the smallest gain in utility. These calculations support the ideas illustrated in Figure 11.1. They also illustrate:

Lesson 1

A. *Using different closures the largest gain in utility from incremental agricultural liberalization is more than a factor of five times the smallest gain in utility. The implication is that in assessing agricultural policy, it is important to imbed the analysis in a general equilibrium framework.*

B. *An incremental cut in the agricultural export tariff will be most effective when imports are covered by a fixed quota premium instead of a fixed quota and the cut makes possible the reduction of a highly distorting tax[17].*

C. *It will be least effective when there is a fixed import quota combined with a rent seeking mechanism, so that the liberalization results in increased rent seeking.*

D. *Liberalization makes possible the reduction of a distorting tax elsewhere when the initial export tax exceeds the maximum revenue tax, as it does in every simulation we performed with fixed world prices.*

Row 2 indicates that the increment to real government revenue is largest with the lump sum tax, smaller with the incremental lump sum tax, and smallest when there is a quota. The increment is largest in the lump sum tax case, because the liberalization of the rest of the economy has increased agricultural exports to a multiple of 1.59 of its initial value (not shown), so the base on which the agricultural tax operates is much larger than in the benchmark equilibrium. The figure for the incremental lump sum tax case is over twice that for the fixed quota case because in the former case AX expands more, raising more revenue from export and import taxation.

Row 3 indicates that cutting the export tax by 1 per cent may cut food consumption by as much as 0.05 per cent or raise it by as much as 0.026 per cent.

Recall from Table 11.3 that our utility function is first degree homogeneous; we define a unit of utility so that the marginal utility of income is unity, and we define a unit of real revenue as that which buys one util at current prices. Row 4 shows the ratio of the utility change to the change in consumption of food, where a unit of food is defined as that amount which costs one unit of domestic currency in the benchmark equilibrium. This implies that the ratios in row 4, like all the other rows in the table, are dimensionless. The large positive figures in columns 5, 6 and 7 imply that for those simulations the current export tax is slightly above the maximum nutritional level. Consequently, incremental export tax reductions raise welfare much more than they do the nutritional level. The other figures imply that an incremental tax reduction raises utility by 1.6 to 7.4 times as much as it cuts the value (at initial prices) of food consumption. The tradeoff is least beneficial to a tax reduction in the rent seeking/fixed quota case of column 8. This is because of the contribution that liberalization makes to increased rent seeking. This analysis yields:

Lesson 2

Cutting the agricultural export tax incrementally may raise or lower food consumption. But even when the maximum nutritional export tax lies above the benchmark level, the marginal welfare gain from trading off the nutritional goal is quite large (163 per cent to 736 per cent of the reduction in food consumption). This implies that it is fruitful to search for more efficient ways to keep nutrition up.

Row 5 shows the ratio of utility change to the change in industrial employment, where a unit of labour is defined as that amount which earns one unit of domestic currency at initial wages. Thus the welfare cost of using incrementally higher agricultural export taxes to raise industrial employment is 0.6 to 4.6 times the value of employment created thereby.

Row 6 shows the ratio of utility change to the change in total real rents accruing to industrial capital (RRK). Thus the welfare cost of using incrementally higher agricultural export taxes to raise real rents to industrial capital is 0.3 to 3.34 to times the real rents bestowed.

The figures in the last three rows lead us to conclude:

Lesson 3

A policy maker who values aggregate real income as well as food consumption, industrial employment, and/or high real incomes for industrial capitalists will find agricultural export tax reduction more appealing, if he is able to eliminate both fixed quotas and rent seeking.

Apportioning the Welfare Gains

In Figure 11.1, we attempted to provide an intuitive treatment of the paper. Now we relate our simulation results to the standard mathematical analysis of welfare change in the presence of incremental tax adjustments, developed by Harberger and modified by Smith (1982) and others.

It follows that the change in developing country real income, measured as the change in consumption at consumer prices can be measured as:

Developing Country Real Income Change =

(1)   The change in exports of agricultural goods multiplied by the export tariff [Export Distortion Effect]

+*(2)*   The change in imports of industrial goods multiplied by the import tariff and the import license premium [Import Distortion Effect]

+*(3)*   The change in consumption of the domestically produced agricultural good multiplied by its tax [Agricultural Consumption Distortion Effect]

+*(4)*   The change in consumption of the traded goods composite multiplied by the excise taxes (+ leakages, i.e. taxes kept by the tax collector)[Excise Tax Effect]

–*(5)*   Resources absorbed in rent seeking [Rent Seeking Effect]

+*(6)*   The change in the explicit transfer to the developing country through increased foreign aid or reduced repayment of principal on its debt [Transfer Effect]

–*(7)*   The change in the implicit transfer from the developing country through reduced agricultural prices, measured as the initial value of its agricultural exports times the change in their world price [Terms of Trade Effect].

Intuitively, any item which is taxed is worth more to the buyer than it is to the seller. Therefore, an increase in the size of a taxed transaction represents movement of items to where they are valued more highly. Consequently, a country's welfare rises whenever it exports more of a taxed good, imports more of a protected good, consumes more of a taxed good, or when resources are released from rent seeking. Welfare also rises whenever the country receives an explicit transfer or an implicit transfer through improved terms of trade.

Now we explain and interpret some of the results from Table 11.5. In these particular simulations, there are no implicit or explicit transfers, so transfer effects are absent. In Table 11.6, we normalize the change in welfare to equal 100 per cent, in order to see what proportion of the welfare gains in each simulation is accounted for by each distortion. This accounting is a measure of the importance of the various distortions.

From Table 11.6 we see:

Lesson 4

If one correctly measures the flows of goods and factors but in the welfare calculations ignores all distortions, except for the agricultural export tax, the estimate of the welfare change ranges from 62 per cent to 286 per cent of the correct value. This is one measure of the importance of considering general equilibrium welfare effects in carrying out such analysis. In particular, in the fixed quota premium cases, 23 per cent to 25 per cent of the total impact of incremental liberalization are accounted for by the effect of import restrictions[18].

It is well known from Krueger and others that import and export taxes combine to create a bias against international trade. Consequently, in the presence of both types of restriction, a reduction in either one can significantly increase welfare. Table 11.6 makes that same point in yet another way.

Optimum Welfare Agricultural Export Tax

Table 11.7 presents the export tax rates which maximise domestic utility under various circumstances. So that the reader can develop a sense of how the model works, we present benchmark (base equilibrium) values for a number of variables (defined in Table 11.3) in column 2. Then in subsequent columns we present the ratio of their values with the optimum agricultural export tax to their initial values. Only for the agricultural export taxes do we present actual *ad valorem* rates. The second row indicates that the utility ranges from 98.4 per cent to 106.8 per cent of its base value. Column 3 shows that if all distorting taxes, except for the agricultural export tax, are removed and replaced by non-distorting lump sum taxes, the optimum value for the export tax is zero, which is what theory predicts, with utility rising by 6.8 per cent above the base value. The lower value than we had anticipated for the utility increase reflects the small initial volume of international trade.

Column 4 indicates that if all other taxes are held in place, the optimum agricultural export tax is a subsidy of 14.6 per cent. This subsidy partially offsets the import tariff/quota wedge on industrial imports of 71 per cent (as well as the other distortions).

Column 5 indicates that with excise tax adjustment the optimum export subsidy is smaller than in column 4, as a lower subsidy enables reduction of the distorting excise tax.

Column 6 indicates that with the fixed import quota and incremental lump sum tax adjustment, the subsidy is still smaller than with the tariff in column 3 or column 4, as there is no benefit from an efficiency standpoint of counterbalancing the tariff with a subsidy.

Column 7 indicates that with the fixed quota and excise tax adjustment, the optimum strategy changes from a subsidy to a tax, because, as in column 5, this permits reduction of the distorting excise tax.

Column 8 finds that the introduction of rent seeking behavior raises the optimum agricultural export tax to 27.7 per cent. This relatively high optimum export tariff reflects the fact that raising the tariff from the level in column 7, lowers the price of food. This lowers the value of the marginal product of labour in agriculture, which lowers the wage rate. This lowers the price of services and causes a shift away from the consumption of the imported industrial good, *J*, into services. This lowers the quota premium on *J*, and drives labour out of rent seeking.

Column 9 finds that if the fixed import quota is replaced with a fixed *ad valorem* equivalent of the initial quota, that the import quota roughly the same at 27.6 per cent. It is interesting to note that this tariff reduction (from the benchmark value of 55.6 per cent) actually reduces rent seeking below its base value. The reason is that the lower export tariff raises the wage by a larger proportion than it increases imports of *J*. Therefore with the fixed *ad valorem* import tariff, labour is drawn away from rent seeking into socially productive activities.

Column 10 investigates a fall of net foreign aid from the initial 5 per cent of GNP to -5 per cent of GNP. We choose to interpret this as paying off foreign debt. Should governments raise export taxes in periods of low net transfer receipts? Putting the same issue differently, does foreign aid give governments an incentive to liberalize? The relevant column for comparison is 4. We see that reduced foreign aid lowers the optimum export subsidy by approximately 1 percentage point, or that increased foreign aid provides an incentive to lower the export tax slightly. To see why this is the case, note that debt repayment lowers domestic real income, which shrinks domestic demand for the non-traded services. This shrinks the price of services, and causes substitution out of goods into services. Since the marginal propensity to spend on J is now lower than before, incremental cuts in the export tax cause fewer imports to enter the country across the tariff/wedge than before. Therefore, the beneficial effects on the import side from export tariff cuts are lessened. Consequently, the optimum export tax is higher (export subsidy is lower) than it would otherwise have been.

This analysis of Table 11.7 leads us to:

Lesson 5

With the ad valorem equivalent of the import quota fixed, efficient taxation at the margin, and no rent seeking, the optimum export tax is negative -- a subsidy of 14.6 per cent. Rent seeking for import licenses reduces the optimum degree of export tax reduction, driving up the optimum export tax to 28 per cent both with the fixed quota and the ad valorem equivalent of the quota fixed.

Maximum Revenue Agricultural Export Tax

Table 11.8 presents the consequences of imposing the maximum (real) revenue agricultural export tax (*MRAXT*). The concept only has a meaning when all other taxes are held constant. Thus we present only the lump sum and incremental lump sum tax calculations. Our values for *REVTOT* are real revenues collected other than through lump sum taxes.

MRAXT is seen to lie between 35 per cent and 49 per cent. Of course, ideally all taxes should be adjusted until all of their marginal welfare costs of tax collection are equalized. When other taxes are unconstrained, the optimum tax structure would consist solely of taxes on primary factor services and/or consumption. Trade should be taxed only if a terms of trade effect is present.

Because of the contribution that import tariffs make to revenue, the *MRAXT* is lower in column 4 than in column 3.

Reducing net foreign aid receipts, as we have done in column 5 raises the *MRAXT* slightly, again because, as in the last table, incremental imports of *J* due to reduced export taxes shrink.

Replacing the *ad valorem* equivalent of the base quota with a fixed quota, but still without rent seeking (going from column 4 to column 6) raises the *MRAXT*, as one would expect, for again increased exports no longer contribute to increased import tariff revenues.

Adding rent seeking to the fixed quota case, in going from column 6 to column 7, raises the *MRAXT* further, as the higher export tax draws down the import quota premium and puts rent seekers back to productive labour.

Replacing column 7's fixed import quota with column 8's fixed *ad valorem* equivalent of the base quota lowers the *MRAXT* as incremental export tax reductions once again contribute to increased imports across the tariff barrier.

An unexpected result is that holding the *ad valorem* equivalent of the base quota constant and introducing rent seeking by moving from column 4 to column 8 actually lowers the *MRAXT*. The explanation is that with rent seeking, incremental lowering the export tax from column 4's maximum revenue level raises wages faster in percentage terms than it raises *J* imports, and this draws labour out of rent seeking.

This analysis of Table 11.8 leads us to conclude:

Lesson 6

The maximum revenue agricultural export tariff is between 35 per cent and 49 per cent. Reducing the agricultural export tax to its maximum revenue level would raise real revenues by figures ranging from 0.3 per cent to 3.4 per cent.

Maximum Nutritional Agricultural Export Tax

The WDR (1986, p. 150) notes that export taxes and quotas are often used in developing countries to keep the price of food low. It then goes on to note: "Small and well-targeted food distribution programs are more effective in promoting specific nutritional objectives in especially disadvantaged groups." Still, it is interesting to ask: "Suppose such ideal programmes are infeasible, what is the food export tax which maximises food consumption?"

Table 11.9 presents the maximum nutritional agricultural export tax (*MNAXT*) under various assumptions. Note that the *MNAXT* ranges from 85.5 per cent of its base value up to 158 per cent. Thus which way the export tax should move to maximise nutrition is indeterminate.

In moving from column 3's lump sum tax case to column 4's incremental lump sum tax, the MNAXT falls. This reflects the role of tax reductions in stimulating imports across a tariff wedge which is welfare increasing and in turn stimulates food consumption.

The MNAXTs were so high that they reached the prohibitive levels ($AX = 0$) in columns 3 and 4.

Column 5 assumes that excise tax adjustment with no leakages to the tax collector is used to balance the government's budget. The marginal welfare cost of tax collection in the base equilibrium was 16.6 per cent. This assumption, as one would expect, drives the maximum nutritional tax down, closer to the maximum revenue level.

Column 6 assumes that for each dollar remitted from excise taxes to the government the tax collector keeps $0.84 for himself, resulting in a marginal welfare cost of tax collection in the base equilibrium of 50 per cent. This drives the *MNAXT* even further down and closer to the maximum revenue level.

Our analysis of Table 11.9 leads us to conclude:

Lesson 7

The maximum nutritional agricultural export tax ranges from 47.5 per cent up to 86.1 per cent. Thus which way the export tax should move from its base value of 55.6 per cent to maximise nutrition is indeterminate. Higher marginal welfare costs of tax collection drive the MNAXT down closer to the maximum revenue levels.

Trading Off Welfare And Nutrition

No reasonable policy maker would adjust export taxes to maximise either revenues or nutrition. Sensible policy making dictates trading off objectives. With GAMS, one can select a vector of policy instruments to maximise an objective function of multiple arguments1.

Table 11.10 presents optimum export taxes generated by maximising alternative objective functions for the policy maker. The policy maker is assumed to maximize an objective function which is a weighted average of welfare and food consumption. Welfare is the equivalent variation of income from the benchmark. Thus food consumption is a component of welfare. Food is the composite commodity consisting of imported "cereal" and domestically produced agriculture. A unit of food is defined as that quantity which a unit of currency would buy at benchmark prices. In row 1 the policy maker cares solely about welfare, so row 1's taxes are optimum welfare taxes. In row 8, the policy maker cares solely about food consumption, so row 8's taxes are maximum nutritional taxes. As before, column 2's LST means that all other distorting taxes and quotas have been eliminated; column 3's ILST means that all other taxes are in place but incremental revenue is raised by non-distorting taxes. Column 4's ETA means that incremental revenue is raised by excise tax adjustment. Column 5's ETA/FIQ/RS means that excise tax adjustment is used in the presence of a fixed import quota and rent seeking.

The data from Table 11.10 are reproduced in Figure 11.3. From analyzing Table 11.10 and Figure 11.3 we conclude:

Lesson 8

The optimum export tax is an increasing function of the weight the policy maker attaches to food consumption relative to that attached to welfare. So long as the relative weight on food is no greater than 5, the optimum export tax is lowest with ILST (for it counterbalances the import tariff), higher with ETA (for it counterbalances the import tariff but revenue considerations are still important), still higher for LST (for there is no import tariff to counterbalance), and highest for ETA/FIQ/RS (for again there is no import tariff to counterbalance and export liberalization draws labour into rent seeking). If we ignore the rent seeking case and assume that the policy maker is unwilling to trade off more than $1 of welfare for $1 of additional nutrition, in no case should the export tax exceed 10 per cent.

Of course, if the policy maker is concerned only with food consumption by the poor, who are potentially malnourished, the objective function should include only food consumption by the poor. Such revised calculations, unless agricultural liberalization markedly increases poverty, would tend to reduce the wight of food in the objective function and therefore, the optimum export tax. Moreover, according to Table 11.7, liberalization increases the real wage (*W/PU*) in each case. If efficiency differs between workers and the poor are characterised as inefficient labour, liberalization would tend to reduce malnutrition.

318

Liberalizing to Pay Off Debt

Table 11.11 answers the question: "Suppose low income developing countries adjusted their tax systems to maximise the repayment of international debt, holding welfare constant. How much debt could they repay each year?" The closure rules are the same as in Table 11.10. We find that when there are no other distorting taxes, the optimum export tax is zero (which is reassuringly consistent with theory). The optimum export tax for ILST is a subsidy. For ETA it is a smaller subsidy. For the fixed import quota with rent seeking it is a tax. All this is consistent with our expectations. In addition, we find:

Lesson 9

Assuming that developed countries take steps to prevent terms of trade deterioration for the developing countries, replacing the distortionary tax system with a distortionless one (the limiting case of ideal tax reform) enables low income developing countries to pay 203 per cent of their debt service costs without a loss of utility, whereas that drops to 19.5 per cent when there is a fixed import quota, rent seeking and excise tax adjustment. Alternatively, with LST tax reform they could pay off $23 billion of debt each year without a loss of utility, but in the presence of a fixed quota, rent seeking and excise tax adjustment, that figure falls to $2.2 billion. These figures amount to 14 per cent and 1.3 per cent of the outstanding external public debt respectively.

Terms of Trade Effects

Table 11.12 compares the agricultural export tax rates which maximise the three objectives, assuming foreign excess demands for agricultural exports of -3 and -5. If there were no other distortions in the model, the standard formula tells us that the optimum export tax should rise from zero in the small economy case to 25 per cent with the foreign elasticity of -5 and to 50 per cent with the foreign elasticity of -3. We would also expect the maximum revenue tax to rise as the foreign elasticity shrinks in absolute value. We had no priors on the maximum nutritional export tax except that if all goods were consumed in fixed proportions, the optimum and maximum nutritional export taxes would coincide. Thus we had a weak prior that the maximum nutritional export tax would rise as the foreign elasticity falls in absolute value.

Our priors hold up for the optimum welfare and maximum revenue export taxes. But the prior is only weakly supported for the maximum nutritional tariff. As the foreign elasticity drops from infinity to -5 the maximizing tax rises from 78.0 per cent (Table 11.9, column 4) to 80.1 per cent and stays at this level as the foreign elasticity drops further to -3. Our most important conclusion is that it is striking how insensitive the *MNAXT* is to variations in the foreign demand elasticity.

Analysis of Table 11.12 leads us to:

Lesson 10

The optimum welfare and maximum revenue agricultural export taxes are decreasing functions of the foreign elasticity of excess demand, and the maximum nutritional export tax is fairly insensitive to that parameter.

Conclusions: Agricultural Tax Reform Versus Ideal Policy Reform: Magnitudes of Gain

Table 11.13 shows the effects of moving the agricultural export tax to its optimal level, assuming government revenue is recouped by a non-distorting lump sum tax. It also shows the effects of elimination of all distorting policies. The welfare changes are equivalent variations in expenditure at base prices, and the food consumption changes are changes in food consumption with these consumption changes valued at base prices.

Analysing Table 11.13 leads us to:

Lesson 11

Assuming that developed countries take measures to prevent the terms of trade of developing countries from declining, the optimal agricultural export subsidy by itself leads to a $16.7 billion gain for the poorest developing countries and a reduction in food consumption of $4.4 billion. Complete liberalization leads to a $20.7 billion welfare gain and an increase in food consumption of $850 million. Thus 81 per cent of the total gain from complete liberalization can be generated through optimal agricultural export policy alone.

The remaining conclusions are summarised in the other "lessons" sprinkled throughout the paper. The results are qualitatively consistent with what we had expected on the basis of *a priori* reasoning. The one surprise to us, was that in order to offset import tariffs, the optimum welfare agricultural export tax is negative. Yet this is simply a manifestation of the Lerner neutrality theorem[20]. In the presence of a tariff on some imports, an export subsidy may be desirable to restore internal relative prices to a level closer to their international counterparts. The magnitudes of gain from liberalization quoted in Table 11.13 are interesting, but of course they are conditional on developed countries simultaneously taking measures to assure that terms of trade of developing countries do not deteriorate. From the standpoint of agricultural liberalization, the study's most important contribution is to quantify how important it is for the success of agricultural liberalization to combine this liberalization with measures to eliminate rent seeking in the competition for import licenses, by reforming the allocation mechanism, or replacing import quotas with tariffs, or eliminating import barriers entirely.

Figure 11.1 **THE WELFARE IMPACT OF AGRICULTURAL LIBERALIZATION**

Figure 11.1a

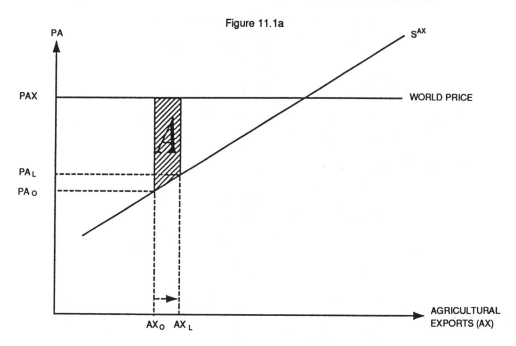

Figure 11.1b

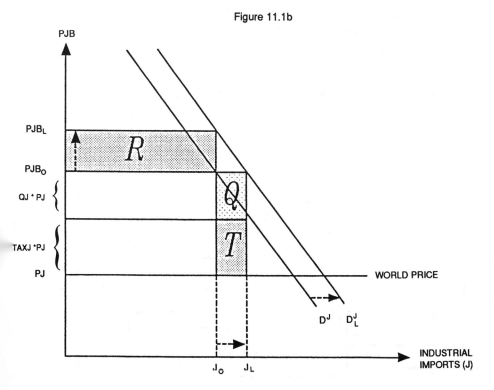

Figure 11.2 A SCHEMATIC MODEL OF A REPRESENTATIVE LDC

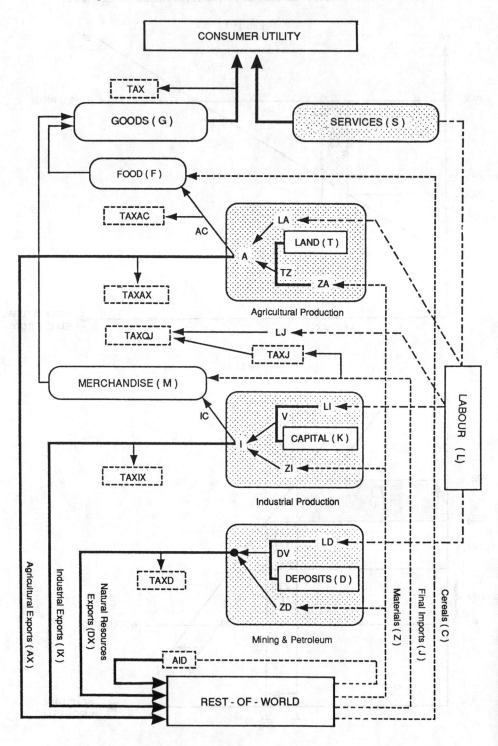

Figure 11.3 **WELFARE VERSUS NUTRITION** (Table 10)

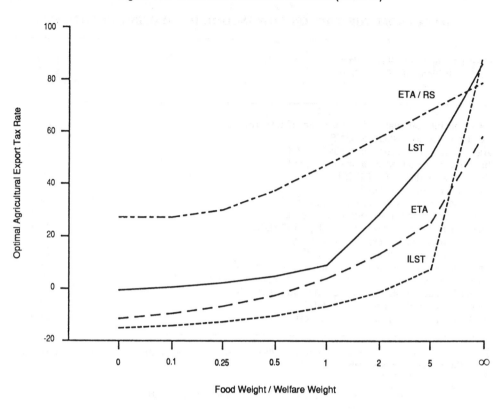

Table 11.1

DATA FROM THE WDR ON LOW INCOME DEVELOPING COUNTRIES[1]

GNP per capita in 1987 dollars	$280
GDP in billions of 1987 dollars	$239
	(Per cent)

Taxes on international trade as a share of total revenue	20.7
Total revenue as a share of GNP	17.8
Agricultural value added as a share of GDP	33.0
Industrial value added as a share of GDP	27.0
Services as a share of GDP [S]	40.0
Exports as a share of GNP	20.0
Trade deficit as a share of GDP [AID][2]	5.0
Share in merchandise exports of agriculture[3]	27.0
Share in merchandise exports of "deposits" [DXS][4]	48.0
Share in merchandise exports of industry[5]	25.0
Share in merchandise imports of food[6]	22.0
Share in merchandise imports of intermediate inputs[7]	48.0
Share in merchandise imports of import competing manufactures[8]	39.0
Labour's share in manufacturing value added $[1 - 0_k]$[9]	29.5
Public debt service as a share of GNP	4.7
Public debt service as a share of exports	21.9

1. All of the data in this table are taken from the *World Development Report 1989*, pp. 164-195. They refer to 1987.
2. This is minus "Resource balance," p. 180.
3. This is "Other primary commodities," p. 194.
4. This is "Fuels, minerals and metals," p. 194.
5. This is "Machinery and transport equipment" and "Other manufactures," p. 194.
6. This is "Food" and "Other primary commodities," p. 192.
7. This is "Fuels" and "Machinery and transport equipment," p. 192.
8. This is "Other manufactures," p. 192.
9. This is the average of "Total earnings as a percentage of value added" in 1986, p. 176.

Table 11.2

TAX AND QUOTA DISTORTIONS

	Effective rate of protection for:	Per cent
AC	Domestically consumed agriculture	-20.0
AX	Exportable agriculture	-40.0
IC	Domestically consumed industrial goods	100.0
IX	Exportable industrial goods	0
	Ad valorem tax rate on:	
AC	Agricultural consumption (*TAXAC*)	20.8
AX	Agricultural exports (*TAXAX*)	55.6
IX	Industrial exports (*TAXIX*)	0.0
J	Import tariff/quota margin (*TAXQJ*)	71.4
J	Import tariff margin (*TAXJ*)	18.0
G	Excise tax on goods consumption (*TAX*)	6.4

Table 11.3

DEFINITIONS

Variable	Definition
TAXAX	Tax rate on agricultural exports as fraction of sellers' price.
U	Aggregate utility defined so initially the marginal utility of income = 1. The benchmark value of 127 is domestic absorption at market prices in the base equilibrium, with domestic income at factor cost in the base equilibrium (GDP) normalised to equal 100. Since utility is first degree homogeneous in consumption, changes in this variable are equivalent variations in income from the benchmark equilibrium.
AID	The trade deficit*.
A	Agricultural production*.
AC	Consumption of A*.
AX	Exports of A*.
C	Cereal imports*.
DX	Oil exports*.
F	Food consumption*. F(.) = F(AC,C). One unit of food is defined as that which costs one currency unit in the benchmark equilibrium. Thus, F is also the value of food consumption measured at benchmark prices.
G	Goods consumption*. G(.) = G(F,M).
I	Industrial production*.
IC	Industrial consumption*.
IX	Industrial exports*.
J	Imports of the non-domestically-produced industrial good*.
L	The labour supply*.
LA	Labour in agriculture*.
LD	Labour in deposits*.
LI	Labour in industry*.
LJ	Labour in rent-seeking*.
M	Consumption of merchandise M(.) = M(IC,J).
PA	Producer price of A.
PAX	World price of A.
PI	Price of I.
PJB	Price of J to domestic buyers.
PU	Price of U. The ideal measure of the C.
REVTOT	Real revenue from taxes plus foreign aid*.
RK	Nominal rental rate on industrial capital.
RT	Nominal rental rate on land.
S	Labour in services*.
TAXQJ	Tariff plus quota premium on J as proportion of sellers' price.
TAXJ	Tariff on J as proportion of sellers' price.
TAX	Excise tax rate on G as proportion of seller's price.
W	Nominal wage rate.
Z	Imports of intermediate inputs*.

Note: A* signifies that the relevant variable is defined as a percentage of base equilibrium domestic income with its price to sellers normalised to equal 1 in the base eqilibrium.

Table 11.4

GENERAL EQUILIBRIUM PRICE ELASTICITIES FOR AGRICULTURE
(Per cent)

Agricultural production	0.627
Agricultural consumption	-0.093
Agricultural exports	8.13

Table 11.5

SELECTED COST/BENEFIT RATIOS FOR INCREMENTAL REDUCTION OF AGRICULTURAL EXPORT TAXES

Cost-benefit ratio: (1)	LST[1] (2)	ILST[2] (3)	ETA[3] (4)	ETA 50% MWC[4] (5)	ILST FIQ[5] (6)	ETA FIQ (7)	ETA FIQ RS[6] (8)
1. $U/[-TAXAX]$	0.065	0.067	0.072	0.082	0.043	0.044	0.014
2. $\dfrac{REVTOT}{-TAXAX}$	0.337	0.163	n.a.	n.a.	0.0671	n.a.	n.a.
3. $F/[-TAXAX]$	-0.029	-0.025	-0.050	0.026	0.00064	0.0089	-0.023
4. $P_U dU/P_F dF$	-589.0%	-736.0%	-388.0%	863.0%	18 233.0%	1 341.0%	-163.0%
5. $P_U dU/wdLI$	-239.0%	-317.0%	-355.0%	-455.0%	-198.0%	-207.0%	-60.8%
6. $dU/dRRK$	-143.0%	-165.0%	-206.0%	-334.0%	-92.2%	-100.0%	-29.9%

1. LST denotes "lump sum taxes."
2. ILST denotes "incremental lump sum taxes."
3. ETA denotes "excise tax adjustment."
4. 50% MWC denotes that the excise tax leakage is set to 84.7 per cent, so that the marginal welfare cost of tax collection is 50 per cent.
5. FIQ denotes "fixed import quota."
6. RS denotes "with rent-seeking." In all tables columns without "RS" refer to simulations in which rent-seeking is absent.

Table 11.6

ACCOUNTING FOR THE WELFARE GAINS
(Per cent)

Effect on welfare of:	LST (2)	ILST (3)	ETA (4)	ETA 50% MWC (5)	ILST FIQ (6)	ETA FIQ (7)	ETA FIQ RS (8)
1. Export distortion	100	72	70	62	96	102	286
2. Import distortion	0	25	25	23	0	0	0
3. Agricultural consumption distortion	0	-4	-3	0	-3	-2	-17
4. Excise tax effect	0	7	8	15	7	0	17
5. Rent-seeking effect	0	0	0	0	0	0	-186
Total	100˙	100	100	100	100	100	100

Table 11.7

OPTIMUM WELFARE AGRICULTURAL EXPORT TAXES
(World prices fixed)

Variable	Bench-mark level (2)	LST (3)	ILST (4)	ETA (5)	ILST FIQ (6)	ETA FIQ (7)	ETA FIQ RS (8)	ETA RS (9)	ILST AID = -5 (10)
TAXAX	55.6%	0%	-14.6%	-11.1%	-0.83%	4.3%	27.7%	27.6%	-13.8%
U	127.	1.068	1.055	1.051	1.024	1.021	1.005	1.033	0.984
AID	5.	1.	1.	1.	1.	1.	1.	1.	-1.
A	39.6	1.423	1.359	1.294	1.232	1.185	1.102	1.141	1.423
AC	36.1	0.990	0.9215	0.904	0.985	0.967	0.966	0.971	0.847
AX	3.47	5.933	5.9096	5.356	3.802	3.457	2.513	2.9061	7.422
C	3.25	1.275	1.6774	1.581	1.543	1.440	1.177	1.184	1.526
DX	9.60	0.850	0.774	0.783	0.822	0.838	0.919	0.925	0.786
F	46.9	1.00755	0.961	0.939	1.016	0.994	0.979	0.985	0.882
G	81.4	1.218	1.137	1.104	1.056	1.039	1.024	1.065	1.055
I	22.8	0.906	0.960	0.943	0.961	0.945	0.919	0.925	0.932
IC	7.8	1.161	1.229	1.208	1.231	1.210	1.177	1.184	1.193
IX	5.00	0.	0.	0.	0.	0.	0.	0.	0.
J	9.75	2.185	1.677	1.581	1.	1.	1.	1.184	1.526
L	75.0	1.	1.	1.	1.	1.	1.	1.	1.
LA	22.0	1.487	1.323	1.245	1.195	1.145	1.090	1.148	1.423
LD	2.36	0.571	0.414	0.431	0.509	0.544	0.746	0.763	0.436
LI	5.60	0.668	0.701	0.679	0.746	0.729	0.746	0.763	0.661
LJ	5.21[1]	n.a.	n.a.	n.a.	n.a.	n.a.	1.273	0.977	n.a.
M	34.5	1.577	1.429	1.376	1.113	1.103	1.088	1.184	1.344
PAX	1.56	1.	1.	1.	1.	1.	1.	1.	1.
PI	1.	1.098	1.364	1.309	1.254	1.190	1.	1.	1.279

Table 11.7 (continued)

PJB	1.71	0.583	1.	1.543	1.440	1.177	1.	1.
PU	1.	1.118	1.590	1.632	1.507	1.485	1.182	1.135	1.551
RK	1.	0.995	1.309	1.234	1.205	1.124	0.919	0.925	1.191
RT	1.	2.214	2.473	2.264	1.930	1.765	1.342	1.391	2.565
S	40.0	0.802	0.897	0.943	0.956	0.984	0.965	0.968	0.847
TAXQJ	0.714	0	1.	1.	2.304	2.055	1.424	1.	1.
TAXJ	0.180	0	1.	1.	1.	1.	1.	1.	1.
TAX	0.067	0	1.	2.349	1.	1.853	1.144	0.842	1.
W	1.	1.489	1.869	1.819	1.614	1.541	1.231	1.212	1.802
Z	12.0	1.646	1.878	1.740	1.553	1.438	1.151	1.181	1.893

1.   The benchmark value of this variable is zero in the non-rent-seeking cases.

331

Table 11.8

MAXIMUM REVENUE AGRICULTURAL EXPORT TAX
(World prices fixed)

Variable	Bench-mark level (2)	LST (3)	ILST (4)	ILST AID = -5 (5)	ILST FIQ (6)	ILST FIQ RS (7)	ILST RS (8)
TAXAX	55.6%	40.9%	35.3%	36.0%	44.9%	48.7%	34.9%
U	127.	1.043	1.023	0.952	1.008	1.002	1.025
AX	3.47	2.530	2.295	3.636	1.556	1.339	2.331
C	3.25	0.967	1.124	1.034	1.068	1.040	1.128
DX	9.60	0.983	0.946	0.958	0.971	0.980	0.945
F	46.91	1.053	0.988	0.913	0.999	0.9664	0.988
IX	5.00	1.039	0.311	0.687	0.627	0.770	0.292
J	9.75	1.659	1.124	1.034	1.	1.	1.128
LJ	5.208	n.a.	n.a.	n.a.	n.a.	1.	1.
REVTOT	22.8	0.452	1.033	0.667	1.007	1.003	1.034
TAXQJ	0.714	0	1.	0.714	1.163	1.095	1.
Z	12.00	1.164	1.117	1.150	1.054	1.031	1.121

Table 11.9

MAXIMUM NUTRITIONAL AGRICULTURAL EXPORT TAX
(World prices fixed)

Variable	Benchmark level (2)	LST (3)	ILST (4)	ETA (5)	ETA MWC = 50% (6)
TAXAX	55.6%	86.1%	78.0%	58.3%	47.5%
U	127.0	0.992	0.976	0.996	1.011
AID	5.00	1.	1.	1.	1.
AX	3.47	0.	0.	0.841	1.519
C	3.25	0.767	0.903	0.984	1.053
DX	9.60	1.095	1.047	1.007	0.981
F	46.91	1.072	1.006	1.00011	1.002
IX	5.00	2.261	1.557	1.086	0.726
J	9.75	1.315	0.903	0.984	1.053
REVTOT	22.80	0.303	0.924	1.	1.
Z	12.00	0.958	0.924	0.987	1.047

Table 11.10

THE AGRICULTURAL EXPORT TAX WHICH MAXIMISES POLICY MAKER'S UTILITY FOR ALTERNATIVE TRADEOFFS BETWEEN WELFARE AND NUTRITION
(Percentages)

Maximand	LST (2)	ILST (3)	ETA (4)	ETA/FIQ/RS (5)
1. U + 0 F	0	-14.55	-11.08	27.73
2. U + .1 F	1.18	-13.55	-9.04	27.73
3. U + .25 F	2.85	-12.1	-6.22	30.41
4. U + .5 F	5.36	-9.98	-2.06	37.81
5. U + 1 F	9.60[1]	-6.33	4.60	47.69
6. U + 2 F	28.78	-0.880	13.52	58.03
7. U + 5 F	51.2	8.016	25.70	68.64
8. F + 0 U	86.07	88.0	58.32	78.90

1.   In this simulation there were multiple optima for the objective function. At an export tax of 16.417 per cent and an export level of 0.695, the same value (183.00) for the maximand was reached. Thus, there are two optima. In the one reported in the body of the paper, exports of the industrial good are completely eliminated. In the one reported in this footnote the country continues to export the industrial good.

Table 11.11

MAXIMUM DEBT REPAYMENT AGRICULTURAL EXPORT TAXES

Variable	Benchmark level (2)	LST (3)	ILST (4)	ETA (5)	ETA FIQ RS (6)
TAXAX	55.6%	0.%	-14.07%	-11.17%	26.65%
U	127.	1.	1.	1.	1.
AID	5.	-0.917	-0.5657	-0.2998	0.8167
IX	5.	0.	0.	0.	0.
AID (billion $)	11.97	-10.98	-6.77	-3.59	9.78
Change in *AID* (billion $)		-22.95	-18.74	15.56	-2.19
Debt repayment as % of:					
External public debt[1]		13.9		9.45	1.33
Debt service		203.5	166.9	138.3	19.5

1. For low income economies other than China and India, external public debt is 68 per cent of GNP and debt service is 4.7 per cent of GNP. This is from p. 210 of the 1989 *WDR*.

Table 11.12

MAXIMISING AGRICULTURAL EXPORT TAXES
(Variable world prices)[1]

Maximise	U		REVTOT		F	
Elasticity	-5	-3	-5	-3	-5	-3
Variable	(2)	(3)	(4)	(5)	(6)	(7)
TAXAX	17.4%	41.4%	52.0%	77.8%	80.1%	80.1%
U	1.0060	1.0004	1.0008	0.9984	0.9945	0.9982
AX	2.3151	1.2532	1.0807	0.7213	0.5907	0.6985
F	0.9758	0.9947	0.9988	1.0051	1.0053	1.0055
REVTOT	0.9617	0.9912	1.0002	1.0038	0.9910	1.0038

1. Using incremental lump sum tax adjustment and constant advalorem equivalent of import quotas.

Table 11.13

THE EFFECTS OF LIBERALIZATION[1]

	Agricultural liberalization	Ideal policy reform
Taxes	Agricultural export subsidy of 14.6%	All taxes 0; no quotas
Utility gain	$16.7 billion	$20.7 billion
Food consumption gain	-$4.4 billion	$0.85 billion

1. This table is based on Table 11.7, columns 2, 4 and 3, plus the estimate of GDP at producer prices for low-income countries other than China and India from the *WDR* (1989, p. 168) of $239.390 billion (1987 dollars).

NOTES AND REFERENCES

1. The authors are grateful to Leonard Cheng, E. Kwan Choi, Pat Conway, Betty Daniel, Al Field, Hal Fried, Tom Hertel, Jim Harting, Allen Kelley, Therese McCarty, Bruce Reynolds, Richard Schwindt, Ed Yurcisin and participants at seminars at the 1989 Southeastern International Trade Conference and Union College for helpful discussions, and to the World Bank and the Walker Foundation of the Pittsburgh National Bank for funding.

2. This is a general equilibrium curve, reflecting adjustments in the export tax.

3. The increase in rent seeking is also likely to steepen both S^{AX} and D^J, as labor is drawn out of agriculture into rent seeking, further reducing any welfare gain.

4. Articles which use a similar approach to rent seeking are Bloomqvist and Mohammad (1986) and Clarete and Whalley (1988). Also see Robinson (1990). Tower interviewed a Nairobi businessman in March 1989 who said that he pays no bribes, but one fourth of his firm's managerial time is spent in explaining to government officials the importance to the Kenyan economy of allocating import licenses to him. If this is the case for rent seeking in general, then rent seeking absorbs skilled labour, whose shadow price may well exceed its market price significantly.

5. The result of our earlier paper, Loo and Tower (1989) that developing countries have much to gain from increases in world agricultural prices, results from the assumption that import protection takes the form of an import tariff combined with a fixed *ad valorem* import license premium with no rent seeking. Had we allowed rent seeking or assumed that import licenses were fixed in quantity, the gains from increased world agricultural prices would be much smaller. This stems from the increased resources spent in rent seeking as well as the reduced responsiveness of the developing countries' economies to the changed world prices induced by quantitative import restrictions and rent seeking.

6. The model could be applied to other developing countries as in Loo and Tower (1989).

7. We are grateful to Sherman Robinson for suggesting this approach, which we follow both here and in Loo and Tower (1989).

8. The *WDR* classifies the following as low-income economies, excluding China and India, for which data is available (listed in increasing order of their 1987 GNPs): Ethiopia, Bhutan, Chad, Zaire, Bangladesh, Malawi, Nepal, Lao PDR, Mozambique, Tanzania, Burkina Faso, Madagascar, Mali, Burundi, Zambia, Niger, Uganda, Somalia, Togo, Rwanda, Sierra Leone, Benin, Central African Republic, Kenya, Sudan, Pakistan, Haiti, Lesotho, Nigeria, Ghana, Sri Lanka, Yemen PDR, Mauritania, Indonesia, and Liberia.

9. This term includes the implicit taxation associated with corrupt official agricultural marketing boards for domestic sales.

10. We modeled this tax as a royalty payment on mineral extraction. With minerals treated as a fixed factor, this tax is distortionless.

11. The ERPs for industrial and agricultural exports are defined as the ratio of value added at producer prices to that at world prices minus unity. We assume that domestically consumed industrial and agricultural goods are imperfect substitutes for their imported counterparts. Thus, their domestic prices are not raised by the full amount of the tariff/quota premia on corresponding imports. We have calculated the ERPs for these goods as if their domestic prices were increased by the full amount of the *ad valorem* equivalents of the import varriers on their imported counterparts. Thus, letting t be the *ad valorem* import barrier on the substitute in consumption and assuming no tariffs on imported intermediate inputs, the ERP is calculated as:

$$ERP = \left(\dfrac{Domestic\ Value\ Add}{\dfrac{Domestic\ Sale}{1+t} - (Value\ Imported\ Intermediate\ Inp)} \right) - 1 \,.$$

We then work back from the ERP calculated this way to calculate the tariff on the import competing good.

12. Our import tariff/quota premium of 71.4 per cent and export tax of 55.6 per cent seem high. Remember, however, that the 71.4 refers to the tariff/quota premium on imports of final industrial goods. Moreover, both tax rates incorporate the effects of multiple exchange rates. We calibrated our import tariff and export tariff rates assuming zero tariffs on intermediate inputs, so as to yield plausible effective rate of protection figures. How plausible are our figures? The ratio of our ERP coefficient (1+ERP) for domestic agriculture to that for industry is 0.4, while the ratio of our ERP coefficient for exportable agriculture to that for industry is 0.3. The 1986 *WDR*, p. 62 presents this ratio for several economies. The only one of that collection which is in our group of low income economies is Nigeria in the 1970s and 1980s with a figure of 0.35. Han and Tower (1988) find a figure of 0.183 for Sudan in 1985. Thus, our figure seems reasonable to us in the absence of better data and more detailed modelling.

13. Conrad (1986, p. 11) writes "A 1970 study by Jap Kim Siong [1971] estimated that in 1971 the total burden of taxes [including side payments] in Indonesia was 18 per cent of GDP compared with only 9 per cent of GDP reported to the Tax Department." In our model we considered the bribes to be transfers, so no welfare cost is attached to the bribes *per se*. The associated costs reflect the effects of the price distortions caused by the existence of bribery.

14. It is interesting to cmpare our elasticity of agricultural production with those in the literature. The *WDR* (1986, p. 68) notes African supply elasticities for individual crops ranging from 1.0 to 24.3. Newbery (1987, p. 377) notes that Binswanger *et al.* (1985) "find rather low own-price elasticities [of aggregate agricultural supply] of between 0.1 and 0.3. Melo and Robinson (1989) assume product differentiation in production to reduce the elasticity of export supply.

15. The calculations in this column were accomplished in two stages. In the first stage, all distorting taxes, except for the agricultural export tax, were eliminated. In the second stage, the agricultural export tax is reduced by 1 per cent. The figures in this column are the differences between the outcomes of the two stages.

16. See for example Smith (1982), Dixit (1984), Tower (1984, Chapter V) and Tower and Pursell (1986), and for the same argument inpartial equilibrium see Corden (1974) and Caves and Jones (1985).

17. Had we simulated agricultural liberalization with the import quota repolaced by a tariff, we would have found that when distorting taxes are used to adjust revenues, agricultural liberalization is more effective when protection is accomplished by tariffs rather than quotas, because of the additional contribution that increased imports generated by liberalization make to revenues.

18. A similar welfare decomposition, but for the case of customs union formation, has been numerically implemented by Harrison, Rutherford and Wooton (1988). They calculate a sequence of general equilibria for different levels of trade taxes and trace the *paths* of the decomposition terms. A caveat is that these decompositions appear not, in general, to be robust to the order in which the various tax changes are implemented. Of course, an alternative measure of the importance of general equilibrium effects is the effect on welfare of liberalization under alternative scenarios, e.g., Table 11.5, row 1 and Clarete and Whalley (1988).

19. For example, David Feldman has suggested to us that one could examine optimum official responses to disturbances under the assumption that the government maximises a Corden-type conservative social welfare function.

20. On the Lerner neutrality theorem, see Kaempfer and Tower (1981).

BIBLIOGRAPHY

BALLARD, C.L., J.B. SHOVEN, and J. WHALLEY (1985). "General Equilibrium Computations of the Marginal Welfare Costs of Taxes in the United States," American Economic Review, March, 1985.

BINSWANGER, H., Y. MUNDLAK, M.-C. YANG, and A. BOWERS, "Estimation of Aggregate Agricultural Supply Response from Time Series and Cross-Country Data," working paper 1985-3, World Bank, Commodity Studies and Project Division, processed.

BLOMQVIST, Å. and S. MOHAMMAD, "Controls, Corruption, and Competitive Rent-Seeking in LDCs," Journal of Development Economics, 21, 1986.

CAVES, R.E. and R.W. JONES, World Trade and Payments, 4th Edition, Boston: Little, Brown and Co., 1985.

CLARETE, R.L. and J. WHALLEY, "Interactions Between Trade Policies and Domestic Distortions in a Small Open Economy," Journal of International Economics, 24, 1988.

CONRAD, R.F., "Essays on the Indonesian Tax Reform," Country Policy Division Discussion Paper No. 1986-S, World Bank, Typescript, 1986.

CORDEN, W.M., Trade Policy and Economic Welfare, Oxford: Clarendon Press, 1974.

DIXIT, A., "Tax Policy in Open Economies," Chapter 6 in Alan J. Auerbach and Martin Feldstein (eds), Handbook of Public Economics, Volume 1, Amsterdam: North-Holland Publishing Co., 1984.

HAN, K. and E. TOWER, "Trade, Tax, and Agricultural Policy in a Highly Distorted Economy: The Case of Sudan," Duke Economics Department working paper, summarised in Tower and Loo (1989), 1988.

HARRISON, G.W., T.F. RUTHERFORD, and I. WOOTON, "The Welfare Effects of Customs Union Accession," working paper No. 8810C, Center for the Study of International Economic Relations, University of Western Ontario, December, 1988.

JUDD, K.L., "The Welfare Cost of Factor Taxation in a Perfect-Foresight Model," Journal of Political Economy, August, 1987.

KAEMPFER, W.H. and E. TOWER, "The Balance of Payments Approach to Trade Tax Symmetry Theorems," Weltwirtschaftliches Archiv, Band 118, Heft 1, 1982.

LOO, T. and E. TOWER, "Agricultural Protectionism and the Less Developed Countries: The Relationship Between Agricultural Prices, Debt Servicing Capacities and the Need for Development Aid," Chapter 2 of Andrew B. Stoeckel, David Vincent, and Sandy Cuthbertson (eds), Macroeconomic Consequences of Farm Support Policies, Durham: Duke University Press, 1989.

de MELO, J. and S. ROBINSON, "Product Differentiation and the Treatment of Foreign Trade in Computable General Equilibrium Models of Small Economies," Journal of International Economics, Volume 27, 1989.

NEWBERY, D., "Agricultural Taxation: The Main Issues," Chapter 13 of David Newbery and Nicholas Stern (eds), The Theory of Taxation For Developing Countries, World Bank, Oxford University Press, 1987.

ROBINSON, S., "Computable General Equilibrium Models of Developing Countries: Stretching the Neoclassical Paradigm," elsewhere in this volume.

SIONG, J.K., De Indonesische Vennootschapsbelasting, Kluwer, Deventer, 1971.

SMITH, A.M., "Some Simple Results on the Gains from Trade, from Growth, and from Public Production," *Journal of International Economics*, 13, November, 1982.

STUART, C., "Welfare Costs of Additional Tax Revenue in the United States," *American Economic Review*, 74, June, 1984.

TOWER, E., Effective Protection, Domestic Resource Cost and Shadow Prices: A General Equilibrium Perspective, World Bank Staff working paper, No. 664, September, 1984.

TOWER, E. and G. PURSELL, On Shadow Pricing,. World Bank Staff Working Paper, No. 792, 1986.

TOWER, E. and T. LOO, "On Using Computable General Equilibrium Models to Facilitate Tax, Tariff and Other Policy Reforms in Less Developed Countries," Chapter 11 of Malcolm S. Gillis (ed), Tax Reform in Less Developed Countries, Durham: Duke University Press, 1989.

WORLD BANK, World Development Report, 1986.

WORLD BANK, World Development Report, 1989.

Chapter 12

GROWTH AND WELFARE EFFECTS OF A GATT AGREEMENT IN AGRICULTURE ON THE LOW INCOME COUNTRIES: AN INTEGRATED MULTIMARKET GENERAL EQUILIBRIUM ANALYSIS

by

Elisabeth Sadoulet and Alain de Janvry

AGRICULTURE AND THE GATT

The September 1986 Uruguay Round of multilateral trade negotiations marked the beginning of an attempt at bringing the trade of agricultural commodities and services under the rules and disciplines of GATT. The objective is to de-escalate government intervention in agricultural markets which has been pervasive in both developed and developing countries. In the MDCs, agricultural protectionism, through direct border measures and farm support programmes, has been rising to ruinous budgetary costs; excess production has led to the rapid accumulation of stocks; surplus production has created sharp declines in international grain market prices; the cost of export subsidies has exceeded all expectations; the benefits from farm programmes have been regressive and eventually nefarious on the welfare of the smaller farmers, making their political legitimacy increasingly unacceptable; and political frictions have developed between the United States, the EC, and Japan on disposing of farm surpluses, as well as with some traditional developing country grain exporters such as Thailand, Argentina, and Uruguay. With growing difficulties for the developing countries to service their foreign debts, there is also pressure for the MDCs to liberalize their imports of tropical products and thus improve foreign exchange earnings of developing countries and their chances of meeting debt obligations. Most developing countries, by contrast, discriminate against their agriculture both directly by export taxes to generate government revenues and indirectly through macroeconomic policy aimed at the protection of the industrial sectors. Negative effects include the stagnation of agricultural production, increasing imports in a period of foreign exchange shortage, the undermining of government efforts to promote agricultural development through investment and technological changes in a context of low private profitability, maintenance or aggravation of rural poverty, and uncontrolled migration which puts in excessive burden on the urban economies.

At least at the level of political rhetoric, there consequently exists a strong desire to change the nature of domestic policies and to seek implementation of the GATT rules. The pressure for liberalizing comes, however, primarily from the more developed economies, and the most sensitive conflicts pertain to temperate-zone products. A few developing countries which export commodities competitive with MDC farm exports strongly support this move as they are especially affected when large powers make bilateral trade deals which exclude them. Most of the developing countries, on the other hand, would benefit from priority given to products other than cereals and would lose from trade liberalization in cereals. And their approach has been to seek preferential treatment on an individual basis rather than through global negotiations (Valdés 1987).

This asymmetry of participation in the negotiations will influence the scope and nature of the liberalization that may ultimately be agreed upon. While there are also potential gains to be found in an extensive liberalization of tropical products, the most likely outcome of the negotiations is likely to be a reduction in protectionism for temperate products in the OECD countries.

The effects of such a liberalization on international market prices have been analysed in a number of studies. Their results are difficult to compare, largely because these studies look at different liberalization scenarios and make different assumptions about the characterisation of the current distorted system (Gardner). In particular, drastically different outcomes on world market prices are obtained depending on whether the developing countries would liberalize or not, and whether liberalization would apply to border measures only or to all trade distorting interventions. These results are also very sensitive to the assumed direct and cross-price supply elasticities, on which information is notably incomplete. Yet, if one considers policy changes in the OECD countries only, there seems to exist an agreement that this would result in an overall world price increase for cereals, meat products, and sugar, of an order of magnitude in the range of 10 to 30 per cent.

Considering the case where trade liberalization is confined to the MDCs and to the temperate goods which they produce, the resulting increase in world prices will affect the developing countries. While a small subset of these countries is composed of net exporters of these commodities that will evidently benefit from rising prices, the vast majority is composed of net importers that may be hurt. Particularly in countries where agriculture is a large sector in the economy, where trade dependency for staple foods is high, where there are limited possibilities for import substitution in agriculture, and where there are large numbers of poor people, the growth and welfare effects may be large. It is the expected consequences of this trade liberalization scenario on the low income developing countries which we analyse in this paper.

The developing countries are highly heterogeneous in terms of levels of income, industrial structure, agricultural comparative advantages, structure of trade, and current levels of price distortions. The implications of trade liberalization will consequently necessarily be highly uneven across them. In addition, some of these implications are simple short-run income effects created by price movements while others are the result of resource reallocation that requires a time lag to materialise. While some of these effects can be captured by partial equilibrium analysis, the most important medium and long-run effects are likely to occur through general equilibrium effects. For these reasons, tracing out the growth, welfare, and trade implications of agricultural liberalization on the developing countries requires distinguishing between different types of developing country economies and analysing the effects that liberalization creates through general equilibrium models and over time.

There are several reasons why the MDCs need to understand clearly the impact that agricultural trade liberalization can be expected to have on the developing countries. First, although for the moment the main actors in the GATT negotiations have been the United States, the EC, Japan, and to some extent the Cairns[2] countries, the other developing countries could mobilise against the GATT negotiations and use their veto power if they feel threatened, as large importers of temperate foods and feeds, by the expectations of rising world market prices. This stand would seriously complicate an already difficult problem of harmonization of policies among many actors. Second, the developing countries are the most dynamic markets for US and EC cereal exports. Rapid expansion in the demand for food grains has occurred in the very low income countries where domestic agriculture has lagged behind the growth in demand and, particularly, in the tropical middle income countries where strong income effects are created by industrialisation or mineral exports but where temperate cereals, wheat in particular, cannot be grown. Demand for feed grains has grown extremely rapidly in the upper middle income and the oil exporting countries where patterns are shifting from the direct consumption of food grains to the consumption of feed-fed animal products (Vocke; de Janvry, Sadoulet, and White). If the GATT agreements redefine the prices of tradable wage goods and the potential role of agriculture in economic development, the resulting income effects will have strong implications for the creation of effective demand for MDCs, farm exports. Third, the growth and income effects created by agricultural trade liberalization will also imply other benefits or costs for the MDCs in terms of foreign aid to alleviate malnutrition and problems of debt repayment. Finally, any multilateral negotiations that affect the world food system cannot proceed, for ethical and political reasons, in the abstract without considering the implications that they may have for food security and the levels of malnutrition and hunger in the low income Third World. For that reason, the negotiators must carefully identify who will be the losers among the world's poor and understand the instruments that could most effectively be used for short-run compensation.

IMPACT OF TRADE LIBERALIZATION ON THE DEVELOPING COUNTRIES: PREVIOUS STUDIES AND SOME HYPOTHESES

Two different types of analyses have been used to look into the impact of OECD country trade liberalization on the developing countries. The first is primarily concerned with predictions about world price changes and, for this, uses world models. Developing countries are included in these models to arrive at a correct accounting of aggregate supply and demand, but this is done from a world perspective rather than a developing country perspective. In particular, the degree of disaggregation of the developing world depends on its importance in world trade for the commodities considered, not on its specific structural features. The second type of analysis, to which our model belongs, takes a single country approach. The rest of the world and the international commodity prices are taken as given. In this case, the developing countries are classified according to their economic structures in order to capture the differential effects that trade liberalization could have on particular classes of developing countries.

The existing world models specify different degrees of completeness in the economic structures, ranging from commodity, to sectoral, and to general equilibrium approaches. They also differ in the coverage and degree of aggregation of agricultural commodities and in the level of aggregation of the individual countries in regions. In a partial equilibrium model, commodities are treated as homogeneous and domestic prices differ from international prices by a tariff wedge. Each country/region is characterised by a system of supply and demand elasticities for agricultural commodities. In a commodity model (Valdés and Zietz, 1980), each commodity is considered independently, and substitutabilities in production and consumption can only be indirectly taken into account, for example by lowering the magnitudes of the direct elasticities. In the sectoral models (Krissoff, Sullivan, and Wainio; Anderson and Tyers), interdependencies among commodities are explicitly characterised by cross-price elasticities. Net imports and exports from all the countries constitute the world commodity markets on which equilibrium world prices are determined. The principal result of these studies is to measure the impact of the removal of some distortions on the equilibrium world market price. They also give, for each commodity and country, the resulting increases in exports or declines in imports. This, in turn, provides, for each country, measures of the changes in foreign exchange earnings and in producer and consumer welfare. While these studies identify some of the important consequences of trade liberalization on the developing countries, and are, as such, important first approximations, they cannot take into account the income effects that trade liberalization may induce, particularly as a result of intersectoral resource reallocations provoked by changes in the terms of trade or readjustments in the exchange rate.

In the general equilibrium models (Fischer, Frohberg, Keyser, and Parikh; Burniaux) each country/region is characterised by a complete general equilibrium model. This is particularly important for developing countries where agriculture has a large share in domestic product, employment, and foreign trade, and where agricultural policy can create important macroeconomic effects. Domestic economies are partially isolated from international markets by imperfect substitution between their domestic products and foreign products. The country models are then linked by matrices of bilateral trade. These models have the potential of providing the greatest in-depth analysis of the impact of trade liberalization on the developing countries. Markets for factors are specified as well as commodity markets, and rigidities can be introduced in any of them. Government budget rules insure that interventions are done in a consistent way. And the macroeconomic balances are insured. The limitation of these models is less theoretical than empirical. Because they are so large and demanding, they have in fact serious limitations in the level of disaggregation and in the completeness that each national model can have. The most common necessary simplification is in the social structure that can be imbedded in each economy, which is generally reduced to an agricultural/non-agricultural contrast.

The country models pursue a very different objective. By nature, they will not answer questions about the overall outcome of trade liberalization on international prices. They focus directly on the impact of given international price changes on the economic performance of specific countries. Emphasis is given in these models to the detailed interactions among the different subsectors of the economy and to the characterisation of different socioeconomic classes, each with differentiated sources of income. In this way they can tell which sectors and social groups will be affected by the adjustments and how. As a result, this type of analysis gives the possibility of designing complementary programmes and compensatory measures to reinforce or diminish the effects of liberalization on the developing countries. Within this class of country models, the same distinction is made between sectoral models and general equilibrium models. The sectoral models (Hammer and Knudsen, in this volume) are simpler than the general equilibrium models but they usually treat the substitutabilities and complementarities in the agricultural sector in a more appropriate and realistic way, while the general equilibrium models focus on the intersectoral relationships and the macroeconomic effects. A first study of the impact of trade liberalization on the developing countries in a single economy general equilibrium context was done by Loo and Tower (see also Center for International Economics, 1988). They partition for that purpose the set of developing countries into six groups: low income, India, lower middle income, upper middle income, oil exporters, and highly indebted countries. While these models focus on relevant links between international prices, government revenues, and levels of distortions, they do not retain some interesting features of the standard CGE models. One is the assumption of imperfect substitution between domestic goods and imports, which implies differential transmission of world prices into domestic prices across sectors and thus relative price changes induced by international price movements. Another is the specification of a social structure with various household income groups. Finally, all six models simplified to the extreme the richness of the differential substitutability effects by assuming the same unitary elasticities for all factors and all commodities.

In this paper, we follow the single country approach and, for the first time, integrate the multimarket and CGE models, thus combining the comparative advantages of both approaches: a better specification of the nature of agricultural production compared to previous CGEs, and a better characterisation of intersectoral relations and macroeconomic linkages compared to multimarkets. There are at least five key features that characterise our analysis in contrast to previous approaches.

The first is a decomposition by products within agriculture that allows clearly to identify which countries may gain or lose from changes in international prices according to the composition of their agricultural trade. MDC trade liberalization in food and feed grains will likely create losses for most developing countries since they are net importers of cereals with the exception of a few developing countries, some of which are members of the Cairns group. We specify for that purpose the following commodity disaggregation: cereals, non-competitive (tropical) agricultural exports, and other farm commodities including livestock in particular.

The second is a decomposition by social actors in order to identify the distribution of the social gains or losses from liberalization, in particular on the weaker segments of rural and urban society. We introduce for this purpose several sizes of farms in agriculture and several levels of income in the urban sector, with each social group characterised by its specific portfolio of sources of income and transfers. The social disaggregation we use is: in the rural sector, rural landless, medium farmers, and large farmers; in the urban sector, poor and rich households.

The third is to make explicit a number of non-price factors that condition the ability of countries to respond to the price adjustments. A key distinction is, on the one hand, those countries which produce commodities that are substitutes in consumption to the imported commodities whose prices rise and, have the ability (the degree of which is determined by non-price factors) to increase domestic production of these commodities, and, on the other hand, those countries which must continue to rely on imports at the higher price. In all cases, effects occur across commodities (e.g., between imported cereals and exported tropical goods) through exchange rate movements.

The fourth is to introduce a time dimension in the intersectoral reallocation of resources and capital accumulation in order to be able to distinguish between the short- and the medium-to-long-run effects of liberalization. The key long-run phenomenon which we want to capture is the differential role of private and public investment in enhancing productivity. Public investment is determined by fiscal revenues and foreign borrowing less current expenditures and changes in public deficit. Fiscal revenues originate in indirect taxes, direct taxes on firms and households, and, importantly, import tariffs and export taxes. In this case, trade liberalization in the developing countries may have the opportunity cost of reducing fiscal revenues and thus the level of delivery of public goods to agriculture and future productivity growth. Foreign aid that complements price movements to enhance the non-price determinants of supply response via public investment (e.g., technology and infrastructure) may thus be an important mechanism by which the number of developing countries able to benefit from trade liberalization can be increased.

Finally, it is unlikely that governments will accept the welfare effects of trade liberalization, if they affect the poor or the politically powerful, without introducing compensatory policies and targeted transfers. Since foreign aid may be called upon to fund some of these compensatory schemes, the forms that these transfers can take, their targeting of particular social groups, and the level of their costs will be studied with the archetype models used.

COUNTRY CLASSIFICATION AND ARCHETYPES

There are two categories of countries on which the impact of trade liberalization can be expected to be large in terms of general equilibrium effects. One is composed of the net cereal exporters, most of which are members of Cairns, that will benefit from rising international prices. The growth and welfare effects on these countries are rather trivial and we consequently do not analyse them here. The other set includes the low income countries which are not oil or mineral exporters. The impact on them of trade liberalization can be significant because the share of agriculture in their total economy is large and because most of them are heavily dependent on cereal imports. In addition, from the standpoint of welfare, there are the countries most exposed to potentially nefarious effects of rising international prices on nutritional standards. We thus focus here exclusively on the low income developing countries. The defining criteria that we use to create a typology of countries on which to build the archetypes are consequently the following:

a) The structure of cereal trade: net exporters or importers in 1985;

b) The level of per capita income, using the World Bank threshold of $500 (1985) between low and middle income countries;

c) The share of fuels, minerals, and metals as a share of merchandise exports, with a threshold of 74 per cent; and

347

d) The degree of substitutability between imported cereals and domestic production. The indicator used for this purpose measures the degree of similarity in the production (Q) and import (M) of cereals (i) as follows:

Average over cereals of $\left| \dfrac{M_i}{M} - \dfrac{Q_i}{Q} \right|$

with a threshold of 0.45.

Use of these criteria gives us five groups of countries. Starting from a data set of 74 developing countries, the composition of the five groups and the main statistics on economic performance and structure, trade, agricultural production, and government revenues of each country and group are given in Table 12.1. We exclude China and India from the construction of the archetypes as their sizes would overwhelm any group in which they would be included and they deserve separate treatment. The composition of the two low income (non-oil or mineral exporter and non-cereal exporter), archetypes is as follows:

I.   Low income cereal importers with high substitution in imports: Mali, Mozambique, Madagascar, Central Africa Republic, Tanzania, Guinea, Sierra Leone, Liberia, and Lesotho, all of which are African countries. Coarse cereals and rice dominate production and imports in all these countries.

II. Low income cereal importers with low substitution in imports: Ethiopia, Burkina Faso, Bangladesh, Togo, Burundi, Benin, Somalia, Rwanda, Kenya, Sudan, Haiti, Senegal, Sri Lanka, Ghana, and Mauritania. Most countries in this group produce coarse grains, and import mainly wheat and some rice. The exceptions are Bangladesh and Sri Lanka which produce rice.

We see from Table 12.1 that only 8 of the 74 developing countries are net cereal exporters. Most developing countries will consequently be hurt in the very short run by the price rises created by MDC trade liberalization. The middle income developing countries import the bulk of the cereals (56 per cent), followed by the mineral exporters (16 per cent). While these countries will consequently bear the burden of most of the price adjustment, the resulting general equilibrium and per capita welfare effects will be small.

The two groups of low income countries are similar in their levels of per capita income ($256 and $213 respectively) and shares of agriculture in GDP (46 per cent and 40 per cent). Even though their combined share of cereal imports is small on a world scale (11 per cent), both groups of countries are heavily burdened by food imports as a share of total merchandise imports (13 and 18 per cent, respectively). Rising prices for cereal imports can consequently have heavy costs on foreign exchange availability and economic growth. They are also highly dependent on agricultural exports for foreign exchange earnings (61 and 59 per cent, respectively). For these countries, a key issue will consequently be how price effects get transmitted from cereal imports to agricultural exports. Because the share of tropical exports in total exports is large, they will benefit if trade liberalization also affects tropical products, a subject which we do not develop here since the consequences on their economies are, like for cereal exporters in group I, rather trivial.

STRUCTURE OF THE SOCIAL ACCOUNTING MATRIX

The social accounting matrix (SAM) constructed in Table 12.2 is based on the aggregate levels for the two groups of low income countries observed in Table 12.1. The two groups of countries are subsequently distinguished by their differential degrees of substitutability between domestic and imported cereals. Details for the interindustry flows, the structures of income and consumption, and government transfers are taken from the SAM for Sri Lanka (Pyatt and Roe). The principal features of the matrix are the following.

Domestic Production

The economy is dominated by agriculture that accounts for 36 per cent of GNP. The agricultural sector is decomposed into three sectors of roughly similar sizes: agricultural exports (tropical products), cereals, and other agriculture (mainly livestock). Non-agriculture includes agricultural processing, industry, a large sector that contains services and trade, and the administration that produces public services.

International Trade

The economy is highly open with 18 per cent of domestic demand satisfied by imports. Food imports account for a large fraction (28 per cent) of total imports, most of which are cereals. These cereal imports represent 25 per cent of domestic supply.

On the export side, agriculture has a large share (61 per cent) in total exports. The agricultural trade surplus is consequently important for the economy as it accounts for 5.9 per cent of GDP. Yet, as we have seen, the country is a net importer of cereals. The total balance of trade is negative, but the deficit is not particularly high as it represents 2.7 per cent of GNP and 17 per cent of the total value of exports.

Government Sector

The government sector is large, accounting for 22 per cent of GDP. Government revenues originate in equal thirds from the trade sector (taxes and tariffs), indirect taxes, and taxes on incomes and profits. The levels of trade distortion are typically high (World Bank, 1986): the rate of taxation on agricultural exports is 22.5 per cent and the tariff rate on industrial imports is 40 per cent.

Government expenditures represent 26 per cent of GDP, with a deficit equal to 4 per cent of GDP. These expenditures are distributed as follows: 48 per cent goes to current expenditures on public services, 18 per cent to public investment, 16 per cent to food subsidies, and the rest to transfers. The rate of food subsidy, which is measured as the cost of the subsidy relative to the total value of food consumption, is high (32 per cent).

Social Structure and Incomes

The population is largely rural (78 per cent). Rural incomes represent 72 per cent of total income while agricultural value added is only 40 per cent of total value added. This indicates the large importance of non-agricultural sources of income for the rural population. The rural population is also the poorest as rural incomes are, on the average, 38 per cent below urban incomes.

In the rural sector, the rural poor are landless workers who derive 94 per cent of their income from agricultural labour and 3 per cent from non-agriculture. The medium income rural households are small farmers with a diversified group of activities: 25 per cent of their income comes from agricultural profits, 24 per cent from agricultural labour, and 49 per cent from non-agriculture, principally services and commerce (42 per cent). Only the high income households are farmers who derive 68 per cent of their income from agricultural profits and 31 per cent from trade. It is this last category of households that captures all the profits from the agro-export sector.

In the SAM, all rural and all urban labour incomes are pooled before being redistributed to households. For the rest of value added, however, we avoid the usual pooling of income by distributing value added directly to households from the sector where it originates, thus keeping a direct connection between levels of sectoral activity and the determination of household incomes.

THE GENERAL EQUILIBRIUM MODELS

The Computable General Equilibrium (CGE) models used here follow, in general, the structure of the standard neoclassical real CGE models (Dervis, de Melo, and Robinson), but with some important modifications for the purposes at hand that we will describe in what follows. Following the standard specification, the relationship between the rest of the world and the domestic economy is determined, for each commodity, by the substitutability between imported goods and domestic goods on the consumption side, and by the substitutability between production for the domestic market and for the international market on the supply side. The tradable/non-tradable division is therefore generalised to a concept of degree of substitutability. Substitutions in demand and supply then occur in response to the relative prices of foreign to domestic market goods, with the former defined by the level of international prices, the exchange rate, and commercial policies (taxes, subsidies, and tariffs). On the supply side, commodities for the domestic and for the export markets aggregate in a constant elasticity of transformation (CET) function and, on the demand side, imports and domestic production aggregate in a constant elasticity of substitution (CES) function. The distinction between the two groups of low income countries introduced earlier in the typology of archetypes, which was based on the degree of substitutability between domestic and imported cereals, is characterised by the corresponding elasticity of substitution in the CES cereals aggregate, with a high value of 3 for the countries with an import-competing cereals sector and a low value of 0.3 for the countries with a non-import-competing cereals sector. The other elasticities of the model are 0.5 for the other commodity CES aggregates, 1.2 for the agricultural export CET aggregate, 0.8 for the industry CET aggregate, and 0.5 for the other commodities.

Within the domestic economy, the CGE consists of a set of behavioural equations for the different institutions that determine demand and supply on the different markets and of reconciliation rules to balance the markets. Specific CGE models are differentiated mainly by the choices of these closure rules on the different markets and by the choices of elasticities of substitution which reflect the relative rigidities of the economy. A brief description of these characteristics for our model follows the specification of the agricultural sector.

An important departure of our model from the usual CGEs is in the specification of the supply of agricultural commodities. The production functions typically used in CGEs are specified independently for each commodity, using either a Cobb-Douglas or a CES with different levels between the primary factors, and with fixed coefficients for intermediate inputs. Substitutions in production among crops only come indirectly from their sharing of common factors, mainly labour. In contrast, agricultural production should be seen as emerging from an income strategy decided at the sectoral level, where the output mix and the demands for inputs are jointly decided. This is the approach taken in the multimarket-type models and this is what we introduce here in the CGE model. This approach captures better the substitutabilities among crops and factors, and allows for the specification of non-attributable inputs and capital. In this way, we combine here the CGE and multimarket specifications, keeping the most attractive features of each approach. The non-agricultural sectors are, however, treated in the standard CGE fashion: rural and urban labour aggregate in a Cobb-Douglas employment index, and the aggregate employment and the fixed capital of each sector aggregate in a CES function to produce output.

The base values for the elasticities of the agricultural supply and factor demand system are derived from the data compiled by Sullivan, Wainio, and Roningen (1989) and from the multimarket model for India developed by Quizón and Binswanger (1986). Table 12.3 gives the elasticities used here.

In the non-agricultural sectors, a medium value of 0.8 is chosen for the CES aggregate of labour and capital.

All the commodity markets in this CGE follow the neoclassical market-clearing price system, in which producer and consumer prices are jointly determined and vary only by given tax and subsidy rates. On the labour markets, urban labour is assumed to be in surplus with an exogenous real wage[3]. For the rural labour force, wages are flexible and clear the competitive market. Public service employees are hired at an exogenous real wage.

The foreign exchange constraint imposes a flexible exchange regime with devaluation endogenously determined for a given level of capital inflow. Indeed, if the government were to use the exchange rate as a policy instrument, debt accumulation would have to be controlled by a rationing system. This alternative is, however, not considered to be available in the current period of debt crisis and adjustment.

The government's budgetary rules are an important characteristic of the adjustment policy, and alternative scenarios will be simulated. Government income derives from domestic revenues raised from different taxes and from foreign net savings (foreign capital inflow net of debt repayments). Expenditures include some commodity subsidies (on cereals), current expenditures on the services provided by the public sector, public investment, and some small transfers to households and firms. These latter are taken as constant in real terms. The food subsidies are non-targeted and consist of a price wedge between the supply price (where supply is, as we have seen, a CES aggregate of domestic production and imports according to the relative levels of the producer and border prices) and the consumer price. The net saving or deficit of this budget leads the government to loan or borrow on the domestic credit market which, in turn, enhances or crowds out private investment. Policy instruments thus include the different tax and subsidy rates and the relative levels of current and investment expenditures.

The foreign exchange shortage imposed on the economy by rising import prices has implications for the government budget. When the government maintains both current and investment expenditures at their pre-liberalization level, the increase in the cost of food subsidies generates a corresponding deficit which needs to be covered by private savings, thus crowding out private investment. The alternative is for the government to cut expenditures and maintain a constant domestic deficit. We will consider the case in which this is achieved by cutting both current and investment expenditures proportionately.

The last closure rule to be considered is the savings-investment equilibrium. Savings are generated by exogenous savings rates for households and firms. Private investment is equal to net savings available after the government budget has been decided upon.

The model only solves for a one period equilibrium, and results have to be interpreted in terms of comparative statics. However, a time frame can be introduced by setting alternative market rules and behavioural relationships that characterise the short and long terms. More specifically, we consider here the impact of investment on productivity growth. Investment has almost no impact on production in the short term, except through the demand effects generated by the demand for investment goods. It is worth noting, in this respect, that private investment includes a large amount of machinery and equipment which has a high import content, while public investment consists mostly of public works which place demands on the labour-intensive construction and services sectors. A shift in the balance between public and private investment will therefore not be neutral on the economy, and on the equilibrium exchange rate in particular, even in the short term. However, the main impact of investment takes place in the longer run through capital accumulation, and the principal effect of private capital accumulation is not in the mere increase in the stock of capital, but in the technological changes and productivity gains imbedded in the renewal of capital. As for public investment, its role materialises in the enhancement of the productivity and profitability of private investment. This is captured by making total factor productivity in the different sectors a function of both total private and public investment. The same elasticities relating productivity to investment have been applied to all sectors, although better knowledge of differential productivity effects across sectors would have allowed use of the intersectoral reallocation of investment as a policy instrument.

IMPACT OF TRADE LIBERALIZATION ON THE LOW INCOME DEVELOPING COUNTRIES: PREDICTED IMPLICATIONS AND ALTERNATIVE POLICY SCENARIOS

Preliminary Observations on the Size of the Effects

Before looking at general equilibrium results, it may be first noted that a simple partial equilibrium calculation indicates that, even in the low income developing countries, the impact of a rise in the international price of cereals on average real incomes will be relatively small. If prices increase by 20 per cent and if 25 per cent of the domestic availability of cereals is provided by imports, domestic prices increase by roughly 5 per cent. If the share of cereals in the average budget is 12 per cent, real incomes fall by only 0.6 per cent. This does not mean, of course, that specific countries where levels of dependency are higher and specific groups of poor whose budget share of cereals is much higher will not bear a higher burden. In Table 12.1, several countries have dependency levels of the order of 40 per cent. The poorest rural poor can have budget shares for cereals as high as 58 per cent (India). This would imply a fall in their real income equal to 4.6 per cent, still not a very large figure even if significant for their welfare. In the following general equilibrium exercises for archetype countries, levels of aggregation hide these extremes. For the country averages by archetype and for the broad social groups as specified, the overall growth and welfare effects will be relatively small. Detailed analyses for specific poverty groups in highly dependent countries consequently remain a necessary complement to the following results.

A second preliminary observation is that a rise in cereal prices, a final consumption good, will have a lesser general equilibrium effect than would a rise in an intermediate product. This is shown by comparing the results in experiments 5 and 6 in Table 12.4. In experiment 5, the import price of cereals increases by 20 per cent. In experiment 6, the price of industrial imports is raised so that the increase in the value of industrial imports would be equal to the increase in the value of cereal imports when their price increases by 20 per cent before general equilibrium adjustments. Exchange rate devaluation is consequently similar in both. However, the resulting negative growth effect is more than three times larger when the price of an intermediate good import rises. Rising cereal prices could also have a negative effect on industry by inducing a rise in nominal wages. Yet this effect is small since real wages are held constant relative to a general price index in which cereal is a relatively small component. Welfare effects on the urban poor are also larger with the rising price of an intermediate product since it affects them through employment effects.

In spite of the relatively small size of overall effects, we will see that the general equilibrium effects are an important part of the total effects that rising cereal import prices induce. In particular, we will see that the exchange rate response has a strong effect on the production of tradables and that the effects on government revenues from trade distortions have a strong impact on investment and long-term productivity gains.

Countries with Import Substitution Possibilities versus Non-competitive Cereal Imports

We compare, in experiments 1 and 2 versus 4 and 5, the two country archetypes representing situations where cereal imports are competitive with domestic production, and hence where import substitution possibilities exist, as opposed to situations where imports are not competitive with domestic production. To show the importance of exchange rate responses in transmitting the effect of a 20 per cent increase in the price of imported cereals, we analyse these effects under a fixed exchange rate regime where adjustment occurs through foreign borrowing (experiments 1 and 4) and under a flexible exchange rate with a constant balance of payments deficit (experiments 2 and 5).

The main difference between competitive and non-competitive imports is that rising international prices will spill over to domestic production directly in the first case and only indirectly, principally through exchange rate effects, in the second. With competitive imports and a fixed exchange rate (experiment 1), domestic producer prices increase by 8 per cent inducing, in the short run with a low elasticity of supply response, a rise in cereal output of 3 per cent. Consumer prices rise by 11 per cent, inducing a decline in cereal consumption. Rising supply and falling demand lead to a sharp fall in the volume of cereal imports (24 per cent) and hence also in the value of imports. Even though agricultural exports fall because of crowding out in production by cereals, the balance of trade deficit is sharply reduced (–15 per cent). This loss of foreign exchange, as indebtedness is reduced, creates a fall in GDP. On the welfare side, the terms of trade for agriculture improve and this benefits the large farmers. All the other social categories are hurt as they are net buyers of food (the rural landless and urban poor) and they lose employment in industry.

The key result of shifting to a flexible exchange rate is that falling imports lead to a revaluation of the exchange rate of 1.4 per cent. Revaluation of the exchange rate lowers the GDP loss, but the loss in absorption is still much larger than that in GDP. Agricultural exports decline a little more as the price of tradables falls and the large farmers do not gain as much as before. The loss to others is also reduced since exchange rate adjustment mitigates both the rise in the price of cereals and the fall in GDP.

For countries where cereal imports are not competitive with domestic production there is no direct spillover on the rest of the economy. Indirect effects are also minimal for as long as the exchange rate can be maintained fixed by rising indebtedness. Consumption of cereals nevertheless falls as their price rises by 4 per cent, while the volume of cereal imports falls only by 6 per cent, as opposed to 24 per cent in the countries with competitive imports, and hence the value of cereal imports increases sharply. The result is that indebtedness increases by 10 per cent, allowing the rate of growth in GDP to remain about constant. Welfare effects are small, although the main losers are the rural households, as agricultural production stagnates since it does not benefit from a passing through of price effects.

With rising indebtedness impossible, the exchange rate needs to be devalued by 2 per cent (as opposed to revalued with competitive cereal imports). This creates a positive spillover on the price of agricultural exports (1.5 per cent) and on their level of production (0.9 per cent) and exports (1.5 per cent). Exchange rate devaluation further reduces the levels of cereal imports and of cereal consumption. Thus while exchange rate adjustment neutralises the overall growth effects of rising international cereal prices (as opposed to competitive imports), the welfare effects remain negative. Only the large farmers gain as they capture all the profits from agro-exports. The other social categories are hurt by rising consumer prices for cereals.

The conclusions on the short-run effects of a rise in the international price of cereals on the two archetype economies are thus, at first sight, paradoxical. The country with more import substitution possibilities is hurt the most both because prices spill over directly to all domestic cereal prices and because of exchange rate revaluation provoked by a sharp fall in the value of cereal imports, with a consequent foreign exchange saving effect. The welfare effects are sharply negative on the poor and are regressive. The key policy implication, which we will explore in the next section, is to increase the elasticity of supply in cereal production if these dire consequences are to be avoided.

The countries with less ability for import substitution in cereals are the least affected in the short run. There is no direct price spillover effect and exchange rate devaluation benefits agro-exports and industry. While negative growth effects are thus avoided, welfare effects are not negligible with the poor losing both absolutely and relatively. In this case, the key policy implication, which we will explore later, is using compensatory transfers, either domestic or through foreign aid, to compensate the losers among the poor until growth effects restore their sources of income.

Role of Non-price Factors for Import Substitution

In the long run, once short-run non-price factors have been readjusted to increase the elasticity of supply response (Binswanger *et al.*), the negative short-run effects of a rising international price of cereals on countries with competitive imports can be mitigated. This is explored in experiment 3 in Table 12.4.

We see that with an elasticity of cereals production equal to 1.2 per cent economic growth can be restored even though exchange rate revaluation still needs to occur as the value of cereal imports falls. Cereal production increases by 6 per cent, allowing the price of cereals to only rise by 5 per cent (as opposed to 7.8 per cent with inelastic supply). Rising cereal prices, however, continue to raise the cost of food subsidies for the government. The gross deficit of the government thus continues to increase (9.6 per cent), crowding out private investment which falls by 2.6 per cent. Even though this is less than with an inelastic supply, the long-run consequences of falling investment on long-term productivity growth can be serious, a subject to which we will return.

While the rise in cereals prices on the domestic market is partially held in check by rising domestic supply, it hurts the poor. Overall cereal consumption is reduced by 2.4 per cent and the welfare of the rural and urban poor falls slightly. Yet their welfare is very directly affected by the level of economic growth which, itself, depends upon the elasticity of the cereal supply. Enhancing the capacity for import substitution will consequently be the principal policy approach to both growth and welfare in these countries.

Whether countries that have the ability to substitute for cereal imports will be hurt by or benefit from rising international prices thus depends on the elasticity of agricultural supply. The magnitude of this elasticity depends crucially upon a number of non-price factors, public investment in agriculture in particular. This includes such things as infrastructure, agricultural technology, and access to markets and credit. The key policy implication here is that if the MDCs want to transform trade liberalization into an instrument of economic development for this category of countries, foreign aid programmes aimed at "elasticising" their supply of cereals for import substitution should be an integral complementary dimension of the GATT negotiations.

Trade Liberalization and Government Revenues: The Short and the Long Run

The level and composition of government expenditures have an effect on growth in both the short and the long run. This is explored in experiments 7 to 10 in Table 12.4.

When cereal imports are competitive, we saw in experiment 2 that the deficit in the government's budget increases sharply as the international price of cereals rises. This is due to falling export taxes and import tariff revenues and to rising costs of food subsidies while the levels of other current expenditures and of public investment remain constant. The result is a strong crowding out effect on private investment as the government's deficit competes with private investment for access to private savings. Since future productivity growth is determined by the level of investment, this crowding out effect can have a strong negative impact on growth.

In experiments 7 to 10, the net government deficit (i.e., the government deficit net of foreign capital inflow) is held constant in domestic currency (changes observed in Table 12.5 are consequently due to exchange rate movements that change the value of foreign borrowing by government). In a period of stabilization policies and structural adjustment, it is indeed unlikely that the level of government deficit can be raised. Maintaining the deficit constant (as opposed to experiment 2) implies cutting current expenditures and/or public investment. In experiments 7 to 10, these cuts are applied proportionately to these two categories of expenditures. While the result is to reduce public investment by 3.8 per cent (experiment 7), it only reduces private investment by 0.2 per cent as opposed to 4.4 per cent before. Yet overall investment falls sharply. The result is that GDP growth falls further, from 0.8 to 1 per cent.

While this is not too serious in the short run, the opportunity cost of falling investment is less productivity growth in the longer run. Experiment 8 represents a situation where investment induces productivity growth with an elasticity of 0.1 with respect to public investment (to reflect the public goods nature of these expenditures) and 0.07 with respect to private investment. Falling investment implies that economic growth is further reduced by 1.6 per cent, cereal consumption falls by 4.6 per cent, and the welfare of all social groups is reduced.

The policy implication is that protecting the level of investment is key to reducing the negative growth effect of rising cereal prices. This can be done by choosing to cut current expenditures to protect public investment. Alternatively, structural adjustment loans and international aid could be directed at helping maintain public investment in a period of fiscal austerity.

Food Subsidies and Food Aid

Since, in both archetypes, the poor are hurt in the short run by rising prices of imported cereals, we can explore different schemes of compensation via non-targeted food subsidies, financial transfers to the poor, and targeted food subsidies backed by international food aid in order to protect their real income levels. This is done in the following six experiments.

In experiments 11 and 12, reported in Table 12.5, the previous scheme of food aid, whereby a wedge was maintained between producer and consumer prices, is replaced by holding consumer price levels for cereals constant at the pre-GATT level. The necessary level of food subsidies is consequently endogenously determined. The results of experiments 11 and 12 are to be compared to the results of experiments 2 and 5, respectively.

With a fixed consumer price the cost of food subsidies increases sharply. This is due to the fact that, as consumption rises, the producer price of cereals and the level of imports both increase greatly. The result is a sharp increase in government deficit and a fall in private investment through crowding out effects. The mix of falling demand for investment goods, falling relative prices for industry and services, and exchange rate devaluation creates a negative effect on the economy, with a loss of one percentage point in GDP and falling output in all sectors other than cereals. This negative effect on growth implies that the scheme of food subsidies fails to achieve its purpose of protecting the welfare of the urban poor. The large farmers gain most, as the producer prices of cereals rise, and the rural poor also benefit from rising employment in agriculture and falling cereal consumer prices. But the real income of the urban poor deteriorates sharply. Thus the conclusion is that fixing the consumer price of cereals in a context of rising international prices and using the government budget to finance the gap between producer/import and consumer prices is an appropriate strategy to protect cereal consumption but not for economic growth or the welfare of the urban poor. For the latter, the opportunity cost of slower growth is too large and it largely overwhelms the benefits from cheap grains.

Before turning to financial and food aid, it should be noted that it is not possible to tax the gainers from GATT-induced price movements, in this case only the large farmers (see experiments 2 and 5), to compensate the losers among the rural and urban poor. The large farmers are too few and do not capture enough income gain from the price adjustments to have the resources to compensate the losers. It is for this reason that we turn to international aid as a source of compensation. The questions we ask are what form this aid should take and what is the magnitude of its cost.

In experiments 13 and 14, a foreign exchange injection is made of an endogenous amount equal to what is necessary to maintain the real income of the rural landless and the urban poor at the pre-GATT level. Their real income is measured relative to the overall consumer price index (CPI) since this is what government uses in the measurement of price effects. The result is that, even if the real income of the landless and urban poor is constant relative to the CPI, the real income of the landless falls and that of the urban poor rises relative to their class-specific CPIs. The foreign resources needed amount to 11 and 9 per cent of the balance of payments deficit.

While the effects are small, the strategy fails in that it leads to an increase in the price of cereals as it focuses on demand management without attention to the supply side. The result is a fall in overall growth, a rise in government deficit, and a fall in private investment. Rising prices largely erase any gain in the consumption of cereals. The welfare of the urban poor is adequately protected, but not that of the rural poor. The medium farmers pay the cost of a backlash effect through rising cereal prices of which they are net buyers. The conclusion is that a foreign transfer to the poor is not the best approach to compensate the effect of rising international prices of cereals on the poor. Supply management is necessary as well, particularly in the countries where domestic cereal production is competitive with imports.

Targeted international food aid thus appears as a better solution. This is done in experiments 15 and 16. The main benefit is that it allows holding in check the rise in domestic cereal consumer prices. While the production of cereals increases less (experiment 15) or falls more (experiment 16) than before, the overall negative effect on the economy is mitigated. The important observation here is that the overall cost of the food transfer that is needed to protect the welfare of the rural and urban poor is small: it is only on the order of 8 per cent of the level of pre-GATT cereal imports or 6 per cent of the balance of payment deficit. Short-run compensatory food aid to the poor in the low income food importing nations thus appears as a highly reasonable possibility that should be considered as an integral component of the GATT negotiations.

CONCLUSIONS

We have argued that the growth and per capita income effects of rising international prices for cereals, induced by eventually successful GATT negotiations in the OECD countries, would be small for most of the developing countries. This does not mean that specific countries, with high levels of cereal dependency and large agricultural sectors competitive with imported cereals, would not be more severely affected.

Also, in all countries, particularly the poorest non-mineral exporters, specific groups of poor people who are net buyers of cereals will be affected by rising prices. Both these countries and social groups require a more detailed level of analysis than can be done with archetype CGEs.

356

We concluded that there is an apparent paradox in the way rising international prices for cereals affect low income countries. Countries with more possibilities for import substitution in cereals are, in the short run, the most negatively affected by rising prices as these spill over directly to all cereal prices, lead to a fall not only in the volume but also in the value of cereal imports, and, consequently, to an exchange rate revaluation, with negative consequences on the other tradable sectors. The welfare effect is highly negative on the poor and regressive. By contrast, countries with a cereals sector that is not as directly competitive with imports fare better: prices do not spill over on all cereals, and exchange rate devaluation benefits tropical exports and industry. While growth effects are therefore minimal, the poor are, however, here also hurt both absolutely and relatively.

The most important policy implication for the countries with the capability of import substitution is to increase their elasticity of cereal supply as rapidly as possible. This requires enhancing public investment in agriculture, at the cost of reduced current expenditures, and the productivity effects of new investments. This calls for programmes of foreign assistance to the non-price determinants of aggregate supply response such as technology, infrastructure, and the removal of credit constraints. Developmental assistance for cereal production in this type of developing country should consequently have a high payoff in helping more developing countries benefit from the international price adjustment and in reducing the time span during which negative growth and welfare effects are felt.

In all countries, but particularly in those with little capacity for import substitution, temporary special programmes of assistance to the poorest net buyers of food should be considered. We have shown that compensation to the poor cannot be made by taxing the gainers (i.e., the large farmers) since their total income gain is less than the loss for the poor. Replacing food subsidies based on a price wedge by a fixed consumer price for cereals has extraordinary costs in terms of economic growth, creating a backlash on the welfare of the poor, urban in particular. International income transfers without supply management are also not effective since they increase the price of cereals and fail to protect the rural poor. The optimum short-run relief policy appears to be food aid targeted on the rural and urban poor. We estimated that the total cost of this aid programme would be small, amounting to no more than some 8 per cent of the level of pre-GATT cereal imports. Compensation schemes of food aid for specific countries, target groups, and time spans should consequently also be explicitly introduced in the GATT negotiations. In addition to obvious welfare considerations, they are key instruments to enlist the support of these countries for a successful outcome of the ongoing negotiations to achieve trade liberalization.

Table 12.1

DEVELOPING COUNTRIES' CHARACTERISTICS

	General Countries' Characteristics							International Trade				Government	
	Number of countries	Population mid-1985 (millions)	GNP per capita 1985 ($)	GDP 1985 (million $)	Agriculture[1]	Industry[1]	Service[1]	Export[1]	Resource balance[1]	Agricul. commod. (exports)[2]	Food (imports)[2]	Total current revenue[3]	Taxes on int'l trade & transfer[4]
Total LDCs	74	3 347.1	558	1 726 510	22	35	42	18	0	28	12	20	13
LDCs excl. India & China													
Net cereal exporters	8	250.2	657	151 690	19	35	47	18	0	64	7	16	19
Mineral exporters	11	364.6	827	296 860	21	39	41	23	4	8	15	24	11
Middle income	29	598.1	1 336	764 080	15	34	50	22	2	29	12	22	9
Low income	24	328.8	222	72 640	41	17	42	14	-10	59	17	19	32
Substitutability in cereals imports													
High	9	69.9	256	17 310	46	14	40	13	-9	61	13	14	39
Low	15	258.9	213	65 330	40	18	42	15	-10	59	18	19	31
Low income; high substitutability in imports													
Mali		7.5	150	1 100	50	13	37	21	-24	81	14		
Mozambique		13.8	160	3 230	35	11	53	4	-10	64	20		
Madagascar		10.2	240	2 340	42	16	42	14	-5	86	12		
Central African Rep.		2.6	260	610	39	20	41	25	-14	64	17		
Tanzania		22.2	290	5 600	58	8	33	7	-10	76	4		
Guinea		6.2	320	1 980	40	22	38	25	4		12		
Sierra Leone		3.7	350	1 190	44	14	42	11	-1	33	27	7	40
Liberia		2.2	470	1 000	37	28	36	43	6	34	24	20	28
Lesotho		1.5	470	260	21	27	52	12	-112			21	71
Low income; low substitutability in imports													
Ethiopia		42.3	110	4 230	44	16	39	12	-16	89	29		
Burkina Faso		7.9	150	930	45	22	33	16	-26	89	23	14	30
Bangladesh		100.6	150	16 110	50	14	35	6	-10	32	24		
Togo		3.0	230	700	30	24	47	41	-11	35	15	37	29
Burundi		4.7	230	970	61	15	24	11	-10	82	9		
Benin		4.0	260	960	48	16	36	24	-15	39	12		
Somalia		5.4	280	2 320	58	9	34	7	-21	98	22		
Rwanda		6.0	280	1 710	45	21	34	9	-9	94	9		
Kenya		20.4	290	5 020	31	20	49	25	-2	65	9	22	20
Sudan		21.9	300	6 930	26	18	57	10	-10	94	11		
Haiti		5.9	310	1 930				16	-8	32	15		
Senegal		6.6	370	2 560	19	29	52	31	-13	72	26	24	32
Sri Lanka		15.8	380	5 500	27	26	46	26	-12	63	15	11	41
Ghana		12.7	380	4 860	41	15	43	13	-2	65	15		
Mauritania		1.7	420	600	29	25	47	60	-17	41	25		

1. Per cent share of 1985 GDP.
2. Share of total 1985 merchandise.
3. Total current revenue of central government as a per cent of real 1985 GNP.
4. Per cent of total current revenue of central government in 1985.
Sources: World Development Report, FAO Trade Yearbook, FAO Production Yearbook.

Table 12.1 (continued)

	Agricultural Trade		Cereal Supply						Index of similarity prod. imports (all cereals)	Net cereal imp. share total domest. cereal supply[5]
	Net cereal imports 1985 ($10 000)	Share sample cereal imports[5]	Wheat[6]	Rice[6]	Coarse grains[6]	Wheat[7]	Rice[7]	Coarse cereals[3]		
Total LDCs	977 847	100	198 157	417 371	263 171	38 768	-2 134,2 594	.51,4.3		
LDCs excl. India & China										
Net cereal exporters	-369 001	2.4	22 842	42 217	31 254	-5 192	-6 158	-14 138	-.15	-36.0
Mineral exporters	266 679	16.4	1 665	42 247	23 531	8 990	393	2 801	.48	15.3
Middle income	850 199	55.6	37 615	36 372	73 990	23 188	2 541	15 695	.20	21.9
Low income	181 549	10.5	2 549	30 175	23 227	5 319	2 082	462	.42	12.3
Substitutability in cereals imports										
High	35 765	2.1	100	4 171	5 751	460	662	471	.19	13.7
Low	145 784	8.4	2 450	26 005	17 477	4 859	1 420	-9	.48	12.0
Low income; high substitutability in imports										
Mali	5 607	0.3	3	222	1 517	37	122	63	.39	11.3
Mozambique	6 300	0.3	5	58	535	115	76	188	.27	38.8
Madagascar	4 309	0.2	0	2 158	148	42	143	-2	.15	7.4
Central African Rep.	691	0.0	0	11	119	17	5	8	.44	18.7
Tanzania	6 033	0.3	78	487	3 140	60	53	138	.20	6.4
Guinea	2 691	0.2	0	474	105	69	75	2	.32	20.1
Sierra Leone	3 150	0.2	0	471	52	30	94	1	.16	19.2
Liberia	4 864	0.2	0	292	0	26	93	1	.15	29.2
Lesotho	2 120	0.2	15	0	135	64	2	73	.25	48.1
Low income; low substitutability in imports										
Ethiopia	18 629	1.2	800	0	4 652	838	11	26	.55	13.8
Burkina Faso	4 166	0.2	0	39	1 700	31	77	34	.49	7.5
Bangladesh	47 844	2.5	1 223	22 836	29	1 530	397	1	.50	7.4
Togo	1 995	0.1	0	18	351	45	20	4	.59	15.7
Burundi	736	0.0	11	20	431	16	1	0	.62	3.5
Benin	1 041	0.1	0	8	507	28	21	5	.59	9.5
Somalia	7 660	0.4	1	5	615	135	106	46	.55	31.6
Rwanda	1 082	0.0	5	5	313	13	11	2	.59	7.5
Kenya	5 895	0.0	270	53	2 994	144	31	-270	1.29	-3.0
Sudan	19 034	1.2	139	2	3 796	835	47	-2	.64	18.3
Haiti	4 478	0.3	0	155	290	177	11	20	.57	31.9
Senegal	8 830	0.7	0	147	923	125	357	38	.53	32.7
Sri Lanka	16 796	1.3	0	2 625	46	711	194	79	.52	26.9
Ghana	3 398	0.2	0	80	763	88	57	0	.60	14.7
Mauritania	4 200	0.3	1	15	72	143	80	8	.52	72.5

5. Average 1985-86 (per cent).
6. Average 1985-86 production (1 000 MTs).
7. Average 1985-86 net imports (1 000 MTs).

Table 12.2

SOCIAL ACCOUNTING MATRIX FOR THE ARCHETYPE POOR ECONOMY

	Activities							Labour		Households					Firms	Gov't. subs.	Trade marg.	Priv. inv.	Publ. inv.	Export taxes	RoW	Total
	Ag. Exp.	Cereals	Other Ag.	Ag. proc.	Ind-ustry	Cons. serv.	Administr.	Urban	Rural	Urb. poor	Urb. rich	Land-less	Med. farm	Large farm								
Ag. exports				321						61	13	146	152	35						267	1 182	2 177
Cereals	78									151	32	371	467	72								1 171
Other Ag.		106		84						329	114	512	685	175							53	2 163
Ag. process		12	38	215	40	49	21			277	84	448	641	144				17	127		103	2 048
Industry	151	40	79	743	646	124	29			354	288	432	920	399				813	475		384	5 542
Cons. serv.	71		75	108	613	681	112			344	198	313	693	233			1 805	970			75	5 664
Administr.							180									1 628						1 628
Labour																						
Urban	27	28	115	96	303	340	210															1 182
Rural	855	719	378	92	355	681																3 080
Households																						
Urban poor								1 182								60						1 792
Urban rich															31							1 132
Landless							68		2 125							72						2 265
Med. farm	154		866	166	1 513	190			955							69						4 033
Large farm	553	176	216	120		432										13						1 390
Firms				334	710											194						1 238
Govt. subs.	-556									121	121		101		376	556				73		1 841
Indirect taxes	48		624	82	189																	669
Import tariffs	267		110																			267
Export taxes	205		219	723	300																	1 805
Trade margins	126									155	282	43	374	226	733							1 813
Private inv.																71		8				602
Public inv.	406	159	103	1 382	325											83					523	2 587
RoW															129							2 320
Total	2 177	1 171	2 163	2 048	5 542	5 664	1 628	1 182	3 080	1 792	1 132	2 265	4 033	1 390	1 238	2 777	1 805	1 813	602	267	2 320	

Table 12.3

PRICE AND FIXED FACTOR ELASTICITIES OF OUTPUT SUPPLY AND FACTOR DEMAND

	Ag exports	Cereals	Other Ag	Urban labour	Rural labour	Fixed factors
Output supply						
Ag exports	0.4	-0.2	-0.1	-0.1	-0.3	0.5
Other Ag	-0.2	0.4	-0.1	-0.1	-0.3	0.5
Factor demand						
Urban labour	0.2	0.2	0.3	-0.6	0.3	0.1
Rural labour	0.2	0.2	0.3	0.3	-0.6	0.1

Table 12.4

SIMULATION OF THE IMPACT OF A 20 PER CENT INCREASE IN CEREAL IMPORT PRICE
(Per cent change over base values)

	Base values	Competitive Cereal Imports[1]			Non-competitive Cereal Imports[1]			Constant Government Net Deficit[4]			
								Competitive cereal imports[1]		Non-competitive cereal imports[1]	
		Fixed exchange rate	Flexible exchange rate	High supply response[2]	Fixed exchange rate	Flexible exchange rate	Ind. imp. price increase[3]	Short run	Long run	Short run	Long run
		(1)	(2)	(3)	(4)	(5)	(6)	(7)	(8)	(9)	(10)
GDP market price	12 807	-1.0	-0.8	0.2	.2	0.0	-0.3	-1.0	-1.6	0.0	0.0
Absorption	13 118	-1.8	-1.2	-0.3	.0	-0.6	-0.9	-1.5	-2.1	-0.6	-0.6
Price index	100										
International Trade											
Exchange rate	100	.0	-1.4	-2.2	.0	2.0	1.9	-1.4	-1.5	2.0	2.0
BOP deficit ($)	523	-8.8	0.0	10.3	0.0	0.0	0.0	0.0	0.0	0.0	0.0
BOT deficit ($)	311	-14.8	0.0	0.0	17.3	0.0	0.0	0.0	0.0	0.0	0.0
Agric. exports	1 502	-2.1	-2.7	-1.3	.3	1.5	1.0	-2.6	-3.0	1.5	1.5
Cereal imports	406	-24.3	-22.2	-23.9	-5.7	-6.8	-5.5	-22.7	-23.0	-6.8	-6.8
Food imports	509	-19.7	-17.7	-18.9	-4.6	-5.7	-4.8	-18.2	-18.6	-5.7	-5.7
Industrial imports	1 382	-2.1	-1.1	0.3	.3	-0.8	-2.1	-0.7	-1.2	-0.8	-0.8
Domestic prices											
Producer price Ag. exports	1	.5	-0.7	-1.8	-.1	1.5	1.0	-0.7	-0.8	1.5	1.5
Producer price cereals	1	8.3	7.8	5.0	-.7	-1.1	-0.1	7.5	7.3	-1.1	-0.1
Producer price industry	1	-1.5	-1.5	-1.0	.2	0.5	0.8	-1.3	-1.2	0.4	0.4
Producer price services	1	-2.4	-1.9	-0.8	.4	0.0	-0.1	-1.7	0.0	0.0	0.0
Cereal consumer price	1	10.9	10.2	7.8	4.4	4.7	0.4	10.0	9.8	4.7	4.7
Ag. prod. (at producer price)											
Total agriculture	4 624	-.3	-.3	1.2	.0	.0	.1	-.3	-.8	.1	.0
Ag. exports	1 657	-1.5	-1.9	-0.8	.2	0.9	0.6	-1.8	-2.2	0.9	0.9
Cereals	1 195	3.0	3.1	6.1	-.2	-0.6	0.1	3.0	2.6	-0.6	-0.6
Other agriculture	1 772	-1.5	-1.2	-0.1	.0	-0.3	-1.3	-1.8	-0.3	-0.3	-0.3
Government budget											
Borrowing requirements	531	13.8	14.0	9.6	2.4	.8	-3.6	-1.4	-1.5	1.9	1.9
Foreign trans. in LCU	523	-8.8	1.4	-2.2	10.3	2.0	1.9	-1.4	-1.6	2.0	2.0,
Import tariffs	669	-2.0	-2.4	-1.8	.2	1.1	4.8	-2.1	-2.7	1.0	1.0
Export taxes	267	-2.1	-4.1	-3.5	.3	3.5	2.9	-3.9	-4.6	3.5	3.5
Food subsidies	556	6.3	6.2	5.8	2.6	2.3	-.9	5.9	5.3	2.3	2.3
Current expenditures	1 628	0.0	0.0	0.0	0.0	0.0	0.0	-3.8	-4.7	0.3	0.3
Public investment	602	0.0	0.0	0.0	0.0	0.0	0.0	-3.8	-4.7	0.3	0.3
Private investment	1 805	-6.9	-4.4	-2.6	2.3	-.1	-0.4	-0.2	-0.8	-0.5	-0.5

Table 12.4 (continued)

Welfare											
Real income											
Rural landless	2 265	-1.2	-1.0	-0.6	-.7	-1.0	-0.9	-1.0	-1.3	-1.0	-1.0
Medium farmers	4 033	-1.7	-1.0	0.4	-.6	-1.4	-1.8	-1.2	-1.8	-1.4	-1.4
Large farmers	1 390	2.4	1.2	2.1	-.7	0.7	0.1	0.0	-0.8	0.8	0.8
Urban poor	1 792	-2.6	-1.9	-0.7	.0	-0.7	-1.1	-2.1	-2.5	-0.7	-0.7
Urban rich	1 132	-1.9	-1.3	-0.3	.0	-0.5	-1.6	-2.2	-2.6	-0.4	-0.4
Cereal consumption	1 093	-4.7	-4.0	-2.4	-1.8	-2.4	-1.4	-4.2	-4.6	-2.4	-2.4

1. Competitive (non competitive) cereal imports are characterised by an elasticity of substitution of 3, (.3) between imports and domestic production.
2. Experiment 3: direct price elasticity of 1.2 for cereals and .3 for the other agricultural sectors, with all cross-price elasticities of -.05.
3. Experiment 6: 6 per cent increase in international price of industrial goods and no increase in cereals price.
4. Experiments 7 to 10: constant net deficit equal to government borrowing requirements minus foreign transfer.
5. LCU: local currency units.

Table 12.5

ALTERNATIVE COMPENSATION POLICIES IN RESPONSE TO A 20 PER CENT INCREASE IN CEREAL IMPORT PRICE
(Per cent change over base value)

| | | Endogenous Food Subsidies[2] | | External Income Transfer to Poor Households | | | |
| | | | | Financial aid[3] | | Food aid[4] | |
		Competitive cereal imports[1] (11)	Non-competitive cereal imports[1] (12)	Competitive cereal imports[1] (13)	Non-competitive cereal imports[1] (14)	Competitive cereal imports[1] (15)	Non-competitive cereal imports[1] (16)
GDP market price	12 807	-1.9	-0.8	-0.9	-0.2	-0.1	0.6
Absorption	13 118	-2.4	-1.4	-1.4	-0.8	-0.6	0.0
Price index	100						
International Trade							
Exchange rate	100	-0.1	2.2	-1.3	2.0	-2.0	2.5
BOP deficit ($)	523	0.0	0.0	10.8	9.2	5.9	6.2
BOT deficit ($)	-311	0.0	0.0	0.0	0.0	0.0	0.0
Agric. exports	1 502	-3.5	0.3	-3.0	1.2	-2.6	1.9
Cereals imports	406	-13.3	-4.4	-21.3	-6.4	-25.6	-3.9
Food imports	509	-10.8	-3.9	-17.0	-5.3	-20.3	-3.3
Indust. imports	1 382	-4.0	-2.5	-1.6	-1.3	-0.3	-1.9
Domestic prices							
Producer price Ag. exports	1	0.9	2.1	-0.5	1.6	-1.2	1.2
Producer price cereals	1	12.7	3.0	8.3	-0.3	5.7	-6.6
Producer price industry	1	-2.8	-0.6	-1.8	0.1	-1.3	2.3
Producer price services	1	-4.2	-1.6	-2.3	-0.4	-1.2	1.2
Cereals consumer price	1	0.0	0.0	10.6	5.3	8.4	-4.3
Ag. prod. (at prod. price)							
Total agriculture	4 624	-.4	-.1	-.3	-.1	-.2	.3
Ag. exports	1 657	-2.4	0.1	-2.0	0.7	-1.7	1.2
Cereals	1 195	4.3	0.7	3.1	-0.4	2.4	-1.2
Other agriculture	1 772	-1.7	-0.8	-1.0	-0.2	-0.6	0.5
Government budget							
Borrowing requirements	531	56.8	26.4	14.3	1.8	8.7	-13.1
Foreign transfer in LCU	523	-0.1	2.2	-1.3	2.0	-2.0	2.5
Import tariffs	669	-3.5	-0.1	-2.7	0.7	-2.2	5.7
Export taxes	267	-3.6	2.6	-4.2	3.2	-4.6	4.3
Food subsidies	556	14.1	7.2	7.0	3.1	3.0	-6.1
Current expenditures	1 628	0.0	0.0	0.0	0.0	0.0	0.0
Public investment	602	0.0	0.0	0.0	0.0	0.0	0.0
Private investment	1 805	-17.4	-7.8	-7.5	-2.9	-2.7	2.5

Table 12.5 (continued)

Welfare			
Real income			
Rural landless	0.6	-0.2	-0.2
Medium farmers	-0.3	-1.0	-1.5
Large farmers	5.4	2.9	0.9
Urban poor	-3.2	-1.6	0.1
Urban rich	-2.6	-1.3	-0.8
Cereal consumption	-0.6	-0.8	-2.2

	2 265	-0.8	
	4 033	-1.1	
	1 390	1.4	
	1 792	0.2	
	1 132	-1.7	
	1 093	-3.7	

1. Competitive (non-competitive) cereals imports are characterised by an elasticity of substitution of 3. (.3) between imports and domestic production.
2. Experiments 11-12: Food subsidies at endogenous rate to maintain consumer price of cereals constant.
3. Experiments 13-14: Foreign income transfer to maintain nominal income of rural landless and urban poor in line with the aggregate consumer price index.
4. Experiments 15-16: Foreign food aid transfer.

365

NOTES AND REFERENCES

1. We are indebted to Ian Goldin and Edward Tower for useful suggestions.

2. The Cairns group includes free-trader agricultural exporters from both the MDCs (Australia, New Zealand, Canada, and Hungary) and the developing countries (Argentina, Uruguay, Brazil, Chile, Colombia, Indonesia, Malysia, Philippines, and Thailand). Among the developing countries of this group, only Argentina, Uruguay, and Thailand are net exporters of cereals.

3. In the experiments for which the CGE is used, the aggregate employment effect of GATT scenarios is sufficiently small, even in the long run, not to exhaust surplus labour. A flexible real wage would dampen the impact of policy scenarios on GDP.

BIBLIOGRAPHY

ANDERSON, K. and R. TYERS, "Agricultural Protection Growth in Advanced and Newly Industrialized Countries," in A. Maunder and A. Valdés (eds)., *Agriculture and Governments in an Interdepent World*, proceedings of the XX International Conference of Agricultural Economists, Aldershot, England: Dartmouth, 1989.

BINSWANGER, H., M. YANG, A. BOWERS, and Y. MUNDLAK, "On the Determinants of Cross Country Aggregate Agricultural Supply," *Journal of Econometrics*, Vol. 36, 1987.

BURNIAUX, J.-M., *Le Radeau de la Méduse: Analyse des Dilemmes Alimentaires*, Economica, Paris, 1987.

CENTRE FOR INTERNATIONAL ECONOMICS, "Macroeconomic Consequences of Farm Support Policies: Overview," Canberra, 1988.

de JANVRY, A., E. SADOULET, and T.K. WHITE, "Foreign Aid's Effect on U.S. Farm Exports: Benefits or Penalties?," Foreign Agricultural Economic Report No. 238, Economic Research Service, US Department of Agriculture, November 1989.

DERVIS, K., J. de MELO, and S. ROBINSON, *General Equilibrium Models for Development Policy*, New York: Cambridge University Press, 1987.

FISCHER, K., K. FROHBERG, M.A. KEYSER, and K.S. PARIKH, *Linked National Models: A Tool for International Food Policy Analysis*, Dordrecht: Kluwer Academic Publishers, 1988.

GARDNER, B., "Recent Studies of Agricultural Trade Liberalization," in A. Maunder and A. Valdés (eds)., *Agriculture and Governments in an Interdepent World*, proceedings of the XX International Conference of Agricultural Economists, Aldershot, England: Dartmouth, 1989.

HAMMER, J., and O. KNUDSEN, "Agricultural Trade Liberalization: Developing Country Responses," Agriculture and Rural Development Department, The World Bank, Washington, D.C., October 1989.

KRISSOFF, B., J. SULLIVAN, and J. WAINIO, "Developing Countries in an Open Economy: The Case of Agriculture", Agriculture and Trade Analysis Division, Economic Research Service, USDA, Washington, D.C., September 1989.

LOO, T. and E. TOWER, "Agriculture Protectionism and the Less Developed Countries: The Relationship Between Agricultural Prices, Debt, Servicing Capacities, and the Need for Development Aid", Durham: Duke University, 1988.

PYATT, G. and A. ROE, *Social Accounting for Development Planning with Special Reference to Sri Lanka*, Cambridge: Cambridge University Press, 1977.

QUIZÓN, J. and H. BINSWANGER, "Modeling the Impact of Agricultural Growth and Government Policy on Income Distribution in India," *The World Bank Economic Review*, Vol. 1, No. 1, September 1986.

SULLIVAN, J., J. WAINIO, and V. RONINGEN, *A Data Base for Trade Liberalization Studies*, Economic Research Service, USDA, Washington, D.C., March 1989.

VALDÉS, A. and J. ZIETZ, *Agriculture Protection in OECD Countries: Its Cost to Less-developed Countries*, IFPRI, Research Report No. 21, Washington, D.C., December 1980.

VALDÉS, A., "Agricultural in the Uruguay Round: Interest of Developing Countries," *The World Bank Economic Review*, Vol. 1, No. 4, September 1987.

VOCKE, G., "U.S. Grain Imports by Developing Countries," ERS, USDA, Agricultural Information Bulletin No. 542, Washington, D.C., May 1988.

WORLD BANK, *World Development Report, 1986*, New York: Oxford University Press, 1986.

Part III

ANALYTICAL ISSUES

Chapter 13

TERMS OF TRADE EFFECTS, AGRICULTURAL TRADE LIBERALIZATION AND DEVELOPING COUNTRIES[1]

by

John Whalley and Randall Wigle

INTRODUCTION

Of late, there has been much speculation about what the implications may be for developing countries of agricultural liberalization resulting from the current GATT Uruguay Round. These countries have tended to divide into the two groups of agricultural exporters and agricultural importers, the latter often being referred as the "fourth force", in contrast to the three other forces of the EC, the United States and the Cairns group. The view from this group (which includes Jamaica, Mexico, Egypt and a small number of other countries), has been that as agricultural net importers, they would likely see an increase in the price of agricultural products as a result of agricultural liberalization. Products previously accumulated in stockpiles by developed countries and sold with export subsidy supports would no longer be available and global prices would increase. They have, therefore, tended to be cautious with respect to agricultural liberalization.

There are, however, a number of considerations which come into play in determining the potential impact on developing countries. One is whether, even for the importers, benefits potentially accruing from their own liberalization and removal of domestic interventions in agriculture could more than offset any losses on the terms of trade front[2].

Another concern is the question of crop coverage. The focus of discussions in agricultural liberalization has been on grains due to the involvement of the EC, the United States and the Cairns Group. Even more pointedly, discussions have focussed on wheat because of the membership of the Cairns Group (Australia, Argentina and Canada are all significant wheat exporters). But if liberalization is largely confined to grains, then countries which are significant exporters of (particularly) sugar and meats, may not see the hoped for gains which they had sought.

There are also questions of the variability of world prices, the effects that agricultural trade restrictions have, and whether liberalization may increase or reduce the price variation on residual markets.

All of these are, of course, quite legitimate sources of concern both for developing countries and researchers trying to disentangle the potential effects of liberalization on them. This paper, however, focuses on the narrower question of whether or not the sign of terms of trade effects can unambiguously be inferred from various liberalization proposals.

In particular, we emphasize a point which we have made in a previous paper (Whalley and Wigle, 1988): namely, that the representation of agricultural support programmes in models of agricultural liberalization can have a substantial bearing upon the model predictions as to the outcome of liberalization experiments. We focussed earlier on the role that endogenous participation decisions and set-aside arrangements in US wheat price supports can play in reversing the sign on the output effect of liberalization proposals involving US support programmes compared to an *ad valorem* production subsidy treatment of programme supports. In this paper, we go one stage farther and argue that changes in model treatment of this type can also affect the terms of trade prediction from such a programme change, since they affect the sign of the output response.

We use our earlier model to evaluate the implications for developing countries of alternative possible liberalizations involving wheat, emphasizing both unilateral and multilateral liberalization experiments involving the United States. Perhaps not surprisingly, we show that compared to more conventional *ad valorem* equivalent modelling of production subsidies, models with endogenous participation in set-aside programmes seem to produce results that are the opposite of conventional thinking as regards the effects on the terms of trade and, therefore, on the implications for developing countries. This is particularly important for those debates which focus on the division between agricultural importers and exporters stressed above.

We do not claim that this is a general result which applies to all agricultural liberalization and all products. We also stress the important changes which have taken place in the US programme since 1985, with the move to decouple partially agricultural supports. Nonetheless, we do very strongly emphasize how the subtleties of agricultural support programmes need to be brought into models and, therefore, the need for careful modelling of programme features in evaluating their effects on developing countries. In addition, these issues are not confined to the modelling of US wheat supports. Paid diversion features of Japanese rice supports, for instance, can produce similar effects.

Thus we argue that many existing numerical models which capture the effects of domestic agricultural support programmes treat them as subsidising production, in effect introducing a series of *ad valorem* distortions or price "wedges" between foreign and domestic prices[3]. However, this price wedge treatment of agricultural supports can, in some cases, seriously misrepresent their welfare and quantity effects. We make our point by focussing on pre-1985 US wheat programmes[4], but features of programme supports in other countries can be cited where there would be comparable pitfalls with the *ad valorem* approach[5]. This line of argument also raises questions over an approach in the multilateral trade negotiations of negotiating on Producer Subsidy Equivalents (PSEs), or some other subsidy-like aggregate measure of support.

Agricultural Liberalization and Developing Countries

Agriculture, as is well known, is an area which since 1947 has largely resisted the application of meaningful GATT discipline. This began with the original drafting which provided for special arrangements for export subsidies under Article 16 and special provisions which apply to agricultural quotas under Article 11. The US waiver of 1955, and the formation of the European Community (EC) in 1958, and its associated Common Agricultural Policy took this process farther. By the time the Kennedy and Tokyo Rounds were launched, although there was a feeling that there was a need for some firmer international discipline in the agricultural area, the attempts made at the time failed. This was largely because of the agreements reached by the United States and the EC towards the end of each of these negotiations which, in effect, kept substantive agricultural discussion off the table in the final stages of the negotiations.

In the current Uruguay Round of negotiations agriculture has taken on a high profile, in part, because of frustration over the inability of the GATT process to deal with the lack of international discipline in the agricultural area in earlier rounds. There are pressures for progress on agriculture this time also because the EC progressively became a net exporter of more agricultural products through the late 1970s, and because of the export subsidy wars between the

EC and the United States in third country markets in the early 1980s. By 1985, agriculture had clearly become the key issue in the Uruguay Round, so that at the time the Round was launched, a strong statement was included in the Declaration which made a commitment to move towards liberalization and firmer international discipline over agriculture trade distortions.

In part, this commitment at the start reflected the activities of middle-size countries which, through the pressures exerted by the Cairns group coalition of 14 agricultural producing countries, were able to insist on a high profile for agriculture in the negotiations[6]. This pressure on agriculture has subsequently been kept up and agriculture has retained the same high profile in the Round up to and beyond the recent Mid-Term Review in Montreal in December 1988. Nonetheless, an interim agreement on how to proceed on agriculture was only achieved in April of last year, with a commitment to freeze levels of agricultural support and to begin negotiations aimed at a sustained reduction in levels of support from 1991 onwards[7].

Each of the participants in these negotiations has a different view at this point. The United States, for instance, is focussing on tariffication proposals with a major thrust to convert the variable levy system in the EC into an *ad valorem* tariff, which the United States hopes it will eventually be able to negotiate downwards. The EC is focussing on broad measures of agricultural support, such as the PSE, Consumer Subsidy Equivalent (CSE) or trade distortion equivalent (TDE), in the hope that it will be possible to place a cap on the broad measure and proceed to negotiate support levels downwards. The Cairns group, in turn, is taking a multi-faceted approach of looking for specific programme disciplines as well as exploring possibilities within broad aggregate measures such as PSEs.

The current negotiations, therefore, are delicately poised and the impacts on developing countries are clearly crucial. The support or opposition of developing countries for the different liberalization proposals coming from each of these groups, has been actively sought. The United States, for instance, tied its offer on tropical products to further progress in agriculture, clearly seeking to obtain support from developing countries for the course it wished to follow in the agricultural negotiating group. Also, the position which has been taken by the so-called fourth force of agricultural net importers has been important in shaping the direction for the group, since it has tended to act as a brake on forward momentum. It has also been a position which Japan and other Asian importers, for which liberalization would create major domestic political problems, tend to support.

Developing countries, therefore, have a crucial role to play in these negotiations, and developed countries are clearly anxious to gain their support and convince them of the virtues of supporting systems of international liberalization in agriculture. This is why the terms of trade issues that are stressed above are so central to this process. If the terms of trade effects are advantageous to one group of developing countries and are clearly seen to be so, then their support may be forthcoming. If, however, the perception runs the other way, their support may be lacking. This, in turn, leads to the central issue of model analysis, how models portray these terms of trade effects and, in turn, the conjecture of this paper that the representation of programme supports in model form can have a significant effect on the perceived outcome of alternative liberalization experiences.

US Wheat Programmes and Programme Participation

The main theme of this paper is that modelling agricultural programmes in a general equilibrium framework is surprisingly complex, and overly simple modelling can be misleading. This can be especially the case for the analysis of terms of trade effects from liberalization, and the impacts on developing countries. We illustrate our point by discussing the modelling of supports paid to US wheat farmers. Supports for producers of wheat (as well as corn, grain sorghum, oats, barley, and rye) in the United States are largely provided through Commodity

Loans and deficiency payments. These jointly have the effect of raising prices received by farmers.

Under the Commodity Loan programme, the Commodity Credit Corporation (CCC)[8] makes non-recourse loans to farmers using commodities (wheat) as security, stored either on the farm or in commercial warehouses. These loans mature on demand, but on or before the loan's maturity date farmers have the option of regaining possession of their crop by paying off the loan plus any accrued interest, or forfeiting the farm- or warehouse-stored commodities to the CCC as full payment of the loan. This component of price supports effectively operates through the setting of the loan rate.

Deficiency payments are based on the difference between the target price and the higher of the national average market price and the loan rate. This difference is multiplied by the established yield of each farmer's land to determine his total deficiency payment. Prior to 1985 established yields were frequently recalculated using a five-year moving average of preceding years' yields on a farm-by-farm basis. Under this system, subject to a lag, higher yields imply higher deficiency payments. In effect, marginal output receives the support (target) price. One of the major changes in the 1985 Farm Bill is the attempt to "decouple" deficiency payments from output by fixing established yields.

Acreage set asides coexist with these two methods of price support as a condition for receiving support. To receive deficiency payments on their harvested acreage, or to gain access to non-recourse loans, farmers are required to reduce their planted acreage by a specified percentage of their base acreage[9].

The aim of these set-aside requirements is to reduce surplus production thought to be generated by the price supports[10]. However, the joint effect of deficiency payments, loans, and set asides on output and prices, and hence, on market prices is uncertain. Producers participating in the programme plant a reduced acreage but face a higher price, giving ambiguous effects on production. Increasing the target price will increase yields of programme participants, but may also increase participation, reducing planted acreage. To assess the net effect, it is necessary to analyse farm participation decisions.

To decide whether or not to participate in support programmes, individual farms compare their profits from participating in both the price support and set-aside programmes with their profits if they do not participate. Thus, if P^W is the target price of wheat designated under price supports, P^Z the price of non-land inputs used by all farms and λ the set aside rate; the participation decision for farm i involves the comparison of the profit functions π_i^N, π_i^P for farm i under participation (P) and non-participation (N).

If, for farm i,

$$\pi_i^N (P^W, P^Z) > \pi_i^P (P_T^W, P^Z, \lambda) \tag{1}$$

then farm i will chose not to participate in the set-aside programme, and will only participate if the inequality is reversed.

Typically farms differ in a range of characteristics, including the crop in which farms have a comparative advantage, land quality, and the ease with which land and other inputs can be substituted. Typically, for any given levels of target and market prices and set-aside rates, it will pay some farms to participate and others not[11].

If farms are ranked by their relative profits from participating and non-participating and are indexed by the subscript i, the distribution of participant and non-participant farms is described by the relative profit functions as represented by Figure 13.1. Changes in programme parameters, such as P_T^W and λ, will shift these relative profit functions, changing the number of participant farms. This emphasizes the importance of capturing endogeneity of programme participation in any modelling of the impacts of agricultural supports.

374

A Numerical General Equilibrium Model Capturing Price Supports, Set Asides, and Endogenous Participation Decisions

To analyse the effects of price supports and set asides for wheat in the United States on output and the terms of trade, we use a numerical general equilibrium model of global trade in wheat which we have used elsewhere (see Trela, Whalley and Wigle, 1987), and into which we embed a richer treatment of both farm behaviour and programme supports in the United States. We first describe how US wheat production, programme supports, and set asides are treated in this new version of the model, and then briefly summarise the rest of the model.

US wheat production, programme supports and set asides

The US wheat sector is assumed to be made up of a number of types of farms, producing a distribution both of average yields, and participating and non-participating farms in the model. As an analytical convenience, we assume that farms differ only in the elasticity of substitution between land and non-land inputs in production. We thus abstract from differences in land quality across farms, location (and thus transportation costs in shipping crops), and difference in comparative advantage across crop types between farms.

The production technology for each farm type, i, is assumed to be constant returns, and to take the constant elasticity of substitution (CES) form,

$$(2)$$

$$g_i = B \left[\delta L_i^{-\rho_i} + (1-\delta) z_i^{-\rho_i} \right]^{\frac{1}{\rho_i}}$$

where g_i is the output of farm type i, L_i and Z_i are land and non-land inputs δ is a share parameter, B a units term taken to be identical across all farms, and

$$\sigma_i = \frac{1}{1-\rho_i}$$

is the elasticity of substitution between inputs[12]. Wheat-producing land (L) and other inputs (Z) are assumed to be the sole inputs in the production of wheat by any farm.

Since acreage available to each farm, L_i, is fixed, producers face a two-level optimization problem. They must first compare their profit under participation in the commodity programme (including any set-aside provisions), to their profit outside the programme. Given their participation decision, they then optimize on non-land inputs and outputs.

The profit functions from participation and non-participation are given by (3) and (4):

$$\pi_i^P = P_T^W \bar{y}_i (1-\lambda) L_i - P^Z Z_i + T_i \tag{3}$$

$$\pi_i^N = P^W \hat{y}_i L_i - P^Z Z_i \tag{4}$$

where:

π_i^N farm i, assuming it does not non-participate in support programmes

π_i^P farm i, assuming it does participate in support programmes

P^W is the free (world) market price for wheat

P_T^W is the US target price for wheat

y_i, $\bar{y}_i$ are the optimal yields under non-participation and participation decisions, respectively

$\bar{L}_i$ is the total acreage available for farm i

P^Z is the price of other inputs

Z_i, $\bar{Z}_i$ are the total amounts of other inputs used under non-participant and participant decisions respectively

λ is the proportional set-aside requirement and

T_i is the lump sum "paid diversion" received by farm i (equal to the rental value of a pre-specified proportion of land set aside when complying with set-aside requirements).

In this formulation, farm profits equal the returns to land net of input costs. Participating farms are assumed to receive the target price for incremental output, although in some later experiments we vary the degree to which deficiency payments are coupled to current yields.

Using (2), input demands for non-participating farms are given by

$$\hat{z}_i = \left\{ \frac{1}{\delta} \left[B(1-\delta)\frac{\frac{W}{P}Z}{P} \right]^{\frac{\rho_i}{\rho_i^{-1}}} + \frac{(\delta-1)}{\delta} \right\}^{\frac{-1}{\rho_i}} \cdot L_i \tag{5}$$

and their optimal yield is

$$\hat{y}_i = \delta[(1-\delta)B]^{\frac{-1}{1-\rho_i}} \left[\frac{P^W}{P^Z} \right]^{\frac{\rho_i}{1-\rho_i}} L_i \tag{6}$$

For participants, their input demands are given by

$$\bar{z}_i = \left\{ \frac{1}{\delta} \left[B(1-\delta)\frac{P_T^W}{P^Z} \right]^{\frac{\rho_i}{\rho_i^{-1}}} + \frac{\delta-1}{\delta} \right\}^{\frac{-1}{\rho_i}} \cdot (1-\lambda) \cdot L_i \tag{7}$$

and their optimal yield is

$$\bar{y}_i = \delta[(1-\delta)B]^{\frac{1}{1-\rho_i}} \left[\frac{P^W}{P^Z} \right]^{\frac{\rho_i}{1-\rho_i}} (1-\lambda)L_i \tag{8}$$

Given the programme parameters P_T and λ, and knowing the market price of wheat P^W, and the input price P^Z, it is possible to solve for the optimal yields and input demands under participation and non-participation. This allows for a comparison of the two profit functions (3) and (4), and a determination of the participation decision. This, in turn, allows input demand and outputs to be calculated.

Whether farms choose to participate in any configuration of programme supports and set asides depends on the level of programme supports, the way marginal cost functions change as land is idled to comply with set asides, and the lump sum costs which set-aside requirements cause. We assume that the elasticity of substitution between inputs across farms is uniformly distributed over a pre-specified interval[13]. Farms with higher elasticities of substitution have higher average yields, and, given that land is a fixed factor for each farm, these farms have more shallowly sloped marginal cost functions. The parameter values we use in the model along with the data to which the model is calibrated, imply that low elasticity (high yield) farms participate in programme support, while high elasticity farms do not.

The Remainder of the Model

As indicated above, this treatment of the US wheat sector has been introduced into a multicountry general equilibrium structure of the global grain market, used by Trela *et al.* (1987) to analyse the effects of global policy interventions in grains. The earlier model uses the same *ad valorem* equivalent approach which we criticise here, and our modification of the treatment of the United States is aimed at highlighting the pitfalls of *ad valorem* modelling which were discussed above. Also, proceeding in this way allows comparisons between the approach used here, and a more conventional "price wedge" approach to be made for comparable data.

Thirteen countries or blocs[14] of countries are identified in both models, with wheat and other goods as the only produced commodities. Demands in each region are based on utility maximising behaviour with a single national consumer assumed who receives all the income originating in the country. This consumer faces domestic consumer prices in making consumption decisions, but the country as a whole satisfies trade balance at world prices, i.e.:

$$P^W \cdot C_k + X^c_k = P^W g_k + X^p_k \qquad k=1,\dots,13 \tag{9}$$

where P^W is the world price of wheat denominated in terms of other goods (whose price is unity). C_k is consumption of wheat in country k, g_k is production of wheat in country k, and X^c_k and X^p_k are country k's consumption and production of other goods.

Production in all regions (all regions other than the United States in the present model) is specified through a constant elasticity of transformation (CET) function between wheat and other goods

$$\tag{10}$$

$$F_k = \left[\delta_k g_k^{\,\rho_k} + (1-\delta_k) X_k^{\,\rho_k} \right]^{\frac{1}{\rho_k}} \qquad k=1,\dots,13$$

where δ_k is the share parameter in the CET function, and

$$\sigma_k = \frac{1}{1+\rho_k}$$

is the elasticity along the transformation surface. Distortions in the wheat sector in these countries are modelled in *ad valorem* equivalent form, typically as *ad valorem* subsidies which produce a difference between producer and consumer prices within the country.

In the present modified model, a CET function is used for the United States to describe the economy's production possibilities for other goods $\left[X^p_{US} \right]$ and non-land inputs into wheat production (Z^{US}).

$$\tag{11}$$

$$F_{US} = \left[\delta_{US} X^p_{US}{}^{\rho_{US}} + (1-\delta_{US}) Z_{US}^{\,\rho_{US}} \right]^{\frac{1}{\rho_{US}}}$$

where δ_{US} is the share parameter the CET function, and

$$\delta_{US} = \frac{-1}{1+\rho_{US}}$$

is the elasticity along the transformation surface, as in equation (2). The separate treatment of price supports and set asides as modelled above also enters the model.

Equilibrium Solution of the Model

The equilibrium structure of this extended model involves three prices: those for wheat, other goods, and non-land inputs into wheat production in the United States. There are three associated market excess demand functions. The first two prices affect behaviour in all regions captured in the model, including the United States, the third price only affects behaviour in the US component of the model.

In regions other than the United States, the relative price of wheat in terms of other goods, along with the *ad valorem* domestic subsidies or taxes allows production and consumption of these two goods to be calculated using the first order conditions for utility and profit maximising behaviour. Knowing producer prices in the country (given by world prices gross of any distortions at producer level), a tangency to the production frontier can be found. The country will then trade along a world price line, such that a tangency of an indifference curve and a domestic price line is found on the world price line through the production point. Solving for production and consumption behaviour in this way implies the net trades for each region in wheat and other goods.

In the case of the United States, information on the prices of non-land inputs into wheat and other goods allows outputs of these two goods in the United States to be determined from the first order conditions from profit maximisation subject to the CET production frontier. The prices of wheat and non-land inputs also allow for solution of programme participation decisions for all the farm types in the model, using equations (3) to (8). This allows both the use of non-land inputs, and the returns to land for all farm types, to be calculated. Knowing the value of production of other goods and non-land inputs, and the return to land for all farm types, allows aggregate income and hence US demands for other goods and wheat, to be determined.

Aggregating across the United States and all the other countries or regions in the model yields the market demands for wheat and other goods. Summing production across all countries yields total supply, and hence excess demand for wheat and other goods. The third excess demand is given by the difference between the demand for non-land inputs into wheat summed across all farm types, and output of Z_{US} from the tangency to the CET production frontier in the United States.

The model thus generates a system of three excess demands involving three prices. Equilibrium occurs in the model when a zero is found for all three excess demands. The model is solved using a modified Newton method, for which the experience has been that convergence is rapid.

DATA, MODEL, CALIBRATION, AND ELASTICITIES

We use the model for counterfactual equilibrium analysis, by calibrating the model to a 1981 microconsistent equilibrium data set, and then computing counterfactual equilibria for a variety of policy changes. The global component of the model has been calibrated to the 1981 data set using the inverse function methods outlined in Mansur and Whalley (1984). This involves solving for values of share and scale parameters in the CES and CET functions so as to produce data on quantities demanded and produced as solutions to optimizing behaviour at 1981 equilibrium prices.

Prior to implementing these procedures, values of substitution elasticities in the CES and CET functions need to be specified. We use estimates reported by Valdés and Zietz (1985) for supply and demand elasticity estimates for wheat by country, and values of the elasticities of substitution are chosen to reproduce these.

The main features of the microconsistent data used in this calibration procedure are displayed in Table 13.1. They show the large net export position of the United States in wheat in 1981, along with the significant wheat export position of the EC. Price data reveal the significant effects of domestic policy interventions by region, especially in Japan. US producer prices are those paid to non-participants, rather than target prices.

To use the inverse function calibration method to determine parameters for the wheat production functions for the US component of the model it would be necessary to know acreage, input use, yields, and the elasticity of substitution between inputs for farms of all types. There is no linked data of this form available.

We therefore iteratively search across combinations of the wheat production function parameters, δ, B, and the mean value of R_i until the following three conditions are met:

a) The US production of wheat from farm optimizing behaviour equals the value of production in the microconsistent data set.

b) Non-land inputs used in the production of wheat as a result of optimizing behaviour equal the value of inputs appearing in the microconsistent data set.

c) The endogenously determined participation rate equals the observed 1981 rate of 42 per cent.

We thus determined values of these parameters such that optimizing behaviour by farmers is consistent with the observed data.

We then assume that the substitution elasticities across farms, R_i are spread over an interval, with a step-size of 0.065. This distribution of R_i leads to a mean supply elasticity of wheat of 0.78, in line with consensus estimates used elsewhere[15]. This 0.065 step-size can then be varied in subsequent sensitivity analysis. These differences in substitution parameters across farms allow an endogenous participation rate to be determined which matches the 1981 observed value of 42 per cent.

Table 13.2 reports both some of the other data we use in implementing these procedures, along with the substitution elasticities by farm class and implied own price elasticities of wheat supply by farm type. The data on programme characteristics are presented largely to provide an indication of the differences between market prices, loan rates and target prices and in a footnote we indicate how these have changed in recent years. The set-aside rate, λ, used in the model is the 1981 value of 15 per cent.

An issue of some controversy in the agricultural economics literature[16] has been the degree of "slippage" in commodity programmes, and it is worth indicating how this was handled in the data and the model. Slippage indicates the extent to which a 1 per cent acreage reduction in the programme due, say, to participation in set asides, leads to a smaller than 1 per cent reduction in both planting and yields. Slippage reflects the response of farmers to a number of substitution margins in response to set-aside requirements. These include more intensive use of remaining land, setting aside the least productive of the land they have available for cultivation, and planting all land and then subsequently ploughing under the least productive once the realised yields on the various parcels of land are known. The "slippage" from farms altering their input use in response to land being idled as a result of set asides is captured in the model, but these other effects are not. To the extent that increased cultivation of non-idled land is the largest source of slippage, making no special modifications to the model to take account of these other factors seems to us a reasonable way to proceed.

Comparing Ad Valorem and Full Programme Modelling of US Wheat Market Intervention

In this section, we report results from the model for two different policy experiments. One is unilateral elimination of the US programme supports for wheat. The other is multilateral liberalization removing all interventions in domestic and international wheat markets. In this we include both the elimination of agricultural support in developed countries, and the elimination of the taxation of agriculture in some developed countries.

In each case, we compare results under two different model treatments. In the first, all policies in all countries are treated in *ad valorem* form as price wedges (PSEs), while in the second, US Commodity programmes are fully modelled as described above (with endogenous voluntary participation). For the United States, we use a PSE at the low end of the USDA's estimates for the period[17].

Unilateral elimination of commodity programme

We have used the minimum of the USDA PSE range in modelling the effects of US intervention in the wheat market, first treating these commodity programmes as equivalent to an *ad valorem* producer subsidy. When modelled in this way, these programmes have an unambiguously positive effect on production, even though our earlier discussion suggests the net effect of commodity programmes is ambiguous. This is because of the offsetting effects of set-aside requirements, and production incentives associated with programme benefits.

With the programmes explicitly modelled, as in earlier sections, the results could hardly be more different, as shown in Table 13.3. When modelled as *ad valorem* subsidies, eliminating programme supports causes US output to fall and the world price to rise. When the policies are explicitly modelled to capture changing participation decisions and acreage set asides, the opposite result occurs[18].

Under explicit programme modelling, output rises when programmes are abolished because the increase in production from the extra acreage planted more than offsets the fall in production due to the decrease in prices received by producers originally in the programme. In the *ad valorem* subsidy case, the output of the US wheat sector must fall when the subsidy is eliminated so long as the world price does not rise by more than the subsidy. The difference in the terms of trade effects, and hence the implications for developing countries, emerge clearly from this table[19].

Other implications also follow from these results. When support programmes are explicitly modelled, budget expenditures of over $250 million have a remarkably small impact on land rents[20]. This is because the idled resources implied by acreage set asides act as lump sum taxes on programme participants. Budget expenditures of $264 million are initially associated with annual land rents of $4 281 million. Elimination of programme supports reduces programme costs to zero, but only reduces annualised returns to land by $75 million, or less than 2 per cent.

Also, the effects of programme elimination are different across farms. Farms that were previously participating experience a loss of programme benefits, plus a decrease in world price. Farms which were not initially participating only experience the effects of the lower world price. Land values thus fall by 3.3 per cent for the class of farms most likely to participate, but by only 1.1 per cent for farms least likely to participate.

Furthermore, the elimination of set asides and paid diversion generates a sizeable welfare gain for the United States, and the world as a whole. The world welfare gain ($245 million) corresponds almost precisely to the value of the land originally idled under the set-aside programme ($253 million). Results in Table 13.3 thus suggest that while adverse terms of trade effects for the United States from abolition of their wheat support programmes do occur, they are not large enough to offset the welfare gains associated with eliminating the waste of domestic resources.

Multilateral liberalization

In Table 13.4 we analyse the effects of multilateral liberalization of wheat supports and interventions in all countries represented in the model. A question of special interest is the size and direction of price changes for agricultural products from multilateral liberalization.

In this case, results are not surprisingly very different, reflecting the fact that all regions, rather than just the United States, remove their intervention policies. The large effects for Japan, for instance, are due to the large PSE equivalent need for Japan and the small production in the base case.

As far as price and terms of trade effects are concerned, the world price of wheat rises, regardless of how US programmes are modelled. The contrast in results between the *ad valorem*

(PSE) and full commodity model treatments is thus not as dramatic as in the unilateral case. Nonetheless, the size of the price increase experienced when programmes are modelled as PSEs are three times the size as those when US programmes are modelled fully.

Furthermore, and of particular interest to low income countries, the welfare effects for both Africa and Latin America (which dominates the Other America group) switch signs, from being negative when US programmes are modelled as wedges, to being positive when they are modelled fully. This is not particularly surprising given the difference in world price effects, and the fact that both blocs are net importers of wheat. Gains come from removing domestic interventions, and losses come from the adverse terms of trade effect. Where terms of trade effects are smaller (as in the full model treatment), the net effect is that agricultural net importers gain from liberalization. Where terms of trade effects come out as larger (the *ad valorem* case), the net effect is reversed.

SUMMARY AND CONCLUSIONS

This paper stresses how the modelling of domestic agricultural support programmes can make a major difference in how agricultural trade models show effects on developing countries of agricultural trade liberalization as it may emerge from the GATT Uruguay Round. We illustrate how, in the case of US commodity programmes for wheat, payments to producers who participate in programmes are linked to non-marginal reductions in total acreage planted. High support prices which might appear to subsidise production can thus also increase participation in support programmes cutting acreage planted, and potentially reducing output. *Ad valorem* modelling will miss these effects.

A numerical general equilibrium model built and calibrated to 1981 data suggests that when fully modelled US commodity programmes can have a positive effect on producer incomes, and a negative effect on total production, which is opposite to the effects which would be portrayed by *ad valorem* equivalent models. The model also highlights the differences in the terms of trade and welfare effects for agricultural net importing developing countries in alternative model-based analyses of agricultural trade liberalization.

We also argue that the features we model in US wheat programmes are not unique. They occur in commodity programmes in other countries, such as the Japanese rice support programme. Thus the use of *ad valorem* equivalent measures of the effects of agricultural programmes obviously needs to be treated with caution, especially where such model-based analyses are used to infer the effects of agricultural trade liberalization on developing countries. This same point also carries over into the current international trade negotiations in the Uruguay Round where much of the technical work is focussed on the construction of *ad valorem*-like measures (Producer Subsidy Equivalents, or PSEs) as negotiable instruments.

Figure 13. 1.

DISTRIBUTION OF FARMS BETWEEN PARTICIPANTS AND NON-PARTICIPANTS
IN PROGRAMME SUPPORTS AND ACREAGE SET-ASIDE PROGRAMME

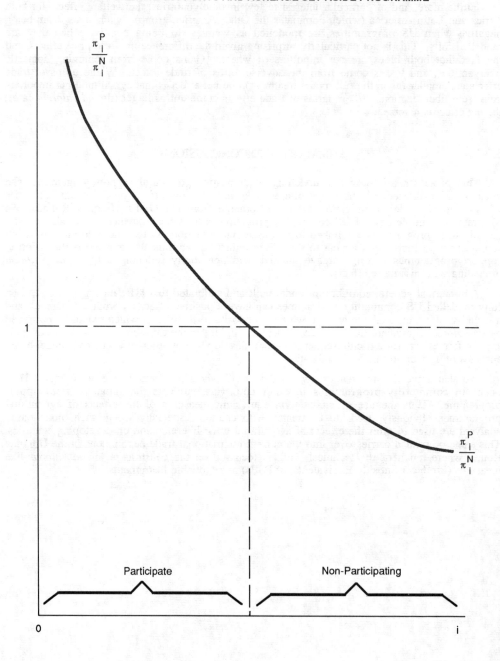

Table 13.1

DATA ON PRODUCTION, CONSUMPTION, AND TRADE IN WHEAT, AND DOMESTIC PRICES USED IN CALIBRATING THE MODEL
(1981 data in $)

Region	Production	Consumption	Net Exports
Consumption, production and trade data[1] ($ billions)			
US	10.9	4.0	6.9
Canada	3.4	0.6	2.8
Argentina	1.3	0.7	0.6
Brazil	0.4	0.4	0.0
Other America	0.7	3.6	-2.9
China	9.7	11.7	-2.0
Japan	0.1	1.0	-0.9
Other Asia	12.6	13.4	-0.8
EC	10.7	8.3	2.4
Other Europe & Oceania	4.4	8.6	-4.2
Australia	2.4	0.6	1.8
USSR	14.7	16.9	-2.2
Africa	1.5	2.9	-1.4
World	72.7	72.7	

Region	Producer prices[2]	Consumer prices[2]
Domestic price data (US $ per metric tonne)		
US	164.0[3]	164.0[3]
Canada	182.2	168.8
Argentina	93.9[4]	150.8
Brazil	319.0	92.8
Other America	220.4	202.5
China	164.0[5]	164.0[5]
Japan	979.0	393.4
Other Asia	235.5	151.1
EC	168.5[6]	168.5[6]
Other Europe & Oceania	164.0[7]	164.0[7]
Australia	152.0	154.0
USSR	123.0	123.0[8]
Africa	227.8[9]	227.8[9]

1. Production data is from *FAO Production Yearbook 1985*, (1979-81 averages); Trade data is from *FAO World Trade Yearbook 1981*.
2. Unless otherwise noted, the source for this price data is Lattimore (1982).
3. Producers price for non-programme participants
4. From Cirio (1986).
5. No data (set to "world" price).
6. EC intervention price. Sources Agricultural Situation in the Community (1981) and Yearbook of Agricultural Statistics (1981), both published by Eurostat.
7. Data used for New Zealand
8. Producers' price data used.
9. Average of data for Kenya, Egypt, Morocco, South Africa, and Nigeria.

383

Table 13.2

DATA ON THE US WHEAT SECTOR USED
IN CALIBRATING THE MODEL

Production Data

Wheat Program Acreage	90.6 million acres[1]
Value of non-land inputs into wheat production	$6.84 billion[2]
1981 participation rate	42%

Farm types	Elasticity of substitution R[i]	Own price elasticities of wheat supply by farm type
0	0.31	0.45
1	0.38	0.60
2	0.44	0.78
3	0.50	1.02
4	0.57	1.32

1981 Programme Support Characteristics[3] (prices are US $ per bushel)[4]

Target price	3.81
Market price	3.66
Loan rate	3.20
Paid diversion	5%
Set-aside requirement	15%

1. Glaser (1986), p. 85.
2. Estimate based on USDA information for Illinois.
3. Coyle et al., p.16.
4. Comparable data for 1986 are $4.38 for the target price, $3.30 for the market price, and $2.40 for the loan rate, showing the large increase in program supports occurring through the 1980s.

Table 13.3

**EFFECTS ON PRODUCTION AND WELFARE FROM ELIMINATION OF US
PRICE SUPPORTS AND SET-ASIDES FOR WHEAT**
(Per cent)

	When US wheat supports are modelled as:	
	(1)	(2)
	Producer subsidy equivalent	Full commodity programme with price supports and set asides
Wheat production in US	-10.3	1.3
World price	+9.1	-1.11
Rental value of land used for wheat production	n.a.	-1.6
Change in US welfare[1] as a per cent of the value of wheat production	6.5	1.4
Change in production in other countries:		
Canada	2.4	-0.3
Argentina	1.8	-0.2
Brazil	1.8	-0.2
Other America	1.8	-0.2
China	0.0	0.0
Japan	0.0	0.0
Other Asia	2.0	-0.2
EC	0.0	0.0
Other Europe & Oceania	1.8	-0.2
Australia	3.9	-0.5
USSR	0.0	0.0
Africa	0.0	0.0
World	-0.8	0.1

1. Welfare is measured as the Hicksian EV in millions of $US (1980) and calculated as a proportion of the original value of production at world prices.

Table 13.4

EFFECTS OF MULTILATERAL LIBERALIZATION
OF WHEAT SUPPORTS AND MARKET INTERVENTIONS
(Per cent)

| | When US wheat supports are modelled as: | |
	(1) Producer subsidy equivalent	(2) Full commodity programme with price supports
Changes in US wheat production	-13.2	+2.9
Change world price	+4.5	+1.5
Welfare[1] effects as a per cent of the value of wheat production		
US	+4.2	+3.2
Canada	+3.5	+1.4
Argentina	+8.6	+6.7
Brazil	+16.9	+21.2
Other America	-4.2	1.4
China	-.9	-.3
Japan	+434.8	+495.9
Other Asia	+1.8	+2.7
EC	+.7	+.3
Other Europe & Oceania	-.7	-.3
Australia	+3.8	+1.5
USSR	+1.3	+1.5
Africa	-1.0	+5.7

1. Welfare is measured as the Hicksian EV in millions of $US (1980) and calculated as a proportion of the original value of production at world prices.

NOTES AND REFERENCES

1. The second author acknowledges support from the Social Science and Humanities Research Council (SSHRC), Ottawa. Earlier versions of the material on which this paper is based have been presented to a conference on "Agricultural Policy Modelling", University of Western Ontario, May 1987, and to seminars at Guelph, Purdue and Western Ontario. We are grateful to conference and seminar participants for their comments, and to Tom Hertel, Marinos Tsigas, Bob Thompson, Karl Meilke, and Tom Rutherford for stimulating discussions.

2. See the discussion and differences in model predictions on this issue between Tower and Loo (1988) and Parikh *et al*. (1987), for instance.

3. See, for example, Chisholm and Tyers (1985), Valdés and Zietz (1980), and Frohberg *et al*. (1987).

4. We concentrate on pre-1985 programmes because of changes in support programmes in the 1985 Farm Bill. These weakened but, as we discuss below, by no means removed the features we stress here.

5. These include the "acreage quotas" used by the Canadian Wheat Board to limit grain deliveries to wheat pools. One can argue in this case that the major constraint on grain production is the transportation system, and these quotas merely ration access to shipment facilities. Another complex situation is the differential exchange rate facing farm exporters in Argentina (see the description in Cirio, 1987). Price supports to dairy farmers in the EC have, since 1984, been accompanied by quotas. Again *ad valorem* equivalent modelling of the price support component alone can be misleading. Also, as mentioned above, rice producers in Japan must comply with acreage diversion requirements in order to qualify for high support prices paid by the government (see Yasuo, 1987, and Naraomi and Takamitsu, 1987).

6. See the discussion of the Cairns Group in Hamilton and Whalley (1989).

7. See Whalley (1989) and GATT Focus (1989) for more details on the outcome of this Mid-Term Review, including the decisions on agriculture in April 1989.

8. This is a government owned and operated corporation established in 1933 to stablize and support farm incomes and prices.

9. Farmers also receive diversion payments to cover part of the foregone earnings on idled land. These apply to required diversions and to voluntary (extra) acreage diverted to approved conservation uses. The sum of deficiency and diversion payments is capped at $50 000 per farm under the wheat and feed grain programmes combined, although this is rarely a binding constraint for wheat producers since until recently there were no restrictions on subdividing acreage covered by the programmes.

10. In periods when price supports (and loan rates) have been high, such as in the 1970s, a sharp growth in stockpiles of wheat and feed grains has occurred. Further policies beyond acreage reductions have been used for stockpile management. One such programme was the Payment-in-Kind (PIK) programme introduced in 1983. Under this programme, farmers who agreed to reduce their acreage by between 10 and 30 per cent more than the amount required to be eligible for loans, purchases, and payments were compensated by the government, in kind, i.e., by payment of commodities out of its own commodity reserves.

11. Also, the more that yields vary across land on any individual farm, the more attractive is the programme, since the lowest yield land can be diverted from production.

12. The assumption that only ρ_i (or equivalently σ_i) varies by farm class also generates a distribution of yields across farms.

13. To simplify the calculations we make with the model, we calculate solutions to farm optimization problems for five elasticity values, and interpolate over a range of elasticities of substitution between land and other inputs.

14. United States, China, Australia, Canada, Japan, USSR, Argentina, Other Asia, Africa, Brazil, EC, Other America, Other Europe and Oceania.

15. Valdés and Zietz' estimate is 0.80.

16. See Garst and Miller (1985) for example.

17. The range of USDA estimates is from +0.25 to +0.49 (see USDA 1987, page 29). Using price data for the period would suggest a smaller number (in the order of +0.10).

18. Increasing our estimated PSE to the middle of the range suggested by the USDA's calculations would only serve to increase the disparity in results between the two approaches.

29. While we do not report them here, sensitivity analysis of these results suggest that they are robust to reasonable variation of the parameters.

20. See also the comparison paper by Rutherford, Wigle and Whalley (1989) which discusses the capitalization effects of agricultural price supports on alternative models.

BIBLIOGRAPHY

CHISHOLM, A.H. and R. TYERS, Food Security: Theory, Policy and Perspectives from the Pacific Rim, Amsterdam: North-Holland, 1982.

CIRIO, F., "Agricultural Trade in Argentina: Impacts on the Global Economy and Strategy for the Next GATT Negotiations", mimeo, 28th June 1986 (on file).

COYLE, B., Robert G. CHAMBERS and Philip L. PAARLBERG, "Measuring the Gains from Trade for US Farm Exports," USDA Economic Research Service (FAER-XXX), Washington, D.C., 1985.

DAM, K.W., The GATT, Chicago: University of Chicago Press, 1970.

de GOERTER, H. and Karl MEILKE, "The EECs Wheat Price Policies and International Trade in Differentiated Products," American Journal of Agricultural Economics, January 1987.

FOOD AND AGRICULTURE ORGANIZATION OF THE UNITED NATIONS, FAO Commodity Review and Outlook 1980-81, Rome 1981.

FOOD AND AGRICULTURE ORGANIZATION OF THE UNITED NATIONS, Production Yearbook 1981, Rome 1982.

FOOD AND AGRICULTURE ORGANIZATION OF THE UNITED NATIONS, World Trade Yearbook 1981, Rome 1982.

GATT, GATT Focus and News of the Uruguay Round; various monthly issues in 1989.

GARST, G.D. and T.A. MILLER, "Impact of the Set-Aside Program on US Wheat Acreages", Agricultural Economics Research, Vol. 27, No. 2, 1983.

GERRARD, C. and G. POSEHN, "Government Intervention in Food Grain Markets in Kenya," Saskatchewan: University of Saskatchewan, mimeo, 1985.

GLASER, L.K., Provisions of the Food Security Act of 1985, Washington, D.C.: USDA, Economic Research Service, 1986.

HAMILTON, C. and J. WHALLEY, "Coalitions in the Uruguay Round: The Extent, Pros and Cons of Developing Country Participation," Weltwirtschaft Archiv, September 1989.

HUFBAUER, G.D. and J.S. ERB, Subsidies in International Trade, Washington, D.C.: Institute for International Economics, 1984.

LATTIMORE, R.G., "World Grain Market Instability and Food Security: An Exporters Perspective," chapter in A.H. Chisholm and R. Tyers, Food Security: Theory, Policy and Perspectives from the Pacific Rim, 1982.

NARAOMI, I. and S. TAKAMITSU, "Rice and the Politics of Protectionism," Japan Echo, Vol. XIV, No. 3, 1987.

PARIKH, K.S., G. FISCHER, K. FROHBERG, and O. GULBRANDSEN, Towards Free Trade in Agriculture, a report on the findings of the Food and Agriculture Program of the International Institute for Applied Systems Analysis, Laxenburg, Austria, April 1987.

RUTHERFORD, T.F., J. WHALLEY and R. WIGLE, "Dilution of Capitalization Effects from Agricultural Price Supports: The US Wheat Case," mimeo, 1989.

SHOVEN, J.B. and J. WHALLEY, Applying General Equilibrium, 1988, to be published by Cambridge University Press.

TOWER, E. and T. LOO, "Agricultural Protectionism and the Less Developed Countries: The Relationship Between Agricultural Prices, Servicing Capacities and the Need for Development Aid," in A. Stoeckel (ed.), The Macroeconomic Consequences of Farm Policy, Durham, North Carolina: Duke University Press, 1989.

TRELA, I., J. WHALLEY and R. WIGLE, "International Trade in Grain: Domestic Policies and Trade Conflicts" Scandinavian Journal of Economics, Vol. 89, No. 3, 1987.

USDA (Economic Research Service), Policy Research Notes, Issue 22, Washington, D.C.: Government Printing Office, November 1986.

USDA (Economic Research Service), Government Intervention in Agriculture: Measurement, Evaluation, and Implications for Trade Negotiations, Washington, D.C.: Government Printing Office, April 1987.

VEEMAN, T. and M. VEEMAN, The Future of Grain: Canada's Prospectives for Grains, Oilseeds, and Related Industries, Toronto: The Canadian Institute for Economic Policy, 1984.

WHALLEY, J. (ed.), The Uruguay Round and Beyond: The Final Report of a Ford Foundation Supported Project on Developing Countries and the Global Trading System, Macmillan, 1989.

YASUO, T., "Rice Policy: The Outlook for Change", Japan Echo, Vol. XIV, No. 3, 1987.

390

Chapter 14

AGRICULTURAL TRADE LIBERALIZATION: DEVELOPING COUNTRY RESPONSES

by

Jeffrey S. Hammer and Odin Knudsen

Many studies have attempted to quantify the gains from either industrial market economies or all world economies liberalizing trade of agricultural commodities. Because the major actors in this liberalization would be the developed countries, much of this modelling effort has been focussed on the intricacies and effects of agricultural trade liberalization of the industrial market economies. Developing countries are usually considered in these models either as passive actors — accepting unflinchingly the effects of the new industrial country trading system — or as enthusiastic adherents of free trade, joining in by liberalizing their own trade regimes. But as is well known, developing countries in reality would not react at all this way[1].

Agricultural policies in developing countries and their accompanying trade regimes are complex, perhaps equally or even more so than those implemented in industrial countries. Although the developing countries may overall disprotect their agriculture through a combination of direct trade subsidies and indirect taxation through macroeconomic policy, within this disprotection there exist great variations in protection and policies.

Some of these agricultural policies serve non-agricultural goals such as collecting tax revenues or redistributing income in favour of urban areas. In other cases, they serve non-economic objectives, for instance, the securing of political support from certain producer or agro-industrial groups. In many developing countries, agricultural trade policy is really food policy aimed at maintaining adequate levels of urban food consumption or of domestic production of staples (as characterised by the rhetoric over food self-sufficiency).

The policy makers who have constructed these policies realise that these policies have costs and that there are tradeoffs among their objectives. They know that collecting tax revenues through export taxes impairs foreign exchange earnings; that maintaining urban consumption requires either subsidies from the budget, foreign exchange to import food or lower producer prices or combinations of these modes. Likewise, achieving food self-sufficiency requires subsidies and trade intervention that impinge either upon the government's or the consumers' budget or both. Furthermore, policy makers have not passively maintained these policies but have adapted them to changing world markets and prices. They have changed taxes and tariffs as world prices changed or, as in the food crisis of 1973-74, built elaborate state enterprises to protect their markets or to distribute food at lower than world prices. Therefore, it would be naive to anticipate that developing countries would behave passively or completely liberalize in the way the modellers assume for their simulations. Certainly the builders of the simulation models of trade liberalization are not so naive as to believe that their models depict the reality of developing country behaviour. In fairness, their results may be argued to bracket the possible outcomes — with the passive result representing the lowest gains and the full free trade results providing the largest gains.

The objective of this paper is to examine possible developing country response to agricultural liberalization of industrial market economies through simulating the policy options or choices open to three types of developing countries when faced with a more liberalized market (as characterised by a set of higher and different relative world prices). The "types" of countries which these examples cover are:

a) Primarily exporters of the agricultural commodities;

b) Primarily importers; and

c) Mixed — those which both import and export.

The comparisons of policy options before and after the anticipated changes in international prices are analysed by a set of simple simulation models for three countries: Argentina (an agricultural exporter), Tunisia (a food importer) and Senegal (an agricultural exporter and food importer). The simulation models are of the multimarket type as described in Braverman and Hammer[2]. These are partial equilibrium in nature but explicitly model some of the substitution possibilities available in consumption and production for the relevant crops. They were originally designed to answer policy questions concerning the effects of proposed reforms within the countries on such outcomes as the government deficits (or revenues), the foreign exchange earnings from agriculture and the real incomes of various groups in society to assess the distributional consequences. Since these models were developed over the last few years to answer specific policy questions, they may be somewhat out of date. Therefore, the results should be considered suggestive of certain types of economies rather than precise analyses of these particular countries. Before we present the results of these simulations, it would be useful to depict through diagrams the possible policy choices and how they are influenced by the higher and different relative world prices caused by industrial country liberalization of agriculture.

A FRAMEWORK FOR EVALUATING TRADE OFFS

We begin with an analytic description of a "typical" exporting country that is taxing its exports, then proceed to depicting an importing country that is subsidising urban consumption, and finally end with an exporting/importing country that attempts to do both. In all cases, we make the "small" country assumption, that is, the country is a price-taker.

In Figure 14.1, we render the options presented to an exporting country. The tradeoff in its export tax policy is shown by the possibility curve AA', representing the tradeoff between government revenues from export taxation and foreign exchange for a given set of world prices for the export products. The frontiers of the curve represent an optimum tax giving the constraints or objectives of the government, for example, with respect to income distribution. Within the frontiers represents tax rates that are non-optimum, that is, where revenues could be increased by changing tax rates without a loss of foreign exchange. The curve begins at the origin representing the case of a prohibitive export tax. As the tax is lowered, export earnings and government revenues rise. As the tax is further reduced in favour of increasing exports, government revenues reach a maximum and begin declining. Finally, when the tax is eliminated, foreign exchange earnings reach a maximum at A'. Assuming some form of well-behaved, convex government preference function pp' between tax revenues and foreign exchange, the government is assumed to have chosen to tax to achieve the point a, or where the indifference curve is tangent to the policy possibility frontier. At this point, government revenues are given by the distance OD and foreign exchange earnings by OD'. If the government abandoned the taxation of exports, it would earn foreign exchange OA' or the free-trade amount.

When world prices rise for its agricultural exports, as would most likely be the case under liberalization, the tradeoff curve expands outward to BB'. If the export commodity were not a single commodity but a composite then it is possible that the lines could cross, depending on the relative price changes; likewise the slope, whether it flattens or becomes more steep depends on the elasticity of the supply response of the export commodities and how the tax is applied between the export commodities. If it maintained the same export tax rates as before the price changes, the government would move to point b and foreign exchange earnings would be OE'. If the government lowers the tax rates so as to maintain the same amount of government revenues, then it would move to c and earn foreign exchange equal to OG'. Of course, if it abandoned taxation of exports, its "free trade" earnings would be OB'. However, in practice it is likely to move to some other intermediate point, say d in Figure 14.1 where a new policy preference curve would be tangent to the possibility curve. In this case, export earnings would be OF' and tax revenues OF.

In this depiction, the foreign exchange gains from a passive response to trade liberalization (where developing countries do not react) would be low, $D'E'$, in our figure, and relatively massive, $D'B'$, if they liberalize their trade by eliminating taxation of this export (however, this would be an overstatement as the gains $D'A'$ are realisable without global liberalization and should be deducted from this amount). The actual gains from the expected policy response (lowering export taxes and passing on some of the windfall to producers) would be much less, $D'F'$, than the free trade solution and higher than the passive solution. If the government has a greater desire at the margin for government revenues than depicted by the policy preference curve, the actual gains could even be smaller.

If the possibility curve BB' steepens as a result of liberalization such that government revenues become "cheaper" in terms of foreign exchange than before the liberalization, then the tangent point would move closer to the y-axis and be inside of point b for a homothetic preference curve. Foreign exchange gains would be smaller than the passive solution and possibly even negative. The technical tradeoff between government revenues and foreign exchange along with the government's choice function are therefore critical to the outcome of trade liberalization. In fact, a conceivable solution is that export earnings might even decline for the agricultural exporter as the government's propensity for government revenues increases. What is critical in this depiction is the changing slope of the possibility curve. If the slope steepens such that the price of government revenues in terms of foreign exchange goes down after the price rise, it is conceivable that export earnings would actually decline even though in a first-best welfare sense the country would be "better-off." Nevertheless, the typically held expectation that export earnings would expand for an agricultural export is not entirely evident *a priori*.

For an importing country, the possible outcomes are more complex. In Figure 14.2, the tradeoffs for a typical importing country are shown. For simplicity, we have depicted a case where all food is imported but it could easily be expanded to a case where only some of the food needs of a country are imported (basically this would involve a shift of the x-axis downward). The tradeoff — given by the curve AA' — is assumed to be between saving foreign exchange and increasing urban consumption financed through government subsidies. The amount of foreign exchange available is assumed to be OA'. If the government decides to increase (decrease) urban consumption, it increases (decreases) the consumer subsidy (for example, by lowering the consumer price) as shown in Quadrant I of Figure 14.2. But this increase (decrease) expands (contracts) imports and reduces (expands) foreign exchange availability as shown in Quadrant II. For example, if the indifference choice between urban consumption and foreign exchange is pp', then the preferred urban consumption and foreign exchange is given by point a. To maintain this level of urban consumption requires a subsidy given by OS. The foreign exchange cost is given by the distance F to A' on the x-axis.

If, as a result of liberalization by developed countries, prices of the imported foods rise, the possibility curve rotates inward and is now shown by the line BA' (for the time being, we assume that the availability of foreign exchange has not changed). Since for any level of subsidy, only a lower level of consumption can now be maintained, the consumption-subsidy curve shifts downward. If we assume that the government maintains urban consumption as before (for instance by holding the consumer price constant) both subsidies and foreign exchange costs dramatically increase to OS' and $F'A'$, respectively. However, if the government decides to maintain the aggregate level of the subsidy as before, urban consumption declines from u to u' and the change in foreign exchange earnings becomes ambiguous — dependent on the price elasticity of consumption (in the diagram we have shown the foreign exchange cost declining to $F'''A'$). If the consumption elasticity is inelastic with respect to price (which is most likely the case), maintaining a constant subsidy means an unambiguous foreign exchange loss as the world price has gone up and the quantity of imports does not change much in response to the adjustment in the consumer price needed to maintain constant subsidies. But indeed if consumption is elastic with respect to price, consumption will fall so dramatically that foreign exchange costs will actually decline. For a preference curve as shown, the government would choose between losses in foreign exchange and urban consumption as given by the point b. Foreign exchange costs and consumer subsidies would go up while the consumer absorbs some of the adjustment through lower consumption of food. In practice, this is the scenario feared by many food importing developing countries and the likely response to it. But a severely constrained government with few government revenues and low foreign exchange reserves could pass on the full brunt of the adjustment to consumers — that is, maintain the aggregate level of subsidies.

For the case of an exporter-importer of agricultural commodities, the story becomes considerably more complex as shown in Figure 14.3. If we assume as before that the export commodity is not consumed domestically and the imported food is not produced domestically, we can add to Figure 14.2, two additional quadrants to show the effect of the changes in world prices on net foreign exchange and net government revenues. In Quadrant IV of Figure 14.3, we add the export-revenue tradeoff RF as in Figure 14.1. As depicted, the maximum foreign exchange OF' available for food imports occurs when exports are not taxed (we are implicitly assuming that these agricultural export earnings are dedicated to food imports). In Quadrant III, we show the transformation between consumption subsidies and government export revenues. The 45 degree line is when the government's agricultural budget is balanced with consumer food subsidies equal to export taxation revenues. To the left of the line the government budget is in deficit; to the right in surplus. The foreign exchange versus urban consumption options are given by line $C'F$ in Quadrant I. If the government choice results in point a in Quadrant II and a balanced budget is required, then the foreign exchange costs depends on the response of export earnings to the raising through export taxes of the amount of revenue needed to meet the consumer subsidies. Foreign exchange costs to import food are given by fF' and foreign exchange earnings by Of. The difference is the surplus or deficit on the agricultural trade accounts.

With liberalization, the results become quite complex and ambiguous. The urban consumption-foreign exchange line shifts outward and rotates downward as shown by line CF'. The consumption-subsidy curve shifts downward and the export-revenue foreign exchange curve shifts outward. The net outcome on foreign exchange and on urban consumption depends now on the relative magnitudes of the price shifts, the initial trade balance, and whether the government will tolerate a budget deficit. The foreign exchange results become equally ambiguous. As shown in Figure 14.3, the government chooses to let urban consumers take a hit even though it increases subsidies from OS to OS'. The downward adjustment in consumption results in a rise of foreign exchange costs of imports to $f'F$. But to pay for the higher consumer subsidies requires that exports be taxed resulting in a decline in export earnings from Oe to Oe'. However, as shown in Figure 14.4, if the government abandons the balanced budget it can improve its export earnings as its revenue needs have decreased, at least in the short term.

The complication of these depictions even after simplifying assumptions demonstrates that an interactive model is needed so that the actual choices could be specified. This model should explicitly represent the tradeoffs between the policy choices and their interactions because it is clear that the outcomes are far from self-evident. We now turn to the modelling results for the three cases studie to indicate how the possible policy choices for these types of countries might evolve.

CASE STUDIES OF LIBERALIZATION

The Exporting Country Example — Argentina

The structure of the Argentina model is quite simple. The country is divided into two regions, Pampas and Non-Pampas. The Pampas produces wheat, feed grains, oilseeds, beef and poultry. The supply of each of these commodities respond to the farmgate prices of every good through elasticities. The Non-Pampas region's only agricultural production involves fruits and vegetables. Demands for each of the commodities are determined by the consumer prices of all six goods as well as income (in the relevant region) which is endogenous in the model (see the appendix for the algebraic formulation). The domestic prices (both farmgate and consumer since transport and processing costs are constant) are determined by exogenous world prices (given in Table 14.1) less the export tax levied on the goods which form the policy variables of the model. Income distribution for the rural sector is not examined as most farms in the Pampas are relatively large.

The principal use of this model is to explore the consequences of different export tax regimes; in particular, the question of how much government revenue is lost (gained) for each unit of foreign exchange earned (lost) as each of the export taxes are changed in turn. Given the pattern of protection and the sets of elasticity estimates available, this number allows for the assessment of one tax versus another, or, identifies desirable directions of reform. In the context of the current question, we want to see, first of all, what are the direct consequences of the anticipated changes in world prices following the GATT reforms and, secondly, to see if the relative tradeoffs between the different tax instruments are much affected by the change in the external environment. Since the taxes are imposed on trade itself, there is a direct influence on the domestic prices from the changes in international market conditions.

Table 14.2 presents the results of the Argentinean case. In the first part of the table we see that the direct effect of the world price changes is to increase the government revenues collected from agricultural exports by 36 per cent and to increase the value of foreign exchange earnings from agriculture by 57 per cent. In one sense, the government has considerable leeway in how this windfall is spent and important policy choices may be involved in the degree of relative sharing of the aggregate gain from the entire set of price increases. If the past is a guide, the government may be expected to take the opportunity of higher world prices to increase the tax rates on agricultural exports. Previous empirical work on Argentina indicates that the government has used tax policy as an instrument of price stabilization, responding to price increases with concomitant tax increases and giving tax relief during times of lower prices. If the price changes due to international trade reform are considered permanent, however, it is not clear what the reaction of policy makers would be.

The second part of Table 14.2 is relevant to the assessment of the relative value of the individual tax instruments. In this part, the cost in terms of government revenue of generating foreign exchange with each of the tax instruments is presented. Note that this is not a welfare measure *per se* as no account is taken of the income effects on the private economy, but it provides guidance on the narrower aims of the government. In this comparison we see that taxes on crops tend to yield more revenue per unit of foreign exchange lost than do those on animal products. That is, taking into account the interactions in production and consumption, revenues from wheat, oilseeds and to a lesser extent feed grains are very sensitive to attempts to increase foreign exchange through reduced export taxation. For example, to increase (decrease) one unit of foreign exchange by decreasing (increasing) the wheat tax results in 5.71 unit loss (gain) in tax revenues in general. For beef, the result is much less, only 0.32 because of the pattern of substitution.

This result is changed little by the new configuration of prices after international trade reforms. Since domestic incomes are functions of domestic prices alone, broader measures of welfare also give this general conclusion: that the policy tradeoffs faced by the government are essentially unchanged by the new set of prices. Therefore, while the extra earning capability of the country can lead to policy questions concerning the overall sharing of the windfall between the public and private sector (or, between agricultural producers and the non-agricultural sector as a whole, including government) there does not appear to be much to change the assessment of the intercommodity pattern of export taxes.

For each policy, however, the marginal cost in terms of government revenue foregone from the higher foreign exchange earnings via export tax reductions is increased after the price changes. This is a direct consequence of the larger share that exports represent in domestic supply[3].

Returning to our initial diagrammatic discussion, the results for Argentina indicate at the margin a steepening of the policy frontier curve. If policy preferences are homothetic (that is, the slope of the indifference curves are equal on any radical from the origin), then it could be expected that government revenues will be somewhat higher and export earnings somewhat lower than the passive result.

The Case of an Agricultural Importer — Tunisia

While Tunisia is an exporter of certain agricultural goods (olive oil, dates, oranges and tomatoes), there is little or no interaction between these sectors and the cereal and livestock sectors which are relevant here. As such, we place Tunisia in the category of a food importer. The institutional details in the Tunisia model[4] make for some complexity in the algebraic formulation (described in the appendix) but the general structure is that the country imports wheat (hard and soft), feed grains, meat and milk products. The government sets the producer and consumer prices for all items except meat which is subject to an import quota. Therefore, there is no automatic transmission of world price changes to the domestic economy and the direct impact of the world price changes is felt entirely in the government accounts and the foreign exchange position. While there are some subsidies to agricultural producers, the overwhelming majority of funds spent are in the form of consumer subsidies on most items, the cost of which are dependent on the world price levels.

Table 14.3 presents both the direct impact of the projected world price changes as well as the effect of policy changes on the government deficits, foreign exchange earnings and the real income of the poorest third in each of five rural and the urban areas. As might be expected, the increase in world prices results in a large extra burden on the government budget when policies remain unchanged. The increase in the deficit for agricultural commodities increases by 33 per cent, the cost of importing those goods by 24 per cent. The big issue facing the government under these conditions is the mirror opposite image of the situation facing exporters such as Argentina. Given a distinctly less favourable external environment, how is the burden to be shared between the government and the beneficiaries of the subsidy programmes? While there might be some scope for rearranging policies to better conserve resources (shifting out of subsidies to bread towards hard wheat for its distributional impact), the relative tradeoff between the policy options is not very sensitive to the projected changes in the world prices.

In terms of our initial discussion through the diagrams, the government, if it chooses to maintain consumption of the poorest third faces dramatic increases in subsidies. The price adjustments required to reduce the deficits are more substantial than before the liberalization and therefore their impact, particularly on urban incomes of the poor is greater. But the instruments — the price of hard and soft wheat — that are the most important in this adjustment remain as before the price changes.

The Case of an Agricultural Exporter/Importer — Senegal

The structure of the agricultural economy and the types of intervention are more complicated in the case of Senegal[5]. Briefly, the structure of the model is as follows. The government sets the price of the main export crops, groundnuts and cotton at farm level which are lower, generally, than world price levels. The profit is earned by the marketing board which we will count as part of the government. The prices of rice at both farm and retail levels are also set by the government at levels which are higher than world prices (this arrangement has varied over time but was true for the year modelled). Senegal is a net importer of rice and therefore earns a profit on the trade. Completing the production side of the model are two commodities, millet and maize, which are principally subsistence crops, are not traded internationally, but are marketed to some extent by the farmers.

Since the government officially set the prices of all internationally traded commodities for the base year of the model, 1982/3, there would not be any direct allocational effects of the change in world prices. The direct impact of the price changes show up entirely in the revenue and foreign exchange accounts. This effect is presented in Part A of Table 14.4. Since Senegal is both an importer and an exporter of agricultural goods, the effects on these accounts *a priori* are ambiguous. However, as Table 14.4 illustrates, the net effect of the price increases for groundnuts, cotton and rice are to change a net government deficit into a slight surplus and to increase net foreign exchange earnings by 6 per cent.

Beyond the direct impact of the price changes, however, is the possibility that the new configuration of prices leads to a reassessment of the policy choices available to the government. The effects of various policy options under both price regimes are presented in Part B of Table 14.4. Since domestic prices are set by the government, and assumed to be unchanged, the effects on real incomes in the five regions (four producing regions and the urban sector represented by Dakar), are the same in both regimes. The main difference comes in the revenue and foreign exchange side of the ledger. Driving the results to some extent is the fact that the change in international prices turns what was a tax on rice consumption into a subsidy. The fact that the world and domestic prices switch order opens up opportunities for improvements in the pattern of government interventions.

How the change in world price patterns can affect the tradeoffs facing the policy maker can be examined in a number of ways. Figure 14.5 shows the effects on two objectives (decreasing the deficit and increasing foreign earnings) for both the original conditions and for the new set of prices of each of the policies examined. Since the effects on the income levels are the same in each case they are suppressed in this diagram. Each vector has been constructed to show the relative impact on government revenue of a one-unit change in foreign exchange earnings (positive for the policies of increasing the producer prices of groundnuts, rice and cotton and negative for raising the consumer prices of fertilizer, oil and rice). The main effect of the new price regime is to rotate all vectors counterclockwise, to reduce the cost in terms of government revenue of increasing foreign exchange earnings. In this respect, the results are similar to the Argentinean case and for the same reason. The general increase in world prices makes savings (or earnings) of foreign exchange relatively easier to achieve in terms of government revenue collected or expended. For any combination of policies which hits a particular target ratio of these two objectives, the new regime would tend to increase the reliance on the raising of producer prices relative to the consumer prices.

A second way of examining the impact of the external environment on policy choices is more comprehensive. This entails describing those combinations of policy measures which can simultaneously achieve all of the objectives of the government examined here. It is similar to the concept of Pareto efficiency in this regard but cannot be strictly interpreted as such due to the aggregation of people into groups which are not strictly homogeneous. In order to, on the one hand, avoid generating arbitrary relative weights on the outcome indicators and, on the other, to keep the exposition simple, we aggregate two regions, Casamance and Senegal Oriental, into one. This gives us six policy objectives (increases in income in four regions as well as reducing the deficit and increasing foreign earnings) and the six policy instruments. We can then solve for the "boundaries" of the region of simultaneous improvements by defining a target of a unit increase in each objective in turn and zero for all others and solving for the combination of policies which can achieve each objective when each policy is changed, i.e. gave the value of do_j / dp_j (where o_i is objective i and p_j is policy j). Calling this matrix "A", the problem is

$$d(Policy) = A^{-1} d(objective) = A^{-1} (1,0,0...)'$$

This is solved for policies described by vectors with 1 in one position at a time and zeros in the others. Thus, the results will show an improvement in one objective with no damage done to the others. When the procedure is repeated for both sets of international prices, it is possible to show the shift in the boundaries of this "critical region" (though, because the region is six dimensional, it is not possible to show it graphically). In two dimensions, this procedure can be illustrated as follows. Figure 14.6 shows the effects of changes in two policy instruments on two objectives. Each of the darkened lines represents the combinations of the policies which maintain the status quo level of the indicated objective. Policy combinations in the shaded side of the line lead to an improvement in the objective. The region which is doubly shaded is the area of policy reforms which leads to simultaneous improvement in both objectives. If this diagram were reproduced when the external environment changes (due to new world prices in our case), the darkened lines would rotate around the status quo point, indicating a new region of preferred policy changes. The task is to see if this change can be characterised in some informative way.

An example of this procedure for the objective of increasing incomes in Dakar without compromising any other objective is shown in Table 14.5. The first numeric column presents the combination of policies under the original prices which will achieve these results, the second under the new price regime and the third the difference between the two. These results indicate that a large switch out of subsidising fertilizer, with the increased food prices compensated by direct reduction in rice prices and indirect reductions via the substitutes for cotton (millet and maize) whose prices fall from increased supply, would be called for under the new set of prices.

Table 14.6 presents the increase in the use of each policy under the new price regime when the objective heading the column is to be increased. To continue the example of Dakar incomes, the third numeric column of the table repeats the information provided in Table 14.5. The specific values of these numbers are not of primary concern. Some generalisations, however, can be made on the basis of the sign patterns of the table entries.

With the exception of the goal of increasing foreign exchange directly, a consistent pattern emerges as to the shape of the critical region. The pattern for revenue generation and income increases in the Groundnut Basin and Casamance/Senegal Oriental reflects the basic ideas with minor differences for Dakar and Fleuve incomes. The general pattern is that increased prices for groundnuts, fertilizer, and rice (both producer and consumer prices) are indicated, with reductions in the prices of cotton and groundnut oil. It is interesting to note that this is the same pattern of relative price increases in the world market. The increases in the prices of rice and groundnuts (other oilseeds) at 14.88 per cent and 9.32 per cent are larger than the price increases for cotton and groundnut oil (other oils) at 8.48 per cent and 6.83 per cent respectively. The

398

boundaries of the critical region change such that prices of rice increase most, groundnuts next, while cotton and oil actually decline. This is the same relative order of the increases in the world markets. This reinforces the interpretation of the two-objective analysis that the new prices make it easier to satisfy tradable commodities when revenue goals are being pursued. Also interesting is the general pattern of substantial reductions in the subsidy (increases in the price) of fertilizer. The increases in world prices make the prices of outputs more attractive as a means of increasing (or protecting) income than the use of fertilizer subsidies.

The critical region does not, it appears, rotate uniformly. For the goals of increasing incomes in Dakar and the Fleuve, the basic pattern above is modified slightly. For the former, the new policy configuration provides lower consumer prices for rice paid for by lower subsidy rates on fertilizer (vis-à-vis the case in Casamance for instance). This makes sense as rice is the principal staple in the city. In the Fleuve, the price of groundnuts falls relative to the basic case described above. Groundnuts are a minor crop in the Fleuve and the fall in groundnut prices is compensated by the substantially smaller increase in fertilizer prices (relative to the other columns), which is more beneficial to incomes in the region. Since Senegal is in the French franc zone, the goal of foreign exchange, *per se,* has not been very important. It is interesting, however, that the change in prices induces the exact opposite change in emphasis on each of the policy instruments relative to the canonical case discussed above. This might be explained by noting that it was the increasing ease of obtaining foreign resources which allowed for the aggressive pursuit of the other goals. When it is foreign exchange, *per se,* that is the goal, this constraint reappears in a different form as an objective and entails essentially the opposite sort of reshuffling of policies as needed in the other cases.

In summary, higher world prices would allow the Senegalese government to attain higher total income from the sale of its exports. This can be shared out among its various objectives according to the weights it places on them. The tradeoffs involved in the construction of policies which simultaneously improve the goals examined here are altered. In the pursuit of increased government revenue and incomes, this entails passing on some of the increase in prices directly to producers.

CONCLUSION

In this paper, we have illustrated how policy choices may be incorporated into estimating the range of effects of trade liberalization on developing countries. To do the simulation, we have used relatively simple models that could be constructed for many developing countries. While the multimarket approach certainly has limitations, it does have the benefit of transparency and low costs in construction. However, because of its partial nature and its relevance for only marginal changes, it would not be appropriate for large policy changes. Thus it could not be used to trace out the policy frontiers of the diagrams presented in the second section of this paper. More complex models, although suffering from their own limitations, could be used in a similar manner as illustrated in this paper to describe the policy choices open to governments. As shown by the simulation for Tunisia, these choices may be limited and painful to some groups in the economy. For the countries that are likely to gain like Argentina and Senegal, the choices are more bountiful but the actual response not at all evident. The construction of boundary regions as done for the Senegal simulation could be used to illustrate the "Pareto optimal" possibilities.

ARGENTINA MODEL EQUATIONS

Commodity markets

$$\Sigma \, S_i^R \, (\overrightarrow{P^R}) = \Sigma \, D_i^R \, (\overrightarrow{P^R}, Y^R) + X_i$$

where:

S_i^R = supply of good i in region R

D_i^R = supply for good i in region R

X_i = Export of good i

$R\varepsilon$ = {Pampas, Non-Pampas}

$i\varepsilon$ = {wheat, feed grains, oilseeds, beef, poultry}

$P^{\overrightarrow{R}}$ = set of prices produced in region R

P_i^R = $(1-t_i) \, (1-V_i) \, P_i^w$ if produced in region R

$\quad = (1-t_i) \, P_i^w$ if not produced in region R

t_i = export tax on i

V_i = transport cost of i between regions

P_i^w = world price of i

Note that for feed grains, demand depends on beef and poultry prices and not on income. For Beef and Poultry, supply relations depend on feed grains as inputs.

Income

$$Y^R = \pi \, (\overrightarrow{P_R}) + \alpha^R$$

where:

Y^R = income in region R

$\pi(.)$ = profits from farming

α^R = other sources of income

{Government Revenue = $\Sigma_i t_i \, P_i^w \, X_i$ }

Foreign Exchange = $\Sigma_i P_i^w \, X_i$

SENEGAL MODEL EQUATIONS

Groundnuts

$$\sum_R SS_G^R (P_P^R) = \sum D_G^R (P^c) + X_G$$

Rice

$$\sum_R S_R^R (P_P^R) + M_R = \sum D_R^R (P^c)$$

Cotton

$$\sum S_T^R (P_P^R) = \sum D_T^R(P^c) + X_T$$

Millet

$$\sum_R S_m^R (P_R^R) = \sum D_m^R (P^c)$$

Maize

$$\sum S_Z^R (P_p^R) = \sum D_Z^R (P^c)$$

where:

S_i^R = Supply of good i from region R

D_i^R = Demand of good i from region R

i = {Groundnuts Basin, Rice, CoTton, Millet, MaiZe}

R = {Groundnut Basic, Fleuve, Casamance, Senegal Oriental, Dakar}

P^c = Consumer prices

P_P^R = Producer prices relevant to region R

M_R = Imports of rice

b = Conversion factor for groundnuts

CROPS BY REGION

	Dakar	Groundnut Basin	Fleuve	Casamance	Senegal Oriental
Groundnuts	(none)	V	V	V	V
Millet		V	V	V	V
Rice			V	V	V
Cotton				V	V
Maize				V	V

	Producer prices	Consumer prices
Groundnuts	Set by government ≠	Set by government (oil)
Millet	Free =	Free
Rice	Set by government ≠	Set by government
Cotton	Set by government ≠	Set by government
Maize	Free =	Free

Figure 14. 1. **POLICY TRADEOFFS FOR AGRICULTURAL EXPORTER**

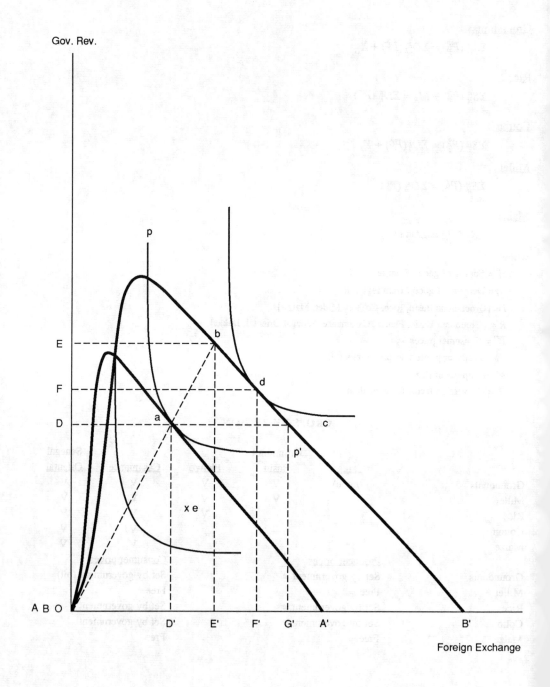

Figure 14. 2. **POLICY TRADEOFFS FOR FOOD IMPORTER**

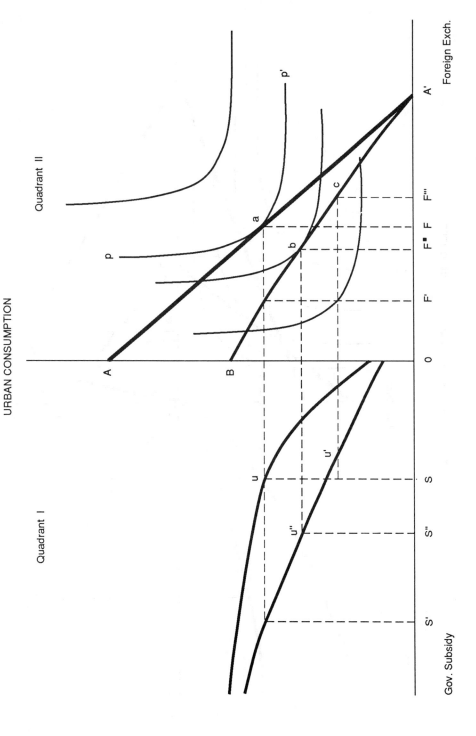

403

Figure 14. 3. **TRADEOFFS FOR AGR. EXPORTER - IMPORTER**

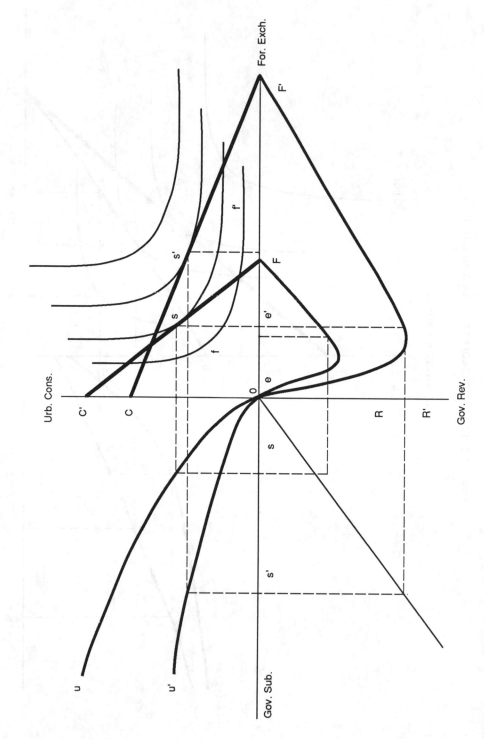

Figure 14. 4. **TRADEOFF WITH AGR. BUDGET DEFICIT**

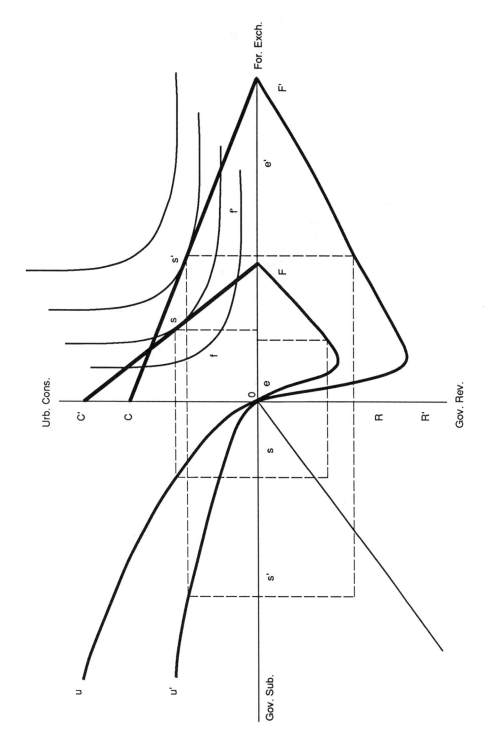

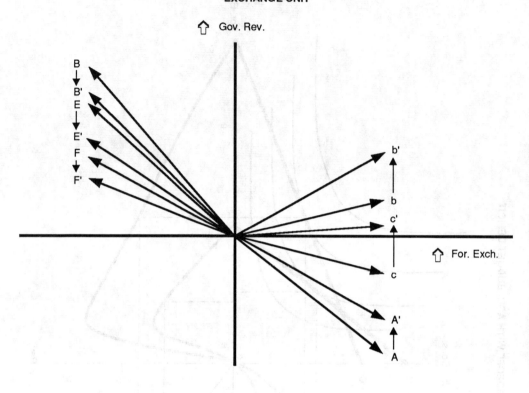

Figure 14. 5. **CHANGE IN GOV. REV. PER FOREIGN EXCHANGE UNIT**

406

Figure 14. 6. **POLICY INSTRUMENTS AND OBJECTIVES**

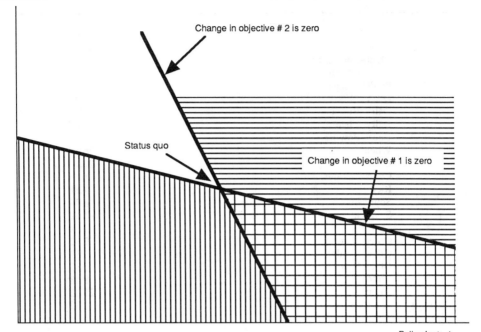

Table 14.1

WORLD PRICE PERCENTAGE CHANGES USED IN MODELS

Beef	16.03
Pork	11.65
Mutton and Lamb	25.74
Poultry Meat	16.12
Poultry Eggs	4.77
Dairy Milk	.00
Dairy Butter	83.64
Dairy Cheese	37.23
Dairy Powder	80.23
Wheat	26.99
Corn	22.25
Coarse Grains	16.03
Rice	14.88
Soybeans	-2.04
Soymeal	-2.62
Soyoil	3.31
Other Oilseeds	9.32
Other Meals	.85
Other Oils	6.83
Cotton	8.48
Sugar	29.33
Tobacco	3.22

Source: USDA/ERS SWOPSIM model runs.

Table 14.2

ARGENTINA : IMPACT OF PRICE CHANGES

Direct impact of world price change on :

Government tax revenues	36%
Agricultural foreign exchange earnings	57%

Government revenue foregone per unit foreign exchange
when the taxes on the commodities below are reduced :

	Original prices	New prices
Wheat	5.71	6.23
Feedgrains	.77	.90
Oilseeds	1.50	1.53
Beef	.32	.38
Poultry	.53	.58

Table 14.3

TUNISIA
POLICY EFFECTS WITH BASE PRICES
(Per cent change)

	Gov't Deficit	Foreign exchange requirements	North-east	North-west	Center-east	Center-west	South	Urban
			Real incomes of the poorest third in					
10 per cent price rise								
A.	7.62	7.64	.233	.871	.984	.912	.214	-.045
B.	2.21	-.36	-.0034	.0039	.179	.147	.047	-.012
C.	3.10	-.39	.154	-.0039	.704	.524	.143	-.0187
D.	3.92	-.24	1.638	1.509	.841	.791	.101	-.025
E.	-5.41	2.12	-1.14	-1.34	-1.43	-1.83	-.895	-.686
F.	-3.47	.78	-.166	-.027	-.238	.014	-.357	-.733
G.	-3.06	-.01	-1.36	-1.37	-.447	-.497	.052	-.0092
H.	-5.93	4.30	.126	.309	.506	.213	.099	-.271
Policy impact with new prices								
A.	3.84	7.65	.233	.871	.984	.912	.214	-.045
B.	1.71	-.33	-.0034	.0039	.179	.147	.047	-.012
C.	2.66	-.60	.154	-.0039	.704	.524	.143	-.0187
D.	2.98	-.21	1.638	1.509	.841	.791	.101	-.025
E.	-4.56	2.09	-1.14	-1.34	-1.43	-1.83	-.895	-.686
F.	-2.8	.78	-.166	-.027	.238.	.014	.357	-.733
G.	-2.26	-.04	-1.36	-1.37	-.447	-.497	.052	-.0092
H.	-5.98	4.72	.126	.309	.506	.213	.099	-.271

A. Producer price of Hard Wheat
B. Producer price of Soft Wheat
C. Producer price of Barley
D. Producer price of Milk
E. Consumer price of Hard Wheat
F. Consumer price of Soft Wheat
G. Consumer price of Barley
H. Consumer price of Milk

Table 14.4

SENEGAL
DIRECT IMPACT OF WORLD PRICE CHANGES

	Before	After
Government accounts (billions CFA)	-1.5	.2
Foreign exchange earnings (billions CFA)	33.1	35.1

Effects of each price by 10 per cent (billions CFA)

	Before		After	
	Change in Govt. deficit (base= 1.5)	Change in foreign exchange (base= 33.1)	Govt. deficit (base= -.2)	Foreign exchange (base= 35.1)
A. Groundnut[1]	4.07	3.06	3.86	3.27
B. Fertilizer[2]	-.27	-.05	-.27	-.06
C. Rice[1]	.08	.61	-.02	.71
D. Cotton[1]	-.08	.32	-.10	.34
E. Groundnut Oil[1]	-.95	-.21	-.93	-.24
F. Rice[3]	-1.90	-.61	-1.89	-.62

Real income changes in both price regimes (percentage)

	Dakar	S. Oriental	Casamance	GN Basin	Flueve
A.	-0.20	1.93	3.92	3.53	-0.58
B.	0.00	-0.18	-0.17	-0.17	-0.05
C.	-0.01	0.30	2.28	0.01	1.11
D.	0.00	0.37	0.87	0.00	-0.02
E.	-0.69	-0.31	-0.88	-0.45	-0.92
F.	-2.11	-0.74	-3.29	-0.72	-3.48

1. Producer price.
2. Price.
3. Consumer price.

Table 14.5

SENEGAL
CHANGE IN POLICIES NEEDED TO ACHIEVE UNIT INCREASE IN PER CAPITA INCOME IN DAKAR HOLDING AFTER OBJECTIVES CONSTANT
(Percentage change)

Product	At original world prices	At new world prices	Difference
Groundnut	.46	1.78	1.32
Fertilizer	-10.69	16.20	26.88
Rice (producer)	-20.52	-19.30	1.23
Cotton	25.15	20.54	-4.61
Groundnut oil	30.78	31.69	.91
Rice (consumer)	-14.75	-15.18	-.43

Table 14.6

SENEGAL
DIFFERENCES IN POLICY EFFORT BETWEEN NEW AND OLD PRICE REGIMES
TO ATTAIN UNIT INCREASE IN EACH OBJECTIVE
(Percentage units)

Product	Revenue	Foreign exchange	Dakar	Real incomes	GN Basin	Flueve
Groundnut	.005	-.004	1.32	.98	7.7	-.02
Fertilizer	.120	-.105	26.88	24.20	203.0	5.21
Rice	.010	-.007	1.23	1.75	16.0	1.08
Cotton	-.020	.018	-4.51	-4.02	-33.4	-.72
Groundnut oil	-.020	.009	.91	-2.71	-30.3	-4.47
Rice	.006	±.002	-.43	.79	9.11	1.46

NOTES AND REFERENCES

1. It is equally unlikely that developed countries will also accept unfalteringly the prospects of free trade in agriculture. So the policy choices approach of this paper will also have applications for industrial countries.

2. A. Braverman and J. Hammer, "Computer Models for Agricultural Policy Analysis", *Finance and Development*, June 1988.

3. For the one commodity case, the marginal cost may be expressed algebraically as:

$$(dGR/dt)/(dFX/dt) = t - (S - D)/[(S' - D')P] = t - (1 - D/S)/(e_s - D/Se_D)$$

where:

GR = Tax Revenue

FX = Foreign Exchange

t = Tax Rate $GR = t*P * (S-D)$

S = Supply (as a function of the domestic price $(1-t)*P$)

D = Demand (as a function of the domestic price $(1-t)*P$)

e_i = Price Elasticity of i (= Supply, Demand)

When the world price rises, D/S is reduced and the second term in the last expression becomes more negative. This relation carries over to our many commodity case.

4. For details see J. Hammer, "An Analysis of Agricultural Price Policies in Tunisia", World Bank, 1987.

5. For a more complete description of the Senegalese agricultural sector, see Braverman and Hammer, "Multimarket Analysis of Agricultural Pricing Policies in Senegal", in Singh, Squire and Strauss, *Agricultural Household Models: Extensions, Applications and Policy*, 1986.

Chapter 15

WORLD COMMODITY PRICES: THE ROLE OF EXTERNAL DEBT AND INDUSTRIAL COUNTRY POLICIES

by

Gordon C. Rausser, Marjorie B. Rose and Douglas A. Irwin

INTRODUCTION

The domestic support of and protectionist policies towards agriculture in major OECD countries has been partly responsible for surplus commodity production and sagging international commodity prices in recent years. Between 1980-87, the International Monetary Fund (IMF) food commodities price index fell by one third in nominal terms and almost by one half in real terms. Although originally undertaken largely for domestic reasons, these policies have led to trade restraints and export subsidies that have reduced prices and aggravated instability in international commodity markets. Attempts to reform policies in OECD countries via GATT negotiations or other means have led only to modest changes in world commodity production and trade patterns.

The adverse effects of these microeconomic policies in the OECD countries have been particularly severe for developing country commodity exporters. In addition, the macroeconomic policies pursued in a number of OECD countries (especially in the United States) have had important ramifications for these developing countries. A restrictive monetary policy coupled with a deficit-financed fiscal expansion in the United States since 1981 has been transmitted via real interest rates and exchange rates to reduce developing country commodity export prices. The monetary shocks of the early 1980s particularly altered the dynamic path of commodity prices (Rausser *et al.*, 1986).

These two sets of policies in OECD countries, one specific to commodity sectors and another more generally macroeconomic, operated in unison to reduce dramatically commodity prices in the 1980s. Over much of the 1970s, by contrast, these two sets of policies frequently operated in unison to increase commodity prices dramatically.

The commodity exporting developing countries, especially those with a large external debt position, were particularly hard hit by the combination of commodity sector and macro policies of OECD countries, and the external debt situation for these developing countries has deteriorated substantially. The United States alone represents nearly 60 per cent of the total developing country export market; not surprisingly it plays a vital role in the economic stability of these developing countries.

Empirical analysis of the commodity sector policies, macroeconomic policies and external debt linkages has until recently been conducted in separate studies. One stream of the empirical literature focuses on supply and demand conditions underlying individual product prices.

415

Several other studies utilise a complementary approach on aggregate commodity price indices to emphasize the factors that determine investment demand for storable primary goods. Still another group of studies focuses on the effects of macroeconomic variables on aggregate commodity prices, neglecting the fundamental forces of commodity supply and demand. Very few studies have been conducted which isolate the impact of the growing external debt position of developing countries on international commodity prices.

One illustrative empirical analysis of the supply and demand fundamentals in the commodities market is Hwa (1979). He finds that most of the price fluctuation in the 1970s can be explained by factors such as industrial production on the demand side, and commodity production and inventory stocks on the supply side. He uses a reduced form of the supply and demand factors for several major product prices to account for structural changes in the pricing relations in the early 1970s.

Bosworth and Lawrence (1982) use a framework much like Hwa for agricultural commodities and similarly support the traditional pricing analysis. In addition, they utilise the variance/covariance structure of real returns of commodities, bonds, and equity to explain the movements in commodity stocks and prices in the 1970s. They conclude that expanding commodities futures, as well as the large variance in commodity prices over this period can be explained, in part, by the speculative activity in the primary product markets.

Lawrence and Lawrence (1981) explicitly analyse the speculative causes for movements in relative commodity prices by examining the linkages to global financial markets. They initially estimate a model of relative prices on individual categories on commodities in separate regressions to see how the behaviour is related to world industrial production, commodity production, and inventory stocks. In a competing set of equations, the addition of monetary effects via interest rates and inflation rates does not add significantly to the explanation of short-term movement in individual commodity prices for the 1961 to 1979 period.

A report by the IMF (1987) surveys the evidence for the more recent episodes in world commodity prices. Low industrial production growth in the industrialised nations, structural shifts in intensity of commodity use in production, and abundant raw material supplies have contributed to the weakness in commodity prices in the 1980s according to this study. Moreover, the significant decrease in secular inflation coupled with the rise in interest rates have been important macroeconomic influences on the drop in commodity prices.

In another stream of literature, following the earlier work of Sachs (1985) and IMF (1983), Dornbusch (1985) derives an empirical model that includes the US real exchange rate, real interest rate and industrial production as the macroeconomic determinants of the aggregate US real commodity prices for the 1970 to 1985 period. Using ordinary least-squares methods, he finds elasticity estimates for the real exchange rates of -1.55; -0.24 for the real interest rate; and 2.27 for industrial production. There are a number of potentially serious problems with this analysis. For example, the real exchange coefficient in this estimation is significantly smaller -1.0. This (absolutely) large parameter estimate implies that the changes in the dollar exchange rate will affect not only the dollar commodity price, but also will be magnified in terms of other countries' currencies as well, i.e. US policies will affect developing countries' export prices directly via the exchange rate, and indirectly via the effect on other countries' prices.

A recent study by Cote (1987) attempts to correct the Dornbusch analysis by comparing the effects of variables such as world industrial production, interest rates and the US dollar real exchange rate on three different commodity price indices, representing the real commodity prices in the industrial world. The results are mixed: on the one hand, the impact of the dollar appreciation on real commodity prices using the *Economist* dollar index confirms Dornbusch's results of a negative impact; on the other hand, two competing indices (from the *International Financial Statistics* and the *Journal of Commerce*) show a positive effect of exchange rate appreciation on movements in commodity prices. Differences in the weighting schemes and the products included in the construction of the various indices are offered as a possible explanation for the divergent results. The selection of particular products and weights in the latter two indices may be an important consideration because certain commodities are produced and traded more heavily by the developing countries than others, and therefore may represent the impact of the variables on prices more accurately.

Gilbert (1989) suggests that both the strong foreign exchange value of the US dollar and developing country debt service requirements are responsible for the low commodity prices in the 1980s. He criticises earlier studies for using an inappropriate real exchange rate variable (US trade weighted instead of OECD country GNP weighted) and for failure to consider developing country indebtedness. In the category of agricultural foods Gilbert finds strong evidence of a debt servicing induced increase in supply that acts to reduce commodity prices. He also finds a smaller elasticity of dollar appreciation on commodity prices than earlier studies.

To be sure, there are a large number of forces that potentially impinge upon world commodity prices in addition to agricultural subsidisation in OECD countries. The dynamic path of commodity prices will also be influenced by the macroeconomic policies in OECD countries, the stock of physical and financial assets of countries throughout the world, and the pattern and spacial distribution of economic growth.

In many of the computable general equilibrium (CGE) examinations of trade liberalization (e.g., Stoeckel and Breckling, 1988, Robinson *et al.*, 1988), a rise in world prices (often 10 per cent or so) is assumed when multilateral liberalization is examined. In some commodities this rise is consistent with the empirical results of Tyers and Anderson. However, any rise that might occur will be dependent on the macroeconomic policies and growth of OECD countries. In this paper we will analyse these issues by first examining the mechanisms by which monetary, fiscal, and commodity sector subsidisation policies in the industrialised countries can impact upon developing countries. This descriptive treatment will be followed by a theoretical framework which is employed to determine the qualitative effects of various forces. The theoretical framework provides the foundation for an empirical model which is estimated and assessed.

INDUSTRIAL COUNTRY POLICY IMPACTS ON DEVELOPING COUNTRIES

The three major considerations in the analysis of industrial country-developing country policy links are the particular combinations of monetary and fiscal policies pursued, the impact of distortionary microeconomic policies, and the differences between the developing countries' own internal economic structure. Essentially, industrial countries' policies can affect the developing country commodity exporters via four channels: overall economic growth, the real interest rate, the real exchange rate, and the primary product stocks. The extent of the impact from changes in these variables will vary with the degree of openness in the developing countries' trade structure and the level of initial indebtedness.

Macroeconomic Policy Linkages

Interest rates play a key role in the performance of developing economies in several ways. If storable commodities are viewed as a portfolio asset, then real interest rates will represent the opportunity cost of holding a commodity and will affect the speculative demand for the good. Higher real rates cause the demand for primary goods to fall. Consequently, the relative price of commodities will decline until the expected rate of change in the product's value is equated with the real interest rate (plus insurance and storage costs). The foregoing analysis, known as the "overshooting hypothesis" (Frankel 1986, Rausser, *et al.*, 1986) explains why the real world commodity prices (i.e., developing country export prices) will remain low as long as the expected future appreciation (due to higher interest rates) remains high.

A second channel through which the developing countries are directly affected by US interest rate disturbances is by changing their debt service obligations. An estimated 80 per cent of all major developing country debt is under variable rate agreements. As real interest rates crept upward in the early 1980s, so did the interest payments' portion of their debt service. Additional principal also accumulated with the occurrence of current account deficits due to falling export receipts (assuming these could be financed externally).

Another burden is placed upon the debtor when the value of the debt is fixed in one currency, and the export receipts are valued in a different currency. In this case, when the debt currency appreciates relative to the export currency, the value of the developing countries' external liabilities rises, a common situation with the huge dollar appreciation in the 1980s.

Higher real rates can also affect the internal performance via the standard substitution effect of reducing investment in favour of increased saving. Capital flows to countries with higher real rates, and it is not uncommon for real differentials to exist between the developing countries and industrial countries due to regulated financial markets in the developing countries. Although not easily quantifiable, this channel may have important consequences for future developing country debt servicing prospects as the capital goods stock (and therefore future production possibilities) dwindles.

US macro policies can also operate on the developing economies by altering their terms of trade. In addition to the interest rate overshooting, the terms of trade can be altered by cyclical shifts in US demand for developing country exports and by real exchange rate movements. In general, business expansions in the industrial nations improve the developing countries' terms of trade and therefore, the net export position, while recessions are transmitted by a fall off in export demand.

A real dollar exchange rate appreciation may also drive down the terms of trade for these primary product exporters. This is because the pass-through of exchange rate changes is relatively higher for primary commodities versus manufactured goods due to differences in market structure (primary product markets are competitive, while manufactures markets have more market concentration). Moreover, the real currency exchange rate of developing countries moves proportionately more than that of the industrial countries. Finally, developing country supply responsiveness for these products is greater than in industrial countries. All of these influences point in the same direction.

From the above discussion, it is apparent that a rise in real interest rates and/or a fall in the terms of trade will reduce the welfare of the developing countries. Consequently, an investigation of the particular policy combinations that will produce either of these results is imperative.

The shift to a more restrictive monetary policy coupled with an unprecedented fiscal deficit expansion in the early 1980s put upward pressure on real interest rates both in the United States and abroad. This rise in rates of return directly enlarged the developing country debt service obligations and indirectly drove down commodity prices via overshooting and dollar appreciation. However, expansionary fiscal policy can also increase demand for developing country agricultural exports, therefore producing an offsetting effect on the terms of trade. The net effect on the terms of trade depends upon the relative strength of the three combined effects: exchange rate, interest rate and relative demand shifts on commodity prices.

Microeconomic Policy Linkages

Government policies can also affect the supply and demand for primary goods (and therefore the price) on a specific product basis. The coupled subsidisation policies of many industrial countries has resulted in excess production and growth in commodity stocks. Although these

418

policies combined with supply management have in some instances increased industrial country domestic prices in the short run, their long-run effects have been to depress commodity prices especially on external or world markets.

The problems for the developing country commodity exporters from these programmes arise when industrial governments dump their stocks onto the world market at prices below the domestic levels, or donate the stocks as aid. In fact, the US Commodity Credit Corporation (CCC), in the face of enormous commodity stockpiles, began to sell off their inventories after the passage of the 1985 US Farm Bill. This move helped cause many already depressed commodity prices to plummet to lows not seen since the Great Depression.

There have been several studies that have attempted to quantify the impact of the industrialised countries' protectionist policies on developing countries. Valdés and Zietz (1980) use a multiproduct partial equilibrium model with prior estimates of world supply and demand elasticities to analyse the effects of a 50 per cent reduction on trade barriers in the OECD countries on developing country export earnings. Their results simulate the effects of reduced protectionism on a large group of developing country commodity exporters by both commodity and by geographic region and conclude that there will be a net welfare gain to the developing countries.

Tyers and Anderson (1986) use a multimarket model to arrive at conclusions similar to those of Zietz and Valdés. They also find significant increases in the world price of commodities, as well as increases in world trade, upon the liberalization of major industrialised countries' markets. Large welfare gains for nearly every producing region accompany these changes in prices and volumes. Of course, significant welfare losses are imposed upon most of the commodity importing countries.

In a more recent study, Zietz and Valdés (1986) analyse the potential welfare and foreign exchange gains for developing countries of complete trade liberalization in four major agricultural products: sugar, beef and veal, wheat, and maize. The results of the numerical analysis are mixed, with substantial gains for the developing countries from trade liberalization in sugar and beef, and a potential net welfare loss for the developing countries with a reduction of barriers of cereals.

Roningen and Dixit (1989) examine the removal of agricultural subsidies in major countries using an 11-region, 22-commodity net trade, partial equilibrium model. They find that the level of government assistance to the production of a particular commodity is closely related to the world price of that commodity. They estimate, for example, that a full liberalization of agricultural policies by industrial countries would increase world agricultural prices by an average of 22 per cent. Liberalization by the EC alone accounts for almost half of the increase. Per capita income gains would be small in the industrial countries, and would be dependent on developing countries for the degree of their net export position.

Loo and Tower (1988) specifically address the impact of a liberalization of agricultural policies on less developed economies with foreign debt servicing requirements. Increased foreign aid or a direct reduction of debt is found to be a weak means of improving the real income and debt servicing ability of developing countries. Their analysis suggests that increased agricultural prices stemming from policy liberalization in the industrialised countries would more effectively meet developing country interests. They ignore the impact, however, of higher commodity prices on net-importing debtor developing countries.

Developing Country Economic Structure

The impact of changes in the industrial country policy variables on developing countries depends critically upon the initial economic structure of the country in question. The two conditions that determine how much industrial country policies are felt within the developing countries are the initial external debt position and the degree of openness in the trade sector. Higher interest rates will increase the debt burden in proportion to the existing liabilities and may increase the net indebtedness. Moreover, the larger the share of exports in total output, and the larger the share of exports that are comprised of primary commodities, the greater the damage from a deterioration in the terms of trade.

The extent of the spillover of industrial country economic policies onto the developing country commodity exporters will depend upon the initial debt position and the proportion of exports in primary products. Table 15.1 reports the portion of exports by country. The country share of total world exports by commodity is recorded in Table 15.2 and a summary of all agricultural exports, as a percentage of total exports, is reported in Table 15.3.

Aggregate developing country borrowers experienced a 5.43 per cent increase in their export to GNP ratios, while many agricultural developing country exporters saw real declines ranging from 8 to 41 per cent of GNP from the years 1980 to 1984 (Rausser and Rose, 1988).

The change in debt and debt service ratios is even more dramatic. The average increase for 1980 to 1984 in debt and debt service for all borrowers was 38 and 23 per cent respectively. By contrast, the largest developing country rice and cotton exporters, Thailand and Egypt, saw rises in their debt service-export ratios of 146 per cent for Thailand and 58 per cent for Egypt. There was even more of a marked decline in the export share of GNP for Argentina, an exporter of wheat and corn, where the debt-export ratio nearly doubled.

Further analysis of the distortionary effects of industrial country commodity policies is necessary to separate the macroeconomic versus microeconomic policy effects on the developing countries. The case of fruits and vegetables offers some further enlightenment (Rausser and Rose, 1988). The Philippines, which has approximately a total market share of 3.5 per cent of world fruit exports, had positive growth in the exports share, but was well above average in the debt and debt service growth. The net welfare tradeoff of a higher debt burden that decreases disposable income and higher exports that increases welfare is not apparent.

Finally, in the case of the US links with developing countries it is especially important also to recognise the inter-relationships between the large current account deficits of the United States and the developing country debt service burdens. Ever since 1982, exports of the United States to debtor developing countries and also of some other large deficit countries have deteriorated greatly. Currency adjustments, the striving for efficiency gains, and other changes are working very slowly to restore balance. However, it must emphasized that balance will not be achieved on the basis of debt relief alone unless stronger trading relations can be restored between some large industrial countries and their traditional developing country partners. For example, US exports to Mexico and Brazil have not regained their former status that existed as late as 1982.

THEORETICAL FRAMEWORK

In this section we provide an extremely simple general equilibrium model to motivate the empirical analysis. Although many details are not incorporated in the formulation, it does capture the mechanisms that structure the relevant linkages. In essence, the formulation presumes an integrated, world market for commodities. These commodities are traded in dollars and are exchanged by countries with various characteristics, exporter and importer, debtor and non-debtor.

Exchange Rates and Commodity Prices

A useful way of initiating the discussion is to consider Dornbusch's (1985) simple model of the world market for a commodity, consisting of the United States and the rest of the world. An exogenous and fixed supply of commodities is matched by domestic US demand and by foreign demand, both of which depend on the relative price of commodities and on income. Thus,

$$S = D\ (P/P,\ Y) + D^*(P^*/P^*\cdot\ Y^*) \tag{1}$$

where * denotes foreign variables, Y is income, p are commodity prices in home and foreign currency, and P are the national price deflators. Dornbusch assumes that commodity prices are perfectly arbitraged such the $p = ep^*$ where e is the nominal exchange rate (home currency per unit of foreign currency). The real exchange rate λ then depends on P and P^*, being the home and foreign GDP deflators, i.e.

$$\lambda = P/eP^*, \tag{2}$$

where, under perfect competition, "exchange rate movements change relative prices one-for-one." Dornbusch then uses (1) and (2) to solve for the real commodity price of the United States as a function of income, the real exchange rate, and exogenous commodity supply:

$$P/P = J\ (Y,\ Y^*,\ :\lambda S). \tag{3}$$

This equation suggests that a real exchange rate appreciation of the US dollar will "lower real commodity prices in terms of the US deflator while raising them in terms of foreign deflators." With a change in the real exchange rate, commodity prices relative to national deflators change but arbitrage ensures that commodity prices themselves are equalised. An increase in the real US exchange rate will decrease real commodity prices by a function of the weighted elasticities of US and foreign demand, as US import prices fall directly and as the relative price of commodities in foreign markets increases.

The Dornbusch model provides a simple framework in which to evaluate the effects of various shocks to the world commodity market. Here we make several modifications to the framework so as to apply it to the situation of developing countries. First, the supply of commodities will not be assumed as exogenous and fixed but will be determined within the model. Supply can be thought to hinge crucially on the relative domestic price and on government policy towards agriculture in developing countries, which in turn depends on the size of foreign currency denominated foreign debt that must be serviced with export revenues.

A further addition to the model will be the inclusion of stocks of commodities held worldwide. A rise in stocks in net importing industrial countries indicates the effect of their government transfer programmes in closing out the market for imports; a similar rise in stocks in exporting countries also leads to market pressures for a fall in world commodity prices.

Four cases will be considered below, based on the economic position of the developing country to the world commodity market: a commodity exporting country with a foreign debt burden, a commodity importing country with a debt burden, an exporting country without debt, and an importing country without debt.

Exporting Debtor Country

For this basic case, it is first assumed that a representative developing country produces both an exportable commodity and a composite importable, faces endogenously determined terms of trade, and must service official debts denominated in dollars. Note that each economic agent in the developing country — producer and consumer — takes the terms of trade to be given, while the country as a whole can affect the terms of trade. In this two-goods framework, we have by the Walras law the condition that the excess supply of its exportable must equal zero (stars denote foreign variables):

$$S\,(p/p, \alpha) - D^*\,(\lambda p, y^*, s^*, \tau^*) = 0. \tag{4}$$

The export supply of the developing country, $S\,(')$, is a function of the relative (domestic) price of its commodity (p/p) and a summary policy instrument of the government toward the industry (α). Foreign import demand is a function of the relative price of the commodity, the real dollar exchange rate (λ) foreign activity (y^*), and the quantity of stocks of commodities held in the industrial world (s^*), and foreign tariff and non-tariff barriers (τ^*). The stock figure indicates the degree of openness in the foreign market, i.e. the extent of its excess demand for commodities, and of market conditions for the developing country's exports.

A word should be said about the government measures embodied in the term α. Government policy towards agriculture usually includes measures that both tax and subsidise the production of commodities. The net impact of the incentives produced by government policy may be negative (i.e. the producers are, on balance, taxed by the government through export taxes or other measures) or positive (i.e. indicating producers receive revenue from the government either through direct payments, subsidised input prices, or other forms of transfers).

We have a specific notion for the endogenous and equilibrium determination of α. Because the exporting country is a debtor, it must service its debt with, we assume, a constant flow of export proceeds denoted δ. The foreign currency earned by the debtor country is simply the revenue from its export earnings. It is presumed that the costs of producing the exports are paid in domestic currency. All foreign currency proceeds must be devoted to servicing the flow δ which has been exogenously determined by history but whose evolution depends on the prevailing world's real rate of interest. Changes in the domestic supply of the commodity, the price of the commodity, or the real dollar exchange rate all affect the export revenue of the country. Changes in the world's rate of interest affect the flow of resources from the country. We assume government policy, α is adjusted to ensure that:

$$pS\,(\bullet) = \delta\,(r).$$

Total differentiation yields:

$$\hat{p} + \hat{S} = \hat{\delta}$$

where hats indicate proportionate changes, i.e. $\hat{p} = dp/p$. $\hat{S}$ can be shown to equal $\varepsilon\hat{p} + k\hat{\alpha}$, where ε is the price elasticity of supply and k is the elasticity of output with respect to government policy incentives. Rearrangement yields:

$$\hat{\alpha} = [\hat{\delta} - \hat{p}\,(1 + \varepsilon)]/k.$$

This equation is the reaction function for the determination of the change in α. Note that this government reaction function is in accord with the stylised facts of the response of many commodity exporting countries. Namely, exogenous shocks that affect a country's ability to service its debt requirements, such as a change in λ or in r, result in a changed government policy to increase export proceeds by encouraging the movement of factors and resources into the sector.

Argentina, for example, reduced direct export taxes in 1987 on agricultural goods from close to 20 per cent to under 5 per cent in an effort to increase export supply. Although some new indirect taxes limited the effectiveness of this direct reduction, the response of the government, and the direction of its action, accord well with the specification we have outlined here.

Totally differentiating the equilibrium condition (1) and, with simple rearrangement of terms, we have:

$$\hat{p} = [n^*\,\hat{\lambda} + \theta y^* + \mu s - \beta\alpha - \varepsilon\tau^*]/[E - n^*], \tag{5}$$

422

where hats represent proportionate changes, n^* is the (negative) foreign elasticity of demand with respect to price or exchange rate changes, θ is the (positive) activity elasticity of demand in foreign countries, μ is the (negative) response of current foreign demand to a change in stocks, β is the (positive) supply response of the exporting country to a change in net government production incentives towards the sector, and ε is the (negative) elasticity of demand with respect to tariffs and other barriers. The denominator is positive because $E>0$ and $n^*<0$.

While we are not formally testing this model, it does highlight the salient features we hope to capture in our empirical work that follows. Equation (5) indicates, for example, as in Dornbusch's model, that an appreciation of the dollar reduces the world prices of the commodity, an increase in foreign activity tends to increase commodity prices, an increase in foreign stocks and tariffs tends to decrease commodity prices, and debtor country encouragement for production tends to decrease commodity prices (through a shift in the supply schedule).

It is important to note that debtor country efforts to increase exports (and thereby preserve its debt payment capacity) in the face of, say, an exogenous terms of trade shock, actually further deteriorate its term of trade. Thus a government responds to an increase (decrease) in the price of its own exportable with policies that reinforce the direction of that movement. Governments can therefore exacerbate the world price instability of their own exports.

Similar effects are also noted for an increase in the world's interest rate (r). An increase in r leads to government efforts to expand export supply to increase foreign currency revenues. At the same time, foreign demand for commodities drops as a result of the movement of stocks from storage to the market. An increase in r then unambiguously leads to a decline in the price of commodities. The stock figure is also dependent on the world's prevailing rate of interest, r, the opportunity cost of holding commodities in stock-form. In writing $s^*(r)$, we note that a higher rate of interest will induce holders of stocks to sell their commodities and thus reduce foreign demand for such produce from the developing country.

Importing Debtor Countries

The second class of countries trading in this world commodity market are net importing countries that have a debt burden. A prominent example is Mexico. This is analytically similar to the above situation with several differences. The example would have to be recast with the country having an excess demand for the commodity under question, thus

$$D\,(p, y, \alpha, \tau) - S^*\,(p, s^*) = 0 \tag{6}$$

where D is the developing countries' import demand function.

In this case, the role of α and τ would be not to promote imports, but to limit them in response to a price or exchange rate shock. Import restrictions in such a case are the result of an effort to stem the loss of foreign exchange. Both α and τ would distort the developing economy by drawing resources into a sector where the country is a net importer of goods, thereby reducing the total volume of trade. A real appreciation of the dollar would in this instance reduce debtor country demand for commodities by raising the foreign currency price of the commodities. This rise reduces demand on the world market generating downward pressure on commodity prices.

Exporting Non-Debtor Countries

A third scenario is the case of an exporting developing country with no debt burden to service. Government policy may then be more flexible in its response to external shocks as it does not have a foreign currency debt to service, and indeed it may have no policy whatsoever.

There may be less of a tendency for government policy to expand supply and exacerbate the downward pressure on commodity prices in the face of an external shock. Otherwise, this country is affected by external shocks the same as an exporting developing country with debt considered previously.

The United States may also be said to fall into this category. As an exporter of many commodities, however, its government is not a passive participant but adjusts its policy parameter to encourage supply and thereby, at times, increases the stock of commodities.

Importing Non-Debtor Countries

A fourth scenario takes an importing developing country without a debt burden (such as Taiwan). This is also analytically similar to the case of an importing debtor country, except there being no debt burden, government policy may not have the protectionist, foreign-exchange saving objective as would a similarly situated debtor.

Inter-Country Linkages

A final stylised version worth considering is the case where the developing country debtor exports in competition with the United States a commodity destined for third-country markets. An appreciation of the dollar in this instance induces a substitution effect in third-country markets between the two suppliers. The appreciation raises foreign prices of the commodity, thus reducing demand. However, the appreciation also increases the price the debtor developing country can receive through exporting. The net effect on the world price is ambiguous.

Summary

The above cases are summarised in Table 15.4 where the signs of changes in the exogenous variables and their effect on commodity prices are shown. An implication of the model is that, regardless of the net trade and external debt position of a country, a real exchange rate appreciation of the dollar, an increase in stocks, and increase in interest rates will decrease commodity prices. Most of the other effects will appear or be muted (zero) depending on the particular case considered (exporter or importer, debtor or non-debtor) and the nature of the shock. Implications about welfare do not necessarily coincide directly with the signs, however, as an increase in the real value of the dollar has a uniform effect on commodity prices with different implications for exporters and importers of commodities.

Any empirical investigation of the world commodity market includes in its sample a number of trading countries whose economic situation is similar to one of the five cases outlined above. In the commodity market, an aggregation of these traders is necessary with implicit weights being the importance of a particular class of countries in world trade. A glance at Table 15.4 suggests that there should be little ambiguity over the signs of the aggregate coefficients, although the significance of some may be at issue.

In addition, as Cote (1987) has noted, there may be no clear signed effect for these shocks on the developing countries' terms of trade. For example, the affect of a real appreciation of the exchange rate can influence both developing country import and export prices. To be sure, a real appreciation of the US dollar can lead to either an improvement or a deterioration in developing countries' terms of trade, depending on the breakdown of developing countries' trade with industrial trading partners.

EMPIRICAL RESULTS

As noted above, the macroeconomic impact of growth in the industrialised countries and the real foreign exchange value of the dollar on agricultural prices for major developing country exports have been previously examined. These factors play a major role in determining the quantity of import demand for agricultural goods; the activity variable through the income effect and the exchange rate through the relative price effect.

On balance, developed country agricultural policies have subsidised their own production, thereby decreasing the excess demand to be filled by foreign suppliers. The summary variable used to characterise these policies is the volume of world agricultural stocks of major commodities. An increase in stocks is a signal that agricultural policies in developed countries have acted to reduce foreign market access. These policies have a depressing effect on world commodity prices, i.e. those for developing country exporters, which must find other less lucrative markets for their products.

Yet under certain conditions, the converse can be argued to hold, namely that a reduction in stocks is indicative of developed country dumping or subsidising its stockpile onto world markets and thereby depressing world commodity prices. However, up until 1988 world stocks were accumulating, meaning that the direct effect of policies in closing developed countries' markets for imports was more significant than the secondary effort to reduce those stocks through export subsidisation.

The foreign indebtness of the commodity exporting developing countries can have a significant impact on commodity prices for several reasons. The burden of servicing debt has manifested itself in government efforts to expand exports of goods, especially commodities, to earn foreign exchange. This expansion tended to depress export prices for those commodities of which developing countries successfully increased production and reduced, but did not eliminate, the gains from exporting those commodities.

Once again, the converse can be said to hold: that as commodity prices fell, developing countries borrowed from major private and public lending institutions in an effort to smooth their income and consumption streams. However, this story is not compatible with the stylised facts of the 1970s and 1980s. The accumulation of debt began in the mid-1970s when commodity prices were rising rapidly. The borrowing was to finance further economic expansion at home through investment in a variety of industries. With the recession in the early 1980s, borrowing came to a halt and the problem of servicing the debt became an issue which required renewed attention to export growth. This growth was all the more difficult in the face of slower growth in developed countries and a higher real dollar exchange rate, and the consequent effort to expand exports acted to reduce commodity prices even further.

In summary, three groups of potential causal forces are examined: macroeconomic policies in the industrialised world as reflected by the real exchange rate for the US dollar, US interest rates, and OECD country industrial production; microeconomic agricultural sector policies as reflected by commodity production and stocks; and developing country economic structure as reflected by the external debt of Latin American and African countries. The empirical analysis reported in this section is designed to allow for differential responsiveness to each of these causal forces. As in earlier work (Rausser et al., 1986), the analysis will provide evidence on the separate effects of monetary and fiscal policies via interest and exchange rates, and of distortionary agricultural policies via commodity production and stocks. The implications of these policies for developing countries are allowed to be altered by a measure of developing country external debt. Dynamic adjustments are introduced to all specifications via various rational distributed lags.

The estimated equations are based on quarterly data over the period from 1977 through 1987. The first set of equations focuses on explaining world commodity prices and world agricultural prices. In Figures 15.1 and 15.3 each of these indices is reported back to 1964 with

425

its corresponding "real" counterparts shown in Figures 15.2 and 15.4, respectively. The deflation of each of these series by the US producer price index is almost indistinquishable from the deflated series using the export unit value index of industrial countries. The real series are used as the dependent variables and are sourced with the International Financial Statistics of the International Monetary Fund.

Various measures of the terms of the trade for non-oil developing countries are reported in Figure 15.5 through 15.8. In Figure 15.5 exporting the basket of food commodities onto world markets and importing the average mix of products have faced a nightmare since the mid-1970s. For the representative developing country, however, events have not been this unfavourable (see figure 15.6).

In Figure 15.6 the ratio of export prices to import prices of non-oil developing countries is depicted since the mid-1960s. For those developing countries that export a basket of only commodities, a similar terms of trade time series is shown in Figure 15.7. Finally, for developing countries that export a basket of agricultural raw materials, the relevant terms of trade time series is shown in Figure 15.8. As can be seen from Figures 15.5 through 15.8, there are some rather large differences facing various non-oil developing countries. Hence to differentiate the impact of industrialised country macro and agricultural sector policies on developing countries, equations are estimated for each of the terms of trade time series appearing in Figures 15.6, 15.7, and 15.8.

In addition to the above equations, individual world commodity price equations are specified for wheat, coarse grains, rice, and cotton. Wheat prices refer to US No. 2 Dark Northern spring, 14 per cent *cif* Rotterdam; coarse grains refer to US No. 3 yellow corn, *cif* Rotterdam; rice is white *fob* Thailand; and cotton is *"A"* index from the *Cotton and Wool Situation Report*, *cif* Northern Europe. For each of these individual commodities, microeconomic policies in the United States play a significant role in determining the path of production, stocks, and worldwide prices.

Explanatory variables for the various estimated equations include a measure of the US real effective exchange rate (based on relative value-added deflators in manufacturing); interest rates, measured by the six month commercial paper rate in the United States; the OECD industrial country production index, seasonally adjusted; as a measure for debt, the private sector external liabilities of Latin America and Africa; as a proxy for commodity stocks, the total world grain stocks, and for the individual commodity equations their corresponding world production and stock levels. Except for the individual commodity equations, the industrial production index variable was entered as an arithmetic lag over the current and previous two quarters with weights of (0.2, 0.5, and 0.3). A geometric distributed lag was imposed on all other explanatory variables.

The empirically estimated equations are partially reduced forms in the case of the aggregate commodity price indices or the terms of trade measures. For each of these equations, ordinary least squares were employed to generate the relevant statistics. For the individual commodity equations for wheat, coarse grains, rice, and cotton, correlation among the individual equation error terms and the nonequivalence of the regressors dictate the use of seemingly unrelated regressions methods. To be sure, many of the explanatory variables in a more general structural model would be treated endogenously. Since our purpose is basically exploratory we will leave for some later application the search for a more complete accounting of macroeconomic variables, microeconomic policies as well as developing country debt.

Real Commodity and Agricultural Price Equations

The mathematical specification for all equations was log linear in the variables, except for the interest rate. Since price indices are the dependent variables, all the estimated coefficients

426

are flexibilities except the coefficient for the rate of interest which is a semi-flexibility. In reporting the estimated equations, the mean estimated level of the effects along with the their associated standard errors as well as the standard goodness-of-fit statistics are presented. For each regression equation we also report the immediate impact or short-run flexibilities as well as the long-run stationary state flexibilities.

An interaction effect is allowed between interest rates and the level of commodity stocks in all of the empirical equations. This interaction effect is represented by the product of interest rate and the level of stock. In essence, it admits the possibility that movement in interest rates will have variable effects depending upon the level of commodity stocks. If stocks are nil or nonexistent the interest rate is expected to have little if any effect on commodity prices. Moreover, if the opportunity costs of carrying stocks as represented by interest rates, are very small the level of stocks is expected to exert less pressure on commodity prices.

As can be seen from Table 15.5, for both the all-commodity and the agriculture raw materials price equations all qualitative effects correspond to *a priori* notions. Both equations are stable and the quantitative magnitude of the effects appears reasonable. In both cases, over 90 per cent of the variation of commodity and agricultural index prices is explained by the set of explanatory variables.

For both equations the real exchange rate is highly significant, the industrial production index is insignificant, interest rates are highly significant only for agricultural prices but not for all commodity prices, the level of grain stocks is virtually significant, the interaction effect of stocks and interest rates is highly significant for agricultural prices but not for all commodity prices, and the external debt measure is more significant for all commodities than for agricultural prices.

The effect of real exchange rates no longer has the unbelievable magnitude reported by Dornbusch. In fact, the magnitude of the elasticity of prices with respect to real exchange rates is approximately equivalent to the elasticity with respect to worldwide grain stocks. For all commodities the impact is largest (absolutely) for the real exchange rate followed by the level of grain stocks, external debts, industrial production, and interest rates. The ordering for agricultural commodity prices is basically the same except for the interest rate, which assumes a much larger importance.

Developing Countries' Terms of Trade Equations

In Table 15.6 the estimated equations for non-oil developing countries' terms of trade, commodity exporting developing countries' terms of trade and agricultural exporting developing countries' terms of trade are reported. In all three cases, the equations succeed reasonably well in explaining the various terms of trade movements over time. Qualitative effects generally correspond to *a priori* notions with a few minor but insignificant exceptions.

Real exchange rates and interest rates are significant at the 5 per cent level only for the agricultural raw materials' terms of trade equations. In some cases the industrial production index is almost significant but in most instances it proves to be insignificant. The commodity stocks variable has the anticipated effect on all terms of trade equations as does the interest rate stock interaction variable. However, only in the case of the agricultural terms of trade are the effects of the latter two variables significant. The external debt variable has the right qualitative effect on all three terms of trade but is significant only for the aggregate non-oil developing country terms of trade.

In constrast to the real commodity and agricultural price equations appearing in Table 15.6, the real exchange rate no longer dominates in the terms of trade equations. This is no surprise given the real exchange rate influences on both components of the terms of trade. Note that this observation does not hold for the agricultural raw materials' terms of trade. Here, the real exchange rate effect once again dominates in terms of its absolute level of influence.

Our results for the terms of trade equation stand in sharp contrast to those reported by Cote. Her results cover the period 1963-1983 and show a significant positive link between the US dollar exchange rate and the non-oil developing countries' terms of trade. The difference between our results can be explained by several factors, including the incorporation of both external debt and worldwide stocks of grains. Even if these variables are excluded, however, the real exchange rate still has a negative effect but is less significant for the total non-oil developing countries' terms of trade. In the case of the agricultural raw materials' terms of trade, the real exchange rate has a significant negative effect regardless of a set of explanatory variables or, for that matter, the mathematical form of the equation.

Individual Commodity Price Equations

The same basic specifications utilised for Tables 15.5 and 15.6 are reported in Table 15.7 for the real world prices of wheat, coarse grains, rice, and cotton. The estimation method for each of these equations recognizes that the error terms are related and thus a generalised least-squares method of estimation is applied. For three of the equations more than 80 per cent of the variation in the real price series is explained by the set of explanatory variables while in one equation (coarse grains) the proportion explained is 78 per cent. Each equation is dynamically stable.

For all equations, the real exchange rate effect is insignificant. This result is not surprising given the importance of the United States as a producer and consumer of these primary commodities. The more important the role of the United States is, the less is the US dollar price adjustment to movements in the real dollar exchange rate.

For most of the individual commodity price equations, stock levels and current production dominate. The effects of interest rates are negative and significant for wheat and coarse grains but insignificant for cotton and rice. In some cases, the interaction between interest rates and stocks is positive and significant and in other cases it is insignificantly negative (rice and cotton).

The results for the external debt variable are as expected for all equations except perhaps for cotton. The external debt variable has a negative effect on wheat and rice prices, but an insignificant and positive effect on coarse grain prices. The quantitatively large and significant effect in the case of rice can be explained in part by the importance of the Philippines in world rice markets. The negative effect, although insignificant, in the case of wheat can be partially explained by the role of Argentina in world wheat markets. It is interesting to note that all three of the external debt variables are highly significant in each of the pricing equations for wheat, coarse grains, and rice when nonlinear trend variables are included in the equations. The outcome for cotton is also not robust under alternative specifications. The incorporation of a time trend will move the effect of the external debt on cotton prices to be insignificantly different from zero and for some specifications the effect of external debt on cotton prices can also be negative.

CONCLUDING REMARKS

In contrast to a number of previous empirical studies that focus only on industrial country commodity sector policies, or only on macroeconomic phenomenon, or only on external debt and economic structures of developing countries, this paper has examined the joint effects of these forces on commodity prices and alternative measures of the developing countries' terms of trade.

428

Except for the individual commodity price equations, the qualitative effects of all three sets of forces are consistent with *a priori* notions and are statistically significant.

The results reported in this paper stand in sharp contrast to those presented earlier by Dornbusch. He focussed only on the macroeconomic linkages with international commodity prices and non-oil developing countries' terms of trade. For the former, he obtained the implausible result that the flexibility of world commodity prices to real exchange rates exceeds unity. Our results also contradict the correction of Dornbusch's work offered by Cote. The most dramatic difference between our empirical results and those reported by Cote relates to the estimated effects of the real dollar exchange rate on developing countries' terms of trade. We obtain a significant negative effect while Cote reports a significant positive effect.

In the final analysis, the reduced form equations in this paper reflect all three major sets of forces that impinge upon world commodity markets:

   a)   Agriculture and food policy;

   b)   Conventional supply and demand forces; and

   c)   Macroeconomic linkages of exchange rates, interest rates, and economic growth.

The previous work of Dornbusch, Cote and others focuses on one or at most two of these major forces.

The simple theoretical framework advanced in the paper can be extended to a large system of dynamic econometric equations to evaluate formally partial or total liberalization of agriculture and food trade regimes in industrialised countries. In contrast to much of the literature on agricultural trade liberalization, however, such an assessment must recognise all three forces mentioned above. In particular, it is crucial to assess the sensitivity of the dynamic adjustment path resulting from any partial liberalization or reduced level of subsidisation of OECD countries to shocks arising from the macroeconomic linkages. The simple theoretical framework presented in this paper provides the foundation for empirical studies that can be conducted to capture the implications of such shocks on the liberalization adjustment paths.

Finally, to complete the empirical analysis conducted in this paper, an expanded set of individual commodities should be examined; particularly sugar, coffee, cocoa as well as other agricultural commodities. It is important to examine the robustness of the individual commodity price equations recorded here for commodities in which the United States is not a major player. In future research, alternative specifications will be evaluated and longer time periods will be investigated to determine how stable or robust the flexibility measures reported here are to different regimes that can be identified. The relevant regimes can be defined in accordance with alternative configurations of the three major forces: commodity policy, macroeconomic policy, and the economic structure of developing countries as it relates to external debt.

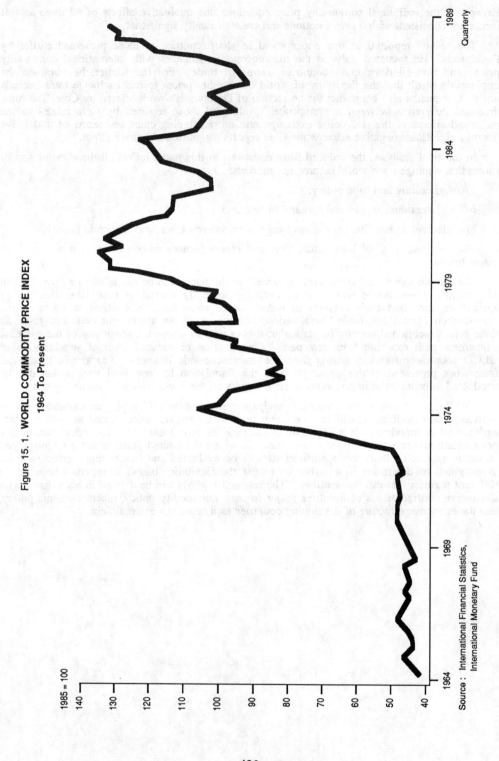

Figure 15.1. **WORLD COMMODITY PRICE INDEX**
1964 To Present

1985 = 100

Source : International Financial Statistics,
International Monetary Fund

430

Figure 15. 2. **WORLD COMMODITY PRICE INDEX DIVIDED BY THE U.S. PRODUCER PRICE INDEX**

1964 To Present

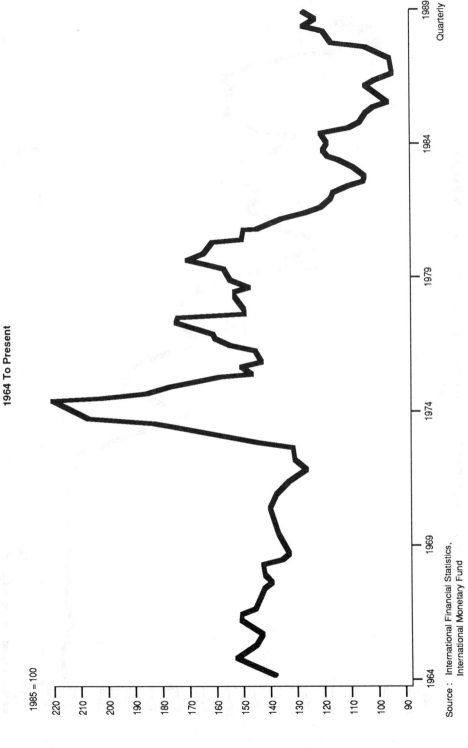

1985 = 100

Source : International Financial Statistics,
International Monetary Fund

431

Figure 15. 3. WORLD AGRICULTURAL RAW MATERIALS COMMODITY PRICE INDEX

1964 To Present

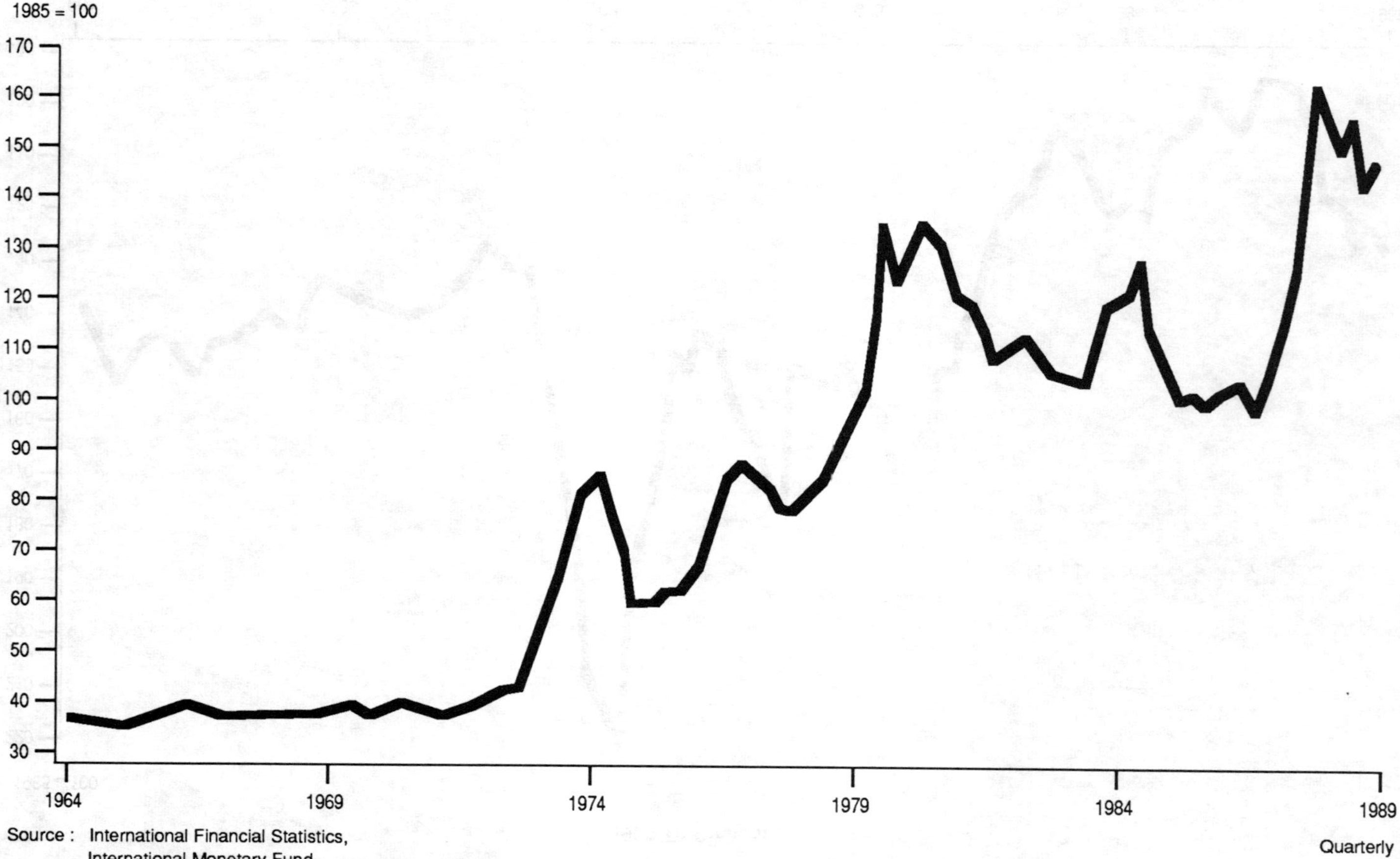

1985 = 100

Source : International Financial Statistics,
International Monetary Fund

Quarterly

432

Figure 15. 4. WORLD AGRICULTURAL RAW MATERIALS COMMODITY PRICE INDEX
DIVIDED BY THE U.S. PRODUCER PRICE INDEX

1964 To Present

1985 = 100

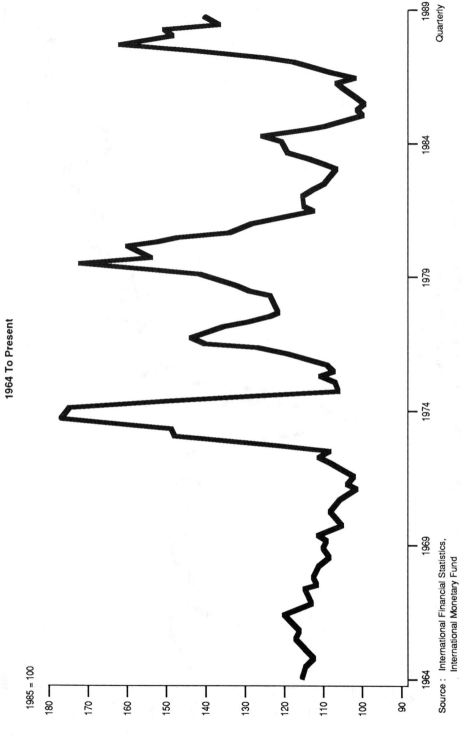

Quarterly

Source : International Financial Statistics,
International Monetary Fund

433

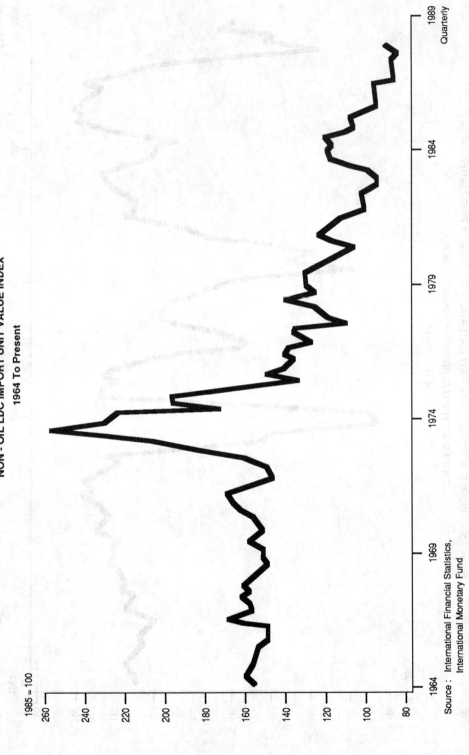

Figure 15. 5. WORLD COMMODITY PRICE INDEX FOR FOOD DIVIDED BY THE
NON - OIL LDC IMPORT UNIT VALUE INDEX

1964 To Present

1985 = 100

Source : International Financial Statistics,
International Monetary Fund

Quarterly

Figure 15. 6. **TERMS OF TRADE INDEX : NON - OIL DEVELOPING COUNTRIES**

1964 To Present

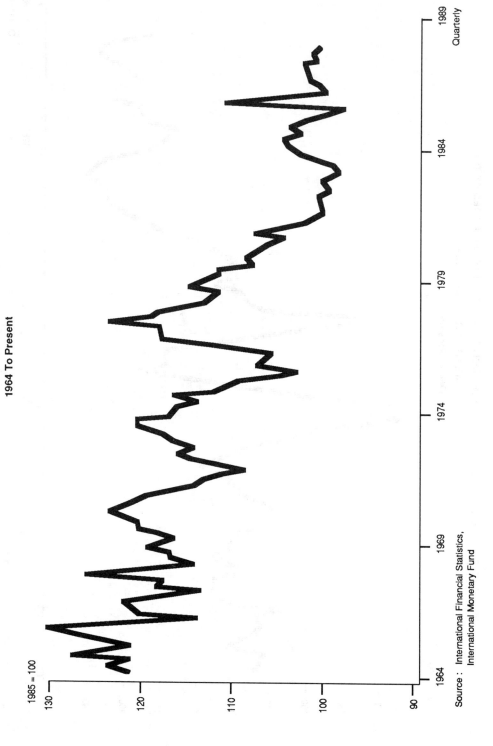

1985 = 100

Source : International Financial Statistics,
International Monetary Fund

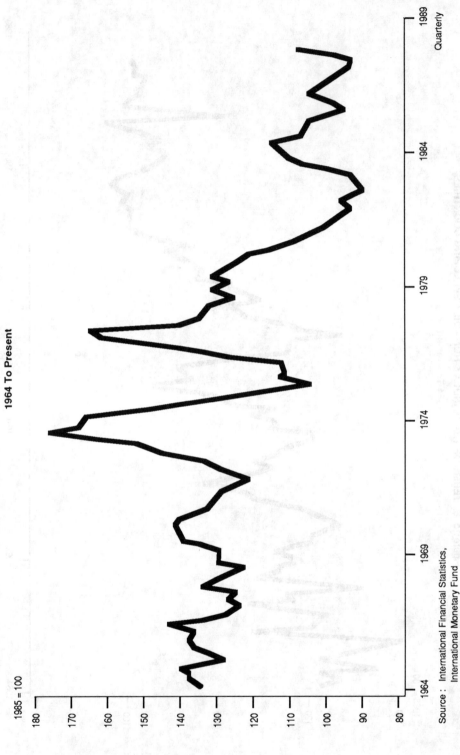

Figure 15. 7. DEVELOPING COUNTRY COMMODITY PRICE INDEX DIVIDED BY THE
NON - OIL LDC IMPORT UNIT VALUE INDEX

1964 To Present

Source : International Financial Statistics,
International Monetary Fund

436

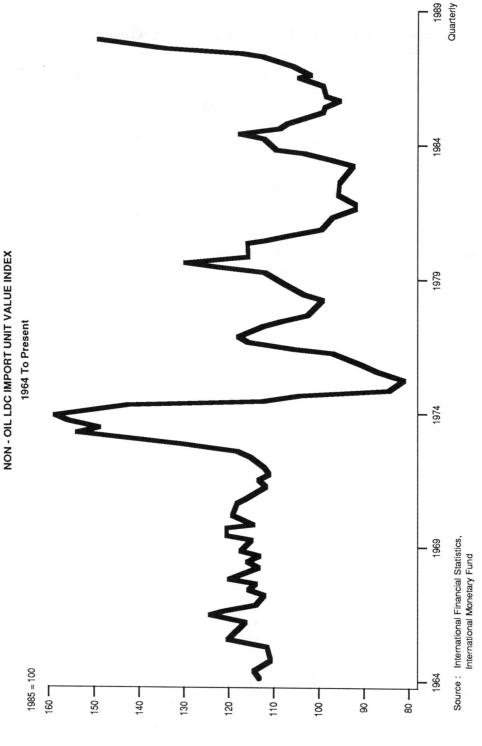

Figure 15. 8. WORLD AGRICULTURAL RAW MATERIALS COMMODITY PRICE INDEX DIVIDED BY THE NON - OIL LDC IMPORT UNIT VALUE INDEX

1964 To Present

1985 = 100

Source :   International Financial Statistics, International Monetary Fund

437

Table 15.1

AGRICULTURAL EXPORTS AS A PERCENT OF MERCHANDISE EXPORTS

	1980	1981	1982	1983	1984	1985
Thailand	33.2	31.1	32.6	33.2	31.4	28.3
Uruguay	21.5	24.6	27.8	22.7	21.2	21.5
Egypt	19.8	20.0	19.4	20.7	22.5	16.6
Guatemala	57.6	51.3	59.6	51.3	--	--
Paraguay	56.9	66.2	69.4	68.7	75.5	--

Source: International Trade Statistics Yearbook, 1986, vol. 1 (New York: United Nations, 1988).

Table 15.2

WORLD EXPORTS BY COUNTRY
(Percent of world exports)

	1980	1981	1982	1983	1984	1985	1986
Wheat							
Argentina	2.1	0.5	0.5	0.5	1.1	1.0	0.3
Corn (maize)							
Thailand	3.1	3.5	4.2	3.7	4.2	3.6	6.2
Argentina	0.8	1.6	1.5	8.2	7.4	9.9	9.7
Soybeans							
Brazil	--	--	1.8	4.6	11.5	16.6	7.3
Argentina	--	--	3.7	4.8	11.8	10.8	9.5
India	--	--	0	.03	.02	1	0
Paraguay	--	--	1.5	--	--	1.8	1.2
US	--	--	94.4	89.3	75.7	69.6	80.0
Rice							
Thailand	22.3	23.7	27.4	25.6	33.1	29.8	29.9
Burma	3.0	3.2	4.1	4.2	2.1	2.5	1.6
Uruguay	1.5	2.1	2.6	2.1	2.2	3.2	0.4
Cotton							
Egypt	6.5	8.2	7.5	8.1	7.8	8.4	11.0
Mexico	4.8	5.2	3.3	2.0	3.3	1.5	1.4
Guatemala	2.5	1.9	3.0	1.9	1.3	1.2	0.6
Paraguay	1.6	2.2	1.3	1.8	2.4	2.7	1.4

Source: International Trade Statistics Yearbook, 1986 (for 1982-86 data updates), vol. 2 (New York: United Nations, 1988).

Table 15.3

AGRICULTURE EXPORTS AS PERCENTAGE OF TOTAL EXPORTS

	1980	1981	1982	1983	1980-83 Average	1984	1985	1986
Argentina	38.7	45.7	40.1	--	41.5	49.0	47	43.3
Brazil	19.9	13.5	16.1	17.6	17.2	--	--	--
Egypt	19.8	20	19.4	20.7	19.7	22.5	16.6	--
Guatemala	57.6	51.3	59.6	51.3	54.4	--	--	--
Paraguay	56.9	66.2	69.4	68.7	61.2	75.5	--	--
Philippines	11.1	10.6	12	--	11.3	10.4	11.3	11.8
Thailand	33.2	31.1	32.6	--	33.2	31.4	28.3	--
Mexico	9.3	7.9	--	--	8.6	--	--	--
Uruguay	21.5	24.6	27.8	22.7	24.1	21.2	21.5	--

Sources : International Trade Statistics Yearbook, 1986 (for 1982-86 data updates), vol. 2 (New York: United Nations, 1988).

Table 15.4

SUMMARY OF SIGNED EFFECTS

Effect on world commodity prices	Shock							
	$\uparrow\lambda$	$\uparrow\alpha$	$\uparrow\tau^*$	$\uparrow y^*$	$\uparrow s^*$	$\uparrow r$	$\uparrow\beta$	$\uparrow y$
Debtor commodity-exporter	—	—	—	+	—	—	0	0
Debtor commodity-importer	—	—	—	0	0	—	—	+
Non-debtor commodity-exporter	—	0	—	+	—	—	0	0
Non-debtor commodity-importer	—	0	0	0	—	—	+	+

Table 15.5

IMPACT AND LONG-RUN FLEXIBILITIES FOR TOTAL COMMODITY AND AGRICULTURAL PRICES

Dependent variables	Constant	Explanatory variables							R^2	DW
		Exchange[a]	Interest[b]	IP[c]	Stocks[d]	Debt[e]	Inter[f]	Lag[g]		
Real commodity price										
Impact	4.12	-0.37	-0.08	0.18	-0.32	-0.19	0.01	0.42	0.94	1.3
(Standard error)	(1.13)	(0.11)	(0.08)	(0.28)	(0.16)	(0.12)	(0.01)	(0.08)		
Long-run		-0.63	-0.13	0.31	-0.55	-0.32	0.02			
Real agricultural price										
Impact	2.31	-0.33	-0.17	0.33	-0.25	-0.12	0.03	0.78	0.91	1.3
(Standard error)	(0.98)	(0.11)	(0.08)	(0.26)	(0.15)	(0.11)	(0.01)	(0.08)		
Long-run		-1.50	-0.77	1.50	-1.13	-0.54	0.13			

a   US real exchange rate.
b   Nominal US interest rate.
c   Industrial production, industrial countries.
d   Stocks of commodities.
e   External debt.
f   Interaction between interest rate and commodity stocks.
g   Lagged dependent variables.

Table 15.6

IMPACT AND LONG-RUN FLEXIBILITIES FOR NON-OIL DEVELOPING COUNTRIES' TERMS OF TRADE

Dependent variables	Constant	Explanatory variables							R^2	DW
		Exchange[a]	Interest[b]	IP[c]	Stocks[d]	Debt[e]	Inter[f]	Lag[g]		
Total terms of trade										
Impact	5.05	-0.20	-0.01	-0.32	-0.11	-0.23	0.01	0.41	0.96	1.3
(Standard error)	(1.26)	(0.13)	(0.09)	(0.45)	(0.17)	(0.12)	(0.02)	(0.06)		
Long-run		-0.34	-0.02	0.54	-0.18	-0.39	0.02			
Commodity terms of trade										
Impact	5.03	-0.24	-0.09	0.06	-0.33	-0.19	0.01	0.05	0.96	1.4
(Standard error)	(1.60)	(0.16)	(0.12)	(0.40)	(0.23)	(0.19)	(0.02)	(0.02)		
Long-run		-0.25	-0.09	0.06	-0.34	-0.20	0.01			
Agricultural/Raw materials terms of trade										
Impact	4.65	-0.44	-0.21	0.30	-0.41	-0.21	0.03	0.51	0.95	1.2
(Standard error)	(1.26)	(0.14)	(0.09)	(0.32)	(0.19)	(0.13)	(0.01)	(0.07)		
Long-run		-0.89	-0.42	0.61	0.83	-0.42	-0.06			

a US real exchange rate.
b Nominal US interest rate.
c Industrial production, industrial countries.
d Stocks of commodities.
e External debt.
f Interaction between interest rate and commodity stocks.
g Lagged dependent variables.

Table 15.7

IMPACT AND LONG-RUN FLEXIBILITIES FOR WORLD WHEAT, COARSE GRAIN, RICE AND COTTON PRICES

Dependant variables	Constant	Exchange[a]	Interest[b]	IP[c]	Output	Debt[d]	Inter[e]	Lag[f]	R^2	DW
Wheat prices										
Impact	2.57	0.02	-0.39	-0.94	0.44	-0.10	0.09	0.36	0.85	1.8
(Standard error)	(1.72)	(0.02)	(0.13)	(0.27)	(0.41)	(0.10)	(0.02)	(0.11)		
Long-run		0.03	-0.60	-1.51	0.68	-1.62	0.14			
Coarse grain prices										
Impact	6.20	0.01	-0.14	-0.34	-0.78	0.08	0.03	0.57	0.78	2.2
(Standard error)	(2.69)	(0.02)	(0.08)	(0.18)	(0.48)	(0.10)	(0.02)	(0.16)		
Long-run		0.02	-0.32	-0.79	-1.81	0.18	0.07			
Rice prices										
Impact	4.65	-0.02	0.15	0.35	-0.33	-0.41	-0.04	0.33	0.87	1.3
(Standard error)	(1.07)	(0.02)	(0.10)	(0.33)	(0.08)	(0.06)	(0.06)	(0.07)		
Long-run		-0.03	0.02	0.53	0.50	-0.62	-0.18			
Cotton prices										
Impact	2.99	-0.02	0.01	-0.26	-0.99	0.27	0.00	0.41	0.84	1.7
(Standard error)	(1.40)	(0.02)	(0.10)	(0.24)	(0.34)	(0.09)	(0.03)	(0.14)		
Long-run		-0.03	-0.02	0.44	-1.67	0.46	0.00			

Explanatory variables

a   US real exchange rate.
b   Nominal US interest rate.
c   Industrial production, industrial countries.
d   External debt.
e   Interaction between interest rate and commodity stocks.
f   Lagged dependent variables.

BIBLIOGRAPHY

BOSWORTH, B.P. and R.Z. LAWRENCE, Commodity Prices and the New Inflation, Washington, D.C.: The Brookings Institution, 1982.

CHAMBERS, R. and R. JUST, "An Investigation of the Effect on Monetary Factors on U.S. Agriculture," *Journal Monetary Economics*, Vol. 9, 1982.

COTE, A., "The Link Between the U.S. Dollar Real Exchange Rate, Real Primary Commodity Prices, and LDCs' Terms of Trade," *Review of Economics and Statistics,* Vol. 44, No. 3, August 1987.

DORNBUSCH, R., "Policy and Performance Links Between Developing Country Debtors and Industrial Nations," Brookings Papers on Economic Activity, Vol. 2, 1985.

FRANKEL, J.A., "Expectations and Commodity Price Dynamics: The Overshooting Model," *American Journal of Agricultural Economics,* Vol. 68, No. 2, December 1984.

GILBERT, C.L., "The Impact of Exchange Rates and Developing Country Debt on Commodity Prices," *Economic Journal*, Vol. 99, September 1989.

HWA, E.C. "Price Determination in Several International Primary Commodity Markets: A Structural Analysis," International Monetary Fund Staff Papers, 26:1, 1979.

INTERNATIONAL MONETARY FUND, Primary Commodities: Market Developments and Outlook, Washington, D.C., May, 1987.

LAWRENCE, C. and R.Z. LAWRENCE, "Global Commodity Prices and Financial Markets: Theory and Evidence," working paper, December 1981.

LOO, T. and E. TOWER, "Agricultural Protectionism and the Less Developed Countries: The Relationship Between Agricultural Prices, Debt Servicing Capacities and the Need for Development Aid," Macro-economic Consequences of Farm Support Policies, Centre for International Economics, Canberra, 1988.

RAUSSER, G.C. and M. ROSE, "The Effects of US Macro and Micro Policies on LDC Debtors: Measuring Commodity Price Linkages," unpublished, University of California, Berkeley, May 1988.

RAUSSER, G.C., J. CHALFANT, H.A. LOVE, and K.G. STAMOULIS, "Macroeconomic Linkages, Taxes, and Subsidies in the U.S. Agricultural Sector," *American Journal of Agricultural Economics*, Vol. 68, May 1986.

ROBINSON, S., M. KILKENNY, and I. ADELMAN, "The Effect of Trade Liberalization in Agriculture on the U.S. Economy: Projections to 1991," Macro-economic Consequences of Farm-support Policies, Centre for International Ecnomics, Canberra, 1988.

STOECKEL, A. and J. BRECKLING, "Some Economy-wide Effects of Agricultural Policies in the European Community: A General Equilibrium Study," Macro-economic Consequences of Farm-support Policies, Centre for International Economics, Canberra, 1988.

TYERS, R. and K. ANDERSON, "Distortions in World Food Markets: A Quantitative Assessment," prepared for the World Bank, World Development Report 1986, Washington, D.C., January 1986.

VALDÉS, A. and J. ZIETZ, "Agricultural Protection in OECD countries: Its Costs to Less-Developed Countries," International Food Policy Research Institute, Research Report No. 21, December 1980.

ZIETZ, J. and A. VALDÉS, "The Costs of Protectionism to Developing Countries," World Bank Staff Working Papers, No. 769, 1986.

Part IV

DISCUSSANT NOTES

Chapter 16

DISCUSSANT'S CONTRIBUTIONS

GLOBAL PARTIAL EQUILIBRIUM MODELS AND THE ANALYSIS OF AGRICULTURAL TRADE LIBERALIZATION

by

David Blandford

In recent years, several world models of agricultural markets have been constructed in order to evaluate the effects of liberalizing agricultural policies. Typically, these models have a partial equilibrium (supply/demand) structure. They differ in country and commodity coverage, in the detail with which they treat individual countries, whether they are static or dynamic, and the way in which they represent agricultural policies. The purpose of this note is to comment on the characteristics of these models and the information which they generate, and to identify future priorities for model development.

Global partial equilibrium models have primarily been constructed to provide insight into the implications for domestic and international agricultural markets of existing and alternative agricultural policies. The models generate information on the effects of such policies on domestic supply, demand, and prices; the volume of international trade and "world market" prices. This information is often used to compute partial equilibrium welfare measures such as producers' and consumers' surplus. An important characteristic of these models is their ability to capture the price effects of policy changes across related commodities, through substitution in supply and demand, and among countries through the trade linkage. The models do not typically analyse the effects of policies on trade flows between individual countries, but on aggregate net imports or exports. The information which different models provide on these factors is determined largely by their structure and the way in which agricultural policies are incorporated.

Structural Characteristics

Major structural differences between models are in four areas:

a) Commodity coverage;

b) Country coverage;

c) Temporal properties; and

d) The "partiality" of their partial equilibria.

In many cases commodity coverage is related to country coverage. Models which have been built primarily to analyse the effects of agricultural policies in industrial countries tend to neglect

449

"minor" commodities, those which have negligible production in these countries or which are not subject to significant government intervention. Only when such commodities are significant substitutes in consumption for those produced in industrial countries (e.g., the fats and oils group, or manioc in the EC) are they usually included. Consequently, many commodities of interest to developing country exporters receive cursory treatment.

The models typically treat commodities as being homogeneous. For an importer, wheat from Canada, for example, is considered to be a perfect substitute for wheat from the EC. This simplification implies that only the behaviour of net trade can be analysed, even though many countries have both imports and exports of a commodity group and imports from different suppliers may not be perfect substitutes. An empirical evaluation of variation in such imports and exports is only possible if commodities are treated as imperfect substitutes. Interrelationships between commodities are reflected by cross-price elasticities, but these do not always meet theoretical restrictions, such as symmetry and homogeneity. Differences in the assumed values of elasticities between models can be an important determinant of differences in results.

Country coverage is often related to commodity coverage. Where the focus is primarily on industrial countries, developing and centrally planned economies often receive cursory treatment. One of the major reasons for this is the difficulty of obtaining information on market parameters and policies in such countries. Work to rectify this problem should be a high priority for the future, a point which is amplified below.

A further important structural characteristic is the temporal property of the models. Many are static with "medium-term" elasticities. Only a few are dynamic. This means that the models as a whole provide limited information on stability, frequently an important concern of developing countries. They also cannot determine the time path of the effects of changes in policy or evaluate the phasing of policy reform. Frequently, it is not only important to know the end result of a particular change in policy, but also what might happen along the way. The phasing of policy change and the implications of alternative policies for domestic and international market stability are important issues for both developed and developing countries.

Finally, there is the issue of how partial are the partial equilibrium assumptions in the models. Static models do not incorporate the effects of changes in such factors as income, except through comparative statistics. Dynamic models have to deal with changes in income and other shift factors, but these are typically treated as exogenous. Changes in input prices are typically excluded, although there is some ongoing work in this area. All models incorporate exchange rates which can be varied exogenously. One particularly important issue in the context of developing countries, is that changes in the agricultural sector may themselves have implications for income and the economy as a whole and hence further second round implications for agriculture. Also macroeconomic policies, particularly exchange rate regimes, have a major influence on agriculture and agricultural trade in many developing countries.

Treatment of Policy

One of the crucial aspects of the partial models is the way in which they represent domestic agricultural and trade policies. The most popular approach has been to express the aggregate effect of policy as a tariff equivalent or wedge between domestic and world prices. One of the simplest approaches is to compute the difference between a domestic price and an international reference price, possibly adjusting for transportation costs and marketing margins, and attribute this difference to the effects of domestic policies. A slightly less crude approach is to estimate the value of producer support (or consumer tax) per unit of output using a combination of domestic/international price comparisons and government expenditure data, and express these as a Producer Subsidy Equivalent (PSE) and a Consumer Subsidy Equivalent (CSE). These can handle instruments whose effects are not reflected directly in market prices, such as input subsidies, but a decision must be made as to how such subsidies actually influence incentive prices. Models differ (and are often obscure) as to how they treat margins between domestic and international reference prices. This is not a trivial issue, since the structure of margins and the level to which model elasticities correspond (retail, wholesale, farm level) can affect substantially the potential response of production, consumption and trade to changes in policy.

All models make explicit or implicit assumptions about the degree to which changes in international prices are transmitted to domestic prices. Such assumptions can have a major impact on the results obtained. The only way to deal effectively with this price transmission question, and the differential effects of policies on incentive prices is to incorporate specific policy instruments into the models. This is time consuming, requires substantial detailed knowledge about the way in which policies operate in individual countries, and can often lead to models which are computationally difficult to solve. It is, therefore, not surprising that progress on the more accurate representation of policies in global models has been limited.

Future Priorities

It is very easy to be critical of existing models. However, these models take a substantial amount of time and effort to construct. Even in their simplest forms they are extremely information intensive. Despite their limitations, the models have made a major contribution to increasing public understanding of the domestic and international implications of agricultural policies. Important cross-commodity and transnational effects of agricultural programmes are highlighted by such models. The inefficiency of many existing programmes is made clear. The particular empirical results obtained differ for numerous reasons, including differences in structure and base period, and in assumptions about the effects of national policies. It is important to examine why such differences arise, particularly when these are in key areas, such as the direction of price changes. Whether it is possible to resolve these differences, typically depends on the ability of analysts to agree on assumptions. Sometimes such agreement is difficult to achieve.

If we are prepared to live with the basic partial equilibrium assumptions of the models (a point which is highly debatable in the context of developing countries) the major priorities for the future are as follows:

a) *Access to information:* it is important to have relatively complete information on a model and the results which it generates, if these are to be useful. If the model is simply a black box, it is of little value to policy makers or to those charged with advising policy makers. Although it is tedious and time consuming to prepare and maintain model documentation and to provide full information on results, particularly when most model builders are prone to regular tinkering with model structure and assumptions, the provision of adequate information is an essential condition for a model to be useful.

b) *Sensitivity analysis:* it is often unclear how sensitive models are to basic assumptions. Although some limit must be placed on sensitivity analysis, it is important for the modeller and potential users to know if particular parameters or policy assumptions, about which there is uncertainty, can cause major qualitative changes in results.

c) *Improved treatment of policy:* the next and most essential phase of development in the models should be an improved representation of policies. Price wedges or PSE/CSEs are simply not enough. They do not capture important discontinuities in the effects of policies nor the differing effects of alternative policies on the linkage between domestic and international markets. Measures of support, such as PSEs, will continue to be useful in their own right, but it is time for modellers to move on to the difficult but potentially rewarding area of incorporating individual policy instruments and instrument combinations in their models.

d) *Better treatment of non-industrial country commodities and markets:* this is a major issue for the relevance of the models for developing countries, and also in improving assessments of the effects of policies in industrial countries. Developing and centrally planned countries are an increasingly important force in many commodity markets. The cursory treatment which they receive in most models limits the ability of the models to capture the effects of changes in policies, either in industrial countries, or in non-industrial countries. Although it is often extremely difficult to obtain the necessary information to be able to model commodity markets and policies in non-industrial countries, it is necessary to tackle this problem if we are to be able to provide more accurate and realistic assessments of the international implications of domestic policies.

THE ROLE OF PARTIAL EQUILIBRIUM AGRICULTURAL MODELS

by

L. Alan Winters

This note is part of a long tradition of comments written in the absence of a paper. It breaks with tradition, however, by seeking not to disguise the fact, but rather to exploit it in order to make an unprovoked defence of the models we have considered in this session. In recent years much effort has been devoted to the development of computable general equilibrium (CGE) models of agricultural policy. Such effort has been well-directed and valuable, but occasionally it seems to have blinded us to the contribution that partial equilibrium models continue to make to policy analysis. This note offers a brief pre-emptive defence of such models. It is not "against" general equilibrium, but it is "for" partial equilibrium.

The past few years have seen several computable general equilibrium analyses of agricultural policy — e.g., Burniaux and Martin (1989), Trela, Whalley and Wigle (1987), and Parikh (1987). Their arrival on the scene stems partly from the growth of computing power (both hardware and software) which has suddenly rendered such models technically feasible, and partly from a belief that agricultural policy is sufficiently distortionary and agriculture sufficiently significant that general equilibrium interactions should be taken into account. I have no quarrel with either point, and would add that general equilibrium has been one of the economics profession's finest contributions to the human intellectual heritage and should certainly be exploited for all it is worth. That said, however, CGE models should not relegate all partial equilibrium analysis to second-class status. Economists, more than any other profession, know that life — including model building — is about tradeoffs. Thus the relevant question is what do partial equilibrium analyses give us that general equilibrium cannot? The answer is focus. In an ideal world it may be possible to build CGE models encapsulating every conceivable detail of the economy — although it could be asked whether we would need to build models at all if we attained such omniscience — but even then there would be a high price in terms of complexity and opacity. Until that point, however, we shall certainly have to trade generality for focus, and the tradeoff depends on the question being posed.

In the terms used by agricultural model builders, the distinguishing feature between general and partial equilibrium is the former's recognition *and quantification* of the consequences of shocks in one sector for outcomes in another, and the possible second round feedbacks from those effects back to the original sector. The difference does not reside in international interactions — which are mechanically analogous to intersectoral interactions — nor does it reside merely in the recognition that other sectors must be affected by agricultural shocks, for that is implicit in agriculture's downward-sloping demand curves and upward-sloping factor supply curves, and also in the welfare calculations that partial equilibrium analysts frequently conduct. The issue resides in the explicit modelling of the non-agricultural sector.

Thus the unique contribution of general equilibrium models of agricultural policy lies in results such as OECD's observation that the *Common Agricultural Policy* (CAP) has increased EC processed food exports by 84 per cent and reduced other exports by 14 per cent, Burniaux and Martin (1989). Such results are inherently interesting and potentially useful in pointing out the (sectoral) distributional consequences of agricultural policy. CGE modelling's contribution is not primarily its overall welfare calculations, for partial equilibrium calculations will be seriously misleading only if agricultural policy causes material changes in the prices of other goods or of factors of production. Now it is likely that some other prices will be significantly affected by agricultural distortions, but in general only the prices of goods and factors intimately related to agriculture — for example, fertilizers and farm machinery. But no CGE model is able to operate at this level. So far as other goods are concerned, the impact of agricultural policy is likely to be rather small, for in most industrial countries — which are the usual concern of CGE modelling — agriculture accounts for less than 5 per cent of GNP, and many goods are traded on world markets, which further insulates their prices from domestic agricultural shocks. However, for developing countries, with their much greater agricultural dependence, CGE modelling is necessary for welfare calculations and probably also for positive analysis.

Returning to industrial countries, partial equilibrium models are able to move down to a fairly detailed level within the agricultural sector. Thus, for example, the model used by Tyers and Anderson and the OECD's MTM model use input/output relationships between agricultural products and the substitutability in production between products (competition for scarce land). Agricultural policy is made at a commodity level, and the spillovers from one sector to another are important, especially when one is exploring international implications. Thus, for example, the transmission of the CAP from cereal protection to beef production to the demand for non-grain protein and thence to vegetable oils is important, but it only involves agriculture.

The simplification of the partial equilibrium framework also allows researchers to model policy more precisely. Thus quantitative restrictions can be modelled directly rather than via tariff equivalents. The existing multisectoral partial equilibrium models adopt PSEs or tariff equivalents too readily, and although the doyen of general equilibrium modellers, John Whalley, has made significant progress on modelling set asides, Whalley (1989), further progress will be easier in a partial, rather than a general, framework. The correct modelling of policy is surely one of the principal issues for future work to address.

A third area on which partial equilibrium allows focus is estimation. By adopting a simpler simulation framework, partial equilibrium modellers sometimes leave themselves more time for the careful estimation of the important parameters of economic behaviour. Such estimation is the only point of contact between policy simulation models and the real world on which they comment, for we have no other means of detecting whether the models' theoretical structures are relevant or their policy prescriptions appropriate. Now CGE modellers are not precluded from careful estimation, nor partial equilibrium modellers obliged to adopt it, but we all face time and resource constraints. Estimation is difficult and frustrating, but that is a reason to devote more, not less, resources to it.

The simplest partial equilibrium model, with no intra-agricultural or international linkages is too simple for most practical policy purposes.

But once such generalisations are made, and when suitable supply functions for factors of production are incorporated, then a partial equilibrium model of the agricultural sector is an excellent tool of analysis. It enables us to understand how agricultural policies distort economies and what it lacks in linkages to other sectors it gains through detailed treatment of agriculture.

To summarise, my comments are not "against" general equilibrium models — an important part of our armoury; they are merely "for" partial equilibrium analysis. We would not denigrate the passenger airliner just because it is possible to send a spacecraft to Neptune.

BIBLIOGRAPHY

BURNIAUX, J. and J. MARTIN, "Economy-wide Effects of Agricultural Policies in OECD Countries: A GE approach Using the WALRAS Model", OECD/World Bank Symposium on *Agricultural Trade Liberalization: Implications for Developing Countries,* Paris, October 1989.

PARIKH, K.S. *et al., Towards Free Trade in Agriculture,* Nijhoff, Amsterdam, 1987.

TRELA, I., J. WHALLEY and R. WIGLE, "International Trade in Agriculture: Domestic Policies, Trade Conflicts and Negotiating Options", Working Paper 8618C, Department of Economics, University of Western Ontario, London, Canada, 1986.

WHALLEY, J. and R. WIGLE, "Terms of Trade Effects, Agricultural Liberalization and Developing Countries", OECD/World Bank Symposium on *Agricultural Trade Liberalization: Implications for the Developing Countries,* Paris, October 1989.

THE USE OF GENERAL EQUILIBRIUM MODELS FOR THE ASSESSMENT OF THE IMPACT OF AGRICULTURAL TRADE LIBERALIZATION

by

K.J. Munk

The Criteria

As a tool for policy analysis within an international governmental institution models should be relevant, transparent, flexible and verifiable.

Relevance

For a model to be relevant as a tool in advising policy makers the model must represent the goal variables which are relevant from the point of view of the value judgements of the policy maker and the policy instruments which the policy maker controls or is able to influence. The model must also represent those variables which are not under the control of the decision maker but which may significantly influence the goal variables. The structure of the model must correspond to the structural characteristics of the system which imposes the major constraints of the decision maker's possibility of obtaining desired values of the goal variables.

Goal Variables

A relevant model must represent the goal variables and the tradeoff between the goal variables which are relevant from the point of view of the policy maker. Generally speaking, policy makers dealing with agricultural policy issues are interested in the problems related to structural adjustment, real income variability due to fluctuating agricultural prices and the impact of policy changes on the real income of producers (farmers), consumers and the government budget (taxpayers). The issues which concern policy makers in developed and in developing countries are, however, quite different. For policy makers in developed countries the major issue is the pressure which rapid technological progress in agriculture combined with small demand price elasticities imposes on the agricultural sector. Government intervention here may be seen as based on the perceived tradeoff between the decrease in adaptation costs in the short term and the increases in distortional costs in the long term. For policy makers in developing countries the major policy issue is food security and the role to be played by the agricultural sector in the growth strategy of these countries.

Policy Instruments

A relevant model must be able to represent the policy instruments which the decision maker controls in a rather faithful way. The government intervenes in relation to agricultural policy issues with a wide range of policy instruments: producer taxes/subsidies, border measures, quantitative restrictions, etc. Government intervention in agriculture relates to a wide range of commodities and is often rather complex. The type of governmental intervention to be represented often differs significantly from one commodity to another.

Major Constraints

A relevant model must represent the major constraints on the decision maker's possibilities of obtaining the desired values of his or her goal variables. The possibilities of policy makers attaining their objectives are clearly constrained by the physical production structure. The information constraints are, however, also important in particular in developing countries. Tax instruments which are desirable from the point of view of their effect on resource allocation are not used in developing countries because the implied costs in information gathering, information processing and enforcement would be prohibitive. This is even the case for certain tax instruments in developed countries. Lump sum taxes based on people's intrinsic possibility for earning income fall in this category. General taxes such as income taxes and value added taxes are often not feasible in developing countries, which are therefore forced to use highly distorting taxes such as border taxes. The budgetary implications of changes in government policies are of major importance for decision makers in developing countries due to the high opportunity cost of government revenue.

The question is to what extent AGE models are relevant in the ways defined above.

Analyses based on the use of applied general equilibrium models are often made in a comparative static framework. Such models may be well suited to deal with the impact of policy changes on consumers, producers and taxpayers in the long run. However, such models are not relevant for assessing the tradeoff between short-term benefits and long-term costs of government intervention nor for the analysis of issues related to uncertainty or the structural changes due to technological progress. AGE models may represent the time dimension, but the costs in terms of further technical complexity are considerable. A question of major policy relevance is whether the trend in agricultural prices in the medium term will be decreasing, as has been the case in the last 200 years, or whether the pressure of an increasing world population will be stronger than the effect of technological changes. Static AGE models contribute very little to answering this question. The same is true for the questions of how the relative prices between tropical products, northern crops and animal products will evolve in the coming years. However, these matters are clearly important for the way world income distribution will develop.

Government policies are often represented in AGE models only by price wedges and often commodities which are treated quite differently are aggregated together. The technical complexity and the data requirements mean that it is difficult in AGE to represent the complexity of government policy intervention faithfully.

The strong point of AGE models is their ability to reflect the physical constraints on government action. AGE models can represent the interaction between different sectors due to the consumption of intermediate inputs and common resource constraints. But even here there are problems in the case of modelling the agricultural sector. Multi-output multi-input production functions used in AGE models in general impose input/output separability, which is not realistic.

Applied general equilibrium models, however, do not represent the constraints in information gathering, information processing and enforcement which are important in assessing the cost of obtaining government revenue. Sometimes even the distortional costs of obtaining government revenue are not well represented either. Certain AGE models, where the government is either assumed to be able to make lump sum transfers or to be able to tax a fixed factor (often total labour supply is assumed fixed), may lead to policy recommendations which are grossly misleading. AGE models, in general, do not represent the fluctuations in the real income of producers and consumers due to agricultural price fluctuation. This limits the relevance of policy recommendations derived using such models for countries with many small farmers who are not well integrated with financial institutions and for poor developing countries where the variance of food costs is an important issue. In judging the relevance of AGE models one would be aware that many partial models have the same pitfalls in terms of relevance as

AGE models. However, the point is that more partial models, by definition, are less complex in terms of representation of the rest of the economy. More *ad hoc* assumptions to represent the various aspects mentioned above may therefore be introduced in partial models without going beyond the point where the models become so complex that they are nearly as difficult to understand as the real world. This is a danger with AGE models if one wants to make them more "realistic".

Transparency

A model is transparent if the policy adviser using the model is able to trace the results generated by the model in the sense that he or she can identify which (simplifying) assumptions are crucial for particular results. All models represent a simplification of reality. Pushed beyond certain boundaries the model will produce unreasonable results. It is important that the policy adviser is able to recognise these boundaries. Theoretical consistency is an important element in making a model transparent. Many AGE models are constructed strictly within a neoclassical paradigm. This tends to make these models rather transparent (at least for the policy advisor with a standard economic background). The structure of a standard AGE model is, however, so complex that even in this case it might be difficult for a policy adviser without profound knowledge of general equilibrium theory and welfare economics to identify the crucial assumptions for certain results. To take an example: AGE models often make the seemingly innocent simplifying assumption that the supply of aggregate labour is fixed. This implies that raising government revenue by a tax on labour has no distortional costs. This in turn implies that a price change replacing price support with deficiency payments increases economic welfare significantly. If the administrative and distortional costs of raising government revenue had been recognised in the model this would not necessarily have been the case. The neoclassical assumptions are widely recognised not to be realistic. Thus there is a temptation to introduce *ad hoc* assumptions to represent aspects of reality about which there is no consensus on how to represent them in a theoretical fashion. Certain AGE models have introduced factor market imperfections in the neoclassical framework. Other models have introduced imperfect competition. Such modifications, which in all cases represent gross simplifications of reality, can therefore be made in a number of different ways with different and important implications for model behaviour. Theoretical consistency is important for parameter specification. In specifying a multi-input multi-output production structure a number of theoretical results may be used to restrict the matrix of elasticities. In general, this is not possible in a partial equilibrium model where elasticities to a certain extent reflect the rate of adaptation of primary factors which are not represented in the model. The implication of *ad hoc* assumptions may, on the other hand, be more transparent in partial equilibrium models.

Flexibility

The search for general equilibrium models which may be used to analyse a broad range of agricultural policy issues has proven to be an incorrect strategy. Smaller models more closely tailored to the policy issue in question have been more useful. But even in the case of small AGE models a considerable amount of work has to be devoted to create a consistent data base. In order to have a suitable CGE model data have to be gathered and parameters specified for parts of the economy not directly relevant for the issue in question. How the economy outside the agricultural sector is modelled may have important implications for the behaviour of the model, as we saw above, and therefore cannot be neglected. The cost of general equilibrium model analysis may be reduced by creating a general data base which may serve as a source of information for several applications. Experience shows, however, that the costs of setting up such a data base are considerable and even with such a data base policy analysis based on an

AGE model is a major exercise. AGE models therefore cannot be considered a very flexible tool for policy analysis.

Verifiability

Most AGE models are static. This poses a major difficulty in confronting results obtained with such models with reality. This is particularly true when such models are used to analyse agricultural policy issues where the effect of technological change is important. The empirical evidence available concerning elasticities are in general not directly relevant for the elasticities to be specified in general equilibrium models. The truth is that the elasticities used in static AGE models may be specified within a broad range without contradicting existing empirical evidence. This might not be a major problem when AGE models are used to illustrate a theoretical point, but it poses a major problem for the credibility of quantitative assessment of the effect of specific policy options on which decisions have to be taken. The validation of AGE models is the major obstacle to the use of AGE models for policy analysis in governmental institutions which, as far as I can see, can only be overcome if AGE models become dynamic. However, it is not clear that this is possible if the complexity of these models is to be kept within reasonable bounds.

Conclusion

The instinct of any theoretical economist is that agricultural policy analysis should be made on the basis of general equilibrium models rather than partial equilibrium models since the interaction between the many agricultural commodities is important. It is thus understandable that there is a considerable interest in general equilibrium modelling. However, the points mentioned above explain why AGE models are not yet used by government agencies on a regular basis for policy analysis, as is the case of macroeconomic models.

It seems that in the immediate future it will not be possible to construct AGE models which can supply results which can form the basis for making decisions on agricultural policy.

It is too difficult to incorporate sufficient details concerning policy instruments and at the same time represent the time dimension. Representing the time dimension implies not only taking into account technological change but also the different adoption speed to price changes for various agricultural products and agricultural sector inputs. On the other hand, it also seems that the limitations of traditional supply and demand models are even more evident than those of AGE models. These models have played a useful role in drawing the attention of policy makers to the economic aspect of agricultural policies, but the theoretical and empirical deficiencies of such models are all too apparent when attempts are made to quantify the effects of agricultural policy changes. The types of models which national and international government agencies need to assess the effects of agricultural policy reform and the impact of international agricultural trade agreements would be a hybrid between the general equilibrium models and dynamic partial equilibrium models. The full representation of the agricultural sector, i.e., modelling of all agricultural products, intermediate input and primary factors requires that such sector models should have a time dimension so that the effect of technical change on the slow adaptation of the primary factors employed in the agricultural sector can be represented explicitly. In order to represent policy instruments adequately and represent the linkages which are the most essential for assessing the effects of agricultural policy changes, it is also important to supplement such agricultural sector models with a representation of the principal upstream and downstream sectors, household consumption, external trade and government budget flows. However, it seems that these supplementary elements need not be modelled with the full rigour of general equilibrium theory.

The appropriate modelling of the agricultural sector is not a trivial task. The agricultural sector needs a multi-input multi-output representation without imposing the unrealistic restriction of output/input separability. There seems to exist no satisfactory functional form which has this property and which globally satisfies all theoretical conditions. However, a lot of progress has been made in formulating and estimating flexible functional forms. From the point of view of creating models to be used for agricultural policy analysis in governmental institutions, it seems more important to attempt to incorporate the results of this effort in dynamic multisector models than to use the resources in constructing static AGE models with an unrealistic representation of the agricultural sector.

POLICY IMPLICATIONS OF MODEL RESULTS

by

Kym Anderson

What have we learnt from the model results that are now available? Leaving aside trade of tropical agricultural products, whose liberalization would obviously benefit developing countries, there are at least four things we can say clearly about liberalization of food policies by the OECD countries:

a) It would cause international food prices to be higher than otherwise would be the case, estimates varying from 15 to 30 per cent on average depending on the range of food commodities included and the period in which the liberalization occurs;

b) It would reduce the instability of prices in international food markets, by as much as one third on average and one half for wheat;

c) If some of the increase in international food prices were to be transmitted to developing country markets, the vast majority of the world's poor, namely farm families in those countries, would be better off following liberalization by OECD countries; and

d) If productivity growth in agriculture is reasonably price responsive, the gains to food producers would more than offset the loss to consumers of food in many developing countries and foreign exchange would increase, so that such countries gain overall in net welfare terms.

Even so, governments of developing countries have been reluctant to support the inclusion of food policy in the Uruguay Round. This is because they give more weight to the interests of their urban industrialists and consumers than to their farmers. This is revealed by the presence in most developing countries of food consumer subsidies and of much higher effective rates of assistance to industrial as compared with agricultural production. Therefore, it has tended to be ignored in the past that most developing countries would gain overall from food policy liberalization by OECD countries, and that the gain would be even greater if developing countries liberalized their own anti-agricultural policies.

There are four features of the current environment, however, which may encourage developing countries to rethink their indifference to or antagonism towards liberalization of world food markets. The first is their chronic debt situation. The massive debt service obligations of many developing countries is forcing them to look for ways to expand rapidly their net foreign exchange earnings. As shown in Table 2.5 of Chapter 2 of this volume, by Anderson and Tyers, and contrary to conventional wisdom, food trade liberalization by OECD countries is likely to add to rather than subtract from most developing countries' net foreign exchange earnings. Needless to say, those earnings would be far greater if developing countries also liberalized their own trade and exchange rate policies.

A second and related point has to do with recent changes in the perceived role of agriculture in economic growth. Traditionally, agriculture has been seen as the lagging sector, as less capable of generating income and export growth than the industrial sector, and therefore unworthy of being promoted by the government. That climate of opinion — which was self-fulfilling because it led to anti-agricultural policies in most developing countries — is gradually changing. One reason for the change is the dramatic productivity growth that has been generated by the so-called Green Revolution during the past quarter century, a phenomenon which has demonstrated clearly that there is substantial scope for income growth by reducing the degree of underinvestment in agricultural research in developing countries. The other major change that is causing governments to reconsider the scope for rapid growth through agricultural development is the success of recent reforms to farm incentives in a number of fast-growing economies. The most spectacular case is of course China, but there are numerous other examples where dramatic agricultural growth has occurred as a direct result of higher producer prices (e.g., Indonesia, South Korea, Taiwan). These experiences are helping developing country governments realise that their policies of low food prices and underinvestment in agricultural research and rural infrastructure have had a very high opportunity cost in terms of lost income and export growth. If OECD countries were to open their markets to imports of farm products from developing countries, that may be enough to stimulate poorer countries to reduce their policy discrimination against agriculture.

Thirdly, in practice, any liberalization of food policies by OECD countries would at best be partial and would be phased in over a number of years. Given the long-term declining trend in real international food prices, such a liberalization is likely to merely slow the rate of decline of that price trend rather than cause food prices to rise in absolute terms. Any concern on the part of developing country governments that agriculture's inclusion in the Uruguay Round reforms will generate urban food riots is therefore misplaced.

The fourth and final point has to do with the fact that the OECD countries are much more serious about including food policy reform as part of the Uruguay Round than was the case in previous rounds of multilateral trade negotiations. If developing countries were to support food's inclusion in this Round by way of liberalizing their own policies, this would (according to the results presented Chapter 2, among others) add to the stability of food prices in international markets and would enhance economic welfare in OECD countries. Developing countries could use this as a bargaining chip in the negotiations in the form of seeking liberalization of the import barriers of OECD countries against tropical processed products and labour intensive manufactures such as textiles, clothing and footwear in return for supporting food trade liberalization.

In short, developing countries have a great deal to gain from supporting the inclusion of food trade liberalization in the Uruguay Round. It is thus in the interests of OECD and Cairns Group countries wanting liberalization to ensure that governments of developing countries are aware of those substantial benefits.

METHODOLOGICAL ISSUES

by

Alberto Valdés

Economic modelling can be a useful tool to assess the relative merits of proposals and issues on agriculture negotiated in the Uruguay Round and in the follow-up to the negotiations. Throughout this conference we have examined various approaches to quantifying the potential effects of policy reforms in industrial as well as in developing countries. These brief remarks offer some reflections on the methodological gaps most relevant for modelling the effect of trade liberalization in developing countries.

On the Composition and Level of the Farm Output Response and the Supply of Exports

Practically all the empirical work that considers a simultaneous change in several products and in several countries ends up using an extraordinarily simple framework for the production response process. It is excessively simple, in fact, particularly for predicting the long-run response. Let me highlight two related aspects of the problem. The first is that our empirical models chain us to a particular output and export mix, which is used as a base, despite evidence that the process of trade liberalization is likely to result in a much more diversified structure of output and exports, including non-traditional exports which could become an important source of export revenues for developing countries. New products, either not in the existing base or at very low values, can have production and export supply elasticities substantially higher than the traditionally traded commodities. Thus the composition and overall value of developing country exports and imports could change significantly, a change which would, in turn, influence the measured costs and benefits of trade liberalization for the developing countries.

The second aspect refers to the aggregate supply response. Most of the empirical work presented at this conference fails to capture the response of the aggregate supply in the long run, a topic for which we lack a solid empirical base, CGE models included[1].

If we accept that economy-wide policies (such as exchange rate misalignment and industrial protection) are the principal forms of price interventions in most developing countries[2], and consider that what is at stake is not only a reform of farm policies but also a reform correcting the real exchange rate misalignment — the case in most developing countries today — then we need to endogenize the effect of the change in the relative price structure of agricultural prices (relative to non-agricultural prices) on intersectoral flows of labour and capital. But today we simply do not have the empirical basis to do this. From my experience in a recent study funded by the World Bank on 18 developing countries in Asia, Africa, Middle East, and Latin America, in which the country authors were asked to estimate the output and trade effects of removing the sectoral and indirect price interventions prevailing in each country during 1960-84, for only two of the 18 countries could an attempt to be made to measure the long-run response with an explicit treatment of the indirect (economy-wide) effects[3]. The two countries were Argentina and Chile, and previous work in those countries by Yair Mundlak and his collaborators on investment functions and labour migration equations made the estimations possible. For none of the 18 countries could we go much beyond a distributed lag approach, commodity by commodity, incorporating cross-price effects and some shifters. Such an approach does not capture the adjustments that take place in factor markets, which are very influential in the final outcome. For example, agriculture in Argentina and Chile requires large amounts of capital (in livestock, orchards, etc.), and some activities, such as horticultural production for export (in Chile), are also very labour intensive. We found that investment opportunities and changes in real wages in the non-agricultural sector can be quite influential in the agricultural sector's response to trade liberalization across the economy, as was the case in Chile during the last ten years. In my opinion, none of the studies presented at this conference approaches what is needed to capture the long-run adjustment process of agricultural output and trade when broad liberalization occurs, which is the outcome we hope for if the Uruguay Round is "successful". We are much better at predicting the very short- and medium-term effects.

Income Response

Something similar occurs in trying to predict the real income effects of a trade liberalization scenario for the various income groups in the urban and rural areas. The instantaneous effects of price changes (given nominal wages and other sources of income) is certainly a computation we do fairly successfully. But again, quantifying longer-run changes in the real income of urban and rural households is a different game. We would need to model the dynamics of the labour markets in rural and urban areas, which is something not found in any of these studies. The CGE models are too *ad hoc* and conditioned by a particular specification that lacks, in most cases, empirical support for a realistic analysis. As in the output and trade questions raised above, our present estimates for income distribution are pretty much restricted to the very short run. The longer-run effects could differ in magnitude and even in the direction of the effects.

Malnutrition

Changes in agricultural price interventions affect the nutritional status in a very complex way, a process on which there is still considerable debate. In analysing the effectiveness on the levels of malnutrition, my plea to the modellers is a simple one: please do not confine the analysis to a simple estimate of the potential effect on nutrient intake (i.e., calories or proteins). As you might know from the work by Behrman and Deolalikar (published in the *Journal of Political Economy* and the *World Bank Economic Review*), by Bouis at IFPRI and by Shah for India, a very small proportion of the additional income generated by expanding agricultural production (or from other sources) is devoted to purchasing calories. Most of it goes to buy more expensive, higher quality foods and to non-food consumption. This behaviour has been observed for very low-income families in rural India, the Philippines, and other countries. There is nothing perverse about such choices by low-income households; they could in fact be raising their longer-run health and nutritional status through improvements in drinking water, sewage disposal, and other household functions (see Schiff and Valdés in *Economic Development and Cultural Change*, January 1990).

In conclusion, enormous progress has been made in the development of an explicit framework for analysing the output and trade effect of trade liberalization in developing countries. Compared to the early 1970s our models today are analytically superior and since then substantial progress has been achieved in quantifying the potential effects of policy changes on farm output, consumption, trade, and income. However, our progress is still pretty much restricted to the estimation of the short-run effects. The challenge now is to extend our analytical framework in order to capture in a more realistic way the dynamic effects that determine the outcome of policy reforms in the longer run.

NOTES AND REFERENCES

1. See Alberto Valdés, discussant comment on "The Policy Response of Agriculture," by Hans Binswanger, forthcoming in the *World Bank Economic Review*, 1989.

2. See A.O. Krueger, M. Schiff, and A. Valdés, "Agricultural Incentives in Developing Countries: Measuring the Effect of Sectoral and Economy-wide Policies", *World Bank Economic Review*, 2:3, 1988.

3. For several of these countries, CGE models had been estimated.

POLICY IMPLICATIONS OF MODELS

by

R.C. Duncan

There were two recent developments in the models presented which, to my mind, should lead to more realistic simulation results. First, is the higher supply elasticity being used in the modelling by Sadoulet and de Janvry. Second, is the inclusion of technical change in the Anderson and Tyers work.

We have learnt a good deal about agricultural supply response in recent years from both empirical analysis and experience with policy reform programmes. We now know that supply response in the short run is very inelastic and in the long run more elastic than previously believed. These facts imply sharply different results from short-run and long-run model simulations. More important, it means that we have to explain to policy makers and their constituencies that responses to policy change in the agricultural sector will take time. Patience in these matters is vital, but is hard to find especially in times when the external environment turns unfavourable.

In the long run, when capital and labour (including intersectoral movements) have fully responded to the relative price changes, the supply response in agriculture can be significantly large. The technical change which Anderson introduces captures some of this response.

A point which has come through loud and clear in the various papers and discussions is that, without liberalization of agricultural policies in the developing countries, the benefits to them of liberalization by the industrial countries will be minimal, or even adverse. This is another point which we have to explain to people in the developing countries. From the perspective of political economy, we have to remember that policy makers generally change policies because of the impact in their own countries, not the impact on other countries.

The use of models will always *underestimate* the "gains from trade" because they cannot include the *potential* activities which are excluded because exchange rates are overvalued or because of other distortions to relative prices.

Finally, there are two points to make on the results from the modelling of the liberalization of agricultural policies in the industrial countries. Contrary to the results we have seen, I do not believe that grain prices will rise, on average, following liberalization. The models which give this result assume that these markets are perfectly competitive. They are not. The grain markets, particularly wheat and maize, are oligopolistic markets with the price-leading United States putting a floor under world prices through its loan rates, acreage set asides, and stocking policies. As an oligopolist, the United States attempts to raise prices, on average, above perfectly competitive prices. World prices will rise on average after liberalization in a market like sugar where countries with price-support policies dump their excess sugar in the world market.

Second, it may be doubted that a reduction in intervention in commodity markets will reduce the variability of prices as the model results show. Price behaviour as modelled presently does not capture the essence of their variability, which is in their nonlinear response to the levels of speculative and transaction stocks. These highly nonlinear reactions are independent of the degree of intervention. We observe them in a market which is close to being perfectly competitive, such as copper, as much as in a market in which there is a large degree of intervention, such as coffee or sugar.

SOME IMPLICATIONS OF TRADE LIBERALIZATION IN CEREALS FOR LOW INCOME FOOD DEFICIT COUNTRIES

by

Panos Konandreas and Richard J. Perkins

There is no real dispute in the trade liberalization debate about the long-term efficiency gains that would accrue to the world as a whole from trade liberalization. This is especially the case if liberalization involves a large number of countries and includes a wide range of commodities.

The debate over trade liberalization is often not related to these long-term effects, but to the distributional effects, both among countries and within countries, and especially during the transition period. This is particularly the case for liberalization of the agricultural and food sectors where past government intervention was widespread and has influenced development strategies and investment decisions in other sectors, in both developed and developing countries. In particular, government intervention in developed countries has not only dominated world food markets but also played an important role in influencing food policies pursued by low income food deficit countries. This note discusses some of the adjustments that the latter group of countries will have to undertake to respond to a situation with a more liberalized regime in the food sector.

Higher Effective Price for Food Imports

While the results of the various studies may not be very conclusive on the precise nature and extent of the effect of liberalization on cereal prices in the world market, the most commonly accepted conclusion of both old and new studies is that at least in the short term cereal prices will rise. The rise in prices could be substantial if it is assumed that liberalization is confined only to OECD countries, whereas when liberalization in developing countries is also assumed, the increase in prices would be much more modest.

From the point of view of low income food deficit countries an important element determining the cost of their cereal imports, aside from the nominal world price level, is the degree of concessionality associated with commercial trade. Besides food aid for which the concessional element approaches 100 per cent, commercial transactions with developing countries also have been subject to some degree of concessionality, especially in the recent past when competition for markets intensified and concessional credit was given by major exporters (e.g., the US export enhancement programme, and EC differentiated export refunds). Such export promotion programmes were offshoots of domestic agricultural support policies. However, trade liberalization implies reduction or elimination of domestic agricultural support as well as the concessionality of commercial trade. The implication of this is an increase in the *effective price* of cereals to be paid by low income food deficit countries, which have depended heavily on concessional imports in the past. The increase in the amount to be paid for their cereal imports could be substantial.

In the short term and in the longer term, in cases where the potential to increase cereal production is highly limited or does not exist, food deficit countries will need to allocate additional foreign exchange to the higher priced cereal imports. Two sets of countries within the food deficit category can be distinguished. First, are those that are net exporters of tropical products for which increases in prices are also foreseen under a generalised agricultural trade liberalization scenario, resulting in foreign exchange gains which would outweigh the increased costs for cereal imports. For these countries, if it is also assumed that they would spend all the increase in foreign exchange earnings to pay for the increased cost of their cereal imports, short-term food security in aggregate terms would not be affected, provided appropriate fiscal, or other redistributional mechanisms are put in place. However, in the context of large debt obligations and an overall scarcity of foreign exchange, competition for its allocation would be strong so that the volume of food imports could indeed decrease.

The second set of low income food deficit countries are those that do not export tropical products and/or have limited export share in such products, inadequate to counterbalance their higher food import bills. For these countries adjustments in the importation of other goods will have to be made. In other words, if these countries were to maintain the volume of their cereal imports, foreign exchange allocated to other non-food consumer items and/or capital goods would have to be decreased.

Both groups of countries, but especially the latter, can legitimately claim some sort of international assistance to mitigate the overall short-term negative effect of liberalization on their food security. The international compensatory assistance required to mitigate these negative effects would be reduced if liberalization has a global character and includes both tropical and temperate products. Conversely, the required compensation would be the highest in the case of liberalization of temperate-zone products only and when liberalization is confined to OECD countries only.

The form of this assistance can be in kind (e.g., food aid or provision of agricultural inputs) and/or in cash. However, as mentioned, since the availability of food aid in the past has been largely an offshoot of domestic agricultural policies in developed countries, liberalization of these policies would also reduce the availability of food aid. Thus if low income food deficit countries were to receive compensatory assistance, the largest part of this assistance would have to be in the form of financial aid, to purchase food from the world market.

Domestic Budgetary Adjustments

The other kind of adjustment that will be required in low income food deficit countries is internal. In many countries the low world food prices of past years have been passed on to consumers and in several cases food consumption has been further subsidised by the government budget. The higher effective price for food imports which food deficit countries would face following liberalization would imply, if passed on to the internal market, benefits to domestic producers and costs to domestic consumers. Depending on the extent of the price increase, the price elasticity of supply and productivity growth achieved through induced innovation, producer gains could be higher or lower than consumer losses. In the case that they are higher and redistribution of gains was possible, society as a whole could gain from liberalization.

Independent of whether overall welfare gains to a food deficit developing country would be positive or negative, to make liberalization politically and socially acceptable, compensation of consumers may be needed. It could be envisaged that part of the producers' gains could be transferred to consumers through some form of taxation. Given that there is no rationale either to tax or compensate subsistence food producers, a redistribution of producers' gains would actually involve a subset of producers, namely those who market their output (less than 25 per cent in a typical Sub-Saharan Africa country). Equally only a subset of consumers would need to be compensated, namely those that purchase food from the market.

It turns out that the lower the proportion of marketed output and the lower the food self-sufficiency ratio of a country, the lower the ratio between producers' gains and consumers' losses. For example, for a typical Sub-Saharan African country, out of 100 tonnes of cereals consumed, about 35 tonnes are marketed, of which about 15 tonnes from imports and 20 tonnes from domestic production, while about 65 tonnes are subsistence production. Producers' gains in this case would amount only to 57 per cent of consumers' losses. Thus compensation of consumers through taxation of producers would be very limited, as otherwise it would amount to a disincentive to increasing domestic output, and thus negate the positive effects of liberalization. There are also practical considerations which would limit the feasibility of a producer-to-consumer compensation. Most low income food deficit countries lack the tax infrastructure, appropriate institutions and trained personnel that would make such a mechanism possible.

Therefore, as transfers from producers to consumers may not be possible or advantageous in a typical low income food deficit country, if compensation of consumers is considered politically and socially necessary, it would be feasible largely through adjustments in the government budget. This can be done either through cuts in other government expenditures, or increases in the government budget. The latter option may be counterproductive as it would fuel inflation which could negate the effect of the government transfers.

Again, as in the case of needed adjustments in the external account, the likelihood of a country being able to effect, on its own, compensatory transfers to consumers is higher the broader the commodity coverage of trade liberalization. In the case of a broad commodity coverage, not only the number of producers who benefit increases but also the marketed share goes up considerably in view of the fact that most of the output of tropical products goes through the market for export. Thus in this case, it would be easier to transfer part of the producers' benefits to consumers without this representing a substantial disincentive to domestic production and marketing.

Distribution of Cereal Stocks and their Adequacy

Theoretically, price instability could be reduced under a liberalized trade regime and this is indeed suggested by models which have examined this aspect of market behaviour following liberalization. However, trade liberalization implies also limited government involvement in stockholding or other supply and demand regulating interventions. Thus the stocks that would exist following liberalization would be largely in the hands of private agents, who would only hold a level that yielded positive returns; consequently carry-over stocks of major exporting countries are likely to be reduced under a liberalized trade regime compared to the levels of recent years.

However, the probability of abnormal supply shortfalls due to climatic factors is likely to remain the same. Variability in world production could change to the extent that liberalization leads to a significant shift of production to regions with substantially different climatic variability. Production fluctuations would increase if there is a major shift in world production to areas with higher than average climatic variability and decrease in the opposite case. *A priori* there is no reason to assume either one of these outcomes; more likely, fluctuations in output due to climatic factors would not change substantially.

In the infrequent years of sharp production shortfalls of the magnitude experienced in the past, private stocks may not be adequate (it does not pay private agents to hold stocks for rare eventualities) and world prices may rise to prohibitively high levels. This could pose serious food security problems in certain years for those low income countries which depend on imports for a large share of total consumption. Having limited foreign exchange available, they will find it difficult during these exceptional years to purchase needed supplies at the world market. To avoid such eventualities, and notwithstanding the costs involved, those food deficit countries that consider themselves more exposed to the world market, may decide to carry larger stocks under a liberalized trade regime than the limited quantities they normally held up to now.

Thus while before liberalization there are large stocks concentrated in the main exporting countries, in a liberalized trade regime stocks are likely to be more dispersed geographically. However, considering the effect of these stocks on the world market, there appears to be an asymmetry between stocks held by traditional exporting countries and those held by low income food deficit countries. As regards the latter, they normally are meant for domestic use and generally they would not respond to a supply shortfall outside the country where those stocks are held. The stocks freely available to the world market — by and large those held by the traditional exporting countries — could be substantially reduced following liberalization. In view of this, the effect on world price of a major shortfall in global output could be much more pronounced.

Stock behaviour following liberalization is an important question for better understanding the implications of liberalization for food security under the extreme situations of supply fluctuations considered above. This question, however, should be researched outside the complex and rigid structure of the trade models that have been used up to now to assess the effects of trade liberalization. Indeed, for such models to be able to incorporate convincingly the stochastic nature of world food markets, a better understanding of stock behaviour relationships is required. For the traditional food exporting countries, a study of the relationship between private and public stocks is a crucial one, as it will allow an assessment of the extent to which the former will make up for a reduction in the latter following liberalization.

ISSUES IN MODELLING

by

W. Tims

Three sets of issues appear to dominate the present discussion on appropriate modelling techniques regarding alternative trade policies. My comments thus focus on three areas: policy instruments, model dynamics and empirical content.

A number of participants, Hertel and Whalley and others, have emphasized the shortcomings of aggregate measures of protection, notably the widely used and abused PSEs and CSEs based on price comparisons. It has been found that they are of limited use by policy makers who must determine which instruments are to be phased out or abolished. They may also misrepresent the actual situation. For example, Srinivasan reminded us that a quantitative restriction cannot be properly reflected in a tariff equivalent. Finally, they may not embrace restrictive measures like area set asides which lead to higher prices, *ceteris paribus*.

There is a broad range of policy instruments which directly or indirectly protect agriculture and in most countries they include more than a subset of agricultural policies. For example, they include fiscal (and financial) policies which discriminate between sectors or social groups. Comprehensive national modelling is especially necessary for countries in which the agricultural sector is large in terms of its output, its share of consumer expenditures and external trade.

The same comclusion can be drawn from Robinson's statement that the effects of changes in trade policy on the economy seem to be larger in terms of sectoral outputs and trade than for the GDP and welfare. Although one needs to be careful with regard to welfare until one has assessed differential effects by socio-economic groups, structural consequences of trade policy shifts point to the need for close attention to the modelling of factor markets. Again this suggests the need for a comprehensive approach.

Others have said much the same, for example, Scandizzo in his remarks on the implications of trade policy changes for public revenue. These should not be used as an argument against such changes, but it is difficult for policy makers to take seriously scenarios which do not explicitly deal with the fiscal aspects of policy. This applies equally, it may be added, to the claims for compensation by the present beneficiaries of protection. Some of those claims which may be justified from a welfare point of view have fiscal consequences whose impact on the public sector needs to be clarified for those receiving compensation and those who pay for it. Few studies have dealt with alternative forms of compensation, but there are obviously other possibilities than annual lump-sum or deficiency payments.

Trade policy analysis appears not to allow disjointed analysis. It is so closely integrated with the entire policy framework that national modelling is needed. In turn, few researchers feel capable of doing this for countries which they do not know intimately. It requires the participation of researchers in each country who are familiar with its structural and institutional characteristics and with the intricacies of local policy making and implementation. As trade policy analysis requires model linkage, researchers must also be ready to adhere to a common discipline. An example of an effort along those lines was IIASA's Food and Agriculture Programme presented earlier by Frohberg; the paper regarding the Food and Agriculture Network (FAN) is an example of a similar effort planned for the years ahead. Financing agencies interested primarily in the trade policy aspects can play an important role, for they can insist on network discipline which renders model linkage possible. The costs can remain limited since national models are usually constructed primarily for domestic use and have their own financing.

Turning now to dynamic features of current modelling, we find ourselves confronted by an unsatisfactory state of affairs. Most of the modelling work does not address issues of changes over time in productive capacities and is limited to what is stated to be comparative static analysis. Obviously this type of analysis cannot claim to compare long-run adjustment to policy change. Still it purports to be more than short-run analysis. Then what is the meaning of comparative static analysis if it is neither a comparison of steady states, nor represents the outcome of investment and development processes over time?

Dynamic models which do describe these processes and at the same time are realistic enough to be policy relevant are needed and there is considerable methodological work required to make progress in this area. It is one thing to say that factor markets need to be included, but it is far from clear whether this is possible with the analytical tools at hand. Frohberg mentioned the problems encountered when estimating migration functions and Scandizzo noted the existing uncertainty regarding technological developments in EC agriculture under different trade policy regimes. For many of the developing countries one may need to start with the question of whether factor markets do exist in reality. Beyond that, the approach to dynamic modelling needs to focus on Pareto-efficiency in an intertemporal sense and to give due emphasis to compensation-related issues.

Several speakers have noted the wide spectrum of empirical work incorporated in the various models. Some use the set of PSE/CSE estimates from the OECD and obtain parameters from the literature. We had a discussion on whether in all cases the use made of these parameters does justice to the restrictions that applied to their (econometric) derivation. More recent modelling work appears to include more "own" empirical work, both in terms of observing macro-balances and construction of SAM-type datasets and in terms of econometric work to establish suitable sets of parameters. Relevant policy modelling requires considerable empirical data work, if only to ensure that users of model results recognise the numbers used to be the same as they are familiar with. One can go further and insist that in equilibrium modelling there should be no sources of "costless" supplies or sinks where goods disappear. But that would put very heavy demands on researchers for which they are not rewarded professionally. It also would need to be explained to the agencies funding such research that this cannot be done quickly and well at the same time, and that the financing is to permit the necessary statistical and econometric work. Alternatively, one can ask to what extent international organisations could orient some of their data work to provide the research community with standardised data sets which constitute an important part of model needs.

Finally, the issue of instability of international markets was raised several times. Armington has noted its link to food security at the national and household levels. I would like to add my observation that developing countries face the dilemma of closer alignment of domestic prices to fluctuating world market prices on the one hand, and the consequences for domestic food price instability on the other. Particularly for lower income groups the latter may be politically unacceptable and the issue is then, what measures governments may take which do maintain linkage between domestic and world prices but at the same time safeguard economically weaker groups from the real income fluctuations which they cannot bear. There is a need for more research on this issue which can provide practicable policy instruments.

Part V

CONCLUSIONS

Chapter 17

THE IMPLICATIONS OF AGRICULTURAL TRADE LIBERALIZATION FOR DEVELOPING COUNTRIES

by

Ian Goldin and Odin Knudsen

REFLECTIONS, IMPLICATIONS AND AN AGENDA FOR THE FUTURE

The papers collected here show that the developing countries will be among the most seriously affected — positively or negatively — by the outcome of the GATT negotiations on agricultural trade liberalization. In developing countries, agriculture is generally much more important as a source of income and employment than is the case in the industrialised economies. Developing countries, because of their relatively large dependence on agriculture, their reliance on agricultural trade and, for many, because of their high dependence on food imports, will be influenced by any outcome of the Uruguay Round negotiations.

The process of agricultural trade reform presents the developing countries with both opportunities and dangers. Their distinct comparative advantages in land, labour, and climate in a number of commodities mean that free trade could boost exports and serve as a significant engine of growth. Many developing countries, however, are large food grain importers. They will be hurt if, as most of the models predict, liberalization does away with cut-price surplus grain from the temperate industrial countries.

The models provide forecasts of the potential effects of liberalization on prices, production, consumption and welfare. Thus their value clearly extends beyond the academic world; their simulations and results provide important perspectives and insights for the negotiating process. It is this policy importance that has motivated the OECD Development Centre and the World Bank to sponsor the development of trade models presented here and review their results.

In this, the concluding chapter, the results of these models are reviewed in order to shed light on the implications of agricultural trade liberalization for developing countries, to yield policy directions and to provide pointers to the agenda for future research. We begin by examining the most critical result — the effect on international prices — then turn to the policy implications and conclude with some thoughts on the future agenda for modelling.

Liberalization in OECD Countries and Food Prices

Of the models presented in this volume, six make predictions regarding the anticipated effects agricultural reform in the OECD countries would have on world food prices (Table 17.1). Price is the key factor influencing production and consumption, and thus provides a rough proxy for the welfare and trade effects of liberalization. All the models point to increases in meat, dairy and sugar prices, and all but one (the OECD's MTM model) forecast rises in food grain prices[1]. For feed grains, the results are more ambiguous, with both the OECD's MTM model and the Zietz/Valdés model pointing to a price decline and the other models forecasting that the prices of feed grains would rise as a result of liberalization in the OECD countries.

There is considerable variation in the magnitude of the price changes particularly for dairy products, meat and sugar. While livestock and sugar price changes will have important implications, particularly for some exporting countries, changes in food grain prices are the most politically sensitive and the primary concern of the coalition of food importing countries that have been vocal in asking for compensation in the Uruguay Round. Given the central importance of food grains in nutrition, it is not surprising that the issue of food grain prices has been a pressing consideration underlying the agricultural negotiations in the GATT.

Although the magnitudes of price changes are of course important, sign differences in the direction of change are even more dramatic because they reverse the policy implications. If grain prices decline as a result of liberalization as implied by the MTM results, the importers and exporters switch sides in liberalization's benefit-cost equation. So, for example, while grain exporters such as Argentina would benefit from higher grain prices, and importers such as Mexico or Egypt would lose, their positions would be reversed were prices to fall as a result of liberalization, although in the case of lower prices, it may be the case that increased demand would allow total revenue of the grain exporters to be maintained.

The results of the MTM and Zietz/Valdés models are important not so much because the models are particularly sophisticated but because they present different results from all the other models. The difference between the MTM results and the USDA/ERS SWOPSIM model, which predicts a rise in grain prices, occurs despite the use of similar elasticity assumptions in the two models.

Examining this disparity in conclusions on price changes it is evident that some of the differences are accounted for by the base year and differing assumptions regarding the initial and final levels of protection. The Zietz/Valdés model uses a base year of 1981-83 and the MTM model uses an average level of protection for 1982 to 1985 while, for instance, the SWOPSIM model has a base year of 1986. Furthermore, whereas the Zietz-Valdés and SWOPSIM models project reductions of 100 per cent, the MTM only forecasts the implications of a 10 per cent reduction in support. In addition to the differences in reference periods (and consequently in the assumed rates of agricultural protection), the comparison of the results, in the case of the MTM, rests on the simple "scaling-up" of a 10 to 100 per cent reduction.

From a modelling and policy perspective, the treatment of the livestock sector in the OECD countries is among the more significant differences between the models. All the models have the livestock sector highly supported in their base, pre-liberalization runs. After liberalization, most of the models predict that livestock production falls substantially in the OECD countries, reducing the demand for animal feed, and it is here where the differences between the models become critical. The MTM model contains the most comprehensive feed sector and this includes forage and non-grain feeds. Moreover, the cross-elasticity effects on food grains are modelled as strong. Therefore, the fall in livestock production reduces derived demand for all feeds and their prices also fall because the supplies of these products are highly price inelastic. For example, in the MTM model, cassava prices decline by 29 per cent and corn gluten prices by 35 per cent. Through the cross-price effect on food grains, this fall in feed grain prices causes a drop in food grain prices[2]. The livestock sector, with its heavy dependence on animal feeds, becomes the driving force in the MTM model in influencing grain prices. Although the USDA/ERS SWOPSIM, the Zietz-Valdés and the Anderson-Tyers models include some of this interaction they do not do so with as much detail as the MTM model.

While the MTM may overemphasize the cross-price effects and does not trace the increased demand for pasture land to a reduction in the land available for food grains, it clearly points to the importance of modelling the livestock sector. A comparison of the simulations reveals that the livestock sector and the degree of liberalization associated with it are critical to the outcome with respect to prices in the partial equilibrium models. The livestock sector is particularly difficult to model because of its intertemporal linkages, but its pivotal role in determining the influence of liberalization on grain prices requires that further work be undertaken in this area.

While the partial equilibrium results show substantial variation in price effects, the general equilibrium models find a more consistent price response of around 15 to 18 per cent for wheat, 8 to 11 per cent for coarse grains and 10 to 18 per cent for meat. In some ways, this similarity in the results of the general equilibrium models is surprising as the models are much less uniform in their specification than the partial equilibrium models. In particular, the non-agricultural sectors of the general equilibrium models are presented in considerably different detail. Given the strong link between these sectors and the agricultural sector, it may have been assumed that the impact of economy-wide liberalization would have had differing effects on agricultural prices, according to the divergent assumptions regarding the modelling of the non-agricultural sectors. On the other hand, to the extent that there is a more muted price response in the general equilibrium models, this is to be expected as the models allow for far greater factor substitution and mobility than is the case with the partial equilibrium models. In examining long-term and gradual changes, such as those which are likely to be associated with agricultural reform, the intersectoral linkages within general equilibrium models make them an appropriate and valuable tool of analysis.

Simultaneous Liberalization by Developing Countries

A message of the models is that liberalization by the developing countries — as well as the industrialised countries — would significantly mute price rises. Including developing countries in the liberalization process implies that international prices will be more fully transmitted to developing country farmers. Their production response to higher prices is the principal factor underlying the difference between the simulation results in Tables 17.1 and 17.2.

The models of developing country liberalization differ in their specification of the agricultural reform process. A number of the models examine only the direct effects of protection of agriculture, that is the effects of measures such as tariffs, quotas and other agriculture-specific interventions. The indirect effects of protection of non-agriculture and from currency controls (which typically imply overvaluation of developing country exchange rates) are, however, also important.

A comparison of the Zietz/Valdés and Anderson/Tyers results with the IIASA and USDA/SWOPSIM results suggests that the coverage of the developing country reforms exercises an important influence over the final result. The Zietz/Valdés and Anderson/Tyers models included in this volume specifically include indirect interventions and simulate exchange rate changes in their modelling. In their analysis, the authors note that these indirect effects are particulary important in developing countries. The reform of these indirect measures underlies the strong production response of developing country farmers to liberalization, which in turn is reflected in lower world prices and increased levels of self-sufficiency in many food-importing countries.

The IIASA and MTM models of world trade liberalization restrict their analysis to the measurement of the removal of direct interventions, that is principally tariffs, quotas and other border distortions. All other distortions and the indirect effect of protection in non-agriculture are kept constant. The IIASA model does however generate income changes. Thus demand responds to both income and price changes. In developing countries, agriculture product demand is generally highly income elastic. These income effects underpin the price projections in the IIASA world liberalization scenario.

In their adaptation of the USDA/SWOPSIM model, Krissoff, Sullivan and Wainio examine both the income effects generated by agricultural reform and the indirect effects of a move to exchange rate equilibrium. Their results are in general consistent with the IIASA findings. Caution should, however, be exercised in the interpretation of their findings as these are premised on the grafting of general equilibrium-type analysis onto a partial equilibrium model. Uncertainty remains both with respect to the interpretation of the exchange rate changes, which in the general equilibrium models favour all tradables and not simply agriculture, (so that the final result depends on the balance between the different tradable sectors), and also the income side, where the general equilibrium effects go far beyond the inclusion of an income in the demand function and the addition of an income multiplier, which are added-on to the USDA/SWOPSIM model.

The inclusion of developing country liberalization in the reform process, as a comparison of Tables 17.1 and 17.2 reveals, will significantly influence the final market and price implications of the liberalization process. The results reaffirm the need for a truly multilateral outcome to the Uruguay Round, with all countries participating in the liberalization of agriculture and the developing countries not insulating their own markets. By acting together, developing countries as a whole, or as groups, will be able to influence the final outcome for themselves and for others. The issue of sequencing of reform is particularly important in this regard; for many developing countries' domestic reforms are likely to cushion substantially any negative implications of international agricultural trade liberalization.

Productivity and Technical Change

An important area largely left open in most of the models that will affect the price implications is the effect of liberalization on technical change. Anderson and Tyers have made a courageous effort at incorporating technology both exogenously and endogenously in their models. Their assumptions on the magnitude and form of technological change determine the nature of their results on the implications of liberalization to developing countries. If technological change continues at historical trend rates, as they assume in their base run, developing countries can expect that any price rises resulting from liberalization will be buffered by the downward trend in real food prices caused by productivity gains from technological advancement. Even if food prices are forced upward by the liberalization, real food prices in the future could be lower than today because of this technological change. If, as Anderson and Tyers assume in their "price-dependent" model runs, technological change is endogenous with respect to price and higher prices induce greater and quicker advances, liberalization would accelerate advances in technology and productivity. The result, as shown in Tables 17.1 and 17.2, would be that all price rises coming from liberalization would be reduced by this endogenous technological change.

The Policy Implications of Liberalization

The general consensus of the modelling is that commodity prices will be higher than they would have been without agricultural trade liberalization. However, real food prices are likely to be lower if the assumption is made that these higher prices will induce more rapid technological change. The magnitude of changes in prices will depend on what happens to livestock production in the OECD countries. If livestock production is sustained through protection and subsidies, the effect on food grain prices of liberalization will be much more significant.

The models provide important insights into the implications of differing liberalization scenarios. To serve as policy guides, they need to be placed in the context of the current negotiations and the associated geo-political policy debate. In this context, two other factors may be introduced into the policy argument: the "liberalization dividend" expected from free and unprotected trade in agricultural products, and the time frame in which the liberalization process is likely to take place.

Liberalization offers the world a potential dividend estimated at well over $200 billion a year in savings to governments — and their taxpayers — and food purchasers[3]. The sheer immensity of this "bonus" is a powerful incentive to liberalize — it also provides a large potential pool of essentially costless resources that can be used to soften the adjustment process.

At the same time, none of the parties to the Uruguay Round is proposing instant removal of all barriers to free agricultural trade. It is universally recognised that the present agricultural trade system is so entrenched that immediate and universal liberalization would wreak politically unacceptable havoc with domestic economies and international trade. Even the most far-reaching proposal, the "zero-option" put forward by the United States in 1988, envisions a ten-year period of phased-in changes.

Money and time — the two basic ingredients of a smooth adjustment process that can bring losers, whether they turn out to be grain importers or exporters, into the winners' circle — thus are both available. There is, however, a third — and dominant — ingredient: political will.

The agricultural trade status quo has strong political constituencies, ranging from subsidised sugar beet farmers in Western Europe to the urban poor in developing countries whose existence depends on cheap food grains. Convincing those constituencies — and, through them, their political leaders — that they too will share in the "liberalization dividend" could be a major task of those who wish to influence the Uruguay Round.

The process of trade liberalization for agriculture will most likely be gradual with the general equilibrium effects of intersectoral movements of resources creating other economic opportunities and muting the overall adverse effects. That is, resources will move between sectors in response to the price changes and mute them in the long run. The implication is that developing countries will have ample time to adjust. This does not mean that there will not be dramatic shocks to the system. Short-term prices do not move only in response to immediate changes in supply and demand; they are also influenced by expectations and speculative impulses. Price booms and busts are inherent in agriculture markets and liberalization will not remove these. Although Anderson and Tyers conclude that instability will be reduced, Duncan in his short note is equally as certain that it will continue and gives a convincing example to support his views.

In practice, we know little of the actual factors that drive the instability in agricultural markets. But we do know that political uncertainty cannot help. The major political actors should define clearly and irrevocably the direction that liberalization is to take to avoid contributing to this inherent uncertainty in agricultural markets. Equally, price booms and busts which are sure to occur must not be used as an excuse to derail the long-term adjustment process and further contribute to uncertainty.

The price effects of all the models are within the normal fluctuations observed within international agricultural markets. The most severe price movements projected by the models have already been experienced at one time or another in the international markets for most of the commodities. Nevertheless, while the price results of the models are within the actual background noise that has historically been observed in the international agricultural markets, domestic producers and consumers in most OECD countries and in many developing countries have been insulated from these world prices. For them, the removal of the barriers to these markets is likely to spell much greater price fluctuation. To the extent that the liberalization process is associated with greater exposure to world prices, it is likely to bring new price levels and greater short-term instability to consumers, producers and food processors. Modelling trade liberalization can point to the likely impact of the changes, providing a framework in which it is possible to evaluate mechanisms for minimisation of risk and the easing of the transition process.

While the models differ on the actual effect on prices, they share the view that developing country liberalization will soften the effects on markets. That is, developing countries can reduce the price effects and enhance the benefits of liberalization by OECD countries if they also reform their agricultural policies. In fact, it appears likely that most developing countries could reap more benefits from unilateral liberalization than even from the multilateral process. It is clear from the Hammer and Knudsen paper that liberalization will change the policy options facing developing countries; but it is also true that the current policies are far from optimal and that there can be gains even without a change in world markets.

Certainly some developing countries will be adversely affected by international price rises, particularly of food grains. In the Sadoulet and de Janvry paper, some of these effects were explored through archetypical models of developing countries. They conclude that paradoxically the countries with more import substitution in cereals will be the most negatively affected in the short run. This result comes out of the general equilibrium effects of the rising import prices with all cereal prices rising, the value and volume of cereal imports falling, and the negative impact of the simulated exchange rate revaluation on other tradable sectors. The welfare of the poor would be highly negatively affected under this scenario. They conclude that the way to mute this effect is to increase the supply response of cereals through public investment in agriculture. While the archetypical nature of their modelling effort induces a cautionary note, their results reveal that the effects on developing countries operating through general equilibrium-type changes may not be so straightforward as the partial equilibrium analysis tends to suggest. Indeed, the analysis of individual developing economies will be necessary to predict what the effects may actually be.

Another implication of the models that should be emphasized is the necessity for the Uruguay Round to achieve liberalization of all product categories. It is clear that the livestock sector is a critical influence on the overall effect on world prices. If the livestock sector remains protected and supported, then the effect on feed grain and consequently food grain prices will be strong. Any upward movement in prices induced by reduced support for food grain production would be enhanced by failure to reduce simultaneously support to the livestock sector. The reduction of support to livestock production in the OECD countries could in fact be more important to developing countries than liberalization in food grains.

Directions for Future Work

Successful negotiations and smooth adjustment to a liberalized agricultural trade regime require a much stronger and more comprehensive information base. The disparities between the model results are, in themselves, a strong argument for further analysis and modelling of the likely effects of liberalization, particularly when the meagre amounts spent on research on the effects of agricultural trade liberalization are compared with the billions of dollars in subsidies that already have been sent to producers. But in what areas should the research and modelling proceed?

The first and immediate conclusion that emerges from an examination of the models is that developing countries still have very partial treatment in all of the work. We still are unable to define very definitively the effects of agricultural trade liberalization on individual developing countries or even subgroups of countries. The partial equilibrium models treat developing countries in a largely aggregate way. Even the more disaggregated and archetypical approaches of de Janvry and Sadoulet, Loo and Tower, and Hammer and Knudsen have only partially investigated the issues related to developing countries. Likewise, many of the general equilibrium models such as the WALRAS model consider the developing world much like a residual where trade and supply and demand are to be brought to closure. Even the IIASA model which has a fairly well-specified depiction of developing countries is still incomplete and requires updating. A high priority in future work is to expand existing models to include more completely developing countries and to further disaggregate their treatment. Furthermore, it is important, as indicated by Mabbs-Zeno and Krissoff, to bring tropical products into the models.

All the modelling work is highly sensitive to assumptions regarding elasticities. In the models, elasticities provide a summary measure of the underlying supply and demand relations. The pivotal nature of the elasticity assumptions remains a problematic feature of the models. This is particularly the case for the estimations of developing country responses, where projecting elasticities into the future is made doubly difficult by the uncertainties regarding past trends.

The issue of stability and price fluctuations remains unresolved. While instability in prices may be an inconvenience to many consumers in developed countries who spend a small part of their income on food, in developing countries price stability is of vital interest to the poor and also for the political stability of many governments. Only Anderson and Tyers have made a stab at trying to deal with the effects on stability and their attempt goes little beyond the results predicted by the Central Limit Theorem[4]. Their result is, however, not borne out by the evidence of existing commodity markets; a comparison of narrow and heavily controlled markets, such as sugar, with freer markets, such as cocoa, indicates that instability is not simply related to market intervention. Other factors, such as market structure (market shares and trading arrangements) are also important, as is the nature of stockholding. While liberalization may well lead to a reduction in stocks, notably in the OECD countries, the evidence is inconclusive on whether reduced stocks held by the public sector would lead to greater or less fluctuations in world markets.

In addition to the unresolved issues with regard to stockholding and stability, much research needs to be done on the question of "natural" protection. While the models generally examine the implications of exposing currently insulated economies to world prices, they do not take into account the implications of transport and other costs which create a wedge between domestic producers and consumers and internationally quoted market prices. These differentials mean that in many countries — most notably those which are landlocked or have poor transport and handling infrastructure — producers and consumers could remain substantially insulated from the world market, with important implications for both domestic and global agricultural markets and prices.

Another important line of research is highlighted by the Rausser et al. paper. Their contribution points to the link between the debt problem, macroeconomic imbalances and commodity prices. The importance of this interrelationship cannot be doubted, but there is still a long way to go before the analysis yields specific results regarding individual countries and commodities. Such research is vital as the macro linkages could well be more important in determining the direction of world agricultural prices than trade liberalization. If the debt overhang persists, how will this affect the projections on future prices even after liberalization? More generally, what is the link between domestic liberalization and international trade liberalization, and how should internal adjustments be sequenced? Domestic adjustments, as the Zietz and Valdés paper finds, may well be more important in determining the direction of world prices than international trade liberalization.

There is certainly much to be gained from modelling more precisely individual commodity programmes. The paper by Whalley and Wigle and Blandford's discussant note emphasize the point that the representation of different agricultural support programmes within models of agricultural trade liberalization is necessary in order to deal effectively with the question of how changes in different support systems will impact on production. Arguing that a summary measure such as the PSE is inherently a blunt tool with which to examine programmes such as dairy, sugar and wheat, where supply and quantitative barriers are important, Whalley and Wigle show the need to move beyond *ad valorem* modelling to models which allow a more detailed measurement of commodity programme and agricultural policies.

Allied to the need for more detailed analysis, is that of more transparent analysis. The usefulness of research can be considerably enhanced by the clear specification of the differing assumptions and by the construction of models which facilitate the revision and updating of the data. The simulation, by means of sensitivity analysis, of differing policy alternatives further enhances the usefulness of the models as policy guides and provides a basis for evaluating the implications of varying assumptions regarding the reform process.

While the Anderson and Tyers work attempts to account for technical change, the incorporation is mainly *ad hoc* and speculative. More work needs to be conducted on the role that subsidies have played in technological change and the possible effects of increased world prices on the rate of technological change. Simulations should also provide the basis for incorporating possible breakthroughs in bio-technology on the supply of agricultural products and in changes in food processing technology and the food system on patterns of demand and trade. Whereas many of these changes are not expected to be widely implemented in the immediate future, they may well impact on agricultural markets and prices within the time horizon envisaged in the Uruguay process.

The general equilibrium models bring to centre stage the issue of sequencing of domestic and international reforms and the importance of understanding the variable impact of the timing of the reform process. The speed of the international reform process and the consequences of different possible scenarios — for example, 10 per cent or 50 per cent reductions in support, or the removal of only some interventions — require explicit analysis in order to ensure the maximisation of the potential gains of liberalization. The general equilibrium models also need to be developed to bring out the point that in all countries the implications of agricultural trade reform will not be confined to the agricultural sector, and that the long-term gains of reform may well be reflected in a changing balance between town and country and more efficient allocation of resources between sectors.

More general equilibrium or even archetypical modelling of developing countries is necessary because of the importance of agriculture to employment and GDP in many developing countries. In developing countries the agricultural sector is much more important to the economy, and accordingly the modelling of labour and factor movements becomes particularly important in assessing the effects of trade scenarios on developing countries and determining the overall costs of current policies. Both the IIASA and RUNS models have had to struggle with this issue of wage determination and, as Hertel's paper points out, the treatment of labour movements and productivity between sectors can substantially influence the models' implications for growth.

The rapidly changing situation in Eastern Europe brings to the fore the need to incorporate the planned market economies in the modelling exercises. The Eastern European economies, despite the fact that they have historically been the greatest beneficiaries of OECD countries' agricultural subsidies, have been either entirely neglected or inadequately dealt with in the models. Similarly, China needs to be fully accounted for in the modelling agenda, for it plays a pivotal role, together with the Soviet Union, in markets for grains and sugar. How will the reform movements in Eastern Europe and the policy changes in China impact on agricultural trade and prices, and, what are the possible consequences for developing countries?[5]

Finally, there are many other issues outside of the modelling agenda that require research. For example, the appropriateness of different structural adjustments in the developing countries in response to different world prices and market opportunities; how should food aid be handled when public commodity stocks are lower; how can risk and uncertainty in developing countries be reduced through market mechanisms such as futures markets or commodity linked financial instruments; how can trade be made more efficient through better information systems; and how do environmental and natural resource issues impinge on trade? Finally, how can developing countries and their concerns be brought more integrally into the GATT system? These are of course issues that will persist beyond the end of the Uruguay Round. They are prime candidates for future collaborative research of scholars from both the developed and developing world as the process of agricultural reform proceeds. The challenge ahead is to ensure that liberalization continues and that as the process moves on the implications of specific proposals are understood, thereby ensuring that the full benefits accrue to developing countries from the levelling of the international agricultural playing field.

Table 17.1

PRICE EFFECTS OF LIBERALIZATION BY OECD COUNTRIES

Model	Wheat[1]	Coarse grains	Meat	Dairy	Sugar
Partial equilibrium models					
Anderson-Tyers[2]: (projected 1995)					
a. Price-independent productivity growth	25	3	43	95	22
b. Price-dependent productivity growth	19	2	39	90	27
Zietz and Valdés[3]: (OECD countries liberalize)	3	-3	10	--	15
OECD/MTM[4]: (OECD counries liberalize)	-5	-10	5	31	9
USDA/SWOPSIM[5] (1986 base)	27	16-22	16	84	29
General equilibrium models					
IIASA[6](projected 2000)	18	11	17	31	--
RUNS[7]	15	8	18	--	57
WALRAS[8]	17	--	10	14	--

NB: The tables draw on the analysis presented in the chapters of this book. For further details regarding the data presented here, refer to the relevant chapters.
1. For some models includes other grains.
2. Partial Price Transmission. Meat is ruminant meat.
3. Meat projection is only for beef.
4. The Ministerial Trade Mandate Model of the OECD Agricultural Directorate forecasts 10 per cent reductions. The numbers presented here are simple multiples of these to provide comparative 100 per cent reductions. Meat projections are average of beef, poultry, pork and sheep price movements weighted by world production of these commodities. The MTM model is discussed in the chapter by Moreddu, *et al.*
5. Meat is only beef and veal, dairy is butter (cheese value is 37, milk powder 81, and fresh milk 0). The USDA/SWOPSIM model is discussed in the chapter by Krissoff, *et al.*
6. The IIASA model is discussed in the chapter by Frohberg, *et al.*
7. The RUNS model is discussed in the chapter by Burniaux, Van der Mensbrugghe and Waelbroeck.
8. The WALRAS model is discussed in the chapter by Burniaux, Martin, *et al.*

Table 17.2

PRICE EFFECTS OF OECD AND DEVELOPING COUNTRY LIBERALIZATION

Model	Wheat[1]	Coarse grains	Meat	Dairy	Sugar
Partial equilibrium models					
Anderson-Tyers[2]: (projected 1995)					
a. Price-independent productivity growth	1	-88	60	-12	
b. Price-dependent productivity growth	1	-7	-2	56	-19
Zietz and Valdés[3]: (OECD countries liberalize)	-12	-24	13	--	1
OECD/MTM[4]: (OECD counries liberalize)	-7	-12	-4	29	7
USDA/SWOPSIM[5] (1986 base)	23	8-19	7	79	7
Generale equilibrium models					
IIASA[6] (projected 2000)	23	13	11	34	--

1. For some models includes other grains.
2. Partial Price Transmission. Meat is ruminant meat.
3. Meat projection is only for beef.
4. The Ministerial Trade Mandate Model of the OECD Agricultural Directorate forecasts 10 per cent reductions. The numbers presented here are simple multiples of these to provide comparative 100 per cent reductions. Meat projections are average of beef, poultry, pork and sheep price movements weighted by world production of these commodities. The MTM model is discussed in the chapter by Moreddu, *et al.*
5. Meat is only beef and veal, dairy is butter (cheese value is 37, milk powder 81, and fresh milk 0). The USDA/SWOPSIM model is discussed in the chapter by Krissoff, *et al.*
6. The IIASA model is discussed in the chapter by Frohberg, *et al.*

NOTES AND REFERENCES

1. Caution should be exercised in the interpretation and comparison of the different modelling results. Readers are referred to the papers in this volume for a fuller description of the assumptions and data sets on which the modelling results rest. As indicated in the papers and Tables 17.1 and 17.2 in this chapter, the models are different in their base periods, time horizons, commodity definition and coverage, methodologies (partial and general and static and dynamic), and in their assumptions regarding the definition, extent and coverage of liberalization.

2. The MTM model treats food and feed grains as similar grains. Their domestic prices are linked to the same world price, although their domestic usage is different.

3. An order of magnitude of the potential dividend comes from the OECD *Agricultural Policies, Markets and Trade: Monitoring and Outlook 1989* (OECD, Paris, 1989), Table IV.6, which estimates the total transfers associated with current agricultural policies in OECD countries alone in 1988 to be valued at $270 billion. This figure includes research and expenditure on extension services and so is in excess of the dividend to be gained from agricultural trade liberalization. On the other hand, the estimate does not include the benefit to be derived from developing countries' trade reforms. Further evidence regarding the liberalization dividend is provided by Zietz and Valdés, Anderson and Tyers and Burniaux, and Martin *et al.* in this volume. See also Chapter 6 in World Bank, *World Development Report 1986* (Oxford University Press, Oxford, 1986).

4. The Central Limit Theorem states that as the sample size increases, the variance declines by $1/n$. The implication is that increased participation in a market may be expected to lead to a decline in the variance.

5. In Eastern Europe, given the already relatively high levels of food consumption, reform to the extent it results in productivity improvements may reduce the demand for temperate imports — notably grains and sugar — and therefore depress these prices. The reform process may, however, provide grounds for optimism for the tropical product exporters, as increasing consumer choice may facilitate the opening of new market opportunities for tropical fruits and beverages. The continued change in China's comparative advantage in favour of manufacturing, may well provide a firm support to the grains and sugar markets, although the extent to which this will underpin prices clearly requires further analysis, not least of the implications for China's balance of payments.

AUTHORS AND DISCUSSANTS

Hassan ABOUYOUB	Director of Commerce, External Trade, Ministry of Trade and Industry, Rabat
Kym ANDERSON	Director, Centre for International Economic Studies, Adelaide
Paul ARMINGTON	Division Chief, International Economics Division, International Economics Department, World Bank, Washington
David BLANDFORD	Professor, Cornell University, Ithaca
Jean-Marc BOUSSARD	Professor, Institut National de Recherche Agronomique (INRA), Paris
Avishay BRAVERMAN	Division Chief, Agricultural Policies Division, Agriculture and Rural Development Department, World Bank, Washington
Jean-Marc BURNIAUX	Economist, Growth Studies Division, Economics and Statistics Department, OECD, Paris
Joe DEWBRE	Senior Economist, Trade Analysis Division, Directorate for Food, Agriculture and Fisheries, OECD, Paris
François DELORME	Economist, Growth Studies Division, Economics and Statistics Department, OECD, Paris
Ronald DUNCAN	Division Chief, International Commodity Markets Division, International Economics Department, World Bank, Washington
Louis EMMERIJ	President, OECD Development Centre, Paris
Gunther FISCHER	Research Scholar, International Institute for Applied Systems Analysis, Laxenburg
Klaus FROHBERG	Senior Economist, Trade Analysis Division, Directorate for Food, Agriculture and Fisheries, OECD, Paris
Ian GOLDIN	Head of Programme, Developing Country Agriculture and International Economic Trends, OECD Development Centre, Paris
Jeffrey HAMMER	Economist, Agricultural Policies Division, Agriculture and Rural Development Department, World Bank, Washington
Thomas W. HERTEL	Professor, Purdue University, Indiana
Bruce HUFF	Head of Division, Trade Analysis Division, Directorate for Food, Agriculture and Fisheries, OECD, Paris
Alain de JANVRY	Professor, University of California, Berkeley
Douglas IRWIN	Economist, Board of Governors of the Federal Reserve System, Washington
Odin KNUDSEN	Principal Economist, Agricultural Policies Division, Agriculture and Rural Development Department, World Bank, Washington
Panos KONANDREAS	Senior Economist, Commodities Division, FAO, Rome
Barry KRISSOFF	Section Leader, Macro Policy, Developing Economies, Economics Research Service, USDA, Washington

Ian LIENERT	Economist, African Department, International Monetary Fund, Washington
Tom LOO	Research Economist, Duke University, North Carolina
Carl MABBS-ZENO	Economist, Food Aid Section, Economics Research Service, USDA, Washington
John MARTIN	Head of Division, Growth Studies Division, Economics and Statistics Department, OECD, Paris
Catherine MOREDDU	Economist, Trade Analysis Division, Directorate for Food, Agriculture and Fisheries, OECD, Paris
Knud Jorgen MUNK	Senior Economist, Commission of the European Communities, Brussels
Kirit PARIKH	Director, Indira Gandhi Institute of Development Research, Bombay
Kevin PARRIS	Economist, Agricultural Trade and Market Division, Directorate for Food, Agriculture and Fisheries, OECD, Paris
Michel PETIT	Director, Agriculture and Rural Development Department, World Bank, Washington
Ewa RABINOWITZ	Assistant Professor, Swedish University of Agricultural Science, Uppsala
Gordon RAUSSER	Chief Economist, USAID, Washington
Sherman ROBINSON	Professor, University of California, Berkeley, California
Marjorie ROSE	Economist, Central Banking Division, International Monetary Fund, Washington
Elisabeth SADOULET	Assistant Professor, University of California, Berkeley, California
Pasquale SCANDIZZO	Professor, University of Rome, Rome
T.N. SRINIVASAN	Professor, Yale University, New Haven
John SULLIVAN	Economist, Agriculture and Trade Analysis Division, Economic Research Service, USDA, Washington
Wouter TIMS	Director, Centre for World Food Studies, Free University of Amsterdam, Amsterdam
Edward TOWER	Professor, Duke University, North Carolina
Rod TYERS	Professor, University of Adelaide, Adelaide
Alberto VALDÉS	Program Director, International Food Policy Research Institute, Washington
Dominique van der MENSBRUGGE	Research Economist, University of California, Berkeley
Jean WAELBROECK	Professor, Free University of Brussels, Brussels
John WAINIO	Economist, Agriculture and Trade Analysis Division, USDA, Washington
John WHALLEY	Professor, University of Western Ontario, Ontario
Randall WIGLE	Associate Professor, University of Western Ontario, Ontario
Alan WINTERS	Professor, University of North Wales, United Kingdom
Joachim ZIETZ	Professor, Middle Tennessee State University, Murfreesboro

WHERE TO OBTAIN OECD PUBLICATIONS
OÙ OBTENIR LES PUBLICATIONS DE L'OCDE

Argentina – Argentine
Carlos Hirsch S.R.L.
Galeria Güemes, Florida 165, 4° Piso
1333 Buenos Aires
Tel. 30.7122, 331.1787 y 331.2391
Telegram: Hirsch-Baires
Telex: 21112 UAPE-AR. Ref. s/2901
Telefax:(1)331-1787

Australia – Australie
D.A. Book (Aust.) Pty. Ltd.
11–13 Station Street (P.O. Box 163)
Mitcham, Vic. 3132   Tel. (03)873.4411
Telex: AA37911 DA BOOK
Telefax: (03)873.5679

Austria – Autriche
OECD Publications and Information Centre
4 Simrockstrasse
5300 Bonn (Germany) Tel. (0228)21.60.45
Telex: 8 86300 Bonn
Telefax: (0228)26.11.04
Gerold & Co.
Graben 31
Wien I   Tel. (0222)533.50.14

Belgium – Belgique
Jean De Lannoy
Avenue du Roi 202
B-1060 Bruxelles
              Tel. (02)538.51.69/538.08.41
Telex: 63220 Telefax: (02)538.08.41

Canada
Renouf Publishing Company Ltd.
1294 Algoma Road
Ottawa, Ont. K1B 3W8 Tel. (613)741.4333
Telex: 053-4783 Telefax: (613)741.5439
Stores:
61 Sparks Street
Ottawa, Ont. K1P 5R1   Tel. (613)238.8985
211 Yonge Street
Toronto, Ont. M5B 1M4 Tel. (416)363.3171
Federal Publications
165 University Avenue
Toronto, ON M5H 3B9   Tel. (416)581.1552
Telefax: (416)581.1743
Les Publications Fédérales
1185 rue de l'Université
Montréal, PQ H3B 1R7 Tel.(514)954-1633
Les Éditions La Liberté Inc.
3020 Chemin Sainte-Foy
Sainte-Foy, P.Q. G1X 3V6
              Tel. (418)658.3763
Telefax: (418)658.3763

Denmark – Danemark
Munksgaard Export and Subscription Service
35, Norre Sogade, P.O. Box 2148
DK-1016 Kobenhavn K
              Tel. (45 33)12.85.70
Telex: 19431 MUNKS DK
              Telefax: (45 33)12.93.87

Finland – Finlande
Akateeminen Kirjakauppa
Keskuskatu 1, P.O. Box 128
00100 Helsinki   Tel. (358 0)12141
Telex: 125080 Telefax: (358 0)121.4441

France
OECD/OCDE
Mail Orders/Commandes par correspon-
dance:
2 rue André-Pascal
75775 Paris Cedex 16   Tel. (1)45.24.82.00
Bookshop/Librairie:
33, rue Octave-Feuillet
75016 Paris   Tel. (1)45.24.81.67
                      (1)45.24.81.81
Telex: 620 160 OCDE
Telefax: (33-1)45.24.85.00
Librairie de l'Université
12a, rue Nazareth
13602 Aix-en-Provence   Tel. 42.26.18.08

Germany – Allemagne
OECD Publications and Information Centre
4 Simrockstrasse
5300 Bonn   Tel. (0228)21.60.45
Telex: 8 86300 Bonn
              Telefax: (0228)26.11.04

Greece – Grèce
Librairie Kauffmann
28 rue du Stade
105 64 Athens   Tel. 322.21.60
Telex: 218187 LIKA Gr

Hong Kong
Government Information Services
Publications (Sales) Office
Information Service Department
No. 1 Battery Path
Central   Tel. (5)23.31.91
Telex: 802.61190

Iceland – Islande
Mal Mog Menning
Laugavegi 18, Postholf 392
121 Reykjavik   Tel. 15199/24240

India – Inde
Oxford Book and Stationery Co.
Scindia House
New Delhi 110001   Tel. 331.5896/5308
Telex: 31 61990 AM IN
Telefax: (11)332.5993
17 Park Street
Calcutta 700016   Tel. 240832

Indonesia – Indonésie
Pdii-Lipi
P.O. Box 269/JKSMG/88
Jakarta12790   Tel. 583467
Telex: 62 875

Ireland – Irlande
TDC Publishers – Library Suppliers
12 North Frederick Street
Dublin 1   Tel. 744835/749677
Telex: 33530 TDCP EI Telefax : 748416

Italy – Italie
Libreria Commissionaria Sansoni
Via Benedetto Fortini, 120/10
Casella Post. 552
50125 Firenze   Tel. (055)645415
Telex: 570466 Telefax: (39.55)641257
Via Bartolini 29
20155 Milano   Tel. 365083
La diffusione delle pubblicazioni OCSE viene
assicurata dalle principali librerie ed anche
da:
Editrice e Libreria Herder
Piazza Montecitorio 120
00186 Roma   Tel. 679.4628
Telex: NATEL I 621427
Libreria Hoepli
Via Hoepli 5
20121 Milano   Tel. 865446
Telex: 31.33.95 Telefax: (39.2)805.2886
Libreria Scientifica
Dott. Lucio de Biasio "Aeiou"
Via Meravigli 16
20123 Milano   Tel. 807679
Telefax: 800175

Japan– Japon
OECD Publications and Information Centre
Landic Akasaka Building
2-3-4 Akasaka, Minato-ku
Tokyo 107   Tel. 586.2016
Telefax: (81.3)584.7929

Korea – Corée
Kyobo Book Centre Co. Ltd.
P.O. Box 1658, Kwang Hwa Moon
Seoul   Tel. (REP)730.78.91
Telefax: 735.0030

**Malaysia/Singapore –
Malaisie/Singapour**
University of Malaya Co-operative Bookshop
Ltd.
P.O. Box 1127, Jalan Pantai Baru 59100
Kuala Lumpur
Malaysia   Tel. 756.5000/756.5425
Telefax: 757.3661
Information Publications Pte. Ltd.
Pei-Fu Industrial Building
24 New Industrial Road No. 02-06
Singapore 1953   Tel. 283.1786/283.1798
Telefax: 284.8875

Netherlands – Pays-Bas
SDU Uitgeverij
Christoffel Plantijnstraat 2
Postbus 20014
2500 EA's-Gravenhage Tel. (070)78.99.11
Voor bestellingen: Tel. (070)78.98.80
Telex: 32486 stdru Telefax: (070)47.63.51

New Zealand –Nouvelle-Zélande
Government Printing Office
Customer Services
P.O. Box 12-411
Freepost 10-050
Thorndon, Wellington
Tel. 0800 733-406   Telefax: 04 499-1733

Norway – Norvège
Narvesen Info Center – NIC
Bertrand Narvesens vei 2
P.O. Box 6125 Etterstad
0602 Oslo 6
              Tel. (02)67.83.10/(02)68.40.20
Telex: 79668 NIC N Telefax: (47 2)68.53.47

Pakistan
Mirza Book Agency
65 Shahrah Quaid-E-Azam
Lahore 3   Tel. 66839
Telex: 44886 UBL PK. Attn: MIRZA BK

Portugal
Livraria Portugal
Rua do Carmo 70–74
1117 Lisboa Codex   Tel. 347.49.82/3/4/5

**Singapore/Malaysia
Singapour/Malaisie**
See "Malaysia/Singapore"
Voir "Malaisie/Singapour"

Spain – Espagne
Mundi-Prensa Libros S.A.
Castello 37, Apartado 1223
Madrid 28001   Tel. (91) 431.33.99
Telex: 49370 MPLI Telefax: (91) 275.39.98
Libreria Internacional AEDOS
Consejo de Ciento 391
08009 –Barcelona   Tel. (93) 301-86-15
Telefax: (93) 317-01-41

Sweden – Suède
Fritzes Fackboksföretaget
Box 16356, S 103 27 STH
Regeringsgatan 12
DS Stockholm   Tel. (08)23.89.00
Telex: 12387 Telefax: (08)20.50.21
Subscription Agency/Abonnements:
Wennergren–Williams AB
Box 30004
104 25 Stockholm   Tel. (08)54.12.00
Telex: 19937 Telefax: (08)50.82.86

Switzerland – Suisse
OECD Publications and Information Centre
4 Simrockstrasse
5300 Bonn (Germany) Tel. (0228)21.60.45
Telex: 8 86300 Bonn
Telefax: (0228)26.11.04
Librairie Payot
6 rue Grenus
1211 Genève 11   Tel. (022)731.89.50
Telex: 28356
Maditec S.A.
Ch. des Palettes 4
1020 Renens/Lausanne Tel. (021)635.08.65
Telefax: (021)635.07.80
United Nations Bookshop/Librairie des Na-
tions–Unies
Palais des Nations
1211 Genève 10
              Tel. (022)734.60.11 (ext. 48.72)
Telex: 289696 (Attn: Sales)
Telefax: (022)733.98.79

Taïwan – Formose
Good Faith Worldwide Int'l. Co. Ltd.
9th Floor, No. 118, Sec. 2
Chung Hsiao E. Road
Taipei   Tel. 391.7396/391.7397
Telefax: (02) 394.9176

Thailand – Thalande
Suksit Siam Co. Ltd.
1715 Rama IV Road, Samyan
Bangkok 5   Tel. 251.1630

Turkey – Turquie
Kültur Yayinlari Is–Türk Ltd. Sti.
Atatürk Bulvari No. 191/Kat. 21
Kavaklidere/Ankara   Tel. 25.07.60
Dolmabahce Cad. No. 29
Besiktas/Istanbul   Tel. 160.71.88
Telex: 43482B

United Kingdom – Royaume-Uni
H.M. Stationery Office
Gen. enquiries   Tel. (01) 873 0011
Postal orders only:
P.O. Box 276, London SW8 5DT
Personal Callers HMSO Bookshop
49 High Holborn, London WC1V 6HB
Telex: 297138 Telefax: 873.8463
Branches at: Belfast, Birmingham, Bristol,
Edinburgh, Manchester

United States – États-Unis
OECD Publications and Information Centre
2001 L Street N.W., Suite 700
Washington, D.C. 20036-4095
              Tel. (202)785.6323
Telex: 440245 WASHINGTON D.C.
Telefax: (202)785.0350

Venezuela
Libreria del Este
Avda F. Miranda 52, Aptdo. 60337
Edificio Galipan
Caracas 106
              Tel. 951.1705/951.2307/951.1297
Telegram: Libreste Caracas

Yugoslavia – Yougoslavie
Jugoslovenska Knjiga
Knez Mihajlova 2, P.O. Box 36
Beograd   Tel. 621.992
Telex: 12466 jk bgd

Orders and inquiries from countries where
Distributors have not yet been appointed
should be sent to: OECD Publications
Service, 2 rue André-Pascal, 75775 Paris
Cedex 16.
Les commandes provenant de pays où
l'OCDE n'a pas encore désigné de dis-
tributeur devraient être adressées à : OCDE,
Service des Publications, 2, rue André-
Pascal, 75775 Paris Cedex 16.

Printed on behalf of the
Organisation for Economic Co-operation and Development
and the World Bank by
OECD PUBLICATIONS, 2, rue André-Pascal, 75775 PARIS CEDEX 16
PRINTED IN FRANCE
(41 90 04 1) ISBN 92-64-13366-6 - No. 45127 1990
ISBN 0-8213-1527-7